Russian Politics and Society: An Introduction

**Pearson
Education**

We work with leading authors to develop the
strongest educational materials in politics,
bringing cutting-edge thinking and best learning
practice to a global market.

Under a range of well-known imprints, including
Longman, we craft high quality print and
electronic publications which help
readers to understand and apply their content,
whether studying or at work.

To find out more about the complete range of our
publishing please visit us on the World Wide Web at:
www.pearsoneduc.com

Russian Politics and Society:
An Introduction

Catherine J. Danks

An imprint of **Pearson Education**

Harlow, England · London · New York · Reading, Massachusetts · San Francisco
Toronto · Don Mills, Ontario · Sydney · Tokyo · Singapore · Hong Kong · Seoul
Taipei · Cape Town · Madrid · Mexico City · Amsterdam · Munich · Paris · Milan

Pearson Education Limited
Edinburgh Gate
Harlow
Essex CM20 2JE
England

and Associated Companies throughout the world

Visit us on the World Wide Web at:
www.pearsoneduc.com

First published 2001

© Pearson Education Limited 2001

ISBN 0-582-47300-4 PPR

British Library Cataloguing-in-Publication Data
A catalogue record for this book can be obtained from the British Library

Library of Congress Cataloging-in-Publication Data
Danks, Catherine J., 1956-
    Russian politics and society : an introduction / Catherine J. Danks.
        p. cm.
    Includes bibliographical references and index.
    ISBN 0-582-47300-4
    1. Russia (Federation)--Politics and government--1991- 2. Perestroæka--Russia
(Federation) 3. Soviet Union--Politics and government--1985-1991.
    4. Democratization--Russia (Federation) 5. Political culture--Russia (Federation)
I. Title.
DK288.D35 2001
320.947--dc21

                                                                        2001036712

Typeset by 43 in 10/12pt Sabon
Printed in Great Britain by Henry Ling Ltd., at the Dorset Press, Dorchester, Dorset

10 9 8 7 6 5 4 3 2 1
05 04 03 02

For

Ernest S. Danks
20 November 1931–12 February 1996

Contents

List of maps

List of boxes

Russia at a glance

Name	Russian Federation or Russia
Status	Federal republic
Location	Europe and Asia
Capital	Moscow
Language	Russian
Religions	Russian Orthodox, Islam, Buddhism, Judaism
Ethnic composition	81.5 per cent Russian, 3.8 per cent Tatar, 3 per cent Ukrainian, 1.2 per cent Chuvash, 0.9 per cent Bashkir, 0.8 per cent Belarussian, 0.7 per cent Moldavian, 8.1 per cent other
Currency	Rouble
National holiday	Independence Day, 12 June (1990)
Constitution day	12 December
Area	17 075 200 sq km (or 6 592 849 square miles)
Agricultural area	2 220 000 sq km
Government-administration	Bicameral Federal Assembly (parliament): the Federation Council is the upper house and the State Duma the lower house
Suffrage	18 years and Russian citizenship
Population	146 338 000 (at the end of 1998)

Bering Strait

UNITED STATES

Arctic Ocean

Bering Sea

U.S.

Lena

Magadan

North
Pacific
Ocean

S i b e r i a

Yakutsk

Sea of
Okhotsk

Kurile
Islands

Lena

Amur

Kholmsk

Khabarovsk

Amur

Irkutsk

Lake
Baikal

JAPAN

CHINA

Nakhodka

MONGOLIA

N. KOREA

Vladivostok

The Russian Federation

Preface

Anybody writing about contemporary Russia is daily reminded of the curse 'May you live in interesting times'. I started studying the USSR during the Brezhnev years when change was slow and academic books did not date so rapidly. Gorbachev's *perestroika* triggered an upsurge of interest in the USSR, precisely because at long last there were new ideas, phenomena and people to discuss. But undergraduate interest in Russia has certainly now fallen from its *perestroika* high. My *vox pop* of 'the student at the back of room' indicates that Russia is interesting but too complex, too difficult to get a handle on, and writing an essay on Russia is like trying to nail jelly to a wall. Unfortunately, the soviet era image of all Russians as dour party functionaries in bad suits has now given way to the equally inaccurate image of all contemporary Russians as drunks and gangsters. Russia is a fascinating and complex country and one of the great challenges in writing this book has been to provide students with the academic tools to understand it while keeping up-to-date. My aim has been to write an accessible book and so I took the conscious decision to avoid using jargon and social science terms as far as possible. This book assumes no prior knowledge of Russia and so short historical accounts are interspersed throughout the text. Each chapter is self-contained but I have indicated where there are useful links to other chapters. Suggested further reading and useful websites are indicated at the end of each chapter.

The text is divided into four parts. Part I examines the making of the Russian Federation. It examines Russia's stated goal to create a capitalist democracy, the reasons for the introduction of *perestroika* and its ultimate failure, the lessons of *perestroika* for post-communist development, problems of the transition process, the impact of the soviet legacy, and the creation or recreation of a Russian identity. The themes of democratisation versus authoritarianism, and of centrifugal versus centralising forces, are introduced. Part II, on the making of the Russian state, picks up on these themes, and stresses the early continuity of Russia's state institutions with their soviet predecessors. It addresses the struggle for supremacy between the president and parliament, to create a unified federation, and the problems of reforming and maintaining civilian control over the armed forces and of creating a law-governed state and an independent judiciary. The struggle and tension between authoritarian and/or centralising tendencies on the one hand, and the aim of democratisation and the fear of disintegration and chaos on the other, is a central theme of Part II. Part III looks at the making of Russian democracy. It examines the development of Russia's civil society, and the organisation and institutions, such as political parties and the mass media, that are supposed to provide the people with a voice. Part IV focuses on reforming Russia. The abandonment of soviet socialism has led to new aims and criteria underpinning policy-making, such as a commitment to open up to the world, the importance of establishing a market economy, and a reassessment of what constitutes and what would best promote the national interest. Russia is having to contend with a wide range of changing realities, such as its changed geopolitical situation, declining economic performance and financial constraints, when framing its foreign, economic and social policies. The final chapter examines President Putin's background, rise to power and policy initiatives and asks whether Russia's democratisation is in danger.

Transliteration

The transliteration system followed in this book is a modified version of the Library of Congress system. In cases where a particular spelling of a Russian name or word has come into general English usage, this spelling is used rather than the direct transliteration. So Yeltsin is used rather than El'tsin, Fyodorov rather than Federov, and the newspaper *Izvestiia* is rendered as *Izvestia*; the first names Igor, Yury, Gennady and Grigory are used rather than Yegor, Yurii, Gennadii and Grigorii. Surnames ending with ii and aia are transliterated by the more common y and aya, so Zhirinovsky rather than Zhirinovskii and Zavadskaya rather than Zavadskaia. Names beginning with 'Iu' or 'Ia' have been transliterated by the more common 'Yu' and 'Ya', so Iavlinskii is transliterated as Yavlinsky. Within the text soft signs have not been transliterated although they do appear in the bibliography and transliterated words in brackets in the text. So Lebed is used rather than Lebed', Belarus rather than Belarus', *glasnost* rather than *glasnost'* and *oblast* rather than *oblast'*. As the spelling of Russian names varies in English language publications, the spelling employed by the text being cited is always employed. So although it is common practice to spell the name of the sociologist as Tatyana Zaslavskaya, she also appears as Tat'iana Zaslavskaia, and similarly Alexander Solzhenitsyn also appears as Aleksandr Solzhenitsyn.

Acknowledgements

This book could not have been written without the financial support of the Department of History and Economic History at Manchester Metropolitan University. I also owe a particular debt of gratitude to Colin Buckley, my former head of department, who gave me the time and the financial support to begin this project. Thanks also go to colleagues at MMU for their support and encouragement, particularly Frank Carr, Geraldine Lievesley, Philip Lloyd, Trish Richards, Melanie Tebbutt and Mike Tyldesley, who all also gave me the most valuable advice any author can be given, 'Get on with it'. I would also like to thank my colleague John Hassan for reading Chapter 11. I owe an enormous debt of gratitude to my students at MMU, who have been some of the most insightful and enthusiastic critics of my work. Thanks must also go to the four readers whose eagle eyes and expertise saved me from some embarrassing errors; any remaining errors are of course my own. I would also like to thank Professor Galina Gribanova for her help in planning this book and her support during my research trips to Russia; Margarita Mudrak of the St Petersburg House of Friendship for helping to organise my trips; and Larissa Smirnova and Tanya Pavlenko for their hospitality and friendship.

Publisher's acknowledgements

We are grateful to the following for permission to reproduce copyright material: Box 1.4 from *The Economist* 4.4.98 © The Economist Limited 1998, London; Box 5.2 from *OECD Economic Surveys 1999–2000 Russian Federation Paris*; Box 5.4 'Back to the USSR' in *The Guardian* 29.5.00 by A. Gentleman and Box 9.4 'Russia's media. All the news that fits' in *The Economist* 15.2.97 © The Economist Limited, London 1997.

Whilst every effort has been made to trace the owners of copyright material, in a few cases this has proved impossible and we take this opportunity to offer our apologies to any copyright holders whose rights we may have unwittingly infringed.

PART 1

The making of the Russian Federation

Introduction: transforming Russia

This chapter examines the Russian Federation's transition from soviet socialism to capitalism and democracy. Russia's first steps towards democratisation and marketisation are introduced and the interrelationship and sequencing of economic and political reform are analysed. The impact of the Imperial Russian and the soviet legacies on the course of the reforms is also examined, as are the continuity of economic and political elites, the continuing importance of network and clan alliances often forged in the soviet era, the power of the oligarchs, and a state corporatist analysis of the Russian state. Finally, stress is placed on the importance of continued state-building in Russia today, especially on the vital importance of developing an independent judiciary to ensure the rule of law.

Introduction

In 1992 under the leadership of President Boris Yeltsin, Prime Minister Igor Gaidar and Foreign Minister Andrei Kozyrev, the Russian Federation (RF) set out to become a capitalist, liberal democracy. This westernising or Atlanticist agenda, as it became known, was influenced by western ideas and institutions. The leading seven capitalist countries (the G7), the International Monetary Fund (IMF), the World Bank and the American economist Jeffrey Sachs were all actively engaged in devising the goals and substance of Russian reform. It may have seemed self-evident in the G7 capitals that the collapse of soviet socialism inevitably meant the victory of its old ideological enemy, capitalism and liberal democracy, but the views of the Russian people were not canvassed in new democratic elections at this crucial time. It is doubtful whether many Russians, even those who had worked for the end of soviet socialism in the name of democracy and the market, truly understood the path their country was about to take. The collapse of the Union of Soviet Socialist Republics (USSR), the loss of its superpower status and the demise of soviet socialism and its certainties left many Russians feeling vulnerable and disoriented. There was no popular consensus about what form Russia's post-communist economic and political systems should take. The coalition of forces that had finally destroyed soviet socialism included reformist communists such as Alexander Rutskoi through to Yeltsin's Atlanticist allies. Once soviet socialism was defeated, the differences, in some cases the chasms, in opinion amongst this loose coalition became increasingly evident. Russia therefore set out on its new course without a supporting popular or elite consensus.

Marketisation and democratisation

Democratisation: reforming Russia's institutions

Russia is now described as post-communist. The Communist Party of the Russian Federation (KPRF) no longer enjoys the monopoly of political power once exercised by the Communist Party of the Soviet Union (CPSU). Marxism–Leninism is no longer the official state ideology and communism is no longer seen as the final, inevitable stage of history. Communism may have collapsed in 1991 but the soviet state, institutions, organisations and ways of thinking did not. In Russia there has been no pro-democratic education, no purges, no Truth and Reconciliation Commission and no putting the old regime on trial. In 1992 President Yeltsin even ordered the soviet secret police (KGB) archives to be closed, so frustrating any investigation into the crimes of the Communist era. The 7 November public holiday in honour of the Bolshevik Revolution remains a holiday, only now it is rather optimistically called National Reconciliation Day. The new Russian state also inherited its personnel and institutions from the Russian Soviet Federative Socialist Republic (RSFSR). It did not have a new constitution, reformed representative institutions and founding elections until 1993. The 1978 RSFSR Constitution with a few amendments provided an inappropriate and contradictory legal foundation for the new democracy during the crucial first two years of democratisation. There was also continuity of political and economic elites at all levels and throughout the country. According to research conducted by the Russian Academy of Sciences (RAN), Institute of Sociology, 75 per cent of the Russian Federation's political elite and 61 per cent of the business elite come from the old soviet elite, the *nomenklatura* (see Box 1.1). Yeltsin was elected chair of the RSFSR Supreme Soviet in May 1990 and only left the CPSU in July 1990. In June 1991 he was elected to the new post of RSFSR president and it was not until 1993 that he was formally elected president of the new Russian Federation. The CPSU was never defeated at the polls and the KPRF, although briefly

BOX 1.1

The continuity between the Soviet and the Russian political and economic elites (in percentages)

	President's inner circle	Party leaders	Regional elite	Government	Business elite
Total from soviet nomenklatura	75.0	57.1	82.3	74.3	61.0
Including from:					
CPSU	21.2	65.0	17.8	0.0	13.1
Komsomol	0.0	5.0	1.8	0.0	37.7
Soviets	63.6	25.0	78.6	26.9	3.3
Economic	9.1	5.0	0.0	42.3	37.7
Other	6.1	10.0	0.0	30.8	8.2

Source: Olga Kryshtanovskaya (1996) 'The Financial Oligarchy in Russia', *Izvestia*, 9 January, 5. Olga Kryshtanovskaya is the head of the sector for the study of the elite, Institute of Sociology, RAN.

banned (from November 1991 until early 1992), remains a potent political force in Russia.

The Congress of People's Deputies (the lower house of parliament) was dominated by communists and nationalists (the Red-Browns) who opposed Yeltsin's Atlanticist orientation and economic shock therapy. Congress and president were soon embroiled in an increasingly acrimonious deadlock. Congress believed that it could legitimately act as the voice of the people in the face of Russia's international decline and mounting domestic problems. This championing of the people mostly took the form of criticism and obstruction of the president, rather than constructive suggestions or a willingness to take any responsibility. Yeltsin for his part would brook no criticism of his reforms and presented himself as the champion and guarantor of democratic and economic reform. In 1993 President Yeltsin declared a state of emergency and opened fire on the recalcitrant parliament (see Chapter 4). The sight of the White House, the Russian parliament building, under fire graphically symbolised the fragility of Russian democracy. It was also a potentially dangerous precedent for the armed forces rather than democratic procedures to be used to settle disputes between president and parliament.

Russia emerged from the 1993 emergency with a new constitution, reformed representative institutions, new elections and an extremely powerful office of president. Although the importance of a separation of executive, legislative and judicial functions was recognised in the 1993 Constitution, in reality it only enshrined a rudimentary system of checks and balances between these institutions (see Chapter 4). There have however been dramatic changes in Russia which reflect the growing pluralism in its society and political system. The development of a federal system has led to the devolution of authority and competence over a wide range of issues away from Moscow (see Chapter 5). Elections are held, political parties organise and put forward competing programmes, and freedom of speech, organisation and the press all exist, on paper at least (see Part III). Guarantees of human rights, the creation of a law-governed state and the maintenance of law and order have proved more intractable problems (see Chapter 6).

Marketisation: the dash to the market

Russia's economic reform programme (see Chapter 11) was developed in accordance with the Washington consensus advocated by the IMF and the World Bank. The Washington consensus combines a neoliberal approach to the economy with a belief that the state's role is to ensure the national security, rule of law and stability that the market needs in order to operate effectively. In Russia this involved a commitment to ending the soviet state's ownership, planning and management of the economy. Economic reform took the form of a programme of shock therapy elaborated under the tutelage of the IMF representative Jeffrey Sachs. Sachs worked with Prime Minister Igor Gaidar on macroeconomic stabilisation policies aimed at stabilising the rouble, eradicating inflation and eliminating the budget and balance of payment deficits. Financial support for these reforms was provided by the IMF on behalf of the G7 countries. Privatisation of state enterprises was initiated, and in January 1992 prices were liberalised, triggering hyperinflation. Shock therapy raises important questions about the sequencing of the components of economic transition. Macroeconomic stabilisation, privatisation and economic liberalisation were initiated before adequate institutional reforms had been introduced. Russia lacked private property, commercial, contract, bankruptcy, taxation, currency and anti-monopoly laws. Also absent or poorly developed were stock exchanges, a banking system to provide credit to new businesses, trained personnel in management and accountancy, and appropriate customs controls. In the face of mounting economic problems shock therapy was largely abandoned in 1993–4.

Latin America and Southern Europe: models of post-authoritarian transition?

In the early 1990s analogies were drawn between the Russian situation and the post-authoritarian experiences of Latin American and Southern European countries. Whilst Russia shared certain similarities with these countries, there are significant differences that render comparisons unhelpful. Certainly in the USSR, Latin American and Southern Europe the authoritarian states tried to control all political activities and to prevent the development of civil societies that might challenge this state dominance. In Latin American and Southern Europe the Catholic Church provided an alternative ideology and organisation that were not successfully controlled by the state. In contrast in the USSR the Russian Orthodox Church was deeply compromised by its symbiotic relationship with the soviet state and was unable to play an independent role. Nevertheless, the USSR did have the beginnings of a civil society which was increasingly active during Gorbachev's Reconstruction period (1985–91). Again while the economies of Latin America, Southern Europe and the USSR shared a general need to modernise, there are more important and profound differences. The Latin American and Southern European countries were already capitalist whilst under authoritarian rule. They began their post-authoritarian modernisation with private property laws for example already in place, and they already had private commercial banks and stock exchanges. The economies also had quite different structures. The Latin American and Southern European countries had small and medium size businesses whereas the soviet economy had a massive military-industrial complex which accounted for approximately one-third of its gross domestic product (GDP). In Russia, therefore, economic modernisation entails a daunting array of tasks such as passing new laws, setting up a range of new institutions and grappling with these giant industrial dinosaurs.

The Asian Tiger economies as modernising dictatorships

The state capitalist model of development employed by Japan and the Asian Tiger economies (South Korea, Taiwan and Singapore) provides an alternative model of economic modernisation. Advocates of state capitalism such as Alexander Rutskoi, who served as Yeltsin's vice-president (1991–3), believe it to be better suited historically and culturally to Russia than the Washington consensus neoliberalism and shock therapy. Rutskoi shares with many Russian nationalists and communists the belief that Russia is a Eurasian rather than a European country (see Chapter 3) and should therefore follow an Asian model of development. In the early 1990s Rutskoi was particularly interested in the lessons that Russia could learn from South Korea. Rutskoi favours gradual reform and also argues that state capitalism is in keeping with Russia's pre-communist tsarist economic development which was characterised by high levels of state intervention in the economy, with the state encouraging investment and even acting as an entrepreneur (Steele, 1994: 333–4). Rutskoi has often praised Pyotr Stolypin, Tsar Nicholas II's prime minister, who advocated economic reform combined with a strong state. The Asian Tigers' policy of protecting domestic markets seems to offer a weakened and vulnerable Russia a better chance of achieving the rapid economic modernisation and restructuring that it so desperately needs, than would opening up to the forces of global capitalism. Amongst the G7 countries it is not surprising that Japan tends to favour a state capitalist model of development rather than shock therapy for Russia (Gill, 1997: 160). Another feature of the Asian Tiger and Japanese model of development is that economic reform took precedence over democratisation. South Korea has achieved tremendous economic modernisation but it is not a democracy. Alexander Rutskoi does not advocate the abandonment of Russia's nascent democratisation in order to be more like South Korea's modernising dictatorship, but he does believe that Russia needs a strong state – a state that stands up for Russian interests in the world, maintains its integrity against internal threats such as crime and ethnic dissent, while forging ahead with economic modernisation.

The interrelationship, sequencing and pace of marketisation and democratisation

Russia's *kamikadze* reformers and the importance of rapid reform

The young Atlanticist reformers in Yeltsin's government such as Igor Gaidar and Anatoly Chubais called themselves *kamikadzes* (kamikazes) to capture the image of their do or die approach to economic reform. Their rhetoric is curiously reminiscent of soviet maximalist, military rhetoric such as 'storming the steel front'. The *kamikadzes* shared their soviet predecessors' belief in the absolute correctness of what they were doing, believing that there was no alternative to shock therapy. Curiously, they also shared the soviet belief in the primacy of economic matters, namely that if they got the economy right then this would have beneficial political and social consequences. They believed that economic reform had to be accomplished as quickly as possible for three main reasons. Firstly, this would break the CPSU's power base in the state owned and run economy. Secondly, the *kamikadzes* feared that the inevitable dislocation generated by economic reform, if prolonged, could lead to social revolt and the danger of a communist party restoration to power. Thirdly, the privatisation of state assets was also supposed to provide the new economic and political system with popular authority and legitimacy. All Russians were issued with vouchers (see Chapter 11) in order to give them the opportunity literally to buy a stake in the new Russian economy. Unfortunately this last reform did not have its intended consequences and the majority of Russians have not been transformed into share-holders.

The Washington consensus: marketisation and/or democracy?

The western bodies involved in Russia's reforms – the IMF, the World Bank, the Organisation for Economic Cooperation and Development (OECD) and the G7 countries – were in favour of the twin goals of liberal democracy and capitalism, but they did not make the receipt of economic aid conditional upon democratisation. In contrast the European Bank for Reconstruction and Development (EBRD), which was set up in the wake of the 1989 revolutions in East-Central Europe, makes a clear commitment to such conditionality. EBRD's 1990 Articles of Agreement state: 'In contributing to economic progress and reconstruction, the purpose of the Bank shall be to foster the transition towards open, market-oriented economies and to promote private and entrepreneurial initiative in central and eastern European countries committed to and applying the principles of multiparty democracy, pluralism and market economics' (Ascherson, 1992: 25). Unfortunately, under its first chair, Jacques Attali, EBRD was slow to disburse funds to former communist countries but quick to spend lavishly on its own London headquarters. It has been suggested that Attali also fell out of favour because he advocated 'a more state capitalist, planned form of reconstruction in the east', in contrast to the neoliberal approach of the Washington consensus (Gill, 1997: 155). Attali was replaced by a former managing director of the IMF, Jacques de la Rosière. In 1996 Alexander Korzhakov, a long-time Yeltsin ally and then still the head of his bodyguards, said that Yeltsin should cancel the scheduled presidential elections as it seemed likely that the KPRF leader Gennady Zyuganov would win. The IMF provided the Russian government, which effectively meant Yeltsin, with funds in the run up to the election. Yeltsin was able to use these funds to promote projects in Russia's regions that helped to swing enough voters his way. The democratic procedure of an election did take place, and the West and Russia's new business elite had their preferred candidate back in office.

Democracy without democrats?

Was Russia ready for democratisation?

Western democracies are the products of long and gradual evolution. Imperial Russia and the USSR were not democracies and soviet socialism was finally destroyed when sections of the CPSU leadership, including Yeltsin, decided it was beyond reform. The Russian people were not mere bystanders in this, but until Reconstruction they had not been able to set up the political parties, interest groups, charitable organisations, free trade unions and religious groups that are the basis of a civil society. The Russian people were also unfamiliar with the culture of gradualism and compromise that enable democracies to work. Since the 1980s when Gorbachev first started democratisation, there have been fears in Russia that once the Russian-Soviet authoritarian state was weakened by democratisation there would be anarchy or chaos (*khaos*). Democracy requires freedom, but freedom requires a sense of responsibility and the rule of law to protect the rights and freedoms of others; their absence risks what Russians call behaviour *bespredel*, literally 'without limits'. Democracy therefore concerns the relations between citizens and between citizens and the state. Democracy is not only about creating new institutions and procedures, it is also about how people think and particularly whether they believe democracy has a substantive value, whether it is literally a 'good thing' in bad as well as good times. Despite mounting problems of economic and personal security, Russians have remained acquiescent. Remarkably between 60 and 70 per cent of the population still bothers to vote in elections. There have been strikes and demonstrations but these have been peaceful and have not presented a threat to the security of the state. The main danger to Russia comes not from ordinary Russians but from the crime and criminality that stretch to the heart of the Russian state; it is here and amongst Russia's criminals that one finds activities *bespredel*.

Affluence and economic reform as prerequisites of democracy

As we have seen, a feature of the Asian state capitalist model is that economic modernisation took precedence over democratisation. Even Japan, which had a liberal democratic constitution imposed upon it following defeat in World War II, operated more as a one-party state than as a liberal democracy until the 1970s. South Korea and Singapore are still not democracies, but have in the course of their economic modernisation developed well-educated populations which now include vocal pro-democracy campaigners. The American political scientist Professor Samuel Huntington, while not advocating dictatorship, argues that economic modernisation promotes the changes in social structure, specifically urbanisation and the development of a bourgeoisie, which in turn create the social base necessary to sustain democracy. He also argues that democracy is best built in conditions of affluence, with poverty as its main enemy (Huntington, 1993: 22). The logic of Huntington's analysis and the Asian Tiger experience is that democratisation should only be initiated once it has the firm social base of a bourgeoisie or a middle class.

The middle class and the social basis of democracy

The *kamikadzes* believed that once Russia had private property a new class of private property owners would be the foundation of a law-abiding, civil society. The Russian sociologist Tatyana Zaslavskaya (Zaslavskaia, 1997: 17) argues that social stability is promoted by the existence of an educated and comfortably off middle class. The USSR did have a middle class of well-educated, largely urban professionals and skilled workers, who tended to favour the reform and even the abandonment of soviet socialism. They could have provided, and might still provide, a solid basis for post-communist developments. The problem is that economic shock therapy largely destroyed this class economically. Their savings in government banks were wiped out by currency reform and hyperinflation, and they are now suffering unemployment or low or unpaid salaries. According to Zaslavskaya the Russian middle class constitutes about 25 per cent of the population (compared to 60–80 per cent in most western countries) and comprises the middle level of the bureaucracy, highly educated and well-paid professionals whose skills are currently in demand, and small and medium size business entrepreneurs (*ibid.*). If the Russian economy begins to expand then the former soviet middle class, with their education and skills, may metamorphose into an expanding post-communist middle class, so providing the new Russian state with a firm social base (see Chapter 8).

Does Russia need transitional authoritarianism?

Russia began democratisation and marketisation under Gorbachev, but even then the interrelationship between the two was hotly contested. The problem is that capitalism does not need democracy, it needs markets and stability. Democracy is not necessarily conducive to capitalism, particularly at a time of heightened expectations but falling standards of living. Russian democrats and capitalists (who are not necessarily the same people) fear that even the legendary patience of the Russian people will run out and that they will vote the Red-Browns into government. The political analyst Andranik Migranyan (1990) argues that Russia needs a form of transitional authoritarianism in order to give the new leadership the time and the powers to push through the reforms that Russia so urgently needs, without the disruption of popular opposition. Once the reforms have been accomplished and the Russian people are reaping their benefits, then authoritarianism can safely be abandoned in favour of democratisation.

Russian public opinion survey data does not support the idea that the Russians are looking for a strong leader like Chile's General Pinochet to push through market reforms with what is euphemistically called a 'firm hand', that is with the suppression of democracy. The public opinion analyst Igor Kliamkin, while equally sceptical about the prospects for both Russian parliamentarism and authoritarianism, specifically takes issue with Andranik Migranyan's advocacy of a transitional authoritarianism. Kliamkin acknowledges that the prerequisites for successful democratisation, such as the existence of private property and a civil society, are not firmly entrenched in Russia (see Box 1.2). At the same time, however, his findings raise doubts about the readiness of the people and influential elite groups such as economic managers, administrators and even the armed forces to push through reform with a 'firm hand'. In a nationwide survey conducted in August–September 1993, respondents were asked to choose the political figures closest to their ideal. Pinochet came second to last with only 1 per cent of the votes, pipped

BOX 1.2

Authoritarianism defined

In the modern understanding of the term, an authoritarian regime is an agreement among influential groups that control the economy and the 'structures of power' to curtail or to restrict political freedoms in order to close the legal channels through which social discontent can be manifested and to break, if necessary with force, the resistance of that segment of the population that prefers the ideal of just distribution to the ideal of economic freedom and efficiency.

Source: I.M. Kliamkin (1994) 'What Kind of Authoritarian Regime Is Possible In Russia Today?', *Russian Politics and Law* 32 (6) November–December, 37. Igor Kliamkin is the director of the Analytical Centre of the Independent Public Opinion Research Foundation.

for last place by Saddam Hussein of Iraq. In the two top spots, separated from the others by a wide margin, were Yury Andropov and Margaret Thatcher. Kliamkin interprets these results as evidence that Russia was ready for a strong leader but that 'It is wavering between the democratic authoritarianism of the "Iron Lady", who improved British capitalism, and the authoritarianism – not at all democratic, but not dictatorial in the Stalin style either – of one of the last Communist general secretaries, who tried to use administrative measures to improve Brezhnev's "developed socialism"' (Kliamkin, 1993: 4).

Kliamkin also rejects the interpretation of the findings that the majority of Russians supported the imposition of the state of emergency in 1993 as evidence that they would support a 'firm hand'. Kliamkin argues that 'Most of the supporters of a "firm hand" in today's Russia envisage it not as a political dictatorship to ensure economic freedom but as something quite different – as authoritarian regulation of the economy and protection of the individual from arbitrariness and lawlessness while preserving political freedoms' (Kliamkin, 1994: 39). Russians do not want a dictatorship, and they do not yearn for a strong state for its own sake. What they want is an effective state that is able to provide stability and law and order.

Democratisation to build consensus, authority and legitimacy

In 1990 the Hungarian economist Janos Kornai (later a colleague of Jeffrey Sachs) stressed the importance of simultaneous democratisation and marketisation, in order to break the communist bureaucratic monopolies and to develop the public support and consensus necessary to see a country through the disruption of economic reform (Kornai, 1990). Kornai rejects the idea that democratisation presents a threat to economic reform through political elites being thrown off course by a discontented electorate. For Kornai democratisation is a vital adjunct to economic reform as it promotes the further development of a civil society, which in turn strengthens a sense of personal responsibility amongst citizens, enhances respect for the authority and legitimacy of the government and laws, and promotes social and political stability. All these factors are vital to the operation of a capitalist economy.

Arguments in favour of a transitional authoritarianism are part of an elitist analysis that sees democracies, especially new democracies, as in danger of 'rotting' from the bottom up. This analysis holds that the people do not understand what is required, that they will be swayed by demagogues, that the elite is rational and disinterested and able to elaborate a coherent and effective reform programme in the interests of all, and that it should not be subjected to popular forces that might drag it off course. The argument that democratisation should be delayed until after economic reform is based on the dubious assumption that an elite is able to identify the national interest and to push it forward. The Russians have rid themselves of the CPSU, a self-appointed elite whose ideology of Marxism–Leninism was claimed to enable the party to identify what was best for the country, but which had such disastrous consequences. Without being subject to democratic controls, no matter how flawed and frustrating they may be, there is no guarantee that a new elite would be any more successful in defining the national interest or interests. Equally without democratic accountability there is nothing to stop the new elite from merely pursuing its own sectional interests in the name of the national interest. The suppression of democracy would not necessarily promote national economic development but it would enable the suppression of any popular objections to the excesses of what Russians call their 'wild capitalism'.

Democracy, crime and corruption

In the long term, democratisation by promoting competition, transparency and accountability should work against the corruption and crime that are plaguing Russia (see Box 1.3). Democratisation, however, also provides greater opportunities for corruption. In Russia today political parties are still poorly developed institutions, often lacking in organisation and funds. At the same time Russia's central and local governments are currently privatising Russia's state assets including industrial enterprises, raw materials and housing. The combination of these two factors has generated tremendous criminal interest in Russia's democratic institutions. In 1997 Mikhail Manevich, the head of St Petersburg's City Property Committee, was assassinated, after attacking insider deals in the privatisation of the city's property. The December 1998 elections to the St Petersburg City Legislative Assembly also demonstrate the interconnection of democratisation and crime. Political parties backed by criminals were openly buying votes, particularly from older voters who have been especially hard hit by the economic reforms. Galina Starovoitova, a co-chair of the reformist Democratic Russia party, was murdered on 20 November

---

BOX 1.3

Democracy and corruption

Democratic systems also provide incentives and opportunities for corrupt behaviour, notably the enormous cost of mounting elections campaigns, the capture of political parties by economic elites, the politicization of the state apparatus by elected officials and the desire of the latter to compensate for political uncertainty by building up a capital stake through corruption ... these phenomena are especially strong in fledgling democracies where a procedural transition has not been accompanied and underpinned by a spread of 'real' or substantive democracy.

Source: Barbara Harriss-White and Gordon White (1996) 'Corruption, Liberalization and Democracy', *IDS* 27 (2) April, 3.

1998 after she threatened to expose the criminal gangs who were trying to take over the running of St Petersburg. An honest and outspoken democrat, Starovoitova's murder sent shock waves throughout Russia. One year after Starovoitova's murder no one had been charged, despite the fact that the Federal Security Bureau (FSB) had questioned 700 people and arrested 18. Her aide Ruslan Linkov, who was also gravely wounded in the attack, stated: 'I believe the people who ordered the killing were extremely powerful, well-connected among the police and the FSB – they know how to put pressure on people to ensure the case is not resolved' (*The Guardian*, 20 November 1999: 22). Criminalisation has subverted the very state institutions that are charged with providing the law and order that democracy needs. Russia does however still have democrats like the late Starovoitova, who are prepared to challenge the subversion of Russian democracy and the criminalisation of the Russian state. As recent scandals in Western Europe have shown, even established democracies are not immune to corruption.

Marketisation without capitalists?

Nomenklatura capitalists

Private economic activity was illegal in the USSR until Gorbachev legalised cooperatives and the leasing of land (see Chapter 2). This, combined with the value of savings being wiped out by currency reforms, meant that there were not many Russian citizens with money to set up new businesses in the early 1990s. Despite the issuing of privatisation vouchers to the Russian people (see Chapter 11), the main beneficiaries of the privatisation of state assets were the former soviet elite, the *nomenklatura*. Membership of the *nomenklatura* was by invitation only and was a prerequisite for the country's top jobs. The *nomenklatura* were well-placed to take advantage of Russia's privatisation process. They had money, know-how and contacts, not to mention control over the privatisation process itself. The directors of state economic enterprises also used Gorbachev's reforms to set up their own businesses. Typically they would set up a cooperative within and parasitical upon their state enterprise, and then channel the enterprise's raw materials and goods through the cooperative to make profits for themselves. The directors then had the finance to buy their workers' vouchers during privatisation and so became the private owners of an enterprise they had formerly managed for the state. Some directors simply took advantage of the chaos of the time to seize state assets. The result is that many newly privatised enterprises are owned by individual members or partnerships of former *nomenklatura* members, using the money and assets they amassed during the soviet era.

In the aftermath of the failed August 1991 coup, a senior CPSU official, Nikolai Kruchina, died in a mysterious fall from his balcony. The KGB were quick to say it was suicide, but the real reason for Kruchina's death undoubtedly lay in his responsibility for CPSU finances. Through its control of the soviet state's assets the CPSU had become extremely rich, 'owning' property, foreign investments and bank deposits. The true extent of what has been called the 'party gold' will probably never be known. Kruchina was killed because he knew too much. The existence of this party gold meant that elements within the former *nomenklatura* were in a financial position to take advantage of the privatisation of state assets. Privatisation provided the *nomenklatura* with a fabulous opportunity to get rich quickly, whether they had access to party gold or not. Through privatisation about one-third of Russia's GDP passed into the hands of members of the *nomenklatura*. So well have they done that Igor Gaidar, the architect of Russia's radical economic reform, refers to '*nomenklatura* privatisation', '*nomenklatura* capitalism' and even somewhat strangely to '*nomenklatura* democracy' (Gaidar, 1995: 104). The December 1992 appointment of Viktor Chernomyrdin as Gaidar's replacement as prime minister marked the arrival of the *nomenklatura* in the Kremlin. Chernomyrdin had made his fortune from his post as minister of the gas industry (Gazprom) which provided him with control of a (perfectly legal) giant monopoly. In the period before price liberalisation *nomenklatura* capitalists were able to buy raw materials such as oil, gas and metals from the state at prices typically less than 1 per cent of the world price, which they then sold on the world market becoming instant billionaires.

The Komsomolers

The Komsomol was the CPSU's youth organisation whose members ranged from teenagers to people in their early thirties. Membership of the Komsomol was a stepping stone to party membership and as such was an important testing ground for the future soviet elite. During Reconstruction some Komsomol members were encouraged to engage in the newly legalised forms of economic activity. The CPSU leadership wanted to develop a cohort of young people with entrepreneurial skills, particularly in the area of new technologies, and to establish small and medium size businesses. In 1987–8 Youth Centres for Scientific and Technical Creation (NTTM) were created under the aegis of Moscow district party committees. The NTTMs were provided with start-up funds of 50 000 roubles, granted a five-year tax holiday and told to make a profit. The NTTMs provided the vehicle for some Komsomol members to become members of the new post-communist financial and political elite. One such NTTM was the Centre for Inter-branch Scientific and Technical Programmes, known by its Russian acronym Menatap, which traded in computers and software. Menatap is now one of Russia's major financial-industrial groups. Crucially NTTMs were the only organisations apart from the state itself which could legally engage in foreign trade. Oneximbank (the United Export-Import Bank) was founded after 1991 by Komsomolers who had got an early start in the highly lucrative import trade. Konstantin Borovoi used NTTM profits to set up his own cooperative in 1987, then went on to set up the Russian Commodities and Raw Materials Exchange (RTSB), one of Russia's first and largest commodities exchanges. Sergei Kiriyenko, who was briefly prime minister from March to August 1998, also began his political and economic career in the Komsomol and the NTTMs (Coulloudon, 1998: 539–40).

The New Russians

The rich in post-communist Russia are known as the New Russians. They include Komsomolers, *nomenklatura* capitalists and others who took advantage of the new opportunities in the late 1980s and early 1990s to get rich. Olga Kryshtanovskaya of the Russian Academy of Sciences (RAN) has found that the New Russians are differentiated by their past experience, educational and cultural levels, lifestyles and political aspirations. There are the not-so-well-educated low-level entrepreneurs, who are inclined to be involved in rather shady or risky business ventures. These include the shuttlers (*chelnoki*) who travel to and from neighbouring countries, bringing back goods for sale in the markets, pavement kiosks or small shops of Russia. According to Kryshtanovskaya these New Russians like to flaunt their wealth and indulge in lavish displays of conspicuous consumption, but they are not interested in politics. There is also a business elite of respectable, highly educated businessmen who hold high-level positions in legal commercial structures. They do not flaunt their wealth but like to live well (Kryshtanovskaia, 1994, 1995). Members of the business elite, which includes the *nomenklatura* capitalists and former Komsomolers, are also marked, according to Kryshtanovskaya, by their efforts to influence the political process.

The oligarchs, clans and state capitalism

The clan system

The *nomenklatura* system encapsulated the patron–client relationships, institutional or corporate pluralism (see Chapter 2), nepotism, clan politics and informal networks that were vital to the functioning of the soviet system. As president and parliament battled for domination of the RF's government and politics in the 1990s, these networks and clans adapted to the new political and economic realities. The clans are not typically family members related to each other by blood or marriage; rather a clan is composed of people sharing a common economic interest. Through their representatives within the government and/or the presidential administration, the clans compete for influence, power, resources and money. There are industry-based clans: for example, Viktor Chernomyrdin is the head of the (oil and gas) Energy clan and Oleg Soskovets heads the Military-Industrial Complex clan. Until 1996 when he was sacked as deputy prime minister, Soskovets was the third ranking figure in the government hierarchy after President Boris Yeltsin and Prime Minister Viktor Chernomyrdin. The government also had a Security clan which is also known as the War Party due to its support for the Chechen war (1994–6). The Security clan included Alexander Korzhakov, the head of Yeltsin's presidential guard of 17 000 men until he was sacked in 1996; Mikhail Barsukov, the head of the FSB; Defence Minister Pavel Grachev; and Oleg Soskovets, whose military-industrial interests chimed with the security-minded Korzhakov, Barsukov and Grachev. There is also a Moscow clan based on shared banking and property interests, and headed by Moscow's mayor, Yury Luzhkov. In addition there are also sub-clans which represent individual regions or less powerful economic interests such as agriculture.

The clan system (although not necessarily the same clans) operates at all levels of the Russian state and in all regions of Russia. In Russia's super-presidential system these groups focus their energies on gaining access to the president's court and in the republics and regions to the presidents and governors. They are quite ruthless and will use compromising materials, blackmail, bribes, threats and even assassination to get their way. They are not committed democrats but see democratic procedures such as elections as useful weapons in their power struggles. The Russian government is very sensitive to this analysis of Russian politics. In November 1995 Thomas Graham, a first secretary at the American Embassy in Moscow, wrote an article for the newspaper *Nezavisimaia gazeta* about the 'warring clans' at the top level of government. The USA received an official protest from the Russian government accusing Graham of violating diplomatic protocol. Graham stated that 'these clans contain few staunch supporters of democracy, and none of these clans are devoted to democratic ideals, despite public assurances to the contrary' (cited in *Izvestia*, 29 November 1995: 3). Further evidence of the clan wars came in 1997 when Chernomyrdin's Energy clan came into conflict with the Western clan headed by Anatoly Chubais and Yeltsin's daughter Tatyana Dyachenko. The conflict was provoked by a new round of privatisations of state oil assets. The competing clans wanted the power to direct these privatisations to their advantage. The economic stakes in the power struggle were enormous, with some of Russia's richest assets literally up for grabs. Korzhakov, who hated both the Western and the Energy clans, claimed to have compromising materials allegedly showing that Chernomyrdin had millions of dollars in Swiss bank accounts. In January 1997 Chubais was accused of tax evasion. During the final years of Yeltsin's presidency the use of such compromising materials (*kompromat*) increasingly became a weapon in these inter-clan battles at the highest levels (see also Chapter 4).

The Russian Oligarchs

(see Box 1.4)

Tremendous economic and political power in Russia has passed to a group of men known as the oligarchs. The leading oligarchs are Vagit Alekperov, Boris Berezovsky, Mikhail Friedman, Vladimir Gusinsky, Mikhail Khodorkovsky, Vladimir Potanin, Alexander Smolensky and Rem Vyakhirev. In the early 1990s the oligarchs established vast financial, industrial and media empires which now control over 50 per cent of the Russian economy in GDP terms. The oligarchs developed a symbiotic relationship with the Yeltsin leadership and particularly close ties to Anatoly Chubais, who in 1992 was a deputy prime minister and the head of the State Property Committee responsible for privatisation. Fearing that a victory by the KPRF leader Gennady Zyuganov would put an end to their power and riches, the oligarchs financed and (with Anatoly Chubais) largely ran Yeltsin's 1996 re-election campaign. During the campaign Chubais's Centre for the Defence of Private Property received an unsecured, no-interest loan of $14 billion from Alexander Smolensky's Stolichny Bank (later SBS-Agro) to help promote a civil society, which in reality meant to help get Yeltsin re-elected. Following Yeltsin's re-election, the oligarchs were repaid for their support with broadcasting and commercial licences and through a further round of privatisation of some of Russia's most valuable assets: energy, transportation and communications. Chubais and four associates also received an extremely generous $450 000 advance for a book on privatisation from a publishing house controlled by Vladimir Potanin's Oneximbank. At the time Oneximbank was a bidder for Sviazinvest, a telecommunications company. All these new privatisations were conducted at absurdly low fixed prices, depriving the government of both assets and funds that would have helped it to weather the summer 1998 economic crash. After Yeltsin's election Anatoly Chubais became the head of the presidential administration, which was an important position particularly given Yeltsin's

BOX 1.4

The oligarchs: Russia's leading financial-industrial groups

Group	Oligarch	Financial interests	Industrial interests	Media interests
Lukoil	Vagit Alekperov	Bank Imperial (with Gazprom)	Lukoil (oil)	*Izvestia* newspaper (with Oneximbank)
Berezovsky	Boris Berezovsky	Obyedinenny Bank Logovaz (a car dealership)	Sibneft (oil) merged with Yukos in 1998 to form Yuksi	ORT television company (with others) *Nezavisimaia gazeta* newspaper *Ogonyok* magazine
Alfa	Mikhail Friedman	Alpha Bank	Tyumen oil and various trading firms	
Most	Vladimir Gusinsky	Most-bank		*Sevodnia* newspaper *Itogi* magazine NTV television company (with Gazprom)
Menatap	Mikhail Khodorkovsky	Bank Menatap	Yukos merged in 1998 with Sibneft to form Yuksi	Independent Media news group
Oneximbank	Vladimir Potanin	Oneximbank	Sidanco (oil) Norilsk (metals) Sviazinvest (telecom)	*Komsomolskaia Pravda* newspaper *Russkii Telegraf* newspaper *Izvestia* newspaper (with Lukoil)
SBS-Agro	Alexander Smolensky	SBS-Agro Bank		*Kommersant* newspaper
Gazprom	Rem Vyakhirev	Bank Imperial Gazprom Bank National Reserve Bank	Gazprom (oil and gas)	*Trud* newspaper *Rabochaia Tribuna* newspaper NTV television company (with Most)

Sources: The Economist, 4 April 1998, 40; *The European*, 25–31 May 1998, 1.

declining health and withdrawal from day-to-day affairs. Chubais championed the appointment of the leading oligarch Boris Berezovsky as a deputy minister for security. Berezovsky is a mathemetician and started his economic empire with the Logovaz car business, and did not have any particular skills for his new post. However, Berezovsky's oil interests meant that he was keenly concerned with the impact of the Chechen war on Russia's oil industry and his new government post gave him access to policy-making on Chechnia.

State corporatism

Russia is developing a system of state corporatism, in which various groupings (primarily the *nomenklatura* capitalists, the clans and the oligarchs) are competing for both economic and political power. The manner in which privatisation was conducted effectively legalised insider trading and led to the creation of private monopolies. It also helped to perpetuate and promote the importance of contacts and networks, particularly those providing linkages between business and the state. Russia has developed a business structure of large financial-industrial groups (FIGs) similar to those in nineteenth-century Tsarist Russia, and to the contemporary Japanese *keiretsu* and South Korean *chaebols*. In Russia today these FIGs literally prosper through their proximity to the state. For example, Russia's banks were often set up with the support of the state and its funds. Banks, particularly those that supported Yeltsin in his 1993 conflict with the parliament, were given the right to handle government funds and to represent the state in export dealings, and had the help of state bodies in obtaining export licences. In 1993, for example, Vladimir Potanin's Oneximbank was commissioned by the government to administer federal budgets. In 1995 Oneximbank became the bank of the State Committees for Bankruptcy and Privatisation and then took on the management of funds allocated for the rebuilding of Chechnia (Coulloudon, 1998: 539). Banks have also made even greater profits out of their handling of state funds by delaying the transfer or payment of state obligations such as salaries or pensions, and then using these funds to provide highly lucrative short-term credits (see Box 1.5).

BOX 1.5

The corporate state defined

A state in which government represents and is answerable, not to individual citizens, but to the various corporations of which the individual is a functional part.

Source: The Oxford Dictionary of Politics (1996) Oxford: Oxford University Press.

The legacy of the Imperial Russian and Soviet states

Imperial Russia and the USSR: the people and the state

Before the 1917 Bolshevik Revolution Russians lived in an autocracy and after the Revolution in a one-party authoritarian state. Historically the Russians have had a rather ambivalent attitude towards the state, seeing a strong state simultaneously as the best guarantor of their security but also as something beyond themselves, to which they held no duty of obedience. The state was protector but also oppressor. The Imperial and the Soviet states could both be completely arbitrary in their dealings with the people. There was no rule of law and no regard for individual rights. Under Stalin, whole categories of peoples – whether they were the so-called rich peasants, the *kulaks*, or nationalities accused of collaboration with the Nazis – could be crushed, physically annihilated or exiled. Certainly, by the 1950s the application of law was largely routinised but the judiciary was not autonomous and when the state or the CPSU decided to intervene in legal procedures, even when this intervention contravened soviet law, the individual had no recourse. The result was that the state commanded fear rather more than respect. The people were used to falling back on their families, friends, networks and communities (or in the case of criminals, their gangs) for support and protection against the state. To this day, this phenomenon encourages people to see the state and its laws as something alien, to be got around and subverted.

From patrimonialism, *kormlenie* to corruption

In both Tsarist Russia and the USSR political power was closely linked to property ownership (see Box 1.6). Imperial Russia was a patrimonial regime, 'where the rights of sovereignty and those of ownership blend to the point of becoming indistinguishable, and political power is exercised in the same manner as economic power' (Pipes, 1977: 22–3). The tsar rewarded nobles with economic privileges in return for their service and support. In 1722 Peter the Great established a Table of Ranks which divided state service into armed services, civil service and court. The CPSU leaders of the soviet state also disposed of political and economic power and authority, and the CPSU also had its own rough equivalent of a table of ranks in the *nomenklatura* system. The Imperial Russian nobility were in effect the elite of the civil service and like all the other civil servants they indulged in *kormlenie* or feeding. They performed their service to the tsar such as tax collection but kept a portion back for themselves. This approach to public service did not disappear with the Bolshevik Revolution. Under Gorbachev, for example, anyone wishing to set up a cooperative or lease land had to pay bribes in order to get the necessary permissions and licences.

BOX 1.6

The patrimonial state defined

In a patrimonial state there exist no formal limitations on political authority, nor rule of law, nor individual liberties. There can be, however, a highly efficient system of political, economic and military organization derived from the fact that the same men – kings or bureaucracies – dispose of the country's entire human and material resources.

Source: Richard Pipes (1977) *Russia under the Old Regime*, Harmondsworth: Penguin, 23. Richard Pipes is a professor of Russian history and the director of the Russian Research Center at Harvard University.

Kormlenie – or, less euphemistically, corruption, the use of public resources for personal gain – also characterises post-communist Russia. The privatisation process provides highly lucrative opportunities for corruption. These include activities that in the West would be classified as a conflict of interest or insider trading but which are not yet covered in Russian law. They also include the illegal use of state funds or the preferential granting of licences in return for a personal reward. The Norilsk loans-for-shares scandal uncovered by the Russian Audit Chamber in 1997 is just one example of such activities. Norilsk is one of Russia's major hard-currency earners, producing 90 per cent of Russia's nickel, 80 per cent of its cobalt and all of its platinum. In 1995 Vladimir Potanin's Oneximbank acquired a 38 per cent share in Norilsk Nikel for a $170 million loan to the government, and in 1997 Oneximbank lent the government a further $250 million. Once the government paid back the loan it had in effect sold a major state asset for only $80 million. The scandal was heightened by the fact that Norilsk workers were not being paid. Potanin is an ally of Anatoly Chubais. In Russia there is an expectation that individuals will use state service for personal gain. Yury Luzhkov has become rich through his business dealings while mayor of Moscow and yet he remains popular with the Muscovite electorate. He was re-elected on 16 June 1996 with a staggering 91.5 per cent of the vote. The explanation is that he looks after his electorate, their salaries and pensions are paid, and Moscow is becoming a prosperous city, so whatever else he might be doing is irrelevant.

Corruption pervades all levels of the Russian state, although it is difficult to gauge the scale of such activities as they are obviously neither recorded nor publicised. The state's and therefore politicians' and civil servants' role in privatisation or tax collection provides ample opportunities for corrupt behaviour. Customs officials do deals with criminals gangs, receiving a cut of the profits in return for not collecting import taxes. The FSB (successor organisation to the KGB), the police and members of the armed forces are all known to sell security services. These services range from performing their normal state function for private reward, to using their capacities (know-how, contacts, weapons) as state functionaries for illegal purposes. The lack of an adequate legal framework, low wages, a loss of mission on the part of the security forces, the state's inability to provide security and the tradition of using positions for personal power have all contributed to this phenomenon.

The Great Criminal Revolution

The greatest threat to Russia's reforms comes not from the Russian people suffering from 'transition fatigue' and voting in the Red-Browns, but from crime and corruption. Capitalist markets and democracy both need the rule of law, and law and order. The soviet legacy and the post-communist reforms have created the conditions in which crime and corruption flourish. The criminal gangs of Imperial Russia survived the Bolshevik Revolution and displayed their contempt for the soviet state by refusing state obligations such as military service. The criminals instead had their own codes and called themselves 'thieves in the law' (*vory v zakone*) and talked of the thieves' world or society (*vorovskoi mir*). After the death of Stalin (1953), but more decisively under Leonid Brezhnev's leadership (1964–82), there was a growth in both criminal organisations and their interconnection with the *nomenklatura*. Criminals and members of the *nomenklatura* used the shortages that were endemic to the soviet economy to make money. The structure and the activities of the *nomenklatura* led the soviet investigative journalist Arkady Vaksberg (1991) to describe the soviet regime itself as a mafia. The result is that Russia is experiencing what Stanislav Govorukhin, a cinema director and a deputy to the State Duma, has called 'the Great Criminal Revolution' (see Box 1.7). General lawlessness, organised crime, corruption and the creeping criminalisation of the Russian state itself are all part of this revolution. It was extremely difficult for the new Russian state to maintain the rule of law and law and order, as the country lacked appropriate laws to enforce. The result

---

BOX 1.7

The Great Criminal Revolution

The new power which established itself in the Kremlin after December 91, committed the inconceivable – it changed the country into a camp of criminals. With criminal laws, with criminal morality ... In the guise of a class of property owners it created a class of thieves.

Source: Stanislav Govorukhin (1993) *Velikaia kriminal'naia revoliutsiia* (The Great Criminal Revolution), Moscow: Andreevskii flag, 35. Govorukhin is a Russian nationalist deputy and film director. His film *The Russia We Lost* showed an idealised picture of Tsarist Russia. He also claims that the Communist terror in the 1930s damaged Russia's gene pool leading to the survival of the least fit. His film *The Great Criminal Revolution* was highly critical of Yeltsin and the storming of the Russian parliament building in 1993.

was that Russian privatisation has taken place in an environment in which there is no clear distinction between legal and illegal activities and so a generally lawless atmosphere. Little wonder then that most Russians use the western word businessman (*biznesmen*) ironically, to mean a criminal. The lack of a legal framework facilitated the criminalisation of economic activities and has also frustrated the development of a market economy. The lack of anti-monopoly legislation, for example, meant that privatisation resulted in the transformation of gigantic state monopolies into private monopolies and the creation of a small group of super-rich businessmen.

The legacy of the over-regulated, soft state

Soviet socialist states have been described by George Schöpflin (1994: 133) as 'over regulated' and 'soft'. These terms provide a timely antidote to the image of the all-powerful soviet state. Firstly, soviet states were over-regulated because the centre issued 'streams of directives, decrees, and other forms of instruction' (*ibid.*). As it was humanly impossible to comply with all the directives, regulation and legality became devalued. Party-state officials became selective about what instructions they implemented and adept at filing reports that made it appear as if they were doing what was required. The capricious nature of Yeltsin's decision-making and his penchant for rule by decree in the face of opposition from the parliament, the form of super-presidentialism that emerged in 1993 (see Chapter 4) and the increasing assertiveness of local elites have all reinforced this soviet tradition of ignoring central directives. The soviet state was also 'soft' as 'the state administration under communism lacked the will and the means to enforce the rules it issued, both politically and practically, thereby encouraging corruption, a lackadaisical approach to regulation, and disregard for the legal sphere' (*ibid.*). Again there are continuities in the RF, most obviously in the sphere of tax collection. These problems began with a long delay in creating new tax codes that reflected the changing nature of the Russian economy. Tax codes were so complicated that it was impossible to abide by them and make a profit. Not surprisingly a 1997 survey found that 61 per cent of Russians believed that tax evasion was not a crime (Anichkina, 1997: 3). In the mid-1990s Russia had a television advertisement to encourage people to pay their taxes which asked, 'Do you want to live a moral life in a decent country where children are properly educated and your grandparents get their pensions on time? Then why don't you pay your taxes?' In 1997 due to the continuing failure to collect taxes there was a dramatic change in tone: 'The tax police have guns and they know how to use them', the new advertisement warned. Russian tax inspectors had also acquired a new Tax Police, a special 500-man SWAT (special weapons and tactics) team armed with AK-47 assault weapons, sniper rifles, tear gas, grenades, shotguns, bullet-proof body armour, heavy-duty saws and mountaineering equipment (*ibid.*). While it may seem counter-intuitive to argue that such paramilitary policing is evidence of a soft state, the SWAT team's existence illustrates the state's inability to frame appropriate legislation and to establish a routinised compliance with laws, decrees and instructions.

The importance of building a strong but democratic state

In the early 1990s, when Russia began its transition from soviet socialism to capitalism and democracy, the Washington consensus held that 'the greatest threat to freedom and capitalism ... came from totalitarian states' (Gray, 1999: 200). The soviet state looked all-powerful: it had nuclear weapons, a large standing army, well-developed coercive institutions including the militia (police) and secret police, and a controlled judiciary. Until Gorbachev introduced reforms to the representative institutions (parliament and soviets) and the electoral system in the late 1980s, elections had always been stage-managed and the parliament always voted unanimously for what the party-state elite put before it. However, the strength of the soviet state lay more in its ability to silence opposition than its ability to elaborate and implement an effective reform programme. Behind this façade of power the soviet state was fundamentally soft or weak. The new Russian state still has a large nuclear arsenal at its disposal but this does not help it to implement its new legislation, collect taxes or combat crime and corruption. The prospects for Russian economic development and the security and well-being of the Russian people are threatened by the weakness of the Russian state. Russian state institutions remain heavily bureaucratic and their authority is poorly defined. The new Russian state, like its soviet predecessor, functions unevenly, both spatially and territorially (Schöpflin, 1994: 133). Russia's federal subjects are differentiated in terms of the revenues they pass to Moscow and the subsidies they receive. The republic of Tatarstan, for example, refuses to allow its military conscripts to serve outside Tatarstan, and the city of Moscow has its own visa system. The creation of a unified, but not centralised, federal state is further complicated by Russia's ethnic divisions (see Chapter 5).

Russia needs a state that is able to maintain law and order and to implement legislation. Attention must be paid to state-building, which inevitably entails strengthening the state. The idea of strengthening the Russian state rings all sorts of alarm bells. The Russians have a tradition of authoritarian and autocratic rulers. The Russians have been an imperial people and so talk of a strong Russian state is potentially alarming to Russia's neighbours and its non-Russian citizens. By the second half of the 1990s the oligarchs already had too much power and to strengthen the state might seem to be strengthening them. A strong state is not necessarily an expansionist or an authoritarian state, however, although the dangers are certainly present. A weak state is not synonymous with democracy but with anarchy and lawlessness. The Russian people need a state that will help to create the conditions in which people can thrive, in which their rights and personal security will be protected.

State-building involves both reforming institutions that still bear a soviet overlay and creating new state institutions (see Part II). The creation of an independent judiciary is a vital component of state-building, for without an independent judiciary there is the danger that a strong state will be an authoritarian state.

Conclusion

Russia's transition to capitalism and democracy has proved a more complicated and prolonged process than was at first anticipated. Russia's difficulties cannot be explained solely in terms of a failure to sequence economic and political reform appropriately, or to create the necessary institutions, procedures and law. The difficulty in identifying appropriate and timely reform measures is complicated by the complex and contradictory forces effecting Russia. These forces have a variety of sources including the communist legacy, Soviet-Russian culture and globalisation. Democratisation is challenged by a strong authoritarian impulse, which may be explained by Russia's lack of democratic experience, outright cultural antipathy towards it and/or a yearning for clear and effective direction during the turmoil of transition. Moves towards the creation of a centralised state are countered by powerful regionalist forces, which may represent a democratic challenge to over-centralisation or the disintegration of the country into mini fiefdoms (see Chapter 5). Globalisation is at once courted to promote modernisation and rejected as destroying Russia's unique identity and culture (see Chapter 3). Given the lack of consensus about the whole goal of transition, the complexity of the process and these contradictory forces, it is little wonder that in the 1990s Russia experienced a decade of turmoil which looks set to continue.

References

Anichkina, Miranda (1997) 'Russian Tax Police Go to Work with AK-47 Rifles', *The European*, 3–4 February, 3
Ascherson, Neal (1992) 'The Bank That Likes to Say "Only on Condition..."', *Independent on Sunday*, 12 July, 25

Coulloudon, Virginie (1998) 'Elite Groups in Russia', *Demokratizatsiya* 6 (3) Summer, 535–549

Gaidar, Igor (1995) *Gosudarstvo i evoliutsiia*, Moscow: Evraziia
Gill, Stephen (ed.) (1997) *Globalization, Democratization and Multilateralism*, Basingstoke: United Nations Press/Macmillan

Gray, John (1999) *False Dawn: The Delusions of Global Capitalism*, London: Granta

Huntington, Samuel P. (1993) 'Democracy's Third Wave', in Larry Diamond and Marc F. Plattner (eds) *The Global Resurgence of Democracy*, Baltimore and London: Johns Hopkins University Press

Kliamkin, Igor (1993) 'Russia Faces a Choice: Thatcher, Pinochet or Andropov?', *Izvestia*, 4 November, 4 (translation available in the *Current Digest of the Post Soviet Press* XLV (45), 19–20)
Kliamkin, I.M. (1994) 'What Kind of Authoritarian Regime is Possible in Russia Today?', *Russian Politics and Law* 32 (6) November–December, 3–41
Kornai, Janos (1990) *The Road to a Free Economy*, New York: W.W. Norton
Kryshtanovskaia, Olga V. (1994) 'Politicheskaia elita i krupnyi kapital uzhe ne mogyt sushestvovat' drug bez druga', *Rossiiskoe Obozrenie* (41) 12 October, 3–4
Kryshtanovskaia, Olga (1995) 'Kto nami pravit?', *Otkrytaia Politika* (1) January, 13–19

Migranyan, Andranik (1990) 'Gorbachev's Leadership: A Soviet View', *Soviet Economy* 6 (2) April–June, 155–159

Pipes, Richard (1977) *Russia under the Old Regime*, Harmondsworth: Penguin

Schöpflin, George (1994) 'Post-communism: Problems of Democratic Construction', *Daedalus* 123 (3) Summer, 127–141
Steele, Jonathan (1994) *Eternal Russia*, London: faber and faber

Vaksberg, A. (1991) *The Soviet Mafia*, London: Weidenfeld and Nicolson (trans: John and Elizabeth Roberts)

Zaslavskaia, Tat'iana I. (1997) 'Social Disequilibrium and the Transitional Society', *Sociological Research* 36 (3) May–June, 6–21

Further reading

Truscott, Peter (1997) *Russia First: Breaking With the West*, London: I.B. Tauris, provides a highly readable and wide-ranging analysis of Russia's identity and state-building

For the economy see:

Gray, John (1999) *False Dawn: The Delusions of Global Capitalism*, London, Granta, and Goldman, Marshall (1994) *Lost Opportunity: Why Economic Reforms in Russian Have Not Worked*, New York: W.W. Norton, for very critical accounts of shock therapy
Johnson, Simon and Kroll, Heidi (1991) 'Managerial Strategies for Spontaneous Privatization', *Soviet Economy* 7 (4), 281–316
Marer, Paul and Zecchini, Salvatore (eds) (1991) *The Transition to a Market Economy*, Paris: OECD, looks at the issues raised by the appropriate sequencing of reform

Skidelsky, Robert (1995) *The World After Communism*, Basingstoke: Macmillan, Chapter 9, provides a useful account of the contrasting approaches to the Russian economy advocated by Jonathan Gray and Jeffrey Sachs

The following articles compare Russia's transitions to the experience of China and the post-authoritarian regimes in Latin America and Eastern Europe:

Croan, Melvin (chair) (1992) 'Is Latin America the Future of Eastern Europe?', *Problems of Communism* 41 (3) May–June, 44–57

Johnson, Juliet (1994) 'Should Russia Adopt the Chinese Model of Economic Reform?', *Communist and Post-Communist Studies* 27 (1), 59–75, provides useful comparison to Communist China which has pursued market reforms while maintaining strict political control

Rosenberg, Tina (1995) 'Overcoming the Legacies of Dictatorship', *Foreign Affairs* 74 (3) May–June, 134–152, is a useful discussion of the differences within and between Latin American and East European authoritarian regimes and how to overcome the legacies

On the interrelationship of economic and political reform see:

McFaul, Michael (1995) 'Why Russia's Politics Matter', *Foreign Affairs* 74 (1) January–February, 87–99

Robinson, Neil (1994) 'From Coup to Coup to . . . ? The Post-Communist Experience in Russia, 1991–1993', *Coexistence* 31 (4), 295–308

Analyses of the conditions necessary for democratisation are provided in:

Bermeo, Nancy (ed.) (1992) *Liberalization and Democratization: Change in the Soviet Union and Eastern Europe*, Baltimore and London: Johns Hopkins University Press

Diamond, Larry and Plattner, Marc F. (eds) (1993) *The Global Resurgence of Democracy*, Baltimore and London: Johns Hopkins University Press

Lipset, Seymour Martin (1959) 'Some Social Prerequisites of Democracy', *American Political Science Review* 53 (1) March, 69–105

Lipset, Seymour Martin (1994) 'The Social Prerequisites of Democracy Revisited', *American Sociological Review* (59), 1–22

Putnam, Robert (1993) *Making Democracy Work*, Princeton: Princeton University Press

On crime and corruption see:

Dempsey, Gary T. (1998) 'Mafia Capitalism or Red Legacy?', *Cato Institute*, 7 January, argues that crime and corruption are part of the soviet legacy; see also an updated version by Lukas, Aaron and Dempsey (2000) 'Mafia Capitalism or Red Legacy in Russia?', *Cato Institute*, 4 March; both are available on the Cato Institute website http://www.cato.org/

Handelman, Stephen (1995) *Comrade Criminal: Russia's New Mafia*, New Haven and London: Yale University Press, presents a comprehensive overview of the problems of crime and corruption and their origins

Holmes, Leslie (1993) *The End of Communist Power*, Cambridge: Polity

Kramer, John (1998) 'The Politics of Corruption', *Current History* 97 (621) October, 329–334, is particularly good on the threat that crime and corruption present to the Russian state

Sherr, James (1995) 'Russia: Geopolitics and Crime', *The World Today* 51 (2) February, 32–36

For further information about the oligarchs and the clans see:

Buzgalin, Aleksandr (1998) 'Russia: Capitalism's "Jurassic Park"', *Prism* 4 (15) July 24, http://www.jamestown.org/

Dinello, Natalia (1998) 'Bankers' Wars in Russia', *CSIS Post-Soviet Prospects* VI (I) February, http://www.csis.org/

Freeland, Chrystia (1997) 'Mercedes Nomenklatura', *Financial Times*, 23 December, 14

Kukolev, Igor V. (1997) 'The Formation of the Business Elite', *Sociological Research* 36 (1) January–February, 23–43

Kukolev, Igor V. (1998) 'The Transformation of Political Elites in Russia', *Sociological Research* 37 (4) July–August, 65–81

Meek, James (1995) 'Moscow Gold', *The Guardian*, 20 September, 12–13

Millar, Peter and Wright, Rupert (1997) 'Boris's Billion Dollar Bankers', *The European*, 25 September–1 October, 8–12

Wolosky, Lee S. (2000) 'Putin's Plutocrat Problem', *Foreign Affairs* 79 (2) March–April, 18–31

For an accessible overview of Russia under Yeltsin see:

Shevtsova, Lilia (2000) 'Yeltsin and the Evolution of Electoral Monarchy in Russia', *Current History* 99 (639) October, 315–320

Boris Yeltsin has written several books about his time as president, including his (1994) *The View From the Kremlin*, London: HarperCollins, and (1994) *The Struggle for Russia*, New York: Times Books, which covers the period 1991–3. Yeltsin's (2000) *Midnight Diaries*, London: Weidenfeld and Nicolson, covers his second term as RF president.

CHAPTER 2

Gorbachev and *perestroika*: reforming the unreformable?

This chapter examines the reasons why Mikhail Gorbachev launched *perestroika* (Reconstruction) and the problems encountered in defining and implementing a coherent reform programme. Particular attention is paid to the interrelationship and the sequencing of economic and political reform and to Gorbachev's 'New Thinking' for soviet foreign policy. The role of nationality as a mobilising force against the continuation of the USSR and soviet socialism is explained. The growing polarisation of soviet politics and Gorbachev's 'drift to the right' in response to his increasing isolation and the mounting disorder in the country are examined. Finally, the failed hardline coup in August 1991, the Minsk Agreement dissolving the USSR and the Alma Ata Agreement establishing the CIS are discussed.

Introduction

In March 1985 Mikhail Gorbachev became general secretary of the CPSU, the leader of the USSR. He launched a 'revolution from above' called *perestroika* or Reconstruction, designed to revitalise soviet socialism. *Perestroika* entailed radical changes in political, economic, social and foreign policies which were supposed to be mutually complementary. 'Gorbymania' spread throughout the world so that in 1987 he was American *Time* magazine's 'Man of the Year' and in 1990 he was awarded the Nobel Peace Prize. In contrast to this adulation, within the USSR *perestroika* was condemned by ideological hard-liners as the abandonment of soviet socialism and by radicals as just tinkering with an economically, politically, socially and morally bankrupt system. The reforms rapidly gained a momentum of their own. Gorbachev lost control over his revolution as the soviet people turned it into a 'revolution from below', making increasingly radical demands that ran far ahead of Gorbachev's more modest reformist aims. Even some members of the soviet *nomenklatura*, such as Boris Yeltsin, started to renounce soviet socialism in favour of western-style democracy and the market. There was a hopelessly botched hardline coup attempt in August 1991 but the reform genie could neither be put back into the bottle nor satisfied by Gorbachev's reforms. By December 1991 Gorbachev, who had set out to reform and and thereby strengthen the USSR, had instead unwittingly overseen the demise of the soviet empire in East-Central Europe (in 1989), the end of soviet socialism and the disintegration of the USSR into 15 independent states, and was himself out of office.

Why did Gorbachev launch *perestroika*?

Gorbachev's explanation

Gorbachev advocated *perestroika* to eradicate the stagnation or *zastoi* that was the legacy of Leonid Brezhnev's long tenure as leader of the USSR from 1964 to 1982. According to Gorbachev, the soviet people had become inert and lacking in initiative, crime rates were rising, corruption was pervasive, labour indiscipline was rife, and drunkenness and alcoholism were endemic. The CPSU was itself culpable as it had lost touch with the people and had not fulfilled its constitutionally prescribed 'leading and guiding role'. Party bureaucrats, who were subjected to neither appropriate party discipline nor democratic oversight by the people and the media, had been able to reduce previous reform attempts to ineffective campaigns and empty slogans. In 1983 two future Gorbachev advisers, the economist Abel Aganbegyan and the sociologist Tatyana Zaslavskaya, produced the Novosibirsk Report (Hanson, 1984) chronicling the precipitous decline of the soviet economy. They argued that the methods used by Stalin to turn the USSR from a backward agricultural country into a great industrial and military power were no longer appropriate. The centrally planned economy (CPE) and the whole soviet command-administrative system needed radical reform.

Gorbachev described *perestroika* as 'a genuine revolution' in all aspects of soviet life and as a 'thorough going renewal' (*Pravda*, 28 January 1987). This did not mean he took office with a clear strategy: although problem areas had been identified, actual solutions were slower to emerge. In 1985–6 there was a lot of discussion about the need for *perestroika* and some new slogans were adopted such as calls for 'acceleration' (*uskorenie*) in the economy, but there were few concrete achievements. Attempts to streamline the bureaucracy through the creation of new super-ministries, such as Gosagroprom for agriculture, in reality only created yet another layer of bureaucracy. A new policy of 'openness' or *glasnost* was introduced into the media and the arts in order to expose the scale of the USSR's problems and to persuade the people to support and participate actively in *perestroika*. Gorbachev resurrected his predecessor Andropov's anti-corruption and discipline campaigns and added an anti-alcohol campaign. Now dubbed the mineral water secretary (*mineral'nyi sekretar'*), Gorbachev seemed to be trying to make the old system work by cleaning and sobering it up. His renewal of party-state bureaucrats or cadres, again a resurrection of Andropov's purge of corrupt and inefficient bureaucrats, also looked like the typical move of a new leader eager to demote opponents and promote allies. In 1987, spurred on by the USSR's escalating problems, Gorbachev launched his radical reforms.

The legitimacy of CPSU rule was supposed to be based upon the ideology of Marxism-Leninism, but Brezhnev had been aware that while ideological exhortations were not unimportant, they were not enough to sustain the regime. He had instituted an unwritten social contract between the people and the party, according to which the people had economic security (such as guaranteed work and cheap food) and in return they were expected to be politically pliant (see Chapter 12). Not all soviet citizens were prepared to abide by this 'contract' and from the 1960s onwards dissident voices challenged the very legitimacy of the soviet system. The soviet state responded to dissent with harassment and force. Gorbachev was committed to reducing the level of state coercion within the USSR and he also realised that in the short term at least, economic *perestroika* would lead to unemployment and a fall in real incomes. *Perestroika* simultaneously broke the social contract and weakened the state's ability to put down the resulting growing discontent. Gorbachev had to develop new mechanisms to persuade the soviet people to support the regime and *perestroika* (see Box 2.1). Gorbachev believed that democratisation would foster a sense of responsibility amongst the people for their own and the leadership's actions, and that the soviet leadership at all levels would be accountable to the people, so combating elite inefficiency, ineptitude and corruption. Gorbachev recognised that although he was the CPSU general secretary, supposedly the most powerful man in the USSR, reform entailed confronting vested interests whether from workers or

---

BOX 2.1

Perestroika: reforming the unreformable?

He [Gorbachev] wanted to restructure 'everything' without touching the socialist foundations of state ownership, the Party's 'leading role', and the regime's Communist goals. It is not hard to see that these goals were not attainable. To restructure everything, and yet to leave intact the foundations laid by Lenin, was a logical impossibility. The Communist system was not reformable. Either it exists, or it does not.

Source: Dmitri Volkogonov (1998) *The Rise and Fall of the Soviet Empire: Political Leaders from Lenin to Gorbachev*, London: HarperCollins, 434. Dmitri Volkogonov was a soviet historian and an adviser to President Yeltsin.

party-state bureaucrats (Zaslavskaya, 1988). In order to reform the economy and maintain a (reformed) soviet socialism, democratisation was imperative.

The systemic and structural problems of the soviet economy

The USSR had a centrally planned economy (CPE) with state or collective ownership of enterprises and farms. In the 1920s and 1930s the USSR was electrified, new coal mines were dug and dams, railways, new steel mills and gigantic heavy industrial centres were constructed. The CPE proved adept at promoting this extensive economic growth by increasing the inputs of labour, energy and materials directed to these sectors. This economic system achieved growth at tremendous human and ecological costs, and created an economy that was structurally skewed towards heavy industry and mineral extraction. From the 1950s light industry, the consumer sector and agriculture received more investment but still remained hopelessly underdeveloped. The USSR needed to move away from its overdependence on the old smoke stack industries and to embrace the technological revolution that was sweeping the advanced capitalist economies. The CPE was less adept at promoting this intensive economic growth which required improving the quality, rather than just the quantity, of inputs. The CPE system also suffered from a lack of reliable data, rigid and unresponsiveness plans, and a general problem of providing incentives. The USSR needed to harness its people's skills by encouraging them to show initiative and by improving their motivation, and it needed new managerial techniques and new technologies such as electronics. By the 1950s the old stress on gigantic factories and the military rhetoric of 'storming the steel front' was no longer appropriate.

Since the 1960s Gorbachev's predecessors had talked about reforming the CPE and restructuring the economy but had achieved little. The logic of reforming a CPE demanded the introduction of some form of decentralisation of decision making away from the State Planning Agency (Gosplan) and the ministries in Moscow. In Czechoslovakia during the 1960s economic reforms which entailed the devolution of some decision-making authority quickly spread over into popular demands for greater political freedoms. This Prague Spring was crushed by Warsaw Pact forces in August 1968. For the Brezhnev leadership in Moscow the message was clear: loss of control over the economy could put communist party rule and hence soviet socialism in jeopardy and reform was dangerous. After a rather half-hearted attempt at economic reform in the 1960s, the Brezhnev leadership shelved reform and sought improved relations with the West through a policy known as détente. In the 1970s the USSR was able to take advantage of rising world energy prices to increase its oil and gas exports and at the same time western bankers provided the USSR and its allies with credits. The USSR temporarily had the funds to buy the food, consumer goods and technology from the West that its own economy was unable to provide. The cost however included increasing trade dependency upon and financial indebtedness to its ideological enemies, the capitalist countries. Meanwhile the underlying need to restructure the economy and to reform the CPE remained unaddressed. In the 1980s Gorbachev decided that it was now too dangerous not to reform the economy and that the best hope for the success of economic reform was to pursue simultaneous democratisation.

Soviet modernisation and the development of a civil society

The CPSU argued that its ideology of Marxism-Leninism gave it a scientific understanding of the inevitable course of historical development towards communism. To attain this goal the CPSU demanded a monopoly of political power: no organisation could legally exist without the party's permission and all structures and institutions were dominated by the party. The *nomenklatura* system was employed to ensure that key positions throughout the country were occupied by people loyal to the CPSU. Strict control of education, media censorship, propaganda and agitation campaigns, the restriction of travel abroad and contact with foreigners, were used to instil the correctness of the CPSU world-view amongst the soviet masses. By the 1980s the soviet people had long since ceased to be masses as the USSR had undergone major social and educational changes. At 54 Gorbachev was young and healthy for a CPSU general secretary. He was a member of what in the USSR was called the sixties generation. This generation came to political maturity after the death of Stalin and so had not been scarred by the experience of Stalinist repression and terror. This generation had benefited from the social mobility and educational opportunities opened up by soviet rule and the somewhat freer political atmosphere of the 1960s. At Moscow State University Gorbachev had befriended the Czech communist Zdenek Mlynar who went on to be one of the leaders of the ill-fated Prague Spring. The 1960s reform debates within the USSR and the soviet bloc were part of the broader education of a new generation. Throughout the country people were better educated than their parents; they looked around themselves and could seen the yawning void between the propaganda images of soviet socialism and reality.

The soviet state aspired to total control over the masses but in the increasingly complex and differentiated society created by soviet modernisation this was more difficult and increasingly counterproductive. Before Gorbachev this pluralism had very few legitimate channels through which to express itself, although a form of institutional pluralism or corporatism was becoming increasingly evident (Merridale, 1991: 16). Soviet professional groups such as the armed forces and economic managers became adept at using their positions and specialist know-how to promote their professional interests. The historian Moshe Lewin argues that by the Brezhnev period soviet modernisation had led to an emerging civil society (see Box 2.2). So when Gorbachev launched his revolution from above, seeking to mobilise the soviet people through *glasnost* and democratisation, sections of the soviet people were quick to take these new

---

BOX 2.2

A civil society in the very fortress of statism?

By 'civil society', we refer to the aggregate of networks and institutions that either exist and act independently of the state or are official organizations capable of developing their own, spontaneous views on national or local issues and then impressing these views on their members, on small groups and, finally, on the authorities ... The concept of a civil society operating in the very fortress of statism – among broad layers of officials, politicians and opinion makers, and the party apparatus – challenges the conventional thinking about the Soviet state.

Source: Moshe Lewin (1988) *The Gorbachev Phenomenon: A Historical Interpretation*, London: Radius, 80. Moshe Lewin was born in Poland and served in the soviet Red Army during World War II. A historian, he teaches at the University of Pennsylvania, USA.

---

opportunities to formulate their own agendas, pursue their own sectional interests, and in some cases push for further democratisation.

The international context of *perestroika*

American Republicans such as Vice-President Bush claimed that Gorbachev's decision to pursue *perestroika* was due to the American government's 'squeeze strategy' (Dumbrell, 1997: 116). During President Ronald Reagan's first term (1981–5) he was influenced by right-wingers such as the historian Richard Pipes who described the USSR as being in economic and political crisis. Pipes argued that the USA should 'squeeze' the USSR and precipitate the collapse of its economy, so provoking economic and political reform. The squeeze entailed a twin strategy of sanctions to deny the USSR western technology imports and an arms race, exemplified by the Star Wars Project (SDI) (Pipes, 1986: 272). Reagan did not pursue this policy consistently however. The grain embargo imposed on the USSR by President Carter after the declaration of martial law in Poland in December 1981 was lifted by Reagan in 1982 and by 1983 technology sales were gradually being encouraged again (Dumbrell, 1997: 70–4). Even while the Americans were applying an economic 'squeeze', the Western Europeans and the Japanese continued to supply the USSR with technology and the Australians, Argentinians and Canadians supplied grain. Although the American squeeze strategy did not lead directly to *perestroika*, other international factors were more relevant. As Michael Cox argues, 'What hurt the Soviet Union after 1980 was not US economic pressure as much as the drop in the price of oil, the devaluation of the dollar, and the economic decision by western bankers not to lend any more money to Moscow's indebted East European allies' (Cox, 1990: 164). With the loss of this beneficial international environment economic reform was thrust back onto the soviet agenda.

Democratisation and openness

Demokratizatsiia and glasnost

Democratisation and *glasnost* involved showing respect for and trust in the people. Previous soviet leaders had proclaimed the unanimity of the soviet people and the CPSU; western sovietologists' suggestions that there was a plurality of opinions in the USSR had been condemned by soviet ideologists as outrageous slurs. According to a CPSU slogan, 'The party and the people are united'. In a profound move away from this thinking, Gorbachev argued that the USSR enjoyed a 'socialist pluralism' and that a plurality of opinion and lively debate under the general leadership of the CPSU would be positive assets. Gorbachev's dilemma was that he believed in the rightness of the CPSU's constitutional monopoly of power and the need for the CPSU to exercise its 'leading and guiding role' as embodied in Article 6 of the 1977 Constitution. At the same time he also recognised that the party had not always provided the USSR with adequate leadership, that it was responsible for much of the country's stagnation and that without democratisation elements within the CPSU would continue to obstruct reform. Democratisation entailed encouraging political participation free from direct party control, in order to develop and channel the people's initiative and sense of responsibility towards the reform of soviet socialism, while simultaneously subjecting party officials or cadres to greater public scrutiny.

The freer political environment encouraged people to set up their own organisations without CPSU permission. These organisations were called informals (*neformaly*) because they initially had no legal status. Most were not overtly political: they ranged from music-cultural groups, through ecological and religious-philosophical groups, to lobby groups for Afghan war veterans. The informals with overt political platforms included the Club for Social Initiatives set up in the autumn of 1989 with the stated aim of transforming *perestroika* from 'reform from above' into 'practice from below'. Another political informal called Democracy and Humanism opposed soviet socialism, and the Trust group advocated a multi-party system. Nationalist and secessionist sentiments were well-represented amongst the informals by groups such as the Lithuanian Freedom League and the Karabakh Committee. The rapid development of these informals meant that the authority and legitimacy of the CPSU was now being challenged by would-be political parties. Once the electoral system was reformed and restructured the informals were able to put forward their own candidates and so the CPSU lost its domination over the composition of the the USSR's representative bodies, the soviets.

Glasnost saw a widening of the parameters of what could be reported, represented and debated in the media and the arts. Like democratisation, *glasnost* was intended to persuade the people to work for *perestroika* and also to provide the leadership with additional sources of information and ideas from the people themselves. Before *glasnost* the soviet media had been so censored and bore so little resemblance to the realities of life in the USSR that they had lost credibility. The media were therefore failing in their basic function of educating and mobilising the soviet people to support the CPSU's policies and goals. In adopting *glasnost* Gorbachev was attempting to improve the media's credibility, to demonstrate his trust in the soviet people and to educate and mobilise the soviet people to support and actively work for *perestroika*. *Glasnost* did not mean a complete end to censorship and anti-reformers continued to dominate the local media and national newspapers such as *Sovetskaia Rossiia*. A new media law in August 1990 enabled the informals to found their own publications and although censorship still existed it became increasingly difficult to enforce. By early 1990 the CPSU's domination of the USSR's political life and media was effectively over.

The institutionalisation of democracy and the separation of powers

Gorbachev believed that a much sharper distinction needed to be made between the functions of the CPSU and the state. The CPSU still oversaw the activities of every institution within the USSR, party membership was a prerequisite of a good career, and through the *nomenklatura* system the CPSU controlled key appointments throughout the country. Gorbachev believed that the CPSU would be better able to perform its leadership role if it were not embroiled in day-to-day governance. In 1987 the USSR had its first multi-candidate elections since the 1930s. Only 5 per cent of the local soviet (council) seats up for election that year had more than one candidate, but despite this modest figure the fact that the CPSU could no longer entirely control the outcome of elections was a major change. At the 19th Party Conference in 1988 Gorbachev announced further radical changes that initiated moves towards a rudimentary separation of executive, legislative and judicial powers. These reforms also weakened the CPSU's ability to dominate all aspects of soviet life. Gorbachev received the Conference's approval for his plan to reform the communist party-dominated and largely powerless soviet parliament. Under the new structure a 2000 (later 2250) member Congress of People's Deputies elected 450 (later 542) members to a new two-chamber Supreme Soviet. In formal terms the Congress was the country's highest legislative body, but as it met only once a year its main function was to elect and ratify the actions of the Supreme Soviet. The soviet people had to wait until March 1989 before they had the opportunity to vote for deputies to the Congress of People's Deputies. Most seats in the 1989 Congress elections were contested by more than one candidate; although the CPSU was still the only legal political party at this time, the informals were very active in putting candidates forward.

The new Congress's first session was televised and the soviet people were presented not with the usual carefully scripted speeches but with politicians arguing and Gorbachev being publicly harangued by radicals and conservatives alike. Igor Ligachev emerged as Gorbachev's leading conservative, communist opponent. Ligachev had initially welcomed reform and while he did not favour a return to Brezhnevite stagnation and corruption, he was deeply troubled by the increasing chaos throughout the USSR and the loss of party control. In late 1990 Ligachev joined Soiuz (Union), a conservative organisation founded in March 1989 to represent the powerful military-industrial complex and ethnic Russians living outside the RSFSR of the USSR. Although the majority of the Congress deputies were anti-reform, the Inter-Regional Group co-chaired by Boris Yeltsin and Andrei Sakharov served as an umbrella organisation for pro-reform and radical deputies who ranged from members of the reforming wing of the CPSU to non-CPSU advocates of western-style democracy and capitalism.

The RSFSR parliament was dominated by the Inter-Regional Group's sister organisation, Democratic Russia. The Inter-Regional Group and Democratic Russia favoured Shatalin and Yavlinsky's '500-Day Programme' of radical economic marketisation against Prime Minister Ryzhkov's more cautious approach. They also advocated the transformation of the USSR into a confederation and the abolition of all central administrative and legislative structures including Ryzhkov's government, the Congress of People's Deputies and the USSR Supreme Soviet. Democratisation, far from encouraging a pro-*perestroika* consensus, revealed the ever-increasing plurality of opinion within the USSR which challenged the very legitimacy and authority of the USSR and the CPSU.

A further step towards a separation of powers came in January 1990 with the establishment of the Committee for Constitutional Supervision. For the first time in soviet history there was now an institution which could declare a law unconstitutional. The committee's powers were limited: for example, it could not annul but only suspend an unconstitutional law for three months. The union republics, fearful that the committee would be used by Moscow to frustrate the work of republican legislatures, managed to restrict the committee's sphere of competence to just all-union legislation. As a result the committee was unable to arbitrate between the rival claims of all-union and republican legislation during the 'Law Wars' of 1990–1. In September 1990 the committee ruled that President Gorbachev's April 1990 decree transferring control of demonstrations and public events in Moscow from the city soviet to the USSR Council of Ministers was unconstitutional. This seemingly modest decision established that the soviet head of state was no longer above the law – a major step in soviet democratisation.

The USSR: national versus soviet identities

The USSR: a soviet federation or a Russian empire?

Lenin had described the Imperial Russian Empire as a prison house of nationalities and believed that after the Bolshevik Revolution nationality would become irrelevant as proletarian internationalism would provide a firm foundation for the new soviet state. In the 1920s the Bolsheviks wanted to create a soviet identity but feared that the Russians would reassert their role as the imperial people and come to dominate the new state. The Bolsheviks therefore chose to recognise the multinational composition of their country by creating a state structure founded on nationality-based administrative areas. The 15 soviet republics comprising the USSR were named after their dominant nationality but none of the republics was nationally homogeneous. The republics were subdivided into autonomous republics, territories (*krais*), areas (*okrugs*) and provinces (*oblasts*). In order to counter possible Russian domination, the Bolsheviks also adopted a policy of nativisation (*korenizatsiia*) which promoted the development of local elites. As education expanded in the 1920s it was conducted in local languages, which helped to foster the USSR's national identities. Soviet internal passports (identity cards) recorded each person's twin identities: firstly their citizenship of the USSR (that is, their soviet identity) and secondly their nationality. As allegiance to soviet socialism and soviet identity weakened during Gorbachev's reforms, it was the second identity – nationality – which provided the mobilising factor and institutional basis for challenging the legitimacy of the soviet state to rule throughout the USSR.

Russians within the USSR

The Gorbachev period also witnessed a rapid development of Russian nationalist sentiments. Many Russians believed that Russian national interests had been damaged within the USSR. Stalin, the commissar (minister) for nationalities in the aftermath of the 1917 revolution, had called the Russians the 'big brothers' and the other nationalities the 'little brothers'. To the little brothers the Russians had rapidly returned as the imperial nationality, dominating key positions throughout the USSR. To the USSR's non-Russians soviet culture, identity and interests were in fact Russian. For their part, many Russians viewed sovietisation as a loss of their Russian identity and a denial of their true culture and history. While the other republics had their own communist parties, broadcasting services, academies of science and encyclopaedias, the Russians only had the all-union organisations not specifically Russian bodies.

There was a very real sense that Russia was being economically, culturally and socially damaged by remaining in the USSR. The central planning system meant that the RSFSR gave the other republics a net subsidy of nearly 67 million roubles a year. In a bad deal for the RSFSR, it had transferred its underpriced energy to the other republics in return for overpriced consumer goods. The republics of Kyrgyzstan, Turkmenistan and Uzbekistan also provided net subsidies to the other republics but these were only worth 0.2, 0.4 and 0.5 billion roubles respectively (Steele, 1992: 19). In 1989 28 Russian nationalist supreme soviet deputies formed a parliamentary caucus to fight what they called the 'reverse discrimination' by the USSR's other nationalities against the Russians. They opposed the use of Russia's natural resources to subsidise the other republics and deplored the fact that ethnic Russians were becoming a minority in the Soviet Union because of the higher birth rates in the Islamic republics of Central Asia. Yeltsin as leader of the RSFSR called on the Russians to emancipate themselves from the USSR, to pursue a policy of 'Russia First' and to establish their own independent Russian state.

The nationalities issue, the soviet state and Law Wars

The 1977 Constitution described the USSR as a unitary federal multinational state, formed as a result of the free self-determination of nations and the voluntary union of equal soviet socialist republics. In reality the 15 union republics were not free to leave the USSR and establish independent nation-states. Within the USSR any manifestation of nationalism was condemned as bourgeois and reactionary. However, in a large multi-ethnic empire in which potentially explosive secessionist sentiments were lying under the surface (Lapidus, 1989), democratisation inevitably led to calls for independence. Electoral reform enabled the soviet peoples to elect nationalist deputies to their republican parliaments. These parliaments now had the authority and legitimacy of democratically elected bodies and one by one, led by the Baltic republics, they started to pass their own legislation which was often at variance with all-union legislation and to declare their independence. The 'Law Wars' between all-union laws passed by Moscow and laws passed by the individual republican parliaments had begun.

Economic *perestroika*

Tackling the systemic problems

Successive CPSU leaders believed that the party's direction of the CPE was vital to their ability to control the country's development. In contrast Gorbachev tried to distance the CPSU from the day-to-day running of the economy. The creation of super-ministries with the danger of even greater centralisation was balanced by the devolution of some decision-making authority to the ministries in each of the union republics. The pervasive problem of poor-quality production was similarly addressed by a combination of centralising and decentralising measures. A new state committee called Gospriemka was set up to monitor and enforce production quality standards. The 1987 Law on State Enterprises gave enterprises greater autonomy but also subjected them to the USSR's still limited market forces. The law began the move away from central plan directives to a less comprehensive system of state orders (*zakazy*). According to the new principle of self-financing (*khozraschet*), enterprises were subjected to the 'discipline' of the market. This entailed an end to automatic state subsidies and enterprises now had to cover their own costs or risk bankruptcy. Such moves scandalised the USSR's ideological hardliners who thought a central plan embodied rational decision-making in contrast to the anarchy and irrationality of the market. The very use of terms such as market, profit and bankruptcy and the idea that unemployment could be necessary to improve efficiency and end overstaffing were alien to traditional soviet economic thinking.

In order to complement increased enterprise decision-making authority, changes were also tentatively introduced to their management. Enterprises were now supposed to operate on the basis of self-management (*samouprav-lenie*) with managers elected by the workforce. Soviet workers were generally sceptical about the purpose of these elections and did not show much interest in them. Gorbachev also called upon trade unions to act independently of management and to champion their members' interests, but they did not have the right to prevent the closure of bankrupt enterprises. In 1990 trade unions became supposedly independent organisations rather than bodies controlled by local party committees and they also now enjoyed full financial autonomy. The official trade unions were slow to adapt to this new status and function, and soviet workers began to establish new independent trade unions to protect them during this time of rising unemployment and falling real wages (see Chapter 12). A very basic problem with economic *perestroika* was that it created an incoherent hybrid of a CPE and a market economy. The sequencing of the various components of economic reform was out of kilter. For example, enterprises could not be self-financing if they could not set their own prices, reflecting the true cost of production. However, price reform was constantly delayed because it was feared that price rises would lead to social discontent that would fuel inflation and undermine *perestroika*. The result was that certain basic goods such as matches, soap and toothpaste disappeared from the shops because enterprises could not 'afford' to make them.

Cooperatives: private enterprise, popular resentment and crime

The May 1988 Law on Cooperatives gave cooperatives equal rights with state sector enterprises. Prime minister Ryzhkov denied that the law marked a retreat from socialism and instead stressed cooperatives' potential positive contribution to the soviet economy. Cooperatives were heralded as small and medium size enterprises that would be flexible and responsive to the market in contrast to the gigantic state enterprises. Most cooperatives were established in the consumer goods and services sectors (cafés, hairdressing salons, house and car repairs services and medical services) rather than in small-scale manufacturing. The cooperatives were not universally popular, their prices were too high for most soviet citizens, and their very existence highlighted the poor state provision of goods and services and the ability of the soviet elite to use their personal spending power to bypass the USSR's shortages. The cooperatives were also popularly associated with crime and corruption. Before cooperatives were legalised there had been a thriving illegal 'second' economy in goods and services and this image of illegality stuck. Cooperatives could also make quick profits by buying commodities at fixed state prices and then selling them on with enormous unearned mark-ups. In order to acquire premises, materials and the various licences and permissions needed to operate, the cooperatives became enmeshed with local bureaucrats in a web of corruption. Cooperatives were also vulnerable to the predation of criminal gangs and protection rackets.

Agriculture: feeding the people

The USSR's inability to feed its people provided Gorbachev with a particularly intractable problem. Previous agricultural reforms had concentrated on bringing more land under cultivation and using fertilisers to increase production, but they did not touch the collectivised ownership and administration of soviet agriculture. The soviet peasants were allowed to work, but crucially not to own, small private plots which per hectare were much more productive than collective land. The peasants could sell the produce from these plots at peasant markets for personal profit and so had a material incentive to produce as much as possible. For Gorbachev the problem was how to provide the peasantry with the same material incentive to produce more without taking the ideologically unacceptable step of introducing the private ownership of land. At the 19th Party Conference Gorbachev talked of 'restoring sovereignty' to the peasantry, of making them the 'real master of the land'. The solution to these questions adopted in mid-1988 was to permit peasants to lease land for up to 50 years and then to work that land as independent farmers. This was an ideological sleight of hand which side-stepped land privatisation but which could lead to effective de-collectivisation. The reform was frustrated by the local agricultural bureaucracies such as the party and soviet bureaucrats, collective and state farm managers and agronomists, who all had a vested interest in maintaining the old system. Peasants were typically only offered unattractive short-term leases; there were also fertiliser shortages and the farm machinery available was expensive and only suitable for large-scale collective farms rather than small family farms. The poorly developed rural infrastructure was another disincentive to abandon the at least minimal security of the collective and state farms. By 1991 soviet food shortages were worse than they had been in 1985, land leasing had not taken off, and most collective and state farms were bankrupt and still dependent on state subsidies to survive.

Opening up to the world economy

An important corollary of domestic economic reform was the commitment to open up the soviet economy to the world economy. Previously all foreign trade had been conducted through the USSR Ministry of Foreign Trade, but in 1986 the ministry lost this monopoly. Other ministries and some enterprises were empowered to deal directly with foreign companies and they could also keep their hard currency earnings. In 1987 joint venture enterprises between soviet and foreign partners were legalised. It was anticipated that much-needed foreign technology, know-how and investment would come into the USSR through the joint ventures. However, joint ventures were so hemmed in by restrictions on ownership, taxation and the repatriation of profits from the USSR, that they were not terribly attractive to foreign investors. The USSR also began moves to join such capitalist institutions such as the General Agreement on Tariffs and Trade (GATT), the World Bank and the IMF; and discussions about moving towards rouble convertibility were also initiated. Opening the soviet economy to the global capitalist economy was ideologically extremely contentious. For conservatives it was tantamount to throwing away the gains of the 1917 Bolshevik Revolution by letting the capitalists into the USSR and subjecting the USSR to the vagaries of capitalism. For reformist socialists such as Boris Kagarlitsky such moves risked the 'Third Worldization' of the USSR (Kagarlitsky, 1989).

The 'new thinking' in foreign policy

From superpower confrontation to interdependence

Gorbachev's domestic reforms were complemented by a new thinking (*novoe myshlenie*) on foreign and security policies. Since the end of World War II soviet thinking had been dominated by the Cold War struggle with the ideological enemy the USA. In contrast the new thinking stressed not this struggle but the concept of interdependence (*vzaimozavisimost'*) borrowed from western social science literature. Interdependence means that a country's security is no longer narrowly defined as solely a military issue, but that it also has economic, political and ecological aspects. Recognition of interdependence stresses countries' shared concerns and interests rather than what divides them. Gorbachev believed that abandoning the Cold War adversarial approach to foreign policy would produce dividends not just for the USSR's security but also for domestic reform. Improved relations would mean that the USSR could end the spiralling arms race, reduce its defence spending and transfer precious resources to the rest of the economy. Access to western credits, technology, know-how and increased external trade would also boost economic *perestroika*. In contrast to the muddle of domestic reforms, Gorbachev proved adept at international diplomacy; by 1988 even President Reagan said that talk of the USSR as an Evil Empire now belonged to another time and another place.

The Common European Home, from Brezhnev to Sinatra doctrines

The division of Europe into two blocs led by the USA and USSR was a key feature of the Cold War. The soviet satellite countries in East-Central Europe served as a buffer zone between the USSR and capitalist Europe. From 1956 the Warsaw Treaty Organisation coordinated the bloc's military activities and soviet troops were stationed throughout the empire. Economically the soviet bloc was united through the Council for Mutual Economic Assistance (CMEA or Comecon) founded in 1949. The CMEA achieved neither the hoped-for soviet bloc autarchy (self-sufficiency) nor the integration of national economic plans. The empire was subsidised with soviet natural resources, particularly oil, which were supplied at well below world prices. In return these countries exported their best quality goods to the West to earn hard currency and supplied the USSR with their shoddier products. The empire was an enormous financial drain on the USSR, whose own interests lay in increasing energy export earnings in order to pay for technology imports from the capitalist West.

The new stress on global interdependence led the USSR to move away from its Cold War-inspired fixation on relations with the USA to re-examine its relations with other countries including Europe as a whole. Gorbachev called for an end to the division of Europe and advocated a Common European Home of all European countries regardless of their political orientation. Gorbachev argued that Europe shared a common cultural heritage and common interests across a range of issues. These issues included developing economic ties, improving communications networks and exchanging information and skills. The Chernobyl nuclear disaster in 1986 highlighted the shared need to combat environmental pollution. Gorbachev also argued that Europeans, East and West, needed to develop a shared military security system. The USA was sceptical of the USSR's motivation, seeing these moves as a device to break the Atlantic alliance between the USA and Western Europe and ultimately to destroy NATO. Nevertheless, the USSR now sought improved relations with the European Community which it had previously reviled as the economic arm of the North Atlantic Treaty Organisation (NATO). This led to a declaration of mutual recognition signed in June 1988 and in 1991 to the exchange of permanent missions between Moscow and Brussels.

In another innovative move Gorbachev abandoned the Brezhnev Doctrine in favour of what became known as the Sinatra Doctrine. The Brezhnev Doctrine had been proclaimed in 1969 to justify the crushing of the Prague Spring, which at the time was depicted as a threat to socialism. Under the Sinatra Doctrine countries were now free, in the words of the song, to declare 'I did it my way', without fear of outside intervention. Under Gorbachev the USSR was now the leading advocate and exponent of reform within the soviet bloc. Gorbachev made it clear that he would prefer Moscow's allies to reform but that he did not propose to intervene either to force reform or to shore up unpopular anti-reform leaderships. Then in December 1988 Gorbachev announced to the United Nations (UN) General Assembly the unilateral withdrawal of 500 000 troops and 10 000 tanks from the USSR's East-Central European empire. Without the threat of soviet intervention first Hungary then Poland, East Germany, Bulgaria and Czechoslovakia left the soviet bloc.

Marshall Aid for the USSR?

In the aftermath of World War II the USA provided the war-damaged countries of Western Europe with economic aid called Marshall Aid in order to finance economic reconstruction and to counter the feared communist expansionism. Gorbachev believed that western economic aid was vital to soviet economic reform and would be tangible proof that opening up to the West had brought economic and political dividends. In the spring of 1990 the leaders of the seven leading capitalist countries (G7) began to talk about the need for a new Marshall Plan to encourage democracy and the transition to a market economy in the USSR. In 1991 Yeltsin's economic adviser Grigory Yavlinsky joined a new group based at Harvard University that included the political scientists Graham Allison and Robert Blackwell and the economists Jeffrey Sachs and Stanley Fischer (see Allison and Blackwell, 1991 and Sachs, 1992). The Harvard group worked on an economic reform programme for the USSR which it believed had to be supported by western economic aid. This was to be the 'Grand Bargain' between the USSR and the West, which was also called the 'Window of Opportunity' and in Russian '*shans na soglasie*' or 'opportunity for agreement'. There were however important differences within the Harvard group, particularly about the appropriate level of western economic aid. While Jeffrey Sachs stressed that the West must commit itself to provide annual financial support for reform of around $30–50 billion for five years, Robert Allison was much more sceptical about the wisdom of the West making such a commitment. The divergence of opinion within the Harvard group typified the diverging and wavering opinions within the G7. German Chancellor Helmut Kohl and French President François Mitterrand were inclined to help Gorbachev in order to encourage reform, while American President George Bush and British Prime Minister John Major favoured aid only once reforms had been implemented.

The Harvard group proposed a 'Grand Bargain' whereby the West would provide $45–60 billion in aid over three years to strengthen Gorbachev's authority and push through the USSR's transition to a market economy (see Allison and Blackwell, 1991 and Sachs, 1992). In return the West was to gain military concessions and influence over soviet foreign and domestic policies. However, western leaders became increasingly alarmed by rumours of an impending coup in the winter of 1990–1 and were troubled by the lack of a consistent approach to economic reform. In July 1990 Gorbachev and Yeltsin had agreed to establish a working group whose task was to elaborate plans for fundamental economic reform. The group was led by Stanislav Shatalin, who was an academician and member of Gorbachev's Presidential Council, and Grigory Yavlinsky. The group produced a plan for the rapid marketisation of the soviet economy which became known as the '500-Day Plan', after the time they believed was necessary to implement their radical changes. Gorbachev however dropped this Shatalin–Yavlinsky plan in favour of a much less radical reform programme devised by Prime Minister Ryzhkov and his deputy for economic reform, Leonid Abalkin. The 'Grand Bargain' had been devised to support rapid marketisation; once this was dropped the bargain's foundations looked distinctly shaky. Talk of a Grand Bargain was, however, overtaken by the August 1991 coup and the demise of soviet socialism.

Authoritarianism versus disintegration, 1990–1991

Who governs?

By 1990 the USSR was in turmoil and rapidly fragmenting. The economy was in chaos, there was a huge budgetary deficit, unemployment was rising, workers were on strike, real incomes were falling and the consumer situation was worse than in 1985. Politically, democratisation combined with aspirations for national self-determination led the republics to declare their sovereignty, so that the Union itself seemed on the verge of disintegration. Democratisation and decentralisation of the economy encouraged not just the union republics but also the regions, provinces and cities to lay claim to the ownership of state assets and to make their own policies. Moscow itself was home to two contending power centres. Yeltsin, who had been the chair of the Russian parliament since May 1990, confronted Gorbachev, who was the president of the USSR. Yeltsin campaigned in the RSFSR's first ever presidential elections in 1991 using the slogan 'Russia First', so harnessing Russian nationalism to democratisation and marketisation, and championing greater autonomy from the soviet state for the Russian republic (see Box 2.3). Whilst Gorbachev was backtracking over reform for the USSR during the winter of 1990–1, parliaments within the union republics passed ever more radical

---

BOX 2.3

The results of Russia's first presidential elections, 12 June 1991

Candidate	Percentage of votes in favour
Boris Yeltsin	57.3
Nikolai Ryzhkov	16.8
Vladimir Zhirinovsky	7.8
Aman-Geldy Tuleev	6.8
Albert Makashov	3.7
Vadim Bakatin	3.4
Invalid votes	4.1
Turnout	74.7

Source: Central Electoral Commission in *Pravda* and *Izvestia*, 20 June 1991, 1.

---

legislation. Given the mounting turmoil of the time very little was actually implemented but a very basic question for any political system, 'Who governs?' or more emotively 'Is anybody governing?', remained unanswered.

Gorbachev had feared that the CPSU Central Committee might unite to oust him from the post of CPSU general secretary and end his reforms. The logic of democratisation's transfer of power and authority from the CPSU to the soviets and government was an end to the CPSU's constitutional monopoly of power, which was finally announced in February 1990. Gorbachev therefore sought simultaneously to secure his own power base and to continue reform by creating a new post of executive president of the USSR. Gorbachev was elected USSR president in March 1990. In institutional terms Gorbachev appeared unassailable, more powerful even than Stalin, and yet in reality he was growing weaker. His power and authority were being challenged by the union republics and he was increasingly powerless to stop the drift and chaos. At the same time the USSR's new democratic institutions, such as the Congress of People's Deputies, were proving unable to mediate the conflicts that now rent the country and indeed seemed to exacerbate them.

Calls for a state of emergency to either halt or secure reform?

As president of the USSR Gorbachev had the power to declare a state of emergency, and in the winter of 1990–1 he came under increasing pressure from CPSU conservatives to halt reform (see Box 2.4). In July 1991 the conservative newspaper *Sovetskaia Rossiia* printed a letter from 12 leading figures, including two of the eventual August coup conspirators, Alexander Tizyakov and Vasily Starodubtsev. The letter entitled 'A Word to the People' called for the declaration of a state of emergency. Even political analysts such

---

BOX 2.4

Was simultaneous economic and political reform impossible?

It is quite likely that simultaneous democratization and marketization of a Leninist polity and a militarized command economy set within a huge multinational empire at a time of economic depression, labor unrest, and both ethnic and ecological militancy is an impossible task. Indeed, even accomplishing the first two elements of this equation without the additional qualifications would be historically unprecedented. If this vision is intrinsically impossible to achieve in the Soviet context, then Gorbachev can hardly be faulted for failing to achieve the impossible. He can, however, perhaps be faulted as quixotic for believing (if he did) that he could, and for trying to do so.

Source: George W. Breslauer (1990) 'Evaluating Gorbachev as Leader', *Soviet Economy* 5 (4) October–December, 302. Professor George Breslauer is a political scientist and chairman of the Center for Slavic and East European Studies at the University of California at Berkeley.

---

as Andranik Migranyan, who favoured market reforms and democratisation, thought that Gorbachev had made a fateful error in trying to pursue simultaneous marketisation and democratisation. Migranyan called on Gorbachev to declare martial law in order to push through radical economic reform and suppress the inevitable ensuing labour unrest. According to Migranyan only once the economy had been reformed and stabilised would it be safe to attempt democratisation (Migranyan, 1990).

Gorbachev was now stranded in the rapidly emptying middle ground of soviet politics: too conservative for the radicals and too radical for the conservatives. In June 1990 at the founding of the Russian Communist Party Gorbachev was accused of weakening the USSR through the loss of its East-Central European empire, subservience to the West and the introduction of capitalism. In December 1990 Gorbachev's long-time ally Eduard Shevardnadze resigned as foreign minister warning of the danger of a hardline coup. Abandoned by the radicals, Gorbachev made concessions to the conservatives in both policies and appointments. The radical '500-Day Plan' for the economy was abandoned in favour of the Ryzhkov–Abalkin plan. The conservative Leonid Kravchenko was appointed head of the central television network, which led to the cancellation and postponement of investigative programmes such as *Vzgliad* (View) and *TSN*. In January 1991 the independent news agency Interfax was closed and its assets were seized by the state. Gorbachev made these concessions to the conservatives but he did resist demands for a state of emergency. Crucially, this meant that the first direct elections for the presidency of Russia went ahead on 13 June 1991, so securing Yeltsin's power base (Kaiser, 1991). It also meant that Gorbachev went ahead with the planned 'Nine-plus-one' meetings with the union republics in April 1991, to negotiate a new union treaty rather than trying to maintain the USSR by force.

The armed forces and the KGB: for or against reform?

At a time of turmoil the allegiance of the armed forces and security services (the KGB) can be decisive. Gorbachev was commander-in-chief of the armed forces, but as political authority was fragmenting where should and did the allegiance of the armed forces and the security services lie? During *perestroika* the armed forces and security services had seen dramatic changes in their status and role. For decades their strength and loyalty to the CPSU were seen as vital to the survival of the USSR and to world communism. Now the reformers within the CPSU seemed to be destroying what they had worked so hard to preserve. Gorbachev had thrown away the USSR's buffer zone in Europe, withdrawn troops from Afghanistan, introduced arms control and troop reductions, and cut defence spending. Under *glasnost* the media subjected the armed forces to unprecedented scrutiny, revealing an unflattering picture of corruption, crime, ethnic strife, drug and alcohol abuse and bullying (*dedovshchina*). On the rising tide of nationalism politicians, particularly in the Baltic republics, supported young men's refusal to answer their call-up. Army officers, used to a high standard of living and status, were returning home from the former Warsaw Pact countries to live with their families in army barracks and even tents.

The political spectrum within the USSR was also reflected within the armed forces and the KGB. Support for *perestroika* came from the Shield (Shchit) informal founded in 1989 by a reformist parliamentary deputy (retd.) Major Vladimir Lopatin and in the 1990 elections 22 military officers stood for the Democratic Platform. In April 1989 hardliners took the opportunity of Gorbachev's absence abroad to use troops against demonstrators in the Georgian capital of Tbilisi. During the 1990–1 drift to authoritarianism OMON riot police and KGB commandos were deployed against the Lithuanian Television Centre and the Latvian Interior Ministry. Elements from the republican communist parties and the armed forces in Latvia and Lithuania formed National Salvation Committees which threatened to wrest control of these republics away from their democratically elected nationalist leaderships. Gorbachev claimed that these committees were established and these attacks carried out with his permission. Factions within the soviet armed and security forces saw themselves as the guarantor of the integrity and security of the USSR and believed that they had a duty to frustrate Gorbachev's reforms. When in 1990 Gorbachev signed the Conventional Forces in Europe (CFE) Treaty, the Soviet General Staff evaded the agreement by secretly moving armoured vehicles, guns and tanks beyond the Urals. This paralysed the soviet rail system during the winter of 1990–1, severely disrupting food distribution and contributing to the chaos in the country.

For the KGB, the USSR's enemies were now more difficult to define. Former political dissidents had been released from prison and exile and were now free to promote their views. The former dissident Andrei Sakharov had even been elected to the new Congress of People's Deputies in 1989 and challenged Gorbachev on live television. The KGB now portrayed itself as the champion of law and order in the face of growing crime, corruption and western subversion. After 1989 the KGB lost its links with fellow security services in East-Central Europe and proved unable to subvert the nationalist independence movements within the USSR. As union republics declared their sovereignty, republican KGB organisations gradually transferred their allegiance from the all-union institutions in Moscow to the leadership within their own republic. In the name of Russian state-building an RSFSR KGB was created for the first time in September 1989 by the Yeltsin-led RSFSR Supreme Soviet.

The draft union treaty: maintaining the union?

Gorbachev denounced the union republics' declarations of sovereignty as unconstitutional, but the new reality was that he could either impose the union by force or negotiate. Force was likely to be unsuccessful and would terminally damage *perestroika* and the USSR's relations with the West. Against a backdrop of mounting chaos and disintegration, Gorbachev tried to negotiate a new distribution of power and authority between the union republics and the all-union centre in Moscow. The result was a draft union treaty which did not even mention socialism and instead spoke of 'human rights and freedoms', of 'the commitment to develop civil society, law-based societies and democracies' with a free choice over the type of their economy. The union was to be a 'sovereign federative state' (Sheehy, 1990: 2). On 17 March 1991 an all-union referendum was held on the future of the soviet state. The question posed was: 'Do you consider it necessary to preserve the USSR as a renewed federation of equal sovereign republics in which the human rights and freedoms of any nationality will be fully guaranteed?' Six republics (Estonia, Latvia, Lithuania, Moldova, Georgia and Armenia) did not hold the referendum. The overall turnout was 80 per cent with a 76.4 per cent 'yes' vote, but given the abstention of six republics and the loaded nature of the question, this was not a very convincing mandate for the continuation of the USSR. Discussions continued and a new draft union treaty was published on 16 August 1991. According to the new draft, membership of the union was to be voluntary, republican law would take precedence over all-union law and taxation was to be devolved to the republics. In effect this would mean that the republics could define central government's 'competencies and capabilities' (Galeotti, 1997: 114). The USSR Supreme Soviet was to be disbanded and the all-union ministries either dissolved or reduced to coordinating bodies between the republics. For CPSU conservatives the treaty was going from bad to worse and the death knell of the USSR and soviet socialism was sounding.

The August 1991 coup and the collapse of the USSR

The August 1991 coup

To preserve the USSR action had to be taken before the Union Treaty was signed by Russia, Kazakhstan and Uzbekistan on 20 August. The coup conspirators were an amalgam of party conservatives, military-security personnel and representatives of economic bodies alarmed by the impact of the reforms (see Box 2.5). The conspirators did not seem to have a very clear idea of what they wanted to achieve beyond a declaration of martial law. They believed that Gorbachev could be persuaded to declare martial law, so making their coup 'constitutional'. On 18 August a delegation went to Gorbachev's holiday villa in Foros to persuade Gorbachev to declare martial law, but he refused. On Monday 19 August the soviet people were told that President Gorbachev was ill and that a State Committee for the State of Emergency was running the country. Gorbachev and his family were effectively under house arrest, cut off from the outside world until they discovered that one of the telephones in the servants' quarters had not been cut off. Gorbachev was able

---

BOX 2.5

The August 1991 coup conspirators

The State Committee for the State of Emergency:

Gennady Yanaev	Soviet Vice-President 1990–1
Valentin Pavlov	Prime Minister 1990–1
Vladimir Kryuchkov	Former head of the KGB's First Chief Directorate, Chair of the KGB 1988–91
Dmitry Yazov	Soviet Defence Minister 1987–91
Boris Pugo	Interior Minister 1990–1
Oleg Baklanov	First Vice-Chair of the Defence Council
Vasily Starodubtsev	President of the Peasants' Union
Alexander Tizyakov	President of the Association of State Enterprises

The main figures in the 18 August delegation to Gorbachev's villa at Foros:

Valery Boldin	Gorbachev's Chief of Staff
General Yury Plekhanov	Head of the KGB's Ninth Directorate (bodyguards), Gorbachev's Chief of Security
General Valentin Varennikov	Commander-in-Chief of Ground Forces 1989–91
Oleg Baklanov	First Vice-Chair of the Defence Council
Anatoly Lukyanov	Chair of the USSR Supreme Soviet 1990–1 (former close ally of Gorbachev, he gave the coup tacit rather than overt support)

to telephone out and let his allies know that he was not ill and that an unconstitutional coup had taken place.

The conspirators also wrongly assumed that the country's armed and security forces would back them. The soviet armed and security forces were as riven by internal divisions as other institutions in the USSR. Decisive opponents of the coup were air force commander Col. Gen. Yevgeny Shaposhnikov and Col. Gen. Pavel Grachev commander of the airborne forces (paratroopers) and generals Chechevatov, Samsonov and Novozhilov of the Kiev, Leningrad and the Far Eastern military districts. Gen. Alexander Lebed refused to storm the Russian parliament – the White House. The conspirators did have some forces at their disposal and three Yeltsin supporters were killed in a clash with a tank, but on the whole the conspirators were indecisive about how to use their forces. Yeltsin was able to come out of the White House, climb on a T-72 tank of the Taman Guards division and denounce the coup as unconstitutional. The State Committee had not acted decisively to arrest potential opponents; this meant that Gorbachev was their only prize and others were free to oppose the coup.

The conspirators' final error was to underestimate the potential opposition to the coup and not to understand that six years of *perestroika* had changed the USSR. Power and authority were much more defuse than before and there were now other institutions such as the Russian parliament which could claim legitimacy and serve as the focus of opposition to the coup. Most citizens did take a wait and see approach but there were instances of vital resistance which snowballed. The radio stations *Eko Moskvy* (Moscow Echo) and *Maiak* (Lighthouse) continued to broadcast in opposition to the coup, the editorial staffs of some of the banned print media produced emergency editions and the new newspaper *Obshchaia gazeta* appeared. Foreign broadcasters such as CNN and BBC provided continuous coverage. As the opposition stood firm and the State Committee dithered, resistance grew. To the union republics the message was clearly that Moscow was defeated.

The end of the USSR: the Minsk and the Alma Ata agreements

On 8 December 1991 at Belovezha near Minsk in Belarus, Boris Yeltsin for Russia, Leonid Kravchuk for Ukraine and Stanislas Shushkevich for Belarus signed an agreement dissolving the USSR and establishing the Commonwealth of Independent States (CIS). This move was specifically designed to take the initiative from Gorbachev and to quash any idea that the USSR could survive in any form. Gorbachev was only told about the Minsk Agreement after Yeltsin had informed President George Bush. On 21 December 1991 the CIS was further strengthened by the Alma Ata Agreement of 11 former soviet union republics to join the CIS. President Gorbachev resigned as president of the USSR on 25 December and the soviet parliament was disbanded. The Soviet Union was formally dissolved on 31 December 1991.

Conclusion

What had begun as reform to reinvigorate and strengthen soviet socialism and the USSR had resulted in their collapse. Increasingly, control of the reform process and with it the country slipped from Gorbachev's grasp. By 1989–91 opposition to soviet socialism was spearheaded by nationalists who wanted independence for their republics and by pro-democracy and market forces. Within this democratic opposition many doubted that reform could be achieved in a country as diverse and geographically vast as the USSR and that its dismemberment was both inevitable and desirable. Elements within the soviet *nomenklatura*, convinced that the soviet command-administrative system was outmoded and often simultaneously seeking personal material benefits, also joined the opposition. Meanwhile other elements within the *nomenklatura* sought to save soviet socialism and the USSR by staging the August 1991 coup. However, had the conspirators held on to power they too would have had to address the reform imperative. The course and fate of *perestroika* highlights the difficulty of formulating and implementing a reform programme, a difficulty compounded by the absence of a united pro-reform elite and popular consensus. The task of formulating a coherent reform programme to transform the Russian Federation from a slightly modified CPE and one-party state into a capitalist, liberal democracy is formidable. The new Russian Federation inherited much of the chaos and the centrifugal forces unleashed by *perestroika* and in these inauspicious conditions President Yeltsin launched his reforms in 1992.

References

Allison, Graham and Blackwell, Robert (1991) 'America's Stake in the Soviet Future', *Foreign Affairs* 70 (3) Summer, 77–97

Cox, Michael (1990) 'Whatever Happened to the "Second" Cold War? Soviet–American Relations: 1980–1988', *Review of International Studies* (16), 15–172

Dumbrell, John (1997) *American Foreign Policy: Carter to Clinton*, Basingstoke: Macmillan

Galeotti, Mark (1997) *Gorbachev and his Revolution*, Basingstoke: Macmillan

Hanson, Philip (1984) 'The Novosibirsk Report', *Survey* 28 (120) Spring, 83–108

Kagarlitsky, Boris (1989) 'The Market Instead of Democracy?', *International Socialism* (45) Winter, 93–104

Kaiser, Robert G. (1991) *Why Gorbachev Happened: His Triumphs and His Failures*, New York: Simon Schuster

Lapidus, Gail W. (1989) 'Gorbachev and the National Question: Restructuring the Soviet Federation', *Soviet Economy* 5 (3), 201–250

Merridale, Catherine (1991) 'Perestroika and Political Pluralism: Past Prospects', in C. Merridale and C. Ward (eds) *Perestroika: The Historical Perspective*, London: Edward Arnold
Migranyan, Andranik (1990) 'Gorbachev's Leadership: A Soviet View', *Soviet Economy* 6 (2) April–June, 155–159

Pipes, Richard (1986) *Survival Is Not Enough*, New York: Touchstone Books

Sachs, Jeffrey (1992) 'The Grand Bargain', in Anders Åslund (ed.) *The Post-Soviet Economy: Soviet and Western Perspectives*, London: Pinter
Sheehy, Ann (1990) 'The Draft Union Treaty: A Preliminary Assessment', *Radio Liberty Report on the USSR* 2 (51), 1–6
Steele, Jonathan (1992) 'Fear and Folly in Moscow', *The Guardian*, 21 February, 19

Zaslavskaya, Tatyana I. (1988) 'Friends or Foes? Social Forces Working For and Against Perestroika', in Abel Aganbegyan (ed.) *Perestroika Annual*, London: Futura

Further reading

There are several good general books on Gorbachev and *perestroika*:

Brown, Archie (1997) *The Gorbachev Factor*, Oxford: Oxford University Press, as its title suggests this book focuses on the role of Gorbachev in initiating and carrying out reform; Archie Brown was the first sovietologist to tip Gorbachev for the top
Sakwa, Richard (1991) *Gorbachev and his Reforms, 1985–1990*, New York: Prentice Hall
Walker, Rachel (1993) *Six Years That Shook The World*, Manchester: Manchester University Press

Insiders' accounts of the *perestroika* period are provided by:

Gorbachev, Mikhail (1988) (2nd edn) *Perestroika*, Nottingham: Spokesman
Gorbachev, Mikhail (1991) *The August Coup: The Truth and the Lessons*, London: HarperCollins
Gorbachev, Mikhail (1997) *Memoirs*, London: Bantam Books
Yeltsin, Boris (1990) *Against the Grain: An Autobiography*, London: Jonathan Cape (trans: Michael Glenny)

The journal *Soviet Economy* carried a useful series of articles by leading sovietologists providing contrasting interpretations of Gorbachev:

Breslauer, George W. (1990) 'Evaluating Gorbachev as Leader', *Soviet Economy* 5 (4) October–December, 299–340
Breslauer, George W. (1991) 'Understanding Gorbachev: Diverse Perspectives', *Soviet Economy* 7 (2) April–June, 110–120

Brown, Archie (1990) 'Gorbachev's Leadership: Another View', *Soviet Economy* 6 (2) April–June, 141–154

Hough, Jerry (1991) 'Understanding Gorbachev: The Importance of Politics', *Soviet Economy* 7 (2) April–June, 89–109

Migranyan, Andranik (1990) 'Gorbachev's Leadership: A Soviet View', *Soviet Economy* 6 (2) April–June, 155–159

Reddaway, Peter (1990) 'The Quality of Gorbachev's Leadership', *Soviet Economy* 6 (2) April–June, 125–40

Goldman, Marshall (1991) *What Went Wrong with Perestroika?*, London: W.W. Norton, also provides an analytical overview of the *perestroika* period and raises important questions about the sequencing of the various components of the reform programme

The following provide a range of analyses of why *perestroika* was introduced and soviet socialism destroyed:

Amalrik, Andrei (1980) *Will the Soviet Union Survive Until 1984?*, Harmondsworth: Penguin, provides an early analysis of the USSR's problems by a soviet dissident

Bunce, Valerie (1993) 'The Gorbachev Reforms in Historical Perspective', *International Organization* 47 (1) Winter, 107–138

Maier, Charles S. (1991) 'The Collapse of Communism: Approaches for a Future History', *History Workshop* (31) Spring, 34–59

Skidelsky, Robert (1995) 'Why did Soviet Communism Collapse?', Chapter 6 in his *The World After Communism: A Polemic for our Times*, Basingstoke: Macmillan

For an account of the 'Grand Bargain' written by two insiders see:

Allison, G. and Yavlinsky, G. (1991) *Window of Opportunity: The Grand Bargain for Democracy in the Soviet Union*, New York: Pantheon Books

CHAPTER 3

Russia and the Russians

This chapter examines the identity of Russia and the Russians. The ethnic Russians have been the people at the centre of two multinational empires: Imperial Russia and the USSR. The collapse of the USSR has raised questions about where Russia's borders should rightly lie and who the Russians are. As the Russian Federation struggles to create a new multinational state this raises vital questions about nationality and citizenship. Broader questions about Russia's identity as either a European, Asian or Eurasian country and the implications of these definitions for Russia's post-communist development are also examined. Imperial Russia and the USSR both had official state ideologies and the Russian Federation is in the process of creating a new state ideology.

Introduction

The Preamble to the 1993 Russian Federation (RF) Constitution begins, 'We, the multinational people of the Russian Federation, united by a common destiny on our land...'. While the Russian Federation bears the name of the numerically dominant nationality, the Russians, the Constitution recognises that Russia is a multinational state. This immediately raises questions about the relationship between the Russian state and nationality and therefore citizenship and nationality. The difficulties of resolving these questions are compounded by the fact that pre-soviet Russia never existed within the Russian Federation's current borders, and so the relationship between nationality, citizenship and territory are highly contentious. Russia was born out of the collapse of one multinational state, the USSR, and if it is to survive it needs to resist the centrifugal forces that tore the USSR apart. The Preamble talks of the peoples of Russia as 'united by a common destiny on our land', implying a shared Russian identity that transcends individual national identities and that provides cohesion and integrity. The Constitution also describes Russia as a democratic, federative republic and its multinational peoples as the bearers of sovereignty (Arts 1 and 3). These democratic principles are supposed to underpin Russian state-building and provide the state with legitimacy and authority amongst all its peoples, all its citizens.

Locating Russia and the Russians

Russia's moving geographical location

The Russian Federation inherited its borders from the RSFSR of the USSR. In 1992 the internal administrative boundaries of the USSR became the borders of 15 new independent states. Geographically Russia is in both Europe and Asia: most of the land mass is in Asia but the majority of the population live in the European area west of the Urals. Russia is a country without natural frontiers and this has meant that through the centuries it has been vulnerable to invasion by the Mongols, Ottoman Turks, Poles, Swedes, French and Germans. Conversely, throughout its history Russia, while sometimes losing territory, has also been able to expand into neighbouring areas. Russia therefore experienced a mixture of vulnerability and expansionism in the course of its state-building. Western European countries only conquered their overseas empires after having developed their nation-states. Russia, by contrast, conducted a simultaneous process of state-building and imperial expansion (Dawisha and Parrott, 1994: 26). The Russian state's geographical centre of gravity has shifted (for example after the Mongol conquest in 1240 from Kiev to Muscovy) and Russia's borders have also been subject to constant change. The response of Ivan III (the Great, 1462–1505), Vasily III (1505–33) and then Russia's first tsar, Ivan IV (the Terrible, 1533–84) to Russia's vulnerability was to conquer surrounding territories and create a centralised, militarily powerful, autocratic state. A weak state and diminished military capabilities laid Russia open to foreign intervention and internal dissension, as exemplified by the Time of Troubles (1598–1613) with occupation by the Poles. Further periods of external expansion brought parts of Poland, the Baltic territories, Central Asia and the Caucasus under Imperial Russian control. The history of the development of the Russian state therefore has two key features: the vital importance of an authoritarian and militarily powerful state and the ethnic Russians as an imperial people.

Russia: a multinational federation or a new Russian empire?

For non-Russians the USSR was another Russian empire. For the Russians the soviet state used and distorted their Russian identity and culture whilst simultaneously discriminating against ethnic Russians (see Chapter 2). The RF still contains parts of Imperial Russia's colonial possessions such as the Islamic areas of Chechnia, Bashkortostan and Tatarstan. Although 83 per cent of the population are Russians, there are over 126 other national groups, including the RF's second largest nationality, the 5.5 million Tatars. In addition many Russian citizens have multiple ethno-cultural identities. A Cossack identifies him or herself as a Cossack but also as a Russian or a Ukrainian. In 1992 Yeltsin drew upon Russia's imperial past and adopted, by presidential decree and without the approval of the Duma, the white, blue and red tricolour and the double-headed eagle as the state emblem. Yeltsin also adopted music by Glinka for a national anthem but he and the Duma did not manage to agree on the words for the anthem. The two-headed eagle appears on the front of Russian passports. Above the eagle are three crowns which symbolise the three Khanates of Kazan, Astrakhan and Siberia which Ivan the Terrible captured from the Tatars in the sixteenth century. The crowns are adorned with Orthodox Christian crosses. For Russia's Islamic Tatar people this literally symbolises their national and religious subjugation. The passport is also only in the Russian language. The problem for Russia today is to create a unified state that not only recognises Russia's national diversity but also incorporates this diversity within its state structures and institutions (see Chapter 5). In choosing Imperial Russian symbols Yeltsin stressed the historical continuity between Imperial Russia and the Russia of today. The problem here is that in the nineteenth-century Imperial Russia adopted aggressive Russification programmes amongst its non-Russian subjects. The resulting alienation of Imperial Russia's subject peoples contributed to the instability and discontent that helped to fuel the 1917 Bolshevik Revolution and the destruction of Imperial Russia.

Nationality and citizenship: who are the people?

As a multinational, democratic state Russia needs to develop a civic identity which includes all its citizens rather than a Russian national identity (see Box 3.1). The Russians have two words which are both translated into English as Russian. *Russkii* refers to the Russian language and nationality, while *Rossiiskii* refers to the Russian state and therefore citizenship. A Russia citizen is a *Rossiianin* from *Rossiiskii*. A Russian citizen (*Rossiianin*) is not necessarily a Russian (*Russkii*) and a Russian is not necessarily a Russian citizen. When talking of the Russian people Yeltsin was very careful to use the term *Rossiianye* (meaning Russian citizens) rather than *Russkie* (the ethnic Russians). As a federal system (see Chapter 5) Russia has continued the soviet practice of creating ethnically designated administrative areas such as the 21 republics, which are named after their main (non-Russian) nationality such as the republic of Tatarstan. The RF has, however, abandoned the soviet practice of recording a person's nationality in their RF passport. In soviet times every

---

BOX 3.1

Who are the Russians: defined by citizenship or spirit?

The legal definition

In May 1996 the Russian Constitutional Court clarified who qualified for Russian citizenship, these are:

1. those born in Russia after the formation of the USSR who did not waive Union citizenship,

2. those formerly resident outside of Russia but within the USSR, who have now returned to permanent residency within Russia and who are not citizens of any other newly independent state of the former USSR,

3. residency outside of Russia does not lead to a loss of Russian citizenship.

Source: East European Constitutional Review, 5 (2 and 3) Spring and Summer 1996, 23.

Russian nationality defined by spirit and consciousness not blood

We are justly reminded that on the expanses of the Russian plain, for centuries open to all migrations, a multitude of tribes blended with the Russian ethnicity. But when we say 'nationality', we do not mean *blood*, but always *spirit*, a *consciousness*, a person's orientation of preferences. Mixed blood does not determine anything. The Russian spirit and Russian culture have existed for centuries, and all those who feel themselves a part of this heritage in spirit, in consciousness, in heartfelt pain – are *Russians*.

Source: Aleksandr Solzhenitsyn (1995) The Russian Question at the End of the 20th Century, London: Harvill Press, 102. Aleksandr Solzhenitsyn is a Russian nationalist and Nobel Prize winner for literature.

---

adult had an internal passport which recorded their citizenship (*grazhdanstvo*) and in the fifth point their nationality (*natsional'nost'*). The information provided by the fifth point was used to discriminate against minorities. Even before the collapse of the USSR Russian democrats were calling for the removal of the fifth point, as an important step in the development of a democratic civic concept of citizenship including all the nationalities of Russia. The Yeltsin government began issuing new passports in October 1997 without the fifth point, but this provoked uproar particularly in Tatarstan. While Russia's democrats and non-Russian nationalities still acknowledge the importance of a civic identity, they also recognise the importance of officially recording a person's nationality. The new fear is that if a person's nationality is not recorded, if the differences amongst Russian citizens are not recognised, this will lead to creeping Russification, assimilation and the undermining of the autonomy of the republics. The background to these fears include increasing calls by Russia's Red-Browns (the communists, fascists and nationalists) to abolish Russia's ethnically based republics and to return to the pre-revolutionary Imperial Russian practice of dividing the country into territorially based provinces (*guberniia*). Relations between the federal government in Moscow and the republic of Tatarstan were agreed in a bilateral treaty in February 1994. Under the provisions of the bilateral treaty and according to the Tatarstan Constitution the people of the Tatarstan republic have dual RF and Tatarstan republic citizenship. The new RF passport gives no sense of this dual nationality and this led to calls within Tatarstan for the republic to issue its own passport. The parliament of Tatarstan with the support of their president Mintimer Shamiyev stopped issuing the new RF passports in 1997 (Khasanova, 1997a).

The lost Russians: the diaspora

The Russian diaspora is the 25 million ethnic Russians left outside the RF in the 14 other former union republics of the USSR (see Box 3.2). The USSR was a highly geographically mobile society and Russians spread out throughout the union to hold key positions in local power structures or simply to augment the local labour force. As the Russian nationality was so closely associated with the soviet state, the Russians were and are still often viewed as imperial colonisers and are now often the unwanted remnants of the soviet empire. In the newly independent states of the former Soviet Union (FSU), in what the Russians call the Near Abroad, ethnic Russians are often viewed as Moscow's fifth column providing Moscow with an excuse to meddle in their now sovereign neighbours' domestic affairs. Russians of the diaspora are vulnerable; they have been subjected to physical harassment, discriminatory laws and treated as second-class citizens and so symbolise Russia's diminished status and its inability to protect ethnic Russians (see Chapter 10). In the early 1990s the diaspora became a political issue within Russia with politicians vying to express their concern. As Russia is a multinational state, the selection of ethnic Russians for protection and not Russia's other peoples in the Near Abroad contradicts the Constitution. Yeltsin spoke of Russia's concerns for its compatriots (*sootechestvenniki*) in the Near Abroad and promised that the Russian government would champion their rights and protect them against persecution. Russian liberals tend to stress the importance of all states adhering to international human rights conventions on the treatment of ethnic minorities. Another solution to the problem of the diaspora advocated by the Red-Browns is to move Russia's borders to incorporate all ethnic Russians. Gennady Zyuganov, for example, has complained that, 'The country has been pushed back to the borders it had in the 16th century. Dozens of millions of compatriots are now second class citizens, living behind the frontiers of the Russian Federation. Checkpoints and customs points are built in places where borders never existed, and where they are needed they don't exist' (*The Guardian*, 27 February 1995: 7).

BOX 3.2

The size and distribution of the Russian diaspora

New state	Total population (in millions)	Russian minority as a percentage of the population
Ukraine	52	22
Kazakhstan	17	36
Belarus	10	13
Moldova	4	13
Latvia	3	35
Estonia	7	6
Georgia	5	6
Uzbekistan	20	8
Tajikistan	5	7
Kyrgyzstan	4	22
Turkmenistan	4	9

Source: Anthony Hyman (1993) 'Russians Outside Russia', The World Today 19 (11), 206.

The lost Russians?: the Eastern Slavs

It was the leaders of Russia, Ukraine and Belarus who signed the December 1991 Belovezha (Minsk) Agreement which brought an end to the USSR. Russia's westernising reformers typically believed that Russia's best hope for reform was if it were no longer at the centre of an empire. Russian nationalists such as Alexander Solzhenitsyn also typically believe that the Russian state should encompass all the Eastern Slavs (the Russians, Ukrainians and Belarussians) and also the Russian population of Kazakhstan. These ideas have a long heritage. In the nineteenth century Russian historians such as Nikolai Karamzin (1766–1826), Sergei Solovyev (1820–79) and Vasily Klyuchevsky (1841–1911) stressed the unity of the Eastern Slavs, the Russians, Ukrainians and Belarussians. Although the Eastern Slavs had certain regional differences they are portrayed as part of one Russian nation. Today there is a sense that Russia has been territorially, economically but also culturally diminished by the loss of the Eastern Slavs. Some 22 per cent of Ukraine's population are Russians, and its independence was a strategic and economic loss to Russia. More importantly for Russian nationalists, Ukraine's capital Kiev was the capital of the mediaeval principality of Kievan Rus, which is the cradle of the Russian state.

On 15 March 1996 the Red-Brown-dominated Duma voted to revoke the Belovezha Agreement, so ringing alarm bells throughout the FSU. Gennady

Zyuganov's programme for the 1996 presidential election demanded the abrogation of what he called the 'Belovezha Putsch'. He tried to assure Russia's neighbours that no new state was going to be forcibly annexed, neither was their sovereignty under attack. Zyuganov did, however, commit Russia, if he became president, to take all necessary measures to restore 'fraternal ties' particularly between Russia, Ukraine, Belarus and Kazakhstan as the foundation for a planned and voluntary restoration of a union state. Yeltsin condemned the Duma vote and instead sought to strengthen the Commonwealth of Independent States (CIS). Ukraine continues to guard its independence jealously but President Lukashenko of Belarus has supported Belarus–Russian integration. In April 1997 Yeltsin and Lukashenko signed an outline union treaty committing the two countries to closer military, economic and social cooperation, while maintaining each country's sovereignty. Further treaties followed in December 1998, culminating in December 1999 with a new union treaty committing Belarus and Russia to form a confederation.

Religion and the Russian state

The Russian Orthodox Church and the Russian state

The adoption of Christianity by Prince Vladimir in Kiev in 988 is the defining moment in the development of Russian culture and statehood. The identification of the conversion to Christianity as the beginning of the Russian state highlights the interrelation of state and church in Russia. From 988 until 1917 Orthodoxy was the state religion. Peter I the Great (1689–1725), the great westerniser seen by some as the enemy of Holy Mother Russia, brought the Russian Orthodox Church within the state apparatus. The Holy Ruling Synod under the leadership of the tsar's representative, the ober-procurator, managed church affairs. The Russian Orthodox Church held a privileged position as the national church, was in a symbiotic relationship with the Russian state and played a major role in the development of a Russian identity. Russian Orthodoxy is not just a religion, it is the cradle of Russian history and culture, a repository of art and music.

The Russian Orthodox Church and the soviet state

The soviet state was officially secular and atheistic. As early as the 1920s, however, the Russian Orthodox Church began to collaborate with the state in return for a limited and controlled existence whilst other religions and religious groups were persecuted. Stalin and the Russian Orthodox Church made common cause during the Great Patriotic War (1941–5) to defend Mother Russia against the Nazi invaders. In 1987 Gorbachev abandoned anti-religious propaganda and instead reinvented himself as a champion of the Russian Orthodox revival. At a time when the USSR seemed to be in imminent danger of collapse and Russians were bemoaning their exploitation within the Soviet Union, the soviet media were full of articles and programmes about the forthcoming millennium of Orthodoxy in Russia and links were also made between the importance of Orthodoxy to Russian culture and the strength of the Russian (Soviet) state. In 1988 Gorbachev took the opportunity of the 1000th anniversary of the baptism of Prince Vladimir to court Russian nationalists and invited the head of the Russian Orthodox Church, Patriarch Pimen, and members of the Holy Synod to the Kremlin. In 1990 a new Law on the Freedom of Religion promised to protect the rights of people of all faiths, not to regulate religious life, and affirmed the equality of treatment of all religions.

The Russian Orthodox Church and the Russian Federation

Article 14 of the 1993 Constitution establishes a secular state. It prohibits the establishment of a state religion, asserts the separation of religious associations from the state and recognises the plurality and equality of religious organisations. Reality is somewhat different, as the Russian Orthodox Church and the Russian state have developed a new mutually beneficial relationship. For Yeltsin, a former communist who had been accused of selling out to the West, association with the national church helped to strengthen his Russian national credentials. In return he consulted the Russian Orthodox Church on certain policy issues especially concerning morality, the family and the role of women. Yeltsin also glossed over any discussion of the Russian Orthodox Church's collaboration with the soviet state. The Russian Orthodox Church is also gradually infiltrating state structures, and it has signed various agreements with the Ministry of the Interior, the Federal Border Service and the Ministry of Defence. In images reminiscent of Imperial Russia Orthodox priests now bless Russian service personnel and equipment. For Russia's Muslims the close association between the Russian state and the Russian Orthodox Church is alarming. In 1989 Russia's Tatars celebrated the 1100th anniversary of their conversion to Islam. The Tatars had their own state from the eighth century until their conquest by Ivan the Terrible in 1552. For Russians 1552 is the turning point in the establishment of a powerful Russian state, but for the Tatars it is the beginning of their Russian yoke (*igo Rossii*). It was Islam which enabled the Tatars to preserve a sense of Tatar identity through the centuries of Russian domination, so the idea of the Russian Orthodox Church serving as a *de facto* state religion is alienating for them.

Only about half of the Russian population are religious believers of some kind and of these 75 per cent are Russian Orthodox. Between 1991 and 1996 the number of Orthodox congregations almost doubled from 3451 to 6709. Over the same period the number of Muslim, Buddhist, Catholic and Protestant congregations grew even faster. The number of Muslim congregations almost tripled from 870 to 2349; Buddhist congregations grew sevenfold from 16 to 113; Catholic congregations grew from 23 to 169; and Protestant congregations tripled (*Moskovskie novosti*, 17–24 March 1996: 34). The growing status of the Russian Orthodox Church as a *de facto* state religion contradicts not only the Constitution but also public opinion. A study by the All-Russia Centre for the Study of Public Opinion in August 1997 found that while 27 per cent of respondents agreed with the statement that Orthodox believers in Russia ought to possess legal advantages over atheists or adherents of other faiths, 40 per cent of respondents disagreed (*Izvestia*, 9 August 1997: 2).

The Russian state, the Russian Orthodox Church and religious protectionism

The close identification of the Russian Orthodox Church and the Russian state is exemplified in the treatment of other religions and specifically of western Christian groups (see Box 3.3). In the 1997 Law on the Freedom of Conscience and on Religious Associations, Yeltsin and the Duma provided the Russian Orthodox Church with a form of religious protectionism. The new law was designed to protect Russia from western religious infiltration and it also constitutes part of a broader resistance to western cultural influences. The influx of western missionaries into Russia after 1991 is seen as part of a general capitulation to and colonisation of Russia by the West. The Russian Orthodox Church, while not in total agreement with the Red-Browns, does share their general belief that Russia should be a great power, that Russia is a unique civilisation and that Europe and the West in general are alien and hostile to Russia. In 1996, for example, Alexander Lebed condemned Mormon missionaries as 'mould and filth which have come to destroy the state' (Whitehouse, 1998: 12).

   The 1997 law severely restricted the educational, publishing and charitable activities of any religious organisations which could not prove that they have existed in Russia for at least 15 years (Meek, 1997: 20). The Russian Orthodox Church, Islam, Buddhism and Judaism are all recognised as fulfilling this requirement. The law was designed to protect Russians from foreign missionaries but also works against Russia's minority faiths, particularly Protestant sects. The Pentecostal Church and the Jehovah's Witnesses who were denied official recognition in the soviet period have been subjected to the restrictions. Baptists and Seventh Day Adventists who have been in Russia since before the 1917 Revolution have been particularly hard hit by the restrictions. Patriarch Alexii II, the head of the Russian Orthodox Church, also claimed that the only Catholics in Russia before the 1917 Revolution were Poles or foreign diplomats, and as such Catholicism should also be restricted. The Russian authorities have since grudgingly given Catholicism the status of a long-established

---

BOX 3.3

The importance of Russian Orthodoxy in uniting the people

Both our 'energetic reformers' and those who are pumping American taxpayers' money into the reformers' pockets are convinced that the traditions of the Russian state and Russian culture are incompatible with democratic values, and that a return of post-communist [former] Soviet Russia to its 'historical roots' and a restoration of Russian national consciousness would inevitably lead to a revival of Russian imperialism.

In reality, however, for millions of ethnic Russians and for the overwhelming majority of people living in the Russian Federation, rediscovering the traditional religious customs of their forebears is the only way they can get in touch with their Russianness. Today, an at least partial restoration of the Orthodox Church's former influence on our way of life offers a chance to shape a new Russian national consciousness and to revive a sense of Russian identity.

Source: Andranik Migranyan and Alexander Tsipko (1997) 'Only Together Can a Weak Government, a Weak Church and a Weak Society Be Strong', *Nezavisimaia gazeta*, 20 August, 2. Andranik Migranyan is a political analyst and advocate of the need for a transitional authoritarianism for Russia (see Chapters 1 and 4). Alexander Tsipko is the executive director of the International Foundation for Socio-Economic and Political Studies, the Gorbachev Foundation.

---

religion, but the activities of Jesuits are still restricted. In Russia's republics local laws regulating religious activities by foreign missionaries have resulted in complex accreditation and licensing systems. In the extreme case of the Udmurt republic, missionaries must pay a £100 fee each month, they are fined £1000 if they hold services outside registered places of worship and they face a £2000 penalty for distributing unsanctioned literature (Hearst, 1996: 8).

Russia between East and West

The nineteenth-century debate about Russia's identity and modernisation

The contemporary debates about Russia's identity and optimum course of development have a long historical precedence. From the time that Peter the Great (1689–1725) adopted western ideas in order to force Russia into breakneck modernisation, the question of the relevance of western ideas to Russia has polarised Russian thinkers. In the nineteenth century the debate about Russia's identity and destiny took the form of a clash between the Westernisers (*zapadniki*) and the Slavophiles (*slavianofily*). The Slavophiles stressed Russia's uniqueness (*samobytnost'*) and its organic history. They condemned both Peter the Great's forced modernisation and his importation of alien western ideas as destructive of Russia. Slavophilism was centred on a belief in the superior nature and supreme historical mission of Orthodoxy and Russia. The Slavophiles depicted western society and culture as divided and western rationalism as a source of evil. The Slavophiles stressed the collectivist nature of Russia, embodied in the patriarchal family, peasant commune (*mir*) and in the religious sphere by the concept of *sobornost'*. *Sobornost'* is usually translated as community, but this does not fully convey its true meaning as an organic, harmonious community of Orthodox Christian believers. Slavophiles believed that only within and by submission to this community can people find love, truth and ultimately freedom. The Slavophiles were profoundly opposed to western notions of individualism and therefore parliamentarism and constitutionalism. Slavophiles such as Ivan Kireevsky (1806–56), Alexei Khomiakov (1804–60), Konstantin Aksakov (1817–60) and his brother Ivan Aksakov (1823–86), rejected westernisation and argued that Russia must proceed along its own path and should not simply replicate the western course of development. In contrast the Westernisers stressed the need to follow a western path of development. The Westerniser Peter Chaadaev (1794–1856) in his *Philosophical Letter* (1836) argued that 'Russia had no past, no present, and no future' (Riasanovsky, 1984: 361), that Russia belonged to neither East nor West and had contributed nothing to culture, and that Russia must westernise in order to fulfil its historical mission. Chaadaev was declared mad by the authorities. Rather than demonising Peter the Great, Westernisers praised his efforts to modernise Russia along European lines. Orthodoxy was also of no great importance to the Westernisers; some were Orthodox in their personal faith but others were agnostic or even militant atheists. The Westernisers favoured political reform including the end of autocracy, the adoption of a constitution and the establishment of a parliament.

Russia as a European country

It is important for reformers to establish Russia's European credentials because of the supposed causal link between European culture and capitalism and democracy. If it can be established that Russia is indeed a European country then whatever problems Russia is currently experiencing can be explained as due to the soviet legacy or as transitional phenomena. The counter-argument is that Russia is historically and culturally ill-disposed towards western liberal democracy and capitalism. If as some Russian nationalists argue Russia is unique, then the political institutions and economic arrangements that work in western countries are likely to be inappropriate for Russia. If this is true then Russia has been on the wrong course since the end of Communism; western-style liberal democracy and capitalism are not just experiencing teething troubles that will eventually pass but are doomed to catastrophic failure. The logic of this argument is that rather than following western models of development, Russia must seek out its own path.

Russia's European credentials seem rather limited. Russia was never part of the Roman Empire, did not directly experience the defining events of European history such as the Renaissance and the Reformation, and took no part in the maritime discoveries and the scientific and technological advances of the early modern period. In the eighteenth century Catherine the Great (1762–96) encouraged the assimilation of Enlightenment ideas, but these only influenced some of the aristocracy and the intelligentsia. Nevertheless in the nineteenth century Russians made significant contributions to European art forms such as the novel, opera and ballet. Gorbachev advocated the concept of a Common European Home and defined the USSR as a European country. He allied himself with the historian Dmitrii Likhachev (1906–99), who combined a liberal Russian nationalism with a firm belief in Russia's European heritage. Likhachev argued, for example, that mediaeval Russia constituted a distinctive civilisation within the European whole, and that Prince Vladimir's adoption of Orthodox Christianity in 988 brought Russia into the Byzantine civilisation which contributed to Europe's pre-Renaissance culture. Therefore, according to Likhachev (1991), Russia experienced the Renaissance but through Byzantium rather than Rome. Following this line of argument Russia combines both Russianness and a European identity. Likhachev was dismissive of notions of a mysterious Russian soul defining and restricting its likely course of development; instead he believed that Russia could create its own destiny.

Russia and Asia

Geographically Russia is predominantly an Asian country but Russians have a rather ambivalent attitude towards Asia, at once recognising Russia's Asian heritage but also disparaging it and depicting it as responsible for the negative aspects of Russian culture. It is easy to overstate the impact of the 1240 Mongol invasion on the Russians. The Mongols respected and tolerated the Russian Orthodox Church, which was able to serve as a rallying point and focus for Russian loyalty. The Mongol invasion did, however, feed the Russian sense of vulnerability and was invoked by Russian tsars and emperors to justify territorial expansion and the need for a strong autocratic state to preserve Russia. Imperial Russia's expansion eastward into Siberia was depicted as part of Russia's manifest destiny to bring civilisation and economic development to Asian peoples. The term Asian tends to be used pejoratively amongst Russians. For example, in 1917 Lenin accused some Bolshevik officials as having a semi-Asiatic mentality. Similarly, Lenin ascribed Stalin's crude behaviour and authoritarian manner to his being an 'Asian'. Stalin was a Georgian and educated at an Orthodox Christian seminary, but evidently Caucasian people were also classified as Asian. Russia's Asianess is blamed for making Russia resistant to modernisation, prone to authoritarianism, with a weak civil society and a dominant state.

Eurasianism

The 1980s saw renewed interest by Russia's Red-Browns in the idea of Russia as a Eurasian country and culture (see Box 3.4). Eurasianism was first developed in the 1920s as an alternative to Bolshevism by Prince Nikolai Trubetskoi, George Florovsky and Pyotr Savitsky in their *Iskhod k vostoku* (Exodus to the East) published in Sofia in 1921. In 1989 Sergei Zalygin, the editor of the influential journal *Novy Mir*, reprinted an article by the Eurasianist thinker Nikolai Berdyaev (1874–1948). Berdyaev believed that material development with its need for a market, private property and scientific-technical progress was a universal value and necessary for Russia. Nonetheless he described the struggle between Russia and the West as one of the 'spirit' versus 'machine'. According to Berdyaev Russians do not worship the golden calf (money and material possessions) and Russian civilisation has not become a world of things, unlike the West (Berdyaev, 1947).

BOX 3.4

Russians as Eurasians

The inconsistency and complexity of the Russian soul may be due to the fact that in Russia two streams of world history – East and West – jostle and influence one another. The Russian people is not purely European and it is not purely Asiatic. Russia is a complete section of the world – a colossal East–West. It unites two worlds, and within the Russian soul two principles are always engaged in strife – the Eastern and the Western.

Source: Nicolas Berdyaev (1947) *The Russian Idea*, London: Centenary Press (trans: R.M. French), 2.

In the 1980s Gennady Zyuganov worked with Russians within the CPSU to elaborate a Russian-oriented form of communism. From 1988 the CPSU began to publish a wide range of non-communist Russian thinkers, including the works of the Eurasianist Lev Gumilev. This seems a very strange partnership as Gumilev was vehemently anti-Marxist and believed that Bolshevism was totally alien to Russians. For Gumilev Marxism and Bolshevism embodied alien western and Jewish values, and so could bring nothing but harm to Russia. In Eurasianism the communists found ideas that stress the differences between Russian and European civilisations, are sceptical of capitalism and depict Russia as a unique historical and cultural fusion of Slav and Turkic, Russian Orthodox and Muslim elements. Zyuganov worked quite closely with Alexander Prokhanov, the editor of the Russian nationalist weekly *Den'* (renamed *Zavtra* in 1993), which had a page devoted to Eurasianism, providing a forum for Russian nationalists and Muslims.

In contrast to the Marxist focus on class, Gumilev argued that history is the history of nations, which he termed *ethnoses*. Gumilev argued that it was possible for two or more nations to unite to form a super-*ethnos* and that 500 years ago the Eastern Slavs, Mongols and Tatars had fused to form a super-*ethnos* (Gumilev, 1992: 10–11). A thousand years before that a Teuton and Latin super-*ethnos* had formed in Western Europe and ever since has presented a constant threat to the Slav–Tatar–Mongol super-*ethnos*. In contrast to the idea that Russia had saved Europe and Christendom from the Mongol hordes, Gumilev argued that it was the military prowess of the Mongols that had saved the Eastern Slavs from the predation of the West. Gumilev's concept of an *ethnos* is not defined in racial terms but rather in terms of the link between an *ethnos* and its ancestral lands. This gives rise to the concept of a parasite *ethnos*, an *ethnos* that has lost its ancestral land and survives as a parasite on another *ethnos* – in Russia this means the Jews. According to Gumilev there are also parasite states which lack their own dynamism and survive by living off the resources and culture of another *ethnos* – the USA is a parasite state. Under Zyuganov the Communist Party of the Russian Federation (KPRF) has found Eurasianism more attractive than Marxism: its anti-westernism is appealing, it provides a concept of a multi-national Russia which condones anti-Semitism, and the idea of a super-*ethnos* can also be used to justify Russia as a great power. In the early 1990s other Red-Browns such as the Russian Party and the National Republican Party also adhered to Eurasianist ideas. Since the mid-1990s Eurasianism has been challenged by more narrowly focused Russian nationalist ideas, which are anti-western, anti-Asian and anti-Semitic. The humiliation of the Russian armed forces in the first Chechen war (1994–6), continuing instability in the Caucasus and fear of Chinese expansionism have provoked a reappraisal of attitudes particularly towards the Islamic world and China. By 1996 even Alexander Prokhanov was no longer such a devoted Eurasianist and now argues that the Islamic and Chinese worlds would really enjoy the dissolution of Russia (Shlapentokh, 1997: 12).

The importance of culture?

The relevance of culture

Capitalism and liberal democracy first developed in the largely Protestant countries of northern Europe. This has led to assumptions that their cultural attributes are conducive to capitalism and democracy and by extension that Roman Catholicism, Orthodox Christianity, Confucianism, Buddhism and Shintoism will either hinder or act as a barrier to their development. In the second half of the twentieth century the Catholic southern European countries of Spain and Portugal carried out successful democratic transitions and have modernised rapidly. Japan and the Asian Tiger economies have also achieved rapid economic development. A problem therefore is to accurately identify what it is about a particular religion or historical-cultural tradition that either promotes or hinders capitalism and democracy. Even if it can be shown that certain cultures are not conducive to democracy and/or economic development, most countries are not monolithic and immutable. The RF encompasses a range of nationalities and religions plus urban and rural lifestyles. The period of soviet rule also brought tremendous changes in terms of economic development, industrialisation, urbanisation and educational attainments. Russia has not stood still in the twentieth century; the problem is to tease out what is relevant and what endures.

Culture and the Russian economy

In the Russian case collectivism with its antipathy to individualism is said to hinder the development of a market economy. Following the abolition of serfdom in 1861, peasants continued to hold their land in common rather than individually. They were still subject to the economic, social, religious and political control exercised by the peasant commune (*mir*). This collectivism was continued by the Bolsheviks, when the peasants' *mir* was replaced by collective farms which also tried to control every aspect of their lives. As Imperial Russia developed in the late nineteenth and early twentieth centuries peasants were beginning to break away from the *mir* and similarly Stalinist industrialisation encouraged urbanisation. Today 75 per cent of Russia's population are urban dwellers. Soviet propaganda stressed collectivism and under Stalin a measure of conformity was gained by coercion and terror. Post-Stalin soviet commentators increasingly complained about negative individual behaviour ranging from crime, teenage indiscipline, alcoholism and drunkenness to high levels of labour turnover. At the same time the soviet economy only survived because individuals were showing initiative to get around the blockages of the centrally planned economy. Behind the propaganda the USSR was not as collectivist as it was depicted; collectivism was and remained more important in the countryside than in the cities and amongst the old rather than the young or middle-aged. Survey data published before the collapse of the USSR found that Soviet and American citizens had remarkably similar attitudes to private enterprise and profit making (Schiller *et al.*, 1991). In the new economy Russians object to crime and corruption, the manner in which the old political and economic elites became the New Russians (see Chapter 1), excess profits and the lack of concern for the ordinary people. It is not capitalism as such that Russians object to but to what they call their 'wild capitalism'.

Culture and politics

Imperial Russia was an autocracy and the USSR a one-party state, so the Russians had no experience of democracy before their country set out to become a liberal democracy in 1991. In contrast Likhachev argued that Russia does have a democratic tradition, such as the daily meetings with the boyars held by the princes of Kiev in the tenth and eleventh centuries. From 1549 until it was abolished by Peter the Great, Russia also had an Assembly of the Land (*zemskii sobor*), which was similar to the gathering of representatives of the estates in other European countries. The *zemskii sobor* placed no limitation on the tsars' powers however and the participants were considered to be exercising a state service, for which they were paid by the Treasury, rather than exercising a right of representation. These are also not examples of popular participation. Another commonly held belief is that Russians tend to have a very personalised view of leadership, that they are looking for a tsar, a CPSU general secretary or a powerful president to knock heads together and to sort things out. This 'bossism' (*vozhdizm*) was used to explain Yeltsin's behaviour as Tsar Boris. Certainly, political parties in Russia today tend to be based more around personalities than political programmes, but this is more the result of the specific conditions of Russia's democratisation than a yearning for a strong boss (see Chapter 8). Russia also has a centuries-long tradition of peasant and later worker revolt, so the Russians will not endure autocracy or authoritarianism indefinitely. This gives rise to a view of Russia as torn between authoritarianism and anarchy, that if the state is weakened then there are no accepted social controls or generally accepted democratic principles and procedures to mediate dissent and conflict. The major divide in Russian politics today is between those such as the Red-Browns who advocate a strong state as part of Russia's tradition and as essential if Russia is to pull itself out of its crisis, and those such as the liberal Yabloko party who fear a strong state (see Chapter 8).

Globalisation and Russia

Russia in a globalised age

In the course of the twentieth century economic activity became increasingly internationalised, and the development of new technologies also meant that individual countries have become increasingly subject to cultural and information flows from other countries. The opening of the first McDonald's in Moscow in 1988 symbolised Gorbachev's wish to open up to the West. In 1992 a nine foot high Coca-Cola tin was erected on Moscow's Tverskaia street and it looked as if Moscow was now part of the globalised McDonald's/Coca-Cola culture. Russia is now more open than it has ever been in its history. Russians travel abroad and Russia receives tourists and migrants. The international broadcast media are no longer jammed and foreign print media are no longer banned. Russians have access to the internet, and foreign videos and films are available, with Arnold Schwarzenegger and Jean-Claude Van Damme action films being particularly popular. Russian television broadcasts Latin American and Mexican soap operas such as *Wild Rosa* and American police shows such as *Hill Street Blues*. Television advertisements exhort teenagers to use Clearasil lotion and cat lovers to buy Whiskas. Cadburys chocolate and the Scottish soft drink Irn-Bru are both now produced in Russia. Western goods including French cosmetics, Finnish Fazer brand chocolate, and Lacoste, Nike and Adidas sportswear are all available. While many Russians welcome the new range of ideas and goods that are entering Russia, this unprecedented foreign influence has also produced some unease. The Russians are trying to find their own identity, shorn of its soviet overlays, just at a time when they are subject to unprecedented external influences. Globalisation has contributed to fears that Russia has lost or is in imminent danger of losing its culture and heritage and of being colonised by the West.

Negative reactions to globalisation and the West

The soviet school curriculum produced generations of Russians who were well-versed in the Russian classics. Soviet achievements, whether in sports or space exploration, were also Russian achievements. Russians have a very strong sense that they have a lot to be proud of but that the West denigrates their achievements and wants to see Russia weakened and destroyed. The adoption of alien western economic and political models and the influence of institutions such as the IMF are blamed by the Red-Browns for the poor condition of their country. Certain beliefs which have some basis in reality, but which have been exaggerated and distorted, have become common currency in Russia. The West is held responsible for destroying Russian agriculture by dumping cheaper western products on the Russian market. Western food stuffs are said to be cheap because they are contaminated by dangerous chemical additives. In reality Russian agriculture was damaged by decades of soviet mismanagement and lack of investment, while Russian entrepreneurs import cheap food that they know they can sell. The West is also accused of wanting to use Russia as a toxic waste dump. There has been some evidence of western companies being involved in illegal dumping activities in Russia, but they were taking the opportunities provided by Russia's general lack of law and order to make some quick money, rather than acting of behalf of their governments in a centuries-long western conspiracy. The West also stands accused by the Russian security services of orchestrating a brain drain of Russia's best people. Given the poor funding of educational and research institutions, scientists are leaving Russia and some are taking up new opportunities in Western Europe and North America. It is doubtful, however, that the West is really pleased by Russian nuclear scientists being recruited to work in Iraq (see Chapter 12).

Embracing globalisation?

It is no surprise given the exaggerated expectations of reform in 1991–2 and in the face of mounting problems that there should be a knee-jerk anti-westernism and a stress on Russianness. The mayor of Moscow, Yury Luzhkov, for example, backed the rebuilding of the Church of Christ the Saviour near the Kremlin which was dynamited on Stalin's orders. He has also insisted that all advertisements in Moscow should be in the Russian Cyrillic rather than in the western Latin alphabet. Luzhkov is no isolationist, though, and he has encouraged foreign businesses to set up in Moscow. Russians are not the hapless playthings of globalisation; they are open to foreign influences, but are also tentatively beginning to domesticate them. There are now fast-food outlets that have adopted McDonald's-style counter service, with menus showing pictures and prices of the food, and young staff in jeans and baseball caps, but selling traditional Russian foods rather than burgers.

Globalisation is not just about westernisation; cultural flows and influences are also coming into Russia from Asia and the Islamic world. Russian Muslims, for example, use the new communications to promote contacts with their co-religionists abroad and to listen to broadcasts from Iran, Turkey and Pakistan. A shared culture also encourages business links between these countries, the Central Asian states of the Near Abroad and Russia's Muslims. The oil-rich republic of Tatarstan has agreed to stay within the RF and while keen to reassert its national identity is also ready to embrace globalisation. The current debate about alphabet reform in Tatarstan shows its people wanting to communicate with as wide a world as possible. Under Stalin speakers of Turkic languages in the USSR were forced to adopt the Cyrillic alphabet but since independence Uzbekistan, Turkmenistan and Azerbaijan have adopted the Latin alphabet. Tatars used the Arabic script from the ninth century until 1927 when they briefly adopted the Latin alphabet until forced to use the Cyrillic alphabet in 1939. In 1997 Tatarstan began to move from the Cyrillic to the Latin alphabet. Advocates of this reform claim that Tatar phonetics are better conveyed by the Latin alphabet but crucially that the Latin script will facilitate the computerising of the Tatar language and the Tatarisation of computer programs (Khasanova, 1997b).

A new state ideology and the Russian idea

The state ideology

In 1992 certain strategic decisions were taken about Russia's future. The Yeltsin leadership committed Russia to become an open society, with a competitive market economy, a civil society (*grazhdanskoe obshchestve*) and a law-governed state (Kortunov, 1995: 5). A continuing problem is that Russian politics are polarised between liberal democrats on one side and Red-Browns on the other, so that the very legitimacy and authority of the state are contested. Alexander Tsipko of the Gorbachev Foundation neatly encapsulates the problem as, 'Old Russia was united by ideology combining Christian Orthodoxy and Russian identity. Soviet Russia was united, at least outwardly, by communist ideology. But what ideology can unite the patriots and the democrats, the Russians with traditional Russian identity and the Russians with Soviet identity?' (Tsipko, 1993: 191). Tsipko believes that Russia's democrats need to offer the Russian people a new national idea to challenge the national ideas and ideologies provided by the communists and the nationalists.

In the new states of the former USSR nationalism was mobilised to promote the legitimacy and integration of the new states. Yeltsin used Russian nationalism and the slogan 'Russia First' (see Chapter 2) in his bid to break free from the USSR, but resisted adopting Russian nationalism as a new state ideology. In a multinational state Russian nationalism would be a divisive rather than integrative force, and it also did not sit easily with Yeltsin's westernising agenda. Once Yeltsin was in power his most virulent critics included Russian nationalists, who believed that he had betrayed Russia to the West. Article 13 of the RF Constitution (1993) specifically forbids the adoption of a state ideology. For Russia's democrats the concept of an official state ideology is too reminiscent of Imperial Russia and the USSR to be appropriate for a new democracy. In the new Russia democratic principles and institutions were supposed to promote a cohesive civic Russian identity which was to provide a firm foundation for the new state. However, after Yeltsin's re-election in 1996 he called for the formulation of a national ideology to unite all the citizens of Russia and set up a commission to investigate Russia's identity.

A new state ideology: back to the future?

In the last 200 years Russia has had two state ideologies: Marxism–Leninism and the Official Nationality Doctrine. The KPRF's ideology is now a potent mixture of Eurasianism and Marxism. Lenin's body remains in his Mausoleum on Red Square in Moscow, despite Yeltsin's repeated suggestions that he should be buried in St Petersburg. In 1997 Communists in the Duma even pushed for the readoption of the soviet red flag and the hammer and sickle as the state emblems. They also wanted to return to Stalin's 1944 anthem by Alexandrov except that the Marxist rallying cry 'Proletarians of the world unite' was to be replaced by the more nationalistic 'Be glorious, Russia'; the proposal was defeated. However, in 2000 Putin announced that Russia would return to Alexandrov's music and a modified version of the soviet anthem. In a move designed to appeal to the Communists but also to Russians' pride in their achievements, Putin explained that no longer would Russian Olympians and sports stars be embarrassed by having a national anthem that no one knew. The message is clear: the glory days are back!

The Official Nationality Doctrine was the Imperial Russian state ideology from 1833 to 1917, although briefly dropped by the reformist tsar Alexander II (1855–81). The Official Nationality Doctrine was elaborated by the minister of education, Count Uvarov, and had three elements, Orthodoxy (*pravoslavie*), autocracy (*samoderzhavie*) and nationality (*narodnost'*). Orthodoxy referred to the pre-eminence of the Russian Orthodox Church, autocracy to the absolute powers of the tsar as the foundation of the Russian state, and nationality placed Russians as the principal people in the empire (Hoskings, 1997: 147). Could the Official Nationality Doctrine provide the basis for a new Russian state ideology updated for the new millennium? Russian Orthodoxy is being revived as the state religion and the numerically and culturally dominant ethnic Russians do seem to be the 'principal people' of the Russian Federation. As for autocracy, there seems no groundswell of support to return to tsarism. In 1991 Yeltsin invited Vladimir Kirillovich Romanov, the father of the pretender to the Russian throne, to St Petersburg. At that time about 20 per cent of the Russian population supported the restoration of the monarchy, but by 1995 only 7 per cent were in favour (Figes, 1998: 102). The last tsar Nicholas II and his family were exhumed from a bog near Yekaterinburg in 1991 and finally interred in St Petersburg's Peter and Paul Fortress on 17 July 1998. In his funeral oration President Yeltsin described the burial as a 'symbolic moment of national repentance and unity' (*ibid.*: 98). This is rather ironic as, when Yeltsin was the CPSU secretary in Sverdlovsk (Yekaterinburg), he had followed Kremlin orders and demolished the Ipatiev house where the Romanovs were executed on 17 July 1918. Russia's Communists objected to this state burial as it could constitute not just an apology for the Romanovs' deaths but also a rejection of the Bolshevik Revolution and the entire soviet era. The Russian Orthodox Church, for whom Nicholas is a saint, boycotted the burial, as despite exhaustive scientific testing, they do not believe the remains are authentic. Autocracy in the form of tsarism would not be part of a new state ideology.

It seems likely that if Russia were to develop a new state ideology it would include the ideas of an updated Russian Idea. Drawing on the ideas of the Slavophiles and the Eurasianists, the Russian Idea holds that Russia is a unique civilisation with its own cultural and historical traditions which set it apart from the West. For advocates of the Russian Idea it is these ideas that will promote stability, harmony and development in Russia. The three main features traditionally associated with the Russian Idea are the Orthodox Church, the tsarist state and the peasant commune (McDaniel, 1996: 31). In Russia today these would be a belief in a strong Russian state in alliance with the Orthodox Church. It would not necessarily mean an end to elections or attempts to quash Russia's developing political pluralism. It would however be a state with a strong emphasis on military might and patriotism, and anyone challenging these values would be given short shrift (see Box 3.5).

BOX 3.5

Recommendations for a new national idea for Russia

It would seem that the following could be components of a national idea: the idea of a strong and flourishing Russia; the idea of statehood, patriotism and solidarity; the idea of freedom; the idea of prosperity; the idea of spirituality; the idea of constitutional order and safety; the idea of justice; the idea of civil peace and accord; and the idea of openness to the world...

Source: Aleksei Kiva (1996) 'Ideas are not Cast on Paper but in the Public Mind', *Rossiiskaia gazeta*, 1 August, 2. Aleksei Kiva is a Russian political scientist.

Conclusion

The debate about Russia's identity is a debate about Russia's future. Those who stress Russia's uniqueness (*samobytnost'*) tend to argue that western models of development are not appropriate for Russia. Conversely, those who stress Russia's European identity do so to support a modernising project based on capitalism and democracy. As a multinational state Russia's Russianness is also highly contentious. So far democratic principles and a civic concept of identity have had little success in integrating state and society. Russia is therefore looking for a new state ideology which is likely to draw upon Russian nationalism. Eurasianists and some Russian nationalists stress that their nationalism is based upon an inclusive concept of Russianness, not upon a 'blood'-based definition, and that it can therefore incorporate all Russia's peoples.

References

Berdyaev, Nicolas (1947) *The Russian Idea*, London: Centenary Press (trans: R.M. French)

Dawisha, Karen and Parrott, Bruce (1994) *Russia and the New States of Eurasia: The Politics of Upheaval*, Cambridge: Cambridge University Press

Figes, Orlando (1998) 'Burying the Bones', in *Russia: The Wild East, Granta* (64), 95–111

Gumilev, L.N. (1992) *Ot Russiia k Rossii: Ocherki etnicheskoi istorii*, Moscow: Ekopros

Hearst, David (1996) 'Orthodoxy Raises Barriers', *The Guardian*, 16 December, 8

Hoskings, Geoffrey (1997) *Russia People and Empire 1552–1917*, London: HarperCollins

Khasanova, Gulnara (1997a) 'Russia's New Identity Document Creates Uproar in Tatarstan', *Prism* 3 (21) 19 December, http://www.jamestown.org/

Khasanova, Gulnara (1997b) 'Language and Sovereignty: The Politics of Switching to the Latin Alphabet in Tatarstan', *Prism* 3 (16) 10 October, http://www.jamestown.org/

Kortunov, Sergei (1995) 'Natsional'naia sverkhzadacha. Opyt rossiiskoi ideologii', *Nezavisimaia gazeta*, 1 October, 5

Likhachev, Dmitrii S. (1991) *Reflections on Russia*, Boulder, CO: Westview Press

McDaniel, Tim (1996) *The Agony of the Russian Idea*, Princeton, NJ: Princeton University Press

Meek, James (1997) 'Russia Cracks Down on Minority Faiths', *The Guardian*, 20 September, 20

Riasanovsky, Nicholas V. (1984) (4th edn) *A History of Russia*, Oxford: Oxford University Press

Schiller, Robert J., Boysko, Maxim and Korobov, Vladimir (1991) 'Popular Attitudes Toward Free Markets: The Soviet Union and the United States Compared', *American Economic Review* 81 (3) June, 385–400

Shlapentokh, Vladimir (1997) 'How Russians Will See the Status of Their Country by the End of the Century', *Journal of Communist Studies and Transition Politics* 13 (3) September, 1–23

Tsipko, Alexander (1993) 'Dialectics of the Ascent of a New Russian Statehood', in Osamu Ieda (ed.) *New Order in Post-Communist Eurasia*, Sapporo, Japan: Slavic Research Centre, Hokkaido University

Whitehouse, Tom (1998) 'Mormons Set Free in Russia', *The Guardian*, 23 March, 12

Further reading

For a fascinating and wide-ranging analysis of Russian history and culture by Russia's leading liberal nationalist historian see:

Likhachev, Dmitrii S. (1991) *Reflections on Russia*, Boulder, CO: Westview Press

On the Russia diaspora the following provide useful accounts of the nature and treatment of the diaspora and how this is viewed in Russia:

Chinn, Jeff and Kaiser, Robert (1996) *Russians as the New Minority*, Boulder, CO: Westview Press

Kolstoe, Paul (1995) *Russians in the Former Soviet Republics*, London: Hurst and Co.

Melvin, Neil (1995) *Russians Beyond Russia: The Politics of National Identity*, London: RIIA, Pinter

On the Russian Orthodox Church see:

Davis, Nathaniel (1996) 'The Russian Orthodox Church: Opportunity and Trouble', *Communist and Post-Communist Studies* 29 (3) September, 275–286
Dunlop, John B. (1989) 'Gorbachev and Russian Orthodoxy', *Problems of Communism* 38 (4) July–August, 96–116
Krasikov, Anatoly (1998) 'From the Annals of Spiritual Freedom: Church–State Relations in Russia', *East-European Constitutional Review* 7 (2) Spring, 75–84

On the debates about Russia's identity see:

'Russian Exceptionalism. Is Russia different?', *The Economist*, 15 June 1996, 21–23, provides a succinct overview of the arguments about Russia's 'exceptionalism'

Becker, Seymour (1991) 'Russia Between East and West: The Intelligentsia, Russian National Identity and Asian Borderlands', *Central Asian Survey* 10 (4), 47–64, looks at what Asianness means to Russians
Ferdinand, Peter (1992) 'Russia and the Russians after Communism: Western or Eurasia?', *The World Today* 48 (12) December, 225–229, provides a concise overview of the debate
Stankevich, Sergei (1992) 'Russia in Search of Itself', *The National Interest* (28) Summer, 47–51, provides a Eurasianist critique from one of the leading democracy campaigners of the Reconstruction period
Yemelianova, G.G. (1995) 'Russia and Islam: The History and Prospects of a Relationship', *Asian Affairs* 82 (3), 278–290, provides a comprehensive overview of this topic

On Russia's European identity and its relationship with Europe see:

Dukes, Paul (1998) 'Globalization and Europe: The Russian Question', in Roland Axtman (ed.) *Globalization and Europe*, London and Washingon: Pinter
Neumann, Iver B. (1996) *Russia and the Idea of Europe*, London: Routledge

On the ideas and development of Russian nationalism see:

Agursky, Mikhail (1987) *The Third Rome: National Bolshevism in the USSR*, Boulder, CO: Westview Press
Allworth, Edward (ed.) (1980) *Ethnic Russia in the USSR: The Dilemma of Dominance*, New York: Pergamon
Barghoorn, F.C. (1983) *Soviet Russian Nationalism*, Princeton, NJ: Princeton University Press
Carter, Stephen K. (1990) *Russian Nationalism: Yesterday, Today, Tomorrow*, London: Pinter

On globalisation see:

Barber, Benjamin R. (1995) *Jihad vs McWorld*, New York: Ballantine Books
Burbach, Roger, Núñez, Orlando and Kagarlitsky, Boris (1997) *Globalization and its Discontents*, London: Pluto Press

Websites

http://www.keston.org/ (Keston Institute, UK, monitors the freedom of religious affairs in communist and post-communist countries)

http://www.stetson.edu/~psteeves/relnews/ (Stetson University, US, 'Russian Religious News')

PART II

The making of the Russian state

CHAPTER 4

The president and the parliament

This chapter examines Russia's post-communist constitutional and institutional crisis which was 'resolved' by the use of armed force in October 1993. Russia's 'super-presidential' system is explained together with the composition and working of the Federal Assembly and its two chambers, the State Duma and the Federation Council. The role of the prime minister, the government and the presidential administration are also examined. This chapter also addresses the nature of Boris Yeltsin's presidency and his successful endeavours to secure the presidency for his chosen successor, Vladimir Putin.

Introduction

Russia began its post-communist transition with some slightly reformed soviet era institutions, which had been created for an entirely different political system. One of the major results of Gorbachev's reforms was that political power within Russia was already very diffuse. The creation of new institutions therefore took place amidst struggles between different power centres: the presidency, the parliament composed of the Congress of People's Deputies and the Supreme Soviet, the government and the increasingly assertive republican authorities. The writing of a new constitution became the focus of a struggle for power between different institutions, each wanting supreme power for itself. These personal and institutional rivalries were conducted against a backdrop of increasing economic problems, growing poverty amongst the Russian people and instability on Russia's borders. The overall atmosphere of the early 1990s was one of chaos, crisis and confrontation.

Escalating conflict between president and parliament, 1990–1993

Russia: maintaining its integrity and challenging Gorbachev

Gorbachev's democratisation included a reduction in the powers of the CPSU and an increase in the powers of the soviets and their chairs at all levels. This apparent de-concentration and decentralisation of power and authority was countered by the creation of a strong executive presidency for the USSR (see Chapter 2). In May 1990 Yeltsin was elected the chair of the Supreme Soviet of the RSFSR, which was the standing body of the Congress of People's Deputies. He now held the most powerful non-party post in the RSFSR and chose Ruslan Khasbulatov as his first deputy. In a move that paralleled the creation of the USSR executive presidency, in a March 1991 referendum the RSFSR agreed to create a new post of RSFSR president. Yeltsin was elected RSFSR president on 12 June 1991 and Khasbulatov became the chair of the Supreme Soviet. Yeltsin argued that the RSFSR needed a strong presidency for two main reasons: firstly, to counter and challenge President Gorbachev's central power, and secondly, to maintain Russia's integrity by preventing its regions from seeking independence. Yeltsin's public pronouncements at this time were rather contradictory. On the one hand he urged the USSR's republics and regions to take as much power and autonomy as they wanted and to challenge Moscow's, that is Gorbachev's, rule. Moscow, however, was also the seat of Yeltsin's power and while he encouraged Russia's regions to challenge Gorbachev, Yeltsin wanted to maintain Russia's integrity. In a move designed to appeal to Russia's regions and its non-Russian peoples Yeltsin in July 1990 had already established a Federation Council within the office of the chair of the RSFSR Supreme Soviet. The Federation Council's members included the 31 chairs of the autonomous republic, *oblast* and *okrug* soviets, as well as a further 31 chairs from selected *oblast*, *krai* and city soviets. From 1991 the Federation Council included the leaders of the 88 (later 89) federal subjects (see Chapter 5). In appointing Khasbulatov, a Chechen, as the chair (prime minister) of the RSFSR Supreme Soviet and establishing a Federation Council, Yeltsin was signalling to Russia's non-Russians and regions that they were to be included in the building of a new democratic but united Russia.

In 1991 Gorbachev's Kremlin was the main enemy for Russia's westernising reformers and those who simply wanted the destruction of the USSR. At this stage Khasbulatov and the Russian parliament accepted the need for a strong Russian presidency. The Congress of People's Deputies even granted Yeltsin emergency powers to rule by decree for one year until the end of 1992. The consensus between president and parliament finally ended in December 1991 once the USSR was no more. The 1978 RSFSR Constitution was amended over 300 times between 1990 and mid-1993 and as a result granted both the legislative and the executive branches supreme state power. Khasbulatov wanted a return to the pre-June 1991 situation in which the chair of the parliament rather than the president was Russia's leader, and there were constitutional grounds to support the argument that Russia was a *de jure* parliamentary republic. The reality however was that the new Russian Federation was a presidential republic. The process of drawing up a new RF Constitution was therefore highly contentious, with the parliament led by Khasbulatov pushing for a parliamentary republic and Yeltsin standing firm on the need for a presidential republic.

1991–1992: Economic shock therapy but no political reforms

Following the defeat of the August 1991 coup Yeltsin appeared Russia's undisputed leader. He was the Russian president who had seen off a hardline coup, delivered Russian independence and was the embodiment of Russian democracy. At this time it seemed impossible to challenge Yeltsin's westernising vision of the new Russia. This was a moment when Yeltsin should have seized the initiative, dissolved parliament, called fresh elections, started work on a new constitution and begun to reform institutions and structures. Instead, in a pattern of behaviour that was to mark his leadership, Yeltsin followed the period of furious activity that had defeated the coup by withdrawing to his dacha for several months. Russia was rapidly slipping into chaos but Yeltsin was playing tennis four or five times a week with his great friend and tennis coach Shamil Tarpishev. When Yeltsin did re-emerge he declared that the important thing was to get down to economic reform and that there was no time to talk. He used the powers granted to him by the Congress of People's Deputies to issue economic policy decrees and appoint key government ministers and regional officials.

During 1992 president and parliament worked together somewhat uneasily. Whilst Khasbulatov was highly critical of shock therapy, he shared Yeltsin's belief in the importance of Russian unity and resisted attempts by the republics to achieve greater autonomy let alone independence. Khasbulatov also ensured that most presidential legislation successfully passed through parliament. Parliament, dominated by communists and nationalists (the Red-Browns), increasingly used its control over the administration of legislation to block the implementation of presidential policies. During 1992 as Russia was plunging deeper and deeper into economic and political chaos, the conflict between the parliament and the president grew. Although Khasbulatov could legitimately find constitutional provisions that supported his advocacy of a parliamentary system, it is clear that he was also personally ambitious and turned parliament into his personal power base. He is, for example, alleged to have distributed perks and privileges such as trips abroad to gain supporters. For his part Yeltsin either ignored, insulted or attacked the Congress of People's Deputies and made little attempt to establish a working relationship with it.

By the late summer of 1992 it was clear that the political institutions had failed to resolve the conflict and in an increasingly volatile atmosphere there were allegations and counter-allegations of coup plots. In October 1992 Khasbulatov was accused of plotting a coup against Yeltsin and of having flown armed Chechens to Moscow to fight alongside the parliamentary guard against the president. Mikhail Poltoranin and Gennady Burbulis, members of Yeltsin's inner circle, used such allegations to justify calls for the suspension of parliament and the introduction of direct presidential rule. Poltoranin and Burbulis made the same accusations in January 1993. For its part parliament accused Yeltsin of seeking dictatorial powers and of failing to implement an effective reform programme. Although failing in a bid to impeach Yeltsin, parliament refused to extend his emergency powers which expired in December 1992. Yeltsin accused the parliament of blocking desperately needed reforms and of being dominated by undemocratic deputies.

December 1992: dropping the architects of reform to save reform?

It would have taken a president of consummate political skills to have worked with the Russian parliament at this time. Yeltsin lacked such skills and had failed to capitalise on his heightened prestige after the defeat of the August 1991 coup. In December 1992 Valery Zorkin, the chair of the Constitutional Court, brokered a temporary compromise solution between Yeltsin and Khasbulatov, which included the sacking of some of Yeltsin's closest allies. Yeltsin replaced his acting prime minister Igor Gaidar with the more centrist Viktor Chernomyrdin. Gennady Burbulis, who had created Yeltsin's presidential administration, Mikhail Poltoranin, the information minister, Galina Starovoitova, the presidential adviser on nationality issues, Igor Yakovlev, the chair of Ostankino TV, and Arkady Murashev, the head of Moscow's police, were all sacked. The Congress of People's Deputies also won the right to approve presidential appointments and dismissals in the key areas of finance and foreign affairs. In return it agreed to drop its demand for constitutional amendments to weaken the presidency and to accept a referendum on a new constitution to be held on 11 April 1993. The referendum would decide whether Russia would have a presidential or a parliamentary system.

Although Yeltsin had sacrificed many of his closest allies in the hope of appeasing his critics, he had not capitulated. Yeltsin began a somewhat belated attempt to build support in the Congress of People's Deputies by forming an alliance with the centrist Civic Union bloc of about 40 per cent of the deputies. Yeltsin also managed to preserve a reformist team in the government. The economist Boris Fyodorov, who had worked closely with Gaidar, was appointed the deputy prime minister for financial and economic policy and was put in charge of economic reform, and Andrei Kozyrev remained foreign minister. Yeltsin also moved to strengthen his own presidential administration. The liberal Sergei Filatov, who had organised Yeltsin's campaign for the June

1991 RSFSR presidential election, was appointed to head Yeltsin's administration. In order to strengthen his influence over the media Yeltsin set up the Federal Information Centre and put two of his supporters, Mikhail Poltoranin and Sergei Yushenkov, in charge. Yeltsin was putting his team together to ensure a win in the April 1993 referendum.

Vice-President Alexander Rutskoi

In 1991 Yeltsin had chosen Alexander Rutskoi as his running mate for the RSFSR presidential elections. Although initially the two men worked closely together, not least in their opposition to the August 1991 coup attempt, after the coup they became increasingly estranged. Rutskoi was the leader of the party Communists for Democracy whose ideas were at odds (see Chapter 1) with those of Prime Minister Gaidar, whose reform team Rutskoi contemptuously dubbed 'boys in pink trousers'. Rutskoi sided with Khasbulatov and by the time of the the April 1993 referendum was in opposition to Yeltsin. The post of vice-president was later abolished in the 1993 Constitution.

The April 1993 referendum

Russia desperately needed a new constitution in order to resolve its constitutional crisis, and yet the process of drawing up the constitution was proving a problem. Yeltsin made it clear that the new constitution should include a strong executive presidency while parliament favoured a parliamentary system with the president as a ceremonial figurehead. Parliament and president were locked in an open power struggle, so Yeltsin sought a personal mandate by appealing over parliament directly to the Russian people. Yeltsin emerged a narrow victor from the April referendum and could take some comfort in the fact that over 67 per cent of the voters favoured early elections to the Congress of People's Deputies (see Box 4.1). The percentage of voters expressing no confidence in Yeltsin and his reforms and wanting early presidential elections was still substantial however. Voters were also consistent in their voting across the four referendum questions. So for example in the regions where the majority expressed no confidence in President Yeltsin, they also did not approve of his socio-economic policies and favoured early presidential elections. Yeltsin's victory was largely confined to the big cities and he fared badly in small towns and Russia's heartlands, which had been particularly hard hit by economic shock therapy. Similarly, he lacked support in those areas of Siberia that were not cushioned by oil, coal and diamonds earnings. Whilst parliament and president were fighting over power in Moscow, Russia's non-Russian republics were demanding greater autonomy or outright independence. Ten of Russia's republics, including the Volga republics of Bashkortostan, Marii El, Mordovia and Udmurtia, passed votes of no-confidence in Yeltsin. In the republic of Tatarstan voter turnout was so low

BOX 4.1

The 25 April 1993 referendum: a mandate for Yeltsin?

Question	Percentage of the vote	
	Yes	No
1. Do you have confidence in the president of the RF, B.N. Yeltsin?	58.7	39.2
2. Do you approve of the socio-economic policies carried out by the president of the RF and the government of the RF since 1992?	53.0	44.6
3. Do you consider it necessary to hold early elections for the president of the RF?	49.5	47.1
4. Do you consider it necessary to hold early elections for the People's Deputies of the RF?	67.2	30.1

Source: *Keesings Record of World Events. News Digest*, April 1993, 39421, adapted.

that its vote was declared invalid. Yeltsin also fared badly in the Caucasus: in the republic of Dagestan only 15 per cent and in Chechen-Ingushetia only 2 per cent of voters expressed confidence in Yeltsin. The referendum results did not provide Yeltsin with a decisive mandate and they did not resolve the stand-off between president and parliament.

The struggle for a new constitution

Attacking parliament to save democracy?

The impasse between president and parliament continued throughout the spring and summer and into the autumn of 1993. Since 1990 work had been under way on drawing up a new constitution, and in May 1993 Yeltsin hastened matters by setting up a special Constitutional Assembly to convene in June. The Constitutional Assembly produced a new draft constitution on 12 July which attempted to draw on both the president's draft produced in April 1993 and the parliament's version. The problem was that president and parliament had such profoundly different concepts of their respective roles that they could not be reconciled. The Constitutional Assembly did not approve the constitution and the constitutional crisis continued. In mid-September Yeltsin's main opponents Ruslan Khasbulatov and Alexander

Rutskoi warned that Yeltsin was planning direct presidential rule and a dictatorship. On 21 September Yeltsin issued decree no. 1400 'On Gradual Constitutional Reform in the Russian Federation', dissolving parliament. Parliamentary powers were to be vested in a new Federal Assembly and the existing Federation Council was to be its upper chamber. Yeltsin ordered the Constitutional Assembly to agree a final version with the parliament's Constitutional Commission. A referendum on the new constitution together with elections to a new parliament were set for 12 December 1993 (see Box 4.2).

An emergency meeting of the Constitutional Court ruled by 9 to 4 that Yeltsin's decree and order were in violation of the Constitution. The Supreme

---

BOX 4.2

Were Yeltsin's actions against the Parliament in October 1993 justified?

Arguments in favour of Yeltsin	Arguments against Yeltsin
The Congress of People's Deputies was dominated by communists and nationalists who opposed reform.	Congress passed the declaration of sovereignty and took the first steps towards a separation of powers and a Constitutional Court.
Congress was elected in March 1990 when the CPSU was the only legal political party and while a truer reflection of public opinion than the previous Congress it was not freely elected.	By 1990 the CPSU was so pluralistic that the party label tells little about deputies' allegiances. The CPSU included Stalinists, Social Democrats, Communists, free marketeers. Yeltsin himself only left the CPSU in July 1990.
Yeltsin was elected with a personal popular mandate. Public opinion polls regularly demonstrated that he had more support than Congress.	Yeltsin's campaign programme for the 1991 presidential elections did not include any of the economic reforms that he introduced after the election. There was no electoral mandate for shock therapy.
Yeltsin was the best guarantor of democracy and economic reform. Khasbulatov and his allies were only interested in power.	Yeltsin should have tried to negotiate with parliament and broaden his support there.
Yeltsin had no choice but to use the armed forces because the Congress rebels used force and would not compromise.	A true democrat does not use force to resolve a deadlock. Yeltsin was only interested in power.
Yeltsin was the only person in 1991 with the stature and support to prevent a hardline restoration. Democratisation could only be achieved by hard measures against those who opposed it.	

Soviet responded by declaring Rutskoi acting president, setting up an alternative government and refusing to comply with the order to dissolve parliament. It also summoned an emergency parliamentary session which was attended by 658 of the possible 1033 deputies. Yeltsin replied by sealing off the Russian parliament building, the White House, and cutting off the electricity and water supply with around 100 mostly Red-Brown deputies left inside. Armed insurrection followed on 3 October when around 15 000 supporters of the parliamentary rebels managed to breach the cordon of Interior Ministry troops and enter the White House. The stand-off between president and parliament had rapidly moved to a stage when it could be resolved only by force. Khasbulatov and Rutskoi, emboldened by the rebels' success, believed that the security and armed forces were deserting Yeltsin and so ordered their supporters to attack the office of Moscow's mayor and the Ostankino television centre. Yeltsin declared a state of emergency that continued until 18 October. The armed forces were reluctant to get involved in this conflict between civilian politicians and institutions, but Defence Minister Gen. Pavel Grachev finally relented and on 4 October the White House was bombarded for ten hours. The rebels surrendered and were arrested; 189 people were killed during fighting in Moscow.

Federal Assembly elections and the referendum on the new constitution, 12 December 1993

Following his victory in October 1993 and with his chief opponents in prison, Yeltsin was able to dominate the framing of the new constitution. The Constitutional Assembly was reorganised and headed by Sergei Filatov, the head of the presidential staff. The final version of the constitution produced on 10 November enshrined Yeltsin's preference for a strong presidency and a weak parliament. Yeltsin decided not to call an early presidential election and only presented himself for re-election in June 1996 when his first term in office came to an end. In contrast elections to the new Federal Assembly (parliament) were held in December 1993 on the same day as a referendum on the adoption of the new constitution. In a somewhat unusual move the parliamentary elections were held as if the new constitution had already been approved. The new constitution's section on 'Concluding and Transitional Provisions' even states that, 'The day of the nationwide vote – 12 December 1993 – is deemed the day of the adoption of the Constitution of the Russian Federation'. It seems to have been assumed that the new constitution would be approved by the referendum. In the event 58.4 per cent of votes cast were in favour of the new constituion, but this represented approval by only 31 per cent of the possible electorate, hardly a resounding endorsement (see Box 4.3). Similarly, the results of the Federal Assembly elections produced a decidedly anti-Yeltsin majority (see Appendix 1). An early sign that relations between president and parliament were not gong to be easy came in early 1994 when the State Duma

BOX 4.3

Referendum on the RF Constitution, 12 December 1993

Question: Do you approve of the constitution of the Russian Federation?

	Percentage of the electorate	Percentage of the valid votes
In favour	31.0	58.4
Against	22.1	41.6
Total votes	54.8	
Invalid votes	1.7	

Source: *Rossiiskie vesti*, 25 December 1993, 1.

(Duma) granted an amnesty to all the rebels who had taken part in 'the events' of October 1993.

The basic provisions in the 1993 Constitution

The 1993 Constitution establishes Russia as a democratic, federative, law-based state with a republican form of government (Art. 1) and the people are described as sovereign (Art. 3). The Preamble refers to the 'multinational' people of the Russian Federation and stresses the equality and self-determination of Russia's peoples. The Preamble also affirms the immutability of the democratic foundations of Russia's sovereign statehood and Article 8 guarantees freedom of economic activity. Russia's post-communist course of development as a democratic, capitalist country is therefore enshrined in the Constitution. The Constitution recognises Russia's ideological diversity and specifically rejects the establishment of a state or compulsory ideology (Arts 13.1 and 13.2). The Constitution attempts to define and limit state power. So for example there are provisions on human and civil rights, a prohibition on the imprisonment of dissidents, and limitations on the state's ability to monitor correspondence and bug phones. Russians may freely travel abroad and may not be sent into exile or stripped of their citizenship. The Constitution also endorses the principle of a separation of legislative, executive and judicial powers (Art. 10) and the independence of these institutions, and it also asserts their duty to supervise each other and to abide by the Constitution. A separation of powers is designed to ensure that power is not concentrated in or monopolised by one person, body or institution and as such it is part of a system of checks and balances that is supposed to prevent the emergence of a dictatorship. The reality is that the 1993 Constitution established a rather imbalanced separation of powers. Its creation of an extremely powerful presidency means that not only is Russia a presidential rather than a parliamentary system, it is a super-presidential system.

The Federal Assembly

The Russian parliament

The Constitution replaced the Congress of People's Deputies and Supreme Soviet parliament with a new bicameral Federal Assembly. The new upper chamber is the Federation Council and the lower chamber is the State Duma (Duma). The Federal Assembly's structure, formation and jurisdiction are set out in Chapter 5 of the 1993 Constitution (see Box 4.4 and websites listed at the end of this chapter). The Duma and the Federation Council sit separately and only meet together to hear messages from the president, the Constitutional Court and addresses from foreign heads of state (Art. 100).

BOX 4.4

The Federal Assembly established in 1993

FEDERATION COUNCIL

178 deputies

2 seats for each of the republics and regions

STATE DUMA

450 deputies

CONSTITUENCY SEATS	PARTY LIST SEATS
225 deputies elected by single-member constituencies	225 deputies elected by Russia-wide party lists
First-past-the-post system	Proportional representation
A valid vote requires a 25 per cent turnout	A party list must receive a minimum 5 per cent of the national vote to gain representation
	If a party list candidate wins a constituency seat, (s)he is replaced by the next on the list

The State Duma

The Duma is the standing body and the more powerful chamber of the Federal Assembly. The Duma elects a chair and has its own apparatus. It also has a system of committees on major policy areas (see Appendix 2) whose task is to review legislation and to make recommendations to government. The committee chairs are distributed according to the representation of the different parties, blocs and groups in the Duma. The jurisdiction of the Duma is set out in Article 103 of the Constitution. The Duma approves the president's choice of prime minister, may register a vote of no confidence in the government, and has the right to review government legislation and to initiate impeachment proceedings against the president. The Duma shares with the president and the Federation Council the right of legislative initiative (Art. 104). Federal laws adopted by the Duma are passed up to the Federation Council for approval and if the Federation Council rejects a bill, a joint commission of the two chambers is set up to try to settle the differences. This has generally proved possible, although a two-thirds majority of the Duma can override the Federation Council's veto. The president must sign all bills into law and the president has the right of veto. The presidential veto may be overturned by a two-thirds majority of both the Duma and the Federation Council. The general weakness of the Duma, and the fact that deputies do not have a significant role in government, means that the Russian electorate has very little input into the legislative process. The Duma's weakness encourages it to be obstructionist rather than to have a constructive relationship with the executive (see Fish, 1997 and Linz and Valenzuela, 1994) (see Box 4.5).

State Duma elections

According to the Constitution the Duma's terms last four years. The first Duma elected in December 1993 was considered transitional and so was elected for only a two-year term. Those who wanted to stress continuity with Imperial Russia's four State Dumas (1906–17) called the 1993 or first Duma the fifth Duma. The Duma's 450 deputies are elected for a four-year term by two different methods. Half the deputies (*deputaty*) are elected in single-member constituencies in a first-past-the-post system. The remaining deputies are elected from federal party lists under a proportional representation system. In order to reduce the party political fragmentation in the Duma and to prevent extremist parties from benefiting from proportional representation, a party has to surmount a 5 per cent threshold in order to achieve representation. Parties that win seats through the party list system automatically acquire the status of a party faction, which may also be joined by deputies elected for the single-member constituencies. Independent and other deputies may join an existing party faction, or if they can gather a membership of at least 35 deputies they may form another faction. All the party factions tend to be quite fluid with

---

BOX 4.5

Explaining the weakness of the State Duma

- The Constitution.
- There was a huge backlog of soviet era legislation that needed to be replaced.
- No single party or block has a majority in the Duma and party discipline is also very weak.
- This fragmentation means that debates in the Duma are often very polarised and makes it difficult to achieve a consensus.
- This fragmentation means Duma legislation tends to be the product of back-room trading. This both slows down the legislative process and produces laws that tend to be fairly general and/or to contain contradictory elements, so making laws difficult to implement.
- Deputy immunity from prosecution encourages corruption and has led to criminals standing for election to benefit from both the immunity and the opportunities to influence legislation that a deputy enjoys.

---

deputies changing factions and/or voting with other factions. In the 1995–9 Duma the Communist Party of the Russian Federation (KPRF) was the largest single faction, followed by Our Home is Russia (NDR), Zhirinovsky's Liberal Democratic Party of the Russian Federation (LDPRF) and then the Agrarian Party of Russia (APR).

The Federation Council

In 1993 Yeltsin established a Federation Council composed of 178 members (*chleny*), two from each of the 89 federal subjects, the republics, regions, districts, and the cities of Moscow and St Petersburg. Each of these federal subjects provided one member from its representative and one from its executive bodies (Art. 95.2). As part of the transitional arrangement the 1993 Constitution required that the first convocation of the Federation Council should be directly elected by the people on 12 December 1993 for a two-year period. The new Federation Council met for the first time on 13 January 1994 and elected Vladimir Shumeiko as its chair. The second Federation Council elected Igor Stroev, a former member of the CPSU Politburo and the governor of Orel *oblast*, as its chair. The Federation Council does not however have an executive body overseeing its activities. Also in contrast to the extensive Duma committee system, it only has 11 committees to review legislation and to make recommendations to the government. In 1995 a new Federation Council Law replaced the direct election of members with the *ex officio* appointment of the heads of executives (governors, presidents and mayors) and the heads of the legislatures (chairs or speakers) from each of the federal subjects to the

Federation Council. The second Federation Council convocation was formed on 23 January 1996 for an unlimited term. The system of *ex officio* appointment means that the Federation Council's composition gradually changes as the heads of the executives and legislatures change throughout the federation.

There were three basic problems here. Firstly, Federation Council members are only part-time parliamentarians who combine full-time, highly responsible posts in their republics or regions with monthly Federation Council sessions in Moscow. Secondly, there is no uniform government structure within Russia's republics and regions: some have a president and a prime minister, while in others there is a collective head of government. The identification of the heads of the executive and the legislature is not as clear-cut as it might at first appear. Thirdly, presidents of the republics and regional governors were initially appointed by the RF president and these posts only started to be elected in 1993. By 1995 only 66 of the 89 regional governors and presidents of the republics had been elected. In constitutional terms, the fact that the Federation Council had a substantial corps of presidential appointees contradicted the principle of a separation of powers. It also meant that the Federation Council contained members who owed their political careers to Yeltsin rather than to the electorate of the area they were supposed to represent. The principle of the separation of powers is also contradicted as members of the Federation Council are involved in the legislative process within the Federation Council and then in the implementation of that legislation in their capacities as heads of the executives (presidents, governors, mayors) in the federal subjects.

The jurisdiction of the Federation Council

The jurisdiction of the Federation Council is set out in Article 102 of the Constitution. The Federation Council is required to review legislation on the budget, taxation and other financial matters, as well as foreign policy issues such as the ratification of treaties and the declaration of war. Not surprisingly given its name and composition the Federation Council has a particular responsibility for nationalities and regional issues, including the examination of any proposed changes to internal boundaries. In addition the Federation Council confirms presidential decrees, the imposition of a state of emergency or martial law, the use of Russian armed forces outside the RF, the scheduling of presidential elections and the impeachment of the president. The Federation Council also had certain judicial functions such as the appointment and removal of the general prosecutor and the appointment of judges to the Constitutional Court, the Supreme Court and the Supreme Arbitration Court. The Federation Council also has a key role in changing the Constitution, which could potentially limit the powers of the president. The Federation Council can also impeach the president but only after a lengthy series of referrals to the Supreme Court and confirmation by a two-thirds majority of both chambers of the Federal Assembly.

The changing Federation Council

Between the presidential elections in June–July 1996 and January 1997 there were elections in 40 federal subjects resulting in 56 per cent of Yeltsin's former appointees failing to be elected as governors. Of their replacements 15 belonged to the opposition, 8 were independents and 12 were Yeltsin supporters. Amongst Federation Council members the KPRF and NDR are the two largest parties. Members of the Federation Council are not allowed to establish party factions and many do not have a specific party allegiance. Even for those Yeltsin appointees who survived the election process, political survival now requires that they promote republican or regional interests and concerns. The governors have substantial executive power in their republics and regions; they control budgets and decide how much money their regions pay into federation coffers. They are therefore politicians of some power and stature, who have their own power bases and are not dependent on presidential patronage. The first signal that the Federation Council was becoming more assertive came in December 1996, when it voted for the return of Sevastopol in the Crimea from Ukraine to Russia, against Yeltsin's wishes. In 1999, Yeltsin's final year as president, the Federation Council twice refused to accept Yeltsin's dismissal of the general prosecutor Yury Skuratov, who had initiated investigations into corruption in the executive branch and the presidential administration, and had even issued a warrant for the arrest of Yeltsin's ally Boris Berezovsky.

Putin and the Federation Council

President Putin is determined to establish federal control over Russia's republics and regions (see Chapter 5). This entails a two-pronged approach of combining republics and regions into new federal districts headed by presidential representatives and changing the composition of the Federation Council. Putin describes these reforms as designed to strengthen and cement the Russian state, to make the executive and legislative branches work more effectively and to realise the constitutional principles of the separation of powers, and the unity of the vertical chain of executive power (*Rossiiskaia gazeta*, 19 May 2000, 3). When announcing his proposed changes to the composition of the Federation Council, Putin pointed out that although the Constitution states that it shall be composed of representatives of the executive and legislative branches of government, it does not state that these representatives have to be the federal subjects' top office holders. Putin argued that these office holders should instead concentrate on their work within their republic or region, rather than trying to combine these tasks with Federation Council membership. Putin proposed that the Federation Council shall be composed of full-time, professional senators chosen by republican presidents, regional governors and the chairs of the parliaments, assemblies and legislatures. Putin's proposal means that Federation Council membership will be through appointment rather than direct popular election, and it also retains the principle of regional representation in its composition. Not surprisingly Putin's proposals met with fierce opposition from the Federation Council but were supported by the Duma.

The president

(see Chapter 4 of the Constitution)

The Constitution and the president

The RF president is the head of state and commander-in-chief of the armed forces. The president is directly elected by the Russian people for a four-year term and no individual may serve more than two consecutive terms in office (Art. 81). The president determines the guidelines for the domestic and foreign policies of the state and 'represents the Russian Federation domestically and in international relations' (Art. 80) and has extensive powers, such as the right to declare a state of emergency (Art. 88), call a referendum (Art. 84), dissolve the Duma (Arts 111 and 117) and issue decrees (*ukazy*) that do not have to be submitted to either the parliament or the people (Art. 90). In addition the president also appoints the prime minister, deputy prime ministers, federal ministers, Security Council members, the Russian Central Bank chair and leading figures in the judiciary, subject to Duma ratification. The president can also preside over sessions of the government (Art. 83), present draft laws to the Duma (Art. 84), veto Federal Assembly laws (Art. 107) and dismiss the government. The president is not untouchable, but rather is subject to the Constitution and may be impeached on the initiative of the Duma, but in a rather cumbersome and slow process. For impeachment to proceed the Supreme Court and the Constitutional Court must confirm that there is evidence of 'high treason' or a similar 'grave crime' (Art. 93) and verify that the correct procedures have been followed. It then requires a two-thirds vote in both chambers of the Federal Assembly to complete the impeachment. In an important provision to support Duma independence the president is not allowed to dissolve the Duma once it has started impeachment procedures (Art. 109.4).

Russian super-presidentialism

Despite its endorsement of a separation of powers, the Constitution created not just a presidential system but a super-presidential system. The components of this super-presidency are a strong executive presidency, a weak legislature and a poorly developed judiciary (see Chapter 6). The justification for this super-presidency is that Russia needs a strong presidency in order to push through reforms and to establish a stable transition. However, parliament exists, elections are held, debates continue and there is a platform for opposition to the president. The Federal Assembly is too weak to act as a countervailing force to the president, particularly as the Duma finds it difficult to take any concerted action. For example, the Chechen war of 1994–6 was extremely unpopular with the Russian public but while there were discussions about impeaching Yeltsin over the war, the proposal did not receive the necessary two-thirds Duma vote. The Constitution embodies liberal-democratic principles, but it also set up a strong presidency. A problem here is that if the incumbent president is not a liberal, he or she has the power to rule by decree and to force through a potentially authoritarian agenda. Another problem is the sheer number of decrees that are issued: for example Yeltsin signed about 1500 decrees a year (Satter, 1997). This has two important implications. Firstly, it would be impossible for even the healthiest of individuals to be actively involved in drawing up so many decrees. The sheer number of decrees and Yeltsin's poor health meant that the real authors of the decrees were members of Yeltsin's presidential administration, rather than an elected body. Secondly, rule by decree is rather capricious, with decrees suddenly appearing and equally quickly being revoked and replaced by another decree. In rule by decree consistency and democracy are the losers.

Amending the Constitution: the lost chance of 1998

Constitutions enshrine the fundamental principles of a political system and should not need immediate or frequent amendments. It is usual to make amending a constitution a complicated process to avoid hasty or ill-thought-out changes. The 1993 Constitution provides a definitive answer to a range of basic questions about the nature of the RF and its government; what it could not do was to create a supporting popular and elite consensus. The Duma has challenged Yeltsin and Russia's super-presidentialism but Yeltsin firmly rejected any need for constitutional amendments. In 1998 the combination of economic and political crisis provided the Duma with an opportunity to challenge this super-presidentialism. Prime Minister Sergei Kiriyenko, who was hated by the oligarchs and the business community for his attempt to enforce tax collection and by the Red-Browns for his economic liberalism, was blamed for the devaluation of the rouble and fired by President Yeltsin on 23 August. The Duma briefly had the opportunity to exact concessions in return for once again confirming Chernomyrdin as prime minister.

On 30 August 1998 Chernomyrdin, seemingly with Yeltsin's approval, negotiated a power-sharing agreement with the Duma leaders that would have required a series of constitutional amendments. Under these draft Political

Accords the Duma would have the right to approve the appointment of government ministers although the president retained the right to appoint the 'power ministers', that is the ministers of defence, foreign affairs, security and interior. The Accords required the president to undertake not to dismiss the government without parliament's approval and not to dissolve parliament for an 18-month period. In return parliament agreed to withdraw its threat to impeach the president and to approve Chernomyrdin as prime minister. These Accords would not have reduced the president to a powerless figurehead but they would have gone some way to redress the power imbalance between the president and the parliament.

In the event Yeltsin refused to sign the Accords as it seems that the Duma viewed them as part of a broader deal that required Yeltsin to stand down as president. The Duma voted against the Accords and Chernomyrdin. Yeltsin then had a choice (see Art. 103). He could propose Chernomyrdin for a third time and if the Duma refused dissolve it and call elections, which might have led to a more hostile Duma. Instead Yeltsin proposed and the Duma accepted Yevgeny Primakov as a compromise prime minister. Yeltsin stood firm in his opposition to amending the Constitution, arguing that it would take at least a year of committee work before it could be discussed by parliament. In effect Yeltsin was preserving the 1993 arrangements and shelving the whole question of constitutional amendment until after the year 2000 presidential elections, when he would be out of office. In a radio address on Constitution Day (12 December) 1998 Yeltsin said that he categorically disagreed with proposals for a redistribution of powers between president and parliament and that the Constitution should be difficult to amend in order to block extremists. At the very heart of the Russian system of government there still remains a basic lack of agreement over the relative powers of the president and the parliament.

The prime minister, the government and the presidential administration

Prime minister

The prime minister (the chair) of the government is appointed by the president, subject to confirmation by the Duma (Art. 83.a), and is responsible for Russia's day-to-day administration (see Box 4.6). The president does not have to select a prime minister from the largest single party within the Duma, although he or she needs to present a candidate that the Duma will endorse. Chernomyrdin remained prime minister after the December 1995 Duma elections, even though his Our Home is Russia party only secured 10 per cent of the vote (see Appendix 1). The prime minister and other government ministers help the president and presidential advisers to formulate policy. The post is, however, more important than a rather bland statement of its formal prerogatives might suggest. It is the prime minister who acts as a bridge between the president and the parliament and who acts as the chief advocate of government policy in parliament. Yeltsin's longest serving prime minister, Viktor Chernomyrdin, proved particularly 'adept at forging agreements and building consensus among executive bodies and with legislators and lobbying groups. As founder of Our Home is Russia Chernomyrdin spearheaded an effort to bridge the institutional and policy interests of regional elites, enterprise directors and other executives who [were] so critical to the fortunes of the Yeltsin–Chernomyrdin regime' (Willerton, 1997: 50).

In his battles with, first, Gorbachev and then with the Congress of People's Deputies Yeltsin concentrated on getting power for himself as RSFSR president and then as RF president. Even when firmly entrenched in the super-presidency after 1993 he was still not prepared to tolerate the emergence of any political figure who might challenge him or who might appear as an heir apparent. Prime ministers also provided useful scapegoats for the failures of presidential policies. Igor Gaidar was the first casualty, being blamed for the excesses of shock therapy. Chernomyrdin was similarly unceremoniously dumped despite absolute public loyalty to Yeltsin, but he was being widely spoken of as a future president. Yeltsin sacked Chernomyrdin in March 1998 on the grounds that the government lacked dynamism and needed new ideas and approaches, but then tried to bring back Chernomyrdin in August–September 1998, arguing that the country needed continuity and stability. Prime Minister Sergei Kiriyenko was blamed for the summer 1998 economic crisis and fired by President Yeltsin on 23 August. The oligarchs wanted Chernomyrdin back as prime minister because it would give him a power base for the presidential elections and at that time he was their preferred post-Yeltsin president. When

---

BOX 4.6

Russia's prime ministers

Prime minister	Date of appointment	Served until
Igor Gaidar*	June 1992	December 1992
Viktor Chernomyrdin**	December 1992	March 1998
Sergei Kiriyenko	March 1998	August 1998
Yevgeny Primakov	September 1998	May 1999
Sergei Stepashin	May 1999	August 1999
Vladimir Putin	August 1999	May 2000
Mikhail Kasyanov	May 2000	

* Gaidar was acting prime minister.
** When first appointed Chernomyrdin was the chair of the Council of Ministers.

Primakov was sacked in May 1999, Yeltsin thanked him for bringing stability but criticised him for failing to restructure the economy. The real reason for getting rid of Primakov was that he was being spoken of as a natural candidate for the year 2000 presidential election, far outshone Yeltsin in popular approval ratings, had not been firm enough in his rebuttal of the Duma's attempts to impeach Yeltsin and was attacking the oligarchs. Primakov was replaced by another Yeltsin loyalist, the interior minister Sergei Stepashin, who was rapidly replaced by Vladimir Putin. The increasingly mercurial Yeltsin had had four prime ministers in 18 months.

The government

(see Chapter 6 of the Constitution)

The government is appointed by the prime minister subject to presidential approval (Art. 112). The government consists of the prime minister, deputy prime ministers and federal ministers (Art. 110). The president may dismiss any member or all of the government. The government manages the system of 60 federal bodies of executive power which include the ministries, state committees, federal agencies, commissions sessions and services (see Appendix 3). In August 1999 Yeltsin issued a decree confirming that the government included 26 ministers, 10 state committees, 3 federal commissions sessions, 14 federal services, 9 agencies, 2 inspectorates and 3 other federal bodies; 15 of these bodies are headed by the president. The government drafts the federal budget for approval by the Duma and ensures the implementation of state policies throughout the federation (Art. 114). Other important government functions include the administration of federal property, the defence of the country and state security, and ensuring the rule of law and public order (*ibid.*). The government also has a Cabinet which includes the prime minister, deputy prime ministers and leading ministers.

The presidential administration: the Kremlin rules?

In Russia executive power is exercised by the president and the government. This raises a very basic question about where power really lies. Is it in the White House and Old Square where the prime minister and the government are based? Alternatively, is it to be found in the Kremlin where the president and the presidential administration are based? The symbolism here is immense as the Kremlin was previously the home of the Politburo, the highest body of the CPSU, and of the party general secretary, the leader of the USSR. In the USSR the parliament and the government were subordinate to the CPSU Politburo. 'It is sometimes suggested that these institutions [the presidential administration and the government] replicate the former division between the Party Politburo and the government – the Council of Ministers' (Minasov,

1992: 2). The presidential administration today bears remarkable similarities to the CPSU Central Committee apparatus, except that it has even more staff. The party apparatus and the presidential administration share complex committees structures, their own security services and draw up policies. The presidential administration includes advisory, policy-making and policy-implementing agencies (see Appendix 4). Crucially, the presidential administration, unlike the government, is not subject to legislative oversight.

The head of the presidential administration is an extremely powerful post and its occupant is the focus of lobbying and has an important role in developing and maintaining a working relationship with the government. While Chubais was head of the administration he 'developed connections with a diversity of government, parliamentary, and private sector elements; his influence increased still further with his appointment in 1997 as one of the country's two deputy prime ministers (the other was the reformist governor of Nizhnii Novgorod, Boris Nemtsov)' (Willerton, 1997: 57). It is important to note here that Chubais was simultaneously a member of the presidential administration and a member of the government, and that 'The ability of Chernomyrdin [the prime minister], Chubais and Nemtsov to work together would be critical both to the cohesiveness of the Yeltsin team and to the ability of the federal executive to function effectively under a physically weaker Boris Yeltsin' (*ibid.*: 57 and 60).

The Security Council

The Security Council is one of the most important decision-making bodies in the Russian executive – and at times the most important. It was established by Yeltsin in March 1992 as a consultative body to the president. The Security Council in April 1993 had five permanent members: Yeltsin (the *ex officio* chair), Alexander Rutskoi (vice-president), Yury Skokov (Security Council secretary), Yury Voronin (first deputy chair of the Supreme Soviet) and Viktor Chernomyrdin (prime minister). It also included six non-permamant (that is, non-voting) members: Sergei Shakhrai (deputy prime minister), General Pavel Grachev (defence minister), Yevgeny Primakov (chief of foreign intelligence), Viktor Erin (interior minister), Dmitri Volkogonov (presidential adviser) and Sergei Filatov (chief of the presidential staff) (Derleth, 1996: 46). The Security Council has gradually been reorganised with the number of non-permanent members being increased. The Security Council is always headed by the president and its membership includes the head of the presidential administration, the foreign, defence, interior, nuclear energy, civil defence and finance ministers, as well as the heads of all the major government agencies and services concerned with internal and external security. Putin has also appointed all the presidential representatives to the new Federal Districts to the Security Council. Under its first secretary, Yury Skokov, the Security Council began to parallel and then supplant the formal government policy-making bodies, particularly but not exclusively in the areas of foreign policy and security. So, for example, the decision to send the Russian Army into Chechnia in 1994 was taken in the Security Council.

The Yeltsin presidency

The 1996 presidential elections

The omens for Yeltsin's election as RF president did not look promising. In January 1996 his popular approval ratings stood at only 8 per cent (Willerton, 1997: 55) and he needed the magical figure of '50 per cent plus 1' in order to win. In his May 1996 manifesto Yeltsin acknowledged that he had made mistakes but claimed that he had pulled Russia back from the brink of catastrophe, preserved Russia's territorial integrity, overseen its reintegration into the international community and created a multiparty democracy. Yeltsin promised to complete his economic reforms, specifically to rewrite the tax code, stimulate small businesses, regulate monopolies and introduce new laws on land ownership. He also promised to reform the armed forces and to strengthen social welfare. That Yeltsin secured 35 per cent of the vote in the first round had more to do with his presidential powers and the support of the oligarchs (see Chapter 1) than this manifesto (see Box 4.7). Before the

---

BOX 4.7

The presidential elections, 1996

The results of the first round of presidential elections, 16 June 1996

Candidate	Percentage of the vote
Boris Yeltsin	35.28
Gennady Zyuganov	32.04
Alexander Lebed	14.52
Grigory Yavlinsky	7.34
Vladimir Zhirinovsky	5.70
Svyatoslav Fyodorov	0.92
Mikhail Gorbachev	0.51
Martin Shakkum	0.37
Yury Vlasov	0.20
Vladimir Bryntsalov	0.16
Votes cast against all candidates	1.54

Number of registered voters: 108 494 533
Turnout 69.82 per cent

BOX 4.7 (CONT.)

The results of the second round of the presidential elections, 3 July 1996

Candidate	Percentage of the vote
Boris Yeltsin	53.82
Gennady Zyuganov	40.31

Turnout: 68.9 per cent

Source: Russian Electoral Commission.

election Yeltsin issued presidential decrees on key economic and social issues. Anatoly Chubais organised Yeltsin's campaign, and Boris Berezovsky and his fellow oligarchs provided the finance. The oligarchs made sure that Yeltsin's chief rival, the uncharismatic Gennady Zyuganov, received little coverage in their media outlets. The third-placed Alexander Lebed was persuaded to drop out of the second round and to endorse Yeltsin to his erstwhile supporters. In return Lebed was appointed to the Security Council in June 1996, a position he held only until October 1996.

The president is above politics

As president of the the RSFSR and then the Russian Federation, Boris Yeltsin liked to depict himself as above politics. He therefore resigned as chair of Democratic Russia when he became chair of the RSFSR parliament in 1990 and as RF president he never established a presidential party. According to Burbulis, Yeltsin deliberately chose not to back any particular pro-reform party or to set up his own party because he believed a strong political party would undermine his pre-eminence. Yeltsin also encouraged divisions within the parliament because this weakened parliament and therefore enhanced his powers. Overall Yeltsin put little if no effort into building support in the Congress of People's Deputies or the Duma and instead tried to ignore them. When Yeltsin did have an empathy with 'an influential parliamentary figure he would recruit him into the executive branch, thus losing any influence he might have gained in parliament' (Haspel, 1998: 183).

Yeltsin the populist

Yeltsin was a populist. Soviet leaders had traditionally held themselves aloof from the soviet people. Yeltsin (like Gorbachev) had a more easy-going style, and ordinary Russians felt they could talk to him, that he was one of them. Yeltsin's wife Naina was a great political asset. Modest and unassuming, she always behaved with great dignity. Russians contrasted Naina positively with Raisa Gorbachev, who was generally viewed as pushy and grasping. Yeltsin's love of his family, fun, a good party, drinking, hunting, going to the bath house with his friends and his sentimentalism struck a chord with the Russian people. He also likes what he saw as practical jokes, such as bottom pinching and playing the spoons with the help of any nearby bald head. During the 1996 presidential election, Yeltsin travelled a great deal throughout Russia, giving the lie to rumours that he was too ill and or drunk to stand upright let alone run for election. He campaigned with some extremely boisterous folk and disco dancing, and seemed genuinely to relish being out amongst his people. Again this is typical of his general approach to politics and government, preferring direct contact with the people without having to bother with intervening institutions such as political parties or parliament.

The president is indisposed

A pattern of behaviour which ran through Yeltsin's political career was that a period of furious activity would be followed by a sudden withdrawal from public view and then an equally sudden return. The withdrawals are explained by health (liver, back and cardiac) problems, deep depression and alleged drinking sprees. Yeltsin's public behaviour became increasingly erratic. He appeared drunk at the 1993 Tashkent CIS summit, when he had to be helped off the plane. At the end of March 1993 as the constitutional crisis grew and he needed to muster all his political skills, Yeltsin made a slurred and disjointed speech to the Supreme Soviet. Following the October crisis and the December 1993 referendum and Duma elections, Yeltsin was absent for most of January and February 1994 and after a brief reappearance disappeared again in March, and then again for most of the summer. Then in September 1994 during a ceremony in Germany to mark the final withdrawal of Russian troops, Yeltsin grabbed the conductor's baton and sang along while conducting the military band in an excited fashion. The withdrawal of Russian troops symbolised Russia's reduced power in Europe and required the president to act with great dignity and as a statesman, not as a buffoon. In October 1994 in the USA he behaved strangely at a press conference and on the return trip he had a stopover at Shannon Airport to meet the Irish president and prime minister but failed to get off the plane. The red carpets were out and the plane doors opened and eventually Oleg Soskovets, the first deputy prime minister, came out to explain the Yeltsin was unwell. Korzhakov later claimed that Yeltsin was drunk. His behaviour then seemed to improve and he behaved impeccably during the visit of Queen Elizabeth II at the end of 1994 and during the celebrations marking the 50th anniversary of the end of the Great Patriotic War in May 1995. At the Ramboillet summit (1995) Yeltsin made shooting gestures at the press, an urge that most politicians manage to control. During a state visit to Sweden in December 1997 Yeltsin made an unscheduled announcement that Russia would cut the number of its nuclear warheads by a further third and mistakenly described Germany and Japan as nuclear powers. Yeltsin's erratic and what Russians call uncultured (*nekul'turnyi*) behaviour tarnished his image and he increasingly became a figure of pity or contempt.

Learning to live with a sick old man

It was General Alexander Korzhakov who said that Russia was having to learn to live with a sick old man, after he had been sacked by Yeltsin in 1996. On Yeltsin's arrival in Moscow in 1986, Korzhakov, who was a member of the KGB, was appointed the head Yeltsin's bodyguards and went on to become a close friend and confidant. Korzhakov witnessed Yeltsin's deteriorating health first hand. In 1987 following his sacking as Moscow's CPSU first secretary by Gorbachev, Yeltsin had fallen into a deep depression and suffered a heart attack. Korzhakov remained loyal to Yeltsin, who had further heart attacks in July and October 1995. Yeltsin's health problems made it increasingly difficult for him to carry out his official functions. Following the 1996 presidential elections Yeltsin once again withdrew from public life. The 1993 Constitution (Art. 92.3) says that if the president is unable to perform his duties he must cede power 'temporarily' to the prime minister. In the event that the president demonstrates a 'persistent inability to exercise his powers for health reasons' the prime minister becomes acting president, and new presidential elections must be held within three months. The problem is that it is the president who decides if he is unable to carry out his duties. The Duma pushed unsuccessfully for a commission to be established that could rule on the health-related competency of all leading politicians. Yeltsin and his entourage stoutly resisted such a commission, which would have been used to remove Yeltsin from office. In September 1996 Yeltsin made a token delegation of power when the foreign, interior, intelligence and defence ministers who normally report directly to the president were told to report to the prime minister, Viktor Chernomyrdin. Then just before undergoing a seven-hour quintuple heart bypass operation on 5 November 1996 Yeltsin ceded full powers and the control of the nuclear button to Chernomyrdin. Yeltsin formally took back the powers and the trigger once the operation was over, but he was still clearly too ill to be an effective president as he suffered double pneumonia in January 1997. At the end of that month the Duma passed the first stage of a communist-authored resolution to remove Yeltsin from the presidency on health grounds. Yeltsin, still clearly unwell, returned to work in December 1998 only to be hospitalised again in January 1999 with a bleeding ulcer. Then again during the autumn of 1999, as the whole Northern Caucasus was disintegrating into violence, Yeltsin was hospitalised. While Russian forces were escalating their attacks on rebel forces in Chechnia and Chechen civilians were fleeing their homes and becoming refugees, Yeltsin was recuperating in Sochi.

BOX 4.8

Two comments on Russia's political elite

Alexander Korzhakov's explanation of Yeltsin's appointments 'system'

Experts work out entire theories, analyse mythical chains of Kremlin relationships, to logically explain this or that staff appointment ... But there was and is no theory ... since 1991 people casually tumbled into positions of power and, with equal ease, tumbled out. And it wasn't even the personal preferences of Mr Yeltsin ... It was a matter of chance.

Source: Alexander Korzhakov, *Memoirs*, quoted by Ian Traynor and James Meek (2000) 'A Man whose Greatest Love was Power', *The Guardian*, 1 January, 8.

The Moscow political commentator Andrei Piontkowsky on the lack of a political elite

The most fundamental reason for the Russian predicament is simply the absence of a political elite in the true sense of the world. All the Russian political class – the presidential family, the prime minister, conservatives, liberal economists, red directors and oligarchs – have been indulging in a carnal orgy of self-enrichment at the expense of the state budget and state property without remorse or excuses.

Source: James Meek (1998) 'A Week that Shook the World', *The Guardian*, 29 August, 4.

The court of Tsar Boris: the Sverdlovsk connection

It is all too easy to dismiss Yeltsin as a clown who was out of his depth, and yet he survived in one of the most demanding leadership posts in the world. An increasingly sick and imperious Tsar Boris was very adept at using presidential patronage, treating members of the government and the presidential administration as courtiers, to be dismissed or rewarded for their loyalty and usefulness. A typical Yeltsin tactic which often followed a period of withdrawal was to have a sudden burst of energy, reappear and start, not quite literally, knocking heads together. He would complain that while his attention was elsewhere mistakes had been made, but that he was back now and he would put things right. This usually involved sacking those he blamed for the mistakes and making new appointments. Yeltsin began to create his own presidential administration while RSFSR president and at first depended on trusted allies from Sverdlovsk where he began his political career. Gennady Burbulis, who laid the foundations of Yeltsin's administration, was a former professor of Marxist philosophy in Sverdlovsk when Yeltsin was the local CPSU *obkom* first secretary. Burbulis ran Yeltsin's 1991 presidential election campaign and remained a close adviser until November 1992 when parliamentary pressure led to his sacking. Yury Petrov, the first head of the presidential administration, was a former Communist Party boss in Sverdlovsk who was replaced in January 1993 by the liberal Sergei Filatov. Another member of the 'Sverdlovsk mafia' was Oleg Lobov, Petrov's former deputy in Sverdlovsk, who became the head of Yeltsin's 'Group of Experts' and later a secretary of the Security Council.

The court of Tsar Boris: the Western clan versus the Security clan

In 1996 the Security clan (also known as the War Party) came into conflict with the so-called Western clan headed by Anatoly Chubais and supported by Yeltsin's daughter Tatyana Dyachenko. The conflict between the Security and the Western clans took place at the very heart of the court of Tsar Boris. In January 1996 Korzhakov engineered the sacking of Sergei Filatov as head of the presidential administration and had him replaced with Nikolai Yegorov. Korzhakov believed that Yeltsin could not win the forthcoming presidential elections and that it should be postponed. Korzhakov was increasingly side-lined by Chubais and Dyachenko, who thought him anti-democratic and even worse a liability. The Security clan plus seven leading generals were all sacked between the two rounds of the 1996 presidential elections. This was at the instigation of the Western clan and also in part to coopt Lebed into government and to persuade him to form an alliance with Yeltsin. Following his sacking Korzhakov turned on Yeltsin and began to talk about Russia learning to live with a sick old man, alleging that Yeltsin was out of touch and that Chubais and Dyachenko were in control. Korzhakov went on in October 1996 to describe Chubais as a regent under a living president.

Mounting scandals and the presidential family

President Yeltsin's leadership, already literally weakened by his health problems, was further damaged in 1999 by mounting corruption allegations against what the Russian media called 'the family'. The family includes Yeltsin's own biological family but also his political associates and friends, including the leading oligarch Boris Berezovsky. Throughout 1999 the family came under increasing pressure from Yevgeny Primakov, who had been appointed prime minister in September 1998, and the general prosecutor Yury Skuratov. In February 1999 Primakov launched an anti-corruption campaign specific-ally targeting the presidential family, the oligarchs and particularly Boris Berezovsky. Berezovsky condemned the campaign as being motivated by an ideological antipathy to business and enterprise. The newspaper *Moskovskii Komsomolets* claimed to have transcripts of a 1997 telephone conversation in which Berezovsky asked Dyachenko to persuade Yeltsin to grant businesses a tax amnesty. On 19 February Skuratov announced investigations into Avtovaz, Russia's largest car maker which was linked to Berezovsky through his Logovaz car distribution company. Then in April the general prosecutor's office issued a warrant for the arrest of Berezovsky and Nikolai Glushkov, a former director of the state airline Aeroflot, on charges of diverting hard currency profits from the airline to Swiss-based companies owned by Berezovsky. Yeltsin's son-in-law Valery Okulov is the managing director of Aeroflot. The anti-corruption campaign was closing in on the family, who used the powers of the presidency and the financial and media might of the oligarchs to try to crush the individuals involved. Berezovsky secured immunity from prosecution by being elected as the deputy for Karachevo-Cherkessia in the December 1999 Duma elections.

In early February 1999 Skuratov resigned as general prosecutor on 'health grounds', but the Federation Council voted on 17 March not to accept his resignation which they believed he had been pressurised into making. It is now clear that Skuratov resigned to try to prevent the release of compromising video footage showing someone who looked like him, naked with two prostitutes. The video was broadcast on Russian television on 18 March and on 2 April Yeltsin suspended Skuratov from office supposedly due to this sex scandal. Throughout 1999 the Federation Council repeatedly refused to accept Yeltsin's dismissal of Skuratov but upheld Skuratov's suspension pending investigations into criminal charges against him. On 1 December 1999 the Constitutional Court similarly ruled that Yeltsin could suspend Skuratov but that he could not overrule the Federation Council's rejection of his dismissal of Skuratov.

On 12 May Yeltsin dismissed Primakov and his government and replaced him with Sergei Stepashin. The family were concerned by Primakov's anti-corruption campaign and also wanted some leverage over the Duma which was due to start impeachment proceedings against Yeltsin on the following day (see Box 4.9). In the event the Duma failed to muster the 300 votes necessary for the impeachment procedures to continue and Yeltsin was saved. Meanwhile investigations initiated by Skuratov on 23 March into corruption linking members of the family with Mabetex, the Swiss company responsible

---

BOX 4.9

The failed attempt to impeach President Yeltsin, 15 May 1999

The charges	Votes for	Votes against
Destroying the USSR	239	39
Illegally destroying the parliament in 1993	263	60
Sending troops into Chechnia	283	43
Undermining the armed forces	241	77
Committing genocide against the Russian people	238	88

Source: Keesings Record of World Events 45 (5) 1999, 42950.

for extensive renovation work to the Grand Palace of the Kremlin, were continued by Yury Chaika, Skuratov's acting successor. Pavel Borodin, the head of the presidential administration office in charge the renovations, was also accused in the Russian media of masterminding the campaign to get rid of Skuratov. In an interview with *Literaturnaia gazeta* on 8 December 1999, the Mabetex chair, Beghjet Pacolli, claimed that Mabetex had paid $78 000 of credit card bills run up outside Russia by Yeltsin and his two daughters. The evidence mounting against the family was becoming increasingly difficult to dismiss and they began to look for a way of securing immunity in the post-Yeltsin era.

The beginning of the post-Yeltsin era

Putin becomes prime minister and heir apparent

Yeltsin had consistently declared his intention to stand for re-election in the year 2000 presidential elections. He argued that the Constitution's prohibition against an individual serving more than two consecutive terms as president did not apply to him as his first election had been to the RSFSR president and so he had served only one term as RF president (see Box 4.10). The Constitutional Court finally ruled against this interpretation in November 1998 and so the post-Yeltsin era was in sight. Yeltsin had always assiduously avoided creating an heir apparent but now he needed to pass his reforms into a safe pair of hands and seek protection for the family. The manoeuvring began with the simultaneous announcement that Duma elections would be held on 19 December 1999 and the naming of the little-known Vladimir Putin as acting prime minister. The Duma approved Putin on the first vote by 232 votes to 84 with 17 abstentions, as they knew that if they endorsed Putin the Duma elections would go ahead as scheduled. In his speech to the Duma before the vote, Putin said the sorts of things that most Russians wanted to hear. He promised to make sure that wages and pension arrears would be paid and that he would also help the farming sector and strengthen the defence sector. He promised that the

---

BOX 4.10

Russia's presidents

President	Date of election	Title of post
Boris Yeltsin	12 June 1991	President of the RSFSR – then RF
Boris Yeltsin	3 July 1996	President of the RF
Vladimir Putin	26 March 2000	President of the RF

elections would be honest, to restore discipline to the country and to fight economic crime. He also vowed to defend the interests of Russians in the Near Abroad and to restore order in the Northern Caucasus, an area that includes Chechnia. The December 1999 Duma elections augured well for Putin. The recently formed Unity Movement (see Chapter 8) which Putin supported gained 72 deputies, coming second to the 113 KPRF deputies. Yeltsin surprised Russia and the world by announcing his resignation on 31 December 1999, making Putin acting president. In his televised resignation address, Yeltsin specifically endorsed Putin for the presidential elections, describing him as a leader who would be able to draw society together and to gain broad political support to ensure the continuation of reform. A few days after Yeltsin resigned, Putin issued a decree guaranteeing Yeltsin and his family immunity from criminal or administrative charges and from being arrested, searched, inter- rogated, or subjected to a body search. In a signal that 'the family' were being distanced from power, Tatyana Dyachenko became the first person to be dismissed from office by acting President Putin.

The March 2000 presidential elections

Putin won the 26 March presidential elections without producing a campaign manifesto or an economic programme. He had already acquired tremendous kudos from the military campaign to bomb Chechnia back into the federation (see Box 4.11) and, given the scale of destruction, back into the Dark Ages. It was an election seemingly without politics; Putin is not a member of a party

---

BOX 4.11

The results of the presidential elections, 26 March 2000

Name	Percentage of the vote
Vladimir Putin	52.77
Gennady Zyuganov	29.28
Grigory Yavlinsky	5.82
Aman-Geldy Tuleev	3.01
Vladimir Zhirinovsky	2.70
Konstantin Titov	1.49
Ella Pamfilova	1.02
Stanislav Govorukhin	0.44
Yury Skuratov	0.43
Aleksei Podbereskin	0.14
Umar Dzhabrailov	0.08
Votes cast against all candidates	1.89

Source: Central Russian Electoral Commission, http://www.fci.ru/prez2000/oitog26/pr_00.htm

and like Yeltsin likes to depict himself as a leader above party politics. In the run up to the election he presented himself as an acting president who was too busy with being an effective leader to take time off to campaign. Even members of the KPRF leadership endorsed Putin despite the fact that Gennady Zyuganov was also standing. Putin managed to be all things to all people and so his support cut across ages and classes. There was a sense that the election result was a foregone conclusion and the only real issue was whether Putin would gain the necessary '50 per cent plus 1' vote on the first round or whether the election would have to go to a second round. Putin won on the first round.

Conclusion

Russia has a democratic Constitution, a new Federal Assembly which debates and criticises the chief executive, and a powerful but directly elected president; these are all major innovations. That these developments have not been easy was graphically demonstrated by the 1993 bombarding of the White House by President Yeltsin's forces. The Duma and presidential elections provide a measure of popular legitimacy to the post-1993 political and governmental system. Under Yeltsin the combination of a super-presidency and an ailing president sounded like a recipe for immobilism, but one of the profound post-communist changes is that both formal and real power and authority are no longer concentrated in the Kremlin as Russia has become an increasingly pluralistic system and country. The 89 federal subjects, for example, have their own governments that make policies and pass laws (see Chapter 5). Russia's institutional developments have not taken place in a vacuum. Economic decisions are no longer the preserve of state planners, but have passed to the oligarchs, financial-industrial groups, small-scale traders and producers. Although Yeltsin's torrent of presidential decrees might have suggested otherwise, it no longer takes a central command to get things moving. In reality Yeltsin's rule by decree was reminiscent of the CPSU's increasingly ineffective rule by decree, when central command overload led decrees to be ignored and weakened the soviet state (see Chapter 1). Here lies one of the great paradoxes of Russia's post-communist development: although the president is powerful, Yeltsin found it extremely difficult to pursue a consistent policy programme and ensure its implementation. The election of Vladimir Putin as president and the Duma's overwhelming confirmation of Mikhail Kasyanov as the new prime minister suggest that the president and the parliament may develop a more constructive working relationship. This will not on its own resolve the problems of consistent policy-making and implementation throughout the RF; this requires the new Putin presidency to address the problem of Russia's 'soft' or 'weak' state (see Chapter 1) and to challenge the power of the republics and regions (see Chapter 5).

References

Constitution of the Russian Federation

Derleth, J. William (1996) 'The Evolution of the Russian Polity: The Case of the Security Council', *Communist and Post-Communist Studies* 29 (1), 43–58

Fish, M. Steven (1997) 'The Pitfalls of Russian Superpresidentialism', *Current History* 96 (612) October, 326–330

Haspel, M. (1998) 'Should Party in Parliament be Weak or Strong? The Rules Debate in the Russian State Duma', *Journal of Communist Studies and Transitional Politics* 14 (1 and 2), 178–200

Linz, Juan J. and Valenzuela, Arturo (eds) (1994) *The Failure of Presidential Democracy*, Baltimore, MD: Johns Hopkins University Press

Minasov, R. (1992) '*Nomenklatura* Prepares to Take Revenge', *Rossiiskaia gazeta*, 4 March, 2 (reprinted in *Current Digest of the Post Soviet Press Soviet* XLIV (9), 22–3)

Satter, David (1997) 'An Accidental Political System', *Commentary* 1 (14) 10 October, http://www.jamestown.org/

Willerton Jr, John P. (1997) 'Presidential Power', Chapter 3 in Stephen White, Alex Pravda and Zvi Gitelman (eds) *Developments in Russian Politics 4*, Basingstoke: Macmillan

Further reading

Willerton Jr, John P. 'Presidential Power' and Remington, Thomas F. (1997) 'From Soviets to Parliamentarism', Chapters 3 and 4 in Stephen White, Alex Pravda and Zvi Gitelman (eds) *Developments in Russian Politics 4*, Basingstoke: Macmillan, provide excellent introductions to the development and workings of the presidency and parliament

For analyses of presidential versus parliamentary systems see:

Colton, Timothy J. and Tucker, Robert C. (eds) (1995) *Patterns in Post-Soviet Leadership*, Boulder, CO: Westview Press

Holmes, Stephen (1993/1994) 'Superpresidentialism and its Problems', *East European Constitutional Review*, Fall, 123

Lijphart, Arend (ed.) (1992) *Parliamentary Versus Presidential Government*, Oxford: Oxford University Press

Linz, Juan J. (1990) 'The Perils of Presidentialism', *Journal of Democracy* 1 (1), 51–70

Linz, Juan J. and Valenzuela, Arturo (eds) (1994) *The Failure of Presidential Democracy*, Baltimore, MD: Johns Hopkins University Press

Moser, R.G. (1998) 'The Electoral Effects of Presidentialism in Post Soviet Russia', *Journal of Communist Studies and Transition Politics* 14 (1 and 2), 54–75

Remington, Thomas F. (ed.) (1994) *Parliaments in Transition: The New Legislative Politics in the Former USSR and Eastern Europe*, Boulder, CO: Westview Press

Stepan, Alfred and Skach, Cindy (1993) 'Constitutional Frameworks and Democratic Consolidation: Parliamentarism versus Presidentialism', *World Politics* 46 (1) October, 1–22

On Russia's electoral system see:

McAllister, Ian and White, Stephen (1999) 'The Mixed Member Electoral System in Russia', available from the website of the Centre for the Study of Public Policy at Strathclyde University, http://www.RussiaVotes.org/

Websites

http://www.gov.ru/ (presidential administration)

http://www.maindir.gov.ru/sbrf/Default.html and http://www.scrf.gov.ru/ (Security Council)

http://www.cityline.ru/politika/e/fs/sf.html (Federation Council)

http://www.cityline.ru/politika/e/fs/gd.html (State Duma)

http://www.departments.bucknell.edu/russian/const/constit.html (information on the Russian constitution in English)

http://www.konstituzia.ru/ (information on the Russian constitution in Russian)

http://www.russianlaw.org/res-const-rus.htm (information on the Russian constitution in Russian)

http://www.nupi.no/ (NUPI Centre for Russian Studies, provides regularly updated information about all Russian state institutions)

CHAPTER 5

The Russian Federation

This chapter examines the development and structure of Russia's federalism and local government. Moscow's relations with the republics and regions are analysed with particular attention to the various devices, such as bilateral treaties, presidential representatives and governors, that the Kremlin has used to assert central control in the face of the powerful centrifugal forces inherited from the soviet period. The variety of systems of government within the republics and regions are introduced. The continuing struggle for supremacy between the president and the republics and regions which has led to President Putin's centralising agenda is also analysed.

Introduction

The Russian Federation is the largest country in the world, slightly over 1.8 times the size of the USA, covering 17 075 200 sq km or one-seventh of the world's land surface, and spanning 11 time zones. The problems of maintaining the geographical integrity of such an enormous and diverse country are immense (see Box 5.1). In Imperial Russia and the USSR the tsars and the communist leadership tried to run the country from the capital and although the country was divided into administrative areas, power resided at the centre. Russia today needs to maintain its territorial integrity, for Moscow to serve as a unifying centre and for the government to operate democratically, effectively and evenly throughout the country. As a democratic federation based on the equality and self-determination of its multinational people (see the Preamble to the 1993 Constitution), the Russian state also needs to be responsive to the wishes of all its peoples. Russia is subject to simultaneous contradictory impulses. Russia's non-Russians do not want to live in an updated Russian empire and so the RF has been confronted by demands for independence and has had to find ways to accommodate nationalist sentiments. At the same time RF presidents are keen to assert the supremacy of their office and to impose their rule throughout the country. Federalism seems to provide an antidote to the dangers of an authoritarian, centralised, unitary state on the one hand and the potential 'Balkanisation' of Russia into myriad unstable, mini states on the other. The strength of federalism lies firstly in its ability to keep a country together and secondly in the regularised and democratic coherence it provides to the relations between the federal government (the centre) and the subjects of the federation. In the RF this coherence was quickly sacrificed in order to maintain Yeltsin in office and to try and counter the centrifugal forces, principally nationalism and regionalism, that threatened to pull the RF apart. Although the RF president is unable to impose his will on the republics and regions this has not necessarily been a victory for local democracy. Challenges to Russia's new democracy come as much from local dictators as from Putin's attempts to reassert Moscow's rule.

BOX 5.1

The structure of the Russian Federation

32 nationality-defined federal subjects

21 national republics:
Adygeya, Altai, Bashkortostan, Buryatia, Chechnia, Chuvashia, Dagestan, Ingushetia, Kabardino-Balkaria, Kalmykia, Karachaevo-Cherkessia, Karelia, Khakassia, Komi, Marii El, Mordovia, North Ossetia, Sakha (formerly Yakutia), Tatarstan, Tyva, Udmurtia

10 autonomous *okrugs*:
Aga-Buryatia, Chukchi, Evenk, Khanty-Mansi, Komi-Permyak, Koryak, Nenets, Taimyr (Dolgano-Nenets), Ust-Ordyn Buryatia, Yamal-Nenets

1 autonomous *oblast*:
The Jewish autonomous oblast

57 territorially defined federal subjects

6 *krais*:
Altai, Khabarovsk, Krasnodar, Krasnoyarsk, Primorskii (Maritime), Stavropol

49 *oblasts*:
Amur, Arkhangelsk, Astrakhan, Belgorod, Bryansk, Cheliabinsk, Chita, Ivanovo, Irkutsk, Kaliningrad, Kaluga, Kamchatka, Kemerovo, Kirov, Kostroma, Kurgan, Kursk, Leningrad, Lipetsk, Magadan, Moscow, Murmansk, Nizhnii Novgorod, Novgorod, Novosibirsk, Omsk, Orel, Orenburg, Penza, Perm, Pskov, Rostov, Ryazan, Sakhalin, Samara, Saratov, Smolensk, Sverdlovsk, Tambov, Tomsk, Tula, Tver, Tyumen, Ulyanov, Vladimir, Volgograd, Vologda, Voronezh, Yaroslavl

2 cities:
Moscow and St Petersburg

Creating the Russian Federation

The myth of soviet federalism

According to each soviet constitution the USSR was 'a voluntary union of sovereign republics, that their borders could not be changed without their consent, that each republic retain[ed] the right of secession, that the powers not specifically assigned to the union government [were] reserved for the governments of the republics...' (Unger, 1981: 274). Although the USSR had a federal structure it did not operate as a true federal system. Nationalist sentiments were suppressed before they could become demands for secession and borders were routinely changed without consultation. The CPSU rather than the government was the real power in the country and it was able to dictate policy from the Kremlin in Moscow. As Gorbachev reformed the USSR, nationalist aspirations grew and the union republics began to turn the USSR's mythical federalism into reality. One by one in a 'parade of sovereignty' the union republics claimed their right to secede from the union.

The Russian Socialist Federative Soviet Republic (RSFSR)

The RSFSR, one of the USSR's 15 union republics, declared its state sovereignty on 12 June 1990. At this time the RSFSR comprised 31 ethno-federal subjects which included 16 autonomous republics, 5 autonomous *oblasts* and 10 autonomous *okrugs*. In August 1990 during a visit to Tatarstan, an autonomous republic of the RSFSR, the newly elected RSFSR chair Boris Yeltsin famously urged Tatarstan to 'Take as much independence as you can'. Yeltsin's support for national self-determination was partly designed to undermine Gorbachev's attempts to negotiate a new union treaty that might have preserved the USSR (see Chapter 2). However, Russia's autonomous republics led by Checheno-Ingushetia, Tatarstan and Bashkorto-stan, and Russia's regions began pushing for greater autonomy from both the USSR and the RSFSR. In December 1990 the RSFSR Constitution was amended and the RSFSR's autonomous republics became simply republics. Then in July 1991 the Supreme Soviet elevated four of the five autonomous *oblasts* (Adygeya, Gorno-Altai, Karachaevo-Cherkessia and Khakassia) to republics, leaving only the Jewish autonomous *oblast*. The republics also unilaterally raised their status by electing their own presidents. Tatarstan elected its own president on 12 June 1991, the same day as Yeltsin was elected president of the RSFSR, and by the end of 1991 Kabardino-Balkaria, Marii El, Mordovia, Chechnia and Tyva all had their own presidents. The privatisation of state assets such as economic enterprises, land and buildings added to these centrifugal forces. Moscow, as the capital of both the USSR and the RSFSR,

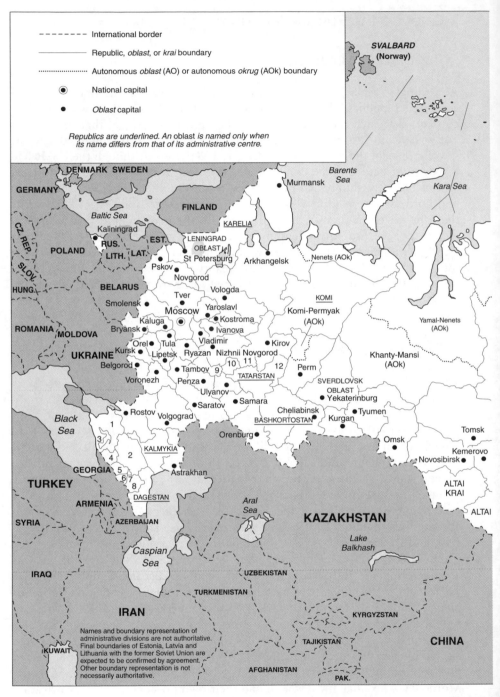

- - - - - - - International border
───────── Republic, *oblast*, or *krai* boundary
· · · · · · · · · · Autonomous *oblast* (AO) or autonomous *okrug* (AOk) boundary
◉ National capital
● *Oblast* capital

Republics are underlined. An oblast is named only when its name differs from that of its administrative centre.

SVALBARD (Norway)

DENMARK SWEDEN
GERMANY
Baltic Sea
Murmansk   Barents Sea
Kara Sea
FINLAND
Kaliningrad
KARELIA
CZ REP.
POLAND   RUS.   EST.
LITH.   LAT.
SLOV.
HUNG.
BELARUS
Pskov
Novgorod
LENINGRAD OBLAST
St Petersburg   Arkhangelsk
Nenets (AOk)
Smolensk
Tver
Vologda
Yaroslavl
Moscow   Kostroma
KOMI
Komi-Permyak (AOk)
Yamal-Nenets (AOk)
ROMANIA   MOLDOVA
Kaluga
Bryansk
Ivanova
UKRAINE
Orel   Tula
Kursk   Lipetsk
Belgorod
Vladimir
Ryazan   Nizhnii Novgorod
Kirov
10   11
9   12
TATARSTAN
Perm
Khanty-Mansi (AOk)
Tambov
Voronezh
Penza
SVERDLOVSK OBLAST
Yekaterinburg
Ulyanov
Saratov   Samara
Cheliabinsk
Kurgan   Tyumen
Black Sea
Rostov   Volgograd
1
BASHKORTOSTAN
Tomsk
3
KALMYKIA
Orenburg
Omsk
Kemerovo
Novosibirsk
4   2
GEORGIA   5
6   7
8   Astrakhan
DAGESTAN
TURKEY
ALTAI KRAI
ALTAI
ARMENIA
Aral Sea
KAZAKHSTAN
SYRIA
AZERBAIJAN
Caspian Sea
Lake Balkhash
IRAQ
UZBEKISTAN
IRAN
TURKMENISTAN
KYRGYZSTAN
KUWAIT
TAJIKISTAN
CHINA
AFGHANISTAN
PAK.

Names and boundary representation of administrative divisions are not authoritative. Final boundaries of Estonia, Latvia and Lithuania with the former Soviet Union are expected to be confirmed by agreement. Other boundary representation is not necessarily authoritative.

Map 5.1

Arctic Ocean

Bering Sea

East
Siberian Sea

Chukchi
(AOk)

Laptev Sea

Koryak
(AOk)

Taimyr (AOk)

KAMCHATKA
OBLAST

Magadan

SAKHA

Petropavlovsk-
Kamchatski

Sea of
Okhotsk

KURIL
ISLANDS

Evenk (AOk)

SAKHALIN
OBLAST

KRASNOYARSK
KRAI

KHABAROVSK
KRAI

Yuzhno-
Sakhalinsk

AMUR
OBLAST

Ust-Ordyn
Buryatia
(AOk)

Lake
Baikal

Aga-
Buryatia
(AOk)

Birobijan
(Jewish AO)

KHAKASSIA

BURYATIA

Blagoveshchensk

PRIMORSKII
KRAI

Chita

Sea of
Japan

Irkutsk

TYVA

CHINA

JAPAN

NORTH
KOREA

MONGOLIA

SOUTH
KOREA

1 KRASNODAR KRAI
2 STAVROPOL KRAI
3 ADYGEYA
4 KARACHAEVO-CHERKESSIA
5 KABARDINO-BALKARIA
6 NORTH OSSETIA
7 INGUSHETIA*
8 CHECHNIA*

9 MORDOVIA
10 CHUVASHIA
11 MARII EL
12 UDMURTIA

* Formerly Checheno-Ingushetia;
  boundary between Chechnia and
  Ingushetia has not been established.

0   250   500 kilometres

0   250   500 miles

The administrative divisions of the Russian Federation

came into conflict with the union republics and Russia's republics and the regions over ownership of these state assets. Tatarstan's declaration of sovereignty on 30 August 1990 was not only about national self-determination but also about securing Tatarstan's ownership of the republic's assets, which included its mighty oil industry. At this time ethnographer Galina Starovoitova, who was also Yeltsin's main adviser on nationality issues, described the USSR as being like a Russian matrioshka, a nest of dolls with each one opening up to reveal an even smaller doll inside. In the early 1990s there were very real fears that the same forces that had led to the disintegration of the USSR would continue and lead to the disintegration of Russia (see Szajkowski, 1993).

The structure of the Russian Federation

In the late 1980s and early 1990s debates about the future structure of an independent Russia produced three broad solutions. Proponents of an Imperial vision of Russia and of the Russians at the centre of a new great power, such as Russian nationalists and Zhirinovsky's fascists, favoured a unitary state. Under this scheme the national-territorial subjects (republics, autonomous okrugs and the one autonomous oblast) would be abolished and the country divided into territorially based administrative regions similar to the tsarist provinces (gubernii). Not surprisingly this approach was vehemently opposed by the republics and by Russia's democrats, who feared that this would create a powerful, centralised state. A second solution that briefly found some support and was enshrined in the 1991 draft constitution favoured the creation of a federal structure with a weak centre (see Map 5.1). Under this scheme Russia would have been divided into nationality-based republics and territorially based lands (zemli) similar to the German Länder. The republics and zemli were to have the same status and rights as federal subjects. This approach was resisted by the republics, who saw it as a diminution in their status and an attack on their sovereignty. The Federal Treaty, signed on 31 March 1992 and ratified by the Congress of People's Deputies on 10 April, enshrined a third approach. The Federal Treaty was incorporated into Chapter 3 of the 1993 Constitution in a slightly modified form, and describes Russia as a federation; it recognises the special status of the republics but also endeavours to enhance the rights of the regions. The Federal Treaty maintains the division of Russia into the 88 (soon to be 89) federal subjects inherited from the RSFSR. These comprise 31 (32 after 1992 division of the Checheno-Ingush republic) nationality-defined subjects: 21 republics, 10 autonomous okrugs and one autonomous oblast. The republics are described as the homelands of non-Russian minorities such as the Tatars, Bashkirs and Udmurts. These nationalities are the titular nationality because their nationality provides the name of the republic (hence Bashkortostan after the Bashkirs and Chechnia after the Chechens). The autonomous okrugs are nationality-based subdivisions of the territorially based *oblasts* and *krais*, so for example Yamal Nenets is an autonomous *okrug* in Tyumen *oblast*. The 57 territorially defined federal subjects are the *krais*, *oblasts* and autonomous *okrugs* (see Map 5.2).

Russia's other peoples

As Yeltsin had endorsed the principle of national self-determination within the USSR it was difficult to resist the declarations of sovereignty by Russia's non-Russian republics. Put simply, if the 1.7 million Estonians could have their own sovereign country then why not the 5.5 million Tatars in Russia? It is easy to see nationalism as the main threat to Russia's integrity and yet with the horrific exception of Chechnia, Moscow has reached peaceful accommodations with 20 of its 21 nationality-based republics. It should be remembered that ethnic Russians comprised barely half the population of the USSR but are 83 per cent of the RF's population; despite Russia's estimated 126 nationalities it is still a fairly homogeneous country. The Tatars are Russia's largest ethnic minority but they constitute only 3.8 per cent of the population. Ukrainians account for 3 per cent, the Chuvash for 1.2 per cent, Bashkirs for 0.9 per cent, Belarussians for 0.8 per cent, Moldavians 0.7 and the other nationalities form 8.1 per cent of the total population. The existence of the nationality-based republics assumes a link between a nationality and a particular geographical area, but just as over centuries ethnic Russians moved across the Eurasian land mass, so did Russia's other peoples. This makes it very difficult to establish clear, indisputable links between a nationality and a territory or a homeland and this contributes to disputes over the RF's internal administrative boundaries. In 1991 the RSFSR passed a law on the rehabilitation of repressed peoples, a laudable piece of legislation designed to address the problems of 12 peoples who had been deported from 'their lands' during the Stalinist repressions. Valery Tishkov, the director of the Institute of Ethnography of the Russian Academy of Sciences, points out some of the very practical problems raised by trying to implement this law (Project on Ethnic Relations, 1992). For example, at the time of their deportation the Ingush were living in a region of Ossetia, but 20 years before that this had been Cossack not Ingush land, and before that it was populated by another nationality.

Within the RF territorial disputes between ethnic groups have been a destabilising factor, particularly in the North Caucasus area, where there has been sporadic fighting between the Ingush and the North Ossetians. In 1991 the Ingush claimed that the North Ossetian region of Prigorodny and also the republic's capital of Vladikavkaz should be part of Ingushetia. In only ten of the RF's 32 nationality-based administrative subjects are the titular nationality the majority in the population. These are Aga-Buryatia, Chechnia, Chuvashia, Dagestan, Ingushetia, Kabardino-Balkaria, Kalmykia, Komi-Permyak, North Ossetia and Tyva. In 18 of the nationality-designated subjects Russians are in

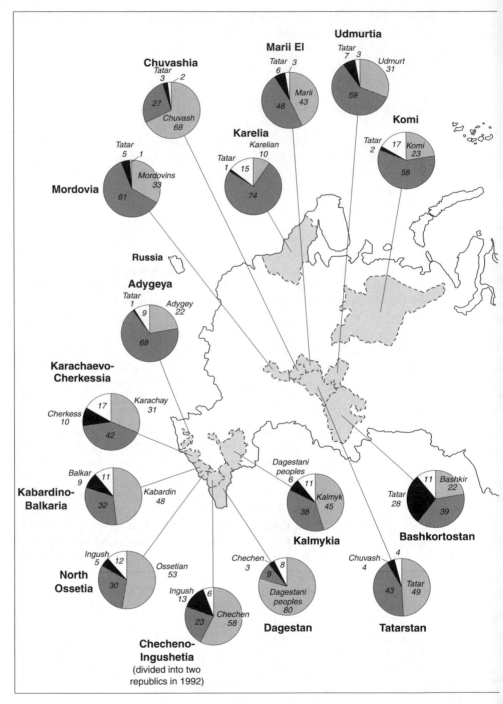

Chuvashia
Tatar 3 2
27
Chuvash 68

Marii El
Tatar 3
6
Marii 43
48

Udmurtia
Tatar 7 3
Udmurt 31
59

Karelia
Karelian 10
Tatar 1 15
74

Komi
Tatar 2 17 Komi 23
58

Mordovia
Tatar 5 1
Mordovins 33
61

Russia

Adygeya
Tatar 1 9 Adygey 22
68

Karachaevo-Cherkessia
Cherkess 10 17 Karachay 31
42

Kabardino-Balkaria
Balkar 9 11 Kabardin 48
32

Dagestani peoples 6 11 Kalmyk 45
38

Kalmykia

Bashkortostan
11 Bashkir 22
Tatar 28 39

North Ossetia
Ingush 5 12 Ossetian 53
30

Checheno-Ingushetia
(divided into two republics in 1992)
Ingush 13 6 Chechen 58
23

Dagestan
Chechen 3 8
9
Dagestani peoples 80

Tatarstan
Chuvash 4 4
Tatar 49
43

Map 5.2

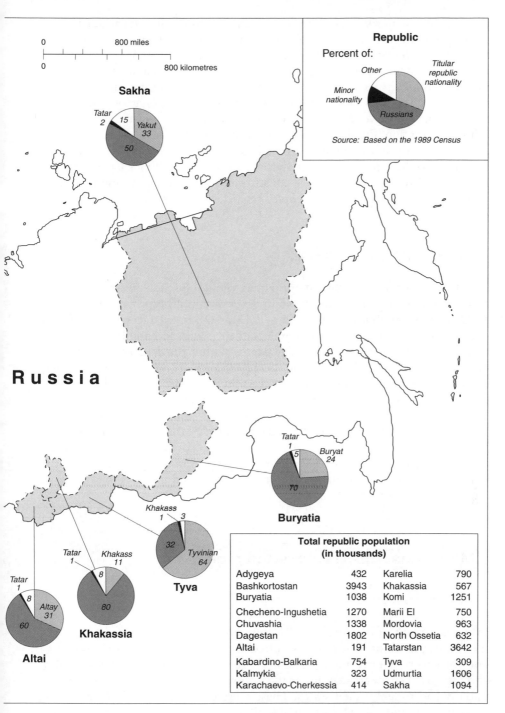

0 | 800 miles
0 | 800 kilometres

Republic

Percent of:

Other

Titular republic nationality

Minor nationality

Russians

Source: Based on the 1989 Census

Sakha

Tatar 2 | 15 | Yakut 33
50

Tatar 1 | 5 | Buryat 24
70

Buryatia

Khakass 1 | 3
32 | Tyvinian 64

Tyva

Tatar 1 | Khakass 11
8 | 80

Khakassia

Tatar 1
8 | Altay 31
60

Altai

Total republic population (in thousands)			
Adygeya	432	Karelia	790
Bashkortostan	3943	Khakassia	567
Buryatia	1038	Komi	1251
Checheno-Ingushetia	1270	Marii El	750
Chuvashia	1338	Mordovia	963
Dagestan	1802	North Ossetia	632
Altai	191	Tatarstan	3642
Kabardino-Balkaria	754	Tyva	309
Kalmykia	323	Udmurtia	1606
Karachaevo-Cherkessia	414	Sakha	1094

Russia

The republics of the Russian Federation

the absolute majority, they are a plurality in three and form substantial majorities in the others. According to data from the 1989 census 51.3 per cent of the people living in the RF's republics are actually Russians and only 48.7 per cent are members of the republics' titular nationalities and others. Within the RF nationality is clearly an important source of individual and group identities, a focus of political mobilisation and the source of inter-ethnic tensions, but the drive to wrest power from Moscow is not just about national self-determination. Ethnic Russians within the republics have also participated in the drive to gain more powers from Moscow for the republics and thus to benefit from the republics' higher status. In turn the republics have generally been careful to recognise in their constitutions that they have multinational populations and that all their people, regardless of nationality, enjoy equal rights.

Russia's asymmetrical federalism

The Federal Treaty established the equal rights and obligations of all the federal subjects, but gave the nationality-based republics special privileges. In 1992 only the republics of Chechnia and Tatarstan refused to sign the Federal Treaty, on the grounds that only independence was acceptable. The Treaty recognises the republics as sovereign states within the federation, that they have their own constitutions and laws, elect their own parliaments and presidents and could have their own supreme courts. The other federal subjects have no such privileges; they are only allowed charters rather than constitutions and initially the regional governors (the heads of the administration) were even appointed by the RF president rather than elected locally. Ilya Glezer describes Russia as an asymmetrical federation in which the 23 million Russian citizens living in the republics live in a federation while the remaining 124 million living in the territorially defined federal subjects live in a unitary state (Solnick, 1995: 52).

Moscow and the republics and regions

Presidential representatives

In the aftermath of the August 1991 coup attempt Yeltsin wanted to prevent the disintegration of Russia and to introduce reform throughout the country, both of which required the assertion of Moscow's control over the republics and regions. Yeltsin created and made appointments to two new posts which initially had roughly equal status. These were the posts of regional governor (*gubernator*) and presidential representative (*predstavitel' prezidenta*) or envoy (PR). In 1991 PRs were appointed to all the *oblasts* and *krais* but not to the republics with the exception of the republic of Chuvashia. By 1998 all the regions and republics had PRs with the exception of the republics of Karelia, Bashkortostan, Tatarstan and Sakha (Petrov, 1998). In the early 1990s most regions were still run by CPSU appointees and so the idea behind the PRs was to introduce a reformer who would monitor what was happening locally and report back directly to the president. As the power struggle between the president and the parliament escalated in 1992 and into 1993 (see Chapter 4) the Supreme Soviet wanted to counter the influence of the PRs by appointing its own representatives in the republics and regions. It however failed to establish a new post of Supreme Soviet representative and then failed to get the PRs abolished. The PRs' continuing role is to ensure that local legislation is compatible with federal laws, they also have the authority to impose presidential decrees directly without consulting the republican-regional leaderships, and they may even recommend the dismissal of any local official they identify as undermining federal policies. The PRs sound very powerful but in reality their effectiveness is hampered by this rather general definition of their functions and because they simply lack the political authority or economic resources that might encourage the republican and regional leaderships to take notice of them. The PRs' duties have been extended to include overseeing the execution of the federal budget, the activities of federal agencies and the use of federal property within their area. The PRs are also supposed to coordinate local government agencies. Despite such attempts to strengthen and define the PRs' role on behalf of the president, the PRs have tended either to be coopted by the republican-regional leaderships or to be actual or former members of the regional executives. Boris Nemtsov even served simultaneously as PR and governor of Nizhnii Novgorod *oblast*. PRs are now more likely to champion the interests and demands of their republic-region to the president than to be presidential representatives.

Regional governors

The establishment of the post of governor was another attempt by Yeltsin to exert presidential control over the regions. Governors, whose role was modelled on that of the tsarist governor-generals, were appointed to head the administration in each of the regions. Most of the governors were not the existing heads of *oblast* or *krai* executive committees and this led to conflicts with local soviets who wanted to have their own chairs appointed governor. The governors, like the PRs, are supposed to ensure that the president's reform programme is implemented in the regions and they were therefore given substantial executive powers such as control over the regional budget. Through their *ex officio* appointment to the Federation Council in Moscow (see Chapter 4) the governors also dominate the Federal Assembly's second chamber. A profound change to the status and function of the governors came with the May 1996 Constitutional Court order that the election of governors (gubernatorial elections) should begin later that year. While the gubernatorial elections did not mark a formal change in the governors' status, they gave the governors greater local legitimacy and authority and removed them from the presidential patronage system. The result is that Russia's governors increasingly became independent voices representing the regions at the national level rather than presidential place men in the regions. By January 1997 elections had been held in 40 regions and 56 per cent of Yeltsin's appointees failed to be elected. Amongst the new governors, 15 were known to oppose to Yeltsin, 8 were independents and only 12 were Yeltsin supporters (*The Guardian*, 1 January 1997: 6). Gubernatorial elections have also provided leading politicians with substantial regional power bases and platforms from which to challenge the federal government. In October 1996, for example, Alexander Rutskoi made a political come-back when he was elected governor of Kursk and in April 1998 Alexander Lebed was elected governor of Krasnoyarsk.

Bilateral treaties with the republics

In the mid-1990s even those republics that had signed the Federal Treaty also concluded bilateral treaties with Moscow. Each bilateral treaty is different and it is the product of prolonged negotiation and horse trading. The treaties typically address such issues as the delineation of jurisdiction between Moscow and the republic, control of exports, levels of taxation and the percentage of tax revenues to be forwarded to the federal government, and the levels of subsidies from Moscow to the republic. The bilateral treaties 'can best be understood not as a consequence of evolving constitutional norms or of latent ethnic conflict, but rather as the product of ongoing political bargaining between federal and regional authorities' (Solnick, 1995: 52). In February 1994 Tatarstan finally concluded a bilateral treaty with Moscow, which described Tatarstan as a state united with Russia on the basis of the constitutions of two sovereign states (see 'Tatarstan's Treaty with Russia', 1994). Tatarstan is surrounded by the RF, so even if it had achieved independence it would have had to come to terms with Moscow, but its great oil wealth meant that it was able to negotiate with Moscow from a position of economic strength. From Moscow's perspective the treaties provide a device to maintain the RF's unity but they have also exacerbated the asymmetry of Russian federalism. The bilateral treaties also contributed to the development of Russia's 'fiscal federalism' which is characterised by 'a significant degree of decentralisation in fiscal authority...' (OECD, 2000: 113). Typically those republics that are rich in natural resources and particularly in oil, gas and diamonds (such as Tatarstan, Bashkortostan and Sakha) negotiated treaties and agreements that enabled them to retain higher percentages of their tax revenues than the other republics and regions. The treaties and fiscal federalism have exacerbated the vast differences that already existed amongst and between the republics-regions. Tatarstan, for example, is able to fund extensive education, health care and welfare services that are the envy of the mostly Russian *oblasts* (see Box 5.2).

Republicanisation: the *oblasts* fight back

Even before Moscow and the republics began to conclude bilateral treaties Russia's regions aspired to the status of republics. Led by their governor Eduard Rossel, members of the Sverdlovsk *oblast* soviet voted in July 1992 to become the Urals Republic and in October 1992 voted to adopt a republican constitution (Levin, 1993). Rossel argued that the nationality-based republics were spurious creations as the titular nationalities were not typically in the majority within their republics, and that their existence encouraged rather

---

BOX 5.2

Indicators of asymmetry in fiscal federalist relations

	Budgetary expenditures per capita (Regional average = 1)		Share of federal aid in total revenues, %		Share of taxes transferred to consolidated regional budgets % of total tax collection	
	1993	1998	1993	1998	1993	1998
Regional average	1.00	1.00	18.10	13.15	62.90	62.93
Tatarstan, Bashkortostan and Sakha	1.46	1.56	0.00	17.18	100.00	84.33
Other republics	0.91	0.77	47.00	35.56	65.60	70.57
Oblasts and *krais*	0.88	0.77	17.60	14.35	62.20	68.13
Cities of Moscow and St Petersburg	1.48	1.80	10.60	1.01	54.60	45.35
Autonomous *oblast* and *okrugs*	2.74	5.48	29.00	7.25	50.30	69.18
of which oil and gas producing[1]	2.98	7.19	5.20	3.45	49.10	68.70
Other	2.27	1.60	79.40	45.18	67.30	79.14

[1] Khanty-Mansi and Yamal-Nenets autonomous *okrugs*.

Source: OECD calculations based on data of the Ministry of Finance in OECD (2000) *OECD Economic Surveys 1999–2000 Russian Federation*, Paris: OECD, 123.

than defused nationalist discontent. Rossel advocated the division of the RF solely on a territorial basis into provinces (*gubernii*), so that no nationality would be perceived as having a privileged status. In 1993 while Yeltsin and the parliament were locked in conflict in Moscow, a growing number of regions followed Sverdlovsk's lead and unilaterally declared themselves republics. Primorskii (Maritime) *krai* called itself the Maritime republic, Krasnoyarsk *krai* and Irkutsk *oblast* formed the East Siberian republic, Cheliabinsk became the South Urals republic, Orel *oblast* joined with other *oblasts* to form the Central Russian republic and in September several Siberian *oblasts* and republics formed the Siberian republic (Teague, 1994: 45). Fresh from defeating the parliamentary insurgents Yeltsin sacked Rossel in November 1993, but Rossel was soon elected to head the Sverdlovsk legislature and in August 1995 he was elected governor of Sverdlovsk *oblast* and threatened to take his case to the Constitutional Court. With the 1996 presidential elections fast approaching and his popularity waning, Yeltsin started to sign bilateral treaties with the regions; the first was signed with Rossel on behalf of Sverdlovsk *oblast*. Rossel had got the deal he wanted for his *oblast* and so he stopped pressing for the creation of a Urals republic and supported Yeltsin in the 1996 presidential elections. The strategically important but economically impoverished Kaliningrad *oblast* was also one of the first *oblasts* to acquire a bilateral treaty. Other regions benefited from patrons within Yeltsin's circle. Orenburg, the home area of Chernomyrdin, was an early recipient of a bilateral treaty, as was Krasnodar *krai*, which had close ties with Nikolai Yegorov, who was then the president's chief of staff.

An assessment of the bilateral treaties

The bilateral treaties stopped the *oblasts'* republicanisation demands and were a useful form of presidential patronage to gather regional support for Yeltsin in the 1996 presidential elections (Zlotnik, 1996). Bilateral treaties were a mechanism by which Yeltsin was able to divide and rule the republics and regions, encouraging them to compete against each other for Moscow's favours rather than to cooperate with each other against Moscow. The result is that only ten federal subjects containing 25 per cent of the RF's population are net donors to the federal budget. Most republics, *krais* and *oblasts* receive subsidies and transfers from Moscow (Mironov, 1999). In extending bilateral treaties to the regions Yeltsin wanted to garner support for his leadership and to overcome some of the discontent in the ethnic Russian areas with the privileges enjoyed by the republics. There were therefore practical reasons for bilateral treaties in a country that seemed on the verge of disintegration and where civil war was raging in Chechnia (1994–6) (see Map 5.3). A constitutional basis for the bilateral treaties is more difficult to sustain. The bilateral treaties contradict Article 5.4 of the Constitution which states that 'All subjects of the Russian Federation are equal with each other in interrelations with federal bodies of state power'. Furthermore the contents of these treaties are usually kept secret and so they evade constitutional review. Another consequence of the bilateral treaties is that although Articles 71 and 72 of the Constitution set out the jurisdictions of the RF and its subjects, the reality is that there are as many versions of relations between Moscow and the republics-regions as there federal subjects.

Ruling or governing Russia's republics and regions?

The complexity of government in the subjects of the federation

There is no uniform system of government in Russia's federal subjects. The 21 republics determine their own system of government. Most of the 89 federal subjects now have a directly elected executive who may be called the governor, president, or sometimes chair of the government, and in the case of St Petersburg and Moscow the mayor. The republic of Udmurtia, however, has a parliamentary system while Samara *oblast* has a presidential system. In the republics of Dagestan and Karachaevo-Cherkessia the head of state is not directly elected. Following the same pattern of a strong president and a weak parliament that exists at the centre, the local legislatures tend to be weaker than the executives. The names of the local legislatures include Duma, Legislative Assembly, City Assembly and State Councils. Again mirroring the pattern for central government, the executives and legislatures usually have their own parallel committees and administrations (see Box 5.3).

The regions march on Moscow

By the late 1990s Russia's federal asymmetry was between the economically powerful republics and regions and the economically less-favoured, rather than between the republics and the regions. The republics-regions were no longer content with taking power from Moscow, they wanted to take control of the federal capital itself, where they already had a strong power base in the Federation Council. In 1998 the republics-regions saw their chance. The federal government was struggling to deal with the economic crisis and the ailing Yeltsin was almost constantly in conflict with the Duma. The republics-regions had their eyes on the December 1999 Duma elections and the year 2000 presidential elections. The president of Tatarstan, Mintimer Shaimiyev, proposed that Russia's next president should be 'one of us', meaning a regional leader rather than a Moscow insider. Konstantin Titov, the governor of prosperous Samara *oblast*, stood in the 2000 presidential elections but was roundly defeated by Putin's electoral steamroller. The republics-regions were particularly keen to capture the Duma and so formed new political parties.

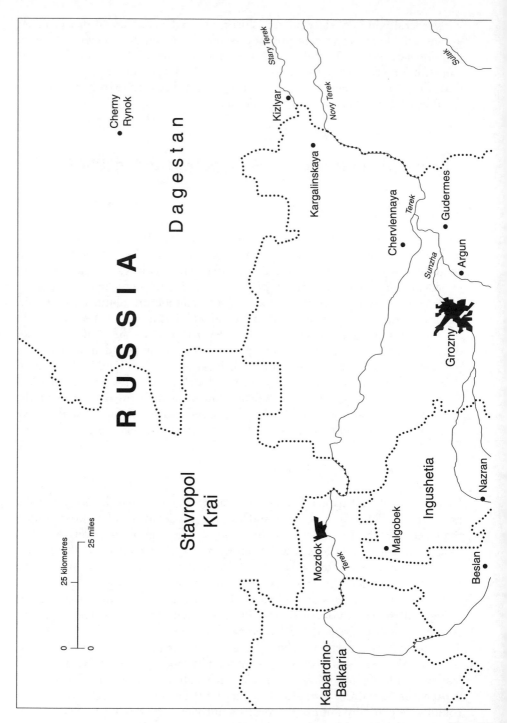

Map 5.3

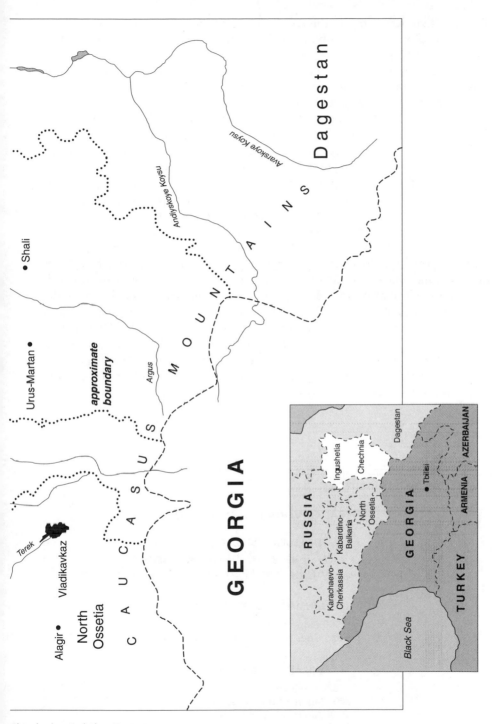

Chechnia and the Caucasus

This is a significant step in the development of the Russian party system as, with the exception of the Communist Party of the Russian Federation (KPRF) and to a lesser extent Chernomyrdin's Our Home is Russia (NDR), Russia's political parties are not organised throughout the country. The lack of all-Russia political parties has meant that candidates for governors or local office form their own parties and once elected these become the local 'party of power', just as NDR was the party of power in Moscow while Chernomyrdin was prime minister. Once elected, regional leaders want Russia to be stable and prosperous but they are not prepared to sacrifice their region's economic prosperity for the greater good. As the economist Philip Hanson has noted, while conflict between regional and national economic policy is not un-common, in Russia 'it has not been moderated, so far, by any effective chain of party loyalties tying the careers of regional politicos to their acquiescence in a particular party's national policies' (Hanson, 1996). In the run up to the 1999 Duma elections the Fatherland-All Russia (OVR) movement, whose leading members included the former prime minister Yevgeny Primakov, Yury Luzhkov the mayor of Moscow and President Shaimiyev, was formed. Konstantin Titov also created Russia's Voice, which was a coalition of the regional 'parties of power' rather than a party with a unified organisation and programme. In the event OVR came a creditable third in the 1999 Duma elections with 66 deputies. OVR's success is a potentially two-edged sword: the deputies want to incorporate the regions' views into the Duma's national policies, but this will require party discipline and a willingness to seek the national good and not just individual regional advantage.

BOX 5.3

Levels of government

FEDERAL GOVERNMENT IN MOSCOW

THE FEDERAL SUBJECTS
21 republics, 6 *krais*, 49 *oblasts*, 1 autonomous *oblast*,
10 autonomous *okrugs*, 2 cities (Moscow and St Petersburg)

GOVERNMENT – DISTRICT LEVEL
2000 (approx.) *raions* (districts),
400 (approx.) cities and towns with district status

LOCAL GOVERNMENT
624 smaller towns and cities
2000 (approx.) urban settlements
2400 (approx.) rural settlements

Chechnia

The Chechens have centuries of resentment of Russian domination. They were conquered by the tsars in the eighteenth century and despite numerous revolts against Imperial Russia and then the USSR they have not regained their independence. The Chechens are an Islamic people with a strong martial ethos and a belief in the principle of the blood feud. Their resentment of alien Russian rule was further fuelled in 1944 when they were declared an enemy people and deported to Kazakhstan and Siberia. As nationalist sentiment grew throughout the USSR in the 1980s Chechen nationalism was also on the rise. In 1991 the Chechens declared their independence and the following year the division of the former autonomous republic of Checheno-Ingushetia into two new republics was formally recognised. The Chechens are the majority nationality in Chechnia but ethnic Russians constitute about 25 per cent of the population. The Chechen leadership was not united however and there was popular Chechen opposition to President Dzhokar Dudaev's rule. Dudaev, a former soviet air force general, was also accused of using Chechen nationalism to his own ends and of supporting the Chechen mafia and various warlords who ran parts of Chechnia. Dudaev dealt with local Chechen opposition by closing the Chechen parliament in the spring of 1992 and armed conflict broke out amongst the rival Chechen groups. Dudaev led a boycott of the constitutional referendum and Duma elections in 1993. For Dudaev only complete independence was acceptable and so he refused to compromise by agreeing a bilateral treaty such as Tatarstan signed in 1994.

For the Russian government Chechnia has major geopolitical significance. Firstly, to have allowed Chechnia to secede was a dangerous precedent to set in the volatile Caucasus region. The other republics of this area – Dagestan, Ingushetia, Kalmykia and North Ossetia – were keenly watching to see what concessions the Chechens might be able to wrest from Moscow, to find out the limits of Moscow's tolerance of dissent and just how far Moscow would go to defend its territorial integrity. Secondly, the 'War Party' seemed to have advised Yeltsin that a show of strength against the Chechens would help his chances of re-election in the 1996 presidential elections. Thirdly, vital railway lines and oil pipelines cross Chechnia. Moscow denied that it was secretly arming anti-Dudaev forces in Chechnia but a failed coup attempt against Dudaev in November 1994 gave Moscow the pretext it needed to intervene in the Chechen civil war. In December 1994 Yeltsin ordered troops to close the Chechen border and to secure the strategically important rail link crossing the republic. Moscow then appointed its own puppet president, Doku Zavgaev, for Chechnia. Instead of providing Yeltsin with a quick victory, the war revealed the inadequacies of the Russian armed forces (see Chapter 7) and dragged on into 1996.

At the end of May 1996 Alexander Lebed, Yeltsin's new security adviser, arrived in Chechnia to negotiate a new settlement. He was hopeful that since the death of Dudaev in a rocket attack on 21 April 1996 the Chechens might be more amenable to negotiation. Aslan Maskhadov, a former soviet army colonel and the former chief of staff of the rebel forces, conducted the negotiations for the Chechens. In Chechen terms Maskhadov was a moderate, a supporter of a secular state, who managed to gather enough votes from Chechnia's Russians, Cossacks and Chechens to be elected Chechen president on 27 January 1997. A deal was struck but the full details were not made public. It is clear that Chechnia was offered amnesties, humanitarian aid and government funds for reconstruction. The oligarch Boris Berezovsky, who has major personal financial interests in Russian oil (see Chapter 1, Box 1.4) and served on the Security Council (October 1996–December 1997), claims that the Chechens were offered special tax and trading privileges and that in turn they agreed to guarantee the safety of oil and gas supplies passing through Chechnia. The vital subject that the peace settlement should have resolved was the question of Chechnia's sovereignty, but it was precisely this issue that was fudged. President Yeltsin records that both sides agreed that 'the question of the status of Chechnia would be postponed until the year 2001; meanwhile there would be a complete withdrawal of forces, and a joint interim governing commission would be created. Essentially, Russia acknowledged the legitimacy of the self-proclaimed Chechen republic. Russian renounced its previous aims – to establish control over the territory of Chechnia, to restore Russian law, and to disband the unlawful army' (Yeltsin, 2000: 62–3). Although the issue of sovereignty was postponed, Aslan Maskhadov and most Chechens clearly believed that the deal signed with Moscow gave them the right to be an independent country which would be called the republic of Ichkeria (Stoner-Weiss, 1997: 244).

Local government

There are two further levels of government below the federal subjects. The next level down, the district level, is subordinate to the federal subjects, and the local level is subordinate to the district level. The town and city mayors at the district and lowest levels head the local administrations and are usually appointed by the regional governor. The mayors work jointly with the municipal councils or dumas, which ratify local budgets and oversee municipal services. It is not possible to provide a clear-cut statement of the jurisdiction and competencies of local government, as this is decided by a complex range of federal agreements and negotiations and again quite simply by what different bodies can get away with. The creation of a single system of local government has also been complicated by disputes between the republican and regional leaders on the one hand and the heads of the local government on the other. These disputes typically centre on the same kinds of jurisdictional and ownership issues that plagued Moscow's relations with the republics and regions. So disputes have seen presidents and governors pitted against the mayor of the capital city of the republic, or the leaders of *krais* and *oblasts* over the budget and/or regional and municipal property. This has happened in the republics of Buryatia and Udmurtia, Primorskii and Krasnodar *krais*, and Arkhangelsk, Omsk and Sverdlovsk *oblasts* (Mironov, 1998). Presidents and governors have responded to these disputes in the case of Tatarstan, Bashkortostan and North Ossetia by trying to abolish local government. In Udmurtia the republican parliament did not abolish local government as such but instead in 1996 abolished the territorial subjects that had a right to local self-government (see Blankengael, 1997). Other tactics employed include just not holding elections to local government bodies or, as in the case of Kursk and Novosibirsk *oblasts*, reducing the status of local government bodies to regional councils and abolishing elected administrations. The result of these developments is that in the second half of the 1990s the number of local government bodies actually decreased threefold (*ibid.*), despite the fact that local self-government is guaranteed by Article 12 of the Constitution.

Federal feudalism?

The leaders of some, but not all, of the RF's republics and regions act more like modern-day tsars or feudal lords than democratic politicians. Following the 1994–6 débâcle in Chechnia Yeltsin had two main concerns: firstly, that local leaders should bring the votes in for him in the 1996 presidential election and secondly, that they should not demand outright independence (Meek, 1998: 14). Yeltsin, the supposed super-president, did not attempt to rein in the republican leaders dubbed the 'little tsars' or the 'feudal lords' by the Russian media. Two of the worst examples of this phenomenon are provided by the republics of Kalmykia and Bashkortostan. In 1993 Kirsan Ilyumzhimov was elected president of Kalmykia and Murtaza Rakhimov was elected president of Bashkortostan. Following Ilyumzhinov's election the republic's Supreme Soviet voted to abolish local soviets (councils) throughout the republic, dissolve the Supreme Soviet and replace it with a 25-member 'professional' parliament. Ilyumzhinov, who calls himself 'the Kalmyk Khan in the Russian Empire', subsequently imposed direct rule through a network of personal representatives (Szajkowski, 1993: 174). In violation of the Constitution Ilyumzhinov was the only candidate in the 1995 Kalmyk republic presidential elections for a new seven-year term of office. He supposedly received 78 per cent of the vote but there were accusations of irregularities and electoral fraud. Having removed rival institutions Ilyumzhinov moved against the republic's democratic opposition. In 1994 the police merely watched while thugs employed by a local bank ejected the staff and took the computer equipment from the republic's one surviving opposition newspaper, *Sovetskaia Kalmykia*. The newspaper was closed down and in order to survive moved to Volgograd (320 km away). The newspaper editor Larissa Yudina challenged the closure through the courts, which ruled in her favour, but Yudina was unable to enforce the court's decision. Larissa Yudina was murdered in June

1998. Although Kalmykia is one of the economically most depressed regions of Russia, the millionaire Ilyumzhinov, who is president of the world chess federation, built a special chess village to host international chess competitions. He has also been accused of corruption and the misappropriation of 10 billion roubles of state credits (Meek, 1998: 12).

President Rakhimov of Bashkortostan is known as Babai (Grandad) and together with other members of his family he runs his republic like a mini fiefdom. By Russian standards Bashkortostan is quite prosperous thanks to its oil industry. As in Kalmykia the media are totally controlled and the local opposition has been reduced to publishing its newspaper in neighbouring regions and smuggling it into Bashkortostan at great personal risk. In defiance of federal law Rakhimov appoints all the republic's judges and prosecutors, and controls the local secret police (FSB) and police force. The president's son runs a holding company that controls the oil industry in the republic's capital of Ufa (Traynor, 2000: 13). When Grigory Yavlinsky of Yabloko tried to campaign in Bashkortostan in 1996, Rakhimov refused his plane permission to land. Ilyumzhinov and Rakhimov through their powers of patronage and coercion got the vote out for Yeltsin in 1996 and Putin in 2000. President Putin now wishes to challenge the powers of such little tsars and feudal lords, and his first specific target was Bashkortostan whose constitution puts Bashkortostan's and federal laws on an equal footing, although the Bashkortostan Constitution should conform with the RF Constitution (*The Economist*, 20 May 2000: 67). In May 2000 Putin wrote to the speaker of the Bashkortostan parliament ordering the republic to bring its republican constitution into line with the RF Constitution, but President Rakhimov has no incentive to comply.

Putin and the assertion of federal authority

Creating a unified state

The RF Constitution and the bilateral treaties might seem to imply that although Russian federalism is very complex there are documents that can be examined in order to understand the relationship between Moscow and a republic or region. However, a republic's or a region's power depends largely on how much they get away with, rather than on a clearly defined and regulated relationship. It is estimated that a staggering 20 000 republican and regional legal acts simply flout the RF Constitution and federal laws (Traynor, 2000: 13). According to Article 71 (j and l), foreign, defence and security policies fall within the jurisdiction of the federal government in Moscow, but North Ossetia has its own army and Bashkortostan conducts its own diplomacy. In the case of Chechnia, even Moscow's superior military might has not so far been able to force the republic into line. Moscow lacks both the authority and the coercive capabilities to make sure that its writ runs throughout the country. Putin came into office as president determined to assert Moscow's control over Russia, take on the feudal lords and put an end to Russia's creeping fragmentation. Putin wants to ensure that Russia is truly what he calls 'a single legal and economic space' (cited *ibid.*).

Putin declares war on Chechnia

Putin's first target, quite literally, was Chechnia. The 1997 Agreements had not brought peace to the area and Moscow has cause to be concerned by Chechnia's potential to destabilise the entire Caucasus region. Sergei Kovalev (2000), who once headed Yeltsin's Presidential Commission on Human Rights but resigned in January 1996 in opposition to the (first) Chechen war, believes that the Maskhadov leadership provided Moscow with all the excuses it needed to send Russian forces into Chechnia in 1999. Since 1997 Maskhadov had done nothing to control the criminal behaviour, including extortion and violence against the Russian population, kidnapping for ransom and slave labour, and the kidnapping of journalists and foreign aid workers, that had become commonplace in the republic. Islamic Law was introduced, including corporal punishment, amputations and public executions broadcast on television. Maskhadov was never in control of Chechnia and it is the so-called 'field commanders' Arbi Baraev and Ruslan Khaikhoroyev and the terrorists Salman Raduyev and Shamil Basaev who control the republic and direct the growing criminal activities. In 1999 Basaev led his self-styled international warriors for Allah in their 'August Liberation' of the neighbouring republic of Dagestan. Dagestan fought back the best it could and the Chechens were finally driven back by the Russian army. At the height of the fighting in Dagestan Prime Minister Stepashin was sacked and replaced by Vladimir Putin. Bomb explosions in Moscow and Volgodonsk in September were blamed on Chechen terrorists so providing a final pretext for the Russian armed forces to move into Chechnia (see Conclusion). Putin sent a clear message that he is prepared to use Russia's full military might to pacify Chechnia and to maintain Russia's territorial integrity.

Putin taking on the regions

Once elected president, Putin turned his attention to reasserting Moscow's control over the republics and regions. In May 2000 Putin ordered the 89 federal subjects to be divided between seven new federal districts – the North Western, Central, North Caucasus (renamed Southern district in June 2000), Volga, Urals, Siberian and Far Eastern. Putin appointed new presidential representatives (see Box 5.4), dubbed governor generals by the Russian media after their tsarist predecessors, to each district. The representatives are

BOX 5.4

The new federal districts

Central Federal District
Presidential representative: Georgy Poltavchenko
Career: former KGB operative; presidential representative to Leningrad *oblast*
District composition: Belgorod, Bryansk, Vladimir, Voronezh, Ivanovo, Kaluga, Kostroma, Kursk, Lipetsk, Moscow, Orel, Ryazan, Smolensk, Tambov, Tver, Tula and Yaroslavl *oblasts*; city of Moscow
Federal district centre: Moscow

North Western Federal District
Presidential representative: Lt.-Gen.Viktor Cherkesov
Career: former KGB operative; first deputy director of the FSB
District composition: republics of Karelia and Komi; Arkhangelsk, Vologda, Kaliningrad, Leningrad, Murmansk, Novgorod, Pskov *oblasts*; city of St Petersburg; Nenets autonomous *okrug*
Federal district centre: St Petersburg

Southern Federal District (formerly North Caucasus)
Presidential representative: Gen. Viktor Kazantsev
Career: commander of the Caucasus military district; senior commander in the Chechen war
District composition: republics of Adygeya, Dagestan, Ingushetia, Kabardino-Balkaria, Kalmykia, Karachaevo-Cherkessia, North Ossetia and Chechnia; Krasnodar and Stavropol *krais*; Volgograd and Rostov *oblasts*
Federal district centre: Rostov-on-Don

Volga Federal District
Presidential representative: Sergei Kiriyenko
Career: oil industry, banking, prime minister
District composition: republics of Bashkortostan, Marii El, Mordovia, Tatarstan, Udmurtia and Chuvashia; Kirov, Nizhnii Novgorod, Orenburg, Penza, Perm, Samara, Saratov and Ulyanov *oblasts*; Komi-Permyak autonomous *okrug*
Federal district centre: Nizhnii Novgorod

Urals Federal District
Presidential representative: Col.-Gen. Pyotr Latyshev
Career: first deputy minister of the interior
District composition: Kurgan, Sverdlovsk, Tyumen and Cheliabinsk *oblasts*; Khanty-Mansi and Yamal-Nenets autonomous *okrugs*
Federal district centre: Yekaterinburg

Siberian Federal District
Presidential representative: Leonid Drachevsky
Career: minister for relations with the CIS
District composition: republics of Altai, Buryatia, Tyva and Khakassia; Altai and Krasnoyarsk *krais*; Irkutsk, Kemerovo, Novosibirsk, Omsk, Tomsk and Chita *oblasts*; Aga-Buryatia, Taimyr (Dolano-Nenets), Ust-Ordyn Buryatia and Evenk autonomous *okrugs*
Federal district centre: Novosibirsk

THE RUSSIAN FEDERATION 139

BOX 5.4 (CONTINUED)

Far Eastern Federal District

Presidential representative: Lt.-Gen. Konstantin Pulikovsky

Career: presidential representative to the Far Eastern District

District composition: republic of Sakha; Primorskii (Maritime) and Khabarovsk *krais*; Amur, Kamchatka, Magadan and Sakhalin *oblasts*; Jewish autonomous *oblast*; Koryak and Chukchi autonomous *okrugs*

Federal district centre: Khabarovsk

Sources: Keesings Record of World Events. News Digest, May 2000, 43582; Amelia Gentleman (2000) 'Back to the USSR', *The Guardian*, 29 May, 2–3; *Rossiiskaia gazeta*, 16 May 2000.

---

expected to reassert the supremacy of the federal constitution and laws, and to manage the local activities of the justice ministry and the 'power ministries' of defence, interior, and security. Putin's appointments reflect the growing use of power-ministry personnel in political and administrative appointments. There are only two civilian presidential representatives and the other five are from the security services or the military. The new presidential representatives have all been appointed to the powerful Security Council. Putin has complemented these reforms by demanding the power to dissolve republican and regional legislatures that have acted unconstitutionally by adopting acts that conflict with federal laws. He has also acquired the right to sack republican and regional leaders and to end their automatic appointment to the Federation Council (see Chapter 4).

Conclusion

Russia's territorial integrity has been maintained by a combination of compromise in the form of bilateral treaties and coercion in the case of Chechnia. The existence of these bilateral treaties have made a nonsense of Russian federalism, but they did make the republics and regions look to President Yeltsin as a source of patronage. Yeltsin's control over the national purse meant that he was able to exploit the rivalries between and within the republics and regions to his advantage. Fear of the potential dangers of life outside the RF also tempered some of the early demands for independence. Primorskii (Maritime) *krai* wanted independence in the early 1990s but rapidly decided that as a thinly populated area next to overpopulated regions of China, it would be safer to stay within the federation. Yeltsin also employed various devices such as the appointment of presidential representatives and governors in his bid to assert the Kremlin's dominance, but they tended to be coopted by the very leadership they were supposed to monitor. President

Putin's response to Russia's anarchic federalism is to try and reassert central control through armed force if necessary. He has also revamped the use of presidential representatives, but this time they are being appointed to territorially rather than nationality designated regions. In appointing new presidential representatives Putin wants the federal government to have disciplined representatives, who will take on the republican and regional leaders within their own fiefdoms and reassert Moscow's rule throughout a unified country.

References

Blankengael, Alexander (1997) 'Local Self-Government vs. State Administration: The Udmurtia Decision', *East European Constitutional Review* 6 (1) Winter, 50–54

Hanson, Philip (1996) 'Russia's 89 Federal Subjects', *Post Soviet Prospects* 4 (8) August, http://www.csis.org/

Kovalev, Sergei (2000) 'Putin's War', *New York Review* XLVII (2) 10 February, 4–8 (trans: Jamey Gambrell)

Levin, A. (1993) 'Provozglashena Ural'skaia respublika', *Gubernatorskie Novosti* (27) July, n.p.

Meek, James (1998) 'Voice of Freedom Stilled by Russia's Local Tyrants', *The Guardian*, 12 June, 14

Mironov, V. (1998) 'Regional Differences in Systems of Local Government: Why Do They Occur?', *Prism* 4 (4) 20 February, http://www.jamestown.org/

Mironov, V.A. (1999) 'A Party of Regional Leaders – Mirage or Reality?', *Prism* 5 (6) 26 March, http://www.jamestown.org/

OECD (2000) *OECD Economic Surveys 1999–2000: Russian Federation*, Paris: OECD

Petrov, Nikolai (1998) 'The President's Representatives: "Moscow's Men" in the Regions', *Prism* 4 (7) 3 April, http://www.jamestown.org/

Project on Ethnic Relations (1992) 'Nationality Policy in the Russian Federation', http://www.websp.com/

Solnick, Steven L. (1995) 'Federal Bargaining in Russia', *East European Constitutional Review* 4 (4) Fall, 52–58

Stoner-Weiss, K. (1997) 'Federalism and Regionalism', Chapter 12 in Stephen White, Alex Pravda and Zvi Gitelman (eds) *Developments in Russian Politics 4*, Basingstoke: Macmillan

Szajkowski, Bogdan (1993) 'Will Russia Disintegrate into Bantustans?', *The World Today* 49 (8–9) August–September, 172–176

'Tatarstan's Treaty with Russia, February 1994' (1994) *Journal of South Asian and Middle Eastern Studies* 18 (1) Fall, 61–67

Teague, Elizabeth (1994) 'Centre–Periphery Relations in the Russian Federation', Chapter 2 in Roman Szporluk (ed.) *National Identity and Ethnicity in Russia and the New States of Eurasia*, Armonk: M.E. Sharpe

Traynor, Ian (2000) 'Putin Redraws the Map of Russia', *The Guardian*, 15 May, 13

Unger, Aryeh L. (1981) *Constitutional Development in the USSR: A Guide to the Soviet Constitutions*, London: Methuen

Yeltsin, Boris (2000) *Midnight Diaries*, London: Weidenfeld and Nicolson

Zlotnik, Marc (1996) 'Russia's Governors and the Presidential Elections', *Post Soviet Prospects* 4 (4) April, http://www.csis.org/

Further reading

For clearly written introductions to the problems of Russia's federalism see:

Mironov, V.A. (1999) 'A Party of Regional Leaders – Mirage or Reality?', *Prism* 5 (6) 26 March, http://www.jamestown.org/ provides a wide-ranging discussion of the issues currently affecting Moscow-regional and inter-regional relations

Stoner-Weiss, K. (1997) 'Federalism and Regionalism', Chapter 12 in Stephen White, Alex Pravda and Zvi Gitelman (eds) *Developments in Russian Politics 4*, Basingstoke: Macmillan

Teague, Elizabeth (1994) 'Centre–Periphery Relations in the Russian Federation', Chapter 2 in Roman Szporluk (ed.) *National Identity and Ethnicity in Russia and the New States of Eurasia*, Armonk: M.E. Sharpe

Tolz, Vera and Busygina, Irina (1997) 'Regional Governors and the Kremlin', *Communist and Post-Communist Studies* 30 (4) December, 401–426, is a very good analysis of the governors' changing role

Zlotnik, Marc (1997) 'Russia's Elected Governors: A Force to be Reckoned With', *Demokratizatsiya* 5 (2) Spring, 194–196, provides a useful analysis of the political orientation of Russia's elected governors

There is an extensive literature on Russia's bilateral treaties and fiscal federalism; particularly worth consulting are:

Dowley, Kathleen M. (1998) 'Striking the Federal Bargain in Russia: Comparative Regional Government Strategies', *Communist and Post-Communist Studies* 31 (4) December, 359–380

McAuley, Alastair (1997) 'The Determinants of Russian Federal–Regional Fiscal Relations: Equity or Political Influence?', *Europe–Asia Studies* 49 (3), 431–444

OECD (2000) *OECD Economic Surveys 1999–2000: Russian Federation*, Paris: OECD

Treisman, Daniel (1996) 'The Politics of Intergovernmental Transfers in Post-Soviet Russia', *British Journal of Political Science* 26 (3) July, 299–335

Treisman, Daniel (1998) 'Deciphering Russia's Federal Finance: Fiscal Appeasement in 1995 and 1996', *Europe–Asia Studies* 50 (5) July, 893–906

On Tatarstan and Chechnia see:

Colarusso, John (1995) 'Chechnia: The War Without Winners', *Current History* 94 (594) October, 329–336
Cornell, Svante E. (1997) 'A Chechen State?', *Central Asian Survey* 16 (2), 201–213
Hanauer, L.S. (1996) 'Tatarstan's Bid for Autonomy: Tatarstan as a Model for the Devolution of Power in the Russian Federation', *Journal of Communist Studies and Transition Politics* 12 (1), 63–82
Khakimov, Raphael S. (1996) 'Prospects for Federalism in Russia: A View from Tatarstan', *Security Dialogue* 27 (1) March, 69–80
Lewis, David C. (1997) 'Ethnicity and Religion in Tatarstan and the Volga-Urals Region', *Central Asian Survey* 16 (2), 215–236
Lieven, Anatol (1998) *Chechnya: Tombstone of Russian Power*, New Haven, CT: Yale University Press
Lieven, Anatol (2000) 'Through a Distorted Lens: Chechnya and the Western Media', *Current History* 99 (639) October, 321–328
Malik, Hafeez (1994) 'Tatarstan's Treaty with Russia: Autonomy or Independence', *Journal of South Asian and Middle Eastern Studies* 18 (2) Winter, 1–36
Menon, Rajan and Fuller, Graham E. (2000) 'Russia's Ruinous Chechen War', *Foreign Affairs* 79 (2) March–April, 32–44
Nichols, Johanna (1995) 'Who are the Chechens?', *Central Asian Survey* 14 (4), 573–577
Nystén-Haarala, Soili (1995) 'Does the Russian Constitution Justify an Offensive Against Chechnia?', *Central Asian Survey* 14 (2), 311–317
Splidboel-Hansen, Flemming (1994) 'The 1991 Chechen Revolution: The Response of Moscow', *Central Asian Survey* 13 (3), 395–407
Tolz, Vera (1996) 'The War in Chechnya', *Current History* 95 (603) October, 316–321

On the creation of political parties to represent the regions see:

Buzgalin, Alesandr (1999) 'Fatherland-All Russia: Governors of all Oblasts, Unite?', *Prism* 5 (18) 22 October, http://www.jamestown.org/
Malyakin, Ilya (1999) 'Gubernatorial Election Blocs: Russia without Moscow or Moscow without Russia?', *Prism* 5 (16) 27 August, http://jamestown.org/
Zherebytaev, Mikhail (1999) 'Russian National Unity: A Political Challenge for Provincial Russia', *Prism* 5 (6) 26 March, http://www.jamestown.org/
Zherebytaev, Mikhail (1999) 'The "Fatherland" Movement and the Formation of its Regional Organizations', *Prism* 5 (9) 7 May, http://www.jamestown.org/

Websites

http://www.incore.ulst.ac.uk/cds/countries/chechnya.html (Initiative on Conflict Resolution and Ethnicity, guide to websites on conflict and ethnicity in Chechnia)
http://www.nupi.no/ (NUPI Centre for Russian Studies, provides short histories and data about all the RF's ethnic groups)
http://www.tatar.ru/english/ (Tatarstan region site)

http://www.mos.ru/ (Moscow city mayor's site)

http://www.amina.com/ (Chechen republic site)

http://library.uraic.ru/~neubert/region.htm (provides an annotated and extensive list of links to sites by and about Russia's regions)

CHAPTER 6

The judiciary and
human rights

This chapter examines the development of the the Russian judiciary, beginning with Gorbachev's attempts to create a law-governed state and a rudimentary separation of executive, legislative and judicial powers. The foundation and evolution of the Constitutional Court and the growing importance of the Constitution as the touchstone of legality, changes in the status of judges and the procuracy, reforms to court procedures and the tentative introduction of jury trials are also explored. The problems of the judicial and prison services in the face of continuing state underfunding and the crime explosion are introduced, together with a discussion of the difficulties encountered in ensuring adherence to Russia's human rights commitments.

Introduction

An independent judiciary is the hallmark of a democracy and a basic requirement for a separation of powers. The Russian-Soviet tradition was that the judiciary served the interests of the state, rather than acting as the protector of the individual and his/her human and civil rights and freedoms. The soviet tradition refused to countenance the existence of an autonomous civil society and also believed that the executive, legislature and judiciary should be fused in a system of monopolistic party control. The creation of a Constitutional Court in 1991 marked a significant departure from this thinking and the tentative beginning of a separation of powers and a more independent role for the judiciary. In Russia's super-presidential system it is vital for democracy that there is an institution such as the Constitutional Court that is able to challenge the president. For the individual an independent judiciary provides a vital antidote to any authoritarian tendencies within the state. Judicial reform entailed replacing the 1978 RSFSR Constitution with a new constitution appropriate to a democratic country with a market economy. This in turn required the passing of additional legislation to complement the Constitution. There is still an enormous legislative deficit in Russia. Institutions still need to be reformed, and lawyers and judges trained to operate in the soviet system need to be retrained. All of these tasks are time-consuming and costly. As with all Russia's reforms, judicial reform has been conducted against a backdrop of escalating crime and in a context of limited state revenues to fund reform.

From party rule to constitutionalism

The creation of a 'law-based state'

Legal reform began in 1986 as part of Gorbachev's democratisation, when he declared that everything that was not expressly forbidden was legal. This seems like a modest innovation, especially in a country where copies of the legal code were not readily available to the average citizen. However, it does entail a recognition of the importance of the rule of law for all people and institutions, including the CPSU. Legal reform began in earnest in 1988 with the stated aim of turning the USSR into what soviet legal scholars called a 'law-based state' (*provovoye gosudarstvo*). This emphasis on a law-based state was part of Gorbachev's endeavours to base the soviet state's legitimacy on legal-rational principles, rather than on the discredited claims of the CPSU and Marxism–Leninism. This legal-rationality entailed putting an end to the arbitrariness of CPSU rule, creating democratic, transparent, routinised and accountable decision-making procedures, and an independent judiciary. At a practical level this required an end to the CPSU's 'telephone law', whereby local party bosses might decide to take an interest in a case and phone the relevant judge with instructions about the required verdict. There is no strong independent legal tradition in Russia and the ruler, whether a tsar or a CPSU secretary, had always been above the law. The difficulties of creating an independent judiciary and the rule of law are therefore compounded by the problems of persuading ordinary people that the reforms are genuine. 'Decades of watching law being used in a crudely instrumental fashion in order to serve the various ends of the Communist Party have taken their toll' (Hendley, 1999: 89). The result is that Russians are generally sceptical both about using the law to protect themselves from the state and about its usefulness in their dealings with other citizens (*ibid.*).

The Constitutional Court, 1991–1993

The establishment of a Constitutional Court in 1991 was one of the great innovations of the *perestroika* period (see Box 6.1). For the first time in

Russian or Soviet history the country's leaders were no longer above the law and their actions could be declared unconstitutional. Formerly, all courts were viewed solely as instruments of state power but the new Constitutional Court was designed to act as a constraint upon state power and marked an important step towards the separation of executive, legislative and judicial powers. Following the collapse of the USSR the Constitutional Court was in the rather bizarre situation of a would-be pillar of Russia's new democracy which had to apply the discredited 1978 RSFSR Constitution and its many contradictory amendments. Nonetheless the Constitutional Court moved quickly to assert itself at a time when Yeltsin was making full use of his power to rule by decree. The Constitutional Court's first post-soviet ruling in January 1992 declared the presidential decree merging the old soviet Secret Police (KGB) and the Ministry of the Interior was unconstitutional. In November 1992 the Constitutional Court, while upholding the president's ban on the Communist Party in the aftermath of the August 1991 coup, ruled that the president could not ban its grass-roots organisations. Under its first chair, Valery Zorkin, the Constitutional Court was engaged in the drafting of the new constitution, which necessarily meant that the Constitutional Court was involved in the power struggle between the president and the parliament (see Chapter 4). In this power struggle both sides could find support for their arguments in the 1978 Constitution and/or its amendments. So, for example, while the Constitution did provide some support for a separation of powers, the amended Article 104 stressed the omnipotence of the Congress of People's Deputies (Nikitinsky, 1997: 84). During the December 1992 constitutional crisis the Constitutional Court was able to mediate a compromise solution between president and parliament, but as 1993 progressed Zorkin seemed to favour the Congress of People's Deputies over the president. On 21 September 1993 Yeltsin responded to the escalating constitutional crisis by suspending the Constitution. Ten of the Constitutional Court's 14 judges voted against

---

BOX 6.1

The Constitutional Court

The first Constitutional Court, October 1991–October 1993
Composed of 13 judges elected for unlimited terms, maximum age 65
Chair: Valery Zorkin

The second Constitutional Court resumed work in February 1995
Composed of 19 judges, 6 new judges elected for 12-year terms, maximum age 70
Judges are nominated by the RF president subject to confirmation by the Federation Council
The composition, functions and jurisdiction of the Constitutional Court are covered in Art. 125 of the 1993 RF Constitution
Chairs: Vladimir Tuman February 1995–7 and Marat Baglay February 1997–

this suspension and in October 1993 Yeltsin responded by suspending the Constitutional Court.

The 1993 Constitution

The 1993 Constitution contains some important statements about the nature of the Russian state. In contrast to its soviet forebears the 1993 Constitution expressly forbids the creation of a state ideology and guarantees freedom of conscience, religion, thought and speech (Arts 28 and 29). Article 1 describes Russia as 'a democratic federative rule of law state', it is multinational (see Preamble), individual rights and freedoms are of supreme value (Art. 2) and the people are sovereign (Art. 3). Robert Sharlet, an American specialist on Soviet and Russian constitutions and law, describes the 1993 Constitution as designed to achieve four objectives for the new Russian political system. Firstly, it establishes the citizen 'as an autonomous person and prime actor of the political universe who is beholden to neither ruler nor ideology' (Sharlet, 1997: 135). Secondly, it buffers 'the citizen from the state in the criminal justice process by creating a durable process of law' (*ibid.*). Thirdly, it empowers 'the citizen for participation in the political life of the society' (*ibid.*). And lastly, 'the new civil/political rights are designed to equip the citizen for involvement in the emerging market economy' (*ibid.*). In a curious continuation of the practice of soviet constitutions, it also provides a variety of social provisions such as a right to housing (Art. 40), health care (Art. 41), education (Art. 43) and even a decent environment (Art. 42).

The post-1993 Constitutional Court

A new Constitutional Court was established in the 1993 Constitution (Art. 125) and its activities were clarified in a 1994 law on the Constitutional Court. Yeltsin and his allies believed that the first Constitutional Court had been too partisan in its judgments and that it had favoured the parliamentary cause. They therefore wanted a less interventionist Constitutional Court which they believed would better serve as a neutral arbiter above the political fray. When the Constitutional Court finally began to operate again in 1995 it did so with a much narrower brief than its predecessor. For example, it could no longer rule on the constitutionality of the actions of top state officials or initiate its own cases. It was also made more difficult for other bodies to ask the Constitutional Court for judgments. Whereas for example any deputy could ask the first Constitutional Court for a judgment, it now requires one-fifth of the deputies or members of one of the parliament's chambers, or a majority vote of the entire Federal Assembly, to agree to a referral (Art. 125.2). The Constitutional Court is empowered to rule on the constitutionality of federal laws, presidential enactments, republican constitutions, regional charters, treaties between the republics and regions and the government in

Moscow, and Russia's international treaties. The Constitutional Court is also charged with resolving jurisdictional disputes between state bodies in Moscow, between the state bodies in Moscow and the republics and regions, and between the highest state bodies of the republics and regions. The Constitutional Court has experienced major difficulties in getting the lower courts to implement its decisions. In 1997 the Constitutional Court declared the Udmurt republic's effective abolition of local self-government (see Chapter 5) unconstitutional, but the Udmurt president ignored the Constitutional Court ruling until put under pressure by President Yeltsin. The Constitutional Court also interprets the Constitution, so for example in 1995 it clarified Article 136 of the Constitution on amending the Constitution, ruling that amendments must take the form of a special legal act, requiring a two-thirds vote of the Federation Council and the Duma, and of the legislative bodies of the subjects of the federation, and be signed by the president. Under its first chair, the legal scholar Vladimir Tumanov, the new Constitutional Court was careful not to become involved in what might be considered political matters. So for example before the 1995 Duma elections the Constitutional Court refused the request of a group of deputies to rule on the constitutionality of the 5 per cent barrier for representation on the party list system. The result is that what might be seen as political cases, such as complaints about election results or the refusal to register candidates for elections, are now taken to the courts of general jurisdiction and the Supreme Court (Nikitinsky, 1997: 85). Since 1996 the republics have been empowered to establish their own constitutional courts and the regions to establish charter courts, to ensure the compliance of republican, regional and local laws and enactments with the republic's constitution or the region's charter (see Box 6.2).

BOX 6.2

Professor Ebeev on the need for a non-political Constitutional Court

In a system where the division of power exists, the Constitutional Court has to be an independent political force, since that is its destiny. This is not a court above the citizens, but this is a court above political power. The real point is that the Court must not, in turn, be politicized. That is, it may not identify itself with any political party, ideology, or faction in the State Duma, although every single judge, as a citizen, has not only the right to have a political affiliation, but may even be obliged to have political convictions.

Source: Boris Ebeev, a professor of law at Saratov Institute and a member of the Constitutional Court since October 1990, quoted in Leonid Nikitinsky (1997) 'Russia, Interview with Boris Ebeev, Justice of the Constitutional Court of the Russian Federation', *East European Constitutional Review* 6 (1) Winter, 85.

The Russian justice system

The Procuracy (prosecutor's office)

The Procuracy was the pre-eminent institution of the soviet criminal justice system, combining three basic functions which in democratic systems are usually but not exclusively carried out by separate bodies. It combined police and prosecution functions which involved investigating cases, signing arrest warrants and presenting the prosecution case in court. This combination of roles was supposed to ensure adherence to the due process of the law. Once a prosecutor presented the 'evidence of guilt', a guilty verdict was a foregone conclusion and in this way the Procuracy acquired its *de facto* third function as the judge of guilt or innocence before a case even came to court. As the prosecutor had already resolved the question of guilt, in the soviet courts the role of judges and defence lawyers tended to be reduced to questions of sentencing. The result was that the Procuracy was part of the soviet state's control system rather than part of a justice system. A 1992 reform began to reform the Procuracy by removing its right to supervise the legality of court proceedings (Mikhailovskaya, 1999: 101), but the 1993 Constitution (Art. 129) and the 1995 Law on the Prosecutor maintained the prosecutor's investigative and prosecuting functions, and preserved his/her role as the supreme supervisor of legality in the RF (see Box 6.3). The Procuracy has also retained its soviet-era role of investigating citizens' complaints against state bodies, a function which since 1992 it has shared with the courts. In contrast to the courts the Procuracy reviews complaints for free and so it continues to deal with most of this sort of work. However, there is a built-in conflict between the Procuracy's supervisory and oversight function and its involvement in the work of bodies such as the police. The Procuracy's investigatory-police function means it shares the police

---

BOX 6.3

The prosecutor's duties under the 1995 'Law on the Prosecutor'

1. General supervision, that is, supervision of compliance with the law – in regulations and administrative acts – by federal ministries, legislative assemblies, and the executive of members of the Russian federation, organs of self-government, and the army.
2. The supervision of the work of the police and criminal-investigation agencies.
3. Monitoring the penitentiary system and detention centres.
4. Prosecuting criminal cases, in accordance with the Code of Criminal Procedure.
5. Coordinating efforts to fight crime.

Source: Inga Mikhailovskaya (1999) 'The Procuracy and its Problems. Russia', *East European Constitutional Review* 8 (1–2) Winter/Spring 101.

interest in seeing cases through to a successful guilty verdict. As a result prosecutors 'often allegedly close their eyes as a police officer uses force against detainees to obtain "results"' (Amnesty International, 1996: 5).

The courts versus the prosecutor and the regions

In the RF there are two main types of courts (see Arts 126 and 127 of the 1993 Constitution). The Supreme Court is the highest of the courts of general jurisdiction, which are concerned with civil, criminal and administrative cases. The Supreme Arbitration Court is the highest of the arbitration courts, which are concerned with economic (and commercial) cases. Below the Supreme Arbitration Court there are ten Interregional Arbitration Courts for the federal districts and 82 Regional Arbitration Courts. The armed forces also have their own courts. Since the early 1990s the courts of general jurisdiction (hereafter courts) have been in competition with the procuracy over jurisdiction. Russian legal reformers generally see the transfer of functions from the prosecutor to the courts as essential to the creation of an independent judiciary and a law-governed state. The 1993 Constitution therefore transferred the authority to approve pre-trial detention (Art. 22.2), telephone bugging, the interception of correspondence (Art. 23.2) and house searches (Art. 25) from the prosecutor to the courts. Even so in 1996 the Supreme Court under its chair, Vyacheslav Lebedev, ruled that a prosecutor had an automatic right to challenge a court's decision to release someone from custody. The prosecutor had argued for this right on the grounds that mafia gangs were either intimidating or bribing lower court judges into releasing criminals. Another problem for the Supreme Court has been to establish itself as the highest court of jurisdiction in the RF. For a while Tatarstan would not allow any cases to be appealed from the republic to the RF Supreme Court and insisted that the Tatarstan Supreme Court was the court of last instance (Solomon, 1997: 54). In April 2000 the Constitutional Court finally resolved a protracted dispute with the Supreme Court over the authority of the courts within the subjects of the federation to examine whether their laws conform to federal law. In 1998 the Constitutional Court ruled that republican and regional courts did not have this authority and that such matters fell within the jurisdiction of the Constitutional Court. In April 2000 the Constitutional Court changed its earlier decision and ruled that local courts may examine regional legislation and suspend it if it contradicts federal law. The fact that the law would only be suspended means that the Constitutional Court, which may only review laws currently in effect, could if requested still examine the law.

Russia's judges

The 1992 federal law 'On the Status of Judges in the RF' was the RF's first assertion of judicial independence. The law recognised that in order for judges to be independent it was vital to address issues such as their appointment, tenure, and personal and professional status. The 1992 law established the principle of lifetime tenure, which was later modified to include a proba- tionary period (Solomon, 1997: 51). This security of tenure is designed to make judges less susceptible to political influences and pressures. The 1993 Constitution (Art. 128.1) gave the president the right to appoint judges to the RF's Constitutional Court, Supreme Court and Supreme Arbitration Court. This power of executive appointment violates the separation of powers, although these appointments do have to be confirmed by the Federation Council. The president also has the right to appoint judges to other federal courts in accordance with federal law (Art. 128.2). The 1992 law also recognised that judges' independence could be compromised by financial inducements and so it guaranteed judges a range of benefits including apartments and access to health care, although it was less clear how these benefits would be funded. According to Article 124 of the Constitution all courts are financed from the federal budget but in reality the Ministry of Justice has not always been able to fund even such basic costs as judges' salaries and benefits, the courts' winter heating bills, electricity and telephone bills, let alone adequate security and hotel bills for juries. The lack of funding was so bad that in 1996 there was widespread talk of a 'crisis in the courts' (see Box 6.4). At this time in Moscow alone 95 of its 450 judges posts were vacant, severely compromising the capital's judicial system. This shortfall in funding means that just as in soviet times, judges are dependent upon republican, regional, municipal and local government to fund their activities, and this makes them vulnerable to pressure or bribery by criminal gangs. The 1992 law on judges gave judges immunity from prosecution (Art. 16.3), as did the Constitution (Art. 122), which was confirmed in a 1996 Constitutional Court ruling. The problem is that judges are now subject to very little supervision and so provisions that were designed to ensure their independence have been used by some judges as a licence to act as if they are above the law. Russia still needs to develop a corps of judges who are uncorrupt, well-trained and understand that they are no longer soviet-style functionaries. Since 1996 the Organisation for Security and Cooperation in Europe (OSCE) has been working with the RF Supreme Court and the Russian Academy of Law on professional training programmes for judges. In 1998 on the initiative of the chair of the Supreme Court, Vyacheslav Lebedev, the Supreme Court and the Supreme Arbitration Court established a Russian Academy of Juris- prudence to provide specialised training for judges.

Trial by jury

Tsarist Russia introduced trial by jury in 1864 but it was abandoned after the Bolshevik Revolution. In soviet trial practice there was a judge and two people's assessors, who were supposed to be independent but always agreed

---

BOX 6.4

The underfunding of the Russian judiciary

...for the last twenty five years the Russian judiciary has faced the problem of not receiving sufficient financial support to cover their current expenses. I do not mean salaries, because judges receive them in time. I speak about financing judicial proceedings and for the functioning of courts. In a number of areas of the Russian Federation courts have practically stopped carrying out their functions. As a result, the constitutional principle, the right to a fair trial, is violated.

Source: V. Lebedev (1996) 'Overview of the Russian Judiciary', OSCE, Office for Democratic Institutions and Human Rights *Bulletin* 4 (4) Fall, http://www.osce.org/. Vyacheslav Lebedev is the chair of the RF Supreme Court.

---

with the judge. The reintroduction of the jury system in the 1993 Constitution (Art. 47.2) requires not just a change in procedures but in legal thinking. In a jury system a clear distinction has to be drawn between 'law' and 'fact', as the jurors decide what are the true facts of a case and the judge decides the law. In the soviet system no such distinction was made and the judge was an inquisitor who had both to ascertain the facts and to apply the law. Jury trials are based on an adversarial rather than this inquisitorial principle of judicial proceedings. The prosecution and the defence have to compete to persuade the jury of the rightness of their version of the facts and this is supposed to ensure that the accused gets a fair trial. Jury trials are not popular with Russia's police and prosecutors as, with some justification, they believe that juries are easily bribed or intimidated by criminals. Russian juries have also proved intolerant of sloppy prosecution cases and have been alert to illegally gathered evidence and in this way they have provided an important guarantee of adherence to the due process of law. The requirement to prove a case means that the police and prosecutors have to put more time, effort and resources into putting a case together at a time when their workload has risen exponentially and their resources have decreased. Jury trials are themselves expensive and time-consuming, the courts do not have funds to reimburse jurors for loss of income, and there is no money to keep juries isolated during a trial.

The police

Perversely, now that the courts increasingly require the police to prove a defendant's guilt, a defendant is more likely to be subjected to police ill-treatment or even torture (see Box 6.5). For the underfunded and undertrained police a confession is the easiest and cheapest way to put a case together and secure a conviction. The methods used include psychological pressure involving threats of violence against detainees or their families, sustained beatings and electroshock treatment. Various asphyxiation techniques are also

---

BOX 6.5

Muscovites fear the police and criminals

During a recent public opinion poll Moscow residents were asked 'Imagine that you are home alone and a person in a police uniform rings the bell. What would be your actions?' 43 per cent answered that they would not open the door under any circumstances, because they generally mistrust the police. On the question of 'who do you fear more – the criminals or the police?', 37 per cent of Moscovites questioned answered they feared them equally.

Source: Sociological centre 'Status' cited in *Komsomolskaia Pravda*, 15 March 1996, quoted in Amnesty International (1997) *Amnesty International Country Report. Torture in Russia. 'This Man-Made Hell'*, http://www.amnesty.org/

---

employed using a plastic bag or sometimes a gas mask; the long breathing tube dangling from the front of the mask has earned this form of torture the name *slonik*, or elephant. Prisoners are also tied into painful positions such as the *konvertnik*, or envelope, where they are forced to sit with their head between their knees with their hands tied to the feet. Another torture position is the *lastochka*, or swallow, in which the hands are cuffed behind the back and then attached to an iron bar or pipe. There is also what the organisation Human Rights Watch (1999) call 'torture by proxy', in which detainees in pre-trial detention centres are used by the police to beat, rape and intimidate other detainees into confessions. While the Ministry of the Interior and the prosecutor deny that torture is used, in his April 1998 annual address to parliament President Yeltsin did acknowledge the need to prevent the degrading and cruel treatment of defendants (*ibid.*). There have been some instances of the police being brought to account, so for example in February 1998 the Supreme Court in Mordovia convicted seven police officers of torturing criminal suspects. The Russian Presidential Human Rights Commission noted that in 1994 more than 20 000 Ministry of the Interior employees were disciplined for breaking the law when conducting investigations and interrogations (Amnesty International, 1996). A Human Rights Watch report entitled 'Confessions at Any Costs' found that police torture had reached epidemic proportions with as many as 50 per cent of all suspects facing anything from beatings to torture using electric shocks (Gentleman, 1999: 19).

The rights of the accused

Russia today has two seemingly irreconcilable aims, on the one hand to combat rising crime and on the other to create a democratic law-governed state. Chapter 2 of the 1993 Constitution on 'Human and civil rights and freedoms' established that no one could be held for more than 48 hours without being charged (*habeas corpus*) (Art. 22.2), there is also a presumption of innocence (Art. 49), the prosecution must prove guilt (Art. 49.2) and the accused has a right to defence counsel (Art. 48). In June 1994 Yeltsin issued a presidential decree 'On Urgent Measures for the Defence of the Population against Banditry and Other Manifestations of Organised Crime', which contradicted the Constitution's *habeas corpus* provision. The decree allowed that anybody suspected by the police of involvement in organised crime could be searched and their documents confiscated, and that they could be held for up to 30 days at the discretion of the prosecutor rather than of the courts. The decree was extended in 1996 to facilitate the work of the Moscow police in their campaign against the so-called 'ethnic mafias', that is criminal gangs from the Caucasus and especially Chechnia. A very basic problem was that simply being a Chechen was taken as evidence enough of criminal activity and therefore used to justify the loss of human and civil rights and freedoms (see Box 6.6). Moscow police also used the decree, which also gave them the right to expel people from Moscow, as a pretext for rounding up the city's homeless. The decree was repealed in 1997.

Pre-trial detention centres and prisons

Following arrest prisoners are taken to pre-trial detention centres where they are held until their case is heard and judgment passed (see Box 6.7). This means that no one in these centres has actually been found guilty of any crime and yet they are held in conditions that are so appalling that they constitute torture. During the soviet period the assumption that everybody arrested was guilty and the summary justice dispensed by the courts meant that prisoners spent only very short periods in these centres. In post-communist Russia the crime explosion, the lengthening of the legal and court processes and the backlog of cases to be heard has meant that the time spent in these centres has lengthened considerably. Periods of over one year in a pre-trial detention centre are not uncommon. Another factor adding to the overcrowding is that even though a bail system has been introduced no one seems quite to understand how it is supposed to work and so it is not used. The result is that even those arrested for quite minor offences will be sent to a pre-trial detention

---

BOX 6.6

Sergei Stepashin on human rights and crime

I am all for the violation of human rights if the human is a bandit or a criminal.

Source: Sergei Stepashin, in 1994 when he was the head of the FSB, commenting on the June 1994 presidential decree 'On Urgent Measures for the Defence of the Population against Banditry and Other Manifestations of Organised Crime', quoted in Amnesty International (1997) *Amnesty International Country Report. Torture in Russia. 'This Man-Made Hell'*, http://www.amnesty.org/

BOX 6.7

Conditions in RF pre-trial detention centres

The first of these quotations is from the UN Special Rapporteur on Torture after a visit to pre-trial detention centres in the RF in July 1994:

The [UN] Special Rapporteur [on Torture] would need the poetic skills of a Dante or the artistic skills of a Bosch adequately to describe the Infernal conditions he found in these cells.

The second quotation is from General Yury Kallnin, head of the Penitentiary Department of the Russian Ministry of the Interior, speaking to a parliamentary committee in 1994:

I have to confess that sometimes official reports on prisoners' deaths do not convey the real facts. In reality, prisoners die from overcrowding, lack of oxygen and poor prison conditions ... Cases of death from lack of oxygen took place in almost all large pre-trial detention centres in Russia. The critical situation in SIZOs (pre-trial prisons) is deteriorating day by day: the prison population grows by 3,500–4,000 inmates a month...

Source: Vivien Stern (1996) 'Penal Reform in Eastern Europe and the Former Soviet Union', OSCE, Office for Democratic Institutions and Human Rights *Bulletin* 4 (4) Fall, http://www.osce.org/. Vivien Stern is the secretary-general of Penal Reform International, an international non-government organisation.

---

centre rather than bailed to appear in court at a later date. Human rights activists dubbed one Moscow pre-trial detention centre, the 'Investigative Isolator No. 2, the Butyrka', as 'the death factory' following the death of 207 inmates in 1995. The Butyrka was built during the reign of Catherine the Great (1762–96) to hold 1500; it now holds five times that number. Inmates sleep on the floor in communal cells in which there is not enough room for all the prisoners to lie down. There is one stinking toilet in the corner of the cell and prisoners are fed watery cabbage soup, bread and porridge (Ash, 1996). Such centres are usually poorly lit and ventilated, becoming dangerously hot in summer. Incarceration in these centres is incentive enough for the prisoners to confess into order to be moved to a penal colony.

The whole of the Russian penal system is grossly underfunded and it is not surprising that it has trouble attracting staff prepared to work in such conditions for low pay. In common with other state employees prison staff have not always been paid regularly; they also receive little training and not surprisingly their morale is extremely poor. Another problem for prison staff and prisoners alike is that the unsanitary conditions, the overcrowding and the lack of basic medical supplies has led to a rapid rise of HIV, scabies and tuberculosis. Approximately 10 per cent of Russia's one million prison population are infected with TB and a third of those have developed multi-drug-resistant TB

(Whitehouse, 1999: 16). Overcrowding means that it is impossible to isolate infected prisoners and there are no funds for basic items such as syringes or aspirin let alone more sophisticated drugs to treat TB. During the 1997 prison amnesty 40 000 prisoners were released early, of whom at least 4000 had TB, which has led to fears that prison amnesties will lead to TB epidemics throughout the RF. Aid provided by western organisations such as Médecins Sans Frontières, Merlin and the Public Health Research Institute has been used in some Siberian prisons to treat TB and has made some inroads into cutting the number of deaths.

Russia has over one million people in prison, which is one of the highest rates of incarceration of any developed country, equal to around 2 per cent of adult males (Ash, 1996). The Russian government has responded to prison overcrowding by periodic amnesties of elderly or terminally ill prisoners and pregnant women, but these are not enough to keep the prison population down. Following an amnesty in June 1999 30 000 prisoners were released and in May 2000 the government announced yet another prison amnesty, this time in order to honour the 55th anniversary of the defeat of Nazi Germany (Gentleman, 2000: 20). Pre-trial detention centre and prison overcrowding will only be solved by reform of the judicial system, including clarification and extension of the bail system, revising sentencing and the use of non-custodial sentences. Until prison numbers are reduced, prisons' function will remain the isolation and control of prisoners rather than rehabilitation. Russian prisons, like their soviet forebears, rely on the use of prisoners to control each other through a complex system of gangs with intricate hierarchies and are a brutalising experience. In 1998 the penal system passed from the jurisdiction of the Ministry of the Interior to the Ministry of Justice. This was one of the commitments the RF made, along with abolition of the death penalty, on joining the Council of Europe in February 1996. The transfer was supposed to signal that Russia's penal institutions are now part of the justice system rather than part of the state's coercive apparatus, but so far this transfer has had little practical impact.

Human and civil rights and freedoms

From the Helsinki Final Act to the 'Year of Human Rights'

The 1977 USSR Constitution gave soviet citizens an impressive range of rights but these were always countered by an even more extensive list of obligations to the socialist state. From the 1960s a small number of soviet citizens struggled to assert their 'constitutional rights' in the face of the soviet authoritarianism. These dissidents were subjected to police and KGB harassment, arrest and imprisonment, and internal exile. Some dissidents were held in psychiatric hospitals where they were subjected to 'treatments' that amounted to torture. In 1975 the USSR signed the Helsinki Final Act, the final document of the Helsinki Conference on Security and Cooperation in Europe (CSCE). The signatories, which included the USA and Western European countries, agreed to a range of principles including a commitment to respect human rights. Within the USSR a Helsinki Monitoring Group was founded by Andrei Sakharov, Anatoly Sharansky and Yury Orlov, but by 1982 the group was all but disbanded following the imprisonment or exile of its leading members. In 1987 Gorbachev freed many of the USSR's political prisoners and human rights activists. Andrei Sakharov returned from exile, quickly becoming a leading voice in the democracy movement, and was elected to the Congress of People's Deputies in 1989. The promotion of human rights was an integral part of the USSR's and Russia's democratising and reforming agendas. In November 1991 the RSFSR parliament adopted 'The Declaration of the Rights and Freedoms of Man and Citizen', which was modelled on international human rights documents. During the process of drafting the new RF Constitution, Chapter 2 on 'Human and civil rights and freedoms' was the least controversial chapter (Sharlet, 1997: 129). Human and civil rights and freedoms are a touchstone of democracy, but states and their agencies do not always respect the rights of individuals or groups who do or say things that while perfectly legal are an irritant or are inconvenient to the state. The soviet tradition was to silence dissent and to deny individuals their rights even if these are enshrined in the Constitution. The RF has made some progress on basic rights and President Yeltsin even called 1998 the 'Year of Human Rights', but in areas such as the penal and criminal justice systems, the fate of the human rights ombudsman Sergei Kovalev, the treatment of conscientious objectors, environmental activists, and asylum seekers, and not least the prosecution of the war against Chechnia (see below), Russia's human rights credentials have been severely damaged (see Box 6.8).

BOX 6.8

Human Rights Watch's assessment of developments in 1998, President Yeltsin's Year of Human Rights

The government imposed further restrictions on freedom of information and freedom of conscience, and did nothing to redress infringements on civil rights by regional leaders. Indeed the only positive developments were the transfer of the prison system to the Ministry of Justice, the ratification of the European Convention on Human Rights and the European Convention for the Prevention of Torture and Inhuman or Degrading Treatment.

Source: Human Rights Watch (1999) *The Russian Federation. Human Rights Developments*, http://www.hrw/hrw/worldreport99/europe/russian.html

Sergei Kovalev – the human rights ombudsman

Sergei Kovalev is a biologist and mathematician who was a dissident during the soviet period. He was editor of the illegal *samizdat* newspaper, the *Chronicle of Current Events*, and was arrested in 1974. Like Sakharov, he only returned to Moscow in 1987 and in 1989 was elected to the Russian Supreme Soviet. In 1989 Yeltsin established a Human Rights Committee which he asked Kovalev to chair. In January 1995 the Duma appointed Kovalev to the post of ombudsman for human rights but sacked him from the post the next month for his opposition to the war in Chechnia. In January 1996 Kovalev resigned as the presidential commissioner on human rights, accusing the president of backtracking on human rights.

Chechnia

The Russian government stands accused of major human rights abuses against civilians in Chechnia and against ethnic Chechens in the rest of the RF. In September 1999 bomb blasts in two Moscow apartment buildings killing more than 200 people were blamed on Chechen rebels and led directly to Russia's military assault on Chechnia and the beginning of the second Chechen war in October 1999. Another bomb in an apartment building was defused by the bomb squad in Ryazan. The would-be bombers were caught red-handed and were found to be carrying FSB identity cards. The FSB is widely believed to be behind the supposed Chechen terrorist threat and to be playing on existing anti-Chechen sentiments amongst ordinary Russians. Certainly, some Chechens are engaged in organised crime, but the bombings were used to justify the widespread denial of civil rights, and led to human rights abuses against anyone who happened to be a Chechen. Following the bombs there was a police sweep in Moscow detaining Chechens, many of whom were subjected to physical abuse to extract confessions of complicity in criminal and terrorist activities. Over 800 Chechens were summarily expelled from Moscow on trumped up charges in the wake of the bombings. The Chechens are Russia's 'enemy within', who have been demonised by the Russian state. The second Chechen war boosted support for the then little known prime minister and former FSB member Vladimir Putin, and catapulted him to victory in the March 2000 presidential elections.

During both the first and the second Chechen wars Russian forces have indiscriminately attacked densely populated residential areas, using weapons of mass destruction such as flame throwers and rockets. Following the resumption of fighting in 1999, Russian forces closed the border between Chechnia and Ingushetia trapping thousands of civilians who were trying to flee the war zone. The refugees were trapped without food, water, medical supplies or basic sanitation. In both Chechen wars the Russian armed forces set up so-called filtration camps to find Chechen fighters hiding amongst civilians. Chechen men and boys are held without trial in these detention centres where, according to Amnesty International and the New York-based Human Rights Watch, they are subjected to physical abuse and torture including beatings, shock treatment and rape. Chechen civilians have also been robbed, attacked and murdered by Russian soldiers.

Environmental activism as treason

Environmental activists are a particular target for harassment by Russian security services. This is despite the fact that Article 42 of the Constitution declares that 'Everybody has a right to a decent environment, reliable information about the state of the environment and compensation for damage caused to his health or property by ecological breaches of the law'. Environmentalists have been active in revealing the continuing damage to the Russian environment caused by its nuclear weapons inheritance. The most high-profile persecution of a nuclear activist is the FSB's campaign against retired naval captain Alexander Nikitin. Nikitin co-authored a book written entirely from open rather than secret sources, called *The Russian Northern Fleet: Sources of Radioactive Contamination*, for the Norwegian Bellona Foundation. Nevertheless Nikitin was arrested by the FSB in St Petersburg in February 1996 and charged under Article 64 of the Russian Criminal Code and two secret Ministry of Defence decrees. In violation of Nikitin's rights not even his defence lawyer was allowed to know what these secret decrees said. The UN High Commissioner on Human Rights, Amnesty International, and the International Helsinki Committee adopted Nikitin as a 'prisoner of conscience' (Nielsen and Gauslaa, 1997: 414). The St Petersburg prosecutor sent the case against Nikitin to court, but the St Petersburg courts refused to be bulldozed by the FSB and the prosecutor, and sent the case back to the prosecutor eight times due to insufficient evidence. When the case came to court in St Petersburg in October 1998 it was heard by a judge and two lay assessors who had to undergo FSB vetting due to the alleged security aspects of the case. The presiding judge, Sergei Golets, in a display of judicial independence, demanded to see the secret laws under which Nikitin was charged. Nikitin was finally found innocent in December 1999. Justice was done, but it was a very protracted process and Nikitin was unusual in having a high international profile and support. The FSB campaign against Nikitin was led by Viktor Cherkesov, whose approach typifies the continuation of soviet-style thinking within the FSB. This is all the more alarming as when Putin headed the FSB he appointed Cherkesov as his deputy.

Conscientious and religious objectors

As the debate about the transformation of the armed forces from a conscript to a professional basis drags on (see Chapter 7), Russian men between the ages of

18 and 27 continue to be liable for military service. Article 59.3 of the Constitution recognises the right of conscientious and religious objection to military service and provides for the substitution of an alternative civilian service. So far an alternative civilian service has not been organised and so conscientious objectors risk arrest for refusing to perform their 'duty and obligation'. Amnesty International (1999) reports the case of Vitaly Gushchin, a Jehovah's Witness and religious objector from Kurchatovo in Kursk region. In December 1997 the Kursk regional court ruled that Gushchin was the member of a sect and his claims to religious beliefs were 'groundless', and he was sentenced to 18 months' detention (see also Chapter 3, section on Religion and the Russian state).

Refugees and asylum seekers

Russia also stands accused of failing to protect the human rights of asylum seekers in the RF. In 1997 the RF forcibly repatriated Elgudzha Khutayevich Meskhia, an opponent of the Georgian government, who had sought political asylum in Russia. According to Amnesty International there were grounds to fear that Meskhia was at risk of torture or ill-treatment in Georgia (Amnesty International, 1997). In March 1998 Guram Absandze, the minister of finance in the government of the former Georgian president, Zviad Gamsakhurdia, and vice-president of the Georgian government in exile, was arrested allegedly at the request of the Georgian authorities and returned to Georgia (Amnesty International, 1999). According to Human Rights Watch (1999), in 1999 Azerbaijani authorities with the collaboration of the St Petersburg police attempted to kidnap Ali Gassanov, whom the UN High Commission for Refugees had recognised as a refugee in Russia.

Conclusion

In the last ten years Russia has made considerable strides towards becoming a law-governed state. The 1993 Constitution and new legislation have pulled Russia away from its soviet past. There remains, however, a large void between the legislation passed and reality. At the highest level the Constitutional Court has a more restricted role than its predecessor but its justices are endeavouring to act as custodians of the Constitution. Russian courts have yet to establish a reputation as impartial, independent arbiters of the law and the police are feared. The government must take action to redress this situation if Russia is truly to become a law-governed state. The judiciary, security services and penal system need to be properly funded and staff given appropriate training. The corruption that is so deeply embedded in the Russian state (see Chapter 1) also poses a threat to the independence of the judiciary. This corruption needs to be rooted out, which is much easier said than done. In the mean time citizens will carry on believing the law will not work for them, and so for example business people will continue to use their own 'security services' to sort out their problems rather than look to the law and the judiciary.

References

Amnesty International (1996) 'Russian Federation: Open Letter From Amnesty International to the Presidential Candidates on the Occasion of the 16 June Presidential Elections', *Amnesty International Report EUR 46/29/96*, http://amnesty.org/

Amnesty International (1997) 'Russian Federation Failure to Protect Asylum Seekers', *Amnesty International Report EUR 46/03/97*, http://www.amnesty.org/

Amnesty International (1999) *Annual Report 1999: Russian Federation*, http://www.amnesty.org/

Ash, Lucy (1996) 'Eurofile. Special Report', broadcast on *BBC Radio 4*, 9 November

Gentleman, Amelia (1999) 'Russian Police Accused of Routine Torture', *The Guardian*, 11 November, 19

Gentleman, Amelia (2000) 'Russia to Release 120,000 from Packed Prisons', *The Guardian*, 27 May, 20

Hendley, Kathryn (1999) 'Rewriting the Rules of the Game in Russia: the Neglected Issue of the Demand for Law', *East European Constitutional Review* 8 (4) Fall, 89–95

Human Rights Watch (1999) 'Confessions at Any Cost – Police Torture in Russia', *HRW Report*, November, http://www.hrw.org/

Mikhailovskaya, Inga (1999) 'The Procuracy and its Problems. Russia', *East European Constitutional Review* 8 (1–2) Winter/Spring, 101

Nielsen, Thomas and Gauslaa, Jon (1997) 'How the KGB Violates Citizens' Rights: The Case of Alexander Nikitin', *Demokratizatsiya* 9 (3) Summer, 407–421

Nikitinsky, Leonid (1997) 'Russia Interview with Boris Ebeev, Justice of the Constitutional Court of the Russian Federation', *East European Constitutional Review* 6 (1) Winter, 83–88

Sharlet, Robert (1997) 'The Progress of Human Rights', Chapter 7 in Stephen White, Alex Pravda and Zvi Gitelman (eds) *Developments in Russian Politics 4*, Basingstoke: Macmillan

Solomon Jr, Peter H. (1997) 'The Persistence of Judicial Reform in Contemporary Russia', *East European Constitutional Review* 6 (4) Fall, 50–56

Whitehouse, Tom (1999) 'Russian Prisoners Incubate Infection', *The Guardian*, 24 March, 16

Further reading

For judicial reform under Gorbachev see:

Barry, Donald D. (ed.) (1992) *Toward the 'Rule of Law' in Russia? Political and Legal Reform in the Transition Period*, Armonk, New York and London: M.E. Sharpe
Berman, Harold J. (1991) 'The Rule of Law and the Law-Based State (*Rechtsstaat*) (with Special Reference to Developments in the Soviet Union)', *The Harriman Institute Forum* 4 (5) May, 1–12
Butler, W.E. (ed.) (1991) *Perestroika and the Rule of Law: Anglo-American and Soviet Perspectives*, London and New York: I.B. Tauris
Juviler, Peter (1991) 'Human Rights After Perestroika: Progress and Perils', *The Harriman Institute Forum* 4 (6) June, 1–9

For general discussion of legal developments see:

Sharlet, Robert (1994) 'Citizen and State Under Gorbachev and Yeltsin', Chapter 5 in Stephen White, Alex Pravda and Zvi Gitelman (eds) *Developments in Russian and Post-Soviet Politics*, Basingstoke: Macmillan
Sharlet, Robert (1997) 'The Progress of Human Rights', Chapter 7 in Stephen White, Alex Pravda and Zvi Gitelman (eds) *Developments in Russian Politics 4*, Basingstoke: Macmillan

For reports on human rights issues consult the Amnesty International and the Human Rights Watch websites listed below.

The journal *East European Constitutional Review* is a particularly good source of articles on legal reform in the FSU and throughout the former soviet bloc.

Websites

http://www.amnesty.org/ (Amnesty International)
http://www.hrw.org/ (Human Rights Watch)
http://www.supcourt.ru/ (Supreme Court)
http://www.arbitr.ru/ (Supreme Arbitration Court)
http://www.friends-partners.org/~ccsi/nisorgs/nislegal.htm (provides links to the websites of human rights organisations throughout the FSU)

CHAPTER 7

The state in uniform

This chapter examines the coercive institutions of the Russian state, their potential as either a source of or support for an authoritarian backlash and whether the conditions exist for the Russian armed forces to usurp the functions of the government. The factors that might predispose them to take up arms against the civilian government are examined. As a former super-power in a changed geopolitical environment during a time of economic constraint, Russia is rethinking what kind of armed forces it needs. The debate about the optimum size for the army, the move from conscript to professional forces, and Russia's other 'power-wielding structures' are discussed. Finally, the first signs that President Putin is attempting to remilitarise Russia are introduced.

Introduction

On 7 May 1992 President Yeltsin issued a decree establishing the Russian Armed Forces. The decree was issued just two days before the Victory Day celebrations on 9 May, so underlining the continuity between the Red Army that had defeated the Nazi invaders in 1945 and the new Russian Army. The 1993 Constitution (Arts 83 and 87) enshrined the president's domination over the armed forces. The president is the commander-in-chief, heads the Security Council, and appoints and dismisses defence ministers and the armed forces' high command. It is the president who has the right to declare states of emergency or war, and to approve the country's Military Doctrine. In Russia's super-presidential system the Constitution established military subordination to the president rather than to a broader system of civilian control. The result was that military–civil relations risk being focused on loyalty to the president rather than a broader loyalty to Russia's government or political system. The

establishment of regularised mechanisms of civilian control over the military
have become embroiled in the broader questions of state-building, institutional
and personal rivalries and central versus regional powers. Russia's armed
forces and security services, like so many of its other state institutions, are
characterised by a considerable continuity with the soviet past. A pressing task
in the early 1990s was the rapid reform of these forces, which had been trained
to serve a different political master and could quite literally turn their guns on
the new leadership. The armed forces and security services also need to be
restructured, modernised, re-equipped and retrained so that they can effectively carry out their professional duties.

Civil–military relations

Civilian oversight of the military

President Yeltsin continued the soviet practice of appointing a soldier as
minister of defence (see Box 7.1). His first defence minister, Gen. Pavel
Grachev, had demonstrated his loyalty to Yeltsin during the August 1991
coup attempt, had a high public profile, and was respected for his role as an
airborne commander during the Afghan war. Following Grachev's sacking in
1996 Yeltsin appointed another general, Igor Rodionov, as minister of
defence. Yeltsin however asked Rodionov to resign his army commission so
becoming Russia's first civilian minister of defence since Leon Trotsky's
resignation as commissar for war in 1925. Rodionov was sacked in 1997
amid allegations of obstructing military reform. He had repeatedly come into
conflict with Yury Baturin, the secretary of the Defence Council, which had
been established in October 1996 to provide a more unified approach to
military issues. Rodionov was replaced by a serving general, Igor Sergeev.
Yeltsin seems to have believed that by appointing military figures he could

---

BOX 7.1

Russia's defence ministers

The Ministry of Defence was formally re-established in March 1992, with Yeltsin
fulfilling the minister's role until Grachev was appointed.

Pavel Grachev (May 1992–June 1996)
Mikhail Kolesnikov (acting defence minister June 1996)
Igor Rodionov (July 1996–May 1997)
Igor Sergeev (May 1997–March 2001)
Sergei Ivanov (March 2001–)

coopt them and so control them. The Security Council (see Chapter 4) includes leading members of the executive and the armed forces and provides an important forum for civilian and military leaders to discuss military and security issues. The Duma has a military oversight function through its security and defence committees, and its discussion of the RF's budget entails discussing military spending.

Timothy Colton and Thane Gustafson on military–civil relations

Colton and Gustafson in their 1990 work on soviet civil–military relations provide useful indicators of the factors that might predispose the military to become involved in politics (see Box 7.2). This is not a simple checklist and they certainly do not suggest that if one or more of these factors exists then the military will automatically undermine, attack or usurp civilian authority. Any or all of these factors may exist but be counter balanced or neutralised by other factors, such as factionalism, regionalism, corruption or straightforward apathy. This also begs the question of what form military involvement or intervention in civilian politics might take and whether it constitutes a threat to the democratic Russian state. The military, as knowledgeable and concerned professionals, should for example be allowed to lobby for better pay and conditions, and to contribute ideas and information about military reform and weapons systems. In a democracy the military should not make these decisions. There is also a wide range of activities that the military might engage in that would not be compatible with democracy. At one extreme would be a military coup, but such activities might also include ignoring the civilian authorities' directions or engaging in unsanctioned activities. What follows is a discussion of Colton and Gustafson's (slightly amended) factors that might predispose the military to become involved in politics applied to the conditions in post-communist Russia.

BOX 7.2

Timothy Colton and Thane Gustafson on civil–military relations

Who rules – the statesman, whose vocation is politics, or the soldier, whose calling is war but who is capable of turning his arms on his own government? How great is military influence in politics, and how complete is the civilians' sway over defence decisions? How weighty a claim does national security exert on the community's resources and on its imagination? Answers to these and unrelated questions tell us much about the nature of the state...

Source: Timothy J. Colton and Thane Gustafson (eds) (1990) *Soldiers and the Soviet State: Civil–Military Relations from Brezhnev to Gorbachev*, Princeton, NJ: Princeton University Press, 3.

Factor 1: The failure to safeguard national security

Colton and Gustafson argue that a crisis in military–civilian relations may occur 'if either side concludes that the other, be it due to mismanagement, denial of resources, or some other reason, is doing an unacceptably poor job of safeguarding national security' (Colton and Gustafson, 1990: 9). During Reconstruction the soviet armed forces had suffered an ignominious withdrawal from Afghanistan (1989), and the end of communist rule in East-Central Europe (1989) also led to the dissolution of their security organisation the Warsaw Pact (1990) and the withdrawal of soviet troops back to the USSR. In 1991 both the armed forces and security services were confronted by the disintegration of the country they had sworn to protect, namely the USSR. The August 1991 coup attempt against Gorbachev was in part to preempt the signing of the Union Treaty which would have signed the death warrant of the USSR. The reduction in defence spending and forces in Europe were all evidence that Gorbachev had failed to safeguard the USSR's security. The great gains of the victorious Red Army that had defeated Hitler and reached Berlin, and then held the mighty USA and NATO at bay for over 40 years, were being squandered. However, only an extremely small number of army officers were directly involved in the coup. Most preferred simply to wait the crisis out, while others actively and decisively opposed the coup. The armed forces were not united, but the deciding factor in deciding their allegiance seems to have been the legitimacy and authority enjoyed by Yeltsin as the democratically elected president.

With the foundation of the RF, it is now Russia's national security not the USSR's that the civilian leadership, armed forces and security services have to protect. Defining national security entails defining the nation. The existence of the Russian diaspora in the Near Abroad has led some Russian politicians and soldiers to see the Russian nation divided by artificial borders (see Chapter 3). Within a month of his appointment as defence minister Gen. Pavel Grachev declared himself ready to fight to protect Russians in the former USSR, so extending national security to include all ethnic Russians and justifying possible military action in the Near Abroad. The Russians were also slow to withdraw from the Near Abroad, partly because it posed major logistical and financial problems, but also due to the reluctance of some senior officers to accept the independence of these states coupled with concern about the ethnic Russians who would be left behind. Russia's senior military leaders have made it perfectly clear that they are deeply troubled by NATO's enlargement into East-Central Europe, but they have so far contented themselves with fiery speeches imploring the politicians to stand up to NATO. While NATO's attacks on Slobodan Milosevic's Serbia in the late 1990s were not direct assaults on Russia's national security, they were attacks on a Russian ally. President Yeltsin and Prime Minister Primakov echoed the military's denunciations of NATO and in March 1999 Foreign Minister Ivanov announced a cessation of RF contacts with NATO due to the bombing of Serbia. This is not to suggest that the military dictated government policy or that Yeltsin–Primakov–Ivanov were forced into an anti-NATO stance with which they disagreed. Civilian politicians and the armed forces share these concerns about national security and slights to Russia's international standing.

Factor 2: Sense of disorientation or loss of mission and status

The long delay in the elaboration of a new Russian Military Doctrine frustrated the armed forces' attempts to define their mission and retain their organisational integrity. The soviet military were a superpower force oriented to defending the USSR against NATO, but since the collapse of the USSR Russian forces have been involved in peacekeeping missions in the Near Abroad and fighting Russian citizens in Chechnia. For the armed forces a very basic question is 'Why are we fighting?' Col. Yury Deryugin, chair of the 'Security of the Fatherland Military Science' society, speaking at the time of the first Chechen war (1994–6) claimed that the army's poor performance was due to the troops' low morale, and that the communists' system of military values had been abandoned but that nothing had been put in its place. According to Deryugin even at the start of the Afghan war (1978–89) soldiers went into battle having first been 'inspired' by the deputy commander for political education; the Russian troops in Chechnia have no such inspiration in contrast to Dudaev's 'deceived followers' who are 'fired up' by a national idea (*Rossiiskiye vesti*, 10 January 1995: 2). The propaganda image of the soviet Red Army was as the valiant defender of the USSR and soviet socialism; young men were conscripted into the armed forces to fulfil their patriotic duty. Conscription took place twice a year and in each town and village throughout the country the conscripts would be given a ceremonial send-off. The realities of life for these conscripts fell far short of the propaganda image and certainly there was a good deal of cynicism about the lofty ideological statements, but they were left in no doubt as to why they were expected to serve. When the government cannot even feed, clothe, pay, equip or train conscripts, why should those conscripts be expected to serve a government that is legendary for its corruption? Whose 'national' interests are being served in Chechnia, those of the Russian peoples or the oligarchs and their oil interests? These questions are linked to the broader question of the very nature and identity of Russia, a question which President Putin is currently seeking to address, by supporting the return to the old soviet anthem and reintroducing military training in schools.

Factor 3: The government's failure to do its job and/or its loss of authority and legitimacy

The prime time for a military coup in Russia would have been 1992–3. The economy was in free fall, people were going hungry, crime was rising and the civilian branches of government, the president and legislature were in conflict. Not only was there no coup but the armed forces were reluctant to intervene, even when both sides were vying for military support. Fears that the military might side with the former air force officer Alexander Rutskoi and the Red-Brown-dominated parliament proved unfounded. The armed forces only reluctantly became involved once fighting had broken out in Moscow. They obeyed President Yeltsin, their commander-in-chief, but Yeltsin records in his *Presidential Notes* that it took several hours to persuade them to attack the White House (Yeltsin, 1994: 382–7). The army's support for Yeltsin also seems to have been partly based on 'the perception that the president enjoyed greater legitimacy and popular support than the parliament and Vice President Aleksander Rutskoi' (Lepingwell, 1994: 118). The danger in using the military to settle a dispute between civilian politicians is that it could set a dangerous precedent. The military could either come to view themselves as the 'king makers', the arbiters between contending civilian factions, or even decide to substitute military rule for ineffective civilian government. Since 1993 there have been important developments in the Russian political system that have reduced the likelihood of the armed forces being asked again to resolve conflicts between the different branches of the civilian government. The RF now has a post-soviet Constitution, a Constitutional Court, the respective powers of the president and the legislature have been decided, and elections are held so confirming the legitimacy and authority of these new arrangements.

The 'man on horseback' is a military leader, a Napoleon Bonaparte figure, who is not born to rule like a king or queen; neither is he an elected leader, he takes power. In the early 1990s Gen. Alexander Lebed seemed to project himself as potential 'man on horseback', as a self-proclaimed clean pair of hands who could sort out the corrupt and ineffective civilian politicians. Lebed professed an admiration for the Chilean dictator Augusto Pinochet, but has since tended to back-pedal on Pinochet and has stated a preference for France's former President de Gaulle (see Box 7.3). After retiring from the army in May 1995 Lebed stood as a candidate for the Congress of Russian Communities (KRO) in the December 1995 Duma elections, but the KRO

BOX 7.3

Alexander Lebed on Pinochet

What did he [Pinochet] do? He led the state from total collapse and put the army in first place ... Now Chile is a prospering country ... This supports the theory that when one thumps his fist on the table once, a hundred men are put [sacrificed] on the altar of the fatherland and the issue is closed. Or is it better with a situation in which five men die every day, seemingly small potatoes, but in time it adds up to a million?

Source: Izvestia, 20 July 1994, 4.

failed to surmount the 5 per cent barrier. Lebed then stood in the 1996 presidential elections, but stood down before the second round so helping to secure Yeltsin's victory.

In return for his timely support, Yeltsin appointed Lebed his national security adviser and a member of the Security Council. This is another example of Yeltsin coopting a potential rival and also hoping to cultivate military support (see Chapter 4). Lebed now had responsibility for overseeing the armed forces, security services and the police. Lebed said he would use the post to crack down on corruption and crime and to reform the army. His first target was the defence minister Gen. Grachev, who was dismissed in June 1996 amid accusations of planning a military coup. The purge continued with the sackings of Gen. Alexander Korzhakov, the head of the Presidential Guard, Col. Gen. Mikhail Barsukov, the director of the Federal Counter-Intelligence Service (FSK), and Oleg Soskovets, the first deputy chair of the Council of Ministers who had close links with the military. They were accused of wanting to cancel the upcoming second round of the presidential elections. One week later Yeltsin dismissed seven army generals, including four high-ranking general staff officers, three officers from the Ministry of Defence and a deputy commander-in-chief of ground troops. Throughout this period Lebed projected himself as the champion of democracy and warned that any mutiny would be crushed. In October 1996 the minister of the interior, Anatoly Kulikov, claimed that Lebed had a 50 000-strong 'Russian Legion' poised to launch a 'creeping coup' and that Lebed was even trying to recruit Chechen rebels to his cause. Lebed was sacked in October 1996. Whatever the rights and wrongs of the various accusations of attempted coups, the second round of the presidential elections did go ahead and Lebed has continued his political career not by staging a coup but by being elected governor for Krasnoyarsk in 1998.

Factor 4: If they are drawn into tasks beyond their usual professional competence, such as internal security

Colton and Gustafson explain that the military's professionalism may be undermined if the military are drawn into preserving civil peace by, for example, being deployed against striking workers, guerrilla bands, or other kinds of dissenters (Colton and Gustafson, 1990: 10). They note that the great soviet dictator Stalin was careful to enhance the Red Army's professional identity and that the task of maintaining internal order was left to the various police and paramilitary forces (*ibid.*: 20). Soviet armed forces were deployed in the Caucasus and the Baltics (1989–91) to counter the nationalist threats to the USSR's integrity, but it was clear that many within these forces found being used against 'their own people' very distasteful. In October 1993 the armed forces were once again reluctant to be deployed against Russian citizens. The first Chechen war provoked what became known as the 'Generals' Crisis' in

1995, when three generals, Boris Gromov, Georgy Kondratyev and Valery Mironov, were removed from the Ministry of Defence for their opposition to the war. Gen. Gromov, a veteran of the Afghan war, was the highest ranking critic of the war, and was popular with both the army and the people amongst whom the Chechen war was generally very unpopular. In contrast to Defence Minister Pavel Grachev, who was one of the leading advocates of the Chechen war, Gromov made it clear that he did not believe that the army should be involved in what was an internal security matter. Furthermore, the RF's Law on Defence restricts the armed forces to external defence. Gromov was moved to the Ministry of Foreign Affairs as its chief military expert, in effect sidelined but not demoted. In contrast to the first Chechen war the second war has proved more popular with the Russian electorate and the army chiefs. Although conscripts show no more wish to fight in Chechnia than their 1994–6 forebears, the army chiefs seem positively to relish the opportunity to overturn the humiliation of their failure to defeat the Chechen fighters and their forced withdrawal from the republic in 1996.

Factor 5: If they are drawn to support a particular faction

The military may be encouraged by politicians, political parties or interest groups to become involved in social, economic and political disputes. Russia has a variety of 'patriotic' organisations and political parties which gather support from members of the armed forces as well as the general public. The patriotic organisations share a commitment to Russia as a great power and the need to fund the armed forces adequately so that they can modernise. Beyond this they disagree: some support the reconstitution of the USSR, others favour a military dictatorship, and the progressive-patriots support Russia's demo-cratisation. The anti-democratic patriotic organisations include some which even have their own paramilitary forces (Thomas, 1995: 542). These include the White Guard, the Living Wheel Union and the Russian National Unity Party whose emblem is a swastika crossed with two blades. The All-Russian Officers' Union, founded in February 1992 and headed by Col. Gen. Vladislav Achalov and Lt. Col. Stanislav Terekhov, believe the USSR should be reconstituted, that democracy is little better than anarchy and chaos, and that it is responsible for Russia's economic decline. They also find civilian control of the military a slight to military professionalism. Both Terekhov and Achalov were briefly imprisoned for their opposition to Yeltsin in October 1993. Such anti-democratic patriotic organisations claim to have high levels of support within the army, but it is very difficult to gauge the real level of support. While there are certainly anti-government attitudes within the armed forces, these are manifested more by apathy, resignation and corruption than covert plans to bring down the government.

In September 1997 the founding congress of the 'Movement in Support of the Armed Forces, Defence Industry and Science' was held in Moscow. The meeting brought together over 40 patriotic organisations with branches throughout the country. The congress was addressed by two high-powered speakers, (retd.) Gen. Lev Rokhlin and the former defence minister Igor Rodionov, who spoke vehemently of the failure to modernise the armed forces and the military-defence industries, the problems of underfunding, the decline in morale and mounting corruption. Rokhlin was careful to project himself as a progressive patriot, who wanted to combine democracy with a pride in Russia and its great power status. He refused to allow Terekhov's Union of Officers to replace the Russian tricolour with the soviet red flag. In December 1995 Rokhlin was elected to the Duma and in April 1998 he was joined by Gen. Andrei Nikolaev. Nikolaev had retired as the head of the Federal Border Guards in December 1997, when Yeltsin proposed merging them with the FSB. Although both Rokhlin and Nikolaev were critical of government policy, they were elected Duma deputies for the pro-Yeltsin 'party of power' Our Home is Russia. Yeltsin moved quickly to coopt these politicised generals: Rokhlin was made chair of the parliamentary defence committee, a post which Yeltsin subsequently offered to Nikolaev.

According to data provided by the Ministry of Defence in the December 1999 Duma elections, the majority of the military electorate voted for the 'party of power' for the first time since the foundation of the RF (see Box 7.4). The party of power is now the Unity party which was endorsed by Putin when he was prime minister. This claim is based on the voting behaviour of a very small sample, the 2 per cent of the military electorate including service personnel, their families, civilians living on military bases and defence industry workers, who voted at their military units rather than at the open polling stations used by the general public. The results also show that military support for the communists (KPRF) while still sizable has fallen by 5–6 per cent since

---

BOX 7.4

Electoral preferences of the military and general electorates in the State Duma elections, December 1999 (as a percentage of those who voted)

	Military	General population
Unity (Medved or Bear)	48	23
KPRF	18	24
Zhirinovsky's Bloc	14	6
Fatherland-All Russia (OVR)	7	12
Yabloko	<1	6
Union of Rightist Forces	<1	9

Source: Andrei Korbut (1999) 'The Army Voted for the Party of Power', *Nezavisimaia gazeta*, 25 December, 3.

the 1995 Duma elections. Similarly, although Zhirinovsky's bloc enjoys greater support amongst the military electorate than amongst the general population, in 1995 Zhirinovsky's party polled 20 per cent of the military electorate vote compared to 14 per cent in 1999. Putin's tough stance on Chechnia and his promise to increase defence spending and to pay military salary and pension arrears all helped to rally military electoral support for the Unity party.

The creation of a professional army

What sort of army does Russia need?

Russia's 1993 Military Doctrine stated that Russia no longer regarded any country as its enemy and did not intend to use military force unless attacked. It has withdrawn its troops from East-Central Europe and the Near Abroad, recognises that NATO poses no immediate threat, and realises that it is more likely to be involved in local conflicts along its borders than battles with a great power. In addition to these changed geopolitical realities, Russia also has to modernise its armed forces at a time of economic constraint. Military reform entails a reassessment of the appropriate size of the armed forces, introducing new military technologies and instituting new forms of training. President Yeltsin designated 1995 as the 'Year of Military Reform', when the tasks included reducing the number of divisions, closing unneeded military installations and bases, destroying superfluous equipment including dismantling old nuclear-powered submarines (see Chapter 12), discharging thousands of officers and providing them with accommodation, and establishing training institutions for career sergeants and other non-commissioned officers. These are all mammoth tasks, which have still not been completed.

Military technology and training

The soviet Red Army in the 1980s was a mass army and the military academies still stressed the importance of the concentrated, mass tank attacks that had helped to bring victory during the Great Patriotic War (1941–5). The Afghan war had already revealed the inappropriateness of these tactics and the Red Army's inability to defeat a highly motivated and American-armed guerrilla force. Unlike the NATO forces in the 1980s, the Red Army did not make the technological leap into the new generation of 'smart' weapons. The Afghan war revealed the USSR's loss of air superiority and that it had nothing to match the highly mobile American Stinger missiles. The air force needs to replace its MiG-29s, Su-24s, Su-27s and the Tu-95 Bears and although there are plans for new subsonic Stealth bombers, intermediate-range joint continental bombers and a new multi-role fighter fitted with a new generation of smart weapons, these remain as yet only plans. Russia's land- and sea-based strategic nuclear forces are also ageing. In December 1988 the army adopted the RS-12M Topol movable ground-to-air missile, and in 1994 a modified version of this, the RS-12M2 Topol-M (or SS27), was developed. Just one Topol-M costs $30–35 million at a time when the government is already in debt to the defence industries. Another result of persistent underfunding is that the armed forces are unable to conduct training exercises. Fuel shortages mean that the Navy cannot conduct manoeuvres and fighter pilots typically log no more than 25 flying hours a year, compared to a western training norm of 180–220 hours (Lambeth, 1995: 89).

Professional or conscript forces?

Conscription's unpopularity, the poor performances in Afghanistan and Chechnia, and the increasing complexity of military technology have all been used to support calls for the creation of professional (or volunteer) rather than conscript forces. Modern high-tech warfare needs high-quality personnel rather than large numbers of conscripts who are not in the forces long enough to become proficient in the use of new technologies. Conscripts are also condemned for being of poor quality. In the early 1990s so many possible exemptions and grounds for deferment were introduced that the lowest rate of conscription was amongst better-educated, urban men. One survey found that of the men who answered the call-up 3 per cent had only an elementary education, 27 per cent had not completed secondary school, 12 per cent had never had a job and 11 per cent had health problems. Other studies have found that as many as one in three conscripts is medically unfit for duty (*Nezavisimaia gazeta*, 1 November 1994: 3). The proliferation of 'power-wielding structures' (see below), conscription evasion, and the small cohort in the relevant age group (see Chapter 12) have all contributed to conscription not bringing in enough troops. In 1991 contract or volunteer service was introduced in the Air Force, Air Defence Force, Strategic Nuclear Forces Command and the Navy and was then extended to other armed forces. The contract personnel were supposed to be well-trained professionals, but in reality they often turned out to be misfits and socially disadvantaged people who could not fit back into civilian life. In addition more than a third of contract personnel were the wives of officers or warrant officers who could not be used in combat roles. A contract soldier also costs four times more than a conscript. The experience of contract soldiers has major implications for the possibility of going over to professional or volunteer forces. Here the Russian armed forces are in a vicious circle: their poor reputation and status, low (or even no) pay, meagre living conditions and reputation for brutality (*dedovsh-china*) do not make them an attractive career choice. At the same time the reforms that are necessary to deal with these problems depend in part on well-educated and motivated, professional personnel.

Living conditions and corruption

The return of troops from East-Central Europe and the Near Abroad

The soviet Red Army was staffed on the assumption that at any time thousands of its troops would be stationed in the other Warsaw Pact countries. Within less than five years Russia had to absorb its troops first from East-Central Europe and then from the Near Abroad. In February 1993 Defence Minister Grachev gave a television interview in which he said that Russia lacked the new bases and housing needed for its returning service personnel and their families, and that at least 155 000 officers and their families lacked adequate housing. To this day army officers are living with their families in tents or in single rooms in barrack blocks, while naval officers and their families are living on their rusting ships. The situation was made worse when funds were diverted from providing service housing and social services to fund the first Chechen war (Lambeth, 1995: 90–1). Some western governments have provided aid to fund the redeployment and retraining of returning service personnel. The German government provided Russia with funds to construct apartments for troops withdrawn from Germany. The British and German governments have also coordinated their efforts to retrain Russian officers for civilian professions such as banking and motor mechanics, and in the skills necessary to set up small and medium size business enterprises.

The armed forces are unable to pay their utility bills

The underfunding of the armed forces has meant that they cannot pay their bills. In 1993 the airline Aeroflot refused military transportation requests because the Ministry of Defence had not paid its bills (Lambeth, 1995: 88). In September 1995 the Arkhangel Power Association cut off the electricity to the Strategic Missile Forces' Plesetsk Test Site, the Plesetsk space centre and the adjacent city of Mirny, on the grounds that they owed the association 12 billion roubles (*Sevodnia*, 16 September 1995: 1). The same month the Northern Fleet, which was owed a staggering 600 billion roubles by the Russian government, was unable to pay its utilities bills. In order to stop the electricity supply being cut off to its nuclear-powered bases and nuclear installations, the fleet put a guard on the Kola Power Station (*Sevodnia*, 23 September 1995: 1). In the same month the electricity supply to garrisons in Moscow, Tambov, Kostroma, Ivanovo, Tver *oblasts* and to the Kaliningrad garrison was cut off (*Sevodnia*, 24 November 1995: 1). The government responded by ordering the power companies not to cut off energy supplies to the armed forces, as this would be a breach of national security. The problem has not disappeared however: in the autumn of 1998 Russia's Baltic Fleet was unable to pay its bakery, electricity and water bills.

'The army needs protection'

Officers' salaries have not kept pace with inflation and during the 1990s many officers were not paid for months on end (Zabosky, 1996: 15). A Moscow bus driver earns more than a fighter pilot and both officers and conscripts spend their time working on allotments and farms to get food and earn money. In order to survive soldiers also moonlight as taxi drivers, hotel doormen and more disturbingly as bodyguards in Russia's growing private security services. The shortfall in conscripts means that officers have to perform menial tasks such as stoking furnaces and standing guard, formerly assigned to conscripts. Suicides among officers rose by 28 per cent in 1996 alone; this is a particular problem in the more remote garrisons where life is already very physically tough. Although the overall size of the armed forces has contracted, it nevertheless has only about 90 per cent of the officers it needs. One-third of officers with over 20 years' service are currently seeking retirement and more disturbingly nearly a half of Russia's lieutenants want to resign on graduation (Jamestown Monitor, 13 October 1999: 1). As a result Russia's officer corps is ageing and it is still dominated by soviet-trained personnel. In order to modernise, the armed forces need to retain these younger officers and provide them with an attractive career. The officer shortage exacerbates other problems such as inadequate training provision and therefore a lack of combat-readiness, corruption and indiscipline. Russian soldiers were sent to Chechnia without appropriate clothing, rations and shelter. In the winter of 1995, naval officers were hurriedly taken off warships and without any rigorous infantry training were sent to Chechnia to fight in marine battalions. Some 25–30 servicemen die daily from training accidents, suicides, or simply bullying. Little wonder then that Aleksei Tsaryov, the adviser to the chair of the State Duma committee on military questions, finds that officers are generally disillusioned with the 'democrats', alienated from politics and do not believe it will prove possible to reform the armed forces. According to Tsaryov, the well-known soviet-era slogan, 'The People and the Army are united', has gradually been transformed by servicemen into another slogan, 'The Army needs protection' (*Rossiiskiye vesti*, 13 January 1995: 2).

The torture of soldiers: *dedovshchina*

The phenomenon of *dedovshchina*, or bullying, was an integral part of army life in the USSR (see Chapter 2), but with the decline of service discipline and morale it has become even worse. The Russian Army has no professional non-commissioned officers and so nineteen-year-old conscripts serve as non-commissioned officers (*Sevodnia*, 18 August 1995: 3). A good deal of the bullying is carried out by these youthful non-commissioned officers but officers have also been found to be involved. The Volgograd military prosecutor found that two conscripts were punished for being absent without leave by being put in a three-metre pit by their regiment commander; they could not escape from the pit where they were beaten daily by both the non-commissioned officers and the officers. The pit caved in burying the conscripts alive; one died and the second was seriously injured (Russian TV, 17 October 1998: 19). The Committee for Soldiers' Mothers monitors and publicises the treatment of Russian soldiers. In one 18-month period the Stavropol Committee for Soldiers' Mothers found that 14 soldiers had been killed by *dedovshchina* in the Budyonnovsk-based 205th Brigade and 350 soldiers had reported torture and ill-treatment to the committee (Amnesty International Report, 1999).

Corruption and the armed forces

Even as soviet forces were preparing to leave Germany, officers began selling or bartering weaponry, tanks and artillery for money, Mercedes cars and electronics. In October 1994 *Moskovskii Komsomolets* military correspondent Dmitry Kholodov was lured to collect a briefcase supposedly containing documentary evidence of high-level military corruption in the army's Western Group (East Germany). Kholodov was killed when the briefcase exploded and it was not until February 2000 that five paratroopers and a security guard were arrested for his murder. The armed forces and their assets were not subject to privatisation like Russia's economic assets. However, just as many soviet economic managers appropriated state assets during the privatisation process and treated them as their own (see Chapter 1), army officers similarly saw military assets as a way to make money for themselves. The military has become involved with criminal gangs by selling them weapons, security and protection, labour and the use of buildings. At the end of 1993 Yeltsin set up a state company, Rosvooruzhenie, which was responsible for Russia's potentially lucrative military exports. It quickly set up offices in over 40 countries, mostly in the Middle East and other countries formerly allied to the USSR. Defence Minister Pavel Grachev's ally Viktor Samoilov was appointed chair, Konstantin Borovoi became deputy chair, Most-bank was authorised to handle the company's transactions, and Yeltsin's bodyguard Alexander Korzhakov was put in charge of overseeing exports. Within a year it was clear that although Rosvooruzhenie was exporting sucessfully, not all the transactions were being properly recorded and profits were being stolen. Another example of this private use of state assets is provided by the activities of Major Rodionov, the commander of a long-range aviation base in the Far East. Rodionov used the base, bomber pilots and crews to transport commercial goods to China so bypassing customs. In 1996 (retd.) Gen. Lebed and the defence minister Gen. Rodionov launched an anti-corruption drive against the allies of the former defence minister Gen. Grachev, with the help of (retd.) Gen. Lev Rokhlin. In an address to the Duma on 5 July 1996, Rokhlin revealed that a firm called Lyukon had a contract with the Ministry of Defence to build apartments for retired officers but that not one had been built.

THE STATE IN UNIFORM

Lyukon's co-founder was a son of Gen. Konstantin Kobets, the chief military inspector (Starr, 1998). Rokhlin also accused three generals of embezzling $30 million from army funds, and a fourth of keeping a 'serf-battalion' of conscript soldiers to build officers' cottages (*dachas*) in the Moscow suburbs. Over the next year Rokhlin continued to attack corruption in the armed forces and in 1997 started to organise opposition to Yeltsin's government within the army. On 3 July 1998 Rokhlin was murdered.

Regionalisation and the armed forces

The regionalisation of the armed forces

The growing power of the republics and regions has been a key feature of Russia's post-communist state-building (see Chapter 5). This raises important questions about where the armed forces' allegiances lie and whether Russia can be said to have a national army. Russia has maintained the soviet-era military administrative districts, which were and still are characterised by close ties between the military and civilian authorities. District military commanders, for example, supplied the local collective farms with soldiers to help with the harvest and soldiers waited on the tables at the local CPSU headquarters. In return, the soldiers were supplied with local products and food. As central funding for the military is now woefully inadequate and in some cases even non-existent, military units have become increasingly dependent on regional authorities to supply the basic requirements for survival. In some cases commanders simply sell their conscripts' labour to local farms and factories and keep the money. According to Dmitry Kholodov, 'A frightening process has begun in the army. District commanders no longer rely on their ministry [but instead] turn to local authorities directly for help. In this way, the army is becoming tied to regions, something that, in the event of a crisis, could break it up into component parts' (*Moskovskii Komsomolets*, 22 March 1994: 10). To date only Chechnia has taken up arms to support its claim for independence. Although individuals have left the RF forces stationed in the republic to fight on the side of the Chechen guerrillas, there have also been cases of whole RF units transferring their allegiance to the Chechen cause.

The 'territoriality principle' of recruitment

Since the 1930s the soviet practice was for conscripts to serve away from their home area in order to help integrate the USSR's nationalities. As Reconstruction progressed and conscription became an increasingly emotive issue, army reformers advocated the introduction of 'national-territorial formations' in the army, enabling conscripts to serve in their home republic (Richter and

Echterling, 1991: 49). In the RF there have been similar demands for a regionally based recruitment system with conscripts serving within a set distance of their home (Lepingwell, 1994: 121). Lepingwell speculates that such a move could have a mixed effect on Russian civilian–military relations. It could promote the formation of regional loyalties with the armed forces having closer ties to the local population. This could reduce the likelihood of military intervention in civilian affairs, because officers and conscripts would be less likely to act against people from their own region. Equally it could also make army units less likely to follow Moscow's orders to suppress local or regional conflicts. Local leaders, secure that Moscow could not impose its decisions on them, may feel free to ignore Moscow and to pursue their own line, which could be reformist, authoritarian or just plain corrupt. The loss of Moscow's control over the regions and the potential loss of military control in the republics and regions could in turn provoke the kind of constitutional crisis that could precipitate military involvement in Russian politics. The presence of military formations with regional loyalties would then become a decisive factor in any conflict. To date the RF has not introduced national-territorial formations into the armed forces, although Tatarstan will not allow its conscripts to serve outside of the republic.

The Cossacks: back guarding the frontiers

The Cossacks are descendants of Russian and Ukrainian peasants who fled serfdom to live in the border areas of the Imperial Russian empire in the Rostov and Volgograd regions, Krasnodar and Stavropol territories, Kazakhstan, Siberia and the Far East. The Cossacks lived as free people and had their own organisations, including military forces (*voysko*) which loyally served the tsars. With the collapse of the USSR the Cossacks have once again found themselves in Russia's border areas and are once again offering their services to Moscow in return for a measure of autonomy. In 1992 Yeltsin defined the Cossacks as amongst the oppressed peoples of the soviet period and therefore they qualify for various benefits and subsidies. The president set up a Council on Cossack Affairs, and in 1994 he promised to restore Cossack units in the armed forces. In the Far East, the Amur and Maritime Cossacks had already created their own forces and the Transbaikal Cossacks, with the agreement of the local Military District Command, had formed their own regiment. By 1995 more than 20 Cossack units and combined units, 12 border troops subunits and two detachments had been formed in the Russian armed forces with a separate Cossack border detachment on Sakhalin. Nikolai Yegorov, who heads the President's Council on Cossack Affairs, stressed that the Cossack units are subordinate not to the Cossack leaders, the Hetmen, but to the armed forces command or officials of the relevant federal agency. The Cossacks have, however, pursued their own agendas and operate freely across Russia's borders. In 1991 Cossack volunteers served in Transdniestr, a

Russian-populated area that had broken away from Moldova. Since then Cossack forces on their own initiative have served in Bosnia and Abkhazia (in Georgia). The Amur and Maritime Cossacks have also made it clear that they would fight any attempt to 'return' the Kuril Islands to Japan. Cossacks are also campaigning for the Russian–Kazakhstan border to be moved so that Russia incorporates all the area's Cossacks. In 1957 Khrushchev had given the Checheno-Ingushetia autonomous republic the Shelkovskaia and Naurskaia district of Stavropol *krai*, which was inhabited by Terek Cossacks. In 1995 while Chechens called for the withdrawal of Russian 'occupation troops' from the district capital of Naurskaia, the local Cossacks demanded the return of these lands to Stavropol *oblast* and resettlement of all local Chechens.

Parallel 'power-wielding structures'

The security services: from the August coup to the Russian Federation

Towards the end of the Reconstruction period the secret police (KGB) chaired by Kryuchkov worked with party conservatives to frustrate and undermine Gorbachev's reforms. Following the August 1991 coup and Kryuchkov's arrest, the all-union KGB bodies were first reorganised and then disbanded along with the USSR in December 1991. Yeltsin tried to create a new Russian Ministry of Security and Internal Affairs (MBVD), which he hoped would bring the KGB under the control of its rival organisation, the Ministry of the Interior. The MBVD was opposed by Russia's democrats and the KGB. The KGB spread rumours that Yeltsin had promised that KGB investigations into corruption by the Ministry of the Interior would be called off if the ministry helped to bring the secret police to heel. For Russia's democrats the creation of such a super-security ministry was too reminiscent of Stalin's dreaded People's Commissariat (ministry) for Internal Affairs. The Supreme Soviet opposed its creation and the Constitutional Court unanimously ruled against it in January 1992.

The proliferation of power-wielding structures

In the USSR there were 8 million men under arms, whereas in Russia the figure stands at around 7.5 million, despite the fact that the RF has only about half of the mobilisation resources of the former USSR. These figures are even more astounding given that the armed forces (army, navy and air force) have been reduced from a soviet figure of 3.9 million to 1.2 million in 1999 (Drummond, 1999). According to Chernomyrdin 5.3 per cent of able-bodied Russian youth are in armed security and if private security guards are included this figure rises to around 10 per cent, compared to 1.8 per cent in the UK (Hosking, 1997). This is explained by the proliferation and expansion of what the Russians call 'power-wielding structures', that is the 20-plus bodies that have some kind of armed forces at their disposal. In addition to the regular armed forces, the Ministries of Defence, Interior, Security and Emergency Situations also have troops. The Federal Border Service which was formerly the KGB's Border Guards Chief Directorate also has troops. The KGB's Eighth and Sixteenth Directorates were merged into the Federal Agency for Government Communications and Information (FAPSI), which also has troops. FAPSI is the RF's high-tech signals intelligence service, which also controls the new fibre optics telecommunications networks, registers securities transactions, provides private companies with encryption software and in St Petersburg controls electronic pagers (Waller, 1997). Then there are the paramilitary State Tax Police, which is a revenue-gathering service but has a large number of staff from the KGB's Fifth Chief Directorate, which had been responsible for tracking dissidents (*ibid.*). In addition to the usual police force (*militsionery*), there is OMON which is a paramilitary police force, and some cities such as Moscow and St Petersburg have their own police forces. Alexander Korzhakov, who was Yeltsin's confidant and chief personal bodyguard, built up his own security and intelligence force with some business sidelines. When Korzhakov was dismissed in 1996 a new Federal Guard Service was set up to provide physical security for Russia's leaders. Other power-wielding structures include the Federal Security Services (FSB) and the Foreign Intelligence Agency (SVR).

Political patronage and the power-wielding structures

Despite having so many people in uniform, Russia has major problems with domestic security and stability. Russian forces have been unable to subdue Chechnia and to combat organised crime. The explanation for the existence of so many power-wielding structures lies in Yeltsin's often precarious political situation and his use of patronage. Yeltsin never created a political party that might have provided him with a firm power base and he was a leader with many enemies. He did not disband the soviet-era security services, but merely reorganised them and changed their names. The existence of parallel structures with duplicate or overlapping functions, competing for missions, budgets and personnel, was part of Yeltsin's policy of divide and rule. Presidential patronage and clan politics (see Chapter 1) therefore played an important part in this proliferation of power-wielding structures. Yeltsin was particularly keen to create new power-wielding structures during his mid-1990s conflicts with Defence Minister Grachev and the 'War Party' (see Chapter 1). In addition to their official duties all these power-wielding structures have their private businesses, which may involve selling their professional skills and contacts for private use as bodyguard, intelligence and protection services. They also have other commercial enterprises which require labour and this is where the conscripts are a valuable free resource. The regular armed forces receive less than 50 per cent of Russia's conscripts and the remainder go to the other power-wielding structures (*Moskovskiye novosti*, 24–31 March 1996: 5). The power-wielding structures are embroiled in the network of corruption that bedevils the development of Russian state structures (*ibid.*).

Russian foreign intelligence service

In 1992 the functions of the KGB were divided between new RF organisations. The KGB's First Chief Directorate's spying and counter espionage role together with its network of foreign agents, electronic monitoring and communications networks and the Space Intelligence Centre were taken over by the Foreign Intelligence Agency (SVR). When in February 1994 the Americans arrested Aldrich Ames, a US citizen, for spying for the Russians, they found out that he had originally been recruited by the USSR and had simply carried on working for the KGB's successors. Speaking in 1995 the SVR's first director, Yevgeny Primakov, said that Russia was no longer a superpower but that the SVR had an even greater role to play in maintaining the country's security than in the past. He described the SVR as having a particular role to play in countering geopolitical threats to Russia's territorial integrity, specifically the enlargement of NATO, and ethnic and nationality conflicts including those within Russia (*Nezavisimaia gazeta*, 22 December 1995: 1). In 1992 the SVR was made subordinate to the president with parliament and the chief prosecutor having some oversight functions, but in December 1995 the SVR was more closely tied to the president.

From Ministry of Security to Federal Counterintelligence Service

The KGB's internal functions and forces, including its border troops, were transferred to the new Ministry of Security (MB). As Reconstruction gathered pace, and its former role of countering internal dissent was less and less required, the KGB had already reinvented itself as the front line fighter against crime and corruption. Under Yeltsin's ally Viktor Barannikov, the MB continued to stress its crime-fighting role but was spectacularly unsuccessful in making any inroads into Russia's soaring crime figures. This together with the failures of the border troops fighting on the Tajik–Afghan border led to Barranikov's dismissal in July 1993. His successor, Nikolai Golushkov, was sacked only three months later in October 1993 for failing to warn about the parliamentary coup. He was replaced by Sergei Stepashin, but the MB was condemned as unreformable and abolished on 21 December 1993 to be replaced by the Federal Counterintelligence Service (FSK). In addition to general internal security matters the FSK was charged with protecting Russia's economic interests. Under the leadership of Stepashin it conducted a covert war against Chechnia and it was Stepashin who ordered the bombing raid in which Dudaev was killed, even though the Defence Minister Grachev had agreed a cease-fire. In six years the RF's internal security services underwent six name changes, six changes of leadership and constant reorganisation. It finally became the Federal Security Bureau (FSB) in July 1995 under Mikhail Barsukov.

Putin and the remilitarisation of Russia?

Putin and reform of the armed forces

President Putin rode to electoral success on the back of the army's campaign in Chechnia. From his appointment as prime minister through to his election as president, Putin has assiduously courted the Russian armed forces and has projected himself as the champion of Russia's great power status. He announced a 50 per cent rise in defence spending and on 23 February (2000), which is the 'Defenders of the Fatherland' holiday, he promoted air force and navy commanders and the three leaders of the Caucasus military campaign. It should not be assumed that Putin's KGB credentials guarantee an easy relationship with the armed forces or that the armed forces present a united front. The Russian armed forces have now experienced ten years of botched reform attempts and there was a bitter and very public power struggle being waged between the then defence minister, Marshal Igor Sergeev, a former rocket forces commander, and the chief of the general staff, Gen. Anatoly Kvashnin, who was one of the architects of the second Chechen war (Traynor, 2000: 1). The rivalry was part personal, part institutional because the roles and competencies of the defence minister and the chief of the general staff have not yet been clearly defined, and part conflict over the type of armed forces that Russia needs today. Kvashnin and the general staff believe that too much of Russia's defence spending, 70 per cent by their calculations, is going on its nuclear arsenal, in a misguided and unnecessary attempt to maintain nuclear parity with the USA. They believe that by 2016 the land-based intercontinental nuclear missile force should be cut from its present level of 756 missiles to 148 and that the strategic rocket forces, which control Russia's land-based nuclear forces, should be transferred to the Air Force. They also believe the funds freed by reducing spending on nuclear weapons should be diverted to spending on conventional forces, but that these should be reduced in number by a quarter from 1.2 million to 900 000 (ibid.). In contrast, Sergeev believed that Russia's nuclear weapons should be grouped together in a new dedicated branch of the armed forces, and claimed that only 17 per cent of Russian defence spending goes on nuclear weaponry. Sergeev held firm to the idea that Russia must develop its nuclear arsenal in order to maintain its international status. Putin has lambasted the lack of reform in the armed forces and has announced that the armed forces will be re-equipped with the latest military technologies. These are general statements of intent and ultimately only President Putin has the authority to resolve the disputes between the minister of defence and the general staff, and to resolve the precise direction of reform. Throughout 2000 Putin tried to isolate Sergeev by sacking six pro-Sergeev generals and publicly opposing his ideas. Finally, in March 2001 Putin sacked Sergeev and sidelined him as an adviser on strategic stability. He was replaced as defence minister by a civilian, Sergei Ivanov, a former KGB member who worked for the Russian foreign intelligence service (SVR) until 2000 and is a Putin loyalist. Putin described these 'personnel changes' as necessary in order to push forward with the long overdue modernisation of the Russina armed forces.

Imperialism and militarism under Putin

Putin has been accused of seeking to remilitarise Russian society. All soviet school students had to attend compulsory military training classes but this was abandoned in 1989. During the soviet period it was not anticipated that this military training would have a direct military use, but it was part of raising disciplined, soviet people who understood the need to defend their country against the ever-present capitalist enemy. On his first day as acting president (31 December 1999) Putin issued a decree on 'The Readiness of Russian Citizens for Military Service', ordering that from 2000 all schools must provide classes to explain the history and contemporary importance of the Russian army. Compulsory military training of two to three hours a week is also being resurrected, so boys between the ages of 15 and 16 will learn drill, how to load and fire a Kalashnikov and army tactics (see Box 7.5). Girls will be taught first aid and non-combat military skills. Young Eagles military youth groups will also be set up in schools. Putin has also called up military reservists for training. Russian military experts estimate that reservists need at least three

---

BOX 7.5

Sergei Kovalev on compulsory military education in schools

This represents a step backwards to a militarised Soviet state. These training classes will have almost no practical use – but they are hugely significant from a psychological point of view, ... It is a clear attempt to manipulate the mood of society – and just one of many instances of the increasing militarisation of society under Putin.

Source: Sergei Kovalev, a human rights campaigner who was sacked in 1995 as Russia's human rights ombudsman for his opposition to the Chechen war, quoted in Amelia Gentleman (2000) 'Back to the USSR', *The Guardian*, 29 May, 2.

months of intensive re-training before they can be deployed. However financial constraints led to the closing down of all military-training courses providing refresher training for reservists in 1991 (*Sevodnia*, 18 August 1995: 3).

Political control of the army

In the soviet armed forces political control was maintained through a system of political commissars inside each unit. The political commissars wore uniforms but their task was to be the eyes and ears of the CPSU and to ensure that the armed forces obeyed their political masters. With the collapse of the USSR the task of overseeing the army eventually passed to the FSB. In addition to countering foreign subversion and spying within the armed forces, the FSB was also charged with rooting out corruption and criminality. A new presidential decree in February 2000 extends these tasks to include the elimination of negative phenomena within the army environment, which sounds very vague but could include monitoring service personnel's political allegiances and dealing with whistle-blowers within the army (see Jamestown Foundation, 2000).

Conclusion

The RF has survived ten stormy years without a military coup. In 1995 there was a rush of retired generals standing for election, but while they wanted to influence government policy, they were prepared to comply with democratic procedures in order to do so. The armed forces seem either to be under adequate civilian control or to be too apathetic or embroiled in their own conflicts or corruption to be concerned with coups. The pressing need to retrain, re-equip and modernise the armed forces has not been met. The standard of living for all but the highest level of personnel is lamentably poor and demoralising, so undermining the military's professionalism. Yeltsin promised, but did not deliver, greater professional rewards and payment. In failing adequately to pay, house, feed and clothe soldiers, the politicians are eroding the soldiers' duty to obey. This has resulted in apathy, suicides, indiscipline, crime and corruption rather than soldiers becoming politicised. President Putin is taking no chances and is seeking to reinforce surveillance of the armed forces while simultaneously courting their support through increased military spending. The armed forces are also subject to undermining factors such as regionalism and corruption. In addition Yeltsin's tactic of creating parallel power-wielding structures both encourages corruption and is wasteful of precious resources. President Putin has depicted himself as the champion of a militarily strong Russia, saying what the armed forces want to hear, but it remains to be seen whether he will be able to deliver.

References

Amnesty International Report (1999) http://www.amnesty.org/

Colton, Timothy J. and Gustafson, Thane (eds) (1990) *Soldiers and the Soviet State: Civil–Military Relations from Brezhnev to Gorbachev*, Princeton, NJ: Princeton University Press

Drummond, Fred (1999) 'Russian Navy Listing but Afloat', *Perspective* 9 (4) March–April, http://www.bu.edu/iscip.html

Hosking, Geoffrey (1997) *Russia Five Years On: A Dialogue with (retd.) Col. Roy Giles*, broadcast on BBC Radio 3, 9 January

Jamestown Foundation (1999) 'Russian Army Continues to Lose Officers', *Monitor* 5 (189) 13 October, http://www.jamestown.org/
Jamestown Foundation (2000) 'Political Commissars for the Military?', *Monitor* 6 (31) 14 February, http://www.jamestown.org/

Lambeth, Benjamin S. (1995) 'Russia's Wounded Military', *Foreign Affairs* , 74 (2) March–April, 86–98
Lepingwell, John (1994) 'The Russian Military in the 1990s: Disintegration or Renewal?', in Douglas W. Blum (ed.) *Russia's Future Consolidation or Disintegration?*, Boulder, CO: Westview Press

Richter, Frank and Echterling, Jobst (1991) 'Military Reform Develops in the Soviet Union', *Aussenpolitik* (English edition) 42 (1), 48–57
Russian TV (1998) 'Buried Alive for Going AWOL', *The Guardian – The Editor*, 17 October, 19

Starr, Richard F. (1998) 'Russia's Military: Corruption in the Higher Ranks', *Perspective* 9 (2) November–December, http://www.bu.edu/iscip.html

Thomas, Timothy L. (1995) 'Fault Lines and Factions in the Russian Army', *Orbis* 39 (4) Fall, 531–548
Traynor, Ian (2000) 'Putin Turns his Fire on the Military', *The Guardian*, 12 August, 1

Waller, J. Michael (1997) 'Russia's Security Services: A Checklist for Reform', *Perspective* 8 (1) September–October, http://www.bu.edu/iscip.html

Yeltsin, Boris (1994) *Zapiski prezidenta*, Moscow: Ogonek

Zabosky, Vladimir (1996) 'Russian Troops Driven to Suicide', *The Guardian*, 30 October, 15

Further reading

Two classic studies of military–civilian relations are:

Finer, Samuel E. (1962) *The Man on Horseback: The Role of the Military in Politics*, London: Pall Mall Press

Huntington, Samuel (1957) *The Soldier and the State: The Theory and Politics of Civil Military Relations*, Cambridge, MA: Harvard University Press

For Russian military–civil relations see:

Mendeloff, David (1994) 'Explaining Russian Military Quiescence: The "Paradox of Disintegration" and the Myth of a Military Coup', *Communist and Post-Communist Studies* 27 (3), 225–246

For Gen. Alexander Lebed see:

Elletson, Harold (1999) *The General Against the Kremlin: Alexander Lebed: Power and Illusion*, London: Warner Books

Lambeth, Benjamin S. (1996) *The Warrior Who Would Rule Russia*, Santa Monica, CA: Rand

For the first Chechen war see:

Gall, Carlotta and De Waal, Thomas (1997) *Chechnya: A Small Victorious War*, London: Pan

Tolz, Vera (1996) 'The War in Chechnya', *Current History* 95 (603) October, 316–321

For conditions in the Russian Armed Forces see:

Amnesty International (1997) 'Torture, Ill-treatment and Death in the Army' *Amnesty International Country Report, Russian Federation*, http://www.amnesty.org/

Amnesty International (1997) 'Russian Federation. The Right to Conscientious Objection to Military Service', *Amnesty International Country Report, Russian Federation*, http://www.amnesty.org/

Herspring, Dale R. (1998) 'Russia's Crumbling Military', *Current History* 97 (621) October, 325–328

Jamestown Foundation (1999) '... But Armed Forces Still Wracked by Social Ills', *Monitor* 5 (138) 19 July, http://www.jamestown.org/

Jamestown Foundation (1999) 'Military Corruption a Growing Concern', *Monitor* 5 (189) 13 October, http://www.jamestown.org/

Traynor, Ian (2000) 'Bogged Down in Chechnya, Russian Returns to Cold War Rhetoric and the Nuclear Option', *The Guardian*, 14 January, 3

Vallance, Brenda J. (1994) 'Corruption and Reform in the Soviet Military', *Journal of Slavic Military Studies* 7 (4) December, 703–724

For the secret police and security services see:

Albats, Yevgenia (1995) *KGB: State Within a State; the Secret Police and its Hold on Russia's Past, Present and Future*, London: I.B. Tauris

Knight, Amy (1996) *Spies without Cloaks: The KGB's Successors*, Princeton, NJ: Princeton University Press
Pustintsev, Boris (1999) 'Kafka's World: FSB and Law', *Perspective* 9 (4) March–April, http://www.bu.edu/iscip.html
Waller, J. Michael (1994) *Secret Empire: The KGB in Russia Today*, Oxford: Westview Press

Websites

http://www.ceip.org/programs/npp/Numbers/russia (Russia: nuclear force information)
http://www.milparade.com (Military Parade, news on Russian defence industry)
http://www.princeton.edu/~ransac/ (Russian–American Nuclear Security Advisory Council)
http://www.nupi.no/russland/RIAtext/National_Security_Concept1997.html (NUPI Centre for Russian Studies, text of the 1997 RF National Security Doctrine)
http://www.scrf.gov.ru/ (National Security Council, in Russian)
http://www.pbs.org/wgbh/pages/frontline/shows/russia (Frontline: Russian Roulette, report on safety and security of Russia's nuclear arsenal)

PART III

The making of
Russian democracy

Democracy and
the Russian people

This chapter examines Russian democratisation, its civil society and the linkages between the people and political elites. Particular attention is paid to the development of the party system and the different orientations of the political parties, surveys of values and orientations, and women's political participation and public activism.

Introduction

Previous chapters have examined different aspects of democratisation from its social prerequisites (Chapter 1) through to democratic institution-building (Part II). Approaches to democratisation that stress its social prerequisites tend to see democracy as a result of modernisation, so that as society modernises it becomes more complex and pluralistic and this creates a demand for greater freedom and opportunities for participation (see Fukuyama, 1989 and 1992; Huntington, 1968 and 1991; Lipset, 1959 and 1994). A second approach to democratisation is to focus on institution-building and the creation of a democratic constitutional order. In 1993 Russia adopted a new Constitution enshrining democratic rights and freedoms, a separation of powers, the people as sovereign, and universal suffrage for all Russian citizens aged 18 and over. There have also been two presidential elections in 1996 and 2000 and three parliamentary elections in 1993, 1995 and 1999. A third approach to democratisation is to stress the importance of a functioning civil society to sustain democracy (see also Chapter 2). Only once there is a civil society and a general belief in democratic values such as human rights and the rule of law, will mere procedural or institutional democracy be transformed into a self-sustaining, substantive democracy.

Civil society

The development of autonomous social organisations

During Reconstruction the CPSU allowed informal groups and organisations to be established without its direction or participation (see Chapter 2), an important step in the creation of a civil society independent of the party-state. There was a proliferation of groups at this time but as Gill and Markwick (2000: 70) argue these groups did not represent a 'mature civil society'. These organisations were weak and 'fragmented and were not part of a web of interactions and relations which constituted an arena of activity which the party-state acknowledged as theirs by right' (*ibid.*). Instead these groups were able to 'carve out niches' in soviet society against a hostile party apparatus. So although the new RF had a civil society it was 'stunted' or 'immature'. Since the late 1980s and through the 1990s Russia has experienced a burgeoning of independent groups; these may be cultural, professional, nationality-based, charitable, ecological or women's groups (see below). However, there seems to be a widespread belief within Russia that such voluntary organisations are more concerned with getting western funding than actually changing things (Malyakin and Konnova, 1999). There is also a tendency for groups to be set up by the existing political elites in a style reminiscent of the soviet practice of setting up what they called 'transmission belts', such as the trade unions or women's soviets, between the CPSU and the people, to serve the party's needs. Russian political parties are not grass-roots organisations set up in order to represent the people in parliament, but instead they have been set up by members of the existing elites in order to harvest votes. Trade unions (see Chapter 12), although now notionally independent organisations, have maintained their soviet role of working closely with management and are not always autonomous organisations. Even though Russia has a political party called Women of Russia, it was based on the soviet women's organisations and such influence as it once had was based on being very firmly tucked under the wing of the party of power, Our Home is Russia (NDR).

The linkages between the state and society

The soviet tradition of authoritarianism and post-communist politics which 'has been shaped overwhelmingly by the dynamics of elite interaction and conflict focused principally on the presidency' (*ibid.*: 205), is not conducive to the development of a mature civil society. It is not so much that Russians are not setting up new groups and networks, as that the points of access between these autonomous groups and the political elites at all levels are limited. Richard Rose (see Box 8.1) has likened Russia to an hour-glass society in which the elites interact and the people interact, but the room for interaction

BOX 8.1

Russia's hour-glass society

In an hour-glass society there is a rich social life at the base, consisting of strong informal networks relying on trust between friends, relatives, and other face-to-face groups. Networks can extend to friends of friends, too. At the top of the hour-glass, there is a rich political and social life, as elites compete for power, wealth and prestige. In the vast Russian state, cooperation within and between elites and institutions is the normal way for individual officials to secure their own goals. Such a society resembles a civil society insofar as a number of informal and even formal institutions are tolerated and now legally recognized by the state. Yet the result is not a civic community but an hour-glass society, because the links between top and bottom are limited.

Source: Richard Rose (1995) 'Russia as an Hour-Glass Society: A Constitution without Citizens', *East European Constitutional Review* 4 (3) Summer, 35. Professor Rose is the director of the Centre for the Study of Public Policy, Strathclyde University, Glasgow.

between the two is very narrow like in an hour-glass. Russia's leaders both in Moscow and in the republics and regions also prefer to interact with the people through elite-established organisations such as political parties rather than through autonomous grass-roots organisations.

The development of the party system

The importance of political parties

The existence of a plurality of political parties is a defining feature of representative democracy. Political parties present the electorate with a choice at the ballot box and their differing programmes provide more or less coherent packages of ideas and policies. For the individual voter party names and manifestos simplify the potentially bewildering task of assessing the relative merits of individual candidates. Political parties also serve important functions for government. Political parties, non-government organisations (NGOs), interest groups and associational groups form an intermediate layer between the people and the government. These parties and groups help to aggregate and filter social demands and interests, so that government is not overwhelmed by a multitude of raw, unprocessed demands. The existence of a small number of disciplined political parties in parliament means that it is possible to anticipate the way in which parliament will behave. In contrast lax party discipline and/or a great number of political parties, with no one party enjoying an overall majority, can be a recipe for instability, unstable voting coalitions, and political decisions taken through back-room deals rather than through open debate.

The development of Russia's many-party system

The development of Russia's party system has been profoundly affected by the experience of soviet politics. In the early 1990s the Communists were the only political party that had a programme, organisation, members, activists and printing presses. Although briefly banned after the August 1991 coup, the Communist Party of the Russian Federation (KPRF) was back in operation the following year and remains the best organised party in Russia. Another feature of soviet politics that has affected the development of the Russian party system is that behind the veneer of the one-party state and ideological unanimity, soviet politics was characterised by institutional and functional lobbying, competing networks or clans, and patron–client relationships (see Chapter 1). These features encouraged loyalty to an individual, rather than to an idea, programme or an institution. This factor combined with the small number of autonomous social organisations and informals in the early 1990s meant that political parties have tended to be established by members of the existing economic and political elite to consolidate their position, rather than by grass-roots social movements seeking to gain access to the corridors of power. Russia's political parties tend to centre on an individual or a small group of allies, so that the differences between parties often have less to do with ideological and programmatic differences than with personal rivalries. Yabloko is inextricably identified with the economist Grigory Yavlinsky, Our Home is Russia with Viktor Chernomyrdin, Forward Russia with Boris Fyodorov and Russia's Democratic Choice with Igor Gaidar. This pronounced tendency towards personality-led political parties is the result not so much of a supposed Russian cultural preference for a single, strong leader (see Biryukov and Sergeev, 1993) but of the specific conditions at the beginning of the 1990s. The result is that political parties are prone to instability and internal rifts, and several political parties may have very similar programmes but will not fight elections together. In the 1999 Duma elections, for example, Yavlinsky's Yabloko refused to form an alliance with the Union of Rightist Forces, even though their programmes were broadly similar. This also means that Russia has a lot of small parties, so rather than having the democratically desirable multiparty system, it has a 'many-party system', which tends to weaken the coherence of the Duma and its ability to counterbalance the powerful presidency. The same factors are at work in the formation of political parties at the republican, regional and local levels, and also political parties that are organised in only one city, region or republic.

The presidential system and the party of power

Depending on the type of political system, political parties also have a potentially important role in the creation of the government. In the British parliamentary system, for example, the largest single party in parliament forms the government and the party's leader becomes the prime minister. In the Russian presidential system, the president chooses the prime minister, who does not have to come from the majority or largest single political party in the Duma. Presidents Yeltsin and Putin were both elected without being a member of a political party but they both supported a party known as 'the party of power' or the 'presidential party'. The party of power is not an autonomous organisation but essentially a government structure set up to provide the prime minister and the government with an organisation with which to contest elections. In 1993 the party of power was Gaidar's party, Russia's Choice, in 1995 Chernomyrdin's Our Home is Russia and in 1999 Sergei Shoigu's Unity party. In 1995 Yeltsin wanted to encourage the development of a two-party system to support the president, while allowing the president to stand above party politics. In May 1995 Chernomyrdin created a centre-right bloc which became NDR. The combination of financial support from Chernomyrdin's gas industry, Gazprom, and support from the government meant that NDR was the best financed political party in the 1995 Duma elections. Ivan Rybkin, the former Communist Duma speaker, established the centre-left Ivan Rybkin bloc, which Yeltsin hoped would act as a loyal centre-left opposition. In the event the Ivan Rybkin bloc failed to unite the moderate centre-left and the idea of trying to institutionalise a two-party system was abandoned, but the concept of the party of power remained.

Political parties, movements and associations

The organisations and activities of political parties in Russia are subject to provisions in the Constitution, a Law on Political Parties (2001) and an earlier 1995 Law on Political Parties. The Constitution requires political parties not to undermine state security or to set up their own armed forces. In accordance with Article 29.2 it is forbidden to establish parties that stir up social, racial, ethnic or religious discord and enmity. During the soviet period the CPSU controlled other institutions by establishing primary party organisations (branches) within them. In order to prevent political parties from trying to control government and state bodies, the 1995 law prohibited the organisation of political parties amongst the staff of any legislative or executive body, and within law enforcement agencies and the armed forces. The 2001 Law on Political Parties is an attempt to reduce the number of political parties contesting elections and to bring them under closer government supervision. Significantly, the 2001 law only allows political parties to contest elections and even requires political parties to participate in elections. The 1995 law categorised political parties according to the number of the 89 federal subjects in which they were organised. So there were federation-wide parties organised in at least 45 republics or regions, inter-regional parties organised in at least two republics and regions, and regional parties organised in only one. In contrast the 2001 law states that a political party must have 10 000 members and be organised in at least half of Russia's republics and regions. The 1995 law allowed a wide range of movements, organisations and associations to contest elections as well as political parties, and it was not unknown for a person to be a member of a number of movements, associations and a political party. The result was that membership of political organisations and parties was quite a flexible affair, which made it difficult to establish notions of party loyalty and discipline, not just amongst members but also amongst their elected representatives. In contrast the 2001 law seeks to encourage smaller organisations and parties to amalgamate by providing new government funds for the period between elections to parties receiving more than 3 per cent of the vote in Duma elections. Such parties will receive a yearly subsidy of 20 kopecks per vote received. This welcome extra funding comes at the price of greater supervision over parties' activities as the 2001 law requires them to submit regular reports on their activities to a range of government agencies, including the Ministry of Justice and the tax authorities. The 2001 law was passed by the Duma by 280 to 109 votes: it was opposed by Zyuganov's Communists, Russia's Democratic Choice and some members of the Union of Rightist Forces, the Agro-Industrial group and Regions of Russia; it was supported by the pro-Kremlin Unity Party, some members of the Union of Rightist Forces and Yabloko.

Russian political parties

(For the 1993–9 election results see Appendix 1)

Defining Russia's political parties

The use of the western 'left–right' terminology to categorise political parties is fraught with confusion. The RF was born out of a political system in which the CPSU, a Marxist–Leninist party which in western thinking would be a left-wing party, was 'the establishment'. Beginning in the 1960s there was a tendency in the USSR to refer to any dissident as a left-winger. This created a bizarre situation in which both Roy Medvedev (Marxist–Leninist) and Alexander Solzhenitsyn (an anti-Marxist Russian nationalist) were classified as on the left. The corollary of this was that as democratisation and marketisation gathered pace, the communists were referred to as right-wingers while Gaidar's free marketeers were referred to as left-wingers. Gradually the western understanding of the terms left and right has been adopted, but this terminology still causes some confusion in Russia. Another problem is that the left–right categorisation of political parties implies that there is a continuum whose two ends have nothing in common. In reality the supposed two extremes of the political spectrum, the communists on the 'left' and the nationalists and fascists on the 'right', share certain basic orientations. The National Salvation Front established in October 1992 brought together nationalists and communists in opposition to Yeltsin's government. The National Salvation Front wanted Yeltsin's economic and political reforms to be reversed, the restoration of the Russia's great power status and the reconstitution of the USSR. Russian democrats coined the term Red-Brown for these groups, taking the Red from the communists and the Brown from Hitler's brown shirts. Although the Red-Browns are not an organisationally or ideologically coherent group, they do share a wariness of the West, capitalism and democratisation. Rather than a left–right divide the main division in Russian politics is between those who favour a strong state (*gosudarstvenniki*) and those who fear that this means an authoritarian state and the end of democracy. The advocates of a strong Russian state include the Red-Browns and also President Putin. They want Russia to be unified, which often leads them to stress the Russianness of the state, to reject Russia's nationality-based federalism (see Chapter 5) and to oppose Chechen independence. They also want Russia to be militarily powerful and believe that law and order is more important than respect for individual and human rights. In contrast the reforming and radical political parties such as Yabloko fear that democratic rights and freedoms will be sacrificed to the higher good of a strong Russia.

Russia's radicals and reformers

Russia's radicals and reformers are distinguished by their commitment to democratisation and marketisation and a broadly westernising agenda. In 1993 Igor Gaidar established Russia's Choice with the backing of Yeltsin and his adviser Burbulis. The idea was to unite reform democrats in a pro-government party, which included an unlikely assortment of Reconstruction-era democrats and Russia's new political and economic elite. The grass-roots movement Democratic Russia that had served as Yeltsin's power base in the dying days of soviet rule also joined Russia's Choice. Its economic programme advocated the radical liberal economics enshrined in the government's programme of shock therapy (Chapter 11). The leaders of Russia's Choice quarrelled during the 1993 Duma election campaign, and many Democratic Russia candidates left to stand as independents. Before the election Russia's Choice had claimed that it would gain 40 per cent of the seats in the new Duma but in the event could only muster 15.5 per cent of the vote, nearly 8 per cent behind Zhirinovsky's fascist Liberal Democratic Party of the Russian Federation (LDPRF). This poor showing was not so much a rejection of democratisation but of the grinding poverty generated by the government's economic policies. In 1994 Gaidar established Russia's Democratic Choice ready to fight the 1995 Duma elections. However, the uneasy coalition that had come together in Russia's Choice could not be reunited to form one party and in 1995 there were a number of parties with broadly similar beliefs. These included Irina Khakamada's Common Cause, the Party of Svyatoslav Fyodorov, the Ella Pamfilova Bloc and Anatoly Sobchak's Russian Movement for Democratic Reform. Boris Fyodorov's Forward Russia, established in 1995, advocated a continuation of shock therapy-type economic policies combined with a stress on patriotism. Fyodorov likens Forward Russia to the American Republican party and Yavlinsky's Yabloko to the American Democrat party.

Yabloko (which means apple) was established in 1993 and takes its name from the initials of its original three founders: Grigory Yavlinsky, Yury Boldyrev (who later resigned) and Vladimir Lukin, the Russian ambassador to Washington. Yabloko identifies itself as the liberal democratic opposition to the Yeltsin and Putin governments. It stands for European values and advocates social-market reforms, combining economic liberalisation with the provision of social safety nets. Yabloko is highly critical of shock therapy, favours a parliamentary rather than a presidential system, condemned Yeltsin's military assault on the parliament in October 1993 and persistently attacked the Yeltsin administration for corruption. Yabloko also includes a social democratic wing. In the 1993, 1995 and 1999 Duma elections Yabloko gained around 6–8 per cent of the vote, which indicates a consistent level of support but an inability to gain new supporters. Yavlinsky is too closely associated with the failed 500-day economic programme at the end of Reconstruction, lacks practical experience and is viewed as a rather arrogant intellectual who is unable to communicate with ordinary voters. Most of Yabloko's supporters are urban, middle-level intellectuals and professionals, who have not necessarily benefited economically from the post-communist reforms but value their new freedoms. Yabloko's anti-corruption stance has also meant that it has not gathered support from Russia's oligarchs (see Chapter 1). However, in the 1999 Duma elections Vladimir Gusinsky, the head of Media-Most who was in conflict with the pro-government oligarch Boris Berezovsky, gave Yabloko access to his substantial national and regional media outlets.

The Union of Rightist Forces (SPS) was established in 1999 by five right-of-centre parties: Sergei Kiriyenko's New Force, Anatoly Chubais's Right Cause, Boris Nemtsov's Young Russia, Igor Gaidar's Russia's Democratic Choice and Konstantin Titov's Voice of Russia. Initially it seemed possible that OVR might join SPS, but Vladimir Ryzhkov, the leader of the OVR Duma faction, and Igor Gaidar reportedly clashed badly. Although Kiriyenko, Gaidar, Nemtsov and Chubais had all served in Yeltsin's governments, the SPS specifically described itself as a right-wing opposition party and not a party of power. The SPS slogan for the 1999 Duma elections – 'Don't you want to live in Europe?' – puts it firmly within the westernising wing of Russian politics. It projected itself as a youthful party and had rock concerts to appeal to young voters but also stressed its experience and professionalism. The SPS favours balancing the budget, the targeting of welfare provision only to those who are unable to support themselves, and better tax collection. It also advocates land privatisation and wants Russia to move away from its dependence on raw materials exports towards becoming an exporter of manufactured goods.

Centrist political parties

In the mid-1990s the leading pro-government, centrist party was Our Home is Russia (NDR). It was established in 1995 by the prime minister Viktor Chernomyrdin, the head of Gazprom and the energy lobby, and the first deputy prime minister Oleg Soskovets, who represented the metallurgy lobby. In Russian the party's name is *Nash Dom – Rossiia* but its base in the gas industry (Gazprom) led to it being dubbed *Nash Dom – Gazprom*, Our Home is Gazprom. The party was established as the centre-right party of power, standing for integration into the world economy but with protection for Russia's domestic economy and state support for industry and agriculture. As the party of power NDR was able to distribute government and municipal contracts to gain support throughout the country. In 1995 the NDR's council included nearly half the heads of regional and territorial administrations, and presidents and prime ministers of the republics. NDR also attracted high-profile supporters such as the film director Nikita Mikhalkov and Gen. Lev Rokhlin, a hero of the Chechen war. The centre-left party of power called the Ivan Rybkin quickly folded (see above); it included Rybkin's Accord Movement, the Union of Realists headed by Yeltsin's former chief of staff Yury Petrov, the Russian Youth Union successor to the Komsomol headed by V. Lashchevsky, the Regions of Russia Association led by Artur Chilingarov and the People's Movement Russia (Rossiia) headed by Igor Shichanin. The Women of Russia party established in 1993 by Yekaterina Lakhova became the women's part of the 'party of power' (see below). There are also political parties designed to appeal to specific constituencies: for example, the Muslim movement Noor was established by pro-government Muslim clergy. The ecological party Kedr (Cedar), headed by Anatoly Panfilov, was established in 1994 by the State Epidemiological Supervision Authority and the Ministry of Ecology. Russia's greens see Kedr as an establishment, pseudo-environmental party.

Once Chernomyrdin was no longer prime minister NDR rapidly lost support. A new party established by Yevgeny Primakov and Yury Luzhkov, the mayor of Moscow, called Fatherland (*Otchestvo*)-All Russia (OVR) looked set to emerge as the leading centrist party. OVR describes itself as a union of strong democratic forces, advocates membership of Asian and European organisations, but also wants Russia's national interests to be defended. It favours a reduction in taxes and a simplification of the tax laws. Its economic programme stresses technological modernisation and the expansion of the domestic market. OVR also believes that Russia is too large to have one standard approach to the economy throughout the country, that regional distinctiveness should be preserved and that the federal subjects should be allowed to decide their own policies on issues such as land privatisation. OVR at first gathered considerable support among republican and regional leaders (see Chapter 5), but accused the federal government of using its financial leverage, such as offering tax breaks for local industries or threatening to cut off oil supplies, to undermine OVR's support and to promote Unity.

The Unity (Yedinstvo) bloc, also known as Medved or Bear, was established in 1999 by Sergei Shoigu, the minister for disaster relief. Within Russia Shoigu's ministry has a good reputation for working efficiently and not being corrupt. Shoigu was asked to establish Unity by President Yeltsin in order to counter Luzhkov–Primakov's OVR. Prime Minister Putin pledged government support for Unity although he did not become a member. The oligarch Berezovsky claims to have provided Unity with ideas and financial support for the 1999 Duma elections, but Shoigu denies this. At first Unity tried to appeal to Russia's regions, the bedrock of OVR's support, by taking an anti-Moscow city and therefore anti-Luzhkov line. Moscow was depicted as a centre of lies, hypocrisy and corruption and Moscow-based politicians as having forgotten the people outside Moscow in their bid to get rich. This was a dangerous strategy for a party supported by Yeltsin, who was the target of mounting corruption charges. Unity's ideas are a strange mixture of nationalist and economic liberal ideas. Like OVR it also favours an expansion of the role of the Duma and its goal for the 1999 Duma elections was to create a pro-Putin majority within the Duma. Unity is the second largest party in the Duma after the KPRF (see Appendix 1). It wants to privatise land, reduce state spending, stop state support for failing industries and reduce taxes. At the same time it also favours greater financial and medical support for pensioners, supports the army, police and military-industrial complex, wants to strengthen state regulation of the economy, and seeks to retrieve Russian capital from abroad and encourage inward investment.

Nationalist and imperial patriots

Russia's patriotic parties range from pro-democracy parties advocating Russia's great power status through to fascist and neo-Nazi parties. They are also divided between Russian nationalists or national patriots who advocate a Russian ethnocratic state and imperial patriots who want the restoration of Russia as a supranational empire, often using Eurasianist ideas to justify their arguments (see Chapter 3). Russian nationalists and Eurasianists share a belief that the West is alien and that Russia is unique. They tend to see western ideas such as democracy and individualism as perniciously divisive and instead favour a strong state, embodying and protecting Russia's national interest against internal and external enemies. The Russian Christian Democratic Movement initially depicted itself as a Western European-style Christian

Democratic party but under the influence of Viktor Aksyuchits it became increasingly nationalistic and alienated many democrats, leading to splits and schisms. In February 1992 Aksyuchits headed the Russian People's Assembly and formed an alliance with Sergei Baburin's imperialist-patriotic organisation, the Russian All Peoples' Union, founded in 1991. Baburin advocated the resurrection of the Russian empire and the spiritual and moral purification of the Russian people. During 1992 Aksyuchits emerged as the leader of the nationalist bloc within the Congress of People's Deputies. In the early 1990s Russian nationalists and Eurasianists also formed the Russian National Council, which had a collective leadership including Valentin Rasputin, Gen. Alexander Sterligov and Gennady Zyuganov. Rasputin is an anti-Marxist Russian nationalist writer who subsequently joined the Agrarian Party, Sterligov is a former KGB general, and Zyuganov was the KPRF leader. Zyuganov also worked with Baburin, the film director Stanislav Govorukhin, Stanislav Terekhov and Ilya Konstantinov in the National Salvation Front.

The Russian nationalist-patriotic bloc, the Congress of Russian Communities (KRO), which had been established in 1993, was expected to monopolise the nationalist-imperialist patriotic vote in the 1995 Duma elections. KRO had three leaders, including two former Yeltsin allies. Yury Skokov was a former Security Council secretary with close links to the military-industrial complex and Sergei Glaziev was the former foreign trade minister who had rapidly rejected shock therapy and resigned in protest over Yeltsin's suspension of the Russian parliament in 1993. The KRO's great asset was retired Gen. Alexander Lebed, the former commander of the Russian 14th Army in the Russian-populated area of Transdniestr in the newly independent state of Moldova. Lebed was a hero of the Afghan war who championed the protection of the Russian diaspora in the Near Abroad and virulently opposed the Chechen war. The KRO was initially established to represent the Russian diaspora, which Lebed had literally defended by force of arms in Transdniestr; it then quickly evolved into a national-patriotic movement, advocating the peaceful restoration of Russia's great power status. The KRO also supports traditional Russian institutions such as the family and the Russian Orthodox Church, opposes Russia's escalating crime and corruption, and condemns Russia's self-serving leaders and its moral degradation. KRO opposes shock therapy and advocates a socially oriented market economy with protection for Russian producers and support for the military-industrial complex. The KRO briefly managed to unite a wide range of groups including moderate Russian nationalists, Russian Orthodox monarchists and even some communists, who opposed the government's economic policies and resented Russia's diminished status. Despite Lebed's charismatic speeches, KRO was unable to compete with the KPRF in 1995 and in 1998 Lebed set up his own patriotic movement called Honour and Motherland (*Chest' i Rodina*).

Russia also has fascist parties. During Reconstruction Alexander Barkashov was involved with the national-historical organisation called Memory

(*Pamniat'*) and went on to found the pro-Nazi Russian National Unity Party. Barkashov used his party's own armed forces to defend the Russian parliament during the October 1993 crisis. The Russian nationalist, neo-fascist National Republican Party of Russia led by Nikolai Lysenko is another remnant of Memory. The Russian National Bolshevik Party is headed by Eduard Limonov, a former ally of Vladimir Zhirinovsky. Zhirinovsky's fascist LDPRF was established in 1989, which suggests that he must have had the active support of anti-reform elements within the CPSU and KGB. Zhirinovsky is typically described as 'mercurial' because his ideas are highly eclectic and volatile, as a 'thug' for picking fights including on the floor of the Duma itself and as a 'clown' for his oafish behaviour. He is also a skilled orator, can work a crowd and should not be underestimated. In economics Zhirinovsky seems to favour a market economy but with protection for Russian producers. He has also argued that criminals should be shot without trial but blames the government for creating the situation in which people are driven to crime. Several of the LDPRF's leaders are known to have links with criminal gangs and have benefited from deputy immunity from prosecution. Following the 1993 Duma elections the LDPRF was the largest single party in the Duma. Zhirinovsky is an imperial patriot: he wants to see Russia restored to its pre-1917 Imperial borders. In the mid-1990s he used Eurasianist ideas to argue that Russia should abandon its pro-western orientation and prioritise relations with the Near Abroad and the Islamic world. He also believes that Russia should be the great power of the Eurasian land mass and such ideas led him to champion aggressively the restoration of Russian control over Chechnia. Zhirinovsky's strident advocacy of the first Chechen war (1994–6) and his penchant for foreign travel at the expense of nurturing support amongst the Russian electorate caused support for the LDPRF to halve its 1993 level in the 1995 Duma elections. In the 1999 Duma election support for the LDPRF almost halved again.

In 1994 members of the LDPR led by Stanislav Terekhov established an electoral bloc called Derzhava (Great Power) in order to unite national and imperial patriots. This coincided with an appeal by the former vice-president Alexander Rutskoi to organise a political movement called Derzhava to unite patriots and support his campaign for the 1996 presidential election. Through the spring and into the summer of 1995 Derzhava experienced internal disputes and conflicts: the Russian Orthodox monarchists left, as did the neo-Nazis. Part of Rutskoi's former political party, the Russian-Social-Democratic People's Party, the successor to his earlier political party the People's Party of Free Russia, joined Rutskoi in Derzhava. Derzhava is an imperial patriotic movement which wants Russia to be returned to its 'historical boundaries', which could mean the reunification of the Eastern Slavs or the pre-1917 empire. It is also advocates a strong and united Russian state. Derzhava has been subject to continuing internal disputes and has not managed to gain a strong popular following.

Communists and agrarians

Russia has a number of communist parties including Nikolai Ryzhkov and Sergei Baburin's Power to the People, Nina Andreeva's All-Union Communist Party and Viktor Anpilov's Russian Communist Workers' Party. The Agrarian Party of Russia (APR), established in 1993 by Mikhail Lapshin on the basis of the Agrarian Union, is also a communist party and has a close working relationship with the KPRF. The APR represents the interests of Russia's as yet largely unprivatised agricultural sector and includes the heads of collective and state farms amongst its members. The KPRF and the APR have mounted a concerted and so far successful opposition to the privatisation of agriculture land, which they want to remain in collective ownership. The APR also emphasises the importance of Russia's regions and village communities to Russian regeneration and wants the soviets to be revived. It favours state control of the economy in order to guarantee the people a stable standard of living.

The largest and most influential communist party is Zyuganov's Communist Party of the Russian Federation, which was originally founded in 1990 within the CPSU. It is difficult to pin down the KPRF's ideology as it has adopted new ideas without jettisoning its old ones and so for example it has managed to assert the legality of private property but at times has also said that it will reverse privatisation. The KPRF is anti-capitalist and anti-western and yet when Zyuganov attended the World Economic Forum in Davos, Switzerland, in 1996 he assured the leading capitalist powers and institutions that if he won the upcoming presidential election he would not reverse Yeltsin's economic policies. The KPRF's maximalist agenda advocates the 'voluntary' restoration of the USSR and its minimum agenda advocates the unification of the Eastern Slavs and Kazakhstan. Although Marx and Lenin are occasionally mentioned, Russian nationalist and Eurasianist ideas (see Chapter 3) are much more important to the contemporary KPRF. Zyuganov is more likely to talk about the shared Russian sense of community (*sobornost'*) than about a Marxist-inspired class struggle, although another leading party member, Aman-Geldy Tuleev, has spoken in favour of restoring the Leninist vanguard communist party. Zyuganov has committed the party to political pluralism and wants the soviets to be restored and a referendum on a new constitution. Zyuganov supports the idea of a restored Russia as the Eurasian great power and not surprisingly such imperialist-patriotic sentiments are disturbing to Russia's neighbours. Domestically, the KPRF advocates guaranteed employment and free education and health care. Within the Duma Zyuganov behaves in accordance with the parliamentary rules of the political game and while often strident in his criticism of the government, he acts like the leader of a loyal opposition party. The KPRF seems to have a solid corps of supporters who are typically older people living in the depressed industrial areas of the the so-called 'Red rust belt'. The skewed age profile of KPRF voters suggests that its share of the vote will decline as its elderly supporters die off. In the 1999 Duma elections the KPRF lost support to Unity, even in regions where it had previously done well such as Kemerovo, Rostov, Volgograd and Voronezh *oblasts*.

Russia's other political parties

Russia also has a number of extremely small political parties. These include parties with serious platforms such the Party of the Scientific and Technical Intelligentsia established in 1995 by Alexander Krasnov and the Supporters of Lower Taxes established in 1995 by Valentin Dyuryagin. There are a number of rather bizarre parties such as the Brownian Movement, which is founded on the principles of the English physicist Robert Brown and stands for the universal harmonisation of living matter and inorganic nature. The Subtropical Party wants the boiling point of water to be reduced to 50 degrees centigrade and Russia to enjoy a constant temperature of at least 20 degrees centigrade. The Beer Lovers Party set up in 1994 by Dmitry Shestakov, the Director of the Institute of Human Rights and Democracy, did manage to secure representation in the 1995 Duma. The Beer Lovers Party believes that beer drinking is able to provide a basis for national consensus. Its members tend to be young business people in medium size businesses, who favour lower taxes and are economic and political liberals.

What do Russians believe?

The rule of law, individual rights, private property and a strong state

Certain statements tend to be said about Russians, both by themselves and foreign commentators, that suggest that Russians typically hold beliefs and values that are not conducive to democracy. Russians are said to be collectivist and not to value individual rights; order and stability are said to be more important than rights, freedoms and the rule of law; and Russians are said to accept authoritarian leaders as necessary to avoid anarchy and chaos. Even if such statements were true in the nineteenth century or when the Bolsheviks took control in 1917, no society stands still. Older generations die off and new generations are born and have different educations and experiences. Igor Kliamkin (see also Chapter 1) has found that the majority of Russians support principles that do not conform to the stereotype of Russian beliefs and culture (see Box 8.2). Although Kliamkin's survey results do show that Russians value a strong state, this does not mean that they want an authoritarian state or a dictatorship. Russians recognise that a weak state is not synonymous with freedom but with the law of the jungle and that states need to be robust

---

BOX 8.2

Russians believe in...

In a May 1996 survey the Institute of Sociological Analysis found that 67–98 per cent of Russians in the nine groups listed in Box 8.3 believe in the following principles:

- the life of an individual is the highest value;
- the law is mandatory for everyone – from president to ordinary citizen;
- a person's property is sacred and inviolable;
- the stronger the state, the greater the well-being of its citizens;
- the stronger the state, the more strictly human rights and freedoms are observed there;
- the most important human rights are the right to life and the right to defend one's personal honour and dignity;
- Russian citizens need freedom just as much as people in the West.

Source: Tatyana Kukovets and Igor Kliamkin (1997) *Nezavisimaia gazeta. Stsenarii* (1) 16 January, 2–3, translation available in *The Current Digest of the Post-Soviet Press* XLIX (3) 1997, 4–7.

---

enough to provide security and protect individual rights through the maintenance of law and order, and the rule of law. Kliamkin also found that there is support for a market economy but that respondents dislike huge income differentials. Kliamkin interprets these findings as indicating that Russians like the idea of the market but do not like the actual consequences of economic reform in Russia.

Western-oriented democrats and restorers of socialism

Kliamkin also found that for the first time in its history Russia has a substantial western-oriented segment, favouring a market economy, democratic freedoms and human rights (see Box 8.3). He also found that only 15–20 per cent of the population favour what he calls 'restorationist ideas', that is support the restoration of either communism or Imperial Russia. Russia's western-oriented democrats (westerners) are exactly that, 'oriented', they are not slavish followers of the West. Kliamkin found that 47 per cent of westerners still believe that Russia has its own path of development that is different from the West's, while 27 per cent favour a western model of development for Russia. This helps to explain the finding of the All-Russian Centre for Public Opinion Research (VTsIOM) that 60 per cent of Russians reject the western capitalist model for their country and believe that in the 1990s Russia was set on the wrong course (Shlapentokh, 1998: 209). This does not mean that Russians reject democracy, capitalism, and individual and human rights, but rather that 60 per cent reject the specific reforms that were introduced in the 1990s

---

BOX 8.3

Post-soviet ideas

Respondents were asked to choose a maximum of three statements from the following list with which they agreed.

Russia should be . . .	Percentage selecting statement
1. a state of ethnically Russian people (Russian nationalists)	16
2. a strong military power (great-power advocates)	21
3. a multinational state of peoples having equal rights (internationalists)	35
4. returned to the socialist system (restorers of socialism)	12
5. a state around which a new and voluntary union of the former soviet republics will form (unifiers)	19
6. reborn as a strong military empire having the same borders as the former USSR (imperialists)	7
7. a state whose strength and might are secured through an increase in citizens' well-being (post-soviet individualists)	52
8. a state with a market economy, democratic freedoms and the observance of human rights (western-oriented democrats)	41
9. an Orthodox Christian country (Orthodox Christians)	13

Source: Tatyana Kukovets and Igor Kliamkin (1997) *Nezavisimaia gazeta. Stsenarii* (1) 16 January, 2–3, translation available in *The Current Digest of the Post-Soviet Press* XLIX (3) 1997, 4–7.

(Shlapentokh, 1998: 209). Russia's westerners support particular principles and values such as individual and human rights, the inviolability of private property and the importance of the market, rather than a specific developmental model. Russia's westerners are also proud of Russia's past achievements and Kliamkin found that this group was characterised by a greater sense of humiliation over Russia's diminished status than any of the other categories. Forty per cent of westerners are humiliated by Russia's brain drain and its status as a raw material exporter to the developed countries. The westerners are well aware of how far short of the western ideal Russia falls.

Amongst those favouring the restoration of socialism 75 per cent believe that Russia must follow its own historical path of development and 54 per cent of restorers believe that soviet socialism was in keeping with Russia's traditions. One unexpected finding is that 78 per cent of restorers believe that human rights were better adhered to under socialism and 80 per cent of the restorers believe that soviet socialism gave people greater opportunities to find their place in life than now. Given that restoration sentiments are stronger amongst those social groups (pensioners, the less educated, rural dwellers and those on low incomes) that have been particularly hard hit by Russia's economic reforms, then it is not so surprising that they value the greater material security of the soviet era. Extreme poverty is also a denial of human rights. Amongst those who identify themselves as Russian nationalists 16 per cent reject the soviet model of development and 54 per cent would like to live like people in the West, but are wary of private ownership and free enterprise. They seem to want an idealised Russian collectivism but with western standards of living. Curiously up to 55 per cent of the imperialists who want to revive the Russian empire want Russia to develop in accordance with western models; they also want guaranteed employment and a staggering 75 per cent want Russia to follow a western model of development, with only 15 per cent preferring soviet socialism. Some 47 per cent of the great power advocates believe that greatness is determined not by strength of weapons but by the well-being of people.

Who supports what ideas?

Kliamkin's survey found that there were marked regional, lifestyle and especially generational differences in the support for the different beliefs and orientations (see Box 8.4). He found correlations between the urban, better educated, higher paid and younger respondents and support for western-oriented ideas. Conversely, the less well-educated, rural, less well-paid and older respondents were more likely to want the restoration of soviet socialism.

BOX 8.4

Who are the western-oriented democrats and the restorers of socialism?

	Western-oriented democrats (%)	Restorers of socialism (%)
Higher education	22	10
Incomplete secondary	11	40
Under 25	17	4
Over 55	18	53
Rural residents	18	40
Large and medium cities residents	50	21
High paid	40	17
Low paid	30	57

Source: Tatyana Kukovets and Igor Kliamkin (1997) *Nezavisimaia gazeta. Stsenarii* (1) 16 January, 2–3, translation available in *The Current Digest of the Post-Soviet Press* XLIX (3) 1997, 4–7.

Democracy without women is not democracy!

Russian women begin to organise

Reconstruction provided an opportunity for women to organise and raise women's issues onto the public agenda. Soviet women began to organise around a range of religious, nationality, social and political issues. In 1990 a coalition of independent women's organisation called the Independent Women's Democratic Initiative was established. Their manifesto declared *Ne Zhdi!* (Don't Wait!) and called for top priority to be given to the struggle for women's economic independence. The academic Centre for Gender Studies was founded in Moscow at this time. In March 1991 the first Independent Women's Forum was held in Dubna, and adopted a slogan from the *Ne Zhdi!* manifesto, 'Democracy without women is not democracy'. The Forum proved a more robust organisation than the Women's Democratic Initiative and at its second forum in November 1992 decided to become a permanent body. The Independent Women's Forum now has 80 regional women's organisations. Another feminist organisation, formed in Moscow during the Reconstruction period, was the League for Society's Liberation from Stereotypes (LOTOS). LOTOS wanted to dispel what it saw as the common myth that feminists hate men, children and the family, and that feminists are unattractive and aggressive. It was and remains common for the Soviet-Russian media to stereotype all women's and feminist organisations as lesbian organisations. The 1991 Dubna conference, for example, was described in the media as a lesbian conference. Women's organisations in Russia have two main image problems to surmount, the first of which is the misrepresentation of their nature and aims. The second problem, according to the Russian feminist Anastasia Posadskaya, is that the CPSU's appropriation of the term 'emancipation' and the tradition of CPSU-controlled women's organisations has left a general legacy of mistrust of women's organisations amongst Russian women (Waters and Posadskaya, 1995: 367).

Women's organisations in the Russian Federation

According to Natasha Stepanova of the Free Association of Feminist Organisations (SAFO), democracy initially seemed to offer women the opportunity to raise previously hidden and ignored problems such as sexual discrimination. This hope rapidly led to disillusionment as the Russian media either trivialised or ignored women's issues. Since the 1980s women's emancipation has been blamed for the high rate of divorce, family breakdown and the demographic crisis (see Chapter 12). There has also been a rise in conservative, nationalist and religious sentiments which believe that women should 'return' to their 'natural roles' as wives and mothers. So while some women are campaigning to preserve the gains of the soviet period, such as their right to paid employment outside the home and for state provision of child care, other women want state support to enable them to be full-time homemakers (see Box 8.5). Women's organisations represent a broad range of opinion and activities: some are feminist, others are based on religious ideas, national identities or professional affiliations, whilst others are focused on specific issues. By the mid-1990s there were around 300 registered women's organisations which included Committees and Unions of Soldiers' Mothers, unions for large families, associations based on professional and creative interests, women's sections in the peace and environmental movements, and business women's clubs (*Izvestia*, 25 October 1995: 7).

Women's organisations also provide a wide range of informational, lobbying, legal and practical services. In Moscow the Russian Consortium unites 70 women's organisations in order to lobby the Duma on women's issues. The Moscow and St Petersburg Centres for Gender Research conduct research into women's issues which they then use to make policy suggestions to the government. The Russian Consortium has also worked on a women's rights programme and on preparing women to participate in the market economy (Human Rights Watch, 1997). The Women's Information Project established in 1993 and reorganised in 1996 with funding from German, Dutch and US bodies, to become the Women's Information Network (*ZhenSet*), gathers, stores and distributes data for women and about women. In Kaluga the women's organisation Liubava provides free legal services to women who have been illegally dismissed from their jobs. One of Russia's most high-profile

---

BOX 8.5

President Yeltsin takes the opportunity of International Women's Day (8 March) to explain the role of Russian women on Russian public television

May all Russian Women receive these warm greetings today, both for those who have fully given themselves to their husbands and children, and those who feel comfortable in the role of a working woman, who value above all independence and autonomy, but they too are first and foremost mothers and wives, . . .

It is a long-established fact that it is the man's work to build a house, to lay the foundations, to put up the walls and the roof, but they will certainly call on you, women, to make that house comfortable . . .

Women's nature is built thus [on the quality of compromise], to think of peace and your children's future, which means the future of the country, and just because of this we must satisfy your whims today. They are like the vagaries of the spring weather, changeable but pleasant, . . .

Source: BBC News Monitoring (1998) 'Yeltsin Extols Virtues of Russia's Women', http://news2.thls.bbc.co.uk/hi/english/world/monitoring/newsid_63000/63182.stm

women's groups is the Soldiers' Mothers Committee, which in 1996 won an alternative Nobel Prize for its work in campaigning against the Chechen war and defending soldiers' rights. There are Soldiers' Mothers Committees throughout the country which gather information about conditions in the army including abuses of human and civil rights; they have also set up rescue missions to retrieve conscripts from Chechnia.

Women campaigning against violence against women

Women's organisations also campaign against the physical and psychological abuse of women and provide refuges for women and children fleeing domestic violence. The phenomenon of violence against women and children was one of the unacknowledged problems of the soviet era, which has now been exacerbated by economic dislocation and increasing alcohol abuse. The Siberian town of Langepas was the first local administration to make funds available to set up a women's refuge following a campaign by local women activists (Human Rights Watch, 1997). The first 11 refuges in Russia were set up by the Russian Association of Crisis Centres for Women (RAKTsZh) in 1994 and by 1997 there were 14 crisis centres throughout the country. Following a campaign by women activists the city of St Petersburg has established a refuge called the Women's House (*Zhenskii Dom*) which can house 60 women and children. The crisis centres also provide telephone advice, individual consultations and legal help. RAKTsZh has also tried to address the Russian police's poor record in dealing with violence against women by organising specialised training for police. In March 1996 RAKTsZh brought over European policewomen and medical experts on sexual violence to help train women police officers. Training was held in Moscow, Murmansk and St Petersburg, and a pilot project was set up in Nizhnii Novgorod to train the local police on domestic violence and the development of crisis centres in Nizhnii Novgorod (*ibid.*). A Moscow organisation called Sisters (Sestry) has produced a pamphlet advising victims of sexual violence on how to take their complaint through the courts; the pamphlets have been distributed to the regional crisis centres and to the police.

The woman deputy – an endangered species?

In the USSR membership of the CPSU and the soviets was governed by an elaborate system of quotas to ensure the representation of women, workers, peasants and the different nationalities. However, throughout the entire soviet period the closer one came to real power in the USSR the fewer women were to be found. At the very apex of soviet power, the Politburo of the CPSU Central Committees there were only ever three women, Ekaterina Furtseva (1957–60) and during Reconstruction Aleksandra Biryukova (1988–90) and Galina Semenova (1990–1). Reforms to the electoral system during Reconstruction meant that the CPSU was no longer able entirely to control the candidate selection process and therefore enforce its quota system. The result was that following the March 1990 elections to the RSFSR Congress of People's Deputies, the percentage of women deputies fell from its quota level of around 35 per cent to only 5 per cent. The removal of quotas revealed the power-lessness of Russian women that had been hidden behind the façade of the large number of women deputies. In 'democratic' Russia women face a substantial range of barriers in standing for election. Firstly, there is the widespread belief amongst men and women that politics is a dirty business best left to men. When selecting candidates political parties tend to view women as a liability and so the overwhelming number of candidates across the political spectrum are men. In addition, as women have to cope with mounting unemployment and declining state child care support, the practical obstacles to political participation of any kind have risen.

Women's political parties

In 1990 under the leadership of Alevtina Fedulova the Soviet Women's Committee (KSZh), which had been established in 1956, became a non-government organisation called the Union of Women of Russia (SZhR). The SZhR inherited the KSZh's organisational infrastructure and rapidly started to campaign for legislation on women's and children's issues and also started to prepare women to stand for political office. In 1993 the SZhR united with the Association of Russian Business Women led by Tatyana Maliutina and the Union of Navy Women chaired by Marina Dobrovolskaya to form a new political party, Women of Russia (ZhR). ZhR recognised the unwillingness of other political parties to adopt women candidates and to promote women's issues. They adopted the slogan 'Democracy without women is not demo-cracy' and selected women candidates to stand in the December 1993 Duma elections. They fought on a centrist platform advocating socially oriented economic policies. Women constituted 13.5 per cent of the deputies elected in 1993, just over 8 per cent of whom were from the ZhR. The number of women deputies and the ZhR have steadily declined from this 1993 peak. In 1995 ZhR won three single-member districts but only only 4.61 per cent of the party-list vote, so failing to overcome the 5 per cent barrier. Overall, following the 1995 Duma elections there were 16 fewer women deputies than in 1993, leaving 46 women deputies or about 10 per cent of the total.

The 1995 elections also included the loss of two high-profile women deputies, Galina Klimantova and Ludmilla Zavadskaya, who had championed women's issues. Klimantova was a leading member of ZhR and chair of the Duma Committee on Women and the Family, who had initiated a draft law on domestic violence. Zavadskaya as chair of the Duma Committee on Human Rights was the author of Article 19 of Constitution which guarantees equal rights and opportunities (Human Rights Watch, 1999). Since 1991 Russia has had only a handful of women ministers. The Russian cabinet in May 1998 contained Oksana Dmitriyeva, the minister of labour and social development, Natalya Dementyeva, the minister of culture, and Tatyana Dmitriyeva, the minister of health. In November 1997 Irina Khakamada, the general secretary of the Party of Economic Freedom, had been named minister of small and medium business affairs. The cabinet in June 1999 contained only one women, the minister of social affairs Valentina Matviyenko, who was also a deputy prime minister. Ekaterina Lakhova, a leading member of ZhR, was the presidential adviser on women's rights for Yeltsin. Yeltsin's daughter Tatyana Dyachenko served on the Commission on the Improvement of the Status of Women, but the commission's director was the deputy prime minister Oleg Sysuev, who previously has shown no interest in women's issues.

Women and politics: the Putin years

ZhR was the female half of NDR, the party of power in the second half of the 1990s. As the NDR vote plummeted in the 1999 Duma elections so did ZhR. Only 7 per cent of the deputies elected to the Duma in December 1999 were women and ZhR failed to get a single candidate elected. They only gained 2.04 per cent of the party-list vote, so failing once again to surmount the 5 per cent barrier. Until Shoigu's Unity party was established, Primakov and Luzhkov's OVR looked set to be the dominant centrist party in the Duma. Yury Luzhkov is reported to have promised ZhR that if it fought the election with OVR, 30 per cent of the bloc's party-list would be women. However, most of the women candidates were placed towards the bottom of the list, so reducing their chance of getting elected (Belin, 2000). ZhR withdrew from the deal and fought the election on its own, although Yekaterina Lakhova, the leader of the ZhR Duma faction, had already left ZhR before the election and stood for Yury Luzhkov's OVR. There is only one woman member in the Federation Council, Valentina Pivnenko, the former head of the legislature in the republic of Karelia, who is backed by OVR.

In August 1998 a new women's political party called the RF Party for the Defence of Women (PRFZZh) held its founding congress. The party is led by Tatyana Roshchina and has about 6000 members in 60 regional branches. Roshchina explained that a new party was needed because the SZhR and ZhR were unable to contest the election at all levels and in every region. The new party is also committed to carrying out charitable programmes and social projects aimed specifically at helping women, families and children (*Nezavisimaia gazeta*, 26 August 1998: 3). The PRFZZh gained only 0.6 per cent of the vote in the December 1999 Duma elections. PRFZZh's programme was virtually identical to ZhR's, as was the programme of Ella Pamfilova's For Civil Dignity bloc. Their programmes advocated socially oriented market reforms, improved care for the elderly and children, and more attention to health issues (Belin, 2000). A proliferation of women's parties has not increased the number of women deputies or helped to push women's issues onto the political agenda. ZhR's alliance with NDR and its support for President Yeltsin did at least ensure that women's issues were represented within government. Increasing the number of women deputies is essentially a non-issue within Russia today. It is also unlikely that individual parties will adopt quotas to increase female representation as these were so thoroughly discredited by their use during the soviet period.

Conclusion

Russia does have a civil society and a growing proportion of the population holds ideas and values that are associated with democracy. Although the clans, which are based on the military-industrial complex or the energy industries for example (see Chapter 1), are able to lobby government, ordinary Russian people organised into autonomous social organisations have fewer points of access to Russian politics. Nevertheless, Russians continue to organise and try to promote their causes. Groups such as the Committees of Soldiers' Mothers even challenged government policy over the first Chechen war. The main impediment to the development of a mature civil society is not so much a lack of willingness on the part of the Russian people to become involved in politics, as an unwillingness by political elites at all levels and throughout the country to communicate with and more importantly to respond to the Russian people.

References

Belin, Laura (2000) 'Fewer Women To Serve In New Duma', *RFE/RL Russian Election Report*, 7 January (8), http://www.rferl.org/
Biryukov, Nikolai and Sergeev, V.M. (1993) *Russia's Road to Democracy: Parliament, Communism and Traditional Culture*, Aldershot: Edward Elgar

Fukuyama, Francis (1989) 'The End of History?', *The National Interest* (16) Summer, 3–18
Fukuyama, Francis (1992) *The End of History and the Last Man*, Harmondsworth: Penguin

Gill, Graeme and Markwick, Roger D. (2000) *Russia's Stillborn Democracy? From Gorbachev to Yeltsin*, Oxford: Oxford University Press

Human Rights Watch (1997) 'Slishkom malo, slishkom pozdno', http://www.hrw.org/
Human Rights Watch (1999) 'Women's Human Rights', http://www.hrw.org/hrw/worldreport99/women/women4.html

Huntington, Samuel (1968) *Political Order in Changing Societies*, New Haven: Yale University Press

Huntington, Samuel (1991) *The Third Wave: Democratisation in the Late Twentieth Century*, Norman: University of Oklahoma Press

Lipset, Martin Seymour (1959) 'Some Social Prerequisites of Democracy', *American Political Science Review* 53 (1) March, 69–105

Lipset, Martin Seymour (1994) 'The Social Prerequisites of Democracy Revisited', *American Sociological Review* 59 (1) February, 1–22

Malyakin, Ilya and Konnova, Marina (1999) 'Voluntary Organizations in Russia: Three Obstacle Courses', *Prism* 5 (8) 23 April, http://www.jamestown.org/

Shlapentokh, V. (1998) ' "Old", "New" and "Post" Liberal Attitudes Toward the West: From Love to Hate', *Communist and Post Communist Studies* 31 (3) September, 199–216

Waters, Elizabeth and Posadskaya, Anastasia (1995) 'Democracy Without Women is No Democracy: Women's Struggles in Post-Communist Russia', Chapter 14 in Amrita Basu (ed.) *The Challenge of Local Feminism: Women's Movements in Global Perspective*, Boulder, CO: Westview Press

Further reading

Useful discussions of the development of Russia's civil society are provided by:

Fish, M. Steven (1995) *Democracy from Scratch*, Princeton, NJ: Princeton University Press

Gill, Graeme and Markwick, Roger D. (2000) *Russia's Stillborn Democracy? From Gorbachev to Yeltsin*, Oxford: Oxford University Press

Lukin, Alexander (2000) *Political Culture of Russian 'Democrats'*, Oxford: Oxford University Press

Weigle, Marcia (2000) *Russia's Liberal Project*, University Park: Pennsylvania State Press

Analyses of Russian voting behaviour and election results:

Carnegie Moscow Center's Project on Russian Domestic Politics (1999) 'Russia's 1999 Duma Elections, Pre-Election Bulletin 1', 2 December, compiled by Tanya Krasnopevtseva, is available on their website http://www.ceip.org/

Radio Free Europe-Radio Liberty Russian Election Report, 7 January 2000, (8) is available on the RFE/RL website, http://www.rferl.org/

White, Stephen; Rose, Richard and McAllister, Ian (1997) *How Russia Votes*, Chatham, NJ: Chatham House Publishers

On women and politics see:

Buckley, Mary (1997) 'Women and Public Life', Chapter 10 in Stephen White, Alex Pravda and Zvi Gitelman (eds) *Developments in Russian Politics 4*, Basingstoke: Macmillan

Hansen, Kristen (1998) 'Aspiring to Equality: An Overview of the RF Duma's Concept Paper On Achieving Equal Rights and Opportunities For Men and Women', http://.glasnet.ru/~womnet/n1/art6.htm

Slater, Wendy (1995) ' "Women of Russia" and Women's Representation in Russian Politics', Chapter 5 in David Lane (ed.) *Russia in Transition: Politics, Privatisation and Inequality*, London: Longman

Sperling, Valerie (1998) 'Gender Politics and the State During Russia's Transition Period', Chapter 9 in Vicky Randall and Georgina Waylen (eds) *Gender, Politics and the State*, London: Routledge

Waters, Elizabeth and Posadskaya, Anastasia (1995) 'Democracy Without Women Is No Democracy: Women's Struggles in Post Communist Russia', Chapter 14 in Amrita Basu (ed.) *The Challenge of Local Feminisms: Women's Movements in Global Perspectives*, Boulder, CO: Westview Press

For an account of a member of the Committee of Soldiers' Mothers, Anna Pyasetskaya's, struggle to find her son see:

Pyasetskaya, Anna and Bradner, Heidi (1998) 'The Lost Boys', *Russia: the Wild East, Granta* (64), 113–132

Websites

http://www.friends-partners.org/~ccsi/nisorgs/niswomen.htm (provides links to the websites of women's organisations throughout the FSU)

http://www.csica.com/selyanka/index.htm (Selyanka, Russian village women's organisation)

http://www.owl.ru/index_e.htl (Women's Information Network)

http://www.friends-partners.org/~ccsi/nisorgs/nisnvir.htm (provides links to the websites of environmental organisations throughout the FSU)

http://www.fci.ru/ (Central Electoral Commission, provides election results)

http://www.nupi.no/ (NUPI Centre for Russian Studies, provides information about political parties, elections and politicians)

http://ceip.org/programs/ruseuras/Elections/elections.htm (Carnegie Foundation for International Peace, provides coverage of the Russian elections 1999–2000)

http://www.RussiaVotes/ (Centre for the Study of Public Policy, University of Strathclyde, provides data on voting behaviour and the results of public opinion surveys conducted by the the All-Russia Centre for Research into Public Opinion)

CHAPTER 9

The mass media

This chapter examines the impact of democratisation and marketisation on the Russian mass media. It establishes that despite a constitutional commitment to media freedom, censorship is continued by a variety of administrative, economic, legal and illegal means. Ownership and control of the media by the oligarchs and republican-regional economic and political elites are analysed. Specific attention is paid to the impact of the two Chechen wars on the role of the media and the role of the media in President's Putin's rise from obscurity. Finally, Putin's concept of the media's role as the servant of the state is introduced.

Introduction

The abolition of censorship and freedom of information were two of the great goals of Russia's pro-democracy reformers. The soviet state enjoyed a near monopoly of the printed and broadcast word and for decades censorship was used to stifle debate, promote CPSU infallibility and hide the inept or corrupt activities of party-state officials. Despite jamming, this monopoly was breached by foreign stations such as the BBC's World Service, Deutsche Welle, the Voice of America, Radio Free Europe and Radio Liberty. Within the USSR illegal *samizdat* (self-published) books and newspapers provided alternative sources of information and views to the official propaganda. The soviet media, foreign broadcasters and *samizdat* were all engaged in an ideological war, each determined to show the superiority of Marxism–Leninism, Russian nationalism or liberal democracy. In the USSR the mass media became one of the great battlegrounds of the Reconstruction period. The Gorbachev reformers did not want impartial media, they wanted media that would support and advocate the pro-Reconstruction message. During Reconstruction the mass media became increasingly pluralistic, reflecting a wide range of opinions from anti-reformers through to those who wanted an end to soviet socialism, and all shades of opinion in between these. With the end of soviet socialism the mass media now operate in a different political-ideological and economic context. The Preamble to the 1993 Constitution describes Russia as democratic and Article 29.5 states that 'The freedom of mass information is guaranteed. Censorship is prohibited'. There is no official state ideology to be promoted and defended and the media should reflect the plurality of views within Russia today. The media have also had to come to terms with the realities of a commercial world without state subsidies. This has led to the growing importance of advertising revenues and since the mid-1990s to the financial support of the oligarchs (see Chapter 1). The Russian media have found their independence increasingly undermined by creeping state censorship and the political and economic machinations of their wealthy proprietors.

The mass media and democratisation

Reconstruction, democratisation and the development of media pluralism, 1990–1993

In June 1990 the USSR adopted a new Law on the Press and Other Media which proclaimed press and media freedom and so signalled the formal end of the the CPSU's already failing attempts to maintain its monopolistic control over the media. Supervision of the media and their activities was thus shifted from the CPSU to the judiciary. The new media law was passed at a time when anti-Reconstruction forces were fighting a rearguard action to frustrate reform and turn back the clock. From 1990 through 1991 Gorbachev appeared to be bowing to these pressures in the face of growing economic, national and political turmoil (see Chapter 2). From 1990 the All-Union State Television and Radio Company (Gostelradio), whose broadcasts from Ostankino reached the farthest corners of the country, dropped its previous pro-Reconstruction stance. Yeltsin persuaded the RSFSR parliament to approve and fund an All-Russia Television and Radio Broadcasting Company (RTV), which was launched in May 1991, under the directorship of Yeltsin's ally Oleg Poptsov. Reform-minded journalists left Ostankino to work for RTV or Leningrad-TV, which was controlled by Leningrad's reformist mayor Anatoly Sobchak. Ostankino, RTV and Leningrad-TV saw themselves as engaged in a battle for the fate of the USSR and they did not aspire to be impartial or to present a range of opinions. Oleg Poptsov played a crucial role in supporting Yeltsin through the August 1991 coup attempt and the October 1993 crisis. Following the August 1991 coup attempt Yeltsin issued a decree transferring all-union (the USSR's) assets such as Ostankino to Russia. Yeltsin replaced the hardline chair of Ostankino, Leonid Kravchenko, with Igor Yakovlev. Yakovlev was the editor of the newspaper *Moskovskie Novosti*, which had constantly challenged and extended the limits of *glasnost*. Yakovlev soon found that Yeltsin wanted a state broadcasting service rather than an independent service. In 1992 Yeltsin dismissed Yakovlev, whom he found too independent and unwilling to follow his orders. Yakovlev founded a new independent newspaper, the *Obshchaia gazeta*. Yakovlev was replaced by the more amenable Vyacheslav Bragin, who was in constant touch with Yeltsin. Bragin's deputy, Igor Malashenko, resigned at the beginning of 1993 in protest at the scale of presidential interference and direction at Ostankino.

Yeltsin also moved quickly to deprive the CPSU of its own media by issuing a presidential decree banning the six CPSU newspapers which had supported the coup; the ban was annulled on 10 September 1991. Between November 1991 and February 1992 the RF discussed new media legislation and passed legislation that guaranteed media freedom and was similar to the 1990 soviet law. These media freedoms could be limited in the event of an emergency, powers which were used by the Yeltsin leadership during the October 1993 crisis (see Chapter 4). Further restrictions were also placed on media freedoms, so for example it was made illegal to incite racial hatred, or to violate national security. The law was used to prosecute the newspaper *Den* (Day) for anti-Semitism and incitement to civil disorder. These restrictions were later enshrined in the 1993 Constitution, which states that 'Propaganda or agitation exciting social, racial, national or religious hatred and enmity is not permitted. Propaganda of social, racial, national, religious or linguistic supremacy is prohibited' (Art. 29.2).

BOX 9.1

President Yeltsin tells the Democratic Press Forum what they want to hear

The Russian state and Russian society have a vital interest in strong, professional and truly free news media. One of the main conditions for this is consistent implementation of the constitutional principle of public freedom of information. First and foremost, this principle assumes noninterference by the state in journalists' professional activity. The journalist has the right to form and set forth his own view of events. The state has a duty to protect that right. Public freedom of information assumes the right of the citizen to seek, obtain and disseminate information. Public freedom of information is the guarantor of the independence of journalistic and editorial staffs.

Source: Rossiiskiye vesti, 2 September 1995, 1.

The 1993 crisis and the media

Even following the demise of the USSR Yeltsin's position was still insecure. The media were once again vital assets in a power struggle, which was now between the president and the parliament. Both sides depicted themselves as the champion of a free media but also used various means to coopt the media to their cause. Yeltsin had a major advantage as he had already placed his supporters in charge of Ostankino and RTV, so depriving the parliamentary cause of positive television and radio coverage. Ruslan Khasbulatov, the parliamentary chair, wanted *Izvestia* to become the Russian parliament's newspaper just as it had been the newspaper of the USSR government. The editorial and journalistic staff at *Izvestia* resisted this loss of independence and so in October 1992 Khasbulatov sent the parliamentary police force to *Izvestia*'s headquarters on Pushkin Square in Moscow to take physical control of *Izvestia* and to force the newspaper to support the parliamentary cause. Yeltsin was able to countermand Khasbulatov's order. In January 1993 Yeltsin announced the establishment of the Federal Information Centre (FIC) under the former media minister and close Yeltsin ally Mikhail Poltoranin. The FIC's stated role was to provide journalists with information about the government, which sounds like a propaganda agency for the presidential cause. Parliament challenged the legality of the FIC and in May 1993 the Constitutional Court ruled it illegal. At the height of the October 1993 crisis parliamentary forces occupied Ostankino, which became the scene of vicious fighting.

NTV, RTV, the Chechen war and censorship

After the 1993 constitutional crisis Ostankino journalists became increasingly concerned by demands that Ostankino should act as the uncritical mouthpiece of the Yeltsin administration. For example, although Ostankino had film showing Yeltsin clearly drunk at a press conference in London, the film was never shown and the tape was wiped (BBC, 6 July 1997). This and other cases of censorship and state intervention led a group of journalists to leave Ostankino and to set up the Independent TV station (NTV). Although independent of the state, NTV has to serve different masters as it is funded by advertising revenues and Media-Most, the oligarch Vladimir Gusinsky's media empire. NTV rapidly developed a reputation for tough reporting during the first Chechen war when its chief correspondent, Andrei Cherkasov, presented his first report from an underground Russian field hospital. These were certainly not the kind of pictures that the Yeltsin administration wanted the Russian people to see. Russian troops imposed censorship on media war coverage by denying journalists access, taking their cameras and confiscating and exposing film. The government also made coverage difficult by not allowing satellite links to be set up in the Chechen capital Grozny so that journalists had to get their video tape out of Chechnia using slow and tortuous routes. NTV journalists persevered and were able to show Russian military aircraft bombing Grozny when the FIC said that no such bombing was taking place. They also showed the coffins of Russian troops coming home and so helped to develop anti-war sentiments amongst the Russian people. In contrast the Chechen side positively courted the Russian media and did everything they could to ease their work, including setting up satellite facilities. The journalist Elena Masyuk later won awards for her interviews with the Chechen leaders such as Shamil Basaev.

The government was also displeased by RTV's coverage of the Chechen war, accusing it of presenting only the Chechen viewpoint. Oleg Poptsov was sacked as the head of RTV in February 1995, a move he believes was partly prompted by the oligarch Boris Berezovsky's manoeuvrings to take over RTV (Poptsov, 1996: 65). When he was sacked Poptsov was also accused of not giving sufficient coverage to the positive developments in Russian industry. Yeltsin appointed Eduard Sagalaev to replace Poptsov and told him to send a film crew to the Magnitogorsk Calibration Plant to record its achievements (*Sevodnia*, 17 February 1996: 2). This sounds all too reminiscent of soviet-era media management to produce celebratory coverage of happy collective farm workers and target-beating industrial workers. RTV's and especially NTV's more independent-minded news coverage won them increased audiences. The viewing figures for RTV's news programme *Vesti* increased by 30–40 per cent during the first Chechen war and both editions of NTV's *Sevodnia* (Today) news programme almost doubled their viewers. In contrast audiences for Ostankino's programmes *Novosti* (News) and *Vremia* (Time) fell and it was left with a mostly older, less educated and conservative audience (*Izvestia*, 6 January 1995: 6). As NTV was independent the government could not sack its head to bring it into line, but it did receive a phone call in 1995 from Oleg Soskovets, President Yeltsin's special representative to the Chechen republic, who warned that if it continued this type of coverage it would have its licence removed and be closed down. NTV went on the offensive by giving interviews to foreign journalists revealing the government's attempts to censor its coverage and it was left alone for a while at least (see Box 9.2).

Subversive puppets

In 1995 NTV started its own satirical puppet programme called *Kukly* (Puppets), which is similar to Britain's *Spitting Image*. On 7 July 1995, the eve of the fourth anniversary of Yeltsin's inauguration, *Kukly* broadcast a satire of Yeltsin's Russia which drew on Maxim Gorky's play about Russian poverty, *Na Dne* (The Lower Depths). The scene takes place in a doss house and begins with Yeltsin depicted as a tramp singing with his bodyguard Alexander Korzhakov presented as a baby. Russia's former prime minister Igor Gaidar is shown as a tramp playing a violin outside an underground station, truly down and out. The prime minister Chernomyrdin is shown wearing a shabby tee shirt and an old cap with ear flaps; in an allusion to his

BOX 9.2

Russia's new methods of censorship

1. *Administrative methods*: Suddenly all sorts of officials take an interest in a publication. The Fire Brigade find violations of fire regulations, tax collectors give accounts a thorough investigation, and there are constant audits and inspections. This attention can lead to (temporary) closures, takes up staff time, and can prove costly through attempts to conform with the latest regulations or fighting matters in court.

2. *The malicious duplication of titles*: The authorities undermine a publication by telling the head of the registering body to register another publication with an identical name and logo but with a different editorial staff and journalists. This happened to *Lyuberetskaia Pravda* and *Sovetskaia Kalmykia*, which both success-fully challenged the duplicate registrations in the courts but could not enforce the judgments.

3. *Legal action*: Accusations of libel or offending the honour and dignity of members of the administration. This method is made easy because the prosecution has no moral or financial responsibility for bringing the case.

4. *Economic measures*: State subsidies are used to enforce political obedience. A new law on advertising means that the media can be fined for dishonest advertising. Threats to use this law can be used by the authorities to influence the content of a newspaper or programme; the threat of its use can also be used as a way get bribes by corrupt officials.

5. *Threats, intimidation, murder*: In 1994–6 19 journalists were killed either to prevent publication of material they had collected or in revenge for what they had already published; threats are also made against journalists' families. The murders of Dmitry Kholodov (see Chapter 7) and Vladimir Listyev are the most high-profile murders of journalists. Those responsible for such acts include criminal gangs, corrupt agencies associated with the Ministry of the Interior, regional authorities and local militias. The Glasnost Defence Foundation (GDF) has docu-mented cases throughout the RF including Vladivostok, Mordovia, Volgograd, Vologda and Voronezh.

6. *Short-term contracts*: Such contracts mean that journalists are constantly under pressure to please their proprietor and wayward journalists are easy to dismiss. At Boris Berezovsky's *Ogonek* journalists typically have two-month renewable contracts. Journalists often have very low official salaries paid in roubles and then receive a dollar 'bonus' in a brown envelope at the end of each month. This practice enables the proprietor to avoid paying payroll tax and makes the journalists vulnerable.

Source: Points 1 to 5: Aleksei Simonov (1996) 'Censorship Yesterday, Today, Tomorrow', *Index on Censorship* (3), 59–64 – adapted. Aleksei Simonov is the head of the Glasnost Defence Foundation. Point 6: Vitaly Korotich (1997) 'The High Cost of a "Free" Press', *Perspective* 8 (1) September–October, http://www.bu.edu/iscip/html

role as the head of Gazprom, he is making money selling the parts of a dismantled gas stove. At the end of the sketch the Chernomyrdin-tramp figure realises that the market economy he has created is no different from a dirty bazaar (*Sovetskaia Rossiia*, 11 July 1995: 4). The general prosecutor Alexei Ilyushenko brought criminal charges against *Kukly* on the grounds that it was disrespectful and an insult to those satirised in the sketch. The charges were condemned by NTV president Igor Malashenko as an attempt to intimidate the media before the upcoming Duma and presidential elections (*Sevodnia*, 19 July 1995: 2). This was a difficult case for members of the government to pursue as not only would it have required them to justify their record, but also prosecuting a puppet show looks ridiculous. The charges were dropped and Chernomyrdin was pictured smiling next to his puppet. Yeltsin ordered Ilyushenko to stop interfering with the media and then sacked him.

The media and Russia's elections

Despite the media's grave concerns at Yeltsin's attempts to censor their activities, the pro-reform media were even more concerned at the prospect of a communist victory in the 1995 Duma and the 1996 presidential elections. An NTV spokesman explained that if the media were 'impartial' this would result in a communist victory, which would put back the clock on reform and end media freedom (BBC, 6 July 1997). This indicates the fundamental lack of consensus amongst the political parties in support of the basic principles of Russia's post-communist political and economic system. The fragility of Russia's democracy has encouraged Russia's beleaguered democrats to behave in anti-democratic ways to preserve the gains of the early 1990s. Another emerging factor was that Russia's oligarchs, who wanted to preserve their economic gains, were beginning to invest in the media, and these new proprietors put their newspapers behind Chernomyrdin and Yeltsin. All the television stations, including NTV, supported Chernomyrdin's party, Our Home is Russia, in 1995 and Yeltsin in 1996. Their opponents found it difficult to get air time and their free air time guaranteed by the electoral law tended to be at times likely to produce the smallest potential audiences. Nevertheless the KPRF and the LDPRF, which were unable to run large-scale media campaigns, emerged from the December 1995 elections as the two largest parties in the Duma. The 'party of power', Our Home is Russia, spent large sums of money on a western-style political campaign and had extensive television and media coverage but it came third.

Selling politicians and the development of Russian advertising

In his 1993 campaign for the Duma elections Vladimir Zhirinovsky had been careful to avoid slick western photography and editing techniques. He talked to camera telling it like it was; he appeared in tune with the people. Gennady

Zyuganov's KPRF's good showing in the 1995 Duma elections was partly due to Zhirinovsky losing support because of his advocacy of the Chechen war and Yeltsin being blamed for Russia's continuing collapse and kowtowing to the West, but also because Zyuganov hardly advertised at all. The slick political western-style advertising campaign run by Prime Minister Chernomyrdin's party only served to alienate voters. The lesson was learnt by the Yeltsin team in time for the 1996 presidential elections. Anatoly Chubais, who with Yeltsin's daughter Tatyana Dyachenko ran the re-election campaign, worked closely with Boris Berezovsky to craft a campaign that would appeal to Russian voters. Berezovsky provided the money and the air time. The primary technique used in the 1996 Yeltsin campaign was to have ordinary people on screen, talking about their lives, their families and their hopes for the future. Seemingly ordinary Russians were shown acknowledging that Russia had problems, but that after all progress had been made. These mini monologues, as they were called, were employed to promote the idea that a return to the past, that is a vote for Zyuganov, would be madness.

Democratisation and the regional-local media

One of the results of Russia's market reforms is that the national press virtually disappeared from the regions due to prohibitively high transportation costs (see Box 9.3). In 1994 subscriptions to the regional press for the first time exceeded subscriptions to the national press, by 22.8 million to 20.8 million (Yasmann, 1995). Between the end of communist rule and October 1993 most of the former republican and regional communist party newspapers were taken over by the soviets (councils) which either did not speak with one voice or were in conflict with the republican-regional executive (Slider, 1997: 262). For a brief time the media had considerable room for manoeuvre, but once the October 1993 crisis was settled in Moscow and the regional-republican soviets were dissolved pending elections, the media came under the control of the regional governors and republican presidents. The appointment of regional and republican station directors is formally made by the Russian Federal TV and Radio Service but with the approval of regional governors or republican presidents (*ibid.*). So a situation developed in which, in contrast to the national media, most of the regional-republican media are either owned or heavily subsidised by the regional-republican authorities. As the central television pays little attention to regional issues, local elites have considerable influence over the information published or broadcast within and about their region or republic. Yeltsin complained to the Democratic Press Forum in 1995 that 'in some regions of the country, administrations have used unlawful directives to dismiss editors-in-chiefs and executives of TV and radio stations for publishing critical articles or airing critical broadcasts. And economic levers have been used to close down publications' (*Rossiiskie vesti*, 2 September 1995: 1 and 3). In November 1995 Yeltsin signed a new law on subsidies to smaller district

BOX 9.3

The press and Russia's place in the world

If one formed a map of the world from one's impressions in the Russian press, it would have a great big Russia in the middle, surrounded by blobs fading to white. The only exemptions would be: Countries visited by Russian officials trying to obtain money for mysterious 'reforms' (subtext: Russia's growing world authority), or Russian criminals (subtext: they might not be scared of our tanks any more, but we've got the baddest criminals).

Source: Fyodor Pogodin (1999) 'The Russian Press and the New Reality', *Business in Russia* (100) April–May, 49–50.

and city newspapers, but allocation of these subsidies was left to the discretion of the regional legislatures and governors, many of whom have clearly used political loyalty as a criterion when allocating funding (Slider, 1997: 262).

Russia as a great power in a disappearing world

As the leaders of a superpower engaged in an ideological battle with the capitalist world, the CPSU believed that it was important for the soviet people to be informed about the evil beyond their borders. The soviet media were highly censored but they did provide extensive coverage of the world beyond the USSR. Astute readers were adept at reading between the lines of the propaganda to be well-informed about the world that they did not have the right to visit. In post-communist Russia, at a time when Russia is more open to the rest of the world than ever before, its media coverage of the rest of the world has contracted. This is partly due to the financial costs of maintaining offices abroad which was made even more difficult by the August 1998 economic crisis. The republican-regional media were especially hard hit in 1998 and many have cut costs by cancelling news services, internet and email provider services, so becoming more isolated (Fossato, 1998). The media cover politics and, in so far as it is safe to do so, crime and corruption, but the world beyond Russia's borders is now only newsworthy in so far as it touches Russia's interests.

The mass media and marketisation

From party-state ownership to the market

The privatisation of the media began in 1990 when most of Russia's central print media were transferred to the ownership of their employees. This was a process similar to the *nomenklatura* privatisation which saw state directors of economic enterprises transformed into the new owners (see Chapter 1). The new proprietors had to confront a rapidly changing economic and political situation. For some titles this new world necessitated a change of name and content: *Agitator* (The Agitator) which was the journal of the CPSU's propagandists became *Dialog* (Dialogue) and more tellingly *Party Life* became *Business Life*. At this time most newspapers and journals still received government subsidies, but for some the spiralling inflation of the early 1990s led to bankruptcy. Newspaper subscriptions fell, while the cost of production and, crucially for such a large country, of distribution rose dramatically (see Box 9.4). In January 1992 alone, 20 newspapers announced that they would cease publication for financial reasons (Korotich, 1997). The 1995 state budget drastically cut newspaper subsidies and only the pro-Yeltsin press continued to receive any state support. The human rights newspaper *Ekspress-Khronika* (Express Chronicle) ceased production in February 1995 after seven years, as grants from foreign foundations had dried up and its readership fell.

BOX 9.4

Russians' reading and viewing habits

Which newspapers do you read regularly?	%	Claimed circulation (millions)
Argumenty i fakty	32	3.4
Komsomolskaia Pravda	14	1.4
Moskovskii Komsomolets	7	0.9
Trud	6	1.4
Izvestia	5	0.6
Rossiiskaia gazeta	4	0.5
Kommersant	2	0.1
Pravda-5	1	0.3
Sevodnia	1	0.1
None	21	

Which television channel do you watch often?	%
ORT	79
RTR	50
NTV	24
TV6	13
Channel 5	9

(Sample 4000 adults nationwide, surveyed June–December 1996)

Source: 'Russia's Media. All the News that Fits', *The Economist*, 15 February 1997, 45–8.

For other publications Russia's entry into the global media world provided new opportunities. The newspaper *Izvestia* formed a joint venture with the *Financial Times* of London to produce *Finansovoe Izvestia* (Financial *Izvestia*), a weekly business news and analysis supplement. Vladimir Gusinsky's glossy weekly news magazine *Itogi* (Conclusions) is a joint venture with American *Newsweek*.

The oligarchs and the media

(See also Chapter 1)

As the 1995 Duma and 1996 presidential elections approached, the oligarchs (see Chapter 1) started to buy media assets. The media desperately needed new sources of finance and the oligarchs were keen to influence the electoral processes and in the process to gain government patronage. *Nezavisimaia gazeta* (Independent Newspaper), which was founded during the *glasnost* period, temporarily stopped publication in May 1995 for financial reasons. *Nezavisimaia gazeta* was bought by Boris Berezovsky and while this meant that the newspaper could resume publication, it also meant that it had to serve the broader interests of Berezovsky's financial-industrial group (FIG). Such purchases immediately led to tensions between journalistic freedom of expression and impartiality on the one side and shareholders' rights on the other. In 1997 the journalists at *Izvestia* came into conflict with Vagit Alekperov, the president of the Lukoil FIG that had bought a share in the newspaper. In March 1997 *Izvestia* reprinted an article from the French newspaper *Le Monde* which alleged that Chernomyrdin had amassed a personal fortune of over $5 billion when running Russia's natural gas monopoly Gazprom (see Box 9.5). Chernomyrdin denied the accusation and claimed to live on his official salary of only $715 a month. Vagit Alekperov and Lukoil had close links with Chernomyrdin and they moved quickly to gain a controlling interest in *Izvestia* and by the end of April they had acquired a 51.3 per cent share. There then followed hostile meetings between the journalists and a new board dominated by Lukoil appointments. The journalists saw the dispute as a struggle against political censorship while Lukoil saw it as a matter of shareholder rights. The imperatives of democratisation and marketisation were in direct conflict. Oneximbank had also bought into *Izvestia* and in July 1997 together with Lukoil sacked *Izvestia*'s editor, Igor Golembiovsky. *Izvestia* had revealed that Anatoly Chubais's Centre for the Defence of Private Property had received a no-collateral, no-interest loan of more than 14 billion roubles from Stolichny Bank. Chubais was then a first deputy prime minister and a close ally of Oneximbank's president Vladimir Potanin. Potanin and Chubais's rivals Vladimir Gusinsky and Boris Berezovsky responded by funding a new newspaper also called *Izvestia* and recruited members of the old editorial staff, including Otto Latsis, Sergei Agafonov and Igor Golembiovsky

---

BOX 9.5

Why do the oligarchs invest in the media?

Sergei Smirnov, head of Gazprom's department for relations to the news media, told journalists that:

The most important thing is to get this whole system to work for our main idea: We are acting in the interests of the state, and the state needs us.

Source: Irina Savateyeva (1996) 'The Russian Press: Beyond Economics', *Novaia gazeta*, 2–8 December, 10–11.

---

as editor-in-chief. The media became embroiled in the shifting allegiances of the oligarchs as they competed for government patronage and offered financial support to politicians.

While supporting the *Izvestia* journalists in their struggle against Potanin, Vladimir Gusinsky still wanted to control the content of *Obshchaia gazeta* in which he had a share. On 6 March 1997 *Obshchaia gazeta* published an article by Anna Politkovskaya, which showed how banks that were empowered to handle government funds used these funds to finance short-term but highly lucrative speculations. Politkovskaya revealed that this kind of speculation by Oneximbank had resulted in the non-payment of workers at the Norilsk Nikel combine north of the Arctic Circle (see Chapter 1). Vladimir Gusinsky was not specifically mentioned in the article but he nonetheless shared his fellow oligarchs' concerns about the shadier side of their financial dealings with government money being made public. Politkovskaya was summoned to the offices of Vladimir Gusinsky, the head of the Media-Most banking and media group, to discuss her article (see Box 9.6). In the course of the discussion it was clear that Gusinsky had information about her personal life which had been gathered by Media-Most's security guards who are former KGB personnel (Satter, 1997).

BOX 9.6

Russia's mass media: who owns what?

BOX 9.6 (CONTINUED)

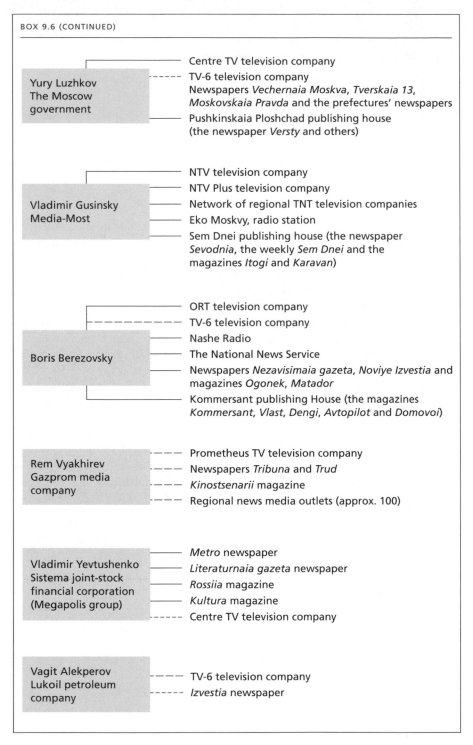

Yury Luzhkov The Moscow government
- Centre TV television company
- TV-6 television company
- Newspapers *Vechernaia Moskva*, *Tverskaia 13*, *Moskovskaia Pravda* and the prefectures' newspapers
- Pushkinskaia Ploshchad publishing house (the newspaper *Versty* and others)

Vladimir Gusinsky Media-Most
- NTV television company
- NTV Plus television company
- Network of regional TNT television companies
- Eko Moskvy, radio station
- Sem Dnei publishing house (the newspaper *Sevodnia*, the weekly *Sem Dnei* and the magazines *Itogi* and *Karavan*)

Boris Berezovsky
- ORT television company
- TV-6 television company
- Nashe Radio
- The National News Service
- Newspapers *Nezavisimaia gazeta*, *Noviye Izvestia* and magazines *Ogonek*, *Matador*
- Kommersant publishing House (the magazines *Kommersant*, *Vlast*, *Dengi*, *Avtopilot* and *Domovoi*)

Rem Vyakhirev Gazprom media company
- Prometheus TV television company
- Newspapers *Tribuna* and *Trud*
- *Kinostsenarii* magazine
- Regional news media outlets (approx. 100)

Vladimir Yevtushenko Sistema joint-stock financial corporation (Megapolis group)
- *Metro* newspaper
- *Literaturnaia gazeta* newspaper
- *Rossiia* magazine
- *Kultura* magazine
- Centre TV television company

Vagit Alekperov Lukoil petroleum company
- TV-6 television company
- *Izvestia* newspaper

BOX 9.6 (CONTINUED)

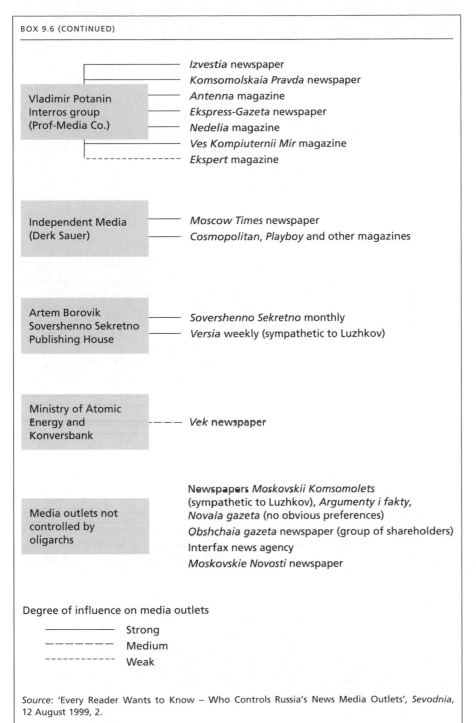

Vladimir Potanin
Interros group
(Prof-Media Co.)

Izvestia newspaper
Komsomolskaia Pravda newspaper
Antenna magazine
Ekspress-Gazeta newspaper
Nedelia magazine
Ves Kompiuternii Mir magazine
Ekspert magazine

Independent Media
(Derk Sauer)

Moscow Times newspaper
Cosmopolitan, *Playboy* and other magazines

Artem Borovik
Sovershenno Sekretno
Publishing House

Sovershenno Sekretno monthly
Versia weekly (sympathetic to Luzhkov)

Ministry of Atomic
Energy and
Konversbank

Vek newspaper

Media outlets not
controlled by
oligarchs

Newspapers *Moskovskii Komsomolets*
(sympathetic to Luzhkov), *Argumenty i fakty*,
Novaia gazeta (no obvious preferences)
Obshchaia gazeta newspaper (group of shareholders)
Interfax news agency
Moskovskie Novosti newspaper

Degree of influence on media outlets

———————— Strong
— — — — — — Medium
- - - - - - - - - - - - Weak

Source: 'Every Reader Wants to Know – Who Controls Russia's News Media Outlets', *Sevodnia*,
12 August 1999, 2.

Advertising in Russia

Advertising comes to Russia

Commercial advertising began to develop during Reconstruction, but despite the changes brought by *glasnost*, the media did not then need advertising revenues in order to survive economically (see Box 9.7). At this time although western companies were allowed to advertise in the soviet media, it was the editors who retained the right to 'dictate the size position, time of appearance – and content [of advertisements]' (Lloyd, 1998: 434). With the end of soviet socialism and the dash to the market this situation rapidly changed as editors realised that advertisements were an important source of revenue. Western companies were eager to sell in the Russian market, and at this time they simply took their existing advertisements created for the Western European or North American market and dubbed them into Russian, with no attempt to adapt them for the Russian consumer. There were also a range of institutions and companies that wanted to advertise their goods and services. Within Russia there was also a very rapid growth in banks and financial houses, new restaurants and shops were also established, and so there was a flourishing domestic market for advertising. The government also needed to advertise each time there was another round of privatisations. The result was that advertising grew from practically nothing in the late 1980s to over $5900 million a year in the mid-1990s (*ibid.*: 435).

BOX 9.7

Russians and advertising

Russians are able to read between the lines:

For decades there was practically no advertising in our country, and whenever an advertising campaign was suddenly launched, we Soviets – well schooled in reading between the lines and quickly grasping ulterior motives – always understood that the intent was to foist something old, shoddy or uninteresting on us. In other words, even when applied to goods marked with the 'seal of quality', our Soviet advertising was essentially anti advertising.

Resentment of foreign advertisements:

Just picture it: In some remote Russian village where there are no roads, no telephones, no newspapers, no network of retail outlets like you have in the capital, but people watch television while they wait for their pensions, a sensuous beauty appears on the screen, swallowing something called Raffaello or Dove chocolate and murmurs in a sultry contralto, 'Now *that's* temptation'. What response could that possibly evoke besides a healthy feeling of resentment?

Source: Vasily Kisunko (1997) 'Commercials Without a Break', *Rossiskiye vesti*, 25 July, 3.

To believe or not to believe?

In 1994 the most frequently aired television commercial was for a financial investment company MMM: in the period March–May it had 2666 advertising spots (Mickiewicz, 1995: 169). The company was really a pyramid investment scheme which used promises of great riches to persuade an estimated 10 million Russians to invest. MMM advertisements showed the Golovkovs, a typical soviet-style family, comprising an industrial worker father, clerical worker mother and two school children living in a cramped flat. The family invest with MMM and suddenly become super rich, buying fur coats and an apartment in Paris, while in another advertisement they are shown enjoying themselves on a Californian beach. MMM also had an advertisement that showed Victoria Ruffo, the star of the immensely popular Mexican soap opera, *Simply Maria*, apparently endorsing MMM. The advertisements were popular because they showed a better life after communism, a life in which people could make their own decisions and get rich (Lloyd, 1998: 422). This was a major part of the appeal of the advertisements, which showed ordinary Russians living life as it actually was (and still is for the majority of the population), but with the hope that they could make life better. The advertisements were the work of Kazakh film director Tilibayev, who well understood the hopes and aspirations of these new post-soviet people. MMM seemed to offer the riches that Russians had expected the market economy to bring. Despite the fact that Russians had been well-trained in the soviet era to read between the lines (see Box 9.6), because MMM's advertisements appeared on public television it was assumed that the company had official backing. Although the government did issue warnings against MMM, when the pyramid finally collapsed in July 1994 and its director Sergei Mavrodi was arrested, it was the government that was blamed by the company's investors for their financial losses.

Advertising and corruption

In the 1990s advertising became associated with crime and corruption. Ostankino beamed its programmes throughout Russia and so was a prime target for advertisers. It was via Ostankino that Russians, even in the farthest, most inaccessible parts of the country, were introduced to American television programmes, Latin American soap operas, Coca-Cola, Snickers bars and BMWs. Advertisers negotiated directly with television producers for access to prime time slots and criminals soon came to see advertising as a way of laundering money, making bribery an integral part of Russia's advertising. The result was that advertising rapidly developed a public image of sleaze, corruption and criminality. In 1994 Ostankino created '*Reklama*-Holding' (*Reklama* is the Russian word for advertisement) as part of an attempt to centralise advertising, to tie advertising revenues to ratings and generally to overhaul the programming schedule. In 1995 Ostankino was partially privatised and the respected journalist Vladimir Listyev was put in charge of the renamed Russian Public Television (ORT). Listyev initiated a four-month ban on advertising in an attempt to clean up Russia's national television station. He was murdered in March 1995 and to date no one has been charged with this crime. Since then ORT has become part of Boris Berezovsky's media empire.

The 'problem of America'

As advertising rapidly became a major source of revenue its very existence started to have a major impact upon television schedules. One of the effects of opening up to the world economy is that Russian television viewers now enjoy television programmes and films from around the world. Advertisers wanted their advertisements to be shown with the most popular programmes and so programme ratings rapidly became a major concern. The result was that the hugely popular programmes like *Love at First Sight* and the Mexican soap opera *Simply Maria* were particularly popular with the advertisers. At the same time venerable political programmes like *Vzgliad* (View) that had pioneered investigative journalism during Reconstruction, but which could no longer attract massive audiences, were axed. New types of television programmes and advertising 'represented a new type of propaganda for an exhausted public; the American-made chocolate bars, Snickers, soon came to symbolise the "problem of America", the overwhelming dominance of US commerce and values in a country attempting to sort out its loss of great-power status' (Mickiewicz, 1995: 168). In 1993 as Russia seemed to be on the brink of collapse, Snickers bars became a symbol of Russia's diminished international standing, its economic collapse and cultural colonisation. Vladimir Zhirinovsky, whose LDPRF polled 22.9 per cent of the vote in the December 1993 elections, capitalised on these sentiments by campaigning for Snickers advertisements to be banned (*ibid.*: 169). The Russian people, while enjoying the soap operas and game shows, were increasingly concerned by Yeltsin's westernising 'Atlanticist agenda' and in 1993 Russia's Red-Browns atrracted the majority of votes.

The development of Russian advertising

Leading personnel from Yeltsin's 1996 re-election campaign, such as Anatoly Chubais's aide Arkady Yevstafyev, have become a major force in the Russian advertising industry. In December 1997 Maxim Boiko, a former deputy prime minister and minister for state property who had been sacked from government, joined the Video International Advertisement Co. (Birman, 1997: 7). The 'mini monologue' technique that had been used so effectively during the 1996 campaign quickly became a staple of Russian advertising, especially on NTV. In NTV advertisements 'ordinary people such as students, dacha owners and farmers do not just try to sell the latest consumer technology, they also offer reflections on daily life, fatigue, recreation, and their sudden craving to see the old Soviet films again' (Kisuno, 1997: 3). There is an advertisement in which three generations of women extol the virtues of an all-purpose cleanser, but their comments on life show them to be normal people wanting a bargain. Aunt Asya is famous all over Russia for her role in advertisements for the Ace brand of bleach. Aunt Asya is unquestionably what the Russian call 'our own' (*nashe*). 'Her intonations are the painfully familiar intonations of the Young Communist League or some or other administrative type who's got the lay of the land now and has honourably taken up some modest but reliable business in the new Russia. The crowning glory, of course, is the almost brilliantly portrayed loathsome neighbour lady who promotes Comet cleaner, which gets out spots and kills germs but, best of all, provides an impeccable excuse to visit the new neighbour and dish her out all the dirt on the old one' (*ibid.*). Neighbours and aunts are now a staple of Russian advertising, which also draw on nostalgia, often for the soviet past, to sell a new world to the Russians.

President Putin and the mass media

The 1999 State Duma and the 2000 presidential elections

In the 1999 Duma elections the pro-Putin Unity (Medved or Bear) party came from nowhere to win over 23 per cent of the vote. Putin was largely unknown before Yeltsin appointed him prime minister in 1998, and Putin's and Unity's electoral successes were in large measure due to the support of the two all-Russia television stations and Boris Berezovsky, who partly owns them. There was absolutely no pretence at impartiality, and both stations shamelessly used compromising materials (*kompromat*) to discredit rival candidates. ORT used its prime time slots to run a slur campaign against Putin's two main rivals. Moscow mayor Yury Luzhkov was portrayed as a crook and even a murderer. ORT also broadcast grisly footage of a hip operation to demonstrate that Yevgeny Primakov, who had only recently undergone a similar operation, would be too weak to run the country. Luzhkov and Primakov both stood down from the presidential race. Boris Berezovsky is reported to have said, 'I was extremely pleased [with ORT's work] ... I believe they helped Russia with a historic task' (Gentleman, 2000: 22). In the run up to the elections, concerns that the candidature of Grigory Yavlinsky might deprive Putin of an outright victory in the first round meant ORT turned its attention on him. Playing on homophobia, Yavlinsky was inaccurately depicted as a homosexual.

The second Chechen war and the return to soviet practices

The second Chechen war played an important role in Putin's path to power as it enabled Putin to depict himself as a strong leader who would stand up for Russia against its enemies. While Putin was acting president he stressed Russian militarism and nationalism and attacked the 'scum' who want to tear Russia to pieces and bring it to its knees (Traynor, 2000a: 17). Chechen rebels and journalists both fall into this category. Putin has made it clear that he will not tolerate the critical reports from Chechnia that dogged the 1994–6 war. Reports on the Chechen war presented on the state-run television channels follow the official line of a war fought nobly against dangerous Islamic rebels and certainly do not include any of the coverage of atrocities or human rights abuses recorded by organisations such as Amnesty International. In contrast to the first Chechen war, during the second war Russian television is not broadcasting interviews with the Chechen rebel leaders, so denying them an important platform for their ideas. NTV has taken an anti-war stance and has tried to continue the objective coverage it pioneered during the first war. NTV has however been put under increasing pressure from the state security services and it is clear that the Kremlin is using 'administrative measures' (see Box 9.2) to bring NTV's coverage into line. NTV soon had its first unexpected visit from the tax inspectors and then encountered problems with a bank loan.

In order to work in Chechnia journalists have to have military accreditation and are only allowed to travel in areas selected by the military and then only if accompanied by a military escort. These restrictions are designed to stop independent investigations and are part of the government's media management. The Russian military also have their own press centres in Makhachkala in Dagestan and Mozdok in North Ossetia. The Chechen rebels are also conducting their own information campaign which is no more truthful or accurate than the information provided by Russian government or military sources. Movladi Udugov, a former local television journalist in Chechnia, has masterminded the Chechen rebels' information campaign in both the first and the second wars. Denied access to the Russian media, Udugov set up a website Kavkaz-Tsentr (http://www.kavkaz.org) to promote the rebel Chechen cause. The FSB has managed to put the website out of action on a number of occasions. There is also a group of Russian hackers, headed by 'Misha Lermontov', who seek out and destroy Chechen websites (Abdullaev, 1999). The choice of the alias is quite deliberate: Mikhail Lermontov (1814–41) was a Russian poet and novelist who served in the Imperial Russian army against the Chechens.

Journalists under attack: Andrei Babitsky and Alexander Khinshteyn

The case of Andrei Babitsky provides a rather bizarre example of the devices that are employed to silence a journalist. In January 2000 Andrei Babitsky, a Russian working for the American-funded station Radio Liberty, was seized by Russian armed forces and accused of lacking the appropriate military accreditation to be in the war zone. After apparently being handed over to the Chechens in return for some Russian prisoners of war, when Babitsky finally re-emerged he was also charged with belonging to an illegal armed group. Babitsky left Russia. It is not clear whether Babitsky's arrest was on the initiative of local officials or the Kremlin, but it was perfectly in tune with official policy. Earlier in January 2000 a foreign ministry official Vladimir Kozin had called for a tightening of the information blockade against western journalists conducting 'subversive work' in Chechnia. The condemnation of investigative journalism as subversion is ominously reminiscent of the CPSU's approach to the media. Another echo from the past is provided by the treatment of Alexander Khinshteyn, a journalist specialising in investigations into government corruption and sleaze. Following attempts to investigate allegations of corruption against Boris Berezovsky and his ally Vladimir Rushailo, the minister of the interior, Khinshteyn was subjected to a campaign of police harassment. He then went into hiding to avoid being committed to a psychiatric clinic by the police.

The campaign against Gusinsky

Putin's campaign to control the media (see Box 9.8) culminated in June 2000 with the arrest of Vladimir Gusinsky, whose Media-Most media empire opposes both Chechen wars, favoured the opposition Fatherland-All-Russia

---

BOX 9.8

Putin's approach to the mass media

According to Mikhail Berger, the editor of Media-Most's daily newspaper *Sevodnia*:

Putin has divided the media into two categories – those organisations that give him total, utter, unquestioning support and those organisations that don't. He views the latter not simply as papers or television companies, but as enemy units which he has to fight ... Under the Soviet Union, everything was categorised either as Soviet or anti-Soviet. Now under Putin, everything is either state or anti-state. Media-Most had been repeatedly accused by the Kremlin of having an 'anti-state' position. In terms of press freedoms, I think we could see a swift return to the Soviet Union, not just to the 70s, but the 40s under Stalin.

According to a leaked Kremlin strategy document:

Opposition media should be driven to financial crisis, their licences and certificates withdrawn and conditions created where the work of every single opposition medium is either controllable or impossible ...

Source for both quotations: Amelia Gentleman (2000) 'Back to the USSR', *The Guardian*, 29 May, 2.

Alliance (OVR) in the December 1999 Duma elections and had openly questioned Putin's democratic credentials. Gusinsky is also locked in a bitter feud with his fellow oligarch Boris Berezovsky, who was then a Putin supporter. NTV's *Kukly* depict Putin in the uniform of the soviet-era youth organisation, the pioneers. Before his arrest Gusinsky had already been subjected to an escalating campaign to silence him using 'administrative methods'. In May 2000 40 tax police armed with machine guns wearing balaklavas and camouflage uniforms raided Media-Most's headquarters, supposedly as part of an investigation into corruption in the Ministry of Finance and allegations that Media-Most was illegally obtaining and disseminating information. Gusinsky sued and a Moscow court ruled that the raid had been illegal. The accusations levelled against Gusinsky include that he had embezzled $10 million during the 1997 takeover of a St Petersburg television company and that he had exploited Gazprom in order to avoid repaying loans (Traynor, 2000b: 20). Gusinsky's arrest is partly due to business rivalries between Berezovsky and Gusinsky, but it is also part of a campaign being conducted by President Putin to crack down on the oligarchs and the media.

The Russian people and the media crackdown

The government's crackdown on the media has disturbed Russia's journalists and foreign commentators, and has even provoked some of the oligarchs to band together to defend Gusinsky. For the oligarchs their freedom to print or broadcast what they want is an important weapon in their battles for economic and political power and not one to be surrendered lightly, whatever they may think of Gusinsky. On 28 January 2000, 200 journalists and human rights activists demonstrated outside Moscow police headquarters in protest at Khinsteyn's treatment, but these are Moscow's intellectuals, its chattering classes. Popular voices of disapproval or demonstrations of concern are conspicuously lacking. A survey of Muscovites conducted by the All-Russian Centre for Public Opinion Research (VTsIOM) found that 33 per cent of respondents had no reaction to Gusinsky's arrest and 25 per cent said they were happy about it. Less than 10 per cent said the arrest was cause for concern and only 4 per cent said the arrest was unjustified. The same survey found that 57 per cent of respondents believed that Gusinsky's arrest was political and 56 per cent thought that pressure from the Russian and international media had helped to secure his release (Lambroschini, 2000). This could be interpreted as evidence that Russians do not care about media freedom but the sociologist Aleksei Levinson of VTsIOM provides an alternative explanation. According to Levinson, ordinary Russians simply do not associate Gusinsky's arrest with press freedom; they do not want to believe that the state could act in such an arbitrary manner. Gusinsky is, after all, an oligarch, so he is probably guilty of something.

Conclusion

The Russian media have shrugged off the role of 'workers on the ideological front' in the service of the CPSU, only to become the mouthpieces of the oligarchs and republican and republican-regional elites. The oligarchs put their media outlets at the service of Yeltsin and then, with the exception of Gusinsky, of Putin in anticipation of economic advantages. This has brought a measure of pluralism to the national media as the interests of these groups do not always coincide, but journalists who try to champion media impartiality, particularly at the republican-regional and local levels, can find professional and personal survival very difficult. Russia is now the most dangerous country in Europe for journalists: during 1999 11 journalists were killed. The dangers come from any individual or group that wants to stifle investigative journalism coupled with the dangers of reporting from Chechnia. Criminals and corrupt officials also want investigative journalists silenced. The vast majority of the Russian political elite continue the soviet approach to the media, viewing investigative journalism and differences of opinion as opposition, which endangers the state and therefore must be crushed. This anti-democratic response rejects pluralism and wants the media to serve the interest of the Russian state. The championing of state security is a useful cloak for the suppression of meddling journalists.

References

Abdullaev, Nabi (1999) 'Moscow Tightly Controls Information on the Chechen Conflict', *Prism* 5 (20), 17 December, http://www.jamestown.org/

BBC (1997) *Breaking the News*, BBC 2 broadcast on 6 July

Birman, Aleksandr (1997) 'Chubais's Team is Going into the Advertising Business. M.B. Will Probably Be Able to Help his Former Boss', *Sevodnia*, 2 December, 7 (English translation in *The Current Digest of the Post-Soviet Press* XLIX (52), 12

Fossato, Floriana (1998) 'Russian Media Empires in Decline. How Russia's Financial Crisis Hurts The Media – An Analysis', *Radio Free Europe/Ràdio Liberty*, 16 October, http://www.rferl.org/

Gentleman, Amelia (2000) 'The Hard Men Behind Putin', *The Observer*, 26 March, 22

Kisuno, Vasily (1997) 'Commercials Without a Break', *Rossiiskye vesti*, 25 July, 3 (English translation in *Current Digest of the Post-Soviet Press* XLIX (31), 20–1

Korotich, Vitaly (1997) 'The High Cost of a "Free" Press', *Perspective* 8 (1) September–October, http://www.bu.edu/iscip/html

Lambroschini, Sophie (2000) 'Russia: Poll Finds General Public Unfazed by Moves Against Media', *Radio Free Europe/Radio Liberty, Features*, http://www.rferl.org/

Lloyd, John (1998) *Rebirth of a Nation: An Anatomy of Russia*, London: Michael Joseph

Mickiewicz, Ellen (1995) 'The Political Economy of Media Democratisation', in David Lane (ed.) *Russian in Transition: Politics, Privatisation and Inequality*, London: Longman

Poptsov, Oleg (1996) 'Capital Television', *Index on Censorship* (3), 64–66

Satter, David (1997) 'Russia's Not So Free Press', *Commentary* 1 (9), http://www.jamestown.org/

Slider, Darrell (1997) 'Regional and Local Politics', Chapter 13 in Stephen White, Alex Pravda and Zvi Gitelman (eds) *Developments in Russian Politics 4*, Basingstoke: Macmillan

Traynor, Ian (2000a) 'Moscow Cracks Down on Media', *The Guardian*, 29 January, 17

Traynor, Ian (2000b) 'Putin's Main Opponent in Jail', *The Guardian*, 15 June, 20

Yasmann, Victor (1995) 'The Fate of the Russian Media', *Prism* 1 (2) 12 May, http://www.jamestown.org/

Further reading

Literature on the media is more limited than on other topics. However, excellent analyses of the early post-communist changes are provided by:

McNair, Brian (1994) 'Media in Post Soviet Russia: An Overview', *European Journal of Communication*, (9), 115–135

Mickiewicz, Ellen (1995) 'The Political Economy of Media Democratisation', in David Lane (ed.) *Russia in Transition: Politics, Privatisation and Inequality*, London: Longman

On attempts to crack down on the media under Putin see:

Abdullaev, Nabi (1999) 'Moscow Tightly Controls Information on the Chechen Conflict', *Prism* 5 (20), 17 December, http://www.jamestown.org/

Gentlemen, Amelia (2000) 'Victim of Russia's Ugly War', *The Guardian – Media Guardian*, 21 February, 2–3

Traynor, Ian (2000) 'Putin's Men Raid Dissenting TV Offices', *The Guardian*, 12 May, 15

Traynor, Ian (2000) 'Putin's Main Opponent in Jail', *The Guardian*, 15 June, 20

Information about Russia's media empires is provided by:

Fossato, Floriana and Kachkaeva, Anna (1998) 'Russian Media Empires IV', *Radio Free Europe/Radio Liberty*, http://www.rferl.org/

Radio Free Europe/ Radio Liberty (1998) 'Russian Media Empires III',
    http://www.rferl.org/

On Russia's satirical television programme, *Kukly*, see:

'The Kuklies. Little Zaches', *Index on Censorship* 29 (6) 2000, 112–117

Viktor Pelevin's (2000) short novel *Babylon*, London: faber and faber, provides a
very funny account of the development of Russia's advertising industry, as Russia
struggles to resolve the struggle between westernisation and Russian nationalism.

PART IV

Reforming Russia

CHAPTER 10

Russian foreign policy: from superpower to great power

This chapter examines the evolution of Russian foreign policy following the end of the Cold War. The institutions engaged in foreign policy are introduced together with the main foreign policy orientations. The evolution of Russia's foreign policy from Andrei Kozyrev's West-First agenda to Primakov and Ivanov's state-realist-centrist approach is explored and the New Security Doctrine and the New Foreign Policy Concept adopted in 2000 are examined.

Introduction

Russia is accustomed to being part of an empire, part of a superpower, and is used to its views being taken seriously in international forums. Russia is no longer a superpower, but it remains a great power with interests stretching across the Eurasian land mass. Soviet foreign policy had been given a certain coherence through its ideology of Marxism–Leninism and the coordinating role of the CPSU. Post-communist foreign policy-making involves defining Russia's national interests, and then elaborating and implementing policies designed to promote them. Addressing these issues goes to the heart of Russia's identity (see also Chapter 3). In 1991 Russia embarked upon a westernising course of economic and political development which defined the western states as its priority allies. This course of development was always contentious and as Russia's honeymoon with the West and its models of development began to turn sour the advocates of alternative reform programmes and alliance priorities gained stronger voices. By 1994, just as a more centrist approach was being adopted towards economic policy, so Russia's foreign policy became increasingly based upon a state-realist-centrist approach. Russia continues to view no country as an enemy, but it has moved away from its early West-First approach to seek allies throughout the world and to challenge what it identifies as US pretensions to global dominance (see Map 10.1).

Map 10.1

Russia and the Commonwealth of Independent States

Russia after the Cold War

From USSR to Russian Federation

After 1945 world politics were dominated by competition for power and influence by the world's only two superpowers, the USA and the USSR. This bipolar world was characterised by a Cold War in which the superpowers competed by all means short of a fighting or 'hot' war directly between them. The Cold War began in Europe in the immediate aftermath of World War II. The USA provided economic aid to its European allies and in 1949 established its military alliance NATO, specifically to counter the soviet threat. The soviet leader Stalin established soviet socialist states or people's democracies in East-Central Europe, which provided the USSR with a buffer zone against the West. In Winston Churchill's memorable phrase, an Iron Curtain had descended across Europe. The superpowers had contending ideologies: the USSR championed Marxism–Leninism while the USA stood for capitalism and democracy. In reality both superpowers were much more pragmatic in their choice of allies and their behaviour towards each other than their ideologies might suggest. Between 1945 and 1989 superpower relations oscillated between direct confrontation over Cuba in 1962 to mutual accommodation and agreement during the détente period in the 1970s, and then back to a new or second Cold War in the early 1980s. During the Cold War the USSR poured vast resources into building up its nuclear arsenal, navy and standing army. It also fostered allies throughout the world, which it provided with economic aid, oil and gas below world prices, military training and assistance, and education programmes in the USSR. The USSR was also a source of inspiration and a model for other countries to follow, its military might and global network of client states a source of great pride to the USSR. It had transformed itself from a backward and isolated state in the 1920s–1930s to a global superpower that was able to keep the USA at bay. The USSR's superpower status was supported by very fragile foundations which finally gave way in 1991, leaving Russia to redefine its national interests and to find new allies.

The end of the Cold War

The first blow to the USSR was struck by the revolutions of 1989 that swept the communist leaderships out of East-Central Europe. In 1991 the bloc's military alliance, the Warsaw Pact, and its economic and trading organisation, Comecon, were both disbanded, and the USSR disintegrated into 15 new states. The collapse of the USSR and soviet socialism was taken by the USA as evidence that it had won the Cold War. In the early 1990s American triumphalism was at its height, while for many Russians there was a strong sense of defeat and vulnerability. Russia is still the largest country in the world, but it is no longer cocooned within a protective empire of socialist republics and people's democracies. Although Russia still has an extensive nuclear arsenal, its armed forces and navy are no longer as powerful as they once seemed (see Chapter 7). In the early 1990s Russia's shrinking resource base and endeavours to balance its state budget led to cut-backs in military expenditure which further reduced its capacity to act as a global power. Economic problems have also meant that Russia is unable to sustain the USSR's external aid programmes and instead Russia has been reduced to going to the IMF with a financial begging bowl. The close identification of Russia with the USSR has had both positive and negative consequences for the RF. On the one hand, it has inherited the USSR's permanent seat on the UN Security Council. However, there is also a sense that Russia aka USSR bears the guilt for the Cold War, that Russia might revert at any moment to its 'natural' aggression towards the West and imperialism towards its neighbours. While the West welcomed the other 14 states of the former Soviet Union as liberated states, Russia found itself being treated much more cautiously by its new western allies.

The new world order

In 1990 in the aftermath of the collapse of soviet socialism in East-Central Europe, American President George Bush declared the end of the Cold War (see Box 10.1). Then the victory of the American-led coalition in the Gulf War encouraged Bush to talk about a new world order, a term that Gorbachev also adopted in the USSR. The new world order was supposed to usher in a new age of stability, free from Cold War conflict. However, almost as soon as the Cold War was over it seemed like a golden, albeit terribly tarnished, age of security and stability. The Cold War system provided a nuclear stalemate between the two superpowers through the doctrine of Mutually Assured Destruction (MAD) and so a measure of certainty in international affairs, at

---

BOX 10.1

President Bush and the new world order

The New World Order ... represented an adaptation of the *Pax Americana* to a world wherein American power did not hold absolute and undisputed sway ... the New World Order recognised that the US could not do everything. American goals – world order, peaceful adjudication of disputes under international law, the advancement of liberal democracy and market economies, the maintenance of liberal economic regimes – would be achieved through collective action (ideally associated with the United Nations) orchestrated by the United States. (Bush's new version conveniently ignored continuing US–UN disputes over the scale of dues owed by Washington to the UN.)

Source: John Dumbrell (1997) *American Foreign Policy: Carter to Clinton*, Basingstoke: Macmillan, 163–4. Dr Dumbrell is a senior lecturer in American Studies at Keele University.

BOX 10.2

Russia's neighbours

Neighbouring country	Length of border with Russia (in km)
Azerbaijan	284
Belarus	959
China (South East)	3605
China (South)	40
Estonia	294
Finland	1313
Georgia	723
Kazakhstan	6846
North Korea	19
Latvia	217
Lithuania (with Kaliningrad *oblast*)	227
Mongolia	3441
Norway	167
Poland (with Kaliningrad *oblast*)	206
Ukraine	1576
Total length of external borders	19 913

Note: Kaliningrad *oblast* on the Baltic is separated from the rest of the RF by Belarus and Lithuania-Latvia.

Source: CIA, *The World Fact Book 1999 – Russia*, http://www.odci.gov/cia/publications/factbook/rs.html

least in superpower relations. For the USA the post Cold War proliferation of new states threatens increased instability, a growth in border disputes, a rise in ethnic nationalisms, religious conflicts and religious fundamentalisms, mass migrations and a growth in cross-border crime – not so much a new order as disorder. The USA is also concerned by the activities of the countries it terms 'rogue states', which include Iran and the former soviet allies of North Korea, Libya, Iraq and Syria. The USA condemns these countries as sources of international terrorism and for their aspirations to become nuclear powers with the attendant dangers of nuclear proliferation and instability.

The making of Russian foreign policy

The Westernisers (*zapadniki*)

During 1991–3 Russia's foreign policy, indeed its whole reform process, was based upon the belief that Russia needed to open up to the West as quickly as possible. In the tradition of the nineteenth-century westernisers (*zapadniki*) and Gorbachev's Reconstruction, the westernisers believed that opening to the West would help to secure democratisation and marketisation against domestic inertia and opposition. Initially, President Yeltsin was one of the leading proponents of this approach together with his foreign minister, Andrei Kozyrev, and deputy prime minister Igor Gaidar. The political parties Democratic Russia and Gaidar's party Democratic Choice were the leading advocates of westernisation. In 1991 when asked by the newspaper *Izvestia* who were Russia's priority partners, Kozyrev enthusiastically replied, 'Rich developed countries, mature democracies with mature economies. This means the United States, Western Europe and Japan' (cited by Hearst, 1996: 21). This thinking led to a 'West-First' or 'Atlanticist' approach to foreign policy and also entailed the dropping of old soviet-era allies like North Korea, Cuba, Vietnam, India, Angola and Ethiopia. The westernisers expected the West-First policy to generate economic dividends by providing Russia with new markets, investment, know-how and humanitarian aid. It was also an ethical or philosophical stance, signifying Russia's acceptance of 'western values' such as democracy, human rights and the rule of law. In January 1996 the Council of Europe voted to admit Russia as its 39th member precisely in order to send positive messages to Moscow and to counter anti-democratic pressures within Russia. The westernisers also believed that Russian security could be secured through active participation in international institutions, particularly the OSCE and the UN. Yeltsin's attempts to extend the role of the OSCE were sidestepped by the leading western powers, which have instead concentrated on enlarging the membership and extending the role of NATO in European security. In the 1990s the USA was in dispute with the UN, which accused it of not paying the organisation the money it was due. The USA has also not been prepared to submit to the UN Security Council, whose five permanent members (the USA, Russia, China, Great Britain and France) all have the right of veto.

Eurasianists

(See also Chapter 3)

Eurasianists believe that Russia, like its crest, the two-headed eagle, looks both East and West. As Russia is simultaneously part of Europe and Asia the Eurasianists believe that Russia should act as a bridge between the two. In the early 1990s Eurasianist ideas were championed by Sergei Stankevich (1992 and 1993), who entered politics as a pro-democracy reformer during Reconstruction and became the deputy mayor of Moscow. In April 1992 Stankevich was appointed to the new State Council, which was supposed to become the new executive body of the government, but which was eclipsed by the Security Council. Stankevich became increasingly critical of the West-First priority in foreign policy and objected to what he saw as Russia's junior-partner relationship to the western alliance and the absence of an independent foreign policy serving Russia's rather than the West's interests. Eurasianists want greater attention to be paid to Russia's relations with the CIS and the Near Abroad, the Middle East, Africa and especially Asia. Eurasianists believe that as Asia and the Pacific Rim are becoming the most dynamic part of the world, Russia needs to orient itself away from the West and towards Asia. Stankevich condemned Russia's westernisers for not supporting Russians in the Baltic states, where according to Stankevich they were being subjected to 'ethnic cleansing' (Buszynski, 1995: 107). In April 1992 Stankevich travelled with Vice-President Alexander Rutskoi to Moldova, where Russians in Transdniestr supported by the Russian 14th Army, headed by Gen. Alexander Lebed, were at war with Moldovan forces. Transdniestr had only become part of Moldova after World War II, when Stalin had decided to compensate Moldavia, as the republic was then called, for Moldavian territory he had transferred to Ukraine. For the Eurasianists Transdniestr was another example of embattled Russians inadequately supported by the westernising Russian government. Eurasianism runs across Russia's political spectrum, from democrats such as Stankevich through to proponents of various forms of authoritarianism, fascists, Stalinists, and the Zyuganov's KPRF, for whom Eurasianism provides a cultural justification for a powerful Russian state and either downgrading the relationship with the West or outright anti-westernism.

Great power (*derzhavniki*) and strong state advocates (*gosudarstvenniki*)

Russia's great power and strong state advocates believe that Russia must be a great power with a strong state in order to maintain its territorial integrity and to prevent anarchy and chaos. The advocates of these views are inspired by a range of concepts including Eurasianism and Russian nationalism. One such advocate is Sergei Karaganov, the deputy head of the Institute of Europe. In August 1992 the Institute's Foreign and Defence Policy Council produced a paper entitled 'Strategy for Russia', which argued that Russia needs a form of transitional authoritarianism and a foreign policy focusing on the stability of its neighbours (Lloyd, 1998: 358). Andranik Migranyan, an advocate of transitional authoritarianism (see Chapter 1), similarly argues against the West-First priority and in favour of the adoption of a much more assertive policy in the Near Abroad. Russia's self-styled national patriots all stress Russia's uniqueness, its distinctiveness from the West, the importance of a strong state and Russia's status as a great power. Zhirinovsky, in his *Last Thrust to the South* (1993) for example, argues that Russia should be the centre of a great Eurasian empire. The Russian nationalist writer Alexander Solzhenitsyn (1995) stresses the alien nature of the West for Russia, bemoans the weakness of the

Russian state and its inability to protect the Russian diaspora, and advocates a union of the Eastern Slavs (see Chapter 3). Gennady Zyuganov (Zyuganov and Podberezin, 1995), inspired by a combination of Marxism and Eurasianism, advocates the reformation of at least part of the USSR. His earlier anti-westernism has been replaced by a more pragmatic approach to the West, while his rhetoric still champions Russia as a powerful state and a great power. In contrast to the westernisers, the advocates of Russia as a great power and certainly the national patriots tend to distrust international organisations and believe that Russia must champion its own interests.

State-realist-centrists

Just as Russia's economic policy moved away from its western-inspired shock therapy towards a centrist economic policy in 1993 (see Chapter 11), so its foreign policy began to move from its West-First priority to a state realist centrism. This approach does not entail a complete rejection of liberalism and the West, but instead advocates a pragmatic approach to managing Russia's democratisation and marketisation combined with a stress on championing Russia's national interests. This approach is based on a realist approach to international relations which sees states in competition and stresses the importance of power, military capabilities and the use of military power as an instrument of foreign policy. Under foreign ministers Primakov and Ivanov Russia has become much more concerned about regional security threats, which has led to greater attention being paid to the CIS and the Near Abroad. Russia has also shown a greater willingness to use economic leverage such as the threat to cut off energy supplies to the other FSU states. Concern about the possible ramifications of instability in the Near Abroad and around its borders has encouraged Russia to pursue good relations with its near neighbours Turkey, Pakistan, Iran and Afghanistan. The state-realist-centrists are also advocates of Russia as a great power which must champion its national interests, even if it means taking part in military ventures in the Near Abroad. International organisations are seen as potentially useful arenas in which to promote Russian interests and while good relations with the West are preferred, this does not preclude tough bargaining to secure Russian interests.

Russian foreign policy-making, 1991–1993

The formulation and implementation of Russian foreign policy was complicated by the political conflicts between the parliament and president which culminated in the October 1993 crisis, and also by the institutional conflicts and rivalries that Yeltsin encouraged as part of his system of presidential rule (see Chapter 4). Russia inherited from the USSR a constitution which gave the Supreme Soviet the right to frame the general direction of its foreign policy. The Supreme Soviet also had the right to approve the appointment of foreign and defence ministers, sanction the commitment of armed forces abroad and ratify international treaties. Through three specialised foreign affairs committees it scrutinised the government's performance in foreign affairs. From the RF's inception in January 1992 to the adoption of the new Constitution in December 1993, the Supreme Soviet was in conflict with the president and the foreign ministry over the basic direction of the country's foreign policy. Kozyrev, Yeltsin and his influential adviser Gennady Burbulis advocated and pursued a westernising foreign policy in the face of mounting Supreme Soviet opposition. While Kozyrev favoured diplomacy to resolve disputes with Russia's neighbours, the Supreme Soviet was much more inclined to be confrontational. So, for example, in May 1992 it annulled the 1954 transfer of the Crimea from the RSFSR to Ukraine and rejected the then current deal over the division of the Black Sea fleet between Russia and Ukraine.

The 1993 Constitution changed the legal foundation of Russian foreign policy making to one based on presidential authority. According to Article 86, the president exercises leadership of foreign policy, conducts talks and signs international treaties, signs instruments of ratification and accepts the credentials and letters of recall of foreign diplomats. The president also approves the RF military doctrine, appoints the RF's plenipotentiary representatives, and forms and heads the Security Council (Art. 83). The Federal Assembly provides legislative support for foreign policy and the fulfilment of international obligations, and retains the right to scrutinise and ratify treaties signed by the president. Only the upper chamber, the Federation Council, has jurisdiction over sending armed forces abroad (Art 102.d). The two Federal Assembly chambers have specialised committees on particular aspects of foreign affairs. The Federation Council has committees on International Affairs, CIS Affairs, and Security and Defence. The Duma has committees on International Affairs, Security, CIS Affairs and Links with Compatriots, and Geopolitical Questions.

The Foreign Ministry and the Security Council

The Russian foreign ministry's role was quickly undermined by financial problems and institutional rivalries within the government. From the early 1990s the foreign ministry's budget was drastically cut, which undermined its ability to fund embassies, conduct research and compete with the growing business sector to employ Russia's well-educated, foreign-language speakers. From the spring of 1992 the foreign ministry's role was increasingly usurped by the Security Council, which had been remodelled along the lines of the US National Security Council (see Box 10.3). The Security Council drafts the president's decisions on defence, foreign and security policy and monitors their implementation. The Security Council was headed by the centrist advocate of Russia's great power status, Yury Skokov (April 1992–May 1993), who had close links with Russia's military-industrial complex and favoured a

> **BOX 10.3**
>
> **Russia's foreign ministers**
>
> Andrei Kozyrev (July 1990–January 1996)
> Yevgeny Primakov (January 1996–August 1998)
> Igor Ivanov (August 1998–)

downgrading of the West-First strategy and a more robust approach to Russia's interests in the Near Abroad. Kozyrev and Skokov therefore headed competing institutions with competing visions of Russian foreign policy. The Security Council's adoption of a harder line on conflicts within the CIS such as in Nagorno-Karabakh, Moldova and the dispatch of Russia special forces to South Ossetia in July 1992 led Kozyrev to accuse Skokov of heading a 'War Party'. Throughout 1992 the foreign ministry continued to lose ground to the Security Council. A presidential decree in 1992 empowered the Security Council to make policy recommendations which then needed to be confirmed by presidential decree. The Security Council has specialised bodies such as the Defence Council and a Foreign Policy Council established in December 1995 to coordinate the work of all the main departments in the foreign policy arena. In January 1996 the little known Vladimir Slavin was appointed to head the Council. Once Kozyrev resigned as foreign minister in January 1996, the role of the foreign ministry underwent a renaissance under the new foreign minister Yevgeny Primakov. A 1996 presidential decree 'On the Coordinating Role of the Russian Federation Foreign Ministry in the Conducting of an Integrated Russian Federation Foreign Policy' asserted the foreign ministry's primacy in coordinating the RF's foreign policy activities conducted by the various agencies of the executive branch.

Russia and the former Soviet Union (FSU)

The Commonwealth of Independent States (CIS)

Russia is the great power of the FSU region. It is distinguished from its neighbours by its geographical expanse, population size and GDP. With the dissolution of the USSR suddenly republics that had been part of the USSR and often before then part of the Imperial Russia Empire became independent sovereign states (see Box 10.4). Russia's relations with these successor states were transformed from relations with another part of the same country to an aspect of foreign policy. These relations are influenced by two contradictory impulses. The 'nationalities question', the aspiration for national self-determination, had played a fundamental role in the dissolution of the USSR

BOX 10.4

Defining the Near Abroad

Near Abroad (*blizhnee zarubezh'e*) – the term used by Russians for the other 14 successor states of the USSR. For these new states this term is evidence of Russian imperialism as it implies that they are not as fully independent of Russia as the countries of the 'Far Abroad'.

and, with the exception of Belarus, none of the successor states wants to be part of a new Russian empire. At the same time the new states had for decades been part of the same country, and so their peoples, economies and armed forces were intertwined. There is therefore a tension between upholding new, hard-won national sovereignty and recognition of the need for some form of institutionalised cooperation. The three Slav states Russia, Ukraine and Belarus founded the Commonwealth of Independent States (CIS) at Belovezha (Minsk) in December 1991. They were soon joined by nine of the other former soviet republics and only the Baltic republics of Estonia, Lithuania and Latvia have not joined. It was agreed that the CIS's administrative headquarters would be in Minsk, the capital of Belarus, to symbolise that this was not to be a Russian-dominated organisation. They also established a Council of the heads of government and a Council of the heads of state, but no central structures as such were established. The CIS was not founded in order to recreate the USSR, but fears that it would be dominated by Russia have meant that it has remained a rather weak organisation. In the early 1990s Russia was engrossed in domestic reform and concentrated on its relationship with the West, to the detriment of clarifying and developing its relations with the CIS.

Problem issues for the Commonwealth of Independent States

As soon as the CIS was founded issues generated by the soviet integration of the FSU's economies and military capabilities came to the fore. In 1992 the rouble was the currency for all CIS countries (the rouble zone), which placed a tremendous burden upon the Russian economy (see Chapter 11). The successor states also expected Russia to continue supplying them with cheap oil and gas, when Russia needed to generate as much income as possible to finance its own reforms. In 1991 the CIS agreed to maintain CIS joint forces, but this was immediately undermined by the creation of national armed forces by several of the successor states including Ukraine. Russia responded by creating its own forces and also claimed soviet military assets located outside Russia. Russia and Ukraine quickly became embroiled in an argument over the ownership of the Black Sea fleet. This argument was fuelled by a territorial dispute over Crimea, which Khrushchev had transferred to Ukraine in 1954 and which Russia now wanted back. In 1993 the Russian Supreme Soviet claimed Sevastopol in Crimea, the home port of the Black Sea fleet, was in Russia. In May 1997 prime ministers Chernomyrdin of Russia and Lazerenko of Ukraine finally agreed that Russia's part of the Black Sea fleet would remain based in Sevastopol for 20 years. The transfer of tactical weapons was swiftly completed by mid-1992, but the transfer of strategic weapons proved more difficult and became yet another point of argument between Russia and Ukraine. The USSR's strategic and tactical nuclear weapons arsenals also had to be divided between the successor states. Ukraine, Belarus and Kazakhstan agreed to transfer these weapons to Russia and to create a somewhat vaguely defined joint command over them under CIS auspices.

The evolution of Russian foreign policy

Andrei Kozyrev: the 'minister for foreign affairs in Russia'

As RF foreign minister Andrei Kozyrev talked about his mission to civilise Russia by bringing it closer to the West. His pro-western foreign policy was a continuation of Gorbachev's approach, which was already undermined by its association with the failure of Reconstruction. Gorbachev had gambled on western support, but the West had proved reluctant to back its verbal support for reform with financial aid. As a result the West was associated with the failed reform that had ultimately led to the collapse of the USSR. Kozyrev's appeasement of the West, perceived failure to defend Russian interests and lack of patriotism earned him the mocking title of the minister for foreign affairs in Russia. A wide range of Russian political orientations, including the communists and nationalists, already viewed the West as not just alien but anti-Russian, and believed that the West wants Russia to be weak. The West's insistence on economic shock therapy, which reduced millions of Russians to poverty, seemed to bear out this interpretation of the West's ambitions. Andrei Kozyrev was the longest serving member of Yeltsin's young radical reforming team that had dominated his first government. The West-First foreign policy line was gradually attenuated amid accusations that it ignored Russia's immediate security and political concerns in the Near Abroad. Kozyrev and Yeltsin were accused of ignoring the fate of the 25 million-strong Russian diaspora (see Chapter 3) and of failing to deal adequately with the conflicts in the Caucasus and Central Asia that threatened to spill over into Russia. At the same time Russians living in Estonia and Latvia were denied citizenship and voting rights, and while the West condemned this discrimination, it did not apply sanctions against these countries. Kozyrev's belief that Russia's security and Russians' human and civil rights would be guaranteed by international law enforced by international organisations had not been borne out. The West's sensitivity to signs of Russian imperialism and to attempts to rebuild the USSR meant that Russia's legitimate need to stabilise its borders were not given adequate support by its western allies. The various centrists believed that Russia could maintain its good relations with the West, while taking a tough stance on problems in its own 'back yard' in the Near Abroad. For the nationalists and communists only a return to Russian dominance over the Near Abroad would resolve these problems and if that meant jettisoning the pro-West line then so be it.

The 1993 Foreign Policy Concept and the realities of Russian foreign policy

Although Russia adopted a new Foreign Policy Concept in 1993 that reflected Kozyrev's westernising approach to foreign policy, as earlier as 1992 while not abandoning westernisation, Yeltsin became increasingly assertive of Russia's interests. Throughout 1992–3 Kozyrev repeatedly came into conflict with the Supreme Soviet over foreign policy. In July 1992 the Supreme Soviet spent three days debating the treatment of the Russian minority in the Baltic states and called for sanctions to be applied against Estonia (Buszynski, 1995: 106). During the summer of 1993, as president and parliament were hurtling towards the October crisis, parliament refused to ratify START II (Strategic Arms Reduction Treaty) and to recognise the 1954 transfer of Crimea from RSFSR to Ukraine, whilst stridently condemning the current plans to divide the Black Sea fleet with Ukraine. In May 1992 Russia voted for sanctions against its traditional ally Serbia in the UN Security Council, which brought Kozyrev into conflict with Yevgeny Ambartsumov, the head of the Supreme Soviet's Committee on International Affairs and External Economic Relations. He also came into conflict with Yury Skokov, who favoured a state-realist-centrist approach, and the Security Council over its July 1992 decision to send Russian special forces into South Ossetia. The Security Council also postponed Yeltsin's trip to Tokyo scheduled for September 1992, because the Supreme Soviet feared that he might agree to return the Kuril Islands to Japan. By early 1993 Russia was calling for sanctions against the Croats, whilst turning a blind eye to the smuggling of weapons, fuel and food to the Serbs in contravention of the UN sanctions that it had voted for only the previous year.

Russia also began to renew relations with former soviet allies such as Iraq and Syria, which are condemned by the USA as rogue states. Russia also strengthened its relations with the Palestinian Liberation Organisation (PLO). Only two years before in 1991 Russia had supported the USA in the Gulf War against Iraq. The strong showing of the KPRF and the LDPR in the December 1993 Duma elections indicated Russian voters' concerns over the westernising domestic and international agenda. These election results and the composition of the new Duma reinforced the shift away from the pro-western approach to foreign policy and Yeltsin increasingly called for a more patriotic foreign policy, putting 'Russia-First'. This entailed support for Russia's traditional allies, so the Serbs Radovan Karadzic and Ratko Mladic, who were con-demned as war criminals by the West, were defended in Russia as the innocent victims of western aggression. In January 1994 Kozyrev also stressed the importance of defending the Russian diaspora, the need for a Russian presence in the Near Abroad and for priority to be shifted from relations with the West to relations with the CIS and Asian countries. Russia also began to open relations with China which had been soured by the Chinese government's support for August 1991 coup.

Russia and NATO

Russia's relations with the West have been strained by NATO's extension into East-Central Europe and its actions in the Balkans. NATO had been founded at the height of the Cold War and so Russia's westernisers anticipated that the end of the Cold War would lead to the end of NATO. Yeltsin and Kozyrev believed that the CSCE (later OSCE) would become the main European security organisation. After 1991 the former soviet bloc countries worked with NATO in the North Atlantic Cooperation Council (NACC), but far from withering away NATO has gone from strength to strength and incorporated former Warsaw Pact countries as members. NATO provides the USA with a powerful security organisation, armed with conventional and nuclear forces stretching from the USA across the Atlantic ocean to Europe. For the leaders of the newly independent states of East-Central Europe, NATO membership is symbolic of their acceptance into the community of democratic states, a recognition that as sovereign states they have the right to decide their own security alliances and also a vital guarantee against possible future Russian imperialist aggression. Despite NATO's assurances that its enlargement is not directed against Russia, Russia nonetheless interprets the extension of Europe's only effective security organisation towards its borders as aggressive. While NATO sees its extension as putting an end to the Cold War division of Europe into East and West, for Russia it puts a new Iron Curtain along its borders, symbolising the fact that Russia has not been accepted by the West as an equal partner and providing further anti-western ammunition for Russian nationalists and communists.

In October 1993 NATO proposed a Partnership for Peace (PfP) to the former members of the Warsaw Pact, which was launched in January 1994. The PfP is a transitional stage to full NATO membership. It provides fairly loose political and security ties, with access to NATO councils, but no decision-making or veto powers. During a visit to Poland in August 1993, Yeltsin described Poland's intention to join NATO as consistent with Russia's long-term interests, but through 1994–5 Russia's attitude towards NATO extension hardened. At this time NATO attempted a series of bridge-building exercises with Russia designed to show that the West recognised Russian security concerns. In 1994 for example there were bilateral joint military exercises between the USA and Russia, which included joint amphibious training at Vladivostok and joint infantry exercises at Totskoye in central Russia. The West also accommodated Russia's security concerns in the Caucasus by relaxing the limits on conventional weapons deployments required under the Conventional Forces in Europe (CFE) Treaty. The Treaty, which had been signed by Gorbachev in 1990 when both the USSR and the Warsaw Pact still existed, had provided for large-scale reductions in tanks, artillery and aircraft in an area stretching from the Atlantic in the West to the Urals in the East. Russia argued that the CFE was the product of a different time before instability in the Caucasus had become such a major security concern. By the end of 1994 23 countries had PfPs with NATO, including ten CIS countries. Each PfP is a bilateral agreement between an individual country and NATO and since 1997 these agreements have been coordinated through the Euro-Atlantic Partnership Council (EAPC) which replaced NACC that year.

Kozyrev signed the accords which formally established Russia's PfP in May 1995. Russia–NATO relations were immediately thrown into turmoil by the US-led bombing of Bosnia in September 1995 (see Box 10.5). NATO and Russia eventually agreed to Russian participation in the Bosnian peace implementation, when NATO took over from the UN in Bosnia in December 1995. Russia participated in the joint consultative commission and the contact group or peace implementation force with the USA, United Kingdom, France and Germany. At the June 1996 NATO defence ministers meeting, the Russian defence minister Pavel Grachev agreed to a formal exchange of senior NATO and Russian military personnel who are now permanently stationed in Moscow and Brussels. They also agreed to work together against terrorism and international crime, and to cooperate on joint weapons development and arms control. Then in May 1997 Russia and NATO signed the 'Founding Act on Mutual Relations, Co-operation and Security between NATO and the Russian Federation' (NATO, 1997). Section I stated that the NATO–Russian partnership is based on the principles of the UN Charter and OSCE documents, which include respect for state sovereignty, independence and the right to choose how to ensure state security. Section II created a new NATO–Russian Permanent Joint Council (PJC) to hold regular meetings and consultations to try to establish consensus between Russia and NATO and then to make joint decisions and if appropriate to take joint action. Section III sets out that NATO and Russia should cooperate in the settlement of conflicts, in peacekeeping, in the prevention of weapons proliferation and in the exchange of information on security and defence forces and policies. Section IV restates NATO's December 1996 statement that it did not intend to deploy nuclear weapons on the territory of its new members in East-Central Europe which was an issue that had been a major stumbling block in Russian–NATO relations. NATO had objected to what it saw as Russia's attempt to establish a veto over its nuclear weapons deployment, while Russia had been angered by the possibility that NATO might move nuclear weapons up to its

BOX 10.5

Andrei Kozyrev: US–Russian partnership in a multi-polar world

The Cold War era is past, but we still have only a vague picture of the international system in which we would live in the next century. The contemporary world is like a driver who knows his place of departure but has no definite destination, no map and no road signs. It is obvious, on the one hand, that there are enormous opportunities for the world to develop along the path of democracy and economic progress. But just as obvious is the danger of chaos and unpredictability in international affairs, and the emergence of new conflicts and schisms within and between states.

One thing is sufficiently clear: the international order in the 21st century will not be a Pax Americana or any version of unipolar or bipolar dominance. The United States does not have the capability to rule alone. Russia, while in a period of transitional difficulties, retains the inherent characteristics of a great power (technology, resources, weaponry). And other rising centers of influence strive for a greater role in world affairs. The nature of modern international problems calls for solutions on a multilateral basis.

Source: Andrei Kozyrev (1994) 'The Lagging Partnership', *Foreign Affairs* 73 (3) May–June, 63.

borders. The charter left the Baltic states outside NATO with no immediate prospect of membership, even though they feel threatened by Russian expansionism. In 1999 the Czech Republic, Hungary and Poland became NATO's first new post-Cold War members. Despite the 1997 'Founding Act' Russian–NATO relations have continued to be aggravated by disagreements over NATO military actions in Yugoslavia. In March 1999 Russian foreign minister Ivanov accused NATO of having violated all the Founding Act's agreements and of being guilty of genocide in Kosovo, and Russia announced a complete cessation of ties with NATO, including the suspension of Russia's participation in the PfP. Yeltsin backed down over Kosovo and in return secured a place at the June 1999 G8 conference in Cologne.

From Andrei Kozyrev to Yevgeny Primakov

In January 1996 Kozyrev resigned as foreign minister; by this time he had few political friends and throughout 1995 the Duma had repeatedly called for his dismissal. Yevgeny Primakov became the new foreign minister, much to the initial alarm of western governments. Primakov's appointment marked a return to an older generation of soviet functionaries. An Arabic speaker and Middle East expert, he had conducted an intensive shuttle diplomacy to Baghdad on Gorbachev's behalf on the eve of the Gulf War, in an attempt to preempt western military action against Iraq. In 1991 Primakov opposed the August coup, which did nothing to endear him to the communists, but encouraged Yeltsin to appoint him to head the Foreign Intelligence Service (SVR). Primakov's security career led to fears that Russian foreign policy might become more hostile to the West. In the event Primakov rapidly proved a tough enough champion of Russia's interests to assuage communist doubts, while establishing good working relations with the West. Russian foreign policy did not undergo a major rethink with Primakov's appointment as foreign minister, as the change to state-realist-centrist approach to Russia's interests and policy had already begun under Kozyrev. The main change was that while Kozyrev's natural impulse was towards the West, Primakov was a statist and a centrist.

Primakov supported a centrist approach towards economic reform (see Chapter 11), which in foreign policy terms he complemented with a continuing commitment to Russian integration in the world economy. Primakov wanted to maintain friendly relations with the West but did not prioritise the West and he saw no need to agree with the USA on crucial international issues. In his first press conference as foreign minister he stated that Russia is a great power and that her foreign policy must correspond to this status. He rejected any return to the Cold War and committed Russia to continuing active participation in international institutions. Primakov confirmed that Russia wished to have friendly relations with the USA, but that these relations must be based on an equitable, mutually beneficial partnership that respects each other's interests. Primakov therefore stridently opposed NATO actions in the Balkans and engaged in extremely tough negotiations over NATO enlargement, but went on to agree the 1997 NATO–RF Founding Act. Primakov also continued to strengthen relations with Syria and Iraq and opposed the US–UK unilateral bombing of Iraq, which had not been sanctioned by the UN Security Council.

Primakov and multi-polarity

Primakov's overt rejection of the West-First strategy was complemented by a commitment to create a multi-polar world in order to stop the USA's post Cold War, unipolar dominance of global politics (see Box 10.6). Under Primakov Russia became increasingly vocal in its opposition to what it saw as US endeavours to maintain a unipolar world and US willingness to use military force to resolve problems. Russia now advocates the creation of an international security system to underpin global multi-polarity, with particular emphasis on the importance of the UN Security Council. Russia also favours strengthened pan-European security and cooperation structures and relationships in order to counter American dominance. In this respect while Russia's membership of the Council of Europe has exposed its human rights records, it has also provided Russia with access to an exclusively European forum. Russia has also pursued good relations with the European Union (EU) and its individual members as desirable goals in their own right, but also to counterbalance the USA. In 1997 Prime Minister Chernomyrdin even announced that Russia wanted to seek full EU membership. It is unlikely that the EU would

BOX 10.6

International institutions

Council of Europe –
founded in 1949 as a European regional group with the aim to coordinate economic, social, cultural, scientific and legal legislation, it is a separate institution to the EU. The Council of Europe established the European Court of Human Rights which considers complaints by citizens against their own governments. Member states are supposed to be based on the rule of law and human rights. Since 1989 the Council has also been engaged in monitoring democratisation in the former soviet bloc. In 1995 Russia's application for membership was temporarily suspended because of the conflict in Chechnia and human rights abuses. Although Russia was admitted as a member in 1996 the Council of Europe is concerned by the renewed conflict in Chechnia, human rights abuses and the continued use of the death penalty.

Organisation for Security and Cooperation in Europe (OSCE) –
originally founded in Helsinki as the Conference on Security and Cooperation in Europe (CSCE) in 1975, it became the OSCE in 1990. CSCE-OSCE members include East and West European States and the USA. The CSCE-OSCE has held a series of meetings and conferences to discuss European security and cooperation, military and trade issues, and human rights. The OSCE provides missions to mediate conflicts and monitor democratisation in Europe. The OSCE has sent missions to Chechnia.

Western European Union (WEU) –
established in 1954 as a European council to coordinate regional defence policy, the USA is not a member. It was largely moribund until the 1980s when some European countries, notably France, became interested in activating the WEU as an embryonic military arm of the EEC. The WEU's remit includes peacekeeping and peace enforcement, humanitarian and rescue missions, and collective defence. The WEU currently has 10 full members and 10 associate partners from East-Central Europe.

accept a membership application from Russia, as its sheer size and the scale of its economic problems would seriously destabilise the union. Nevertheless the EU is the main source of investment and grants for Russia and also a major trading partner (Ivanov and Pozdnyakov, 1998). Russia has also accepted the 1997 Brussels Agenda 2000 timetable for the admission of ten East-Central European countries to the EU.

Russia also supports EU endeavours to develop a shared EU foreign policy and defence identities, distinct from the USA. In 1996 it briefly seemed as if the Western European Union (WEU) would finally be invigorated after decades of inertia, but this did not happen. At the NATO foreign ministers meeting in Berlin in June 1996, the establishment of a European command structure within NATO was agreed. This new structure meant that NATO's European members could organise their own humanitarian and peace-keeping missions. However, the Europeans have proved reluctant to get involved in Kosovo, for example, on their own and instead prefer to work with the Americans in

NATO. Russia also wants Europe's largest organisation, the OSCE, to be reinvigorated and for it to adopt a European Security Charter. However, the Western Europeans while respecting the OSCE as a forum for discussion, view it as too unwieldy to provide a realistic security organisation.

Multi-polarity: Russia and Asia

Relations with Japan have been strained by Japan's insistence that Russia return what Japan calls the Northern Territories and Russia calls the Kuril Islands, a volcanic archipelago between Russian Kamchatka and Japan, seized by the USSR at the end of World War II. The islands became a measure of Yeltsin's commitment to stand up for Russia, and local Cossacks have sworn to fight if there is any attempt to return the islands to Japan. Despite this deadlock Japan and Russia have established a working relationship and managed to conclude fishing agreements. Russia has also pursued improved relations with both North and South Korea. Gorbachev initiated better relations with South Korea when he visited Seoul in May 1991 and in February 2000 Foreign Minister Ivanov visited the North Korean capital of Pyong-Yang to strengthen relations with North Korea that had been downgraded in 1991–2 in order to appease South Korea. Ivanov drew up a Russian–Korean Friendship Treaty, which the Duma ratified in July 2000 while Putin was in Pyong-Yang, the first Russian leader to visit North Korea since 1956. In July 2000 Putin was also able to take to the G8 meeting in Okinawa, Japan, a document signed by the North Korean leader Kim Jing Il stating that he would not launch missiles.

China shares Russia's concern over America's dominance in a unipolar world, its tendency to unilateral action and particularly its decision to create a National Missile Defence System (NMD) or 'son of star wars', and the enlargement of NATO. In 1999 Russia and China jointly opposed the US-led bombing of Yugoslavia. Although there are potential points of conflict between Russia and China, such as Russia's belief that China wishes to expand into the Russian Far East, Sino-Russian relations improved considerably during the 1990s and China is a major importer of Russian military hardware. Russia and China also share concerns about security in Asia and Central Asia. China has substantial Islamic-Turkic populations in its southeastern regions who are increasingly challenging Beijing's rule. Russia is also concerned by instability amongst the Islamic-Turkic peoples of Central Asia and has intervened militarily in the civil war in Tajikistan in order to prop up the Tajik government. President Putin has also indicated that Asia occupies an increasingly important place in Russian foreign policy and visited China (plus North Korea and Japan) in July 2000. This led to the 'Beijing Declaration' which established a shared commitment to the creation of a multi-polar world and set out the basic guidelines for future Sino-Russian relations and strategic cooperation, which included talks over the disputed border areas.

Russia and China are both permanent members of the UN Security Council and want the UN to be reinvigorated as part of the creation of a multi-polar world and as a mechanism to rein in American ambitions. Russia and China have also produced a joint statement on NMD. The USA intends to deploy its nuclear missile defence umbrella over itself and its allies including Taiwan and Japan. Russia and China argue that such a system violates the 1972 Anti-Ballistic Missile Treaty, which they see as the foundation stone of nuclear stability. In February 1995 Yeltsin had offered to begin negotiations on START III in an attempt to preempt American actions, even though the Duma had not ratified START II. The Duma finally ratified START II in May 2000. Russia's Foreign Policy Concept (July 2000) states that Russia is willing to reduce its own nuclear arsenal on the basis of bilateral agreements with the USA and multilateral agreements with other nuclear powers, provided these maintain nuclear stability. Russia is desperate to begin START III talks.

Ivanov, Putin and the continuing commitment to multi-polarity

When Primakov became prime minister he was succeeded as foreign minister by Igor Ivanov, a former career diplomat and first deputy foreign minister. Ivanov has continued in this post under President Putin. Ivanov and Putin's approach to foreign policy is essentially a continuation of Primakov's state-realist-centrist orientation with a continuing commitment to multi-polarity. Ivanov and Putin have produced a new Military Doctrine approved by the Security Council in April 2000 to replace the 1993 Military Doctrine, which had been revised in 1997. The new Military Doctrine contrasted Russia's commitment to multi-polarity with US attempts to establish a unipolar superpower domination committed to resolving world problems by armed force. It identified ten basic features of the current military-political situation which include 'the declining threat of a world war, the appearance and strengthening of regional centers of force, growing national and religious extremism, the escalation of local wars and armed conflicts, the aggravation of propaganda confrontation' (NUPI, 1999). The new Military Doctrine bemoans the ineffectiveness of the world's existing security mechanisms, specifically the inability of the UN and OSCE to deal with these problems. The Doctrine notes that NATO went ahead with the bombing of Yugoslavia in 1999, without seeking the approval of the UN Security Council. The Doctrine also lowers the threshold at which Russia would launch first strike nuclear weapons. While the 1997 Doctrine envisaged the use of nuclear weapons if there was a threat to the very existence of the RF as a sovereign state, the new doctrine envisages the use of a first strike when all other means to settle a crisis have been exhausted or proven ineffective, but does not specify that the RF must be threatened. The 2000 Doctrine is also much cooler in its language towards the West than the 1997 Doctrine: the 1997 Doctrine's statement of the importance of Russia's 'partnership' with the West is replaced by the importance of 'cooperation' with the West.

The new Foreign Policy Concept (July 2000) describes Russia's geopolitical position as the largest Eurasian power with a responsibility to maintain world security at global and regional levels (see Box 10.7). The Concept continues Primakov's advocacy of a multi-polar system of international relations and commits Russia to conduct bilateral foreign policy activities with individual countries and complementary activities within multinational frameworks such

---

BOX 10.7

The general provisions of Russia's new Foreign Policy Concept, announced by Foreign Minister Igor Ivanov, 10 July 2000

The highest priority for Russia's foreign policy is to protect the interests of the individual, society and the state. Within the framework of this process, the principal efforts must be directed toward achieving the following basic goals:

- ensuring the continuing security of our country, preserving and strengthening its sovereignty and territorial integrity, and maintaining and enhancing strong and authoritative positions in the world community that best serve the interests of the Russian Federation as a great power and a centre of influence in today's world – positions that are essential to the growth of its political, economic, intellectual and spiritual potential;

- influencing world processes with the aim of forming a stable, just and democratic world order that is based on the generally accepted norms of international law, including, first and foremost, the goals and principles of the UN Charter, and on equal partnership relations among states;

- creating favourable external conditions for Russia's continuing development, its economic progress, the improvement of its people's living standards, its successful implementation of democratic reforms, the strengthening of its constitutional order, and the protection of human rights and freedoms;

- establishing a ring of good-neighbourly relations with the states along Russia's borders and working towards the elimination of existing sources of tension and conflict and the prevention of new ones from arising in the regions bordering the Russian Federation;

- seeking accord and a commonality of interests with foreign countries and international organisations in pursuit of the objectives dictated by Russia's national priorities, and building, on that basis, partnerships and alliances that will improve the condition and scope of international cooperation;

- comprehensively protecting the rights and interests of Russian citizens and compatriots living abroad;

- promoting a positive perception of the Russian Federation in the world, and popularising the Russian language and the culture of Russia's peoples in foreign countries.

Source: Nezavisimaia gazeta, 11 July 2000, 1.

as the UN or regional alliances such as the OSCE. The Concept states that only by active cooperation with Europe, USA, China, India and other power centres will it be possible for Russia to uphold its interests. It condemns reliance on specifically western institutions and forums which have limited memberships, for the resolution of fundamental problems of international security. Russia continues to champion the UN, which it believes needs to be reformed so that it can respond quickly and effectively to crises around the world. Russia also believes that the UN Security Council should bear the principal responsibility for maintaining international peace and security and that it needs to be made more representative by introducing new permanent members from amongst the developing states. Putin and Ivanov maintain that peace and security will only be secured through the recognition of international interdependence and respect for the sovereign equality of all countries. They oppose what they see as US endeavours to refashion international laws through concepts such as 'limited sovereignty' and 'humanitarian intervention', which were used to justify NATO military operations in the Balkans and to bypass the UN Security Council. While stressing the role of the UN the Concept still advocates the creation of an all-European security and cooperation system based on the OSCE and the European Council. Russia also wants the CFE to be transformed into an effective instrument to maintain European security. The Concept also states Russia's continuing commitment to deepen integration in the world economy in order to boost Russia's economic potential and to advance Russia's domestic agenda (see also Chapter 11). While Russia is actively pursuing new allies throughout the world and taking a robust stance in its relations with the West, its continuing need for western economic aid means that the West will be able to exercise some leverage over Russian foreign policy.

Conclusion

Russia has travelled a long way from its westernising domestic and foreign agenda of the early 1990s. This does not mean that Russia has reverted to some kind of knee-jerk anti-westernism as a result of the lingering soviet legacy or a resurgent, retrograde Russian nationalism. Certainly, Yeltsin increasingly used the language of Russian nationalism in order to define Russian interests, but all governments claim to be promoting the best interests of their country. At no point has Russia defined the West in general, or the USA in particular, as 'the enemy'. Russia has challenged the USA's concept of the new world order, championed multi-polarity and, much to the alarm of its neighbours, asserted its right to establish and maintain stability around its borders. President Putin also uses the language of Russian nationalism and his statements are very assertive of Russia's needs and interests, but he also wants to integrate Russia into the world economy and for Russia to become more open than before. During 2000 Putin showed his commitment to Russia as a great power, with world, not just regional, interests, by paying official visits to Asian and European countries.

References

Buszynski, Leszek (1995) 'Russia and the West: Towards Renewed Geopolitical Rivalry?', *Survival* 37 (3) Autumn, 104–125

Hearst, David (1996) 'How the East was Won – and Lost', *The Guardian*, 19 October, 21

Ivanov, O. and Pozdnyakov, V. (1998) 'Russia and the European Union', *International Affairs* (Moscow) 44 (3), 49–55

Lloyd, John (1998) *Rebirth of a Nation: An Anatomy of Russia*, London: Michael Joseph

NATO (1997) 'Founding Act on Mutual Relations, Cooperation and Security between NATO and the Russian Federation', http://www.NATO.int/docu/
NUPI (1999) 'Russia Updates Military Doctrine', 11 October, http://www.nupi.no/cgi-win/Russland/

Solzhenitsyn, Aleksandr (1995) *The Russian Question at the End of the 20th Century*, London: Harvill Press
Stankevich, Sergei (1992) 'Russia in Search of Itself', *The National Interest* (28) Summer, 47–51
Stankevich, Sergei (1993) 'Rossiia: mezhdu aziatskim molotom i evropeiskoi nakoval'nei', *Rossiiskoe Obozrenie* (6) 8 September, 1–2

Zhirinovsky, Vladimir (1993) *Poslednii brosok na iug*, Moscow: LPD
Zyuganov, G.A. and Podberezin, A.I. (eds) (1995) *Rossiia pered vyborom*, Moscow: Obozrevatel'

Further reading

On the end of the Cold War see:

Deudney, D. and Ikenberry, G.J. (1992) 'Who Won the Cold War?', *Foreign Policy* (87), 123–38
Gaddis, J.L. (1992) *The United States and the End of the Cold War*, New York: Oxford University Press
Garthoff, R.L. (1994) *The Great Transition: American–Soviet Relations and the End of the Cold War*, Washington, DC: Brookings

For an authoritative analysis of American foreign policy see:

Dumbrell, John (1997) *American Foreign Policy: Carter to Clinton*, Basingstoke: Macmillan

A thorough introduction to Russian foriegn policy is provided in:

Shearman, P. (ed.) (1995) *Russian Foreign Policy since 1990*, Boulder, CO: Westview Press

Contending view of Russia's place in the world and on Russian–American relations are provided by:

Brzezinski, Zbigniew (1994) 'The Premature Partnership', *Foreign Affairs* 73 (2) March–April, 67–82

Brzezinski, Zbigniew (1997) 'A Geostrategy for Eurasia', *Foreign Affairs* 76 (5) September–October, 50–64

Galeotti, Mark (1995) *The Age of Anxiety: Security and Politics in Soviet and Post Soviet Russia*, London: Longman, provides a clear account of the Russia's security and foreign policy concerns in the early 1990s

Garthoff, Raymond L. (1997) 'The United States and the New Russia: The First Five Years', *Current History* 96 (612) October, 305–312, a useful overview of US–Russian relations

Kozyrev, Andrei (1994) 'The Lagging Partnership', *Foreign Affairs* 73 (3) May–June, 59–71

Pipes, Richard (1997) 'Is Russia Still an Enemy?', *Foreign Affairs* 76 (5) September–October, 65–78

'The Case against Nato Expansion', *Current History* 97 (617) March, 132–136

Wallander, Celeste A. (2000) 'Russia's New Security Policy and the Ballistic Missile Defence Debate', *Current History* 99 (639) October, 339–344, provides a useful introduction to security and defence issues under Putin

For Russia relations with the CIS and the other former soviet republics see:

Webber, Mark (1996) *The International Politics of Russia and the Successor States*, Manchester: Manchester University Press

Websites

http://www.mid.ru (Russian Foreign Ministry)
http://www.europa.eu.int/index-en.htm (European Union)
http://www.weu.int (Western European Union)
http://www.osce.org/ (OSCE)
http://www.nato.int/ (NATO)
http://www.nupi.no/ (NUPI Centre for Russian Studies, provides English translations of key documents such as the Military Doctrine and the National Security Doctrine)

CHAPTER 11

Reforming the economy

This chapter examines Russia's initial conditions and the development of its pro-western team of liberal economic policy makers. The components of shock therapy, their sequencing, interrelationship and speed of introduction, are discussed, together with the missing dimension of microeconomic reform. The abandonment of shock therapy and the continuing contradictory pulls of centrist and liberal approaches to the economy under Chernomyrdin, in response to the 1998 economic crisis and under President Putin are also examined.

Introduction

President Yeltsin did not understand economics, but he did like seemingly simple solutions to complex problems. A team of young, liberal economists headed by Igor Gaidar provided Yeltsin with the magic formula to transform Russia from a centrally planned economy (CPE) to capitalism at breakneck speed. In January 1992 the Russian government introduced a programme of shock therapy combining price and trade liberalisation with measures aimed at macroeconomic stabilisation. The CPE had destroyed Russia's capitalist institutions and so shock therapy was introduced into a country without commercial banks, stock exchanges, a labour market, an adequate distribution system, trained managers and accountants, appropriate taxation regulations and an adequate legal framework for a market economy. In addition, although private trade was first partially legalised in 1987, there was a lingering, general wariness of entrepreneurial activity. Decades of soviet condemnation of capitalist exploitation, the illegality of the soviet second or shadow economy and the corruption enveloping the new cooperatives during Reconstruction (see Chapter 2) meant that entrepreneurial activity had a rather disreputable image. Gaidar believed that macroeconomic reform would stimulate micro-economic reform and restructuring, so that appropriate laws would be passed as needed, individuals would be encouraged to acquire new skills and engage in new kinds of activities, and enterprises would restructure in order to survive in the market. Gaidar was an admirer of monetarist economists such as Milton Friedman and the economic policies pursued by the US president Reagan and UK prime minister Margaret Thatcher. If one considers that Thatcher took a decade to privatise just 5 per cent of the UK economy, in a country that already had well-established capitalist institutions and behaviour, then the colossal scale and rapidity but also the lack of institutional under-pinning of Russia's reform become even clearer.

Russia's reforms have also involved opening the economy to external influences on a scale unprecedented in Russian or soviet history. While the soviet economy was in its self-imposed, semi-isolation from the capitalist world, the capitalist world economy had changed. At the end of World War II new institutions had been established to manage the global capitalist system. These include the World Bank, the IMF and the General Agreement on Tariffs and Trade (GATT), which in 1995 was superseded by the World Trade Organisation (WTO). These institutions promote a liberal agenda which stresses the importance of freeing markets and reducing the role of national governments within their economies. In 1991–2 Gaidar enthusiastically accepted the advice of the IMF-appointed economist Jeffrey Sachs. In return for introducing shock therapy the Russian government anticipated IMF loans and help with debt rescheduling.

From RSFSR to RF: the initial conditions

The economic structure

In 1991 Russian reformers inherited an economy that had already experienced a long period of stagnation followed by the disruption of half-hearted market reforms under Gorbachev (see Chapter 2). As the USSR hurtled towards disintegration and the CPE teetered on the brink of collapse, its GNP in 1991 dropped by 13–15 per cent. The soviet economy was dominated by techno-logically outdated, inefficient and ecologically destructive heavy industry. Agriculture, light industry and the service sector were poorly developed. For decades the soviet state had directed a disproportionate amount of investment into its gigantic military-industrial complexes, heavy industry, machine build-ing, extraction and metallurgical industries. Even these favoured sectors of the economy were plagued by a growing technology gap with the West, and to this day are unable to match the quality of foreign-made products (see Box 11.1). Russia is rich in uranium, gold, diamonds, and also has 13 per cent of the world's oil and 26 per cent of its natural gas reserves (*The Guardian*, 27 March 2000: 18). Unfortunately, by the 1990s, the easily accessible fields had been worked out and considerable new investment is now needed in order to access the more remote fields.

Changing trade patterns

The disintegration of, first, the soviet bloc in East-Central Europe and then the USSR precipitated a change in Russia's trading partners. In June 1991 Comecon was formally abolished and the USSR's former allies made the strategic decision to look to the West for political, military and economic partners. Within the former USSR the Baltic states similarly oriented themselves towards the West, while the new Central Asian states have increasingly looked towards the Middle East, Turkey, Iran and Pakistan. In addition to these strategic decisions, economic restructuring in all the former CPEs was bound to lead to a restructuring of trade relations. In the soviet period trade decisions served the CPSU's political, military and economic aims, but trade has become increasingly decentralised and liberalised. The result of these developments is that in 1990–1 trade within the former soviet bloc collapsed by two-thirds (Åslund, 1992: 48). Russian exports to the former Comecon countries fell by around 60 per cent and imports from them dropped from $46 billion in 1990 to $14 billion in 1991 (Frydman *et al.*, 1993: 14). Trade between the former republics of the USSR underwent a similar collapse. In 1990 70 per cent of Russia's exports worth $157 billion had been to the other soviet republics, but the following year this fell to $142 billion. Russian imports from the other former soviet republics also fell from $129 billion to $99 billion (*ibid.*).

Government spending and hidden inflation

The soviet legacy included expectations that the government would provide subsidies to industry and fund extensive welfare provisions. The collapse of soviet industry therefore created even greater demands upon the government budget. During the 'Law Wars' between the RSFSR and the USSR (see Chapter 2) Yeltsin made specific promises to raise wages and pensions, and reduce taxes, which further increased demands upon the budget. The result was that in 1991 Russia had a budget deficit that was equivalent to 31.9 per cent of GDP and there was already considerable hidden inflation (Illarionov cited by Hedlund, 1999: 153). Following the collapse of the USSR, Russia's ability to control its money supply was also compromised by the activities of the other former soviet republics. Although the republics established their own central banks they initially still used the Russian rouble as their currency. When the countries of the rouble zone issued credits to keep their enterprises afloat, it was the Russian Central Bank that was called upon to print more roubles. In

1991–2 Russia's money supply was growing rapidly, leading to further inflationary pressures.

Russian debt

Sachs believed that western economic aid, external debt forgiveness and new loans were essential to help the CPEs become capitalist market economies. Following Sachs's advice, the Polish government introduced shock therapy and its soviet-era debt was written off. In October 1991 Yeltsin announced to parliament that shock therapy would be introduced in January 1992, but Russia's inherited external debt has not been forgiven. Sachs has described this lack of debt forgiveness as the West's 'betrayal' of Russia (Sachs, 1994: 15) and Richard Layard and John Parker (1996: 83) are equally scathing about the G7 decision to send in the 'debt collectors' in November 1991. That month David Mulford, US Treasury undersecretary for international affairs, arrived in Moscow at the head of a G7 mission and in December 1991 Russia agreed to assume responsibility for 61 per cent of the USSR's external debt worth $37.2 billion. The debt service both on the repayment of the principal (the original sum borrowed) and on the interest was estimated at $12.3 billion for 1992 alone (Frydman *et al.*, 1993: 14). The G7 countries insisted that Russia must service the debt until a rescheduling agreement could be worked out, but in December 1991 Russia suspended payments claiming that it simply did not

---

BOX 11.1

Economic terms

- *economic structure* – the share of the different sectors (agriculture, industry and services) within an economy
- *market* – a system of exchange in which buyers' demands interact with the sellers' supply; the existence of a market is a prerequisite of capitalism, but markets may also exist in socialist systems
- *free market* – exists when the interactions between buyers and sellers are not subject to external interventions such as the government setting minimum or maximum prices or by the operation of cartels or monopolies
- *market forces* – these are principally supply and demand which determine the prices and the quantities bought and sold
- *inflation* – exists when a sustained rise in the prices of goods and or services reduces the buying power of a currency
- *hyperinflation* – inflation over 50 per cent a month
- *monetarism* – the advocacy of control of the money supply in order to control inflation
- *money supply* – the amount of money within an economy

have enough dollars to cover the payments. In a letter to the *New York Times* on 4 July 1992, Sachs revealed that although in 1990–1 Russia had received $15.6 billion in western aid, $13.1 billion of that sum had been used to service Russia's debt. The result was that most of the western aid that reached Russia was simply returning to the West as debt repayments, and was not available for investment within the Russian economy. By 1993 Russia's external debt stood at around $80 billion and the debt service in 1994 was expected to reach $15 billion (Goldman, 1996: 115).

From Yavlinsky's gradualism to Gaidar's shock therapy

In 1990 Grigory Yavlinsky and Stanislav Shatalin had worked with Sachs on a radical 500-day economic programme that was designed to change the USSR into a market economy. Although Gorbachev rejected the programme for the USSR Yeltsin adopted it for the RSFSR, but given the disorder and confusion of the times very little was achieved. Following the August 1991 coup Yavlinsky was appointed to the commission charged with drawing up a new economic programme for Russia. He proposed a continuation of the 'Grand Bargain' ideas (see Chapter 2) and believed that Russia's transition to a market economy would take until 1997. Devising an economic programme also entailed putting Yeltsin's election slogan 'Russia First' into practice, but quite how this could be achieved without precipitating even further economic dislocation proved highly contentious. Yavlinsky argued that following decades of central planning, the economies of the 15 former soviet republics were so integrated that some union structures would have to be retained (Hedlund, 1999: 148–9). In contrast, Yeltsin wanted a programme that would transform Russia as quickly as possible and release it from any residual soviet-era constraints and responsibilities. Yeltsin dropped Yavlinsky in favour of the liberal economist Igor Gaidar, who only joined Yeltsin's circle after going to the White House during the August 1991 coup. Gaidar was supported by Yeltsin's influential aide Gennady Burbulis, who after the coup provided Gaidar and his team with a government dacha where they worked on their plan for an independent Russian economy. Gaidar advocated a programme of shock therapy that would take just six months to kick-start Russia's transition from a CPE to a market economy. Gaidar also believed that all remaining union structures should be dismantled. These ideas were exactly what Yeltsin wanted to hear and so it was Gaidar and his team who wrote the economic part of Yeltsin's opening speech to the Russian parliament in October 1991, in which which he announced shock therapy.

The development of 'Gaidar's gang'

Gaidar's team were erudite, spoke foreign languages and were well-versed in the theories of the western liberal economists that they admired. They had no practical experience but did have a wealth of self-confidence and an unwavering belief in the correctness of their ideas. In contrast to the old men who had dominated the soviet scene they were also very young, typically only in their early thirties. Their youth and do or die approach earned them the nickname Gaidar's gang, after the popular soviet children's book *Timur and his Gang* written by Gaidar's grandfather. Gaidar's gang had not worked on the various soviet economic reform programmes designed by Aganbegyan, Shatalin, Petrakov, Abalkin and Yavlinsky. Instead they had spent the 1980s in covert, informal, radical but theoretical discussions about how to transform a CPE into a western-style, capitalist economy. As Reconstruction progressed, these discussions gradually became more open and in 1990 Gaidar was able to establish an unofficial think-tank called the Institute of Market Reform. By the late 1980s Gaidar's gang also had increasing contacts with like-minded soviet bloc economists such as Janos Kornai from Hungary, Vaclav Klaus from Czechoslovakia and Leszek Balcerowicz from Poland. Following the 1989 revolutions the former soviet bloc countries finally abandoned the constraints of the soviet economic model and began their transition to capitalism. In Poland Jeffrey Sachs worked with Leszek Balcerowicz, who was the new finance minister, to formulate an economic programme that became known as the Balcerowicz Plan, which was implemented in January 1990. To Russia's radical economic reformers the Balcerowicz Plan's shock therapy provided a ready-made, tried and tested programme to transform a CPE into a capitalist economy.

The Russian government's economic team

In November 1991, despite opposition from the Russian parliament (see Chapter 4), Yeltsin appointed the leading members of Gaidar's gang to key economic positions within the government. Gaidar was appointed finance minister and Alexander Shokhin a deputy prime minister with responsibility for social affairs, Vladimir Lopukhin became energy minister (a post he lost to Chernomyrdin in 1992), Pyotr Aven became foreign trade minister and Anatoly Chubais became the head of the State Property Committee (GKI), which was established in October 1992 to supervise privatisation. In April 1992 Gaidar also brought in Andrei Illarionov as the first deputy director of the government's Working Centre for Economic Reforms. Then in June 1992 Gaidar became acting prime minister with responsibility for economic affairs and Anatoly Chubais was promoted to one of the deputy prime minister posts. Yeltsin also acquired a growing number of western economic advisers who included Jeffrey Sachs, Anders Åslund, the director of the Stockholm Institute of East European Economics at the Stockholm School of Economics, and the British economist Professor Richard Layard of the London School of Economics, who had advised Thatcher.

Shock therapy, 1992–1993

The pace and sequencing of reform: shock therapy or big bang

Drawing on the Balcerowicz Plan, the Russian government introduced shock therapy or the big bang (see Box 11.2). A slower or gradualist approach was specifically rejected in the belief that it would only create a mismatched hybrid economy in which the remnants of the CPE would undermine and frustrate the market reforms, and allow the communist elites to retain too much power (see also Chapter 1). Sachs advised that shock therapy should begin with price and trade liberalisation combined with macroeconomic stabilisation focusing on control of the money supply. On 2 January 1992 foreign trade was liberalised together with 80 per cent of domestic prices. Trade was duly liberalised later that month and the streets were immediately full of people selling handicrafts, household possessions, imported goods and reselling goods bought in state stores. After the shortages of the soviet era suddenly everything was for sale, but industrial and agricultural production continued to decline. The future prime minister Chernomyrdin dismissed the economic reforms as having turned Russia into a gigantic bazaar.

Macroeconomic stabilisation

The financial strategy of the G7, IMF, World Bank and therefore Gaidar put inflation as the greatest enemy of economic stability and growth. It was feared that high levels of inflation would distort all the signals within the economy and undermine popular support for Yeltsin's leadership, and therefore the value of the rouble had to be stabilised. Gaidar anticipated that price liberalisation would lead to an initial surge in inflation, but that this would stabilise along with prices after 3–5 months. In reality the first month of price liberalisation led to hyperinflation of 460 per cent, which was followed by monthly inflation rates of 20–25 per cent. The inflation rate for 1992 was a staggering 2600 per cent (Lane and Ross, 1995: 12). In order to stabilise the rouble the government needed to control the money supply which in turn entailed cutting government spending and balancing the budget. Controlling the money supply was made more difficult when under pressure from the centrists in parliament, Viktor Gerashchenko was appointed in July 1992 to head the Russian Central Bank. Viktor Gerashchenko had headed the Central Bank under Gorbachev, opposed shock therapy and rejected the IMF equation that printing money that was not justified by the country's productive capacities would fuel inflation. Gerashchenko believed that without subsidies Russian enterprises would simply collapse causing untold misery for millions. He also supported emergency winter aid, particularly to those living in the Arctic and Siberia who were in danger of freezing or starving to death. In

BOX 11.2

The main components of shock therapy

- *macroeconomic stabilisation (or adjustment)* – controlling inflation and stabilising the value of the currency, it also entails balancing the budget and the balance of payments

- *balance of payments* – the balance between a country's international spending and earnings

- *price liberalisation* – abandoning the state's setting of prices and allowing market forces (supply and demand) to determine prices

- *trade liberalisation* – removing barriers to trade such as trade restrictions, import or export quotas and tariffs

- *currency convertibility* – the free exchange of one currency for another

- *privatisation* – a form of institutional reform, ending the state ownership of economic concerns and replacing it with private ownership by individuals, companies, investment groups

- *enterprise restructuring* – entails a variety of reforms which include breaking up enterprises into economically viable units, reducing the labour force, retraining workers and management and bringing in new management techniques

- *structural-institutional reforms* – the reforms necessary to establish a market economy, including legal reforms, anti-monopoly regulations, changes to the taxation system, establishing new accounting systems, the development of new pro-market attitudes

the first quarter after Gerashchenko's appointment, the money supply tripled. Throughout 1993 Gerashchenko and the finance minister Boris Fyodorov, who had wanted to chair the Russian Central Bank himself, were in constant conflict over the failure to control the money supply.

Foreign trade liberalisation, currency convertibility and capital flight

In the early 1990s in return for support from the IMF, Russia committed itself to trade liberalisation which entailed the eventual removal of quotas, licences and other bureaucratic restrictions on the free movement of goods, services and capital. It was anticipated that liberalisation would provide farms and enterprises with the stimulus to restructure, and that it would help to bring in capital, new ideas and techniques. Despite the IMF–WTO's championing of free trade, the EU and the North American Free Trade Association (NAFTA) erected barriers to imports from non-members. So neither were the world's markets open for Russia to conquer nor were Russian producers in any fit condition to meet competition within their own domestic markets, let alone conduct an export drive. The exceptions to this somewhat bleak picture are the oil and gas sectors, which dominated soviet exports and continue to dominate

Russian exports. Russia has a comparative advantage in raw materials such as oil, gas, gold, diamonds, other minerals and timber products, which the western industrialised countries are eager to buy. The export of raw materials raises important security issues and concerns about Russia's 'Third Worldisation' as 'a semi colony, raw material source of the world economy' (Rutkevich, 1998: 10). The Russian government maintains strict controls over crude oil exports and uses export licences, taxes and quotas to ensure that oil is available to the domestic market at below world prices. It has also maintained centralised control over the sale of arms and defence-related equipment (Gregory and Stuart, 1998: 393–4), although organised gangs have been extremely active in the illegal export of weapons and uranium. In 1996 the Russian government moved to protect sectors of the economy that had been hard hit by competition from imports. Agriculture has found it difficult to compete with EU agricultural products which are subsidised through the common agricultural policy (CAP). In 1996 the Russian government introduced import quotas on agricultural commodities and then import taxes were increased and extended to cover commodities such as textiles that had previously been tax free. Some 40 per cent of Russian trade is with Europe, making the EU Russia's largest trading partner, and 5 per cent of Russia's trade is with the USA (*The Guardian*, 1 October 1998: 1). A considerable but under-recorded amount of trade is also conducted with Russia's neighbours such as China, Turkey, Iran and East-Central Europe by the shuttle traders. The shuttlers tend to import textiles, clothing and manufactured goods and try to avoid attracting the attention of customs officials and tax men.

In July 1992 Yeltsin, under IMF prompting, stated that the rouble would become a convertible currency, which could be freely traded on the international money markets. The first step towards convertibility had been taken on 2 January 1992 when it became legal within Russia to buy foreign currency at the market prices. This, in effect, meant that the rouble was convertible but only within Russia itself. The immediate result was to undermine the stabilisation of the rouble as it plummeted from the official, but greatly overvalued exchange rate of 0.6 of a rouble to the US dollar, to 100 roubles to the dollar. The continuing difficulties in stabilising the rouble and the growing problem of capital flight which have depleted Russia's foreign currency reserves have contributed to the seemly indefinite postponement of currency convertibility. Yeltsin's first decree on currency liberalisation in November 1991 required Russians to sell a percentage of any foreign currency earning they may make to the Russian Central Bank at the official exchange rate. The required percentage has since varied according to the government need for foreign currency, but in July 1992 was raised to a staggering 30 per cent. Exporters see this requirement as an export tax by another name and have responded by variously attempting to conceal their foreign exchange earnings, concluding barter deals or simply keeping or sending their earnings abroad. In his 1995 state of the nation address Yeltsin explained the problem of capital flight as partially due to administrative problems such as the failure to establish strict customs, banking and currency controls but also that Russia was not an attractive place for investors (*Rossiiskie vesti*, 17 February 1995: 3). The result is that between mid-1994 and the beginning of 1998 a total $80 billion left Russia (Hawkins *et al.*, 1998: 11). According to Yevgeny Gavrilenko of the Bureau of Economic Analysis in Moscow, a major problem is that 'the Russian economy is open at the exit points and remains fairly closed at the entry points' (cited by Elliott, 2000: 15). Money leaves Russia but it does not readily enter. Currency convertibility would greatly facilitate foreign trade but as yet the government believes the rouble is too vulnerable to be subjected to the vagaries and predation of the international financial markets.

Microeconomic reform: delayed institutional reforms

Russia's shock therapists and their IMF advisers believed that macroeconomic stabilisation should precede microeconomic or structural reforms. Macroeconomic stabilisation would create an environment in which market-oriented institutions would more or less automatically develop. Macroeconomic stability would create the conditions in which it was possible to make informed and rational economic decisions and so encourage entrepreneurial behaviour. These new entrepreneurs would then create new businesses, set up new banks and stock exchanges, and demand new laws. Shock therapy was introduced into an economy which lacked the basic capitalist institutions of property, shareholder, bankruptcy, anti-monopoly and commercial laws. It also lacked capital markets, stock exchanges and a commercial banking system and the tax system needed to be completely revised. The 1993 Constitution provided Russia with a general legal framework for its market economy (see Arts 8, 9, 35, 36 and 37), by recognising both private property rights and the right to engage freely in economic activity. These rights were then enshrined in the new Civil Code passed in November 1994 and gradually more specialised laws have been passed. To this day, however, property rights are inadequately protected and it is still difficult to enforce contracts. The criminal and the corrupt are still able to exploit the legal confusion or vacuum in which so much economic activity is conducted. Passing appropriate laws has proved a time-consuming and complex process and their implementation is frustrated by the weakness of the judiciary and the state's law enforcement agencies (see Chapter 6).

The delay in microeconomic reform has undermined macroeconomic stabilisation. For example, in June 1995 a Federal Anti-Monopoly Commission was created to enforce the new anti-monopoly law. But by 1995 enormous individual fortunes had already been made from Russia's monopolies and great tranches of the country's wealth had already been spirited abroad, so denying Russia the capital that would have helped to stabilise the rouble and promote economic development. The banking system also suffered from a dearth of relevant regulations and a laxity in the application of the regulations that do exist. The Russian Central Bank is responsible for registering, licensing and monitoring new banks, but as new commercial banks have emerged they have tended to concentrate on currency speculation. This has contributed to a general air of instability and criminality that surrounds so much of Russia's emerging banking system. Even the long-established state-owned Russian Savings Bank (Sberbank) has found it difficult to persuade the ordinary Russians who have traditionally kept their savings with the bank, that it is stable and safe. The result is that many Russians prefer to keep their money, preferably converted into a stable currency such as the US dollar, at home. These savings evade tax and are not available for commercial investment. The 1998 economic crisis led to the closure of many banks.

Microeconomic reform: the missing enterprise restructuring

In the early 1990s Yavlinsky argued that macroeconomic stabilisation, far from creating the necessary conditions for microeconomic restructuring, would itself prove elusive without some preliminary microeconomic restructuring. For example, as soviet enterprises were gigantic often monopolistic or near monopolistic concerns, when prices were liberalised the absence of competition meant they simply put up their prices without having to improve their production or productivity. Prices rose dramatically, fuelling inflation and undermining macroeconomic stabilisation. Guy Standing of the ILO similarly argues that in early 1992 while Yeltsin still enjoyed popular support and the soviet directors and their political allies were on the defensive, he should have grasped the opportunity to break up Russia's gigantic enterprises. According to Standing the failure to do so was 'a failure of monumental proportions' (Standing, 1996: 6).

Prior to privatisation enterprises were required to transform themselves into joint stock companies, but this was largely a paper exercise that made no change to how enterprises were managed and organised. There was no general attempt to restructure enterprises such as through the closure of their loss-making sections. This would have enabled an enterprise to concentrate on the potentially salvageable parts of its operation so making it more attractive to investors. It was assumed that the combination of privatisation and marketisation would force enterprises to restructure, but this has not proved the case. Russia's economic development continues to be held back by the survival of the gigantic soviet industrial dinosaurs. Russia needs more small and medium size enterprises to provide greater flexibility within its economy, but so far these are a negligible component of its industrial and agricultural production capacities.

Voucher privatisation, October 1992–June 1994

The privatisation of state enterprises was both an important microeconomic reform and an attempt to generate popular support for the economic reforms.

Anatoly Chubais, the chair of the State Property Committee (GKI), introduced a modified form of the voucher privatisation scheme that had been introduced in Czechoslovakia in 1990. In autumn 1992 Russian adults were issued with 10 000 roubles worth of vouchers which were worth the equivalent of $20. Some 90 per cent of adults collected their vouchers, which they could then use to buy shares at auction or invest in mutual funds. Many of these funds turned out to be sham financial pyramid schemes that eventually collapsed (see Chapter 9 on the MMM fund). Stock exchanges only gradually developed, but mostly after rather than before privatisation. Nearly 75 per cent of enterprises opted for a worker buy-out model of privatisation, through which workers had special access to 51 per cent of the shares and a minimum of only 29 per cent of shares had to be sold to outsiders for vouchers. In this way most privatisation was conducted as a form of insider (management and worker) privatisation, which kept the existing management in place and maintained the status quo in management–worker relations. By the end of 1993 45 per cent of enterprises had been privatised and by 1996 this figure had risen to 70 per cent. Under a December 1991 presidential decree the privatisation of shops and cafés was the responsibility of the municipal authorities. The city of Nizhnii Novgorod under Boris Nemtsov, which has been hailed as one of the most successful and go-ahead examples of economic reform, was the first city to privatise its retail outlets. In April 1992 the shops and cafés of Nizhnii Novgorod were auctioned for cash. Throughout Russia some 60 per cent of shops and cafés had been privatised by August 1992 either through auctions or by direct sale to the retail management and workers.

Privatisation, corporate management and demonetarisation

The privatisation of state enterprises was supposed to initiate a change not just in their ownership but also in their structures, organisation and management. In most cases privatisation has not brought any new skills or know-how into an enterprise; the same management teams remain in place and behave as before. They still provide social and welfare facilities, have shied away from sacking staff and continue to expect subsidies or at least cheap credits from the government. Enterprises are also slow to pay each other, which has led to a growing problem of inter-enterprise debt and there is a growing problem of demonetarisation within the Russian economy. Workers are paid in the goods they produce and enterprises trade with each other using various forms of barter. The lack of investment money, the instability of the rouble, and the desire to avoid the attention of the tax collectors or the police have all contributed to a situation in which a large part of economic activity is conducted outside the official money economy. This shadow economy is variously estimated as anywhere between a quarter to a half of all Russia's economic activity (Phillips, 2000: 129). Direct foreign investment into Russia remains negligible in the face of political instability, crime and corruption, the uncertain legal environment, the complex tax system and Russia's continuing poor international credit rating. There have been some moves to support enterprise restructuring by western governments. US President Clinton created the US–Russian Investment Fund chaired by Michael Blumenthal with a $440 million budget to help existing enterprises and create new businesses. The British government provides advice and some funding to help restructure existing businesses and set up new ones through its Know How Fund.

The coming Russian boom and the 1998 crisis

The rise of the centrists

Throughout 1992 and into 1993 opposition to shock therapy and Yeltsin's leadership began to mount. In 1993 production fell by 25 per cent compared to 1992 and enterprise debt stood at 30 trillion roubles (Lloyd, 1998: 57). Gaidar was sacrificed as prime minister in December 1992 and replaced by Chernomyrdin, but this did not mean that liberal policies were immediately abandoned in favour of more centrist policies. Even at the height of the liberals' influence in 1991–2 they had never managed to dominate economic policy completely, as was shown by perpetual struggle with Gerashchenko over the control of the money supply. Andrei Illarionov later complained that Russia could have been a textbook example of economic liberalism if only the Yeltsin government had continued the reforms begun on 2 January 1992. Despite Gaidar's ouster, the liberals were not completely removed from government, neither was the liberal approach to the economy entirely abandoned even after the December 1993 Duma elections. Chubais retained his post as head of the GKI and Boris Fyodorov returned from a senior executive post at EBRD in London to become Yeltsin's chief economic strategist as deputy prime minister for finance and economic policy (March 1993–October 1994). Rather than liberal economics being abandoned in favour of a centrist approach, it is more accurate to think in terms of the balance of economic policy shifting towards the centrists.

The centrists are typically industrial enterprise managers who enjoyed the greater autonomy and control over their enterprises that they had acquired under Gorbachev, but were alarmed by what they perceived as a lack of state support for industry under Yeltsin. In mid-1992 the leading centrist, Arkady Volsky, brought together his Russian Union of Industrialists and Entrepreneurs (RUIE) and other centrist parties, including the Democratic Party and the People's Party of Free Russia (the heir to Rutskoi's Democratic Communists), to form a new political party called the Civic Union. The centrists are believers in a strong state (*gosudarstvenniki*) which immediately puts them at odds with the economic liberals' Washington consensus ideas on the desirability of a minimal role for the state (see Chapter 1). For the centrists the state needs to be strong to protect Russian interests in the global arena and to counter the centrifugal forces within Russia itself. They also believe that the state should maintain subsidies and provide soft credits to enterprises and reduce their tax burdens, to prevent them from going bankrupt and to maintain high levels of employment. In what might initially seem a strange alliance but one that makes perfect sense in the Russian industrial environment, the managers' organisation the RUIE worked closely with the new Federation of Independent Trade Unions (FNPR) in order to lobby for the maintenance of real wage levels, state support for industry and extensive welfare provision. The centrists also believe that Russia should have a strong military and that the defence industries should receive state protection and support. So while Yury Skokov was the chair of the Security Council, true to his centrist orientation he lobbied hard for the maintenance of defence spending and subsidies for the defence industries, despite the fact that he was a Yeltsin appointment and ally going back to his Sverdlovsk days.

Viktor Chernomyrdin and the coming Russian boom

The new prime minister, Viktor Chernomyrdin, projected himself to the G7 and IMF as a responsible custodian of the economy, and persuaded them that Russia was serious about reform and that the IMF should continue to support Russia (see Box 11.3). He was also able to overcome the West's reservations about supporting Russia while it was conducting a war against Chechnia (1994–6). Although Chernomyrdin came to power as a representative of the energy lobby with a centrist orientation, as prime minister (1992–8) he pursued a pragmatic combination of liberal commitment to market reforms and centrist policies. In October 1994 Russia suffered a major financial crisis when the rouble lost 20–27 per cent of its value in one day. This precipitated the sackings of Gerashchenko, the chair of the Russian Central Bank, Sergei Dubynin, the acting finance minister, and the economics minister Sergei Shokhin. The leading liberal Chubais was appointed a first deputy prime minister in charge of the economy and his ally Tatyana Paramonova became the new chair of the Russian Central Bank. Chernomyrdin now championed a liberal agenda which stressed control of the money supply, balancing the budget and pressing on with privatisation. In return the IMF agreed to provide further loans but insisted that its personnel would monitor Russia's adherence to the economic targets agreed by the IMF and the Russian government. By the end of 1995 inflation had fallen to 3 per cent a month and two years later it was down to 15 per cent a year. At last Russia seemed to have achieved macroeconomic stabilisation, but at the expense of plunging Russians into even greater poverty, as in 1995 real wages fell below even the January 1992 level. Russia's economy seemed set for a boom, but while some economic indicators were very good, the Russian economy was being damaged by

---

BOX 11.3

The coming Russian boom

Inevitably the record is mixed. There are two big successes: Markets have replaced the command economy, and most of industry and trade have been privatized. In four years that is quite an achievement. But high inflation persisted for most of that period, and the financial environment remained unpredictable. During the transition real incomes inevitably fell in line with output, and, since wage inequality increased, some people suffered greatly...

   But perhaps the greatest problem in the economy now is the lack of a clear legal framework, upheld by the courts. Apart from that, Russia is now poised for a sizable economic upsurge. It has natural resources unparalleled in the world, a well-educated work force, and plenty of liquid finance waiting to be invested.

Source: Richard Layard and John Parker (1996) *The Coming Russian Boom: A Guide to New Markets and Politics*, New York: Free Press, 310–11. Richard Layard is a professor at the London School of Economics and John Parker is a former Moscow correspondent of *The Economist*.

---

corruption at all levels, the lack of a sound institutional environment and ill-thought-out government policies.

The collapse in production

Between 1987 and 1996 Russia's GDP fell by 38 per cent (Rutkevich, 1998: 9) and Russia moved from 5th to 14th place in the world economic hierarchy, behind developing countries such as Brazil, India, Mexico and Indonesia. Between 1989 and the 1998 crisis, the Russian economy shrank by 40 per cent. Steel production has fallen by nearly 50 per cent, lorry production by 80 per cent, the production of metal-cutting machines by nearly 90 per cent and electricity generation by more than 20 per cent. These general figures mask the dramatic collapse of production in certain regions. In the heavily industrialised area of Eastern Siberia industrial output is now only 10 per cent of its soviet level (Atkinson *et al.*, 1998: 4). At the beginning of 1997 the State Statistical Committee (Goskomstat) reported positive growth in GDP for the first time since 1989. The reported growth was only 1 per cent but after years of collapse the Russian economy seemed to have at last come out of its downward spiral. Goskomstat's statistics were, however, partly the result of a change in the way the economic data was calculated. Goskomstat had decided to change the estimated contribution of the shadow economy to GDP from 20 to 25 per cent. In the current conditions, which include routine tax avoidance, demonetarisation and capital flight, then it makes sense for individuals and producers to hide or underreport their economic activity. This means that most official Russian statistics are inaccurate and that the collapse of production, while undoubtedly dramatic, has not been quite as bad as the statistics suggest.

Agriculture

In November 1990 the RSFSR abolished the state monopoly on land, approved private agriculture and then in December granted the right to land ownership to anyone who was prepared to work the land for ten years. The gigantic state and collective farms that had dominated Russian agriculture since the 1930s seemed set to disappear, but ten years on Russia has yet to experience a radical change in land ownership. In November 1992 a very limited form of land privatisation allowing the purchase of land for horticultural production or for house building was passed and in July 1995 a new Land Code was introduced. However, the Duma has mounted a stubborn resistance to the privatisation of agricultural land with a right to resale. Without the right of resale the supposed private ownership of land is really a form of leasing. In the face of the continuing impasse at the centre some of Russia's regions have taken the initiative on land privatisation. In 1998 Saratov *oblast* held Russia's first post-communist private land auction with buyers having the right to resale the land. Tatarstan has also followed Saratov's example.

The uncertain legal situation throughout most of Russia, the soviet legacy of environmental degradation and the poorly developed rural infrastructure and food-processing facilities act as major disincentives to the would-be independent farmer. To these have been added new problems, such as the lack of investment money and the rising cost of fertilisers and fuel. Organised crime gangs now control many of Russia's retail outlets and they can either deny an independent farmer an outlet for his/her products or charge a prohibitively high fee for access to the gang's shops and kiosks. Again, the picture is quite regionalised as some regions have begun to reintroduce official price controls and Saratov's land privatisation has been complemented by a system of fairs where growers can sell their produce (Serova, 1999: 8). Overall, the general picture of Russian agriculture is rather bleak. In most areas the state and collective farms struggle on in the revised guise of joint stock companies, state subsidies have been slashed and agricultural production has slumped. The devaluation of the rouble in August 1998 provided a lifeline to Russian agriculture as it made food imports more expensive and has even encouraged some investors to turn their attention to agriculture and the food-processing industries (*ibid.*).

Loans-for-shares privatisation

In the first round of privatisation (1992–4) a lot of the privatised enterprises were so outdated that they had very little real value. In this controversial second round of privatisation (1995–6) the GKI auctioned the state's shares in selected companies in return for cash loans. This privatisation focused on the gigantic coal, gas and electricity monopolies, and on the oil and mineral industries. The oil industry was already divided into a dozen separate companies in which the government had majority stakes. When the loans were not repaid the firms were auctioned so that huge tranches of the country's most valuable assets were sold to Russia's oligarchs and emerging financial-industrial groups at bargain prices. The auctions were characterised by corruption at all stages and at all levels; most of the auctions were won by the bank that was running the auction or by a subsidiary of the company being sold (see Chapter 1 on the privatisation of Norilsk Nikel). When Surgutneftegaz (Surgut Oil and Gas) in Tyumen in Siberia was auctioned, the whole city was effectively closed for the day to prevent their dreaded rivals Rosneft (Russian Oil) from bidding. The airport was closed, telephone lines were cut off and just in case any outsider had managed to slip through, armed guards were put on the doors of the auction building (Lloyd, 1998: 251). In this way Boris Berezovsky acquired Russia's ninth largest oil concern Sibneft for just $100 million. It was during this round of privatisation, conducted in advance of the 1996 presidential elections, that the oligarchs' economic and political power was consolidated and their support for Yeltsin assured (see Chapter 1).

Taxation

Russia has experienced major problems in elaborating new and consistent tax regulations and in collecting taxes. The tax system has gone through a series of changes that have changed it from a profits and turnover based system to one based on VAT, income and excise taxes. Despite these reforms the tax system remains inconsistent and there is also an elaborate maze of tax allowances and reliefs. The tax regulations are subject to varying interpretations and so tax payment has become more a matter of negotiating the best possible deal than paying a clearly calculated sum. By the mid-1990s the IMF made the release of further funds to Russia conditional upon improved tax collection. Chernomyrdin was able to persuade the IMF that he would deal with Russia's taxation collection problems and to this end established the Temporary Extraordinary Committee in October 1996. Paramilitary tax police conducted highly publicised swoops upon recalcitrant tax payers, which also encouraged others to pay their taxes before the tax man came knocking with his Kalashnikov. These changes trebled tax collection between September and December 1996, but the overall total for that year was still only 81.1 per cent of projected revenue (Hedlund, 1999: 225).

The irony is that Chernomyrdin, Chubais (who masterminded Yeltsin's 1996 re-election) and the oligarchs (who had funded Yeltsin's campaign) were and still are amongst the country's most reluctant taxpayers. Chernomyrdin, the head of Russia's largest company, Gazprom, got away with filing a tax return for 1997 claiming earnings of just $8031 (Hawkins et al., 1998: 12). Gazprom owes $600 million in taxes and Chubais's Unified Energy System company (UES) also owes several million dollars in tax (Crace, 1998: 10–11). Some of Russia's largest companies have also benefited from the under-valuation of their assets for tax purposes. In 1997 Boris Berezovsky got away with claiming that his oil, media and banking empire was only worth $40 000. Yeltsin responded to the continuing problem of tax collection and the resulting IMF delay in releasing further tranches of money by sacking the head of the state taxation service, Alexander Pochinok, and arresting head of the Goskomstat, Yury Yurkov, for helping companies to falsify their value and so evade tax. The continuing problems of tax collection reveal the level of corruption that was at the very heart of government under President Yeltsin. It also reveals the continuing impact of the lack of microeconomic reform such as a clear and transparent accountancy system, which would facilitate an accurate assessment of a company's true value and thereby tax collection, while discouraging management theft and corruption.

Russia's international debts

Russia's external debts fall into two main categories. There are official credits provided by other governments and commercial credits which often have government guarantees. The Paris Club represents Russia's governmental creditors and the London Club represents the 600 plus commercial banks that had made loans to the USSR. Russia has repeatedly asked the Paris and London Clubs to reschedule the loans, that is to extend the period of time it has to repay the interest and the original sum (the principal) of the loans. Russia's inability to service these debts is due to a variety of factors, which include its general economic malaise, the failure to collect taxes, and the shortage of foreign exchange which has been exacerbated by capital flight and in 1993–4 by the diversion of funds away from debt repayment to prop up the rouble. Debt repayment has placed a major burden on the state budget and undermined its international credit-worthiness, so exacerbating its lack of investment capital. In April 1996 Chernomyrdin concluded a debt reschedul-ing deal with the Paris Club and in October 1997 with the London Club, which gave Russia a much-needed breathing space and went some way to enhance its commercial credit-worthiness.

State short-term bonds (GKOs)

Beginning quite modestly in 1994 the Treasury and the Ministry of Finance began to finance the state's budget deficit by auctioning short-term rouble-denominated bonds (GKOs), which were similar to US Treasury Bills. As GKOs did not lead to an increase in the money supply they were not inflationary, but they were to prove a major factor in Russia's financial collapse in 1998. As the bonds were only short term they had to be redeemed by the government after a matter of only a few months and their buyers had been promised extremely high rates of return. The GKOs became an enormous government-backed financial pyramid in which earlier bonds were redeemed through the Treasury selling more bonds, often at ludicrously high interest rates. The selling of GKOs escalated in 1995 and in that year foreigners were allowed to purchase GKOs. This brought more money into Russia but in the form of financial speculation not as investment in Russia's enterprises. By 1996–7 Russia was already experiencing trouble servicing the GKOs and responded by selling further GKOs, some of which were due for redemption after only a few weeks. Yet another new GKO scheme was launched in the summer of 1998, and many Russians and foreigners holding rouble-denominated GKOs, fearful that the rouble was in imminent danger of collapse, swapped them into dollar-denominated GKOs. The GKO pyramid finally collapsed in August 1998 when the government announced that it could not redeem them.

The August 1998 economic crisis

A government reshuffle in March 1997 brought liberal economists to prominence once more. Chubais, who had been sacked in 1996, was brought in as the minister responsible for financial dealings with the IMF, and Boris Nemtsov became the oil and gas minister with Sergei Kiriyenko as his deputy. Mikhail Zadornov was the finance minister and Boris Fyodorov oversaw tax collection. Chernomyrdin was fortuitously sacked as prime minister in March 1998 and replaced by Kiriyenko who became the fall guy for the August 1998 economic crisis. The Asian economic crisis contributed to Russia's economic crisis as it led to a fall in world crude oil prices from $22 for a barrel in 1997 to $12 in August 1998. The fall in the price of crude oil lost the government an estimated $43.5 billion in tax revenues (Crace, 1998: 11) so depleting Russia's gold and hard currency reserves. The economic success story of the previous three years had been the stabilisation of the rouble. On 1 January 1998 the rouble was relaunched, with new notes issued minus all those embarrassing zeros that testified to the earlier hyperinflation. However, foreign banks began to dump the rouble and its value was only maintained by increasing interest rates to 42 per cent and the Russian Central Bank spending $2 billion to support it. In May 1998 Kiriyenko announced a sweeping 40 billion rouble or 8 per cent reduction in federal spending and regional budgets were also to be scrutinised. By July 1998 Chubais had negotiated a new IMF rescue package of $22.6 billion designed to support to rouble and avert devaluation, and to boost Russia's foreign currency reserves which were down to less than $15 billion (Hawkins *et al.*, 1998: 10). The IMF believed that the new loan would also encourage Russian and foreign investors to buy new lower interest GKOs and that Moscow would be able to meet the payments on earlier bonds and have enough funds to cover its budget spending. George Soros, the influential international financier, attacked the IMF's solution, arguing instead that the rouble should be devalued (see Box 11.4). Soros's statement further

---

BOX 11.4

The international financier George Soros's letter to the *Financial Times*

The meltdown in Russian financial markets has reached a terminal phase ... The trouble is that the action that is necessary to deal with a banking crisis is diametrically opposed to the action that has been agreed with the IMF to deal with the budget crisis ... The best solution would be to introduce a currency board after a modest devaluation of 15 to 25 per cent ... The alternatives are default or hyperinflation.

Note: Soros is reported to have lent the Russian government several hundred million dollars in 1997 when its faced a liquidity crisis. In June 1998 Soros invested $980 million in the Sviazinvest Russian telecommunications company (see Chapter 1) announcing that Russia was ready for economic growth and political change.

Source: Financial Times, 13 August 1998, 18.

---

undermined confidence in the rouble. In the first six months of 1998 the value of the Russian stock market fell by 50 per cent and by the end of Black Thursday, 13 August 1998, the total value of the Russian stock market had fallen by 84 per cent. The Russian stock market was now worth less than the supermarket Sainsbury's valuation on the London Stock Exchange (Elliott *et al.*, 1998: 1). On 17 August 1998 Kiriyenko finally ignored IMF advice and announced that the rouble would be allowed to fall by 20 per cent and introduced new currency controls. He also announced a moratorium of the payment of Russia's foreign debts and the GKOs.

The Russian economy after 1998

Primakov and the rejection of IMF advice

Kiriyenko was replaced as prime minister by the centrist Primakov and Gerashchenko was reappointed to the Russian Central Bank to replace the liberal Dubynin. Primakov rounded on the IMF, on Russia's liberal reformers and particularly on Chubais, accusing them of making a fetish of macro-economic stability above all other economic goals (see Box 11.5). Against IMF advice he introduced tighter currency controls, raised government spending on investment in industry and agriculture, and increased duties on imported goods. The devaluation of the rouble made exports cheaper and imports more expensive, which helped to protect domestic producers. In August 1998 Russia's chief diamond producer Almazy Rossii-Sakha concluded a deal with de Beers to market Russian gems until 2001. The trebling of the price of crude oil in 1999 provided Russia with the opportunity to replenish its hard

---

BOX 11.5

Prime Minister Primakov criticises Russia's economic reformers

It was the reformers who laid the Russian banking system waste, spat on their international obligations and introduced a unilateral moratorium ... It was they not us, who organised all sorts of financial pyramids, drawing in speculative capital with a short life-span and an inclination to flee the country.

   They didn't pay the slightest attention to the social aspects of the economy. But as one American newspaper perceptively noted, you can't carry out Monetarism without people.

Source: quoted in James Meek (1998) 'Primakov Savages Russia's Reformers', *The Guardian*, 21 November, 19.

---

currency reserves, but Russia cannot rely on its oil earnings alone to boost its economy.

Putin and the Russian economy

Putin's approach to the economy is characterised by a combination of liberalism and nationalism. Gerashchenko has remained in post at the Russian Central Bank where he continues to champion an interventionist role in the economy. In April 2000 Putin brought in Andrei Illarionov, the leading liberal, as an economic adviser to counter Gerashchenko's influence. Putin's budget for 2001 demonstrates Illarionov's continuing concern with macroeconomic stabilisation, by its commitment to end the budget deficit and to cut subsidies and government spending (*Kommersant*, 13 April 2000: 1). Putin has also stated his intention to deal with some of the continuing problems of microeconomic reform (see Putin in Box 11.6) through the development of the legal and institutional environment that capitalism needs in order to operate effectively. Putin's belief that the Russian state needs to be strengthened puts him at odds with the Washington consensus, but in the last five years the IMF and the World Bank have recognised the need for capacity building. Passing and crucially enforcing new laws, collecting taxes and sorting out the customs system are all part of capacity building. Putin's nationalism is not about abandoning Russia's integration into the global economy, but about making sure that Russia's international dealings serve Russia's interests (see Ivanov in Box 11.6). Russia still has to deal with the international organisations that dominate global capitalism. It still has to negotiate with the IMF (on behalf of the G7) over its debts and in order to gain loans. The WTO cannot simply be ignored and Russia is currently waiting to find out if it will be admitted as a member. Russia is not about to retreat into isolationism but it does not see its place in the international division of labour as being merely a raw materials exporter.

BOX 11.6

Economic priorities under President Putin

Putin sets out the six fundamental principles to deal with Russia's economic crisis in his state of the nation address 8 July 2000:

- guaranteeing property rights;
- stopping the preferential treatment of some businesses over others, and ending unnecessary state intervention in business;
- lowering the tax burden;
- simplifying the customs system;
- developing banks and other economic infrastructure;
- reorganising the welfare system by reducing the number of benefits.

Source: Amelia Gentleman (2000) 'Putin Turns the Heat on Yeltsin', *The Observer*, 9 July, 24.

Foreign Minister Igor Ivanov on Russia's International Economic Relations:

The chief priority of Russia's foreign policy in the area of international economic relations is to foster the development of its national economy. In the context of globalisation, accomplishing this objective is inconceivable without Russia's broad inclusion in the system of world economic relations. Attaining this goal requires:

- achieving favourable external conditions for the establishment of a market-type economy and for readjusting the Russian Federation's foreign-economic specialisation so as to ensure maximum economic benefits from its inclusion in the international division of labour;
- minimising the risks entailed in Russia's further integration into the world economy with a view to ensuring our country's economy security;
- promoting the creation of an equitable system of international trade in which the Russian Federation's full participation in economic organisations ensures that our country's national interests are defended within them...

Source: 'Document: The Foreign Policy Concept of the Russian Federation', *Nezavisimaia gazeta*, 11 July 2000, 1 and 6.

Conclusion

In 1992 Russia began its transition to capitalism by introducing a programme of shock therapy. The initial conditions were not very propitious and as Gorbachev's reforms had already demonstrated, any attempt at reform was bound to lead to further disruption of an economy that was already on a downward spiral. Gaidar's reform team prioritised macroeconomic stabilisation over microeconomic reform and believed that it was essential to move as quickly as possible to create the optimum conditions of economic modernisation and growth. Ten years on Russia is still changing, but it is difficult to see it as engaged in a transition process that will inexorably lead to the creation of a western-style, capitalist economy in the short or medium term. The macroeconomic environment is quite positive with inflation running at around 2 per cent a month, and the rouble is stable, but most Russians still have more confidence in the US dollar or the Deutschemark than in the rouble. The cities of Moscow and St Petersburg are now prosperous showcases for capitalism, the shops are full, the number of private cars is growing, and there are new banks, cafés and restaurants. Beyond the city centres and out in the Russian provinces, the picture is very different. The lack of microeconomic reform, enterprise restructuring and investment means that large swaths of Russian industry and agriculture struggle on in a worse condition than at the end of the soviet period. The adoption of shock therapy was as much a political as an economic decision and the political environment continues to impact upon the economy. The political instability in some regions, the corruption and lawlessness that characterise so much of Russian life, together with the difficulties in framing and implementing appropriate economic policies, constitute major barriers to Russian economic development. Russia's new Foreign Policy Concept (July 2000) recognises that the globalisation of the world economy provides opportunities for socioeconomic progress but also a risk of economic and financial crises for countries that are already economically weakened, and that Russia's 'economic system and information space' will become dependent on outside influences (*Nezavisimaia gazeta*, 11 July 2000: 6). The Concept also recognises that growing state interdependence has led to the increasing role of international institutions and mechanisms such as the G8, IMF and the World Bank in order to make the international system more manageable. Russia remains fully committed to further integration into the world economy and 'to participate fully and equally in the development of the basic functioning principles of today's world financial and economic system' (*ibid.*).

References

Åslund, Anders (ed.) (1992) *The Post-Soviet Economy: Soviet and Western Perspectives*, London: Pinter

Atkinson, Mark, Elliott, Larry and Meek, James (1998) 'Russia in Crisis', *The Guardian*, 28 August, 1 and 3–5

Crace, John (1998) 'Rouble trouble', *Guardian Education*, 16 June, 10–11

Elliott, Larry (2000) 'Russia in Limbo', *The Guardian*, 30 August, 15

Elliott, Larry, Atkinson, Mark and Meek, James (1998) 'Panic Grips Global Markets', *The Guardian*, 28 August, 1 and 3

Frydman, Roman, Rapaczynski, Andrzej and Earle, John S. (1993) *The Privatization Process in Russia, Ukraine and the Baltic States*, Budapest, London and New York: Central European University Press (CEU Privatization Reports, 2)

Goldman, Marshall I. (1996) *Lost Opportunity: What Has Made Economic Reform in Russia so Difficult?*, New York and London: W.W. Norton
Gregory, Paul A. and Stuart, Robert C. (1998) (6th edn) *Russian and Soviet Economic Performance and Structure*, Harlow: Addison Wesley Longman

Hawkins, Paula, Wright, Rupert and Krushelnycky, Askold (1998) 'Rouble on the Run', *The European*, 9–15 February, 9–12
Hedlund, Stefan (1999) *Russia's 'Market' Economy: A Bad Case of Predatory Capitalism*, London: UCL Press

Lane, David and Ross, Cameron (1995) 'From Soviet Government to Presidential Rule' in David Lane (ed.) *Russia in Transition: Politics, Privatisation and Inequality*, London: Longman, 3–20
Layard, Richard and Parker, John (1996) *The Coming Russian Boom: A Guide to New Markets and Politics*, New York: Free Press
Lloyd, John (1998) *The Rebirth of a Nation: An Anatomy of Russia*, London: Michael Joseph

Phillips, Anthony (2000) 'The Political Economy of Russia: Transition or Condition?', Chapter 6 in Mike Bowker and Cameron Ross (eds) *Russia After the Cold War*, London: Longman

Rutkevich, M.N. (1998) 'Protsessy sotsial'noi degradatsii v rossiiskom obshchestve', *Sotsiologicheskie Issledovaniia* (6), 3–12

Sachs, J. (1994) 'Betrayal' *The New Republic*, 31 January, 15
Serova, Evgenia (1999) 'Russian Agrarian Sector: Development and Prospects', *Russian Economic Trends. Monthly Update*, 20 January, 1–8
Standing, Guy (1996) *Russian Unemployment and Enterprise Restructuring: Reviving Dead Souls*, Basingstoke: Macmillan

Further reading

The best introductions to the Russian economy that are accessible to non-economists without losing the complexity of the subject are provided by:

Stuart, Robert C. and Gregory, Paul A. (1995) *The Russian Economy: Past, Present and Future*, New York: HarperCollins and in their (1998) (6th edn) *Russian and Soviet Economic Performance and Structure*, Harlow: Addison Wesley Longman

The Financial Times and *The Economist* both carry in-depth analyses of the Russian economy. The Journal *Russian Economic Trends* published by Blackwell (Oxford) for the European Commission on behalf of SITE (Stockholm Institute of Transition Economics and East European Economies) provides up-to-date analyses of the Russian economy.

Critical analyses of shock therapy and the sequencing of the various elements of the economic reform process are provided by:

Goldman, Marshall I. (1996) (new edn) *Lost Opportunity: What Has Made Economic Reform in Russia so Difficult?*, New York and London: W.W. Norton. Also see his (1995) 'Is This Any Way to Create A Market Economy?', *Current History* 94 (594) October, 305–310 and his (1997) 'Russia's Reform Effort: Is There Growth at the End of the Tunnel?', *Current History* 96 (612) October, 313–318

Other critical accounts of Russia's economic reforms are provided by:

Afanasyev, Yuri N. (1994) 'Russian Reform Is Dead. Back to Central Planning', *Foreign Affairs* 73 (2), 21–26
Arnot, Bob (1994) 'The Continuing Disintegration of the Russian Economy', *Critique* (26), 11–54
Birman, Igor (1996) 'Gloomy Prospects for the Russian Economy', *Europe–Asia Studies* 48 (5), 735–750
Nelson, L.D. and Kuzes, I.Y. (1995) *Radical Reform in Yeltsin's Russia: Political, Economic and Social Dimensions*, Armonk, NY: M.E. Sharpe
Yavlinsky, G. (1998) 'Russia's Phony Capitalism', *Foreign Affairs* 77 (3), 67–79

For more positive assessments of Russia's economic reforms see:

Åslund, Anders (1994) 'Russia's Success Story', *Foreign Affairs* 73 (5), 58–71
Åslund, Anders (1995) *How Russia Became a Market Economy*, Washington, DC: Brookings Institute
Goldman, Marshall (1994) 'Letters to the Editor, Marshall Goldman on Russia', *Foreign Affairs* 73 (6) November–December, 195–196, challenges Åslund's ideas
Layard, Richard and Parker, John (1996) *The Coming Russian Boom: A Guide to New Markets and Politics*, New York: Free Press

On Putin and the Russian economy see:

Millar, James R. (2000) 'Can Putin Jump-Start Russia's Stalled Economy?', *Current History* 99 (639) October, 329–333

Websites

http://www.cbr.ru/eng (Central Bank of the Russian Federation)
http://www.imf.org (IMF, provides regular reports on world economies)
http://www.worldbank.org (World Bank, provides regular reports on world economies)
http://www.ebrd.org (EBRD, provides regular reports on world economies)
http://www.oecd.org (OECD, provides regular reports on world economies)
http://www.usaid/gov/countries/ru/egrussi.htm (USAID, the US's main dispensing agency for aid)

CHAPTER 12

The Russian people: degraded and insulted?

This chapter examines the health of the Russian people and their land. It analyses Russia's demographic crisis, its fears of 'national genocide' and ecological crisis. The social polarisation into the rich 'New Russians' and the pauperised majority of the population, the government's endeavours to reform the social security and health systems, the peoples' survival strategies and the role of trade unions are also analysed.

Introduction

Russians describe themselves as 'degraded and insulted' (*unizhennye i oskorblennye*) (see Box 12.1). According to Gennady Zyuganov, under Yeltsin Russians had just three 'human rights' – to steal, to be irresponsible and to get drunk. In the same vein the Russian sociologist Galina Morozova argues that 'the degradation of the nation is today already a real danger, raising the alarm of all society' (Morozova, 1994: 22). The word degradation (*degradatsiia*) is frequently employed within Russia to encapsulate both its domestic crisis and its diminished international status. While there is agreement across the Russian political spectrum on the existence of domestic crises or less emotively problems, there is no consensus on their origins. For advocates of the new Russia the crises are the legacy of decades of soviet mismanagement and only in part a regrettable but temporary by-product of the transition period. For communists and nationalists Gorbachev's Reconstruction and then shock therapy have brought a once great people to the edge of the abyss. There are also fears of a moral and spiritual collapse exemplified by the growth of crime, corruption (see Chapter 1), prostitution and pornography. Russia's population is falling so precipitously that there is talk of a Russian genocide. The increased incidence of infectious diseases, escalating suicide rates, and rising drug and alcohol abuse are literally killing Russians. Russia is also an ecological disaster area; its land, water and air are so polluted that they threaten the health of both its current and potential citizens.

With the introduction of shock therapy inflation soared with prices increasing 1700-fold between December 1991 and December 1996, and unemployment and poverty began to rise precipitously (Gray, 1998: 147). Russian society rapidly became extremely polarised, with a small number of super-rich known as the New Russians (*Novye Russkie*), a small middle class (see Chapter 1) and the majority of the population who are either just getting by or are in poverty. Russia's current crisis seems all the more intractable because its components are interrelated. So, for example, the growing number of sick and disabled is partly due to ecological problems, while the social dislocation generated by the economic reforms has exacerbated alcohol and drug abuse. At the same time the RF's ability to frame, implement and fund social, welfare, health and

---

BOX 12.1

The Russians: degraded and insulted

Russian degradation

At the end of 1991 the state declared an economic policy known as 'shock therapy' which was continued in the following years with 'voucher' privatisation, permitting the bacchanal of financial 'pyramids', the new redistribution of property, the sale of the most strategically important concerns (the Norilsk combine, aluminium factories, oil companies, 'Communications investments' etc.) which have led the country into a continuously deepening crisis, which has a *systemic character*, that is – it envelops all aspects of the life of society ... We believe that one cannot now restrict oneself to a statement of the crisis, but may and must in the interests of truth identify the deepening of the processes of THE SOCIAL DEGRADATION OF RUSSIAN SOCIETY.

Source: Mikhail Rutkevich (1998) 'Protsessy sotsial'noi degradatsii v rossiiskom obshchestve', *Sotsiologicheskie Issledovanie* (6), 3 (emphasis in the original). Rutkevich is a corresponding member of the Russian Academy of Sciences.

The Russian catastrophe

The Catastrophe entails above all – our dying out. These losses will only increase: how many women will risk giving birth in today's abject penury? Handicapped and sick children also will augment the Catastrophe, and their numbers are multiplying from the miserable living conditions and the boundless drunkenness of their fathers. And the utter collapse of our schools, incapable today of rearing a moral and learned generation. And a meagerness of housing conditions long forgotten by the civilised world. And the teeming grafters in government – some of whom even cheaply sell off our oil fields and rare metals in foreign concessions.

Source: Aleksandr Solzhenitsyn (1995) *The Russian Question at the End of the 20th Century*, London: Harvill Press, 104.

ecological policies is severely constrained by its continuing difficulties in state-building (see Part II) and economic problems which were compounded by the August 1998 economic crisis (see Chapter 11). Funding questions are also caught up in the broader issue of federal versus republican-regional sources of financing and fiscal federalism (see Chapter 5). The RF is also under pressure from the IMF and the World Bank to reduce state spending in order to receive loans from these organisations. The 1993 Constitution however continues the 1978 RSFSR Constitution's commitments to state social spending. The RF is described as a 'social state', which guarantees a minimum wage plus a system of social services and protection (Art. 7).

The demographic crisis

Russia's genocide?

The Russian population is falling, life expectancy is plummeting and the population is ageing (see Box 12.2). There are very real fears that by 2040 the Russian population may have fallen to only 80–90 million, just over half the population of the 1990s (*Nezavisimaia gazeta*, 14 November 1998: 1–2). Russia's demographic crisis became increasingly evident after 1989 when there was a sharp fall in population growth. Between 1991 and 1995 the birth rate

---

BOX 12.2

Explanations of Russia's demographic crisis

There are many reasons for this [the decline in Russia's population] the drastic deterioration in medical services, mass poverty, a poor diet for tens of millions of citizens, growing unemployment, stress, anxiety over an uncertain future, drunkenness, and so on.

Source: Vitaly Golovachov, political commentator, in *Trud*, 20 January 1995, 2.

...unemployment growing, population rapidly ageing and decreasing in numbers, people's health, their production skills and intellectual level – and perhaps their morality as well – are getting worse. ... The overall fertility index for Russian women has fallen to one child and is continuing to fall – that is: it is only one half to one third of the figure below which a people begins to die out...

Source: Yury Kobishchanov, doctor of history, in *Nezavisimaia gazeta*, 10 February 1995, 1–2.

We have laid waste to the air, the land and the seas ... What do we do about biological and nuclear genocide?

Source: Aleksei Yablokov, former ecological adviser to President Yeltsin, in *The Guardian*, 23 April 1993, 8–9.

dropped by 23.2 per cent and the overall death rate increased by 31.6 per cent (*ibid.*). In 1993, even though some deaths had been offset by immigration, Russia's population fell by 307 000 and in 1994 by another 124 000 (Skripitsyna, 1995: 11). The rapid decline stopped in 1995 and in the first half of 1998 the population declined by only 0.2 per cent to 146.5 million. The Russian population also began to age in the 1960s (Skripitsyna, 1995: 12) and by 1996 20 per cent of the population was over 60 years old (*Sevodnia*, 8 February 1996: 12). With the continuing decline in the birth rate the over-sixties will constitute an ever-growing percentage of the total population, so a contracting pool of economically active people will be supporting a growing number of economically inactive people requiring medical, financial and social support.

The falling birth rate

The falling birth rate is the result of a combination of factors. Russia's population structure is still distorted by the tremendous losses of the 1920s, 1930s and the Great Patriotic War (1941–5). Raisa Skripitsyna, the chair of the Duma Subcommittee on Family Affairs and Demographic Policy, points out that the most active child-bearing age is between 20 and 29. At the beginning of 1994 there were only 9.6 million women in this age group compared to 11.8 million at the beginning of 1987 when the number of births was the highest for the previous 30 years (Skripitsyna, 1995: 11). In 1990 there were 40 million Russians aged 17 and under but only 37 million in this age cohort at the end of 1996 (Elizarov, 1998: 55), so there are and will continue to be fewer prospective mothers.

Abortion remains the most common form of birth control in Russia. In 1991 state medical institutions performed 3.5 million abortions, that is twice the number of births for that year. As the result of multiple abortions half of Russian women experience complications in pregnancy, which between 1980 and 1991 contributed to a twofold increase in stillbirths (Morozova, 1994: 25). In 1990–3 infant mortality rose from 17.4 to 19.9 per thousand births, that is three to four times higher than in North America and Western Europe (Elizarov, 1998: 55). By the mid-1990s 18 per cent of Russian marriages were infertile, half due to male infertility associated with sexually transmitted diseases contracted when young (*Izvestia*, 28 September 1995: 5). The rise in alcohol and drug abuse is also linked to infertility and stillbirths. In the 1960s the soviet geneticists Timofeyev-Resovsky and Dubinin had warned about the genetic damage being done by chemical and radioactive pollution, and their unheeded warnings have led to a situation in which congenital birth deformities are increasing faster than other health problems.

Social pessimism is another important factor in the falling birth rate. Morozova blames social pessimism for changing peoples' attitudes towards marriage and the family, so that between 1980 and 1991 the number of marriages fell by 12.8 per cent and divorces grew by 3 per cent (Morozova, 1994: 25). Skripitsyna cites a survey of Muscovites which revealed that one-third of respondents thought they lacked adequate accommodation and living conditions to have a child. Socio-demographic research conducted by Goskomstat (State Statistical Committee) similarly found that Russians do want children, but they feel unable to have them in the current conditions (Skripitsyna, 1995: 12). The fall in the birth rate is not uniform across the RF. In the non-ethnic Russian republics of Tyva, Dagestan and Kalmykia, for example, the birth rate is sufficient to reproduce the population, and amongst Russia's Islamic peoples the birth rate is significantly higher than the death rate. In contrast in the predominantly Russian populated areas of the North-West, Central and Central-Black Earth regions deaths are 2 to 2.6 times greater than births. Amongst ethnic Russians only religious minority groups such as the Baptists, Adventists and Pentecostalists have higher birth rates than death rates (*Nezavisimaia gazeta*, 10 February 1995: 1–2).

Falling life expectancy

Reform first under Gorbachev and then under Yeltsin, is popularly blamed for Russia's plummeting life expectancy. Yevgeny Andreyev of Goskomstat argues that this a misrepresentation and that life expectancy actually began to decline as early as 1965. Between 1965 and 1981 life expectancy for men in the RSFSR fell by four years. There were temporary improvements in life expectancy during the 1980s anti-alcohol campaigns, which means that what appeared to be a major jump in the death rate in 1993 was actually a return to the trend which had begun in 1965. In 1994 average life expectancy in Russia was 64.2 years, 1.4 per cent less than in the previous year; life expectancy for men was 57.3 and 71.1 for women (*Argumenty i fakty*, 30 July 1995: 13). There are clear and growing gender and regional differences in life expectancy. In the early 1980s women's average life expectancy was ten years longer than men's and by the mid-1990s this gender gap had increased to 11–13 years (*Sevodnia*, 27 January 1995: 6). In some regions life expectancy is 1.5 to 2 years below the age of pension eligibility. Male life expectancy is only 54.4 years in Pskov (68.4 for women), 56.4 years in Moscow *oblast* and 57.1 years in Ivanovo *oblast* (*Nezavisimaia gazeta*, 13 January 1996: 4). In the last six years two-thirds of the increase in the death rate is accounted for by a rising death rate amongst the working population, with the death rate amongst working age men being four times higher than amongst working women (Skripitsyna, 1995: 12). Between 1987 and 1993, the mortality rate for children under the age of 14 increased by 71.3 per cent, the rate for young people under the age of 20 rose by 60 per cent, and the rate for those up to the age of 30 rose by 80 per cent (*Sevodnia*, 27 January 1995: 6). The rising death rates amongst the working population and children under 1 are the most important factors in the overall fall in Russian life expectancy.

Suicide

The suicide rate also began to climb dramatically in the 1990s. Irina Orlova blames this alarming trend on social and socio-psychological problems such as the loss of social ties, depression, frustration, alcoholism, family disruptions, unemployment and the loss of hope (Orlova, 1998: 69). According to the World Health Organisation (WHO) a suicide rate of more than 20 suicides per 100 000 people is considered high; the Russian figure in 1992 was already high at 31 per 100 000 and by 1996 the figure had risen to 39.4. There are also marked regional and gender differences in suicide rates. In the republics of Altai, Udmurtia, Buryatia, Marii El and Bashkortostan, the *oblasts* of Arkhangelsk, Kemerovo and Chita, and the Jewish Autonomous *oblast*, there were a staggering 69–85 suicides per 100 000 inhabitants in 1994. Working-age men form the vast majority of suicides (see Box 12.3).

Immigration and emigration

Discussions of immigration into and emigration from Russia tend to be couched in highly emotive language. The 25 million Russians left outside Russia on the breakup of the USSR are spoken of as being forced to flee 'back to' Russia to avoid persecution. At the same time Russians are also described

---

BOX 12.3

The dynamics of Russian suicide in the 1990s

The number of suicides per 100 000 of the population

	1990	1991	1992	1993	1994	1995	1996
Of the whole population	26.4	26.5	31.0	38.1	42.1	41.4	39.4
Of the urban population	24.1	24.7	28.9	34.9	37.9	37.7	35.4
Of the rural population	32.8	31.7	36.9	47.2	53.7	51.4	50.3

The number of suicides per 100 000 people of working age

	1990	1991	1992	1993	1994	1995	1996
Of the whole population	33.9	34.2	41.2	51.3	56.9	56.1	53.0
Of men	56.4	57.2	69.3	87.1	96.8	94.9	90.2
Of women	9.8	9.6	10.9	12.5	13.2	13.5	12.2

Source: I.B. Orlova (1998) 'Samoubiistvo – iavlenie sotsial'noe', *Sotsiologicheskie Issledovaniia* (8), 71 and 73 (adapted). Irina Orlova is the head of a department of the Institute of Sociopolitical Research of RAN.

as being driven to seek a better life abroad. In reality only 1.7 million ethnic Russians have 'returned' to the RF since the collapse of the USSR, representing only a slight acceleration of a migration trend which began back in the 1960s (*Rossiiskaia gazeta*, 22 March 1996: 2–5). In the 1990s Russian Jews emigrated to Israel and the USA, and Russian Germans to Germany, but most ethnic Russians do not have the necessary foreign connections nor countries willing to accept them. Russia does seem to be experiencing a brain drain (*utechka mozgov*) of some of its best educated and skilled people. The funding crisis in education, science and technology means that Russia has hundreds of thousands of highly skilled but underpaid or unemployed people who have very marketable skills (Loescher, 1992). The danger is that Russia is losing precisely those people it needs to maintain the safety of its nuclear and chemical establishments and for its future scientific and economic development. Morozova cites Russian Academy of Sciences (RAN) research indicating that 13 per cent of educated people were ready to go abroad at the first opportunity and that 40 per cent had not ruled out that possibility (Morozova, 1994: 26). Up to 10 per cent of Russia's scientists have already emigrated. The brain drain also feeds into Russia's sense of its diminished international standing and of being undermined by external forces. The FSB for example has accused America of organising a brain drain that threatens Russia's national interest and the army's combat readiness.

The health of the people

Health care in Russia

Plans to reform health care funding were initiated in a 1991 Law on Health Insurance in Russia, which envisaged health care funded by compulsory and voluntary insurance contributions rather than from the state budget. Most Russians are insured through the compulsory medical insurance system. For private sector employees this is levied by the employer (see below), and the revenues are then divided between federal and local compulsory medical insurance funds in a proportion of 1 to 8 (Yudaeva and Gorban, 1999: 5). The federal government transfers funds to the republican and regional budgets to fund the health care of federal government employees and the non-working population (*ibid.*). The federal government is responsible for the RF's health policy, provides a regulatory framework for the pharmaceutical and medical industries, and monitors the quality of medical care (Green, 1998: 2.79). The 89 republics and regions are responsible for environmental health protection, the control of infectious diseases and the administration of their own health systems which include hospitals, polyclinics, sanatoria and the clinics of scientific centres (see Box 12.4). Local government finances and administers

BOX 12.4

The incidence of major illnesses per 1000 people

	1990	1995	1997
All illnesses	651	679	674
Infectious and parasitic diseases	35	47	42
Tumours	6	7	7
Endocrine, nutritional, metabolic and immunity disturbances	4	6	7
Blood disorders	1	3	3
Diseases of the nervous system and sense organs	46	58	60
Circulatory diseases	11	13	14
Diseases of the respiratory organs	336	295	298
Diseases of digestive organs	27	36	31
Urogenital diseases	20	29	32
Pregnancy and perinatal complications	37	38	41
Dermatological and subcutaneous fat diseases	35	48	44
Osteomuscular and connective tissue diseases	25	27	28
Congenital anomalies (developmental defects)	1	1	1
Injuries and poisonings	85	88	84

Source: Goskomstat cited in Ksenia Yudaeva and Maria Gorban (1999) 'Health and Health Care', *Russian Economic Trends* 8 (2), 27.

a range of primary services provided by polyclinics, hospices and nursing homes (*ibid.*). All levels of the Russian health care system are severely underfunded, so compromising their ability to modernise and to deliver the free health care promised by Article 41.1 of the Constitution. The republics and regions complain that they do not always receive the necessary allocations from the federal budget, while hospitals are increasingly asking patients for payment to cover the costs of a hospital stay, medicines and treatment. A legacy of the soviet period is that nurses expect 'presents' such as money, food, alcohol or sweets from patients in return for performing their nursing functions. Doctors, who like other public employees suffer from low salaries, are also increasingly asking for personal payments.

Contagious and sexually transmitted diseases

Russian health services have worked hard in difficult circumstances to avert epidemics. In 1995 when a major polio myelitis epidemic was forecast only 33 per cent of the under-fives were immunised, but an emergency immunisation campaign in early 1996 averted the epidemic (*Izvestia*, 20 January 1996: 1). A polio epidemic in Chechnia in 1995 was precipitated by the virtual destruction of Chechnia's own health care system and the war meant that Moscow could no longer carry out its annual immunisation programme (*Izvestia*, 3 August 1995: 1). Polio continues to be a major problem in Chechnia. In the mid-1990s a cholera epidemic was also averted, but it nevertheless remains a particular problem in Dagestan and in Astrakhan *oblast*. In the mid-1990s the incidence of measles was also down by 73 per cent, whooping cough by 55 per cent and diphtheria declined for the first time since 1991.

Against notable successes there are continuing major problems. In 1995 there was a further increase in intestinal diseases, registering 147 outbreaks of dysentery, salmonellosis and viral hepatitis A. Almost all the 14 800 people involved were infected through poor-quality water or through food products (*Sevodnia*, 29 February 1996: 9). Over the same period hepatitis rose by 31.7 per cent, again due to contaminated water supplies (*Argumenty i fakty*, 11 March 1996: 13). In Moscow the death rate from tuberculosis increased by 80 per cent in 1992–6, while the incidence of the disease among children nearly doubled (*Sevodnia*, 29 February 1996: 9). The USSR had an effective quarantine system for tuberculosis patients, but this has broken down at a time when drug-resistant forms of tuberculosis are on the rise. Tuberculosis thrives in conditions of poverty and amongst those whose immune system is already suppressed by a poor diet and living conditions. There are considerable geographical variations in the incidence of tuberculosis, the Far East and Western Siberia being particularly badly hit, as are the previously unaffected areas of North West Russia and Kaliningrad *oblast*. According to Alexei Karpeyev, head of the Ministry of Health's venereal diseases department, sexually transmitted diseases have reached near epidemic proportions (*The Guardian*, 23 October 1996: 13). The number of officially recorded cases of venereal disease has been doubling from one year to the next (*Sevodnia*, 29 February 1996: 9). Cases of syphilis increased 57-fold in just seven years from 8000 cases in 1990 to 450 000 in 1997 (Shenfield, 1998). Other venereal diseases such as gonorrhoea, chlamydia and genital herpes are also increasing dramatically.

According to official statistics the RF had only 158 HIV positive people in 1994. This rose to 1500 in 1996, 4400 in 1997 and 8300 in 1998 (Shenfield, 1998). In 1995 the real number of HIV positive people was probably nearer 10 000 (Hearst, 1995: 10) and the total is now closer to 40 000 (Shenfield, 1998). The spread of HIV and AIDS is in part the result of a reticence to discuss sexual matters and the lack of an adequate public health education programme. Lax hospital procedures, with needles routinely reused but poorly sterilised, and the use of untested blood in transfusions, have also played a role in the epidemic. There is also a widespread misconception that HIV and AIDS are not Russian problems and that foreigners, especially African students, are the main source of infection in Russia. The Duma appeared to support this notion when it passed a law in 1995 introducing compulsory AIDS testing for non-nationals staying for more than three months. In reality 80 per cent of those tested HIV positive are intravenous drug users (*ibid.*).

Drug abuse

According to official statistics the number of registered drug addicts doubled to 28 300 between 1985 and 1990. In 1998 there were 260 000 registered addicts but the real figure is somewhere in the millions (*Kommersant Daily*, 20 August 1998: 2). Domestic drug production is on the increase, heroin and opium come into Russia from Central and South East Asia, and cocaine comes in from Latin America. In Russian law dealing, possession and use of drugs are all illegal, so anyone who tests positive for drug use could be imprisoned. In reality the Ministry of the Interior has only 4000 staff to combat drug crime and drug-related crimes rose by 13.2 per cent in 1997–8. Drug use amongst the young is not just a criminal issue, it is also seen as a danger to Russia's 'gene fund' by exposing young Russians to a variety of health risks. Research has found that 8 per cent of young Russians periodically take drugs, 1 per cent regularly use them and 25 per cent have tried them (Popov and Kondratyeva, 1998: 65).

Alcohol abuse, crime and corruption

Vodka is at the centre of colossal health, crime and tax-dodging problems. Dr Alexander Nemtsov, a leading Russian expert on alcoholism, has calculated that the average Russian man drinks almost half a pint of vodka a day and that the number of deaths caused by alcohol doubled between 1988 and 1995. There are half a million deaths from alcohol-related cirrhosis, accidents, murders and suicides every year and Russia has about five million chronic alcoholics (Clark, 1995: 26). Rising unemployment and poverty have contributed to a rise in alcohol abuse, but it is not only those who have been left behind by Russia's 'dash to the market' who are seeking solace in alcohol. Alexander Krivenko, the head of a private Moscow drying-out clinic, is seeing more clients from what he terms 'the creative part' of the population. In contrast to the securities of the soviet period, many Russians are having to contend with a working day that has virtually no limit and are constantly under pressure to make their businesses work (Meek, 1996: 12). Their response to life's difficulties is to resort to the Russian tradition of a vodka binge (*pianka*).

In 1992, as part of Russia's move to a market economy, the state monopoly of vodka production was lifted. This had appalling consequences for both the quality of the alcohol sold and the growth of criminal activity surrounding alcohol production and distribution. Private vodka workshops are supposed to be licensed but in reality most are not subject to any controls. The vodka produced in these workshops is frequently adulterated and often highly toxic, especially as after 1992 it became cheaper to distil moonshine (*samogon*) from industrial grade ethyl alcohol rather than from sugar. President Yeltsin contributed directly to this criminal activity by granting valuable customs duties and tax exemptions to favoured charities. In the early 1990s the National Sports Fund set up by Yeltsin's tennis coach Shamil Tarpishev rapidly cornered 90 per cent of the Russian market in imported alcohol, providing a quarter of Russia's total consumption worth £3 billion a year (Clark, 1995: 26). Tax exemptions for 'charities' robbed the state of an estimated $200 million a month in unlevied duties; it also led to the cost of a bottle of the cheapest vodka being the same as the cost of a loaf and a half of bread. In 1996 Yeltsin dismissed the senior official responsible for regulating the alcohol industry and in 1997 finally began moves to remove the tax privileges enjoyed by charities, but there are no plans to reinstitute a state alcohol monopoly and Russia's alcohol problems continue to worsen.

Violence against women and the sex trade

Statistics for the incidence of violence against women are notoriously inaccurate, as victims may not report crimes and the authorities may discourage reporting and may not even gather statistics. In 1996 RF government statistics recorded almost 11 000 complaints of rape or attempted rape, but the government does not record assaults by husbands or family members (Human Rights Watch, 1997). According to Russian women's rights activists only around 5–10 per cent of rape victims go to the police and the victims of rape by a husband or family member are even less likely to report the assault. This lack of reporting is explained by a range of factors. The police are quite tolerant of violence against women. They often simply refuse to record a complaint or do not bother to conduct a proper investigation. There is also evidence that the police and prosecutors do their best to dissuade victims from proceeding with their complaint and that victims are accused of fabricating or provoking assaults (*ibid.*). Police investigations are themselves quite traumatising and police procedures particularly in gathering medical evidence need to be reformed. According to Ekaterina Lakhova, who was President Yeltsin's adviser on women's affairs, every year 14 000 women are killed by their husbands or family members (*ibid.*). A major problem for the victims of domestic violence is the lack of refuges and police protection. This is one area in which the Russian women's movement has been particularly active (see Chapter 8) and in 1999 the European Union provided funds to the Russian Association of Crisis Centres for Women to help them set up refuges (Human Rights Watch, 1999). The combination of rising female unemployment and the lack of career opportunities, especially in the provinces, has led to a rise in prostitution throughout the RF. Organised criminal gangs also traffic in women from the former Soviet Union. These women are led to believe that they will have jobs in Western Europe as domestics, but once in the West discover that they are expected to work as prostitutes. These women are very vulnerable as they may not speak the local language, the criminal gang takes their passport away and they are usually in the country illegally (Gentleman, 2000: 23).

The ecological crisis

The soviet legacy

The USSR left a lamentable legacy of environmental degradation so that for many Russians the air they breathe, the water they drink and the soil in which their food is grown are polluted. Soviet agricultural practices caused ecological damage through the misuse of fertilisers, over-ploughing and inappropriate irrigation schemes. Nuclear accidents, the legacy of nuclear and chemical weapons testing and unstable chemical and nuclear weapons stocks present a continuing threat to Russians and their neighbours. Russia's environmental problems are also partly explained by the priority given to heavy industry, mining, and the metallurgical and chemical sectors during the soviet period, together with the focus on fulfilling production targets at the cost of all other considerations. As the Russian economy modernises and restructures away from these 'smokestack' industries to high-technology production and as enterprises have to pay a market rather than a subsidised price for energy, pollution may be reduced. As yet, however, most of Russian industry struggles along unable to invest and restructure. Article 42 of the 1993 Constitution declares that 'Everybody has the right to a decent environment, reliable information about the state of the environment and compensation for damage caused to his health or property by ecological breaches of the law'. The Russian government has proved unable to enforce its ecological legislation and President Putin has abolished the official environmental watchdog the State Duma Committee on the Environment.

Radioactive and chemical pollution

Radioactive pollution caused by accidents and nuclear weapons testing is a problem that will not be easy to eradicate and poses a continuing long-term threat to the country's health and its 'gene fund'. In the 1950s and 1960s there were three atomic accidents in Cheliabinsk which polluted the South-Urals region. The accident on 26 May 1986 at the Chernobyl reactor in Ukraine caused radioactive pollution of 15 Russian *oblasts* with a population of over two million people. It is estimated that Chernobyl will continue to pose a threat for the next 70 years, not just to these two million but to the 75 million people living in European Russia, which is still experiencing rising levels of radioactivity (Morozova, 1994: 24). The RF also has 11 RBMK reactors of the type that malfunctioned at Chernobyl, four in Kursk with an additional one planned, three in Smolensk and four in St Petersburg. In the 1990s there were also two little-known nuclear accidents which were on a scale comparable to the Chernobyl disaster. An explosion at the Mayak Radio-Chemistry plant spread cesium-137 over large areas of the Urals *oblasts* of Cheliabinsk and Kurgan (Shenfield, 1998), and in the summer of 1993 a radioactive leak from the Tomsk-7 chemical combine polluted 135 sq km of Siberia (Morozova, 1994: 23). Parts of Siberia are also still struggling with the legacy of nuclear weapons testing which began in the 1950s at the Semipalatinsk firing ground. This has resulted in nuclear contamination affecting the nearly two million people living in Altai *krai* and Novosibirsk *oblast*. To the north, nuclear weapons testing on the Novaia Zemlia archipelago during the 1960s–1980s, led to the radioactive pollution of the Kara and Barents seas with appalling health consequences for the people of Murmansk and Arkhangelsk *oblasts*.

The end of the Cold War has led to international agreements to reduce nuclear and chemical stockpiles but Russia is unable to fund their safe disposal. It is estimated that 17 nuclear submarines, some with their nuclear fuel still on board, have been dumped in the Kara Sea (*Sevodnia*, 16 August 1995: 12). Alexander Yablokov, Yeltsin's former ecology adviser, has described Russia's 100 decommissioned nuclear-powered submarines as 'floating atomic bombs' and claims that 30 are moored with their fuel still aboard. The Norwegian government has provided Russia with financial and technical assistance to make these nuclear submarines safe. The safe disposal of chemical weapons presents an additional problem. According to official data Russia has 40 000 tonnes of chemical weapons, but Yablokov has estimated that a further 150 000 to 200 000 tonnes had already been burned or inadequately buried and need to be redisposed of safely (*Izvestia*, 17 March 1995: 1).

Air, water and soil pollution

Only 15 per cent of Russians have air that is safe to breathe. In total 96 million Russians live with emissions over 5–10 times the permitted levels (Morozova, 1994: 24). This scale of toxic and carcinogenic air pollution has a major impact on people's health, leading to problems of the respiratory, circulatory and digestive systems, and skin and eye problems. In the first half of the 1990s the amounts of nitrogen dioxide, sulphur dioxide and carbon monoxide in the air increased in most cities and towns (*Sevodnia*, 16 August 1995: 12). Additional air pollution problems have also arrived with capitalism. The low levels of private car ownership in the USSR mean that vehicle pollution is a new problem. In Moscow private car ownership is increasing by 20–25 per cent a year. So while in 1988–9 only the main inner city ring road (the Sadovaia Ring) had dangerously high traffic emissions, now most traffic-carrying roads in Moscow pose a danger to people's health.

In Moscow *oblast* 60 per cent of the water supply is extremely polluted. The capital's effluents pour into the Moscow river, parts of which are now so polluted that they have stopped freezing in winter. Russia has many lakes but 75 per cent of them cannot be used for drinking water and 30 per cent of underground water sources are poisoned. Half a million people in Irkutsk *oblast* suffered mercury poisoning from polluted water in the Bratsk reservoir (Shenfield, 1998). Overburdened and outdated facilities result in 100 to 120 million tonnes of largely toxic sediment accumulating at water treatment plants each year (*Sevodnia*, 16 August 1995: 12). This picture is replicated throughout the country. Ineffective water treatment means that almost half of Russia's drinking water does not meet the required standards (Morozova, 1994:24). There are also problems with bacterial pollution of hundreds of times the permissible levels in the Volga, Oka, Kama, Don and Kuban river basins, leading to a constant danger of epidemics of intestinal infections. In addition soil pollution with heavy metals, chemicals and pesticides is affecting food quality. About 5 per cent of food products contain heavy metals and about 3 per cent of meat and milk products are polluted with pesticides (Morozova, 1994: 25). The lax production and transportation practices prevalent in the oil industry have also wreaked ecological disaster. It is estimated that during the soviet period 1 per cent of the country's annual 400 million tonnes of oil production was lost from oil pipelines. In 1995 100 000–150 000 tonnes of oil accidentally leaked from the pipeline near Ussinsk in the Komi republic and pipelines in Chechnia were seriously damaged during the 1994–6 war. In Chechnia this led to the accumulation of 700 000–800 000 tonnes of petroleum products in the Sunzha river bed and concentrations of petroleum products in the Terek river of 50–137 times the maximum permissible levels (*Sevodnia*, 20 December 1995: 12).

Russian society: the rich and the poor

The polarisation of Russian society

Russian income levels have become increasingly polarised. According to official Russian statistics the ratio between the income of the top 10 per cent and the bottom 10 per cent of the population increased from 8:1 in 1990 to 13:1 in 1996. The 'New Russians' are rich and able to indulge in conspicuous consumption, buying imported cars, jewellery, clothes and cosmetics (see Box 12.5). In stark contrast the majority of Russians have seen their standard of living fall precipitously. Currency revaluation in 1992 wiped out the value of savings overnight and 80 per cent of Russians now have no savings (Gray, 1998: 147). The lack of an adequate social security system and the non-payment of pensions, benefits and wages mean that the Russian poor are an ever-increasing group. Poverty is notoriously difficult to define and measure. Subjective factors such as expectations and a sense of relative deprivation are as important as objective, measurable factors such as wage and pensions payments. Russia has a minimum wage which first was introduced in 1975 and

---

BOX 12.5

A joke at the expense of the New Russians

First New Russian: I like your tie, how much did it cost?
Second New Russian: $500.
First New Russian: You fool, you can get the same tie for $1000!

Note: There must be hundreds of New Russian jokes, their common themes being the New Russians' avarice, stupidity and lack of culture.

---

a minimum subsistence level was introduced in 1992. The minimum wage is supposed to guarantee a minimum income for all those in employment and the levels of most benefits were set in relation to the minimum wage. The minimum subsistence level was established 'as the level of monetary income that was sufficient for physiological survival in crisis conditions . . . and this has become the standard Russian poverty measure' (Clarke, 1999: 11). Even using the same criteria, measurements of poverty still differ quite widely. In 1995 Goskomstat calculated that 25 per cent of the population were living on less than the government's minimum subsistence level. In 1996 the World Bank, using the same Russian government minimum subsistence levels, found that 43.1 of Russians were living below this level and that 15 per cent of households were living in extreme poverty (*Trud*, 1999). A survey conducted by the RAN in August 1997 found that 41 per cent of respondents had an income that was just adequate to feed themselves but 17 per cent were unable to feed themselves adequately (Rutkevich, 1998: 6). The Russian poor includes pensioners, the disabled, the unemployed, large families, nearly half of Russia's six million single-parent families and thousands of Russians who are in employment. According to the World Bank almost half of one-child households are in poverty and 16 per cent are in extreme poverty, 61 per cent of two-child families are poor and 30 per cent are extremely poor (*Trud*, 1999).

Poverty and the non-payment of wages and pensions

A feature of the Russian poor is that it includes thousands of people who are in employment. The employed poor are poor because their salaries have not kept pace with inflation and/or because they quite simply have not been paid. Taking 1990 as the base year with a value of 100, in 1997 Russian real incomes were 67.6 per cent and pensions 52.6 per cent their 1990 level (see Box 12.6). Pensions are the same throughout the country although the actual cost of living varies tremendously. In March 1998 an estimated 54.2 milliard roubles of wages were owed to Russians, 10 milliard roubles of which were owed to doctors, teachers, civil servants and the armed forces (Rutkevich, 1998: 10). The reasons for the non-payment of these state wages and pensions

BOX 12.6

The development of nominal and real incomes, 1990–1997

	1990	1991	1992	1993	1994	1995	1996	1997
Average per capita money incomes	0.215	0.466	4.0	45.2	206.3	515.4	761.9	922.8
Real incomes (1990 = 100)	100.000	116.000	60.9	70.4	78.8	66.1	65.8	67.6
Average wage	0.297	0.548	6.0	58.7	220.4	472.4	805.9	954.9
Real wage (1990 = 100)	100.000	98.600	66.2	66.5	61.2	44.1	50.0	52.4
Average pension (annual averages)	0.102	0.266	1.5	19.4	78.4	187.8	302.6	328.2
Real pension (1990 = 100)	100.000	139.200	47.1	64.0	63.5	51.1	55.7	52.6

Source: UNDP, Human Development Report 1998, cited by
http://www.trud.org/ilo_conf/ilo_conf11_end.htm

are a combination of tax collection difficulties and the financial activities of the republican-regional authorities and the commercial banks. The federal government transfers funds to the republican and regional authorities through commercial banks. Many republican and regional authorities and banks then use the money earmarked for wages and pensions to provide credits and to fund other money-making activities, while blaming Moscow for not providing the necessary funds. In its turn the federal government blames the non-payment problem on the failure of republic and regional authorities to collect and transfer tax revenues to the federal government. The non-payment of wages is also due to the basic problem of outdated and uncompetitive enterprises which are simply unable to pay their workers.

Unemployment and suppressed unemployment

In soviet times everyone had the right to employment and anyone unemployed for more than three months could be accused of parasitism. Unemployment was a largely hidden phenomenon estimated at around 4 per cent of the working age population (Åslund, 1991: 18). The transition to a market economy requires the development of a labour market with a reserve pool of labour and therefore unemployment. Between July 1991 and February 1992 the number of unemployed quadrupled, reaching 93 100. By September 1992

294 200 Russians were officially registered unemployed (Morozova, 1994: 27). In reality unemployment is far more extensive than these official figures suggest. According to Guy Standing (1996) of the ILO, Russia suffers from an acute problem of 'suppressed unemployment' affecting about one-third of the industrial workforce. The low level of unemployment benefits, which in 1997 were on average only 24 per cent of the average wage and only 5 per cent of the minimum subsistence level, discourages workers from registering as unemployed (*Trud*, 1999). It is also to the advantage of most workers to remain employed even if they are not paid, as they retain access to crucial benefits provided through the workplace such as subsidised shops, coupons for use in canteens, food parcels and hospitals. They may also receive payment in the goods they produce which they can then sell or barter. For the enterprises, maintaining workers on their books enables them to avoid additional tax and redundancy payments. As a result workers are put on reduced hours or sent on what is known as administrative leave, which means they are formally employed but not expected to turn up to work and are, of course, unpaid. In 1998 4.7 million workers were on administrative leave and working hours were shortened for another 4.3 million workers. This was equal to 2.3 billion 'lost' working hours or the equivalent to 1.1 million full-time workers being unemployed for one year (Nesporova and Ghellab, 1999). So while in 1996 Goskomstat statistics put unemployment at 3.4 per cent, according to ILO research the figure was really 9.5 per cent. In 1998 Goskomstat calculated unemployment at 2.7 per cent, but ILO calculations put it at 10.6 per cent (*Trud*, 1999).

Women and the 'feminisation of poverty'

Women have been particularly hard hit by the collapse of soviet socialism. Women formed over half the soviet labour force and 90 per cent of working age women were either studying or in employment. As restrictions and controls in the economy have now been lifted, equal opportunities and pay have come under attack. According to Alena Nesporova and Youcef Ghellab (1999) of the ILO, soviet women on average earned 70 per cent of a male wage in 1989 but by 1997 their earnings had fallen to 55 per cent of the male wage. Soviet women complained of their heavy 'double burden' of paid employment and housework, but now Russian women are being pushed out of the labour force. Twenty per cent of women are the family's sole bread-winner and, as women are the first to be made unemployed, 'poverty in the new Russia predominantly has a female face' (Bridger *et al.*, 1996: 74).

Women constitute 70 per cent of the Russian unemployed, in 12 regions more than 85 per cent of the unemployed are women and in seven regions over 90 per cent are women (*Izvestia*, 25 October 1995: 7). Women also constitute 62.4 per cent of the rural unemployed (*Sevodnia*, 18 February 1998: 3). Women are not unemployed because they lack skills and education.

In Moscow and St Petersburg, for example, 80 per cent of unemployed women have higher education qualifications. Russian women are being hit by a combination of factors. The demographic crisis is being used to support the contention that a woman's primary role is as a wife and mother. In July 1996 the government also extended the list of jobs forbidden to women on health grounds and specifically cited the need to protect women's reproductive health. In 1993 the minister for labour, Gennady Melikian, remarked, 'Why should we give work to women when there are so many unemployed men in our country?' There were no protests even though this contradicted Article 19.3 of the Constitution which declares gender equality (cited in Bridger *et al.*, 1996: 51). Women have also lost the structures that enabled them to work. Pre-school child care facilities, which in soviet times were provided by the state or employers for free or for only a small fee, have become increasingly rare and expensive.

The high levels of female unemployment are also explained by the impact of reform on the highly feminised sectors of the country's administration and economy. Despite soviet proclamations of gender equality the USSR developed pronounced gender segregation within the labour force. Women constituted 98 per cent of the bookkeepers and 93 per cent of the accountants employed by soviet state planning departments. With the transition to a market economy these posts and and their occupants are redundant (Bridger *et al.*, 1996: 43). Textiles and clothing manufacture were also highly feminised sectors of the economy and these have been particularly hard hit by foreign competition. According to Goskomstat 7.6 million or 20 per cent of 'women's jobs' have been lost since the collapse of communism, compared to a loss of only 1.6 per cent of men's jobs (Human Rights Watch, 1997). The expanding sectors of the economy are now in banking, finance and services, which were feminised sectors under state socialism but as their status and prestige have grown under market conditions they have become increasingly masculinised (Einhorn, 1993: 132). The new economy requires new skills but women are being pushed out of the sectors that require training in the new technologies and are experiencing discrimination in retraining programmes.

Housing and homelessness

The shortage and low standard of housing was a perennial problem in the USSR. It was not uncommon for families to live in hostels provided by their employer or in one room in a communal apartment sharing kitchen and bathroom facilities with other families. Most Russians still enjoy highly subsidised housing and utilities (electricity, gas, heating, water and sewage). Those who cannot afford to pay their rent and utilities bills are rarely subjected to any penalty such as eviction or court action. In 1998 St Petersburg did begin to move tenants who have fallen behind in their payments to less desirable accommodation in dormitories and hostels (Shenfield, 1998). The RF is under pressure from the IMF and the World Bank to reduce state spending, which includes ending subsidised housing and utilities. So far only a few local authorities such as St Petersburg have begun to privatise their housing stocks, so making former tenants the owners of their accommodation. Since 1992 the number of new apartments being built has fallen and market rents for private apartments are up to 50 per cent higher than for state-owned apartments (*Trud*, 1999). It is difficult to see how the RF can live up to its constitutional commitment (Art. 40) to honour everyone's right to housing, to encourage federal and local authorities to promote housing construction and to provide those on low incomes with free or low-cost housing.

In the USSR everyone had to have a residence permit (*propiska*) which stated where they had a right to live. This enabled the state to control population movement and to curb unplanned urban development. Although Russians now have a constitutional right (Art. 26.1) to decide their own place of residence, Moscow and St Petersburg have been allowed to retain a permit system to prevent uncontrolled growth. Nevertheless economic dislocation in the provinces has led to a growth in economic migration within the RF. By Russian standards Moscow and St Petersburg are prosperous and despite the best efforts of the cities' authorities their populations are growing without any corresponding growth in their housing stocks, so both cities have a growing homeless population. As in the soviet era the majority of homeless, around 60 per cent, are former prisoners who have been deprived of their residence permits on conviction. Ethnic conflicts within the RF and in the other states of the FSU have led to a growth in refugees who swell the ranks of the homeless. Housing privatisation has also contributed to homelessness, as Russia's vulnerable people such as the elderly, alcoholics and the mentally ill have been tricked out of their homes. In the mid-1990s the Russian press carried stories of elderly ladies who thought they had swapped their run-down but prime-site city centre apartments for new ones in the suburbs. Criminal gangs would promise to take people to their new homes but would just dump them by the side of the road. St Petersburg had several gangs specialising in this kind of apartment fraud and in 1995 alone 10 000 people fell victim to these scams (Varoli, 1997).

The exact number of homeless people is difficult to calculate but in 1997 it stood at around 1.5 million, including 300 000 to 600 000 children (*ibid.*). The growth in homeless children who often live without any kind of adult care or supervision is a particularly worrying phenomenon. These children are the victims of family breakdowns and violence. In Russia analogies have been drawn between the growing number of street children and the homeless children (*bezprizornye*) of the 1920s. Both the birth of communism and its collapse have resulted in children suffering from the social and economic dislocation and the simultaneous inability of the state to address these problems. These children survive through the work of charitable organisations, selling newspapers, washing windscreens, theft, begging, scavenging and prostitution. Homeless children are pitied but they are also feared. The fires set by homeless children to try and keep warm are blamed for the rise in apartment block fires. Their alcohol and drug abuse, glue sniffing and theft are part of the general rise in lawlessness and insecurity experienced by all Russians.

How do Russians survive?

Non-financial incomes

It seems inconceivable that millions of Russians can survive on low incomes or without pay for months on end. In the early 1990s the sight of Russians, particularly the elderly, standing on pavements selling their meagre possessions in order to survive provided a startling image of the impact of shock therapy. Russian enterprises, including those who do not have the money to pay their workers in cash, still provide a range of non-financial benefits (see above). The soviet-era practice of heavily subsidising cultural facilities and goods intended for children or for educational purposes has also not entirely disappeared. Russians also survive by growing food for personal consumption. The Russian peasantry had small private plots during the soviet period which continue to provide them with an economic lifeline. During the soviet period urban Russians would often spend their spare time at their dacha, that is, a cottage, but more usually a hut with a small garden attached. At the dacha they would grow and bottle fruit and vegetables, and gather mushrooms to dry. This produce provided a welcome supplement to the limited range and shortages of basic foods in the soviet shops and in post-communist Russia this produce is vital to survival. Spare land in towns and cities has now been turned into allotments which provide a lifeline to Russia's poor. As Russia's collective and state farm system has virtually collapsed, the private plots, allotments and gardens are now all that stands between two-thirds of Russians and starvation. These plots and allotments produce 90 per cent of Russia's potatoes, 7 per cent of other vegetables, and 55 per cent of meat and poultry (Shenfield, 1998).

The social security system

Price reforms and attempts to reduce state spending have led to the near abandonment of the soviet era free services. Soviet enterprises provided a range of social benefits, including subsidised holidays and cheap loans, but these have largely disappeared and most enterprises have reduced their social provisions (see Box 12.7). Many of the larger enterprises that used to provide medical services (including hospitals) are now trying to transfer these costly facilities to the local authorities. Government policy is to encourage private insurance schemes to work in parallel with state funding to provide retirement pensions and health care. Given rising poverty levels very few Russians are

BOX 12.7

The four elements of Russia's social security system

1. Employment-related social insurance benefits provided for employees and their dependants: pensions, employment injury benefits, unemployment benefits, health insurance benefits and short-term cash benefits such as sickness and maternity.

2. Universal benefits: public health care system, family benefits and social pensions.

3. Social assistance benefit provisions, benefits of last resort for the poor without other or insufficient income: provision of clothing, free meals, cash income support. Administered by regional or local government.

4. Supplementary schemes: voluntary pension schemes, private health insurance, private pension provision, help provided by NGOs such as charities.

Source: Trud (1999) 'International Conference on Social and Labour Issues: Overcoming Adverse Consequences of the Transition Period in the Russian Federation', http://www.trud.org/ (adapted).

able to make such private provision, although there are the beginnings of industry-based insurance schemes such as the one for gas industry workers. The RF's unemployment, sickness, health and maternity benefits and pensions are largely funded through a payroll surcharge of 39.5 per cent. The employers are responsible for 38.5 per cent and employees for 1 per cent of this figure. The benefits are administered by the Employment Fund, the Pension Fund, the Health Insurance Scheme, the Social Insurance Fund and a new Employment Injury Fund. Each of these funds or schemes have their own federal and regional structures, and federal-regional financial relations (*Trud*, 1999).

As with all revenue-gathering in Russia, the social security system is bedevilled by non-payment or avoidance, administrative inefficiencies and the issues raised by fiscal federalism (see Chapter 5). The non-payment of wages has an inevitable knock-on effect on the ability to gather the payroll surcharge. In addition all the republics and regions, but especially those that are net donors to the federal budget, are acutely aware of the discrepancy between the revenues they raise, what they receive from Moscow and what they pay out in benefits. Those republics and regions that have high wages gather the most revenues (as this is a payroll surcharge) and then find that these revenues are transferred (redistributed) by the federal government to the low wage areas. This provides a growing area of dispute between the federal and the republican-regional governments. The sub-federal levels of government do have some of their own tax income, but most of their finance comes via the federal government and there are frequent complaints that the federal government is slow to transfer funds (*ibid.*). The result is that the poorer areas are unable to fund the social security, pensions and health care, and the richer areas have to divert funds from other schemes to cover the delays or shortfalls in transfers. For its part Moscow complains that funds are transferred but that they are misappropriated by the local authorities (see Chapter 1). In June 2000 the Duma approved a government proposal to replace the workplace insurance contributions into the state social funds with a single social tax (Labour Russia on the Net, 2000). While recognising the difficulties of the current system, Russian trade unions oppose this proposed reform and reject any attempt to depict it as a purely technical matter needed to simplify the collection of insurance funds. Russian trade unions instead see this proposed change as an attempt to replace a system of employee social protection (insurance) in which funds are dedicated to health and social security, with a system that depends on what is available in the dwindling and hard-pressed state budget. The trade unions fear that this will lead to a worsening rather than an improvement in the social security system.

Trade unions and workers

Growing trade union militancy, 1989–1991

In the USSR trade unions were not independent organisations; their activities were controlled by the CPSU and their leaderships were part of the *nomen-klatura* system. Any attempt at independent worker organisation, activity or strikes was ruthlessly suppressed. In the late 1980s under the impact of the freer political atmosphere and economic dislocation, there was a rise in worker militancy particularly by the coal miners. In 1989 miners in the Kuzbass and Vorkuta in Russia, the Donbass in Ukraine and Karaganda in Kazakhstan elected their own union leaders and went on strike. The strikes were used by the miners, but also by local party bosses and the mine managers, to put pressure on the CPSU and the coal ministry in support of demands for better conditions, but also in favour of economic and political reform. In 1990 the miners went on strike calling for the resignation of Prime Minister Ryzhkov and radical reform. Overall the strike movement of 1989–91 met with little resistance from the authorities, long overdue concessions were made to the miners and there was unanimous public sympathy for their cause. New independent trade unions such as the Independent Miners' Union and the Union of Socialist Trade Unions (Sotsprof) were established. By 1991 the strikes had become an important factor in destabilising the soviet system; the miners supported Yeltsin and called for Gorbachev's resignation. A new Federation of Independent Trade Unions of Russia (FNPR) was established in March 1990 to challenge the official trade union umbrella organisation, the All-Union Central Council of Trade Unions (VTsSPS). During the August 1991 coup the VTsSPS was fatally compromised by siding with the communist hardliners and so there was no place for it in the new Russia. The FNPR inherited the considerable assets of the Russian branch of the VTsSPS, which included offices, rest homes and holiday facilities. The FNPR also took over the VTsSPS's monopolistic role in the distribution of social security benefits. The result was that the FNPR soon had over 60 million affiliated members out of a total Russia labour force of 72.5 million.

Russia's 'independent' trade unions, tripartism and social partnership

The development of independent trade unions at the end of the soviet period suggested that, at long last, Russian workers and employees would have organisations that represented their views and interests. A basic problem for the trade unions was that while recognising that soviet rule had not adequately promoted their members' material well-being, the new Russia promised democratisation but also, in the short term at least, reduced standards of living. Sotsprof, the largest new independent trade union, at first called itself 'socialist' and then 'social', but in 1991–3 was closely allied to the government radicals who were pushing forward shock therapy. Not surprisingly, it soon became riven by internal disputes and rapidly lost members. Many of the old soviet trade unions changed their names and proclaimed their independence of government and management. They have slowly changed as the soviet-appointed leaders have either retired or been voted out of office and replaced by new leaders elected by the members. These unions retain many of the characteristics of the soviet trade unions. For example, they enjoy high levels of membership, partly because they have retained the right to deduct union dues from members' wages. These unions are not autonomous, grass-roots organisations, but work closely with management to promote the interests of their industry or professional group. Yeltsin's approach to trade unions was set out in the November 1991 edict 'On Social Partnership and the Resolution of Labour Disputes', in which he proposed an annual socioeconomic agreement between unions and government. In 1992 Yeltsin established the 'Tripartite Commission on the Regulation of Social and Regulation Relations', in order to bring the government, management and trade unions together to mediate labour disputes, monitor working conditions and review wage levels. These agreements put a great strain on the government budget and managements claimed they placed too big a burden on their enterprises. The trade unions had to sign a no-strike pledge in return for being allowed to participate in the Tripartite Commission. In addition from the perspective of workers and employees the minimum wage levels were set too low and were immediately undermined by inflation. This formal tripartism has not become an enduring feature of government–management–trade union relations.

Why aren't Russians in revolt?

Given the level and effectiveness of labour militancy during 1989–91 and the establishment of new independent trade unions, it seems all the more astonishing that at the height of shock therapy in 1992–3 the number of strikes actually fell. Throughout the 1990s poverty levels increased, real wages halved and many workers were not paid for months at a time, and yet Russia has not experienced an increase in worker militancy. According to Kolganov (1999), workers have little experience of organising themselves rather than being organised by the official trade unions. They also believe that industrial action has very little chance of success while the economy is in crisis and so they have pursued a strategy of compromise with all authorities from the enterprise directors to the federal government. Sarah Ashwin (1998) of the London School of Economics, has identified two broad explanations of the USSR's social stability which may be used to explain Russia's continuing lack of labour militancy. According to the 'social contract' explanation (see Hauslohner, 1987), Soviet workers traded their compliance for job and material security. David Lane's (1985) concept of 'incorporated' workers similarly stresses material security, close worker–manager relations, management tolerance of labour indiscipline and the cooption of workers' natural leaders into the party or trade unions, to explain stability. In contrast Viktor Zaslavsky (1982) stresses that the pervasive threat of coercion prevented worker solidarity so that resistance took the individualised forms of absenteeism, drunkenness and frequent job changes. Given that the threat of coercion is no longer so prevalent and the economic reforms have broken the social contract, then one might expect an upsurge of worker militancy but this has not happened.

For Ashwin, the explanation lies in the nature of the soviet enterprise as a basic unit of soviet society which provided a range of social and welfare benefits, child and health care and housing. The enterprises simultaneously encouraged atomisation as workers engaged in competition with each other for the enterprise's discretionary benefits. In this way workers were both incorporated into the enterprise collective but their relations with each other were atomised or individualised. The result is that even though the economic and political circumstances have changed, workers' relationship with the work collective has remained the same. Trade unions have generally not become independent organisations representing workers interests, but instead tend to have very close relationships with management. Workers and management see themselves as sharing common interests and take concerted action to gain support from regional and federal authorities. Workers also engage in individual survival strategies such as taking on additional jobs and growing their own food. According to Ashwin, the result is that even when workers engage in collective action over wage arrears, the action tends to be small scale and/or spontaneous, leaving no organisational legacy. For example in 1997 protests and strikes lasting more than one shift took place in only 8278 enterprises with the participation of 660 000 workers (Buzgalin, 1998) and during 1996–7 workers periodically blockaded transport routes including the Trans-Siberian railway, in protest at the non-payment of wages. Another characteristic of this collective action is that, although it is organised by the trade unions, it usually has the support of the enterprise management and sometimes even regional authorities, who want to put pressure on the federal government (Ashwin, 1998: 195).

Challenging management: the beginnings of labour militancy?

The privatisation process is gradually changing worker–management relations. In the early 1990s the managers of state enterprises were able to use their official positions to transform themselves into new capitalists (see Chapter 1). In manager and worker buy-outs, the workers rarely gained any more control over the enterprise and often sold their shares to the management. Workers tolerated management self-enrichment in return for no mass redundancies. Privatisation has brought workers' control to only around twelve factories in Russia (Kolganov, 1999). There are signs of growing but as yet isolated worker militancy. Kolganov gives the examples of the Yasnogorsk Engineering Plant in Tula where in 1998 workers elected new worker-directors and were able to block the old management's illicit business deals. In 1993 the Vyborg Pulp and Paper Mill in Leningrad *oblast* was privatised and in a process that involved numerous illegal actions the workers lost any stake in the mill. In 1995 the factory was artificially bankrupted so it could be sold cheaply, but Leningrad *oblast*'s prosecutor declared the sale illegal and the workforce occupied the factory, elected their own manager and ran the mill. The workers were attacked by two paramilitary units, OMON riot police and Typhoon, which is usually used against prison riots, on behalf of the 'illegal owners' of the mill. The workers managed to regain control of the factory, but worker militancy is now being met by paramilitary actions.

Conclusion

The transition to democracy and capitalism is supposed to lead to the regeneration of Russia, to provide opportunities for material prosperity, political and social participation and inclusion. For the majority of Russians, however, the reform process begun under Gorbachev and accelerated by Yeltsin has brought only increasing despair and poverty. The fear of a Russian genocide is very real and provides ammunition to Russia's Red-Brown political forces. In his first state of the nation address in July 2000, President Putin stated that the Russian population is falling by 750 000 annually and that in 15 years' time there could be 22 million fewer Russian citizens. He believes that if this trend continues Russia's very survival as a nation will be in jeopardy (*Rossiiskaia gazeta*, 11 July 2000: 1 and 3). The state's continuing difficulties in raising revenues and the disputes generated by attempts to transfer funds from the richer to the poorer areas are manifestations of

Russia's profound and continuing difficulties in state-building, which undermine attempts to address the very real social, health and ecological problems facing Russia today.

References

Ashwin, Sarah (1998) 'Endless Patience: Explaining Soviet and Post-Soviet Social Stability', *Communist and Post-Communist Studies* 31 (2), 187–198

Åslund, Anders (1991) 'Gorbachev, *Perestroyka*, and Economic Crisis,' *Problems of Communism* 41 (1) January–April, 18–39

Bridger, Sue, Kay, Rebecca and Pinnick, Kathryn (1996) *No More Heroines? Russia, Women and the Market*, London: Routledge

Buzgalin, Aleksandr (1998) 'The People are Silent?', *Prism* 4 (20), 16 October, http://www.jamestown.org/

Clark, Victoria (1995) 'Killer Vodka Runs Riot in Russia', *The Observer*, 26 November, 26

Clarke, Simon (1999) 'Poverty in Russia', *Problems of Economic Transition* 42 (5) September, 5–55

Einhorn, Barbara (1993) *Cinderella Goes to Market*, London: Verso

Elizarov, V.V. (1998) 'Demograficheskaia situatsiia i problemy semeinoi politika', *Sotsiologicheskie Issledovaniia* (2), 55–61

Gentleman, Amelia (2000) 'Russians Launch Crackdown on "Sex Slave" Traffickers', *The Observer*, 12 November, 23

Gray, John (1998) *False Dawn*, London: Granta

Green, Geoff (1998) *Health and Governance in European Cities*, London: European Hospital Management Journal Limited for the WHO

Hauslohner, P. (1987) 'Gorbachev's Social Contract', *The Soviet Economy* 3 (3), 54–89

Hearst, David (1995) 'Russians Could Face Aids Explosion', *The Guardian*, 30 September, 10

Human Rights Watch (1997) 'Slishkom malo, slishkom pozdno', http://www.hrw.org/

Human Rights Watch (1999) 'Women's Human Rights', *Human Rights Watch World Report 1999*, http://www.hrw.org/

Kolganov, A. (1999) 'The Labor Movement in Russia: Changes Ahead', *Prism* 5 (19) 19 November, http://www.jamestown.org/

Labour Russia on the Net (2000) 'Position of the FNPR on the Issue of Introduction of a Single Social Tax', 14 June, http://www/trud.org/

Lane, David (1985) *Soviet Economy and Society*, Oxford: Blackwell

Loescher, Gil (1992) 'Refugee Movements and International Security', *Adelphi Papers* (268) Summer

Meek, James (1996) 'Vodka Scourge Crippling Russia', *The Guardian*, 24 February, 12

Morozova, G.F. (1994) 'Degradatsiia natsii – mif ili real'nost'?', *Sotsiologicheskie Issledovaniia* (1), 22–30

Nesporova, Alena and Ghellab, Youcef (1999) 'Labour Market Impacts of the Economic Crisis in the Russian Federation', http://www.trud.org/

Orlova, I.B. (1998) 'Samoubiistvo – iavlenie sotsial'noe', *Sotsiologicheskie Issledovaniia* (8), 69–73

Popov, V.A. and Kondratyeva, O. Iu. (1998) 'Narkotizatsiia v rossii – shag do natsional'noi katastrofy', *Sotsiologicheskie Issledovaniia* (8), 65–68

Rutkevich, M.N. (1998) 'Protsessy sotsial'noi degradatsii v rossiiskom obshchestve', *Sotsiologicheskie Issledovaniia* (6), 3–12

Shenfield, Stephen (1998) 'On the Threshold of Disaster: The Socio-Economic Situation in Russia', *Labour Russia on the Net*, http:www.trud.org/

Skripitsyna, Raisa (1995) 'Demograficheskaia situatsiia ne vnushaet optimizma', *Prezident-Parlament-Pravitel'stvo* (8), 11–13

Standing, Guy (1996) *Russian Unemployment and Enterprise Restructuring: Reviving Dead Souls*, Basingstoke: Macmillan

Trud (1999) 'International Conference on Social and Labour Issues: Overcoming Adverse Consequences of the Transition Period in the Russian Federation. Moscow 6 October', http://www.trud.org/

Varoli, John (1997) 'The Problem of Homelessness is Growing in Russia', *Prism* 3 (20), 5 December, http://www.jamestown.org/

Yudaeva, Ksenia and Gorban, Maria (1999) 'Health and Health Care', *Russian Economic Trends. Monthly Update*, 14 July, 3–10

Zaslavsky, Viktor (1982) *The Neo-Stalinist State: Class, Ethnicity and Consensus in Soviet Society*, Brighton: Harvester Press

Further reading

Tat'iana Zaslavskaia, one of Russia's leading sociologists, presents data on her research project entitled 'Monitoring Economic and Social Change in Russia' in her (1997) 'Social Disequilibrium in the Transitional Society', *Sociological Research* 36 (3) May–June, 6–21

For a thorough overview of Russia's environmental problems see:

Feshbach, Murray (1998) 'Environmental and Health Problems in the Former Soviet Union: Does it Matter to the United States?', *Post-Soviet Prospects* 6 (2) August, http://www.csis.org/

For accessible analyses of Russia's current social problems see:

Buckley, Mary (1994) 'The Politics of Social Issues', Chapter 8 in Steven White, Alex Pravda and Zvi Gitelman (eds) *Developments in Russian and Post-Soviet Politics*, Basingstoke: Macmillan
Critchlow, Patricia (2000) 'First Steps: AA and Alcoholism in Russia', *Current History* 99 (639) October, 345–49
Manning, Nick and Davidova, Nadia (2000) 'Social Policy after the Cold War: Paying the Social Costs', Chapter 8 in Mike Bowker and Cameron Ross (eds) *Russia after the Cold War*, London: Longman

On gender issues see:

Bridger, Sue, Kay, Rebecca and Pinnick, Kathryn (1996) *No More Heroines? Russia, Women and the Market*, London: Routledge
Thornhill, John (1997) 'Ivan the Terribly Lost', *Financial Times* (*Weekend*), 29–30 November, 1
Zdravomyslova, Olga (1995) 'The Position of Women' in David Lane (ed.) *Russia in Transition: Politics, Privatisation and Inequality*, London: Longman

On health care and the health system see:

Powell, David E. (1998) 'The Dismal State of Health Care in Russia', *Current History* 97 (621) October, 335–341
Shapiro, Judith (1997) 'Health and Health Care Policy', Chapter 9 in Steven White, Alex Pravda and Zvi Gitelman (eds) *Developments in Russian Politics 4*, Basingstoke: Macmillan
Yudaeva, Ksenia and Gorban, Maria (1999) 'Health and Health Care', Russian Economic Trends. Monthly Update, 14 July, 3–10
Yudaeva, Ksenia and Gorban, Maria (1999) 'Health and Health Care', Russian Economic Trends, 8 (2), 27

On trade unions and labour relations see:

Ashwin, Sarah (1998) 'Endless Patience: Explaining Soviet and Post-Soviet Social Stability', *Communist and Post-Communist Studies* 31 (2), 187–198
Cook, Linda (1994) 'Russia Labor Relations: Consolidation or Disintegration?', Chapter 5 in Douglas W. Blum (ed.) *Russia's Future Consolidation or Disintegration?*, Boulder, CO: Westview Press

Websites

http://www.trud.org/english (provides information on Russian trade unions)
http://www.csv.warwick.ac.uk/fac/soc/complabstuds/russia/russint.htm (Professor Simon Clarke, Warwick University, includes articles about trade unions, the concept of poverty, different ways of calculating levels of poverty, and the issues surrounding the system of social support in contemporary Russia)

CHAPTER 13

Conclusion

This chapter examines Putin's rise to power from his early career in the KGB, through his participation in democratic politics in Leningrad/St Petersburg, to his transfer to Moscow. Putin's power base, concept of the Russian state and authoritarian tendencies are analysed. Putin's attacks on the Chechens, oligarchs, republican and regional leaders, investigative journalists and environmentalists are explored as part of his strategy of strengthening the Russian state.

Introduction

Putin has made it clear that there cannot be any return to the soviet past and he describes socialism as a 'spent force'. Russia's future is as a democracy with a market economy and it will become further integrated into the world economy. Putin uses the language of a nationalist who wants a strong and unified Russia to be restored to its natural greatness, but at the same time he is also a westerniser. Putin is reminiscent of Tsar Peter the Great (1682–1725), who travelled extensively in Europe bringing back new ideas and technologies, modernised Russia by establishing a powerful state and army, and secured and extended Russia's borders. Peter also ruthlessly suppressed opposition to his vision of Russia within court circles and amongst the boyar nobility (Riasanovsky, 1984). Since becoming prime minister in August 1999 Putin has travelled extensively throughout the world and hosted world leaders in Moscow, and he believes that Russia will be strengthened by adopting western economic ideas. Putin has also moved against groups that he sees as endangering or weakening Russia. While still only prime minister he initiated a new war against the Chechens. Once elected president, Putin turned his attention to the republican and regional leaders and made it clear that he intends to assert the authority of the Moscow federal government throughout the county. He then turned his attention on the oligarchs and leading members of the business community who were told to repay their ill-gotten gains and back taxes, or face arrest. Then elements within the armed forces came under scrutiny and were sacked for frustrating Russia's much-needed military reforms.

While Peter the Great recruited allies and advisers from outside Russia's traditional ruling circles, Putin has turned to the security services to provide him with the institutional support and personnel needed to carry out his reforms. In Putin's first state of the nation address as president in July 2000, he warned that Russia was on the verge of becoming a Third World nation unless its economic problems were urgently addressed. At the root of so many of Russia's problems, not just in the economy, but also its rampant crime and corruption, and the lack of cooperation and even conflict between Moscow and the republics and regions, is the profound weakness of the Russian state. In his address Putin also began to distance himself from his predecessor by attacking the Yeltsin legacy of an ineffective state. The question that hangs over Putin is whether he will create a modern, strong, efficient and democratic state or whether he will try to modernise Russia through an increasingly efficient but authoritarian state.

Putin: from KGB functionary to president

From law student to KGB functionary

In 1998 most people in Russia had not heard of Vladimir Putin, but within a year he was appointed prime minister and six months later elected president. In 1997 when Yeltsin was frequently absent due to ill health, the Russian and western media were full of speculations about who would succeed Yeltsin but none identified Putin as a possible successor at this time. Putin was therefore an enigma not just to western commentators but also to most Russians. Putin was not a career politician like Yeltsin; instead his career was in the secret world of the KGB. He decided that he wanted to join the KGB while still a teenager, but had to wait until he had completed his law degree at Leningrad State University before he was invited to join (Tolstaya, 2000: 9). Putin joined the KGB in 1975, a period of Brezhnevite stagnation at home but détente in international relations. At this time the KGB was headed by Yury Andropov, who became general secretary of the CPSU on Brezhnev's death. As the chair of the KGB Andropov ruthlessly suppressed soviet dissidents, some of whom were incarcerated in psychiatric hospitals and subjected to unnecessary and barbaric treatment. Throughout, Putin was a loyal KGB functionary serving mainly in Leipzig and Dresden in the then GDR.

Will the real Vladimir Putin please stand up?

Following the fall of the Berlin Wall, Putin was sent by the KGB to act as the international liaison assistant to the president of Leningrad State University. In March 1990 Putin's university law professor, Anatoly Sobchak, became Leningrad's first democratically elected mayor (chair of the Leningrad soviet) and Putin accepted Sobchak's invitation to work for him. At this time Leningrad was one of Russia's main centres of anti-communist, radical dissent and Sobchak was one of the leading figures in the democratic movement. Quite how Putin, the KGB functionary, fitted into this environment remains unclear. It is quite possible that the KGB wanted to have one of its men working on the inside, keeping an eye on what the democrats were doing. As this was the time of the 'law wars' (see Chapter 2) when alliances and allegiances were shifting from the all-union level to individual republics, it is also possible that the Leningrad KGB was not sure where its allegiance should lie and wanted to have one of its men within the new city administration. (In September 1991 Leningrad reverted to its old name St Petersburg.) Wherever Putin's loyalties lay at this time, in the future Putin and Sobchak would remain loyal to each other. In 1999 Putin had corruption charges against Sobchak dropped. In the murky world of St Petersburg politics the charges were probably the malicious concoction of Sobchak's political enemies. Sobchak returned from self-imposed exile and died of a heart attack in February 2000, while campaigning for Putin's election as president.

This is the Putin conundrum: he spent the first 15 years of his career working for the KGB, which was charged with preserving the USSR and soviet socialism, and the next six years working for Sobchak, one of Russia's leading democratic liberals who contributed to the dissolution of the USSR and soviet socialism. During 1990–1 Sobchak was in constant conflict with the city soviet, which was still dominated by CPSU conservatives. During August 1991 Sobchak and his team sided with Yeltsin and ordered the military to stay in their barracks, which they willingly did. Throughout these momentous events Putin kept a low profile; he did not turn himself into a politician or an orator, but seems to have diligently got on with his job, whatever that might have been. In 1994 Putin became first deputy chair (mayor) of the city government, a post that involved dealing with western businessmen and investors. Amid accusations of corruption Sobchak lost the mayoral elections in 1996 to Vladimir Yakovlev, one of the city's other deputy mayors. Putin was immediately brought into Yeltsin's administration in Moscow by his fellow Leningrader Anatoly Chubais, the Kremlin chief of staff. Putin was clearly seen as reliable and loyal, and in July 1998 became a secret policeman again, when he was appointed the director of the FSB. Putin's rise from obscurity was then extremely rapid: he was appointed prime minister in August 1999 and named Yeltsin's preferred successor as president. On Yeltsin's resignation as president on 31 December 1999, Putin became acting president and was elected president on 26 March 2000.

The rise of President Putin

Putin's power base – a break with the past?

By the time that Yeltsin resigned as president the Russian public had become exasperated by his antics, his failure to address Russia's mounting problems and the corruption that went to the heart of the presidential family and administration. Putin is anxious to depict his presidency as a break with the past and particularly with the vacillation and corruption that increasingly surrounded Yeltsin's rule. As acting president Putin's first decree was to sack Yeltsin's daughter Tatyana Dyachenko as a presidential adviser, but he also granted the Yeltsin family immunity from prosecution. This does not suggest that Putin is determined to wipe out corruption, unless the immunity is viewed as a purely tactical move to take over Yeltsin's power base. Alexander Voloshin, the head of the presidential administration, resigned with Yeltsin but was immediately reinstated. Putin also inherited the support of Russia's leading businessmen, the oligarchs (see Chapter 1). Whilst Putin was prime minister and then acting president, there is no evidence that he distanced himself from the oligarchs who had bankrolled Yeltsin's election in 1996. As Putin does not have a political party, in order to get elected he needed the funds, personnel, organisation and publicity that the oligarchs could provide. It is clear that the oligarchs were less enthusiastic in their support for Putin in 2000 than they had been for Yeltsin, but they nonetheless put their vast media empires at his disposal. The one notable exception was Vladimir Gusinsky, the head of Media-Most, who had fallen out badly with Boris Berezovsky following the 1996 presidential elections. In the run up to the 2000 presidential elections, Putin declared that he was too busy with affairs of state to campaign, but while not formally campaigning he was shown on television every night working on behalf of Russia (see Box 13.1).

BOX 13.1

Putin in an interview with American ABC television on 24 March 2000

The right of ownership must be a priority in Russia ... We will strive to make the position of the state crystal clear in its legislation. We need to make the state strong enough to guarantee the implementation of these rights. I am bringing into my inner circle people from the law enforcement bodies who are in no way connected with the people and structures which may be associated with any form of corruption.

I have known them for many years and I trust them. It has nothing to do with ideology. It's simply a matter of their professional qualities and personal relationships.

Source: quoted by Ian Traynor (2000) 'Putin Puts his Trust in KGB Honesty', *The Guardian*, 25 March 2000, 15.

The creation of Vladimir Putin

Putin's public image has been carefully groomed simultaneously to distance him from Yeltsin and to calm fears about having a former secret policeman in the Kremlin. The secret policeman has been humanised by presenting him as a loving, family man. His wife Lyudmila has accompanied him on a number of official visits, but generally plays the role of 'the supportive wife in the background', as adopted by Yeltsin's wife Naina. Whilst eager not to appear as a would-be tyrant, Putin presents an image of a tough, incorruptible and decisive leader. Putin is shown as young, healthy, energetic, virtually teetotal, a judo black belt and a skier. Putin was 47 when he was elected president, the youngest Russian leader since Stalin. Whilst Yeltsin was keen to be seen as a westerniser and was shown opening a McDonald's, that symbol of western capitalism in Moscow, during Easter 2000 Putin was shown eating Russian *bliny* (pancakes). The message is clear: Putin is a Russian who will be able to restore Russia's pride and stand up for Russian interests at home and abroad. A major breakdown in the creation of Putin's tough-guy public image occurred when journalists revealed that the Putin family has (horror of horrors) a toy poodle called Toska. Putin eventually appeared in public with Toska but claimed that it was his children's dog and that he used to have a much more ferocious one but it died (Tolstaya, 2000: 8). Evidently, tough presidents do not have pet poodles. The flip side of the careful presentation of a positive image of Putin for the presidential elections was that Grigory Yavlinsky, who it was feared might attract enough votes to prevent Putin from winning outright in the first round, was subjected to a sustained campaign of compromising materials playing on homophobia and anti-Semitism. In the macho world of Russian politics, members of a supposedly gay group, Blue Heart, were shown endorsing Yavlinsky (blue, *goluboi*, is the Russian word for gay). ORT ran a report that Yavlinsky was being backed by the prominent Jewish oligarch Vladimir Gusinsky, who has dual Russian–Israeli citizenship (see Chapter 9). The report was designed to appeal to anti-Semitic sentiments and used images of Jewish people wearing skullcaps. RTV also reported that Yavlinsky had had plastic surgery.

Putin's power base – the security services and state in uniform

Putin's former career in the KGB and as head of the FSB have provided him with a power base within the security services. Putin also made a bid for the support of the armed forces by sacking some generals, but also by promising higher defence spending and new weapons systems. For the security services and armed forces the new Foreign Policy Concept and Military Doctrine both strike the right tone of standing up for Russia. While Putin used the support of the oligarchs and their media to raise his public profile in the run up to the presidential elections, the FSB and the 'state in uniform' provided him with the means to win public support and to consolidate himself once in office. The FSB are implicated in the explosions in Moscow apartment blocks in September 1999 and in a failed bomb plot in Ryazan (see Chapter 6) that were used to justify the assault on Chechnia. A subsequent interrupted attempt at planting a bomb was quickly described as an FSB training exercise, but this supposed exercise involved planting real explosives with a real detonator in a residential area. Russian public opinion had been fiercely opposed to the first Chechen war (1994–6) and so it had to be carefully prepared to support a new military assault and elements within the media whipped up anti-Chechen sentiments. Putin's identification with the war helped to create his public image and sent his popularity rising. The cost is 200 people killed in the Moscow bombings, the untold number of people killed in Chechnia, and large-scale human rights abuses in Chechnia including mass executions of civilians, arbitrary detentions of Chechens, torture and rape.

The continuing personalisation of political power

Putin depicts himself as above politics and like Yeltsin has not founded or joined a political party. In the run up to the 2000 presidential election Putin did not produce a manifesto or a programme, which means that voters were asked to vote for Putin the man. This personalisation of politics enabled Putin to appeal to voters across a wide range of party allegiances and ideological orientations, from pro-market liberals through to communists and nationalists. In the absence of a political party Putin did have 'reception points' such as at the Mining Institute in St Petersburg (Traynor, 2000a: 20). The reception point staff received electors' requests which included complaints about the non-payment of wages and pensions, and requests for housing and financial support. This is reminiscent of courtiers collecting petitions from the people to pass on to a tsar. This indicates a broader problem of institutional development within Russia, which has been exacerbated by both Yeltsin and Putin's personalised approach to political leadership. In democracies, while voters do approach their representatives with individual problems, most popular demands are processed by political parties, autonomous social and political organisations, and parliament, not by *ad hoc* groups of election workers.

The continuing creation of the Russian state

Putin's concept of the strong Russian state

Putin's early career in the KGB led to speculation that Russian democratisation was in peril. In his first speech as acting president Putin was quick to assure Russians that there would be 'no backsliding on any of the key political liberties gained in the past decade' and that 'Freedom of speech, freedom of conscience, freedom of the press, the right to private property – these basic principles of a civilised society will be protected' (http://news unlimited.co.uk/Russia). At the same time Putin also believes that Russia is a great power (*derzhava*) and he is an advocate of a strong state (*gosudarstvennik*) (see Chapter 9), which seems to contradict his commitment to democratic freedoms. Putin has continued Yeltsin's stress on 'Russia First' and its identification of the state with Russia. For Putin, the Russian state is unified, there are identifiable national interests and there can be no interests that are more important than these. All policies both foreign and domestic must promote Russia's interests and strengthen the Russian state; all other concerns are of secondary importance. The Chechen rebels want to weaken the Russian state by diminishing its territorial expanse. As the Chechen rebels are not taking Russia's interests into account, the Russian state is justified in using all means at its disposal to oppose Chechen independence. Human rights issues and democratic freedoms are of secondary importance to the maintenance of the Russian state.

Putin is adamant that only a strong state is able to defend civil, political and economic freedoms (see Box 13.2). It is certainly true that if a state is unable to provide security and law and order, then the result is not freedom but instability and anarchy. Putin's concept of a strong state goes beyond these basic requirements. Even though the president already has extensive powers under the 1993 Constitution, Putin is seeking ever greater powers for the president and the security services. He wants the right to suspend political parties, to close the media, and to monitor emails and the internet. Then at the end of November 2000 he persuaded the Duma to vote by 282 to 130 to give not only Yeltsin and his family immunity from prosecution, but also all future Russian presidents such immunity. This measure was opposed by political parties as diverse as Yabloko and the KPRF, on the grounds that it infringed the Constitution which declares that all Russian citizens are equal before the law, whereas this law would put Russian presidents above the law. This bill needs to pass two more Duma votes before becoming law. In August 2000 leading Russian public figures produced a liberal manifesto in which they warned of Putin's creeping authoritarian tendencies. Berezovsky was one of

---

BOX 13.2

A strong and democratic state?

Putin in his state of the nation address in July 2000 declared that:

Only a strong, an effective state – if someone doesn't like the word 'strong', we'll say 'effective' – an effective state can protect civil, political and economic freedoms and create the conditions for people to live prosperously and for our homeland to flourish.

Source: *Rossiiskaia gazeta*, 11 July 2000, 1.

the signatories and it is clear that he would take any opportunity to attack Putin. Other signatories included Alexander Yakovlev, the architect of Gorbachev's policy of *glasnost*, and leading figures from the arts such as the novelist Vasily Aksenov and the theatre director Yury Liubimov.

Russia as a unified state

Putin has clearly targeted any group that he perceives as a threat to the Russian state and its territorial integrity. A profound problem for Russia today is that while the USSR had the ideology of Marxism–Leninism and the all-pervasive presence of the CPSU to give it some albeit spurious cohesion, Russia lacks this ideological and institutional glue. Although there is increasing support for democratic values (see Chapter 8), Russian state institutions are perceived as ineffective and often corrupt. The Chechens also challenge the very legitimacy of Moscow's authority over Chechnia. For his part, Putin describes the first Chechen war (1994–6) as a 'crime' and a Russian 'defeat'. Chechnia is the extreme example of the Yeltsin administration's inability to assert Moscow's authority over the regions. Putin's creation of new federal districts and the imposition of presidential representatives, drawn mostly from his security institutions power base, is a clear attempt to recentralise the power that drifted to the republics and regions during the Yeltsin presidency. While some of the republican and regional leaders are very far from being democrats (see Chapter 5), it seems that Putin is more interested in imposing Moscow rule than in imposing democracy. Any ousting or undermining of a local dictator would be a by-product of this greater goal. Although Putin recognises that Russia is a multinational state, the presidential representatives are allocated to large territorially designated areas which include Russia's territorial- and nationality-based federal subjects. This could be a way of submerging the nationality-based units within larger Russian state institutions and so an attempt to block the potentially centrifugal effect of providing Russia's non-Russian peoples with their own designated areas. Russia's republics and regions will not just accept this centralisation and so the relations between them and the Putin administration in Moscow look set for a series of confrontations, particularly over Putin's plans to create a centralised system of tax collection. Russia still faces the problem of creating a unified state that recognises that a constructive and democratic pluralism is necessary in such a vast and varied country.

Pluralism, freedom of speech and traitors to Russia

Putin's use of the term 'traitors' to describe not just Chechen rebels, but also journalists and environmentalists (see Chapters 6 and 9), implies a concept of patriotism that does not sit well with democratic pluralism and the rule of law. Putin has shown a lasting allegiance to former heads of the KGB, by paying friendly visits to Vladimir Kryuchkov, who was one of the leaders of the anti-Gorbachev August 1991 coup, and having the plaque dedicated to Yury Andropov put back in its place at the FSB headquarters in Moscow (Traynor, 2000b: 17). Kryuchkov and Andropov were men dedicated to the preservation not just of soviet socialism but crucially also the soviet state. Putin is also alleged to have raised a toast to Stalin, under whose rule the USSR became a powerful monolithic state. The problem is that while Putin describes freedom of speech as one of the unshakeable values of Russian democracy, his understanding of freedom of speech is one which does not countenance any challenge to the state. So the Russian journalist Andrei Babitsky's reports from Chechnia were dismissed because he was a 'traitor', reporting from an allegedly pro-Chechen perspective, and because he was employed by the western propaganda organisation Radio Liberty (see Chapter 9). Similarly, while Putin was the head of the FSB and then prime minister he did nothing to rein in the campaign against environmentalist campaigners such as Captain Alexander Nikitin, who was not even allowed to know under which laws he was charged (see Chapter 6). Russia's environmentalists and anti-nuclear campaigners are condemned as western spies and subjected to harassment. In March 2000, for example, the Moscow offices of Greenpeace were ordered to close because a partition wall supposedly infringed planning regulations. Curiously, the closure order originated in the Anti-Terrorism Commission in Moscow, indicating that environmental organisations are viewed as security risks and covers for western spying. Then, in May 2000, the Duma Committee on the Environment, the official environmental watchdog, was disbanded and its functions transferred to the Ministry of Natural Resources. This ministry is responsible for the licensing and the commercial exploitation of natural resources. Russia's powerful timber, mining and oil lobbies now have no agency within government to challenge their activities and environmental groups are dismissed as traitors. The future prospects for the Russia environment do not look good as commercial interests are taking precedence over environmental concerns.

Putin and the oligarchs

Putin clearly owes his election to the oligarchs, principally to Boris Berezovsky, and yet one of Putin's most popular campaign promises (so far as he made any promises) was that he would destroy the oligarchs as a class. Much of the oligarchs' assets were acquired by methods of dubious legality, they siphon their wealth abroad and avoid paying taxes. With their wealth comes political clout, which undermines Russia's democratisation. Whilst Putin was prime minister and then acting president there is no evidence that he distanced himself from the oligarchs and he even relied on them during the presidential election (see Box 13.3). The experience of prime ministers Primakov and especially Kiriyenko shows that any attempt to take on the oligarchs could

---

BOX 13.3

Putin and the oligarchs: two views before the March 2000 presidential elections

The oligarchs will cease to exist as a class. (Vladimir Putin)

For me personally, little is going to change. The role of the oligarchs will grow. The term oligarch means simply big capitalists in Russia. And big business is going to play a bigger and bigger role in Russia. (Boris Berezovsky)

Source: quoted by Amelia Gentleman (2000) 'The Hard Men Behind Putin', *The Observer*, 26 March, 22.

---

seriously damage a political career. The oligarchs have acted as king makers and will not readily relinquish their substantial powers and economic assets so that Putin can make good his campaign promises. On 24 March 2000 the leading oligarch Boris Berezovsky took the unusual step of holding a breakfast meeting with journalists where he stressed that he and Putin had friendly relations and spoke each day on the phone, but warned that Putin would not survive without the oligarchs' support. For western politicians and potential western investors in Russia, Putin's readiness to take on the oligarchs is a test of his readiness and ability to introduce much-needed economic reforms and to clean up Russia's business environment.

Destroying the oligarchs as a class?

In order to challenge the oligarchs Putin had to have the support of Russia's security services, law enforcement agencies and the tax police. These agencies quite literally have the files and the information necessary to conduct such a campaign. Putin's first oligarch target was Vladimir Gusinsky, who was arrested in June 1999 and charged with defrauding the state of an estimated $10 million during his acquisition of the Russian Video-Channel 11 (see Chapter 9). Gusinsky is Berezovsky's main business rival and they are also vying for control of the Russian branch of the World Jewish Congress which is currently headed by Gusinsky. In addition to being Berezovsky's rival, Gusinsky also opposes government policy in Chechnia and was one of the few public figures in Russia to support NATO's actions in Yugoslavia in 1999. Had the attack on the oligarchs stopped with Gusinsky then it could be dismissed as paying back Berezovsky for his support, but throughout the summer of 2000 one after another the oligarchs came under attack. Russian oligarchs were variously ordered to repay money illegally acquired during privatisation and/or charged with tax evasion. For example the general prosecutor ordered Vladimir Potanin's Norilsk Nikel to make reparations of $140 million to cover for losses incurred by the state during the 1995 loans-for-shares privatisation of Norilsk Nikel (see Chapter 1). The general prosecutor's office also accused Alfred Kokh, who was the chair of the State Property Committee at the time, of acting in collusion with Potanin by underestimating the value of Norilsk Nikel by a disputed $140 million. Vagit Alekperov has been charged with embezzling $500 million and the tax service also launched criminal proceedings against Mikhail Friedman's Lukoil for tax evasion. In July the tax police raided the Volga Automotive Plant (AvtoVaz), and accused the firm of producing cars with duplicate serial numbers in order to under report production and so avoid tax.

Putin and Russia's leading business people

The tax police raids and court actions were part of Putin's campaign to put Russia's business people on the defensive. Having frightened his target group, Putin then called them to a meeting in July 2000. The meeting was between Putin and 21 of Russia's richest business people, although Gusinsky and Berezovsky did not attend. Significantly, Putin told the meeting that he did not intend to modify the outcome of privatisation in the near future, that is, he does not mean to take back into state hands some of the country's most valuable assets that were privatised in suspicious circumstances during the 1990s. The message seemed to be that provided the oligarchs and business people who are under investigation pay the fines, they will be allowed to keep the assets they acquired. So, for example, if Gusinsky pays the $10 million for Video-Channel 11 and Potanin the $140 million for Norilsk Nikel, they will keep these assets. Putin told the meeting that he wants to strengthen private property and that the law enforcement agencies have been ordered to fight crime not business people. Putin therefore warned the meeting that Russia's business people need to clean up their act, pay their taxes and stop siphoning money abroad. Putin also announced plans to create a government council of industrialists and entrepreneurs, which sounds as if Putin is seeking to continue Yeltsin's corporatist approach to government. The attacks on corrupt business practices continued and on 10 August 2000 tax police raided Berezovsky's oil company Sibneft and by November 2000 Berezovsky was wanted for questioning about his alleged involvement in embezzling $1 billion from the national airline Aeroflot. Berezovsky has made counter-allegations that Putin was the beneficiary of money embezzled from Aeroflot and that it was used to finance the Unity party during the 1999 Duma elections and Putin's presidential campaign. By the end of 2000 Putin had not destroyed the oligarchs as a class, but he had certainly sent a loud warning shot across their bows. In July 2000 Berezovsky resigned as the Duma deputy for Karachaevo-Cherkessia, saying that he had opposed Putin's 'reforms' from the very beginning, that government was out to destroy big business but that he did not intend to hide behind his deputy immunity from prosecution. By the end of 2000 Berezovsky and Gusinsky were refusing to return to Russia, claiming they were victims of a political vendetta.

The state and the economy

The collapse of soviet communism coincided with the height of the Washington consensus which tended to see states as impediments to markets and economic growth (see Chapter 1). The powerful soviet state, with its collective ownership of the means of production and five-year economic plans, showed just how badly wrong states could get things when they meddled in the economy. In the RF in the early 1990s policies were adopted at the prompting of the IMF that were designed to get the state out of the economy. Prices and trade were liberalised and privatisation was pushed through. States do, however, have a role to play in the economy, not least in providing the rule of law and an appropriate legal environment in which the market can operate. States are also needed to mediate between the domestic and the international economies. Russia is currently suffering from a collapse in manufacturing, speculative economic activities and financial flight. In the mid-1990s Russia rather belatedly began to reintroduce protection for its domestic industrial and agricultural producers, and it also needs to introduce controls over its financial markets. Overall, the Russian economy needs more productive and less speculative activities, and this requires the Russian government to engage in greater strategic planning. In the course of the 1990s the IMF and the World Bank turned their attention to state capacity building, that is ensuring that states were able to act efficiently and effectively in support of the market. Capacity building means that Russia needs competent and incorrupt civil servants at all levels; a first step here would be to improve salaries to discourage corruption. Russia also needs to have coherent institutions pursuing the same broad policy goals and not for example the situation in the 1990s when the Russian Central Bank printed more and more money, while Gaidar was trying to control the money supply. Russia has also suffered from the different levels of government pursuing contradictory interests, particularly demonstrated by the continuing disputes over the levying and control of tax revenues between Moscow and the republics and regions. The simplest way to achieve the coherence needed to kick-start the Russian economy would be by imposing a new dictatorship. Pyotr Aven, a former foreign trade minister and president of Alfa Bank, has called upon Putin to model himself on Chile's Augusto Pinochet, combining Reaganomics (free market policies) with dictatorial control, arguing that totalitarian methods should be used to push though radical economic reform and that the state should force people to obey the law (Traynor, 2000c: 17).

The *Kursk* disaster and the Ostankino fire, August 2000

In August 2000, barely a year after Putin had been appointed prime minister, there were two incidents that graphically demonstrated just how far Russia has come in the last 10–15 years and how much further it has to go. First, the submarine *Kursk* sank in the Barents Sea killing the 118-strong crew. Putin has committed himself to addressing the much-needed reform and modernisation of the armed forces that this accident so tragically illustrated. Certainly, delays in accepting help from other countries seemed to indicate the disregard for human lives already graphically shown in Chechnia, plus the persistence of a certain Cold War mentality and a sense of inferiority in regard to the West. It took a suntanned Putin ten days to end his summer holiday and travel to the disaster site, which perhaps reveals more that he is not an experienced, populist politician, than any lack of concern. The fact that the disaster was shown on Russian television, that officials were shown being berated by the victims' families and that one highly distressed women was shown being forcibly sedated, would not have been revealed on Russian television even ten years ago. Then at the end of August the Ostankino television tower in Moscow caught fire, putting Russian national television broadcasts off the air. Putin said the fire was symptomatic of Russia's poor infrastructure and lack of investment. The *Kursk* and Ostankino accidents indicate the vast scale of investment and technological modernisation that Russia needs to undertake.

And finally...

Putin was elected president and Yeltsin left office peacefully. This is a major change for Russia, a country where until now leaders have either died in power or been ousted in a coup or a revolution. Elections are being held, public debate is open and freewheeling, and the media are more pluralistic than at any time in Russian history. This is also a country that economically, culturally and politically is more open to the rest of the world than ever before. There will be no going back to a soviet socialist past but what the future holds is still unclear. Putin says he is committed to democracy and free speech, but he has been prepared to abandon them when he perceives the interests of the Russian state to be endangered. Democratic rights and freedoms are just that, rights and freedoms; they cannot and should not be made contingent upon the views of the president, even an elected president. In Chapter 1 the arguments in favour of transitional authoritarianism were introduced. It remains to be seen in the next few years whether such a system is being established by President Putin, and the parallels between Putin and Peter the Great will grow stronger.

References

Riasanovsky, Nicholas V. (1984) (4th edn) *A History of Russia*, Oxford: Oxford University Press

Tolstaya, Tatyana (2000) 'The Making of Mr. Putin', *New York Review of Books* XLVII (9) 25 May, 8–11 (trans: Jamey Gambrell)

Traynor, Ian (2000a) 'Weary Russia turns to Putin', *The Guardian*, 16 March, 20

Traynor, Ian (2000b) 'KGB Veteran says Putin's Rule is Return to Soviet Era', *The Guardian*, 24 March, 17

Traynor, Ian (2000c) 'Putin Urged to Apply the Pinochet Stick', *The Guardian*, 31 March, 17

Further reading

For interesting speculations on how Russia might develop see:

'Feature: Putin's Russia', *East European Constitutional Review* 9 (1–2) Winter/ Spring, 51–91 contains a number of short articles on elections, the media, the strong state ideal, corruption, foreign policy, national security and law and order by leading specialists

Yergin, Daniel and Gustafson, Thane (1993) *Russia 2010 and What It Means for the World: The Cera Report*, London: Nicholas Brealey Publishing

For a positive assessment of the Russian economy originally published in the newspaper *Nezavisimaia gazeta*, 4 April 2000 see:

Åslund, Anders (2000) 'Putin's Boom: After a Decade of Chaos the Russian Economy is Finally Starting to Recover', *Carnegie Endowment for International Peace: Russian and Eurasian Affairs Program*, http://www.ceip.org/

McFaul, Michael (2000) 'Putin in Power', *Current History* 99 (639) October, 307–314 argues that far from the Russian state being weak, Putin has been able to use 'the tremendous power' of the Russian state

The dynamics of State Duma elections, 1993–1999

	1993		1995		1999	
	% Support	No. of deputies	% Support	No. of deputies	% Support	No. of deputies
Communist Party of the RF (KPRF)	12.4	62	22.3	157	24.3	113
Unity (Bear) Medved					23.2	72
(Otchestvo) Fatherland–All Russia (OVR)					12.1	66
Union of Rightist Forces (SPS)					8.6	29
Russia's (Democratic) Choice	15.5	101	3.9	9		
Liberal Democratic Party of Russia (LDPRF)/Zhirinovsky Bloc (ZB)	22.9	66	11.2	51	6.0	17
Yabloko	7.9	28	6.9	45	6.0	21
Women of Russia (ZhR)	8.1	25	4.6	3	2.1	0
Our Home is Russia (NDR)			10.1	51	1.2	7
Agrarian Party (APR)	8.0	49	3.8	20		
Party of Russian Unity and Accord	6.7	27	0.4	1		
Democratic Party of Russia	5.5	17				
Others/Independents	13.0	75	35.8	36	16.5	125

Source: http://www-public.rz.uni-dusseldorf.de/-nordsiew/russia.html

The State Duma committees

Committee on Agricultural Questions
Committee on Security
Committee on Budget and Tax
Committee on Local Government
Committee on Government Building
Committee on Women's Affairs, the Family and Young People
Committee on Nationalities' Affairs
Committee on Social and Religious Organisations
Committee on the CIS and Links with Compatriots
Committee on Federal and Regional Policy
Committee on Legislation
Committee on Information Policy
Committee on Credit Organisations and Financial Markets
Committee on Culture and Tourism
Committee on International Affairs
Committee on Defence
Committee on Education and Science
Committee on Health Protection and Sport
Committee on Natural Resources and the Use of Natural Resources
Committee on the Problems of the North and the Far East
Committee on Industry, Construction and High Technology Research
Committee on the Regulation and Organisation of the State Duma
Committee on Property
Committee on Labour, Social Policy and Veteran Affairs
Committee on Ecology
Committee on Economic Policy and Enterprise
Committee on Energy, Transportation and Communications

Source: http://www.duma.gov.ru/deputats/committee.htm

The federal organs of executive power of the Russian Federation

Federal ministries

Ministry for Antimonopoly Policy and Support for Enterpreneurship
Ministry for Atomic Energy
Ministry of the Interior
Ministry for Property Relations
Ministry for Civil Defence, Emergency Situations and Natural Disasters
Ministry of Public Health
Ministry of Foreign Affairs
Ministry of Culture
Ministry of Taxes and Assessments
Ministry of Industry, Science and Technology
Ministry of Foreign Affairs, Nationalities' Policy and Migration Policy
Ministry of Defence
Ministry of Education
Ministry of Natural Resources
Ministry of Communications
Ministry of Regional Policy
Ministry of Agriculture and Food
Ministry of Fuel and Energy
Ministry of Trade
Ministry of Transportation
Ministry of Labour and Social Development
Ministry of Finance
Ministry of Economic Development and Trade
Ministry of Justice
Ministry of Railroads

Note: In May 2000 President Putin abolished four ministries (Economics, Trade, Science and CIS Affairs) and created two new ministries (Economic Development and Trade; and Science, Industry and Technology).

State committees of the Russian Federation

State Committee for Young People's Affairs (abolished May 2000)
State Land Policy Committee (abolished May 2000)
State Committee for the Northern Regions (abolished May 2000)
State Cinematography Committee (abolished May 2000)
State Environmental Protection Committee (abolished May 2000)
State Fisheries Committee
State Standardisation and Metrology Committee
State Statistics Committee (Goskomstat)
State Committee for Construction, Housing and Municipal Services
State Customs Committee
State Committee for Physical Culture and Tourism

Note: State Committees for State Reserves, the Management of State Property, the Press, and Communications and Information were abolished during Yeltsin's presidency. The functions of the committees and agencies abolished in May 2000 were distributed amongst the remaining committees and agencies.

Federal commissions of Russia

Federal Securities Market Commission
Federal Energy Commission

Federal services of Russia

Foreign Intelligence Service
Aerospace Service (abolished May 2000)
Archive Service
Railway Service
Geodesy and Cartography Service
Railway Forces Service
Migration Service (abolished May 2000)
Hydro-meteorology and Environmental Monitoring Service
Federal Security Service (FSB)
Hard Currency and Export Control Service (abolished May 2000)
Forestry Service
Federal Service for the Protection of the Russian Federation
Bankruptcy and Financial Protection Service
Federal Border Service
Television and Radio Service
Road Agency (abolished May 2000)

Russian state agencies

Russian State Agency for Patents and Trade Marks
Russian Space Agency
Federal Agency for Government Communications and Information (FAPSI)

Federal inspectors of Russia

Federal Mining and Industry Inspectors
Federal Atomic and Radioactive Security Inspectors

Other federal organs of executive power

Administration of the President of the Russian Federation
State Administration of Special Programmes of the President of the Russian
   Federation
State Technical Commission for the President of the Russian Federation
Committee for the Conventional Problems of Chemical and Biological Weapons for
   the President of the Russian Federation

Source: Russian Government website – http://www.gov.ru/ministry/ (updated and amended)

The presidential administration of the Russian Federation

The administration of the President of the Russian Federation
The protocol office of the President of the Russian Federation
The press service office of the President of the Russian Administration
The secretariat of the head of the administration of the President of the Russian Federation
The chief state-legal office of the President of the Russian Federation
The chief supervisory office of the President of the Russian Federation
The chief office of the President of the Russian Federation for regional policy and local self-government
The apparatus of the Security Council of the Russian Federation
The office of the President of the Russian Federation for foreign policy
The office of the President of the Russian Federation for internal affairs
The office of the President of the Russian Federation for state awards
The office of the President of the Russian Federation on citizenship issues
The office of the President of the Russian Federation for Cossack affairs
The office of the President of the Russian Federation for pardons
The office of informational and document security of the President of the Russian Federation
The personnel office of the President of the Russian Federation
The office of the President of the Russian Federation for work with communications from citizens
The office of the President of the Russian Federation for ties with the community and culture
Organisational office of the administration of the President of the Russian Federation
Executive office of the administration of the President of the Russian Federation
Economic office of the President of the Russian Federation

Source: Russian Government website – http://www.gov.ru/ministry/

Russia's republics

* Territorial size is expressed in thousands of square kilometres
** Population is expressed in thousands

Adygeya
Capital: Maikop
Territorial size: 7.6*   Population: 442**
Administrative divisions: 2 towns
Urbanisation: 53.9 per cent
Industry: food, forestry, wood, machine building, gas extraction
Agriculture: grain, sunflowers, sugar beet, tobacco, vegetables, melon growing, wine making, animal husbandry

Note: until 1992 the republic was part of Krasnodar Territory

Altai
Capital: Barnaul
Territorial size: 261.7   Population: 2851
Administrative divisions: 60 *raions* and 11 towns
Urbanisation: 52.2 per cent
Industry: non-ferrous metals, machine building, light industry
Agriculture: grain

Bashkortostan (formerly Bashkiria)
Capital: Ufa
Territorial size: 143.6   Population: 3984
Urbanisation: 64.49 per cent
Administrative divisions: 54 *raions* and 17 towns
Industry: oil production, petroleum chemicals, machine building (oil industry apparatus, chemical equipment, machine tools and motors), metal working, metallurgy, building materials, wood products, light industry, food, oil extraction, coal, iron and copper-zinc ores, military-related industries
Agriculture: grain, sugar beet, sunflowers, vegetables, livestock, poultry, bee keeping

Buryatia
Capital: Ulan-Ude
Territorial size: 351.3   Population: 1056
Administrative divisions: 20 *raions* and 6 towns
Urbanisation: 59.2 per cent
Industry: mineral extraction (tungsten, molybdenum, gold, coal, nickel, aluminium, coal), machine building, forestry, wood products
Agriculture: livestock, grain, fur farming, fur trade

Chechnia

Capital: Grozny
Territorial size: 10   Population: 800
Administrative divisions: not ascertained
Urbanisation: not ascertained
Industry: oil, oil processing, petroleum
  chemicals, energy, machine building,
  food forestry, wood products
Agriculture: horticulture, grain, sugar beet,
  livestock

Note: from 1934 Chechnia was part of the
Checheno-Ingush automous republic of the
USSR; an independent Chechen republic was
declared in November 1991 and formalised in
1992

Chuvashia

Capital: Cheboksary
Territorial size: 18.3   Population: 1353
Administrative divisions: 21 *raions* and 9
  towns
Urbanisation: 42.9 per cent
Industry: machine building, chemicals, light
  industry, wood products, food
Agriculture: grain, horticulture, hops, flax,
  makhorka, livestock

Dagestan

Capital: Makhachkala
Territorial size: 50.3   Population: 1890
Administrative divisions: 41 *raions* and 8
  towns
Urbanisation: 42.5 per cent
Industry: oil and gas extraction, machine
  building, metal working, food, light
  industry, craft industries (coins and
  carpet making)
Agriculture: grain, wine, horticulture

Ingushetia

Capital: Nazran
Territorial size: 9   Population: 500
Administrative divisions: not ascertained

Urbanisation: 42.9 per cent
Industry: chemicals, oil processing, light
  industry
Agriculture: livestock

Note: from 1934 Ingushetia was part of the
Checheno-Ingush autonomous republic of the
USSR; it formally separated from Chechnia to
1992 to become the Ingush republic or
Ingushetia

Kabardino-Balkaria

Capital: Nalchik
Territorial size: 12.5   Population: 784
Administrative divisions: 8 *raions* and 7
  towns
Urbanisation: 59.8 per cent
Industry: machine building, metal working,
  non-ferrous metallurgy, food, light
  industry, building materials, extraction
  and processing of tungsten,
  molybdenum, chromium, nickel and
  gold ores
Agriculture: grain, sunflowers, livestock,
  horticulture, wine

Kalmykia

Capital: Elista
Territorial size: 76.1   Population: 328
Administrative divisions: 13 *raions* and 3
  towns
Urbanisation: 37.4 per cent
Industry: machine building, metal working,
  building materials, food, extraction of
  natural gas, oil
Agriculture: grain, livestock mostly sheep

Note: adopted the name Kalmykia-Khalmg
Tangch in 1992–6, then reverted to
Kalmykia

Karachaevo-Cherkessia

Capital: Chekessk
Territorial size: 14.1   Population: 431
Administrative divisions: 4 towns
Urbanisation: 47.7 per cent

Industry: petroleum, chemicals, light industry, machine building, metal working, electrical, wood products, coal extraction

Agriculture: livestock, grain, sunflowers, sugar beet, vegetables

Karelia
Capital: Petrozavodsk
Territorial size: 172.4   Population: 799
Administrative divisions: 15 *raions* and 12 towns
Urbanisation: 74.1 per cent
Industry: forestry, furniture, cellulose-paper, wood products, machine building, metallurgy, mineral extraction (iron ore, mica)
Agriculture: livestock, poultry, fur farming, fisheries

Khakassia
Capital: Abakan
Territorial size: 61.9   Population: 570
Administrative divisions: *raions* not ascertained, 5 towns
Urbanisation: 72.3 per cent
Industry: material extraction (coal, iron ore, non-ferrous metal ores, copper, molybdenum, marble), light industry, machine building, non-ferrous metallurgy, forestry, wood products, food
Agriculture: grain, livestock (sheep and goats)

Komi
Capital: Syktyvkvar
Territorial size: 415.9   Population: 1265
Administrative divisions: 16 *raions* and 10 towns
Urbanisation: 74.7 per cent
Industry: heating energy, forestry, cellulose-paper, wood products, building materials, metal working, food, light

industry, extraction and processing of oil and gas
Agriculture: livestock, reindeer farming

Marii El
Capital: Ioshkar-Ola
Territorial size: 23.2   Population: 762
Administrative divisions: 14 *raions* and 4 towns
Urbanisation: 62 per cent
Industry: dominated by military industries, machine building accounts for 40 per cent of industrial output, metal working, pulp and paper, wood products, light industry, pharmaceuticals
Agriculture: livestock, flax, grain

Note: Marii El is dependent upon the federal authorities for its energy supplies

Mordovia
Capital: Saransk
Territorial size: 26.2   Population: 964
Administrative divisions: 21 *raions* and 7 towns
Urbanisation: 58.2 per cent
Industry: machine building, metal working, chemicals, light industry, food, building materials; contains the Rossiiskii Svet complex, the largest lighting equipment site in Europe
Agriculture: grain, sugar beet, hemp, livestock, dairy, poultry, bee keeping

North (Severnaia) Ossetia
Capital: Vladikavkaz (Ordzhonikidze until 1990)
Territorial size: 8.0   Population: 695
Administrative divisions: 8 *raions* and 6 towns
Urbanisation: not ascertained
Industry: non-ferrous metallurgy, machine building, wood products, light industry, chemicals, glass

Agriculture: vegetables, grain, horticulture, wine, livestock

Note: South Ossetia is a part of neighbouring Georgia

Sakha (formerly Yakutia)
Capital: Yakutsk
Territorial size: 3103.2   Population: 1109
Administrative divisions: 34 *raions* and 11 towns
Urbanisation: 62.5 per cent
Industry: mineral extraction (gold, diamonds, tin, mica, antimony, coal), forestry, wood products, food
Agriculture: livestock, reindeer farming, fur farming, hunting, fisheries

Tatarstan
Capital: Kazan
Territorial size: 68   Population: 3696
Administrative divisions: 39 *raions* and 18 towns
Urbanisation: 73.5 per cent
Industry: oil and gas production, chemicals, petroleum chemicals, machine building, light industry, food
Agriculture: grain, livestock, horticulture, fur farming, poultry, bee keeping

Note: in the mid-1990s eight new oil fields were found in Tatarstan

Tyva (formerly Tuva)
Capital: Kyzyl
Territorial size: 170.5   Population: 310
Administrative divisions: 14 *raions* and 5 towns
Urbanisation: 48 per cent
Industry: mineral extraction (asbestos, cobalt, coal, mercury), forestry, wood products, light industry, building materials, metal working, food
Agriculture: livestock (sheep, yaks and cattle), hunting-fur skins

Note: Tyva has a particularly poorly developed infrastructure

Udmurtia
Capital: Izhevsk
Territorial size: 42.1   Population 1637
Administrative divisions: 25 *raions* and 6 towns
Urbanisation: 69.9 per cent
Industry: machine building, metal working, metallurgy, timber, wood products, oil, chemicals, glass works, light industry, food, peat extraction
Agriculture: livestock, grain, flax

Note: also produces Kalashnikov vodka named after the rifle which is also produced in Izhevsk

President Putin's Government Cabinet and Security Council (May 2000)

Cabinet

Mikhail Kasyanov	Prime Minister
Ilya Klebanov	Deputy Prime Minister (or vice-chair)
Aleksei Kudrin	Deputy Prime Minister (or vice-chair) and Minister of Finance
Valentina Matviyenko	Deputy Prime Minister (or vice-chair)
Viktor Khristenko	Deputy Prime Minister (or vice-chair)
Aleksei Gordeev	Deputy Prime Minister (or vice-chair) and Minister of Agriculture
Ilya Yuzhanov	Minister for Antimonopoly Policy and Support for Enterprises
Yevgeny Adamov	Minister of Atomic Energy
Vladimir Rushailo	Minister of the Interior
Sergei Shoigu	Minister for Civil Defence, Emergency Situations and Natural Disasters
Yury Shevchenko	Minister of Health
Farid Gazizulin	Minister for Property Relations
Igor Ivanov	Minister of Foreign Affairs
Igor Sergeev	Minister of Defence
Mikhail Shvydkoi	Minister of Culture
Gennady Bukaev	Minister for Taxes and Duties
Vladimir Fillipov	Minister of Education
Mikhail Lesin	Minister for the Press, Television and Radio Broadcasting and the Mass Media
Alexander Dondukov	Minister of Science, Industry and Technology
German Gref	Minister of Economic Development and Trade
Boris Yatskevich	Minister of Natural Resources
Nikolai Aksyonenko	Minister of Railways
Leonid Reiman	Minister for Communications and Information Technology
Sergei Frank	Minister of Transport
Alexander Pochinok	Minister for Labour and Social Development

Alexander Blokhin	Minister of Federation Affairs, Nationalities' Policy and Migration Policy
Yury Chaika	Minister for Justice
Alexander Gavrin	Minister for Energy
Igor Shuvalov	Head of the Presidential Administration; Minister without Portfolio

Cabinet meetings are also attended by the Chair of the Russian Central Bank and the President of the Academy of Sciences.

Note: The first four deputy prime minister posts were abolished by Putin in May 2000.

Source: *Keesings Record of World Events. News Digest*, May 2000: 43581 and *Rossiiskaia gazeta*, 20 May 2000: 1

Security Council

Vladimir Putin	Chair

Permanent members:

Sergei Ivanov	Secretary
Mikhail Kasyanov	Prime Minister
Igor Ivanov	Foreign Minister
Igor Segeev	Defence Minister
Nikolai Patrushev	Head of the FSB

Members:

Alexander Voloshin	Head of Presidential Administration
Gennady Seleznyov	Chair of the State Duma
Igor Stroev	Chair of the Federation Council
Vladimir Rushailo	Minister of the Interior
Yury Chaika	Minister of Justice
Sergei Shoigu	Minister for Emergency Situations
Vladimir Ustinov	Prosecutor General
Vladimir Matyukhin	Head of the Federal Agency for Government Communications and Information
Sergei Lebedev	Head of the Foreign Intelligence Service
Konstantin Totsky	Head of the Federal Border Guards Service
Yury Osipov	President of the Russian Academy of Sciences
Georgy Poltavchenko	Presidential Representative to the Central district
Viktor Cherkesov	Presidential Representative to the North Western district
Viktor Kazantsev	Presidential Representative to the Southern district
Konstantin Pulikovsky	Presidential Representative to the Far Eastern district
Leonid Drachevsky	Presidential Representative to the Siberian district
Pyotr Latyshev	Presidential Representative to the Urals district
Sergei Kiriyenko	Presidential Representative to the Volga district

Source: *Keesings Record of World Events. News Digest*, May 2000: 43581–2

Abbreviations and acronyms

APR	Agrarian Party of Russia
CAP	Common Agricultural Policy
CFE	Conventional Forces in Europe Treaty
CIS	Commonwealth of Independent States
CMEA	Council for Mutual Economic Assistance (Comecon)
CPE	centrally planned economy
CPSU	Communist Party of the Soviet Union
CSCE	Conference on Security and Cooperation in Europe (later OSCE)
DPCR	Democratic Party of Communists of Russia
EAPC	European-Atlantic Partnership Council
EBRD	European Bank for Reconstruction and Development
EU	European Union
FAPSI	Federal Agency for Government Communications and Information
FIC	Federal Information Centre
FIG	financial-industrial group
FNPR	Federation of Independent Trade Unions of Russia
FSB	Federal Security Bureau
FSK	Federal Counterintelligence Service
FSU	former Soviet Union
G7	Group of 7 leading capitalist countries (Canada, France, Germany, Italy, Japan, UK and USA), which hold annual leaders' meetings which are often attended by the EU president and the IMF managing director
G8	G7 plus the Russian Federation
GATT	General Agreement on Tariffs and Trade
GDF	Glasnost Defence Foundation
GDP	gross domestic product
GDR	German Democratic Republic (East or Communist Germany)
GKI	State Property Committee (Goskomimushchestvo)
GKO	government treasury bills (>*gosudarstvennye kratkosrochnye obiazonnosti* or *obligatsii*)
GNP	gross national product
IMF	International Monetary Fund
KGB	Committee for State Security (*Komitet gosudarstvennoi bezopastnosti*)

KPRF	Communist Party of the Russian Federation
KRO	Congress of Russian Communities
KSZh	Soviet Women's Committee
LDPR	Liberal Democratic Party of Russia
LDPRF	Liberal Democratic Party of the Russian Federation
LOTOS	League for Society's Liberation from Stereotypes
MB	Ministry of Security (*Ministerstvo bezopastnosti*)
MBVD	Ministry of Security and Internal Affairs (*Ministerstvo bezopastnosti i vnutrenykh del*)
NACC	North Atlantic Cooperation Council
NAFTA	North American Free Trade Association
NATO	North Atlantic Treaty Organisation
NDR	Our Home is Russia
NGO	non-governmental organisation
NMD	National Missile Defence System, nicknamed Son of Star Wars
NTTM	Youth Centres for Scientific and Technical Creation
NTV	Independent Television
OECD	Organisation for Economic Cooperation and Development
OMON	Special Purpose Militia (*Otdel militsii osobovo naznacheniia*) Department, the Black Berets: regular army troops transferred to the Ministry of the Interior to be used against internal enemies
ORT	Russian Public Television (formerly Ostankino)
OSCE	Organisation for Security and Cooperation in Europe (formerly CSCE)
OVR	Fatherland-All Russia
PfP	Partnership for Peace
PR	presidential representative
PRFZZh	Russian Party for the Defence of Women
RAKTsZh	Russian Association of Crisis Centres for Women
RAN	Russian Academy of Sciences
RF	Russian Federation
RSDLP	Russian Social Democratic and Labour Party
RSDP	Russian Social Democratic People's Party
RSFSR	Russian Socialist Federative Soviet Republic
RSP	Russian Socialist Party
RTSB	Russian Commodities and Raw Materials Exchange
RUIE	Russian Union of Industrialists and Entrepreneurs
SAFO	Free Association of Feminist Organisations
SDI	Strategic Defence Initiative (Star Wars)
SDRF	Social Democratic Party of the Russian Federation
SPR	Socialist Party of Russia
SPS	Union of Rightist Forces
START	Strategic Arms Reduction Treaty
SVR	Foreign Intelligence Service (*Sluzhba vneshnoi rezvedky*)
SZhR	Union of Women of Russia
UES	Unified Energy System
UN	United Nations
USSR	Union of Soviet Socialist Republics
VTsIOM	All-Russian Centre for Public Opinion Research
VTsSPS	All-Union Central Council of Trade Unions (soviet era)

WEU	Western European Union
WHO	World Health Organisation
WTO	World Trade Organisation (successor organisation to GATT)
Yabloko	Yavlinsky–Boldyrev–Lukin bloc
ZhR	Women of Russia

Biographies

Boris Berezovsky

Born 1946 in Moscow. Graduated from the Institute of Forestry at Moscow State University in 1967 and holds a science PhD. Worked as an associate member of the Academy of Sciences in its Institute for Problems of Management. 1991 founded the car import business Logovaz, which in 1995 bought a 16 per cent share of ORT. 1995 bought *Nezavisimaia gazeta* and narrowly avoided an assassination attempt. 1996 became a member of the board of the Sibir Oil Co. One of Russia's leading oligarchs. Supported Yeltsin's 1996 presidential election campaign and in October 1996 was appointed to the Security Council but was dismissed in November 1997. April 1998 appointed executive secretary of the CIS. Elected to the Duma in 1999. Supported Putin's election as president but since then the two men have come into conflict. Holds Russian and Israeli citizenships.

Vladimir Bryntsalov

Born 1946 in the town of Cherkessk in the Karachai-Cherkess autonomous region (now republic) of Stavropol territory. A Russian. 1969 graduated from the Novocherkassk Polytechnic Institute and taught at a Cherkeesk technical college, then headed a construction organisation. 1979 expelled from the CPSU for petit bourgeois trends for building his own house. 1987 set up a bee hive cooperative supplying the pharmaceutical industry. 1989 headed the AgroBioApis firm. 1990 headed a new joint stock company called Verein (later Ferane). Failed to be elected to the Duma in 1993. 1995 Duma elections stood for the Ivan Rybkin bloc and elected as the deputy for the Orekhovo-Zuyevo constituency. January 1996 joined the Social Democratic Party of the Russian Federation (SDRF). March 1996 announced the establishment of the Russian Socialist Party (RSP). A candidate in the 1996 presidential elections.

Gennady Burbulis

Born 1945. Lecturer in Marxism-Leninism in Sverdlovsk when Yeltsin was the *obkom* first secretary. A member of Yeltsin's inner circle of economic and political advisers, drafted and vetted Yeltsin's speeches and was the architect of Yeltsin's late 1991 reform strategy. Headed Yeltsin's campaign staff for the June 1991 presidential election. November 1991 appointed deputy prime minister and came under sustained attack by the parliament. Supported Gaidar's Russia's Choice and shock therapy.

Viktor Chernomyrdin

Born near Orenburg, South Urals, in 1938. Attended a technical school and then began work as an oil refinery mechanic. Worked his way up through the state oil and gas ministry. 1982–92 minister of oil and gas. 1989 the gas and oil industries were split and Chernomyrdin became the head of the gas industry, Gazprom, which was Russia's biggest enterprise and the world's largest gas company. Chernomyrdin made his fortune through Gazprom, which was his economic and political base. Summer 1992 appointed to the government as a representative of the industrial lobby. 1995 founded the centrist political party NDR. December 1992–March 1998 prime minister. Had been increasingly accused of using his position to promote the energy lobby at the expense of manufacturing and other industries. April 1998 Yeltsin appointed Chernomyrdin as Russian special envoy to Yugoslavia during the Kosovo crisis. The Duma blocked Yeltsin's attempts to have Chernomyrdin reappointed as prime minister in August 1998.

Anatoly Chubais

Born 1955 and educated at the Leningrad Institute of Technology and Engineering. A radical economist, an advocate of shock therapy and a close ally of Yegor Gaidar. Appointed a first deputy prime minister and the chair of GKI in charge of privatisation reforms, devised Russia's voucher system of privatisation. January 1996 fired as first deputy prime minister after Yeltsin made him the scapegoat for the hardships generated by economic reform. 1996 returned to head Yeltsin's staff, and masterminded Yeltsin's election campaign, working closely with Boris Berezovsky and Tatyana Dyachenko. Acted as 'regent' during Yeltsin's illnesses. Put in charge of economic policy after the 1996 election. November 1997 fired from post as finance minister for taking an advance on a book about privatisation from a company that benefited from privatisation. April 1998 named head of the Unified Energy System (UES) electricity monopoly and became government liaison representative with the IMF. Fired from government for the third time following the August 1998 economic crisis but remains head of UES.

Dzhokar Dudaev

Born 1944, a Chechen. Joined the soviet air force and trained at military academies in Tambov and Moscow. 1990 commanded a strategic bomber base near Tartu in Estonia where he allowed the Estonian flag to be flown; his wife was Estonian. 1990 returned to Grozny and elected chair of the first All-National Congress of the Chechen People which was supported by Muslim clergy, clan elders and criminal gangs. Following the August 1991 coup the Congress seized power forcing Zavgaev to resign; this was declared unconstitutional by Yeltsin. Dudaev claimed to win the October 1991 Chechen presidential elections with 85 per of the vote with a 77 per cent turnout. Dudaev became increasingly linked to criminal gangs and opposition to his rule grew within Chechnia. 1993 Chechnia adopted a new constitution, abolished the parliament and dismissed the constitutional court. December 1994 Russia committed troops to Chechnia. Killed in a Russian air strike in 1995.

Tatyana (Tanya) Dyachenko

Born 1960. Yeltsin's second daughter. A mathematician. February 1996 joined Yeltsin's re-election campaign working closely with her allies Anatoly Chubais and Boris Berezovsky. During Yeltsin's prolonged illnesses Tatyana started to exercise informal political power by vetting who had access to Yeltsin and what documents he received. Persuaded Boris Nemtsov to join the government. From July 1997 formally appointed as a presidential adviser with responsibility for public relations. The first person to be sacked by Putin when he became acting president. Tatyana, her husband and son (also called Boris Yeltsin) live with her parents.

Umar Dzhabrailev

Born 1958, a Chechen. 1973 studied at a higher technical college in Moscow. 1985 graduated from the Moscow Institute of International Relations, and 1986–8 worked at the Institute. 1989 left the CPSU. 1989–92 worked for various western companies in Moscow. Became a businessman, in 1992 acquiring the Danako oil company. The general manager of Moscow's Radisson Slavianskaia hotel where he was the business partner of the American Paul Tatum; the two men were vying for control of the hotel. 1996 Tatum accused Dzhbrailev of plotting to kill him, and later that year Tatum was assassinated. Dzhbrailev was repeatedly questioned by the militia over Tatum's death but never arrested. 1996 became the deputy director of the Manezhnaia Ploshchad company and in 1997 became the president of the Kremlin Plaza group. The richest candidate in the 2000 presidential elections. Supports the Russian military operation in Chechnia.

Boris Fyodorov

Born 1958 in Moscow, a Russian. Attended the International Finance Institute, which trained people to deal with the capitalist world. 1985 defended his thesis on 'The organisation and economic role of modern produce exchange in advanced capitalist countries'. 1987–90 research fellow at the Institute of World Economy and International Relations of the USSR Academy of Sciences. Worked in the Central Bank, the CPSU Central Committee finance department and was an adviser to the Finance Ministry during Reconstruction. Worked with Yavlinsky on the 500-day reform programme. 1990 became finance minister. 1991 executive of EBRD in London and advised the Russian government on financial issues. October 1992 appointed by Gaidar as the Russian director of the World Bank which Russia had just joined. Resented that Gaidar did not appoint him to be the chair of the Russian Central Bank; although his economic ideas are close to Gaidar's he was never one of 'Gaidar's gang'. December 1992 appointed deputy prime minister for finance. 1993 appointed finance minister. 1993 elected to the Duma as a Russia's Choice candidate. 1994 out of government. 1995 elected to the Duma for a single mandate district for his party, Forward Russia. May 1998 appointed to head the federal tax service.

Svyatoslav Fyodorov

Born 1927 in the town of Proskurovo (now Khmelnitsky) in Ukraine. A Russian, his father was a Red Army division commander purged in 1938. Graduated from the Medical Institute in Rostov-on-Don in 1952. 1957–90 a member of the CPSU. Worked as an eye surgeon. 1960 carried out the first ever implant of an artificial lens. 1989 elected to the Congress of People's Deputies. 1990 joined the Democratic Party of Russia. June 1992 joined the Economic Freedom Party, but resigned in June 1993 due to the party leader Borovoi's support for the strong presidency in the draft constitution. 1993 candidate on the Russian Democratic Reform Movement party list but not elected. September 1994 member of the organising committee of the United Russian Democratic Movement but did not join the resulting SDRF which was founded in 1995. January 1995 presided over the founding congress of the Workers Self-Government Party. Established the Svyatoslav Fyodorov Party for the 1995 Duma elections. Contested the 1996 presidential elections. Died 2 June 2000 in a helicopter crash.

Igor Gaidar

Born 1956. The grandson of a civil war hero and son of a senior naval officer who became *Pravda*'s military commentator. 1981–7 worked as a research analyst at the Faculty of Economics, Moscow State University. 1983 served as a junior member of a state commission for economic reform set up by CPSU General Secretary Andropov, and through the commission he met Anatoly Chubais and Sergei Glaziev. 1987 appointed columnist for the reformist party weekly *Kommunist* and economics editor for *Pravda*. 1990 established a think-tank called the Institute of Market Reform. November 1991 appointed Russian finance minister and went on to be the architect of Russia's shock therapy. Appointed first economics minister and then in June–December 1992 acting prime minister. He was dropped as acting prime minister to appease the parliament but was briefly economics minister in 1993. 1993 helped found the political movement Russia's Choice which won 94 seats in the 1993 Duma elections. Lost his Duma seat in 1995.

Mikhail Gorbachev

Born 1931 in Privolnoi village, Stavropol, in South Russia, the son of a tractor driver. 1945 joined the Komsomol and the CPSU in 1952. 1950–5 law student at Moscow State University. On graduation returned to Stavropol where he worked in the Komsomol and then the CPSU apparatus. 1971 became a full member of the CPSU Central Committee and in 1978 CPSU secretary for agriculture. 1979 candidate and then in 1980 a full member of the CPSU Politburo. 1979 elected to the USSR Supreme Soviet and in 1980 to the RSFSR parliament. March 1985 elected and in July 1990 re-elected general secretary of the CPSU. 1988 elected chair of the Supreme Soviet Presidium and in March 1990 the Congress of People's Deputies elected him the first executive president of the USSR. 1985 launched *perestroika* (Reconstruction), a comprehensive reform programme, which precipitated the collapse of soviet socialism. Popular abroad where his visits were greeted by Gorbymania but increasingly unpopular at home, charged with either being too radical or not radical enough.

August 1991 held under house arrest during a hardline coup attempt and released by Yeltsin and his allies. Returned to Moscow to find the USSR was disintegrating and political developments were dominated by Yeltsin. Stood in the 1996 presidential elections but received only 0.5 per cent of the vote.

Andrei Illarionov

Born 1961. Graduated from Leningrad State University in 1983 with a doctorate in economics, became a close ally of Igor Gaidar. 1990–2 senior research associate and section head at the Regional Economic Problems Laboratory of the St Petersburg Institute of Finance and Economics. First deputy to Sergei Vasiliev, the director of the government's Working Centre for Economic Reforms. Studied at Birmingham University in UK and participated in the formulation of the government's programme approved in summer 1993. 1993 appointed head of the prime minister's Analysis and Planning group with the rank of economic adviser to the prime minister. February 1994 resigned accusing Chernomyrdin of an economic coup and opposed Gerashchenko's appointment as chair of the Russian Central Bank; two days later sacked for violating labour discipline for giving lectures in the UK without the prime minister's knowledge or approval. Since 1994 director of the Institute for Economic Analysis. In 1998 warned that GKOs would collapse and called on Kiriyenko to devalue the rouble. June 1998 one of the founders of the ultra-liberal Northern Capital movement and joined the government's Commission on Economic Reform. April 2000 appointed presidential economics adviser. May 2000 appointed presidential envoy to G7.

Igor Ivanov

Born 1945 in Moscow. 1969 graduated from the Moscow Pedagogical Institute for Foreign Languages then 1969–73 worked as a junior researcher at the Institute for the World Economy and International Relations of the Academy of Sciences before becoming a diplomat in 1973. 1973–83 rose from second secretary to counsellor-envoy at the soviet embassy in Madrid. 1983–91 worked at the Foreign Ministry. 1991–4 Russian ambassador to Spain. 1994–September 1998 first deputy foreign minister. January 1995 also appointed state secretary. September 1998 succeeded his mentor Primakov as foreign minister and joined the Security Council in October.

Mikhail Kasyanov

Born 1957 in Solntsevo near Moscow, a town synonymous with the Russian mafia. Graduated from the Moscow Automobile Institute and Gosplan's Higher Economic Programme. 1981–90 worked for Gosplan as an economist and financial expert, a fluent English speaker. 1991 appointed head of foreign economic relations in the Ministry of Finance. 1993–5 head of the department of foreign credit and debt in the Ministry of Finance, negotiated Russia's debt repayments with the IMF and western officials. 1995 appointed deputy minister of finance and from December 1996 appointed a member of the Intergovernmental Commission on the Council of Europe. May 1999 minister of finance with responsibility to negotiate with the London and Paris Clubs. August 1999 reappointed to Putin's government. January 2000 appointed first deputy prime minister and continued as minister of finance. February 2000 renegotiated the terms of Russia's commercial debt to western banks, getting more than one-third written off. May 2000 appointed prime minister by Putin.

Ruslan Khasbulatov

Born 1942 in Grozny, a Chechen. In 1944 as a child he was deported to Kazakhstan along with most other Chechens who were accused of disloyalty to the USSR. Raised on a collective farm which his father chaired. Studied at the Kazakhstan State University in Alma-Ata and then Moscow State University. 1965 awarded a doctorate in economics. 1965–7 secretary of the Komsomol committee at Moscow State University. 1966 joined CPSU. Became an academic and 1979–90 was a professor at the Plekhanov Institute in Moscow. 1990 elected to the RSFSR parliament for the Chechen capital Grozny, first deputy chair of RSFSR Supreme Soviet and from October 1991 chair of the RSFSR Supreme Soviet. August 1991 one of the defenders of the White House, resigned from CPSU. Quickly came into conflict with Yeltsin over the powers of the chair and the president and the reform programme. After the October 1993 crisis he was arrested and imprisoned for refusing to disband the legislature and for inciting violence. 1994 released from prison in an amnesty.

Sergei Kiriyenko

Born in 1962. An engineer, graduated from the Gorky Institute of River Transport in 1984. From 1987 served as a Komsomol secretary, then first secretary of Gorky Komsomol, and a member of the Gorky *oblast* soviet. 1993 educated at the Academy of Economics specialising in the market economy and management. 1991–4 president of Kontsern AMK. January 1994 founded and became president of the commercial bank Guarantiia Bank in Nizhnii Novgorod (formerly Gorky). 1996–7, on the recommendation of his mentor Boris Nemtsov, appointed head of the Nizhnii Novgorod oil refinery company Norsi-oil, which he turned into a success. 1997 appointed first deputy minister of fuel and energy and from November 1997 succeeded Nemtsov as minister of fuel and energy. Nemtsov wanted Kiriyenko's support in confronting the energy lobby headed by Chernomyrdin. December 1997 appointed chair of the committee of representatives of the government in Gazprom. 23 March 1998 appointed acting prime minister and from 24 April appointed prime minister on the third Duma vote. Blamed for Russia's inability to weather the 1998 economic crisis and for devaluing the rouble, he was sacked as prime minister on 23 August 1998. Came second to Yury Luzhkov in the December 1999 Moscow mayoral elections with 11.4 per cent of the vote. Heads the Union of Rightist Forces (SPS) party of economic liberals, which backed Putin in the 2000 presidential elections.

Alexander Korzhakov

Born 1951, educated at the All-Union Institute of Law. 1970–89 KGB officer assigned in 1985 as Yeltsin's (then the Moscow party boss) chief bodyguard. He became Yeltsin's close friend and confidant and remained loyal to Yeltsin even when he was sacked by Gorbachev in 1987. 1990–1 head of the RSFSR Supreme Soviet Security Service. August 1991 stood on a tank with Yeltsin to defy the coup. 1992 head of the presidential bodyguards. May 1996 promoted by presidential decree to rank of minister, but on 20 June 1996 sacked. In a May 1996 interview with *The Observer* Korzhakov said that he believed the presidential elections should be postponed. He was already unpopular with Chubais and Dyachenko; they accused him of wanting to wreck the presidential elections. He was sacked on charges of wanting a coup and for corruption. In a February 1997 by-election he was elected as the Duma deputy for Tula, the second poorest region of Russia. Claimed that Chubais had masterminded a multi-million dollar campaign to stop him getting elected.

Andrei Kozyrev

Born 1952 in Brussels, the son of a soviet diplomat, he has an excellent command of foreign languages. Worked at the Kommunar machine-building factory in Moscow before going to university. 1974 graduated from the prestigious Moscow Institute of International Relations, where he then worked 1974–90. 1977 defended his doctorate on 'The role of the UN and the development of détente'. 1990–January 1996 worked at the Foreign Ministry of the USSR. 1991 resigned from the CPSU. Appointed foreign minister of the RSFSR in July 1990 and became the leading advocate of Russia's Atlanticist, westernising policies, although from 1993 Russian foreign policy became increasingly centrist rather than Atlanticist. Kozyrev remained foreign minister until January 1996. 1992–6 member of the Security Council. 1993 elected to the Duma for Russia's Choice. 1995 elected to the Duma.

Ekaterina Lakhova

Born 1948 in Sverdlovsk, a Russian. Trained as a paediatrician at the Sverdlovsk Medical Institute, worked as a paediatrician and then the deputy head of the Health Department of Sverdlovsk *oblast* executive committee on mother and child health care. 1990 elected to RSFSR Congress of People's Deputies, and headed the Committee on Women's Affairs, Protection of the Family and Demographic Questions. August 1991 resigned from the CPSU. 1991–4 state adviser and presidential adviser on family matters. 1993 chair of Women of Russia party. 1993 elected to the Duma for Women of Russia party. 1993 appointed by the president as chair of the Presidential Commission on Women, Family and Demography. 1995 elected to the Duma for Women of Russia, member of the Duma Committee on the Regulation and Organisation of the State Duma's work.

Alexander Lebed

Born 1950 in Novocherkassk, Rostov region, into a working-class family. A Russian with a Don Cossack mother and a Ukrainian father. In 1937 his father was imprisoned for being late for work and then sent to serve in a penal battalion during the Russo-Finnish War. Graduated from school in 1967 and worked in a factory. Joined the army in 1968 and trained as a paratrooper. 1981–2 commanded the first battalion 345th special paratroop regiment in Afghanistan and in 1982 entered the prestigious Frunze Military Academy in Moscow and graduated with first class honours in 1985, then commanded airborne troops in Kostroma, Pskov and Tula. At the 28th CPSU Congress in July 1990 he criticised Alexander Yakovlev, a Gorbachev ally and leading reformer.

September 1990 elected to the KPRF Central Committee. During the August 1991 coup attempt he seems to have sided with Yeltsin's forces and was thanked by Yeltsin for his support. June 1992 took control of the 14th division and attacked the Moldovan army which he accused of genocide against Russians in the breakaway Transdniestr Moldovan Republic. September 1993 elected deputy to the Transdniestr Moldovan Republic Supreme Soviet for Tiraspol with 87.5 per cent of the vote. During the October 1993 crisis he refused appeals for support from both Yeltsin and Rutskoi–Khasbulatov, citing the need for the army to remain neutral. 1994 there were rumours that the Russian Defence Ministry wanted to remove Lebed from Transdniestr and send him to Chechnia or Tajikistan. Lebed opposed the December 1994 commitment of Russian forces to Chechnia, which enhanced his popularity. April 1995 Lebed joined the Congress of Russian Communities (KRO) and was elected its deputy chair. June 1995 following disagreements over the reorganisation of the 14th division he resigned from the army. October 1995 the founding congress of Honour and Motherland, an all-Russian movement, elected Lebed its chair. January 1996 KRO nominated Lebed to stand as its candidate for the presidential elections; he came third in the first round and stepped down, endorsing Yeltsin's candidacy. In return he was appointed to the Security Council but was sacked in 1996. Relations between Lebed and KRO leader Skokov deteriorated; although Lebed did not leave the KRO he no longer speaks for them. 1998 elected governor of Krasnoyarsk in Siberia. Claims he gave up drinking alcohol on 25 December 1993 because the country needs a sober person.

Yury Luzhkov

Born 1936 in Moscow, a Russian. Educated at the Gubkin Institute of Oil, Gas and Chemical Industries. 1964–87 held a series of managerial positions in the Chemical Industry Ministry. 1977–90 deputy to Moscow city soviet. When Yeltsin became Moscow party boss in 1987 Luzhkov was appointed to the full-time post of first deputy chair of Moscow's executive committee and head of the Moscow Agro-Industrial Committee. March 1990 Gavriil Popov became mayor of Moscow and Luzhkov the head of the Moscow executive committee. June 1991 Popov resigned as mayor and Yeltsin appointed Luzhkov mayor. August 1991 played a leading role in resisting the coup. Became mayor of Moscow in June 1992, and re-elected mayor in mid-1996 and December 1999. 1992–7 rebuilt the cathedral of Christ the Saviour near the Kremlin; the original cathedral was blown up in 1931. Luzhkov has encouraged economic reform and inward investment into Moscow, has a close working relationship with the Russian Orthodox Church and is a Russian nationalist. (Moscow has a reputation as a corrupt city.) Fairly close to Yeltsin until he began to develop his own presidential aspirations. November 1998 formed the centrist Rodina (Homeland) political movement. Helped to form Fatherland All-Russia (OVR) for the 1999 Duma elections.

Aslan Maskhadov

Born 1951, a Chechen. Joined armed forces in 1969 and served in the Soviet Far East. 1972 graduated from the Tbilisi Artillery Military Academy and 1981 from the Kalinin Artillery Academy. 1990 while serving in Vilnius, Lithuania, took part in the storming of the Vilnius Television Centre. 1991 headed civil defence force when Dudaev declared independence, then appointed deputy chief of staff. 1995 appointed chief of the general staff after organising the defence of the Chechen presidential palace in Grozny. 1996 negotiated the peace treaty with Russia and in May signed on behalf of Chechnia. January 1997 elected president of the Chechen republic.

Boris Nemtsov

Born 1959 in Sochi. Graduated in radio-physics from Gorky State University in 1981 and completed his dissertation on radio-physics in 1984. 1981–91 a researcher at the Radio-Physics Institute in Gorky. Following the Chernobyl accident in 1986 he led a group that successfully lobbied against the building of a new atomic power station in Gorky. 1990 elected to the RSFSR Congress of People's Deputies, became a member of the Supreme Soviet legal committee. August 1991 appointed by Yeltsin as the presidential representative and in November 1991 the governor in Nizhnii Novgorod (previously Gorky), holding the two posts simultaneously. Nemtsov employed Yavlinsky's consultancy organisation Epicentre to make reform suggestions and under Nemtsov Nizhnii Novgorod gained a reputation as a laboratory and a showcase of radical economic reform. November 1995 elected governor of Nizhnii Novgorod. March 1997 appointed first deputy prime minister in charge of social welfare reform. April 1997 appointed minister of fuel and energy. May 1997 appointed to the Defence Council. November 1997 resigned as minister of fuel and energy but remained a deputy prime minister. 1998 reappointed deputy prime minister in the new government. August 1998 in the wake of the economic crisis he resigned from the Yeltsin administration.

Ella Pamfilova

Born 1953 in Tashkent. 1976 graduated from Moscow Energetics Institute, an electronics engineer. 1976–89 worked as an engineer-technologist and headed a trade union committee at the Mosenergo energy production unit in Moscow. 1989 elected to the USSR Congress of People's Deputies on a trade union quota. 1990–1 member of the Union Chamber in the USSR Supreme Soviet, secretary of the Benefits and Privileges Commission. 1991–4 Russian minister for social security. One of the founders of the Russia's Choice electoral bloc. First woman to run for the presidency in 2000, established her own political movement Civic Dignity (or Worth).

Yevgeny Primakov

Born 1929 in Kiev. 1959–91 CPSU member. Graduate of the Moscow Institute of Oriental Studies with a doctorate in Economics from Moscow State University. A Middle Eastern specialist and an Arabic speaker with considerable academic, diplomatic and intelligence experience. An academician of the USSR Academy of Sciences and from 1991 of the Russian Academy of Sciences. One of Gorbachev's chief foreign policy advisers, reputed to have been one of the architects of Gorbachev's 'New Thinking' in foreign policy, served as a member of Gorbachev's Presidential Soviet 1990–1. September 1991 appointed first deputy chair of the KGB USSR by Gorbachev, and appointed director of the Russian Federal Intelligence Service in December 1991 which he left in January 1996 to become foreign minister. 1995 appointed to the Foreign Policy Council of the President of the RF. Championed a state-realist-centrist approach to foreign policy. Appointed prime minister in September 1998 as a compromise candidate when the Duma rejected Chernomyrdin. As prime minister he earned respect across the political spectrum for standing up for Russian interests; he nevertheless established business-like relations with western leaders and stood in for Yeltsin on a number of foreign visits. His moves to stamp down on corruption alienated the oligarchs and his presidential ambitions alienated Yeltsin. He was sacked as prime minister in May 1999. Yeltsin thanked him for bringing stability after the 1998 economic crisis but criticised him for not initiating economic reform. A leader of the Fatherland-All Russia party together with Luzhkov. His 2000 presidential campaign was undermined by compromising material about his health.

Vladimir Putin

Born 1952 in Leningrad. Graduated in law from Leningrad State University. Served in the KGB for 15 years mainly in Leipzig and Dresden in the GDR. Left the KGB in 1990 to return to St Petersburg (formerly Leningrad) where he worked in the city adminis- tration for the liberal mayor Anatoly Sobchak, who had been his university law professor. In 1994 became first deputy chair (mayor) of the city government. In 1996 Sobchak lost the mayoral elections and Putin was brought into Yeltsin's administration in Moscow by Anatoly Chubais, the Kremlin chief of staff. Held the posts of head of the control department, deputy manager of the property department and deputy head of the presidential administration. He was also charged with dealing with the Kremlin's relations with the RF's 89 subjects of federation. July 1998 appointed the director the FSB and in March 1999 became a secretary of the Security Council. Appointed prime minister in August 1999. On Yeltsin's resignation as president on 31 December 1999, Putin became acting president. Elected president 26 March 2000.

Alexander Rutskoi

Born 1947 in Kursk. 1970 joined the CPSU. 1971 completed the Barnaul War Aviation College. 1975 entered the Gagarin Air Force Academy. 1985 commanded an air assault regiment and served in Afghanistan where he was wounded in 1986. Became head of a Military Air College in Lipetsk. 1988 volunteered for active service in Afghanistan where he was shot down and captured by the Mojahedin. He was exchanged for a number of Mojahedin fighters and made a Hero of the Soviet Union. 1989 nominated as a candidate for the Congress of People's Deputies of the USSR, he was supported by the CPSU, Russian Orthodox Church, *Otchestvo* and *Pamniat*. In 1990 he was elected to the RSFSR Supreme Soviet for Kursk and first he voted with the communists but by the third congress was voting with the democrats. 1990 left Otchestvo. From March 1991 he led a reformist faction of the CPSU called Communists for Democracy, which led to the founding of the Democratic Party of Communists of Russia (DPCR), chaired by Rutskoi. Selected by Yeltsin to stand as his vice-president in June 1991 election, a post he held until October 1993. August 1991 announced the DPCR had left the CPSU. Worked closely with Yeltsin to oppose the August 1991 coup. October DPCR renamed People's Party of Free Russia, chaired by Rutskoi. May 1992 formed the Civic Union with Travkin and Volsky. Relations between Yeltsin and Rutskoi rapidly deteriorated and by early 1992 Rutskoi openly opposed Yeltsin and his reform programme and in 1993 he announced his intention to stand for the presidency if Yeltsin resigned. During the October 1993 crisis the Supreme Soviet declared Rutskoi acting president. Rutskoi was arrested and imprisoned for his role in the violence of 3 October, but was released in an amnesty issued by the Duma in March 1994. 1994 established Derzhava (Great Power) Social Patriotic Movement. 20 October 1996 elected governor of Kursk with 79 per cent of the vote.

Yevgeny Savostyanov

One of the founder members of Democratic Russia. The man who locked the doors of the CPSU Central Committee building after the collapse of the August 1991 coup. The former head of the Moscow branch of the FSB, and in 1997 deputy head of Yeltsin's presidential staff. As a candidate in the 2000 presidential elections presented himself as the candidate who would complete Russia's unfinished democratic revolution; wants the state to be reformed and increased cooperation with the West.

Martin Shakkum

Born 1951 in Krasnogorsk Moscow region to a Lett father and a Russian mother. Had to abandon his military career in 1975 due to an arm injury. Began working as an engineer. Since 1991 the director-general then vice-president of the Reforma or Shatalin Foundation. In the 1995 Duma elections he was originally on the list of the Ivan Rybkin bloc but was finally put on the My Fatherland list, but failed to get elected. Contested the 1996 presidential elections.

Yury Skuratov

Born 1952. Graduated from Sverdlovsk Legal Institute in 1973. A specialist in constitutional law, he wrote his doctoral dissertation on local self-government. Headed the CPSU Central Committee's Department for Legislative Initiatives and Legal Questions. Consultant on legal matters for the Russian Ministry of Security in 1991–3. In 1993 he became head of the Institute of the Problems of Strengthening Legality and Law and Order. 1995 appointed general prosecutor but then became involved in prolonged battles with Yeltsin over investigations into corruption within the presidential council. The victim of compromising materials to ruin his reputation. Ran in the 2000 presidential elections.

Anatoly Sobchak

Born 1937 in the Siberian town of Chita near the Chinese border. His grandfather was an Old Bolshevik who died as a result of imprisonment. Graduated in law from Leningrad University and worked as a lawyer in Stavropol before returning to Leningrad to teach law. 1981 became Leningrad's first professor of economic law. Entered politics during the Reconstruction era when he also joined the CPSU. Elected to the Congress of People's Deputies of the USSR in 1989. Ran Yeltsin's presidential election campaign in Leningrad in 1991. During the August 1991 coup he first went to Moscow to support Yeltsin and then returned to Leningrad to lead the resistance to the coup. Mayor of (Leningrad) St Petersburg 1991–6. In 1997 he fled to France following corruption allegations, returning in the summer 1999 once the charges were dropped. It is alleged that Putin, Sobchak's former protégé, had the charges dropped. Sobchak died in Kaliningrad 20 February 2000 following a heart attack while campaigning for Putin in the presidential elections.

Alexander Solzhenitsyn

Born 1918 in Rostov-on-Don. Studied mathematics and science at Rostov-on-Don University and then completed a correspondence course in literature from Moscow State University. At this time Solzhenitsyn was a Marxist–Leninist. 1941–5 served as the commander of an artillery battalion and was twice decorated for bravery. 1945 arrested for writing in a letter that only Stalin seemed to be spoken about in the USSR and that Lenin had been forgotten. 1945–53 imprisoned without trial in the *gulag* (prison camp). 1953–7 in Siberian exile where he survived cancer. 1957 officially rehabilitated. Taught mathematics and science at a secondary school in Ryazan. 1962 his short novel *One Day in the Life of Ivan Denisovich*, about life in the *gulag*, was published in the USSR. His other novels such as *Cancer Ward* and the *First Circle* were not accepted for publication in the USSR but were published abroad. 1968 wrote a widely publicised letter to the Writers' Union complaining about his ostracism. 1969 expelled from the Writers' Union. 1970 awarded the Nobel Prize for literature but was refused permission to attend the ceremony. December 1973 the first volume of his *Gulag Archipelago* was published in the West. 1974 arrested and deported. 1974–91 lived in exile mostly in Vermont, USA. He attacked both the USSR and western values and culture, from a Russian nationalist perspective. 1994 his citizenship was restored and he returned to Russia but was clearly disappointed by what he found. He briefly had a prime time television spot on ORT but the television executives pulled the plug on his programme because they said viewers found him boring.

Galina Starovoitova

Born 1946 in Cheliabinsk in the Urals. Graduated from the Leningrad College of Military Engineering. 1966 attained a candidates degree in social psychology from Leningrad State University and then a doctorate in social anthropology from the Institute of Ethnography of the USSR Academy of Sciences where she worked for 17 years. Her doctoral dissertation was on the Tatars in Leningrad. 1989 elected to the USSR Congress of People's Deputies and in June 1990 to the RSFSR parliament for a Leningrad constituency. She was co-chair of the pro-Yeltsin Democratic Russia group and 1991–2 she was Yeltsin's adviser on nationalities issues. 1992 sacked by Yeltsin for criticising Moscow's backing for the Ossetians against the Ingush. 1993–4 Peace Fellow at the Institute of Peace in Washington, then a year as a visiting professor at Brown University, Rhode Island. Opposed Yeltsin's policy towards Chechnia. 1995 elected to the Duma for a St Petersburg constituency, served on the parliamentary committee on social and religious organisations. Her registration for the 1996 presidential election was rejected amid accusations that some of the supporting signatures were forgeries. November 1998 condemned the Duma for not taking a firm line on anti-Semitism. Took a tough stance on corruption and condemned corruption in the St Petersburg housing privatisation. She was planning to participate in the December 1998 election for the City Assembly in St Petersburg but was murdered in the entrance to her flat in St Petersburg on 20 November 1998. No one has been charged with her murder. Her funeral on 24 November 1998 at the Alexander Nevsky monastery in St Petersburg was attended by thousands of mourners. Russia had lost one its most consistent advocates of democratic reform and human rights.

Sergei Stepashin

Born 1952 on a military base in Port Arthur, China. A Russian. 1973–90 served in the Interior Ministry troops. 1981 graduated from the Higher Political College of the USSR Interior Ministry and Military Academy. 1986 awarded doctorate. 1990 deputy chair of the Institute of Political History in Leningrad. 1990–3 elected as a deputy to the Russian Supreme Soviet and served as chair of its Security Committee. 1991–2 deputy minister of security in Russia. September 1993 first deputy minister of security. 1993 member of the Security Council. December 1993 first deputy director of the Federal Agency for Counterintelligence. March 1994–July 1995 appointed director of the FSB, but resigned/dismissed due to the failed attempt to rescue Russian hostages in Budyonnovsk in June. Became head of the government's administrative department. 1997–8 minister of justice. March 1998 appointed minister of the interior in which capacity he was attacked by Amnesty International for his support for capital punishment and his involvement in the military campaign in Chechnia. In May 1998 he was sent by Yeltsin to Chechnia to negotiate with the Chechens and seems to have been taken hostage. A Yeltsin loyalist, in April 1999 he was appointed to the additional post of first deputy prime minister. In May 1999 he was a surprise appointment as prime minister. In June 1999 he took Primakov's post as a permanent member of the Security Council. Dismissed as prime minister in August 1999 although no reasons were given for his dismissal. Supported Yabloko in the December 1999 Duma elections.

Konstantin Titov

Born 1994 in Moscow. 1962–70 worked at the Kubishev Aviation factory where he also started to work for the Komsomol. 1968 attended Kubishev Aviation Institute. 1978 postgraduate studies in Industrial Economics. 1970–88 worked at the Kubishev Planning Institute and for the Komsomol. 1988–90 deputy manager of the Informatika Research Centre. 1990–1 chair of the Soviet of People's Deputies of Samara (formerly Kubishev) city. September 1991 appointed governor of Samara *oblast* on the Volga river. 1996 elected governor of Samara *oblast*. Titov is widely credited with making Samara one of the most prosperous regions in Russia; he pioneered land privatisation there even though the RF did not have land privatisation legislation. Deputy chair of NDR. April 2000 resigned as governor following his poor performance in the presidential elections. July 2000 re-elected governor. 1999 joined SPS. Although Titov stood in the 2000 presidential election SPS supported Putin.

Aman-Geldy Tuleev

Born 1944 in the town of Krasnovodsk in Murkmenistan. A Kazakh who has lived in Kemerovo (Siberia) since 1964 and worked in the railway industry, rising to become the chief of the Kemerovo railway in 1988. Joined the CPSU in 1968. 1990 elected a RSFSR people's deputy for Gorno-Shorsky national-territorial district and was a member of the deputy group Communists for Russia, then the Industrial Union. 1990 elected a deputy to the Kemerovo regional soviet. May 1990 elected chair of the regional Soviet. January–August 1991 he was also chair of the executive committee of the Kemerovo regional council, thereby combining both representative and executive roles. Supported the Siberian miners' strikes in 1991. June 1991 ran for the RSFSR presidency advocating greater autonomy for Russian's regions and greater social spending. 1991–2 simultaneously a member of the Smena and Fatherland factions. April 1992 became the leader of the opposition Russian Unity bloc. October 1992 elected to the political council of the National Salvation Front. December 1993 as governor of Kemerovo joined the Federation Council. August 1995 joined the electoral association of the KPRF and in December 1995 was elected to the Duma, although he did not take up his seat but instead remained chair of the Kemerovo regional parliament and hence a member of the Federation Council. 1996 stood in the presidential elections but withdrew his candidacy in favour of Zyuganov. August 1996–July 1997 minister for relations with the CIS in Yeltsin's government. October 1997 elected governor of Kemerovo. Contested the 2000 presidential elections.

Yury Vlasov

Born 1935 in the town of Makeyevka, Donetsk region of Ukraine. A Russian. His father was a prominent China specialist who worked as a diplomat and intelligence agent in China. 1957–67 a member of the Olympic weight-lifting team. Joined the army in 1959 and resigned his commission in 1968. Left the CPSU in 1989, the same year he was elected to the Congress of People's Deputies and joined the Inter-Regional Group of deputies. 1993 elected to the Duma but failed to be re-elected in 1995. Contested the 1996 presidential elections.

Grigory Yavlinsky

Born 1952 in Lvov, Ukraine. A Russian whose father was an army officer. Dropped out of school and worked as an electrical fitter, completing secondary school at evening classes. 1969–73 studied at the Plekhanov National Economy Institute in Moscow and in 1978 awarded a Candidate of Economics degree. 1977–84 a senior researcher then a sector chief of the Labour Research Institute in the State Committee for Labour and Social Issues (Goskomstrud). In 1982 his paper 'Problems of improving the economic mechanism in the USSR', which predicted the USSR's economic crisis, was confiscated and destroyed. Believes that the treatment he received supposedly for 'tuberculosis' in 1984–5 was part of a campaign of official persecution against him provoked by the paper. 1985–91 a member of the CPSU. Summer 1989 joined the Abalkin Commission on economic reform. 1990 worked on the '500-day programme' designed to turn the USSR into a market economy. Supported Yeltsin during the August 1991 coup although has since had an uneasy relationship with Yeltsin. Described the 1993 dissolution of the Supreme Soviet as unconstitutional. October 1993 created the electoral association Yabloko. Elected to the Duma for Yabloko in 1993, 1995 and 1999. 1998 supported the appointment of Primakov as prime minister. Has a reputation as an arrogant outsider, whose ideas and skills have never been tested in the real world.

Boris Yeltsin

Born 1931 into a peasant family in Butka, a village in the province of Sverdlovsk (Urals). 1955 graduated as a construction engineer from the Urals Technical Institute and began work as an engineer in the construction industry. Joined the CPSU in 1961. 1976–85 CPSU first secretary in Sverdlovsk. 1976 elected as a deputy to the USSR Supreme Soviet. 1986 joined the CPSU Politburo. 1986 appointed by Gorbachev as the first party secretary of Moscow. He attacked *nomenklatura* privileges and corruption. Sacked and humiliated by Gorbachev, he suffered a heart attack. 1987 left the Politburo. March 1989 won a seat in the USSR Congress of People's Deputies with 89.6 per cent of the vote. Yeltsin rapidly became the figurehead for liberal Russian nationalism and a leading member of the Inter-Regional Group. March 1990 elected to the RSFSR Congress of People's Deputies for Sverdlovsk. May 1990 elected chair (president) of the RSFSR. July 1990 left the CPSU. June 1991 became directly elected president of Russia, receiving 58 per cent of the vote. 1991 led the opposition to the August 1991 coup and organised Gorbachev's return from Foros. Elected president of the RF on 3 July 1996. 31 December 1999 resigned as president, naming Vladimir Putin his chosen successor.

Doku Zavgaev

Headed the Chechen administration at the end of the soviet period. September 1991 the Chechen Congress seized the Supreme Soviet and forced Zavgaev to resign. Late 1995 returned as head of a Russian-appointed government. Stood for NDR in the 1995 Duma elections. 1996 joined the Federation Council.

Vladimir Zhirinovsky

Born 1946 in Alma-Ata (now Almaty), the capital of Kazakhstan. When asked about his nationality he famously replied 'My mother is a Russian while my father is a lawyer'. Zhirinovsky was the surname of his mother's first husband who died 18 months before he was born. The only lawyer in his family was an uncle. Until 1964 Zhirinovsky had his father's surname which was Eidelstein, but Zhirinovsky is vague about his background and denies his Jewish heritage. 1964 became a student at the Institute of Oriental Languages in Moscow, graduating in Turkish. In 1967 his Komsomol Committee refused to support his application for CPSU membership. 1969–70 sent to Turkey but was expelled by the Turkish government for Communist propaganda. 1970–2 military service in Tbilisi. Studied law at Moscow State University at evening classes, graduating in 1977. 1977–83 on the staff of the Ministry of Justice of the USSR. 1983–90 senior legal consultant to the Mir Publishing House. Founded the Liberal Democratic Party of Russia (LDPR) in 1989, and from November 1990 has received a salary from the party. He contested the June 1991 RSFSR presidential elections, coming third with 7.8 per cent of the votes. The LDPR fared much better in the 1993 Duma elections, polling more votes (24 per cent) than any other political party. He lost popular support over his backing of the 1994–6 Chechen war.

Gennady Zyuganov

Born 1994 in the village of Mymrino in Orel province. A Russian, his parents were teachers. 1961–2 worked as a teacher in a rural secondary school. 1962 enrolled at the

Department of Physics and Mathematics of the Orel Pedagogical Institute, but his studies were interrupted 1963–6 by service in military intelligence. 1966–91 member of the CPSU. From 1967 also worked for the Komsomol and then the CPSU in Orel province and later Orel city. 1969 began teaching at the Orel Pedagogical Institute. 1970–8 a people's deputy on the Orel regional and city soviets. 1983–9 worked as an instructor and 1989–90 as a deputy head of the CPSU Central Committee's Propaganda Department. 1978–81 studied at the CPSU Academy of Sciences. 1980 defended his candidate's dissertation on 'The basic principles of planning the development of the socialist urban way of life (based on major cities)'. April 1995 defended his doctoral dissertation entitled 'The main trends of social and political development in Russia and its mechanisms in the 1980s–1990s'. 1989–91 Zyuganov became increasingly popular amongst the anti-Gorbachev forces in the CPSU. June 1990 elected as chair, member of the Central Committee and Politburo of the new RSFSR Communist Party (KPRF). On vacation during the August 1991 coup and did not take part in any capacity. Autumn 1991 helped to establish the Russian People's Union, headed by Sergei Baburin. June 1992 elected co-chair of the Duma of the Russian National Sobor. October 1991–spring 1994 a leader of the National Salvation Front. December 1993 elected as a Duma deputy. September 1994 participated in a congress of Russia's patriotic forces. Spring 1995, along with Alexei Podberyozkin, became a leader of the Organising Committee of the Spiritual Heritage Movement, a national patriotic movement. July 1995 elected member of the Council and Political Executive Committee of the Union of Communist Parties. Came second to Yeltsin in the 1996 and second to Putin in the 2000 presidential elections.

Chronology

7 February	CPSU renounces its constitutional monopoly of power.
29 May	Congress of People's Deputies of the RSFSR elects Boris Yeltsin chair of the Supreme Soviet, that is president of the RSFSR.
12 June	Congress of People's Deputies declares the RSFSR a sovereign state.
21 June	Communist Party of the RSFSR is founded (KPRF).
12 July	Yeltsin resigns his membership of the CPSU.
30 August	Supreme Soviet of Tatarstan declares Tatarstan the 16th union republic of the USSR and no longer part of the RSFSR.

17 March	In an all-union referendum 76.4 per cent vote to preserve the USSR. The referendum is boycotted by Armenia, Latvia, Lithuania, Estonia, Georgia and Moldova. In the RSFSR an additional question on the creation of an executive presidency is supported by over half the registered voters.
23 April	Novo-Ogarevo 9+1 pact signed by Gorbachev and nine of the union republics including the RSFSR.
6 May	A separate RSFSR KGB is created.
12 June	Yeltsin elected president of the RSFSR, receiving 57.3 per cent of the votes cast; Alexander Rutskoi becomes vice-president.
28 June	Comecon (CMEA) abolished.
10 July	Yeltsin sworn in as president of the RSFSR.
18 August	A self-appointed State Committee for the State of Emergency sends representatives to persuade Gorbachev to support them, but he refuses.
19 August	*Coup d'état* launched in Moscow.
20 August	New Union Treaty due to be signed.

21 August	Coup collapses.
24 August	Gorbachev resigns as general secretary of the CPSU.
29 October	Constitutional Court is elected to oversee the constitutionality of Russian laws and of its treaties with foreign states.
6 November	Yeltsin becomes prime minister.
	Presidential decrees ban the CPSU and the KPRF.
28 November	Supreme Soviet passes a law giving citizenship to Russians living outside the RSFSR.
8 December	RSFSR, Belarus and Ukraine sign the Belovezha (Minsk) Agreement creating the CIS.
25 December	RSFSR renamed the Russian Federation by the Supreme Soviet. Gorbachev resigns as president of the USSR.
31 December	USSR is formally dissolved.

1992

2 January	Prices liberalised.
17–18 February	US Secretary of State, James A. Baker, visits Moscow to discuss nuclear disarmament.
	Yeltsin asks for $600 million in loan guarantees to enable Russia to buy grain.
20 March	Kiev CIS summit discusses collective peace keeping but fails to create an integrated military system.
6–21 April	Sixth Congress of People's Deputies votes 447 to 412 with 70 abstentions against a motion of no confidence in Yeltsin's radical economic reforms, and fails to adopt a new constitution.
22 April	The opposition Russian Unity bloc is formed by communists and nationalists.
29 April	Russian Federation officially admitted to the IMF and EBRD.
7 May	Yeltsin creates RF Armed Forces and appoints himself commander-in-chief.
15–16 May	Tashkent CIS summit.
20 May	First session of the RF Security Council.
21 May	Supreme Soviet votes to abrogate the 1954 decree ceding the Crimea from the RSFSR to Ukraine.
30 May	Vladimir Lopukhin replaced as minister for energy by Viktor Chernomyrdin, who is also appointed a deputy prime minister.
4 June	Supreme Soviet passes a law creating the Ingush Republic within the RF, thus splitting the Checheno-Ingushetia Republic.
5 June	Gavriil Popov resigns as mayor of Moscow and is replaced by his deputy Yury Luzhkov.
15 June	Gaidar is appointed acting prime minister by Yeltsin.
21 June	Civic Union opposition group formed.
26 June	Minsk CIS summit agrees exit from the rouble zone.
4 July	Democratic Choice, a pro-Yeltsin bloc, formed.
6 July	Constitutional Court begins proceedings against the CPSU.
6 July	Moscow CIS summit.

7 July	Cease-fire in Transdniestr in Moldova.
3 August	Yeltsin and Ukrainian President Kravchuk agree to divide the former Soviet Black Sea fleet after a three-year period of joint control.
11 August	Liberal Democratic Party of the Russian Federation is banned by the Ministry of Justice for falsifying its membership list.
4 September	Russia, together with Kazakhstan, Kyrgyzstan and Uzbekistan, sends troops into Tajikistan.
1 October	Beginning of voucher privatisation.
8 October	Presidential decree establishes the Interdepartmental Commission for Fighting Crime and Corruption, headed by Vice-President Rutskoi.
9–10 October	Bishkek CIS summit.
21 October	Supreme Soviet rejects Yeltsin's proposal that the scheduled winter session of the Congress of People's Deputies be postponed to the spring.
28 October	Presidential decree bans the neo-communist and nationalist National Salvation Front.
2 November	Yeltsin declares a state of emergency in RF's North Ossetia and Ingushetia republics due to ethnic conflicts.
30 November	Constitutional Court upholds Yeltsin's decrees banning the CPSU and the KPRF but rules that their (local) primary organisations should not have been banned.
1–14 December	Seventh session of the Congress of People's Deputies.
9 December	Congress of People's Deputies rejects Gaidar as prime minister by 486 votes to 467.
10 December	In a compromise agreement brokered by Valery Zorkin, the chair of the Constitutional Court, Yeltsin and Khasbulatov agree to a nationwide referendum on the basic principles of the new constitution to be held on 11 April 1993.
14 December	Congress of People's Deputies elects Chernomyrdin as prime minister.
17 December	Yeltsin appoints Gaidar as his presidential adviser on economic policy.
	German Chancellor Helmut Kohl visits Russia. Russia agrees to speed up the withdrawal of former Soviet troops from Germany and Germany promises $318 million to build housing for returning soldiers and $11.2 billion debt relief.
23 December	Yeltsin approves the cabinet put together by Chernomyrdin.

1993

3 January	Moscow Yeltsin–Bush summit; START-II Treaty signed.
22 January	Minsk CIS summit.
10–13 March	Eighth Congress of People's Deputies.
20 March	In a televised address, Yeltsin declares special rule for five weeks and a referendum to be held on 25 April.

23 March	Constitutional Court rules that the presidential decrees establishing special rule are unconstitutional and violate the Federation Treaty.
26–29 March	Ninth Congress of People's Deputies votes 617 to 268 to impeach Yeltsin but this falls short of the necessary two-thirds vote in favour; it strips Yeltsin of most of his remaining powers.
3–4 April	Vancouver Yeltsin–Clinton summit. Clinton commits America to support Yeltsin.
25 April	Nationwide referendum held. Its four questions concern confidence in Yeltsin, approval of his socio-economic policies, and the need for new presidential and Congress of People's Deputies elections.
30 April	Yeltsin reveals a new draft constitution with a popularly elected president to be head of state and government, and a new two-chamber parliament.
5 June	A Constitutional Conference meets in Moscow to approve the president's draft constitution, but instead produces a compromise constitution.
15 June	Russia's Choice a 'Democratic Bloc of Reformist Forces', founded by Igor Gaidar, Alexander Yakovlev and Mikhail Gorbachev.
July–August	Several regions unilaterally adopt the status of republic and some republics stop transferring tax money to Moscow.
12 July	Constitutional Conference accepts the text of the draft constitution by 433 votes (74 per cent) to 62 (10.6 per cent) with 63 (10.7 per cent) abstentions.
27 July	Yeltsin fires Security Minister Viktor Barannikov.
13 August	A meeting of the Council of the Heads of the Russian republics and representatives of regional associations held in Petrozavodsk approves the draft of legislation to implement the federative treaty.
18–24 August	Yeltsin's Anti-Crime and Corruption Committee produces evidence implicating Vice-President Rutskoi.
31 August	Last RF troops leave Lithuania.
1 September	Yeltsin issues a decree suspending Vice-President Alexander Rutskoi and First Deputy Prime Minister Vladimir Shumeiko.
3 September	Supreme Soviet suspends President Yeltsin's decree suspending Rutskoi and Shumeiko.
17 September	Yeltsin visits internal security troops division in the Moscow area.
17–18 September	Rutskoi and Khasbulatov warn that Yeltsin is planning direct presidential rule and a dictatorship.
21 September	Yeltsin dissolves parliament and calls for parliamentary elections on 12 December. Constitutional Court in an emergency meeting rules by 9 to 4 that Yeltsin's statements are in violation of the Constitution. Parliament goes into emergency session, forms its own government and Rutskoi is sworn in as 'president'. The Russian parliament building, with about 100 deputies inside, is sealed off by troops, and electricity and the telephones are cut off.
24 September	Moscow CIS summit agrees to form an economic union.
3 October	Armed clashes take place between forces loyal to Yeltsin and those loyal to Rutskoi and Khasbulatov. The Rutskoi–Khasbulatov

	forces attack the Moscow mayor's office and the Ostankino television centre. Yeltsin declares a state of emergency.
4 October	Yeltsin deploys armed forces against parliament, which is bombarded and set on fire. The rebels surrender and Rutskoi, Khasbulatov, Barranikov, Dunaev, Achalov, Makashov plus 24 others are arrested.
	Opposition publications *Pravda*, *Narodnaia gazeta*, *Sovetskaia Rossiia*, *Shield* and *Den'* are suspended, as are various Red-Brown movements including the National Salvation Front, the United Front of Russian Working People, the Officers' Union and Russian Communist Workers' Party.
6 October	Valery Zorkin resigns as chair of the Constitutional Court. Yeltsin lifts press censorship and calls on local soviets to disband pending elections on 12 December.
7 October	The funerals are held for the 189 victims of the fighting in Moscow.
9 October	Yeltsin extends the state of emergency in Moscow until 18 October.
11–13 October	Yeltsin visits Tokyo and signs the Tokyo Declaration on the Northern Territories.
15 October	Yeltsin decrees that a referendum on the draft constitution will be held on 12 December.
17 October	A Russian navy tanker dumps 900 tons of liquid radioactive waste into the Sea of Japan.
19 October	Yeltsin issues a decree banning a number of parties and movements from participation in the Federal Assembly elections.
20 October	Yeltsin changes the members of the Security Council.
22 October	Yeltsin decrees new elections are to be held for regional legislatures between December 1993 and March 1994.
23 October	Georgia joins the CIS.
26 October	Yeltsin decrees new elections are to be held for local councils (districts and towns) between December 1993 and June 1994.
27 October	Yeltsin signs a decree on land ownership which removes restrictions on the sale and ownership of land.
28 October	The Sverdlovsk *oblast* soviet adopts a constitution naming the region the 'Urals republic'.
2 November	Security Council approves the New Russian Military Doctrine.
6 November	Yeltsin approves the draft constitution and amended electoral regulations are issued.
4–6 December	Miners strike in Vorkuta and other regions. Yeltsin almost doubles the minimum monthly wage for government workers.
12 December	Elections to the Federal Assembly and a referendum on the new constitution are held.

1994

11 January	Federation Council and Duma meet for the first time.
13 January	Sixty-five deputies form the New Regional Policy bloc.

14 January	Ivan Rybkin elected chair of the Duma.
16 January	Igor Gaidar resigns from the government.
23 February	Duma grants an amnesty to those imprisoned for their participation in the August 1991 coup and the October 1993 conflict.
24 February	Yeltsin presents his State of the Nation address to parliament.
15 April	Moscow CIS summit.
28 April	Liberal Democratic Union formed by 39 Duma deputies.
23 May	Alexander Rutskoi's People's Party of Free Russia renames itself the Russian Social Democratic People's Party (RSDP).
27 May	The novelist and nationalist writer Aleksander Solzhenitsyn returns to Russia after 20 years in exile.
8 June	Russia and the OECD sign a Declaration on Cooperation aimed at helping Russia through the transition process.
12–13 June	Pro-reform bloc Russia's Choice formally reconstitutes itself as a party called Russia's Democratic Choice.
22 June	Russia signs a Partnership for Peace Framework Document with NATO.
31 August	Last RF troops leave Germany and Latvia.
30 September	Returning from the USA Yeltsin fails to leave his plane at Shannon Airport to meet Irish Prime Minister Reynolds.
5 October	Russia signs an outline agreement with the London Club of commercial creditors to reschedule $24 billion of its debts over 15 years.
17 October	Dmitry Kholodov, a journalist for *Moskovskii Komsomolets*, is murdered.
21 October	New Civil Code is passed.
26 November	Russia's covert operation in Chechnia fails.
11 December	Federal forces enter Chechnia and begin a military campaign to reintegrate the Chechen republic into the RF.

1995

5 January	Valentin Kovalev is appointed justice minister, becoming the first member of the Communist Party to serve in a government under Yeltsin.
January	Federal troops gradually gain control of most of Grozny (capital of Chechnia).
6 February	Alexander Rutskoi is dismissed as the chair of the RSDP by its board.
1 March	Vladimir Listyev, a journalist and head of the Russian Public Broadcasting, is murdered.
10 March	Duma votes the Human Rights commissioner Sergei Kovalev out of office.
	Duma passes a vote of no confidence in the interior minister, Viktor Yerin.
15 March	Duma passes the 1995 Budget.

1 April	Russian Public Television (ORT) begins broadcasting.
5 April	Centrist United Industrial Party is founded, chaired by Arkady Volsky.
11 April	IMF approves a huge 12-month standby loan worth about $6.8 billion to support the Russian government's 1995 economic stabilisation and reform programme.
12 May	Prime Minister Chernomyrdin founds the pro-Yeltsin reform movement, Our Home is Russia.
14 June	Southern Russian town of Budyonnovsk is attacked by Chechen rebels led by Shamil Basaev.
21 June	Duma passes vote of no confidence in the government over its handling of the Chechen situation.
1 July	Second Duma vote of no confidence in the government fails.
17 July	RF signs an interim trade accord with the EU.
20 July	Customs Union between Belarus, Kazakhstan and Russia comes into force.
2 August	Dzhokar Dudaev, the rebel Chechen leader, signs a cease-fire agreement with Chernomyrdin ending the eight-month civil war in Chechnia.
12 August	First gubernatorial election since 1993 is held in Yeltsin's home region of Sverdlovsk. It is won by Eduard Rossel, who defeated Aleksei Strakhov of the pro-Yeltsin Our Home is Russia party.
17 September	Presidential decree sets elections for the heads of regional administrations for December 1996 and for most regional parliaments for December 1997.
11 October	Duma passes a law under which the heads of local executives and parliaments should form the Federation Council.
29 October	Electoral Commission rejects the registration of Yabloko and Rutskoi's Derzhava movement for the Duma elections. Both appeal to the Supreme Court which overturns the decisions.
1 November	Chechen Supreme Soviet unanimously elects the Moscow-backed Prime Minister Doku Zavgaev as the republic's head of state.
11 November	Yeltsin vetoes the 11 October Duma law on the composition of the Federation Council.
15 November	Federation Council unanimously decides that presidential elections will be held on 16 June 1996.
17 November	CFE Treaty comes into force; Russia has an extra three years to comply with its provisions.
23 November	Shamil Basaev directs Russian journalists to where Chechen rebels have buried a radioactive parcel in Moscow's Izmailovsky park.
6 December	Duma passes 1996 budget.
14 December	Elections are held in Chechnia. The turnout is 74.8 per cent and almost half the votes go to Our Home is Russia. On the same day Prime Minister Doku Zavgaev is elected president with 93 per cent of the votes cast.
17 December	Duma elections.
18 December	In the first engagement since the signing of the 30 July Peace Agreement federal troops launch heavy artillery and missile attacks on the city of Gudermes in Chechnia.

21 December	Rebel commander Aslan Maskhadov withdraws his troops from Gudermes, saying they had achieved their primary objective of disrupting local and parliamentary elections.

1996

January	In response to the strong KPRF showing in the Duma elections, Yeltsin reshuffles the Council of Ministers dropping prominent reformers. Liberal reformers including Otto Latsis and Igor Gaidar also resign over Yeltsin's handling of the Chechen crisis.
5 January	Andrei Kozyrev resigns as foreign minister and is replaced by Yevgeny Primakov.
9 January	Chechen rebels seize the hospital in Dagestan city of Kizlyar taking around 3400 hostages and killing up to 30 people.
12 January	Bilateral treaty signed between the federal government and Sverdlovsk region.
13 January	Sergei Filatov, a leading reformer, resigns as head of the presidential staff, and is replaced by the more hawkish Nikolai Igorov.
15 January	Federal troops attack the Chechen rebels who have fled from Kizlyar to the city of Pervomayskoye still holding more than 100 hostages.
16 January	Anatoly Chubais dismissed as first deputy chair of the Council of Ministers in charge of economic policy.
16 January	The first meeting of the new Duma is dominated by the Pervomayskoye hostage crisis. Communists and reformers criticise Yeltsin's handling of the situation.
17 January	Duma elects Gennady Seleznov, a Communist and a former editor of *Pravda*, as its chair.
19 January	Chechen hijackers holding over 200 hostages on a Black Sea ferry surrender to Turkish authorities.
23 January	Federation Council elects Igor Stroev, the governor of Orel, as its chair.
24 January	Sergei Kovalev resigns as head of the Presidential Human Rights Commission and as a member of Yeltsin's Advisory Council, citing the lack of judicial reform, the extra-legal powers of the security services, the civil war in Chechnia, the lack of military reforms, secret decrees and closed institutions.
25 January	Alexander Kazakov, a former aide to Anatoly Chubais, is named deputy chair of the Council of Ministers and the chair of the State Committee for the Management of State Property (the Privatisation Agency).
1 February	Yeltsin celebrates his 65th birthday.
1–2 February	500 000 coal miners strike due to non-payments of wages.
2 February	Chernomyrdin approves a financial package of 10 400 billion roubles for the coal industry.

3 February	Government promises to pay the miners' back wages.
5 February	General Prosecutor Yury Skuratov announces an investigation into the privatisation of some of the country's most valuable enterprises including Norilsk Nikel.
8 February	IMF approves a $1.05 billion loan to Russia, the final instalment in a $6.3 billion loan package approved for Russia last year.
	Russian Interior Ministry troops in Grozny surround more than 1000 peaceful demonstrators calling for the departure of federal troops from Chechnia.
9 February	Three of the Grozny protesters are killed and seven injured in an explosion. There are now over 2000 demonstrators. Protests end on 11 February.
10 February	Foreign Minister Primakov holds his first round of talks with US Secretary of State Warren Christopher in Helsinki.
13 February	Film crews from NTV, Russia's only nationwide independent television station, are banned from the Kremlin following the broadcast of an interview with former presidential press spokesman Vyacheslav Kostikov, in which he criticises Alexander Korzhakov.
13 February	Captain Alexander Nikitin is arrested by the FSB and charged with espionage for work carried out for the Norwegian environmental group the Bellona Foundation.
14 February	Vladimir Kadannikov, a first deputy chair of the Council of Ministers and presidential candidate, announces that wage arrears total 13 400 billion roubles.
15 February	President Yeltsin announces that he will seek a second presidential term.
18–21 February	German Chancellor Helmut Kohl visits Russia for talks with Yeltsin.
22 February	Russia and the IMF reach an agreement on a $10.2 billion loan to assist Russia in its transition to capitalism. The loan is formally approved by the IMF on 26 March.
28 February	Russia becomes the 39th member of the Council of Europe.
March	Civil war in Chechnia escalates throughout the month.
29 March	Yeltsin signs a Quadripartite Treaty with Kazakhstan, Kyrgyzstan and Belarus designed to create a community of integrated but sovereign states.
31 March	In a nationally televised speech Yeltsin announces a unilateral and immediate cessation of major military operations in Chechnia and begins peace talks with the rebel Chechen leader, General Dzhokar Dudaev.
2 April	Bilateral Union Treaty signed by Russia and Belarus committing them to greater cooperation and integration while preserving their state sovereignties.
21 April	Chechen President Dzhokar Dudaev is killed in a Russian rocket attack.
22 April	Zelimkhan Yandarbiev becomes president of Chechnia.
24–27 April	Yeltsin visits China and meets President Jiang Zemin.
28 April	Russia, Kazakhstan and Oman agree to build a major oil pipeline from the Tengiz oil field in Kazakhstan to a Russian Black Sea port.

29 April	Paris Club agrees to reschedule over $40 billion of Russia's debt. Chechen rebel field commanders vote for Shamil Basaev as their chief of staff to replace Aslan Maskhadov.
16 May	Russian government announces a new exchange policy in order to help stabilise the rouble.
19 May	First round of mayoral elections in St Petersburg.
2 May	Second round of mayoral elections in St Petersburg. The incumbent Anatoly Sobchak is defeated by 45.8 per cent to 47.7 per cent by his deputy Vladimir Yakovlev.
27 May	Yeltsin and Chechen President Zelimkhan Yandarbiev sign a peace treaty putting an end to the 18-month Chechen conflict.
28 May	Yeltsin makes a short trip to Chechnia.
7 June	Valery Shantsev, a candidate for Moscow's deputy mayor, is seriously injured when a bomb explodes in front of his home.
11 June	A bomb explodes near a Moscow train station, killing four people and injuring 12.
16 June	First round of presidential elections. Yeltsin comes first but fails to get the 50 per cent plus one vote necessary to win outright. Luzhkov is re-elected mayor of Moscow with 89 per cent of the vote.
18 June	Yeltsin dismisses Defence Minister Pavel Grachev and appoints Alexander Lebed, an outspoken critic of the Chechen war, to the post of national security adviser. Lebed drops out of the second round of the presidential elections and endorses Yeltsin.
20 June	The 'War Party' in the Kremlin (Soskovets, Korzhakov and Barsukov) are sacked.
25 June	Continuing the attack on the 'War Party', Yeltsin sacks seven generals.
28–29 June	G7 Summit in Lyon (France) includes Russia, becoming the G8.
3 July	Second round of presidential elections; Yeltsin wins with 53.8 per cent to Zyuganov's 40.3 per cent of the vote.
4 July	Yeltsin reappoints Viktor Chernomyrdin as prime minister.
8 July	RF Central Bank takes control of the TverNoversal bank, amid fears of the instability of the Russian banking system.
12 July	Yeltsin deploys 1000 elite troops in Moscow after two bombs explode. Chechens are blamed for the bombings.
14–16 July	Yeltsin meets American Vice-President, Al Gore, in Moscow.
22 July	IMF announces it will delay the disbursement of this month's $330 million payment, citing the Russian government's tax collection problems.
July–August	Fighting escalates in Chechnia.
9 August	Yeltsin is inaugurated as RF president in the Kremlin.
10 August	Parliament approves the reappointment of Chernomyrdin as prime minister. Yeltsin's national security adviser Alexander Lebed replaces Oleg Lobov as the presidential envoy to Chechnia.
21 August	IMF disburses $330 million to Russia as part of the three-year, $10.2 billion loan approved in February.

22 August	Lebed and the Chechen military commander Aslan Maskhadov sign a peace agreement.
September	Beginning of two months of elections for the posts of regional governors.
7 September	Yeltsin and German Chancellor Helmut Kohl meet informally in Moscow.
17 October	Yeltsin dismisses Lebed, saying that the administration needs to be united.
20 October	Rutskoi is elected governor of Kursk with 79 per cent of the vote.
30 October	The oligarch Boris Berezovsky is appointed deputy secretary of the Security Council.
3 November	Paul Tatum, a US businessman, is shot dead. He had been involved in a legal battle over the ownership of the Raddison-Slavianskaia Hotel in central Moscow.
5 November	Chernomyrdin assumes presidential powers while Yeltsin undergoes a seven-hour multiple by-pass heart operation. Federation of Independent Trade Unions organises a Russia-wide day of action including strikes and rallies to protest against the government's failure to pay wages.
10 November	A bomb explodes at a memorial service in Moscow for Afghan war veterans.
16 November	Bomb explodes in a building housing Russian army officers in Kapisk (Dagestan); Chechen separatists are blamed.
4–6 December	400 St Petersburg nuclear power plant workers protest over unpaid wages. The government sends one billion roubles to St Petersburg.
4–11 December	Nationwide coal miners' strike. Government promises to pay back wages.
15 December	IMF resumes partial disbursement of a $10.1 billion loan to Russia it suspended in October.
20 December	Yeltsin meets Chinese Prime Minister Li Peng in Moscow.
27 December	Lebed announces the formation of a new opposition party called the Russian People's Republican Party.
29 December	Last federal troops withdrawn from Chechnia.

1997

1 January	Yeltsin meets with the German Chancellor Helmut Kohl to discuss NATO expansion and other issues.
14 January	Impeachment proceedings against Yeltsin are initiated by Viktor Iluyukhin, the chair of the Duma Security Committee, due to Yeltsin's persistent inabilities to perform his duties.
20 January	Yeltsin is discharged from hospital.
22 January	Yeltsin reappears in the Kremlin. Duma passes a non-binding resolution by 229 to 63 votes calling for Yeltsin to resign.
27 January	Aslan Maskhadov is elected president of Chechnia.

1 February	Yeltsin meets with French President Jacques Chirac outside Moscow.
3 February	Andrei Vavilov, the deputy finance minister with responsibility for tax collection, survives a bomb attack on his car.
4 February	Interior Minister Anatoly Kulikov is appointed a deputy prime minister in charge of economic crime.
7 February	IMF disburses two tranches totalling $647.2 million of the three-year loan agreed in March 1996. These tranches were withheld in November and December 1996 due to Russia's poor tax collection record.
10 February	Alexander Korzhakov is elected to the Duma for the Tula region.
14 February	State Duma abandons its attempt to impeach Yeltsin on health grounds and instead votes to ask the Ministry of Health and Yeltsin's doctors to report on his health before 1 March.
21 February	IMF mission leaves Moscow refusing to release the latest tranche of its loan to Russia agreed in March 1996, citing continuing failure to collect taxes and effect structural reforms.
6 March	Yeltsin delivers his State of the Nation address live and criticises the performance of the government.
7 March	Government reshuffle begins. Anatoly Chubais is appointed Yeltsin's chief-of-staff and a first deputy prime minister.
17 March	Yeltsin appoints Boris Nemtsov, the governor of Nizhnii-Novgorod region and an ally of Chubais, as a first deputy prime minister.
20 March	Helsinki Yeltsin–Clinton Summit.
27 March	Federation of Independent Trade Unions organises a day of protest over wage arrears.
28 March	CIS heads of state summit held in Moscow. Yeltsin is re-elected chair of the CIS Council of Heads of State.
2 April	Treaty on the Union of Belarus and Russia is signed by Yeltsin and Lukashenko.
11 April	Yeltsin dismisses four senior military officers under investigation for corruption since December 1996.
23 April	Moscow summit of Yeltsin and Chinese President Jiang Zemin.
8 May	State of emergency is declared in Vladivostok due to power cuts of up to 20 hours a day. Coal miners protesting over wage arrears are stopping coal getting to the power stations.
12 May	Yeltsin and Chechen President Aslan Maskhadov sign a formal peace treaty that officially ends the war between Russia and Chechnia.
18 May	Deputy Defence Minister and Chief Military Inspector Gen. Konstantin Kobets dismissed for corruption.
19 May	Government issues a programme to tackle corruption, social inequality and the lack of popular confidence in the government.
22 May	Yeltsin dismisses Defence Minister Igor Rodionov and Chief of General Staff Viktor Samsonov, citing their failure to carry out defence cuts and to restructure the military.
23 May	Yeltsin and President Lukashenko of Belarus sign a Charter of Union in Moscow.

28 May	In Kiev prime ministers Chernomyrdin and Lazerenko (Ukraine) agree that the Russian Black Sea fleet will remain based at the Ukrainian port of Sevastopol for 20 years.
10 June	Presidents Yeltsin and Lukashenko sign a Russia–Belarus Union Treaty.
23 June	Duma angrily condemns Yeltsin's suggestion that Lenin's body should be removed from Moscow.
24 June	Gen. (retd.) Lev Rokhlin, the chair of the Duma Defence Committee, accuses Yeltsin of destroying the Russian army and of being responsible for its defeat in Chechnia.
27 June	Three people are killed by a bomb on the Moscow–St Petersburg train; the government accuses Chechen separatists.
29–20 June	The *Admiral Vinogradov* visits Tokyo, the first Russian warship to do so since 1905.
3 August	Yeltsin announces that the Russian rouble will be relaunched on 1 January 1998. A new one rouble note will replace the current 1000 rouble note.
18 August	Yeltsin and Chechen President Aslan Maskhadov meet to appoint a joint commission to draw up a treaty for future relations between Moscow and Chechnia.
18 August	Mikhail Manevich, the deputy governor of St Petersburg and chair of the city's state property committee, is shot dead. His assassination is thought to be related to his role in the privatisation of city property in St Petersburg.
1 September	Yeltsin announces he will not run for re-election in 2000.
15 September	Yeltsin meets with the oligarchs in an attempt to stop disputes over the privatisation of state assets and their attacks on Chubais and Nemtsov.
17 September	Russia joins the Paris Club of creditor countries; this means that it will be able to recover some of the estimated $140 billion which had been lent by the Soviet Union.
20 September	Gen. (retd.) Lev Rokhlin chairs the founding congress of the All-Russian Movement in Support of the Army, Military Service, and the Defence Industry.
6 October	Russia and the London Club of commercial creditors agree a deal to restructure Russia's $33 billion debt to commercial banks which it took over from the USSR in 1991.
22 October	Russia rejoins the de Beers diamond cartel. De Beers agree to buy 40 per cent of the production of the Almazy Rossii-Sakha mining company.
4 November	The 15 per cent ceiling on foreign ownership of shares in Russian oil companies is lifted by presidential decree.
5 November	In a move described by Boris Nemtsov as an important step in the ending of oligarchy capitalism, Yeltsin dismisses Boris Berezovsky from his post as deputy secretary of the Security Council.
9 November	The Chechen section of the oil pipeline linking the Caspian Sea fields with the Russia port of Novorossiisk reopens following damage during the 1994–6 Chechen war.

20 November	Yeltsin drops Nemtsov as minister of fuel and energy and Chubais as minister of finance due to a scandal over a publisher's advance. Replaced by Mikhail Zadornov and Sergei Kiriyenko respectively.
1 December	Chechen President Aslan Maskhadov dismisses the Chechen government.
2–3 December	Yeltsin makes a state visit to Sweden.
10 December	Yeltsin enters a sanatorium with an acute viral inflection.
14 December	In elections to the Moscow City Duma 27 of the 35 seats are won by members of Luzhkov's list.
18 December	Yeltsin signs the first post-Soviet National Security guidelines.

1998

1 January	New redesignated rouble notes are launched.
8 January	IMF announces it will release the October 1997 tranche of the $665 million loan which had been held back due to Russia's poor tax collection record.
14 January	Eduard Rossel, the governor of Sverdlovsk region, escapes an assassination attempt by a regional crime gang.
15 January	Shamil Basaev, Chechnia's first deputy prime minister, forms a new cabinet.
16 January	Government reshuffle: Chernomyrdin extends his responsibilities to include direct oversight of the Ministries of Finance, Interior, Defence, Foreign Affairs, and Fuel and Energy.
19 January	Yeltsin returns to work after almost a month's absence. In a televised broadcast Yeltsin criticises Chernomyrdin, Nemtsov and Chubais for failing to deal with the 1997 public sector pay arrears. Yukos and Sibneft merge to form Yuksi, Russia's largest oil company.
27 January	Inaugural session of the EU–Russia Cooperation Council opens in Brussels to discuss bilateral trade issues.
30 January	Russian government commission recommends the burial of the remains of Tsar Nicholas and his family in St Petersburg on 17 July.
2 February	Government submits a revised draft tax code to Duma.
9–11 February	Yeltsin makes a state visit to Italy.
19 February	IMF Managing Director Michel Camdessus announces that the IMF's three-year $10 billion fund facility to Russia would be extended by a further year until 2000.
23 February	Japanese Foreign Minister Keizo Obuchi meets Yeltsin in the Kremlin.
19 March	CIS summit is postponed indefinitely due to Yeltsin's ill health.
23 March	Yeltsin dismisses the government and Prime Minister Chernomyrdin, citing the slowness of reform. Yeltsin temporarily and unconstitutionally assumes prime ministerial duties.
26 March	Informal one-day summit meeting of the presidents of Russia and France, and the chancellor of Germany at Bor, south of Moscow.

27 March	Yeltsin names Sergei Kiriyenko as acting prime minister.
28 March	Chernomyrdin announces he will be a candidate in the presidential elections in 2000.
9 April	Federation of Independent Trade Unions organises a nationwide day of protest against unpaid wages.
10 April	Duma rejects Kiriyenko as prime minister by 186 votes to 143.
17 April	Duma votes 271 to 115 (with 11 abstentions) against Kiriyenko.
24 April	Duma votes 251 to 25 in favour of Kiriyenko as prime minister.
30 April	Chubais elected chief executive of Russia's electricity monopoly Unified Energy System with Yeltsin's approval.
1 May	Yeltsin's personal envoy to Chechnia, Valentin Vlasov, is kidnapped by gunmen.
5 May	Embezzlement charges are brought against the former state property minister Alfred Kokh. Kiriyenko appoints a government presidium from the cabinet.
12 May	Trans-Siberian railway is blocked for more than two weeks by coal miners protesting over unpaid wages.
13 May	A bomb explodes at the Lubavitch Marina Roshcha synagogue in Moscow.
17 May	Lebed is elected governor of Krasnoyarsk.
27 May	RF Central Bank trebles its main interest rate to 150 per cent.
29 May	Yeltsin replaces his chief tax collector Alexander Pochinok with the former finance minister Boris Fyodorov to spearhead Russia's tax collection.
2 June	Yeltsin (with Kiriyenko) has his first meeting with the oligarchs since 15 September 1997.
8 June	The head and deputy head of the Russian Statistics Committee are arrested on charges of helping companies to falsify their books in order to evade taxes.
9 June	Boris Fyodorov, the new director of the federal tax service, says he will purge his agency of corrupt officials.
17 June	Chubais is given responsibility for coordinating Russia's relations with the international financial organisations.
18 June	IMF delays a $670 million tranche of a loan due to Russia's poor tax collection. It is released on 25 June.
23 June	Government submits an anti-crisis programme to the Duma.
25 June	Russian shares fall.
July	Miners striking over wage arrears block the main railway lines, bringing the country to a standstill.
13 July	International lenders pledge a further $22 billion (including an additional $11.2 billion from the IMF) in extra credits to Russia. Share values begin to rise.
14 July	Announcement of a voluntary restructuring scheme for Russia's short-term debt.
17 July	Burial of Tsar Nicholas and his family in St Petersburg. Duma partially approves the anti-crisis programme but rejects its revenue-raising measures.
20 July	First $4.8 billion tranche of the new IMF $11.2 billion loan is released.

23 July	President Aslan Maskhadov of Chechnia survives a car bomb attack; the Islamic Fundamentalist Wahhabi sect is blamed.
August	Armed security forces prevent miners from resuming their protests after the government reneges on its promises to pay back wages.
10 August	Markets plummet amid fears of debt default and/or rouble devaluation.
11–13 August	Share prices plummet.
13 August	IMF and the Russian government have emergency talks to prevent the collapse of the stock market and devaluation of the rouble.
14 August	Yeltsin says the rouble will not be devalued.
17 August	Rouble is devalued and the government announces a three-month moratorium on the repayment of Russia's $140 billion foreign debt.
23 August	Yeltsin dismisses Kiriyenko and the government, and recalls Chernomyrdin.
25 August	Announcement of a restructuring of short-term rouble-denominated debt held in treasury bills (GKOs). The rouble suffers its worst fall in nearly four years. Oneximbank, Menatap and Most-bank announce a merger.
26 August	RF Central Bank halts rouble–dollar trading. Russians withdraw their savings from banks.
27 August	Inkombank and the National Reserve bank plan to merge. Avtobank, Mexhkombank and Alfabank plan to merge. RF Central Bank takes over SBS-Agro after it collapses.
30 August	Chernomyrdin and the opposition agree a draft compromise on constitutional changes to reduce the powers of the president but Zyuganov's Communists pull out at the last minute.
31 August	Duma votes 251 to 94 (with 105 abstentions) against Chernomyrdin becoming prime minister. He is immediately renominated by Yeltsin and announces that he will form a government.
1–2 September	Moscow summit with Clinton, who offers more assistance to support reform.
4 September	Federation Council votes by 91 to 17 to support Chernomyrdin as prime minister, after he promises to introduce an 'economic dictatorship' on 1 January 1998 and to print more roubles.
7 September	Duma votes by 273 votes to 138 (with one abstention) against Chernomyrdin's candidacy as prime minister.
10 September	Yeltsin nominates Primakov as prime minister.
11 September	Duma endorses Primakov as prime minister by 317 votes to 63 (with 15 abstentions). Russia admits that it has defaulted on the interest payments on the $40 billion of soviet-era debt restructured by the Paris Club in April 1996, which had fallen due on 20 August.
7 October	Federation of Independent Trade Unions organises a nationwide day of protest organised over wage arrears.
28 October	Kremlin acknowledges that, due to poor health, Yeltsin has relinquished much of the day-to-day running of the country.

30 October	Yeltsin leaves to convalesce in the Black Sea resort of Sochi.
	IMF delegation arrives in Moscow.
31 October	Anti-crisis measures developed by government ministers and the RF Central Bank are approved by the government.
4 November	Duma votes 121 to 107 not to censure KPRF deputy Albert Makashov for anti-Semitic remarks made in October.
5 November	Constitutional Court rules that Yeltsin may not seek a third presidential term.
6 November	USA agrees to supply food and food credits to Russia.
	Russian government and foreign creditors agree the restructuring of Russian government treasury bills (GKOs) market.
12 November	Moscow summit meeting between Yeltsin and Japanese Prime Minister Keizo Obuchi.
13 November	Valentin Vlasov, Yeltsin's personal envoy to Chechnia who had been kidnapped on 1 May, is released.
	Russia asks the EU for food aid.
15 November	Government releases its economic rescue plan entitled 'On Measures of the Russian Government and Central Bank to Stabilise the Socio-economic Situation in the Country'.
	Yury Luzhkov, the mayor of Moscow, announces the formation of a new centrist political movement called Otchestvo (Fatherland).
20 November	Russia appeals to the Paris and London Clubs to reschedule the soviet-era debt for the second time.
	Amid fears of a collapse of the Russian banking system, Prime Minister Primakov establishes a new agency with a charter capital of 10 billion roubles to restructure the banking system.
	Galina Starovoitova, Duma deputy, human rights activist and anti-corruption campaigner, is assassinated.
23 November	Yeltsin is hospitalised with pneumonia.
1–2 December	IMF Managing Director Michel Camdessus visits Moscow but does not release the IMF loans suspended after the August rouble devaluation and debt repayment default.
7 December	Yeltsin dismisses four senior aides including the head of presidential administration, Valentin Yumashev.
25 December	Russia and Belarus sign a 'Declaration on the Further Unification of Russia and Belarus', a 'Treaty between the Russian Federation and the Republic of Belarus on the Equal Rights of Citizens' and an 'Agreement between the Russian Federation and the Republic of Belarus on Creating Equal Conditions for Economic Entities'.
29 December	Russia defaults on a $362 million payment on soviet-era debt to foreign commercial banks, and asks for it to be rescheduled.

1999

17 January	Yeltsin is hospitalised with a bleeding stomach ulcer.

25 January	Yury Kobladze, head of the information sector of the external security service, is appointed as first deputy director of the Itar-Tass news agency.
20 January	IMF mission arrives in Moscow for talks.
25–27 January	US Secretary of State, Madeleine Albright, visits Moscow.
27–29 January	Nationwide teachers' strike over unpaid wages.
31 January	Primakov announces that he is stepping up his campaign against the oligarchs.
2 February	Yeltsin dismisses four of his advisers, leaving only his daughter Tatyana Dyachenko and Mikhail Zubarov. General Prosecutor Yury Skuratov raids the offices of Berezovsky's company Sibneft and claims to have found evidence that Berezovsky had ordered Yeltsin's family to be bugged. General prosecutor resigns on 'health grounds'.
3 February	Russia is ranked amongst the ten most corrupt countries in the world.
4 February	Captain Alexander Nikitin, the environmental activist, loses his appeal against treason charges. A report by General Prosecutor Skuratov highlights irregularities and corruption in the RF Central Bank's financial dealings and in the selling of state property. Special troops raid offices affiliated to Aeroflot, whose managing director is Yeltsin's son-in-law, Valery Okulov. The government releases figures showing that the economy shrank by 4.6 per cent in 1998, the biggest drop for four years.
10 February	A fire at the Samara regional police headquarters kills 67, injures 6 and destroys the city's crime archives. It is thought to be the work of criminal gangs.
17 February	Ministry of Food announces that due to a poor harvest in 1998 Russia is short some 10 million tons of grain.
19 February	EU agree a food aid package for Russia.
27 February	Yeltsin is hospitalised with stomach pains, discharged 18 March.
4 March	Boris Berezovsky is dismissed as an executive secretary of the CIS.
5 March	RF Interior Ministry's representative in Chechnia, Major-General Gennady Shpigun, is kidnapped in Grozny. The Russian government evacuates its remaining officials from Chechnia.
16 March	Nikolai Bordyuzha is dismissed as head of the presidential administration and secretary of the Security Council.
17 March	Federation Council rejects General Prosecutor Skuratov's resignation.
19 March	A bomb explodes in Vladikavkaz, the capital of the southern Russian republic of North Ossetia, killing 60 and injuring more than 100.
21 March	Chechen President Aslan Maskhadov escapes assassination when a bomb explodes near his motorcade in Grozny.
23 March	General Prosecutor Skuratov begins investigations into allegations of corruption involving Mabetex and the presidential administration. Presidential offices in the Kremlin are sealed off by investigators and documents removed.

26 March	Foreign Minister Ivanov announces an end to contacts with NATO due to NATO's actions in Yugoslavia.
29 March	Putin becomes secretary of the Security Council and remains director of the FSB.
	IMF agrees to make new loans of up to $4.8 billion available to Russia to be disbursed in four tranches of $1.2 billion between April 1999 and February 2000.
2 April	CIS heads of state summit in Moscow.
	Yeltsin suspends General Prosecutor Skuratov.
3 April	A bomb explodes outside an office of the FSB in central Moscow.
6 April	General Prosecutor's office issues warrants for the arrest of the oligarchs Boris Berezovsky and Alexander Smolensky, and also for Nikolai Glushkov, the former commercial director of Aeroflot.
	General Prosecutor Skuratov submits his resignation to the Federation Council.
10 April	Prime Minister Primakov appeals to the Duma to drop impeachment proceedings against Yeltsin.
13 April	Yeltsin expands the Security Council to include the chairs of the two chambers of the Federal Assembly: Igor Stroev, the Federation Council chair, and Gennady Selesnyov, the Duma chair.
14 April	Duma postpones until 13 May a vote to impeach President Yeltsin.
18 April	Arrest warrant against Boris Berezovsky is withdrawn and he returns to Moscow.
21 April	Federation Council votes not to accept Skuratov's resignation.
24 April	A bomb explodes outside the buildings holding the US and UK consulates in Yekaterinburg.
26 April	General Prosecutor's office reactivates criminal charges against Berezovsky for laundering money.
	Bomb explodes outside the Intourist Hotel near the Kremlin in Moscow.
28 April	IMF Managing Director Michel Camdessus announces a new loan of $4.5 billion to be paid to Russia over the next 18 months.
12 May	Yeltsin dismisses the government headed by Primakov and appoints Sergei Stepashin as acting prime minister.
15 May	Impeachment of Yeltsin by the Duma fails to get enough votes.
18 May	RF Central Bank revokes the licences of 12 failing banks, including Menatap.
	Russia's sixth largest oil company, Sidanko, is declared bankrupt.
19 May	Duma approves Stepashin as prime minister by a vote of 301 to 55 with 11 abstentions.
1 June	Stepashin forms the new government presidium.
3 June	Stepashin establishes a new government economic council headed by himself.
14 June	Yeltsin makes new appointments to the Security Council including Stepashin.
29 June	RF Central Bank revokes the licences of Oneximbank, Mosbiznesbank, Promstroibank and Mezhkombank.

7 July	Renovations to the Grand Kremlin Palace are completed at a cost of $335 million.
28 July	IMF approves a $4.5 billion standby credit for Russia to be released in seven instalments over 17 months.
1 August	Russia agrees with the Paris Club to restructure the $7.5 billion payments due on Russia's $38 billion soviet-era debt.
3 August	Chernomyrdin resigns as Yeltsin's special envoy to Yugoslavia.
9 August	Yeltsin dismisses his fourth government in 17 months. Appoints Vladimir Putin, the head of the FSB and secretary of the Security Council, as prime minister-designate and names him as his preferred successor as president. Putin is replaced as head of the FSB by his first deputy, Nikolai Patrushev.
10 August	Rebel leaders in Chechnia declare it an independent Islamic state.
12 August	According to Putin Chechen rebel incursions into Dagestan mean Russian forces must retaliate.
16 August	Duma approves Putin as prime minister by 232 votes to 84 with 17 abstentions.
	Chechen president, Aslan Maskhadov, declares a one-month state of emergency in Chechnia.
17 August	Yeltsin issues a decree confirming the structure of the Russian government: the government now includes 26 ministries, 10 state committees, 3 federal commissions, 14 federal services, 9 agencies, 2 inspectorates and 3 other federal bodies.
19 August	Membership of the new cabinet is confirmed.
26 August	New government presidium is appointed.
31 August	A bomb explodes at the Manezh shopping centre in central Moscow; Muslim militants are blamed.
9 September	A bomb explodes in a Moscow appartment block killing 94 and injuring 200; the Chechens are blamed.
21 September	Putin announces that all pension arrears have been paid in full.
23 September	Russian warplanes bomb Grozny, marking the beginning of the second Chechen war.
1 October	Federal troops cross into Chechnia.
5 October	Chechen President Aslan Maskhadov calls on Russia to negotiate peace with the rebels.
8 October	Council of CIS prime ministers meets in Yalta to discuss the introduction of a CIS free trade zone.
12 October	Defence Minister Sergeev tells reporters that federal troops are in control of Chechnia and are liquidating terrorist bands.
13 October	Suspended General Prosecutor Yury Skuratov addresses the Federation Council and denounces Yeltsin's 'entourage' as corrupt criminals. The Federation Council then votes to overturn Yeltsin's dismissal of Skuratov for the third time by 98 to 52.
15 October	Dmitry Vasiliyev, the chair of the Federal Securities Commission, resigns, citing his frustration at his inability to control the oligarchs.
20 October	Viktor Novosyolov, a senior St Petersburg politician, member of the St Petersburg City Legislature and candidate for its chair, is assassinated by a bomb placed on his car. He had lost both legs in a 1993 assassination attempt.

21 October	Federal troops are within 10 km of Grozny.
22 October	EU leaders meet with Putin in Helsinki and call on Russia to negotiate with the Chechen rebels. Putin stresses Russia's need to combat terrorism.
24 October	The main route from Chechnia to the border with neighbouring Ingushetia is closed, trapping Chechen civilians in the war zone.
2 November	Prime Minister Putin announces that an OSCE aid mission will be allowed into the Chechnia–Ingushetia region to help refugees displaced by the renewed fighting in Chechnia.
4 November	Federal troops open the border between Chechnia and Ingushetia which has been closed for two weeks trapping fleeing civilians.
9 November	Russia closes all access roads to Chechnia, bans trade with and suspends international flights to Chechnia.
12 November	International Red Cross withdraws its workers from Chechnia to focus its relief efforts on the refugees in Ingushetia.
15 November	President Yeltsin officially endorses Putin's presidential candidacy.
30 November	FSB detains Cheri Leberknight, an American diplomat, on charges of spying for the USA. This follows the arrest of the US Navy officer, Daniel King, by the Americans on charges of spying for Russia.
3 December	RF government helicopter fires on a refugee convoy leaving Grozny, killing 14 refugees.
7 December	IMF announces the postponement of $640 million credits, on the grounds that Russia has not reached its economic targets.
13 December	Duma refuses to debate the ratification of START II.
14 December	OSCE chairman, Knut Vollebaek, arrives in Russian-held Chechnia to monitor the situation.
19 December	Duma elections. Luzhkov is re-elected mayor of Moscow.
30 December	Captain Alexander Nikitin is finally cleared of treason by a St Petersburg court.
31 December	Yeltsin announces his resignation as president and Putin becomes acting president.

2000

3 January	Putin dismisses Yeltsin's daughter, Tatyana Dyachenko, from her post as presidential adviser.
6 January	Gennady Zyuganov announces his candidacy for the presidential elections.
7 January	Russian military announces the suspension of its assault on Grozny so that civilians may leave.
9 January	Chechen rebels attack the government-controlled towns of Argun and Shali south-east of Grozny.
10 January	Defence Minister Igor Sergeev lifts the suspension of air artillery attacks on Grozny. Acting President Putin signs a new national security strategy.

	Pavel Borodin is dismissed as the Kremlin's facilities manager. Government reshuffle results in the prime minister having seven deputies, including one first deputy, instead of two first deputies and four deputies.
13 January	Putin announces his candidacy for the presidential elections.
18 January	Federal troops re-enter Grozny following massive and sustained air strikes.
	Newly elected Duma convenes.
	Gennady Seleznyov (KPRF) is re-elected speaker (chair) of the Duma in a power-sharing deal between the KPRF and the pro-Putin Unity party. This deal leads to a nine-day Duma boycott by the Union of Rightist Forces, the Fatherland-All Russia faction and Yabloko.
22 January	On Putin's orders Gen. Ovchnnikov is replaced by Col. Tikhomirov as the commander of government forces in Chechnia.
26 January	Pavel Borodin is named as state secretary for the Russia–Belarus union.
27 January	International arrest warrant is issued by the Swiss for Pavel Borodin on charges of money laundering.
	Putin announces plans to double arms spending in 2000.
28 January	Russian government authorities confirm that they have detained the journalist Andrei Babitsky.
1 February	Chechen rebels flee Grozny.
6 February	Putin announces that Grozny has been captured by federal troops.
9 February	Russia signs a friendship treaty with North Korea.
11 February	First Deputy Prime Minister, Mikhail Kasyanov, and the London Club agree to restructure $1.8 billion of Russia's soviet-era debt payments.
13 February	Deadline for the registration of presidential candidates.
16 February	Putin meets with the NATO secretary general, George Robinson, in Moscow and agrees to renew diplomatic ties with NATO which were severed in spring 1999 in protest at NATO's air attacks on Yugoslavia.
17 February	Vladimir Kalamanov is appointed the president's representative for human rights in Chechnia.
20 February	Anatoly Sobchak, the former mayor of Leningrad–St Petersburg, dies.
9 March	Russian government announces that it will sign the 1996 Geneva treaty banning landmines.
10–11 March	British Prime Minister Tony Blair pays a private visit to St Petersburg to meet Putin.
15 March	Six suspects are charged with the Moscow bombings.
26 March	Putin wins the presidential elections on the first round.
16 April	Duma approves the START II nuclear arms reduction treaty, seven years after the agreement was signed with the USA and four years after it was ratified by the US Senate.
17 April	President-elect Putin visits London for talks with Tony Blair and tea with HRH Queen Elizabeth II.

19 April	Federation Council votes 122 to 15 with 7 abstentions to approve START II.
21 April	Security Council approves a new Military Doctrine.
22 April	Putin approves Russia's new Military Doctrine.
7 May	Vladimir Putin is sworn in as president, and names Mikhail Kasyanov as prime minister.
11 May	NATO is condemned for failing to protect Serbs from Albanian attacks in Kosovo.
	The Moscow headquarters of Gusinsky's Media-Most is raided by police and federal agents.
13 May	Putin issues a decree dividing Russia into seven federal districts.
17 May	Putin proposes to reform the Federation Council.
	The Duma confirms Kasyanov as prime minister with 325 votes in favour and 55 against with 15 abstentions.
	The Federation Council confirms Vladimir Ustinov as general prosecutor by 114 votes to 10.
18 May	Foreign Minister Igor Ivanov and Defence Minister Igor Sergeev are reappointed.
20 May	Putin issues a decree restructuring government and abolishing the post of first deputy prime minister.
26 May	Government approves an amnesty for up to 120 000 convicts convicted of minor offences to mark the 55th anniversary of Russia's victory in the Great Patriotic War in 1945.
3–5 June	President Clinton visits Moscow for talks with Putin.
6–7 June	Putin pays an official visit to Italy.
7 June	Mikhail Katyshev is dismissed by the Federation Council as a senior prosecutor. Katyshev had been pursuing cases against Kremlin officials alleged to be involved in the Mabetex scandal.
8 June	Putin imposes 'temporary' direct presidential rule in Chechnia in order to restore constitutional order.
12 June	Putin appoints Akhmed Kadyrov, a local Muslim leader, as the head of administration in Chechnia.
13 June	Vladimir Gusinsky is arrested and held until 16 June.
13–14 June	Putin pays an official visit to Spain.
15–16 June	Putin pays an official visit to Germany.
21 June	Yabloko and the Union of Rightist Forces (SPS) announce plans to merge.
23 June	Putin issues a decree renaming the North Caucasus Federal District the Southern District.
27 June	Vyacheslav Trubnikov, a former member of the FSB, is appointed first deputy foreign minister and presidential envoy to the CIS.
28 June	Federation Council rejects by 129 votes to 13 with one abstention Putin's plans to reform the institution.
8 July	President Putin makes his first state of the nation address since his election.
17–18 July	Putin visits Beijing for a summit with Chinese President Jiang Zemin.

19 July	Putin has talks with North Korean leader Kim Jong Il in North Korea.
21–3 July	Putin attends the G8 conference in Okinawa, Japan.
28 July	Putin meets with Russian business people at the Kremlin.
8 August	A powerful bomb explodes in a pedestrian underpass by the Pushkin monument on Tverskaia street in central Moscow during the evening rush hour.
12 August	*Kursk* nuclear submarine sinks in the Barents Sea with 118 crew on board.
14 August	Russian Orthodox Church canonises the last Tsar Nicholas II, Tsarina Alexandra and their five children and 1100 Christians persecuted during the 70 years of communist rule.
27–28 August	A fire at the Ostankino tower kills four people and closes Russian National TV broadcasts. Putin says that this shows the state of Russian infrastructure.
1 September	Putin announces the formation of a new state body, the State Council.
13 September	Captain Alexander Nikitin is finally cleared.
19 September	Chinese President Jiang Zemin visits Russia.
8 September	Defence Minister Igor Sergeev announces plans to cut the armed forces by up to one-third by 2003.
27 September	Putin postpones scheduled military cuts.
5 October	Putin pays an official visit to India.
13 December	Russian prosecutors announce the closure, due to lack of evidence, of investigations into corruption involving the Yeltsin presidential family over Kremlin refurbishments.
14 December	Putin pardons US citizen, Edmund Pope, who had been convicted of spying and sentenced to 20 years of hard labour.
14–17 December	Putin pays an official visit to Cuba to renew ties broken with the collapse of the USSR. Putin criticises the US economic embargo against Cuba.

2001

1 January	Introduction of a new flat rate of income tax at 13 per cent replaces the former graduated income tax system.
6–7 January	German Chancellor Schroeder visits Moscow.
15 January	US president, George W. Bush, tells the *New York Times* that aid to Russia should be limited to help to dismantle nuclear weapons.
16 January	Russian and Japanese foreign ministers meet in Moscow. Russia stresses it will not 'return' the disputed territories.
17 January	Pavel Borodin, the secretary of the Union of Belarus and Russia, is arrested in New York on a warrant issued by Swiss authorities investigating the Mabetex scandal.
24 January	Russian Federal Securities Commission sues Norilsk Nikel.
25 January	Duma approved by 280 votes to 130 the bill granting former presidents immunity from prosecution.

26 January	At the World Economic Forum in Davos Russia promises the Paris Club that it will service its US $48 billion debt.
	Emergencies Minister Sergei Shoigu goes to Primorskii *krai* to deal with the power cuts that have been troubling the region throughout the winter.
28 January	The head of Norilsk Nikel is elected governor of the Taimyr autonomous *okrug* beating the incumbent candidate.
30 January	A new political party called Entrepreneurial Development is founded, aimed at middle-class voters.
1–10 February	At the Annual Politico-Military Forum in Munich Foreign Minister Ivanov reiterates Russia's opposition to any modification of the 1972 Anti-Ballistic Missile Treaty.
5 February	A bomb explodes at the Belorusskaia metro station in Moscow.
6 February	Yevgeny Nazdratenko, the governor of Primorskii *krai*, resigns. Energy Minister Alexander Gavrin is sacked.
8 February	Duma votes by 280 votes to 109 in favour of Putin's bill on political parties.
9 February	Anatoly Chubais, the head of UES, goes to Primorskii *krai*, following complaints from Putin about the power cuts in the region.
10 February	Reports that Boris Berezovsky is in talks to sell his 49 per cent share in ORT to Roman Abramovich, the governor of the Chukchi autonomous *okrug*.
12 February	Putin orders an investigation into how the general prosecutor acquired a spacious Moscow apartment.
13 February	The Budget for 2001 is amended so that government is able to service its debts to the Paris Club.
16 February	Putin sacks Andrei Zadernyuk, the chair of the Federal Energy Commission.
	Putin sacks Sergei Samoilov, the head of the presidential staff's chief administration for the regions. Andrei Popov replaces him.
20 February	FBI agent Robert Hanssen is arrested and charged with spying for Moscow for 15 years.
21 February	Putin announces deadline of 1 April for the completion of a new Land Code.
24 February	Colin Powell, the US secretary of state, holds his first talks with Igor Ivanov in Cairo.
12 March	Iranian president, Mohammad Khatami, meets with Putin in Moscow; they sign a cooperation and security agreement, discuss arms sales, nuclear cooperation and the exploitation of Caspian Sea oil.
13 March	Russian oil company, Severnaia Neft, wins the licence to exploit three oil fields in the Komi republic.
15 March	A Russian airliner is highjacked by Chechens and taken to Medina in Saudi Arabia.
22 March	50 Russian diplomats are ordered to leave the USA; four immediately and 46 by 1 July.
23 March	Four American diplomats are told to leave Russia for 'activities incompatible with their status' – a euphemism for spying.

25 March	Three car bombs explode in southern Russia killing 21 and leaving 130 wounded; senior Kremlin officials blame Chechen terrorists.
26 March	A Madrid court rejects a Russian request to extradite Gusinsky, who has been under arrest since 12 December 2000.
28 March	Putin replaces defence minister, Igor Sergeev, with the secretary of the Security Council, Sergei Ivanov, and Boris Gryzlov, the parliamentary leader of the pro-Kremlin Unity Party, is appointed minister of the interior. Putin also appoints a woman, Liubov Kudelina, as deputy defence minister, the first woman in his cabinet.

Bibliography

General texts and collections on post-communist Russia

Bater, James H. (1996) *Russia and the Post-Soviet Scene: A Geographical Perspective*, London: Arnold

Blum, Douglas W. (ed.) (1994) *Russia's Future Consolidation or Disintegration?*, Oxford and Boulder, CO: Westview Press

Bowker, Mike and Ross, Cameron (eds) (2000) *Russia after the Cold War*, London: Longman

Lane, David (ed.) (1995) *Russia in Transition: Politics, Privatisation and Inequality*, London and New York: Longman

Löwenhardt, John (1995) *The Reincarnation of Russia: Struggling with the Legacy of Communism, 1990–1994*, London: Longman

Sakwa, Richard (1996) (2nd edn) *Russian Politics and Society*, London: Routledge

Steele, Jonathan (1994) *Eternal Russia*, London and Boston: faber and faber

White, Stephen, Pravda, Alex and Gitelman, Zvi (1997) *Developments in Russian Politics 4*, Basingstoke: Macmillan

The American journal the *Current Digest of the Post-Soviet Press* provides a digest of the Russian press in English

Chapter 1. Introduction: transforming Russia

Baev, Pavel K. (1996) 'A New Look at Russia in Transition', *Journal of Peace Research* 33 (3), 371–376

Blasi, J.R., Kroumova, M. and Ruse, D. (1997) *Kremlin Capitalism: The Privatisation of the Russian Economy*, Ithaca, NY: Cornell University Press

Brovkin, Vladimir (1998) 'Fragmentation of Authority and Privatization of the State: from Gorbachev to Yeltsin', *Demokratizatsiya* 6 (3) Summer, 504–517

Chalidze, Valery (1977) *Criminal Russia: Essays on Crime in the Soviet Union*, New York: Random House (trans: P.S. Falla)

Coulloudon, Virginie (1997) 'The Criminalization of Russia's Political Elite', *East European Constitutional Review* 6 (4) Fall, 73–78

Diamond, Larry and Plattner, Marc F. (eds) (1993) *The Global Resurgence of Democracy*, Baltimore and London: Johns Hopkins University Press

Frisby, Tanya (1998) 'The Rise of Organised Crime in Russia: Its Roots and Social Significance', *Europe–Asia Studies* 50 (1), 27–49

Galkin, A. and Krasin, Iu. (1995) *Kritika Rossiiskogo Avtoritarizma*, Moscow: Institute of Sociology, Russian Academy of Sciences and the Gorbachev Fund

Gill, Graeme (1996) 'Russian State-building and the Problems of Geopolitics', *Arch. europ-sociol* 37 (1), 77–103

Govorukhin, Stanislav (1994) *Strana vorov v doroge svetloe budushchee*, Navra: Firma Shans

Haggard, Stephen and Kaufman, Robert R. (1995) *The Political Economy of Democratic Transitions*, Princeton, NJ: Princeton University Press

Handelman, Stephen (1994) 'The Russian "Mafiya"', *Foreign Affairs* 73 (2) March–April, 83–96

Islam, Shafqul (1993) 'Russia's Rough Road to Capitalism', *Foreign Affairs* 72 (2) Spring, 57–66

Janos, Andrew C. (1991) 'Social Science, Communism and the Dynamics of Political Change', *World Politics* 44 (1) October, 81–112

Kaufmann, Daniel and Siegelbaum, Paul (1996) 'Privatization and Corruption in Transition Economies', *Journal of International Affairs* 50 (2) Winter, 419–458

Kirpichnikov, A.I. (1997) *Vziatka i korruptsiia v Rossii*, St Petersburg: Al'fa

Kliamkin, Igor (1987) 'Kakaia ulitsa vedet k khramu?', *Novyi Mir* (11), 150–188

Kliamkin, I.M., Lapkin, V.V. and Pantin, V.I. (1995) 'Mezhdu avtoritarizmom i demokratiei', *Polis* (Moscow) 2, 57–87

Kukolev, Igor V. (1997) 'The Formation of the Business Elite', *Sociological Research* 36 (1) January–February, 23–43

Lucky, Christian (1997) 'Public Theft in Early America and Contemporary Russia', *East European Constitutional Review* 6 (4) Fall, 91–98

McFaul, Michael (1997) 'Democracy Unfolds in Russia', *Current History* 96 (612) October, 319–325

Maltsev, Yuri (1992) 'Toward a Postcommunist Economy', *Problems of Communism* 41 (1–2) January–April, 106–113

Migranian, A.M. (1987) 'Vzaimootnosheniia individa, obshchestva i gosudarstva v politicheskoi teorii marksizma i problem demokratizatsii sotsialisticheskogo obshchestva', *Kommunist* (8), 75–91

Migranian, Andranik (1989) 'Dolgiy put' k yevropeyskomu domu', *Novy Mir* (7), 166–184

Migranian, A. (1990) 'Demokratiia v teorii i istoricheskoi praktike', *Kommunist* (1), 33–42

O'Donnell, Guillermo, Schmitter, Philippe and Whitehead, Laurence (eds) (1986) *Transitions from Authoritarian Rule: Prospects for Democracy*, Baltimore and London: Johns Hopkins University Press

Remnick, David (1997) 'Can Russia Change?', *Foreign Affairs* 76 (1) January–February, 35–49

Rutland, Peter (1994–5) 'Has Democracy Failed Russia?', *The National Interest* (38) Winter, 3–12

Sajo, Andras (1998) 'Corruption, Clientelism, and the Future of the Constitutional State in Eastern Europe', *East European Constitutional Review* 7 (2) Spring, 37–46

Tikhonova, Nataliia E. (1998) 'The Dynamics of Social Stratification in Post-Soviet Society', *Sociological Research* 37 (50) September–October, 6–19

Weiner, Myron (1987) 'Empirical Democratic Theory and the Transition from Authoritarianism to Democracy', *PS* 20 (3) Fall, 861–866

Williams, Phil (ed.) (1997) *Russian Organized Crime: The New Threat?*, London: Frank Cass

Yavlinsky, G. (1995) *Ekonomika Rossii: nasledstvo i vozmozhnosti*, Moscow: EPItsentr

Zaslavskaia, Tat'iana I. (1998) 'The Social Structure of Contemporary Russian Society', *Sociological Research* 37 (1) January–February, 5–31

Chapter 2. Gorbachev and *perestroika*: reforming the unreformable?

Aganbegyan, Abel (1988) *The Challenge: Economics of Perestroika*, London: Hutchinson

Aganbegyan, Abel (1988) 'The Soviet Economic Crisis', *New Left Review* (169) May–June, 89–95

Armacost, Michael (1989) 'Implications of Gorbachev for U.S.–Soviet Relations', *Journal of International Affairs* 42 (2) Spring, 445–456

Åslund, Anders (1991) (2nd edn) *Gorbachev's Struggle for Economic Reform*, London: Pinter

Bahry, Donna (1991) 'The Union Republics and Contradictions in Gorbachev's Economic Reform', *Soviet Economy* 7 (3), 215–255

Boldin, Valery (1994) *Ten Years that Shook the World*, London: Basic Books/ HarperCollins (trans: Evelyn Rossiter)

Breslauer, George W. (1989) 'Linking Gorbachev's Domestic and Foreign Policies', *Journal of International Affairs* 42 (2) Spring, 267–297

Chechkel, J. (1993) 'Ideas, Institutions, and the Gorbachev Foreign Policy Revolution', *World Politics* 45 (2) January, 271–300

Dyker, David (1992) *Restructuring the Soviet Economy*, London: Routledge

Ellman, Michael and Kontorovich, Vladimir (eds) (1992) *The Disintegration of the Soviet Economic System*, London and New York: Routledge

Ericson, Richard E. (1989) 'Soviet Economic Reforms: The Motivation and Content of Perestroika', *Journal of International Affairs* 42 (2) Spring, 317–331

Galeotti, Mark (1995) *The Age of Anxiety: Security and Politics in Soviet and Post-Soviet Russia*, London: Longman

Gregory, Paul R. and Stuart, Robert C. (1998) (6th edn) *Russian and Soviet Economic Performance and Structure*, Harlow: Addison Wesley Longman

Hill, Ronald J. (1990) *Communist Politics under the Knife*, London: Pinter

Hoskings, Geoffrey A., Aves, Jonathan and Duncan, Peter J.S. (1992) *The Road to Post-Communism: Independent Political Movements in the Soviet Union 1985–1991*, London: Pinter

Kaiser, Robert G. (1991) *Why Gorbachev Happened: His Triumphs and his Failures*, New York: Simon Schuster

Lapidus, Gail W. (1989) 'Gorbachev and the "National Question": Restructuring the Soviet Federation', *Soviet Economy* 5 (3), 201–250

Lapidus, Gail W. (1989) 'State and Society: Toward the Emergence of Civil Society in the Soviet Union' in Seweryn Bialer (ed.) *Politics, Society, and Nationality Inside Gorbachev's Russia*, Boulder, CO: Westview Press

Laver, John (1997) *Stagnation and Reform: The USSR 1964–91*, London: Hodder & Stoughton

Lewin, Moshe (1989) '*Perestroika*: A New Historical Stage', *Journal of International Affairs* 42 (2) Spring, 299–315

McCauley, Martin (1990) *Gorbachev and Perestroika*, London: SSEES

Mau, Vladimir (1996) 'The Road to *Perestroika*: Economics in the USSR and the Problems of Reforming the Soviet Economic Order', *Europe–Asia Studies* 48 (2) March, 207–224

Medvedev, Zhores (1986) *Gorbachev*, Oxford: Blackwell

Nolan, Peter (1995) *China's Rise, Russia's Fall: Politics, Economics and Planning in the Transition from Stalinism*, Basingstoke: Macmillan

Olcott, Martha B. (1989) 'Gorbachev's National Dilemma', *Journal of International Affairs* 42 (2) Spring, 399–434

Pearson, Raymond (1998) *The Rise and Fall of the Soviet Empire*, Basingstoke: Macmillan

Remington, Thomas (1990) 'Regime Transition in Communist Systems: The Soviet Case', *Soviet Economy* 6 (2) April–June, 160–190

Roxburgh, Angus (1991) *The Second Russian Revolution: The Struggle For Power in the Kremlin*, London: BBC Books

Sakwa, Richard (1989) *Soviet Politics*, London: Routledge

Sakwa, Richard (1992) 'The Revolution of 1991 in Russia: Interpretations of the Moscow Coup', *Coexistence* 29 (4) December, 27–67

Sakwa, Richard (1993) 'A Cleansing Storm: The August Coup and the Triumph of Perestroika', *Journal of Communist Studies* 9 (1) Spring, 131–149

Scanlon, James P. (1988) 'Reforms and Civil Society in the USSR', *Problems of Communism* 37 (2) March–April, 41–46

Schmidt-Häuer, C. (1986) *Gorbachev: The Path to Power*, London: Pan

Sestanovich, Stephen (1988) 'Gorbachev's Foreign Policy: A Diplomacy of Decline', *Problems of Communism* 37 (1) January–February, 1–15

Shmelev, N.P. and Popov, V. (1990) *The Turning Point*, London: I.B. Taurus

Sixsmith, Martin (1991) *Moscow Coup: The Death of the Soviet System*, London: Simon and Schuster

Smith, Graham (ed.) (1990) *The Nationalities Question in the Soviet Union*, London: Longman

Surovell, Jeffrey (1994) 'Gorbachev's Last Year: Leftist or Rightist', *Europe–Asia Studies* 46 (3), 465–87

Wettig, Gerhard (1988) ' "New Thinking" on Security and East-West Relations', *Problems of Communism* 37 (2) March–April, 1–14

White, Stephen (1988) *USSR – A Superpower in Transition*, Glasgow: Pulse Publications

White, Stephen (1993) *After Gorbachev*, Cambridge: Cambridge University Press

White, Stephen (1994) 'Pluralism, Civil Society, and Post-Soviet Politics' in Carol R. Saivetz and Anthony Jones (eds) *In Search of Pluralism: Soviet and Post-Soviet Politics*, Boulder, CO: Westview Press

Wilson, Andrew and Bachkatov, Nina (1988) *Living with Glasnost*, Harmondsworth: Penguin

Yakovlev, Alexander M. (1996) *Striving for Law in a Lawless Land: Memoirs of a Russian Reformer*, Armonk and New York: M.E. Sharpe

Chapter 3. Russia and the Russians

Acton, Edward (1995) *Russia: The Tsarist and Soviet Legacy*, London: Longman

Clark, Bruce (1995) *An Empire's New Clothes*, London: Vintage

Clark, Bruce (1996) 'Nationalist Ideas Move from the Margins', *The World Today* 52 (5) May, 119–121

Davis, Nathaniel (1996) 'The Russian Orthodox Church: Opportunity and Trouble', *Communist and Post-Communist Studies* 29 (3) September, 275–286

Dunlop, John B. (1985) *The New Russian Nationalism*, New York: Praeger

Hammer, D.P. (1989) *Russian Nationalism and Soviet Politics*, Boulder, CO: Westview Press

Hughes, Michael (1993) 'The Never-Ending Story: Russian Nationalism, National Communism and Opposition to Reform in the USSR and Russia', *Journal of Communist Studies* 9 (2) June, 41–61

Jones, Lucy (1997) 'Buddhist Revival in a Post-Soviet Nirvana', *The Guardian*, 21 October, 10

Krasnov, Vladislav (1991) *Russia Beyond Communism: A Chronicle of National Rebirth*, Boulder, CO: Westview Press

Laqueur, Walter (1992/3) 'Russian Nationalism', *Foreign Affairs* 70 (5) Winter, 103–116

Mudarian, A. (1992) ' "Evraziiskaia" kontseptii-model' obshchestvennogo razvitiia Rossii?', *Problemy Dal'nego Vostoka* (1–2), 49–60

Nikonov, Aleksandr (1993) ' "Russkii vopros" sevodnia', *Svobodnaia Mysl'* September (13), 15–26

Solchanyk, Roman (1992) 'Ukraine, The (Former) Center, Russia, and "Russia" ', *Studies in Comparative Communism* 25 (1) March, 31–45

Szporluk, Roman (1989) 'Dilemmas of Russian Nationalism', *Problems of Communism* 37 (4) July–August, 15–35

Szporluk, Roman (ed.) (1994) *National Identity and Ethnicity in Russia and the New States of Eurasia*, New York: M.E. Sharpe

Walicki, A. (1978) *The Slavophile Controversy*, Oxford: Oxford University Press

Walicki, A. (1980) *A History of Russian Thought from the Enlightenment to Marxism*, Oxford: Clarendon Press

Ware, Timothy (1985) *The Orthodox Church*, Harmondsworth: Penguin

Wimbush, Enders (1978) 'The Great Russians and the Soviet State: The Dilemmas of Ethnic Dominance' in Jeremy Azrael (ed.) *Soviet Nationality Policies and Practices*, London: Praeger

Chapter 4. The president and the parliament

Alyushin, Alexy (1995) 'Political Consequences of Parliamentary Rules. Russia', *East European Constitutional Review* 4 (2) Spring, 61–66

Brudny, Y.M. (1997) 'In Pursuit of the Presidency: Why and How Yeltsin Won the 1996 Presidential Election', *Communist and Post-Communist Studies* 30 (3), 255–275

Bush, Keith (2000) 'President Vladimir Putin?', *Russian and Eurasian Expert Brief* 3 January, http://www.csis.org/ruseura/

Fish, M. Steven (1995) 'Democracy Begins to Emerge', *Current History* 94 (594), 317–321

Koshkareva T. and Marzikulov, R. (1998) 'Administrative Chaos and the *Nomenklatura*'s Revenge', *East European Constitutional Review* 7(4) Fall, 85–88

McFaul, Michael (1997) 'Democracy Unfolds in Russia', *Current History* 96 (612) October, 319–325

Ostrow, Joel, M. (1996) 'Institutional Design and Legislative Conflict. The Russian Supreme Soviet – A Well-Oiled Machine Out of Control', *Communist and Post-Communist Studies* 29 (4) December, 413–433

Ostrow, J.M. (1998) 'Procedural Breakdown and Deadlock in the Russian State Duma: The Problems of an Unlinked Dual-channel Institutional Design', *Europe–Asia Studies* 50 (5), 793–816

Pushkov, A.K. (1998) 'Constitutional Reform as a Struggle for Power', *East European Constitutional Review* 7 (4) Fall, 77–80

Sharlet, Robert (1993) 'Russian Constitutional Crisis and Politics under Yel'tsin', *Post-Soviet Affairs* 9 (4) October–December, 314 and 328

Sharlet, Robert (1997) 'The Politics of Constitutional Amendment in Russia', *Post-Soviet Affairs* 13 (3) July–September, 197–227

Shevtsova, Lilia (1996) 'Parliament and the Political Crisis in Russia, 1991–1993' in Jeffrey W. Hahn (ed.) *Democratization in Russia: The Development of Legislative Institutions*, Armonk, NY, and London: M.E. Sharpe

Urban, Michael E. (1992) 'Boris El'tsin, Democratic Russia and the Campaign for the Russian Presidency', *Soviet Studies* 44 (2), 187–207

White, Stephen (1995) 'The Presidency and Political Leadership' in Peter Lentini (ed.) *Post-Communist Russian Elections and Political Order in Russia: The Implications of the 1993 Elections to the Federal Assembly*, Budapest, London and New York: Central European University Press

Chapter 5. The Russian Federation

Abdulatipov, Ramazin (1992) 'Kak sovershenstvovat' rossiiskii federalizm', *Parlamentskii vestnik* (2), 1–3

Akhmetov, Rashid (1998) 'Presidential Elections in Chuvashia – Martial Arts, Eastern-style', *Prism* 4 (4) 20 February, http//www.jamestown.org/

Avak'in, S.A. (1996) 'Mestnoe samoupravlenie v Rossiiskoi Federatsii: kontseptsii i resheniia novogo zakona', *Vestnik Moskovskogo Universiteta Seriia* 11, *Pravo* (2), 3–33

Bachkatov, Nina and Wilson, Andrew (1995) 'Fallout from Chechnya', *The World Today* 51 (5) May, 92–95

Barabanov, Igor and Filatov, Vladimir (1996) 'Problemy sovershenstvovaniia vneshnee ekonomicheskoi deiatel'nosti federatsii', *Federalizm* (1), 57–72

Blandy, Charles (1996) 'Cutting the Chechen Knot', *The World Today* 52 (6) June, 147–149

Boltenkova, Liubov' (1996) 'Sootnoshenie zakonodatel'stva rossiiskoi federatsii i ee sub"ektov: osnovnye protivorechiia', *Federalizm* (1), 73–92

Brovkin, Vladimir (1998) 'Fragmentation of Authority and Privatization of the State: From Gorbachev to Yeltsin', *Demokratizatsiya* 6 (3) Summer, 504–517

Buchanan, Sandra (1999) 'National Identities: Russia, Chechnia and the War 1991–97', *Slovo* (11), 23–46

Busygina, Irina (1996) 'Predstaviteli prezidenta', *Svobodnaia mysl'* (4), 52–61

'Constitution Watch. Russia' (1996) *East European Constitutional Review* 5 (4) Fall, 22–23

'Constitution Watch. Russia' (1996) *East European Constitutional Review* 5 (1) Winter, 24–25

'Diskussii po natsional'nomu voprosu' (1993) *Vestnik Moskovskogo Universiteta Seriia* 11, *Pravo* (4), 30–53

Evans, Alfred B. (1997) 'Civil Society and Political Authority in the Semenov District', *Demokratizatsiya* 5 (2) Spring, 197–221

Goble, Paul A. (1995) 'Chechnya and its Consequences', *Post-Soviet Affairs* 11 (1) 23–27

Goodrich, Susan (1997) 'Islam and Ethnicity in the Republics of Russia', *Post-Soviet Affairs* 13 (1) January–March, 78–103

Guznov, Aleksei (1993) 'Sovremennyi federalizm i Rossiia', *Dialog* (3), March, 22–30

Hahn, J. (1997) 'Democratization and Political Participation in Russia's Regions' in K. Dawisha and B. Parrot (eds) *Democratic Changes and Authoritarian Reactions in Russia, Ukraine, Belarus, and Moldova*, Cambridge: Cambridge University Press

Hanson, Philip (1993) 'Russia: Economic Reform and Local Politics', *The World Today* 49 (4) April, 64–66

'Kak sovershenstvovat' federal'noe ustroistvo Rossii' (1994) *Parlamentskii vestnik* (3), 12–15

Kuzio, Taras (1995) 'The Chechnya Crisis and the "Near Abroad"', *Central Asian Survey* 14 (4), 553–572

Leksin, B.N. and Shvetsov, A.N. (1997) *Gosudarstvo i regiony*, Moscow: URSS

McIntyre, Robert (1996) 'Regional Variations on Russian Chaos: Price Controls, Regional Trade Barriers, and Other Neo-classical Abominations', *Communist and Post-Communist Studies* 29 (1) March, 95–102

Mandelstam Balzer, Majorie and Vinokurova, Uliana Alekseevna (1996) 'Nationalism, Interethnic Relations and Federalism: The Case of Sakha Republic (Yakutia)', *Europe–Asia Studies* 48 (1) January, 101–120

Maryniak, Irena (1996) 'Of Blood and Votes', *Index on Censorship* (3), 78–83

Medvedev, Oleg (1996) 'Are Governors in the President's Pocket?', *Business in Russia* (69) September, 12–13

Medvedev, Oleg (1996) 'Federation Council Plays Stabilizing Role', *Business in Russia* (69) September, 16 and 18

Meek, James (1996) 'Local Treaties Undermine Moscow's Authority', *The Guardian*, 31 January, 9

Meek, James (1996) 'Poor Pskov, Trapped Between the Soviet Devil and the Baltic Sea', *The Observer*, 17 November, 12

Michnik, Beth A. (1991) 'Territoriality and Regional Economic Autonomy in the USSR', *Studies in Comparative Communism* 14 (2), 218–224

Mikhaleva, N.A. (1995) 'Konstitutsionnye reformy v respublikakh – sub"ektakh Rossiiskoi Federatsii', *Gosudarstvo i Pravo* (4), 3–10

Pain, Emil' (1994) 'O vzaimosviazi etnonatsional'noi i regional'noe politiki Rossii', *Federal'nye novosti* (49) December, 1–2

Panico, Christopher (1995) 'Conflicts in the Caucasus: Russia's War in Chechnya', *Conflict Studies* (281) July, 1–25

Rotar, Igor (1998) 'Development, Bashkir-style: Ufa's Internal Policy Benefits the Kremlin', *Prism* 4 (2) 23 January, http//www.jamestown.org/

Rotar, Igor (1998) 'Chechnya on the Brink of Civil War', *Prism* 4 (20) 16 October, http://www.jamestown.org/

Sheehy, Ann (1993) 'Russia's Republics: A Threat to its Territorial Integrity?', *RFE/RL Research Report* 2 (20), 34–40

Solnick, Steven L. (1998) 'Gubernatorial Elections in Russia, 1996–1997', *Post-Soviet Russia* 14 (1) January–March, 48–80

Sullivan, Stefan (1992) 'Hunting for a Heritage: Post-Soviet Yakutiya', *The World Today* (48) March, 56–58

Sutherland, Douglas and Hanson, Philip (1996) 'Structural Change in the Economies of Russia's Regions', *Europe–Asia Studies* 48 (3) May, 367–392

Tolz, Vera (1993) 'The Role of the Republics and Regions', *RFE/RL Research Report* 2 (15), 1–8

Tolz, Vera (1993) 'Regionalism in Russia: The Case of Siberia', *RFE/RL Research Report* 2 (9) 26, 1–9

Treisman, Daniel S. (1997) 'Russia's "Ethnic Revival": The Separatist Activism of Regional Leaders in a Post Communist Order', *World Politics* 49 (2) January, 212–249

Troyakova, Tamara (1995) 'Regional Policy in the Russian Far East and the Rise of Localism in Primorye', *Journal of East Asian Affairs* 9 (2), 428–461

Valentei, Sergei (1996) 'Rossiiskie reformy i rossiiskii federalizm', *Federalizm* (1), 23–36

Valiullin, Shamil M. (1998) 'Bashkortostan and the Search for a National Identity: The History and Politics of Bashkir Separatism', *Slovo* 10 (1–2), 149–177

Vogel, Heinrich (1995) 'Partnership with Russia: Some Lessons from Chechnya', *The World Today* 51 (4) April, 64–67

Walker, Edward W. (1995) 'Designing Center–Region Relations in the New Russia', *East European Constitutional Review* 4 (1) Winter, 54–60

Walker, Edward W. (1997) 'Constitutional Obstacles to Peace in Chechnya', *East European Constitutional Review* 6 (1) Winter, 50–54

Whitmore, Brian (1997) 'Yeltsin's Man in Petersburg Grows Stronger', *St Petersburg Times*, 13 May, 1 and 6

Zhukovkaya, Natalya L. (1995) 'Religion and Ethnicity in Eastern Russia, Republic of Buryatia: A Panorama of the 1990s', *Central Asian Survey* 14 (1), 25–42

Chapter 6. The judiciary and human rights

Amnesty International Country Report, Russia (1995) 'Armed Conflict in the Chechen Republic: Seeds of Human Rights Violations Sown in Peacetime', http://www.amnesty.org/

Amnesty International Country Report, Russia Federation (1996) 'Torture and Ill-treatment', http://www.amnesty.org/

Amnesty International Country Report, Russian Federation (1997) 'Russian Federation Failure to Protect Asylum Seekers', http://www.amnesty.org/

Ascher, Ivan (1996) 'Russia's Constitutional Court and the Birth-Pangs of Democracy', *The World Today* 52 (1) January, 13

Bahry, D., Boaz, C. and Burnett Gordon, S. (1997) 'Tolerance, Transition and Support for Civil Liberties in Russia', *Comparative Political Studies* 30 (4), 484–510

Berman, Harold J. (1991) 'The Rule of Law and the Law-based State', *The Harriman Institute Forum* 4 (5), 1–12

Boiko, T. (1997) 'Sudebnaia reforma, kotoraia kasaetsia vsekh', *Eko* 3 (273), 166–180

Hendley, Kathryn (1997) 'Legal Development in Post-Soviet Russia', *Post-Soviet Affairs* 13 (3) July–September, 228–251

Hendley, Kathryn (1999) 'Rewriting the Rules of the Game in Russia: The Neglected Issue of the Demand for Law', *East European Constitutional Review* 8 (4) Fall, 89–95

Human Rights Watch World Report (1999) 'The Russian Federation: Human Rights Developments', http://www.hrw.org/

Jordan, Pamela (1998) 'The Russian *Advokatura* (Bar) and the State in the 1990s', *Europe–Asia Studies* 50 (5) July, 765–791

Kholenko, Andrei (1995) 'Hell on Earth: Prisoners in Vladivostok City Jail', *East European Constitutional Review* 4 (4) Fall, 75–76

Lawyers Committee for Human Rights (1993) *Human Rights and Legal Reform in the Russian Federation*, New York: Lawyers Committee for Human Rights

Lawyers Committee for Human Rights (1995) *The Price of Independence: The Office of Ombudsman and Human Rights in the Russian Federation*, New York: Lawyers Committee for Human Rights

Lawyers Committee for Human Rights (1995) *Justice Delayed: The Russian Constitutional Court and Human Rights*, New York: Lawyers Committee for Human Rights

Lunev, Stanislav (1998) 'Changes in Russia's Law Enforcement Agencies', *Prism* 4 (1) 9 January, http://www.jamestown.org/

Martyshin, O.V. (1994) 'Rossiiskaia Konstitutsiia 1993g. i stanovlenie novoi politicheskoi sistemy', *Gosudarstvo i Pravo* (10), 32–37

Mikhailovskaia, Inga B. (1995) 'Constitutional Rights in Russian Opinion', *East European Constitutional Review* 4 (1) Winter, 70–76

Mironov, Oleg O. (1997) 'Legal Reform in Russia: A View from the State Duma', *Demokratizatsiya* 5 (2) Spring, 281–290

Ovsepian Zh.I. (1995) 'Konstitutsionnyi Sud Rossii: Reforma Pravovogo Statusa', *SShA-EPI* (8), 96–103

Ovsepian Zh.I. (1995) 'Konstitutsionnyi Sud Rossi: Reforma Pravovogo Statusa', *SShA-EPI* (9), 74–82

Reisinger, William M., Miller, Arthur H. and Hesli, Vicki L. (1997) 'Russians and the Legal System: Mass Views and Behaviour in the 1990s', *Journal of Communist Studies and Transition Politics* 13 (3), 24–55

Rhodes, Mark (1993) 'What do Russians Think about the Constitutional Process?', *RFE/RL Research Report* 2 (29), 13–15

Sheliutto, N.V. (1997) 'Voprosy sudebnoi vlasti v ustavakh sub"ektov Rossiikoi Federatsii', *Zakonodatel'stvo i Ekonomika* 3/4 (145–146), 3–7

Shul'zhenko, Iu.L. (1995) 'Zakon o Konstitutsionnom sude Rossiiskoi Federatsii 1994g', *Gosudarstvo i Pravo* (7), 3–10

Slater, Wendy (1993) 'Head of the Russian Constitutional Court under Fire', *RFE/RL Research Report* 2 (26), 1–5

Solomon Jr, Peter H. (1997) 'The Persistence of Judicial Reform in Contemporary Russia', *East European Constitutional Review* 6 (4) Fall, 50–56

Sukhanov, E.A. (1993) 'O Proekte Novogo Grazhdanskogo kodeksa Rossii', *Vestnik Moskovkogo Universiteta Seriia* 11, *Pravo* (5), 3–11

Thaman, Stephen C. (1995) 'Trial by Jury and the Constitutional Rights of the Accused in Russia', *East European Constitutional Review* 4 (1) Winter, 77–80

Walker, Edward W. (1997) 'Constitutional Obstacles to Peace in Chechnya', *East European Constitutional Review* 6 (1) Winter, 50–54

Wishnevsky, Julia (1993) 'Constitutional Crisis Deepens after Russian Congress', *RFE/RL Research Report* 12 (13), 1–7

Wishnevsky, Julia (1993) 'Russian Constitutional Court: A Third Branch of Government?', *RFE/RL Research Report* 2 (7), 1–8

Chapter 7. The state in uniform

Busza, Eva (1996) 'Transition and Civil–Military Relations in Poland and Russia', *Communist and Post-Communist Studies* 29 (2), 167–184

Colton, Timothy J. (1979) *Commissars, Commanders, and Civilian Authority: The Structure of Soviet Military Politics*, Cambridge, MA: Harvard University Press

Erikson, John (1995) 'The Russians Are Coming – But Not Just Yet', *Queens Quarterly* (102/2) Summer, 297–311

Galeotti, Mark (1995) *The Age of Anxiety: Security and Politics in Soviet and Post-Soviet Russia*, London: Longman

Hersping, Dale R. (1995) 'The Russian Military: Three Years On', *Communist and Post-Communist Studies* 28 (2) June, 163–182

Jamestown Foundation (2000) 'Russian Armed Forces' Holiday Highlights Military Politics', *Monitor* 6 (37) 22 February, http://www.jamestown.org/

Knight, Amy (1990) *The KGB*, London: Unwin Hyman

Knight, Amy (1990) 'The KGB and Civil–Military Relations' in Timothy J. Colton and Thane Gustafson (eds) *Soldiers and the Soviet State: Civil–Military Relations from Brezhnev to Gorbachev*, Princeton, NJ: Princeton University Press

Knight, Amy (1996) 'Internal Security and the Rule of Law in Russia', *Current History* 95 (603) October, 311–315

Mathers, Jennifer G. (1995) 'The Generals Manoeuvre on the Political Battlefield', *The World Today* 51 (12) December, 231–234

Nichols, Thomas M. (1995) ' "An Electoral Mutiny?" Zhirinovsky and the Russian Armed Forces', *Armed Forces and Society* 21 (3) Spring, 327–347

Schiff, Rebecca L. (1995) 'Civil–Military Relations Reconsidered: A Theory of Concordance', *Armed Forces and Society* 22 (1) Fall, 7–24

Thomas, Timothy L. (1995) 'The Russian Armed Forces Confront Chechnya: I. Military-Political Aspects 11–31 December 1994', *Journal of Slavic Military Studies* 8 (2) June, 233–256

Yasmann, Victor (1991) 'Law on the KGB Published', *Radio Free Europe/Radio Liberty Report on the USSR*, 2 August, 12–18

Chapter 8. Democracy and the Russian people

Alexander, James (1997) 'Surveying Attitudes in Russia: A Representation of Formlessness', *Communist and Post-Communist Studies* 30 (2) June, 107–127

Babkina, M.A. (ed.) (1991) *New Political Parties and Movements in the Soviet Union*, Commack, NY: Nova Science Publishers

Bahry, Donna, Boaz, Cynthia and Gordon Burnett, Stacy (1997) 'Tolerance, Transition and Support for Civil Liberties in Russia', *Comparative Political Studies* 30 (4) August, 484–510

Berezovskii, B.N. and Krotov, N.I. (eds) (1990) *Neformal'naia Rossiia*, Moscow: Molodaia Gvardiia

Christensen, Paul T. (1998) 'Socialism After Communism?: The Socioeconomic and Cultural Foundations of Left Politics in Post-Soviet Russia', *Communist and Post-Communist Studies* 31 (4), 345–357

Dallin, Alexander (ed.) (1993) *Political Parties in Russia*, Berkeley, CA: International and Area Studies, University of California

Gregor, A. James (1998) 'Fascism and the New Russian Nationalism', *Communism and Post-Communist Studies* 31 (1) March, 1–15

Hill, Ronald J. (1994) (3rd edn) 'Parties and the Party System', in Stephen White, Alex Pravda and Zvi Gitelman (eds) *Developments in Russia and Post-Soviet Politics*, Basingstoke: Macmillan

Hill, Ronald J. (1997) 'Parties and Organisations', in Stephen White, Alex Pravda Alex and Zvi Gitelman (eds) *Developments in Russian Politics 4*, Basingstoke: Macmillan

Kipp, Jacob W. (1994) 'The Zhirinovsky Threat', *Foreign Affairs* 73 (3) May–June, 72–86

Lentini, P. (1992) 'Post CPSU Communist Political Formations', *Journal of Communist Studies* 8 (4), 280–292

Lentini, Peter (ed.) (1995) *Elections and Political Order in Russia*, Budapest, London and New York: Central European University Press

Lester, Jeremy (1994) 'Zhirinovsky's Liberal Democratic Party: A Profile', *Labour Focus on Eastern Europe* (47), 17–30

Löwenhardt, John (ed.) (1998) 'Party Politics in Post-Communist Russia', *Journal of Communist Studies and Transition Politics* 14 (1 and 2) March–June, Special Issue

Mendras, Marie (1996) 'Yeltsin and the Great Divide in Russian Society', *East European Constitutional Review* 5 (2–3) Spring–Summer, 51–57

Mikhailovskaya, Inga (1996) 'Russian Voting Behavior as a Mirror of Social-Political Change', *East European Constitutional Review* 5 (2–3) Spring–Summer, 57–63

Miller, Arthur H, Hesli, Vicki L. and Reisinger, William M. (1997) 'Conceptions of Democracy Among Mass and Elite in Post-Soviet Societies', *British Journal of Political Science* (27), 157–190

Moser, Robert G. (1997) 'The Impact of Parliamentary Electoral Systems in Russia', *Post-Soviet Affairs* 13 (3) July–September, 284–302

Myagkov, Mikhail, Ordeshook, Peter and Sobyanin, Alexander (1997) 'The Russian Electorate, 1991–1996', *Post-Soviet Affairs* 13 (2) April–June, 134–166

Novikova, Elvira (1994) 'Zhenshchiny v politicheskoi zhizni Rossii', *Preobrazhenie* (4), 13–18

Pirani, Simon (1998) 'State Patriotism in the Politics and Ideology of Gennady Zyuganov', *Slovo* 10 (1–2), 179–197

Pribylovskii, Vladimir, Sloan, Dauphine and Helmstadster, Sarah (eds) (1992) *Dictionary of Political Parties and Organizations in Russia*, Moscow: PostFactum/ Interlegal and Washington, DC: Center for Strategic and International Studies

Racioppi, Linda and O'Sullivan, Katherine (1995) 'Organising Women Before and after the Fall', *Signs* 20 (4) Summer, 818–850

Remington, Thomas F. (1995) 'The Development of Parliamentary Parties in Russia', *Legislative Studies Quarterly* 20 (4) November, 457–489

Remnik, David (1996) 'Hammer, Sickle, and Book', *New York Review*, 23 May, 45–51

Sautman, Barry (1995) 'The Devil to Pay: The 1989 Debate and the Intellectual Origins of Yeltsin's "Soft Authoritarianism" ', *Communist and Post-Communist Studies* 28 (1) March, 131–151

Shalin, Dmitri (ed.) (1996) *Russian Culture at the Crossroads: Paradoxes of Postcommunist Consciousness*, Boulder, CO: Westview Press

Sokolova, Ekaterina (1995) 'Feminism v Rossii: Mezhdu proshchlym i budushchim', *Preobrazhenie* (3), 22–25

Solov'ev, Vladimir and Klepikova, Elena (1995) *Zhirinovsky: The Paradoxes of Russian Fascism*, London: Viking

Temkina, Anna (1995) 'Feminizm: Zapad i Rossiia', *Preobrazhenie* (3), 5–17

Vainshtein, Grigory (1994) 'Totalitarian Public Consciousness in Post-Totalitarian Society: The Russian Case in the General Context of Post-Communist Developments', *Communist and Post-Communist Studies* 27 (3) September, 247–259

Vainshtein, G. (1995) 'The Authoritarian Idea in the Public Consciousness', *Journal of Communist Studies and Transition Politics* 11 (3), 272–285

Weigle, Marcia A. (1994) 'Political Participation and Party Formation in Russia, 1985–1992: Institutionalizing Democracy?', *Russian Review* (53), April, 240–270

White, Stephen (1979) *Political Culture and Soviet Politics*, London and Basingstoke: Macmillan

White, Stephen and McAllister, Ian (1996) 'The CPSU and Its Members: Between Communism and Post Communism', *British Journal of Political Science* (26), 105–122

White, Stephen, Rose, Richard and McAllister, Ian (1997) *How Russia Votes*, Chatham, NJ: Chatham House Publishers

White, Stephen, Wyman, Matthew and Kryshtanovskaya, Olga (1995) 'Parties and Politics in Post-Communist Russia', *Communist and Post-Communist Studies* 28 (2) June, 183–202

Women and Russia (1980) London: Sheba Feminist Publishers

Chapter 9. The mass media

Androunas, Elena (1993) *Soviet Media in Transition: Structural and Economic Alternatives*, Westport, CT and London: Praeger

Anichkina, Miranda (1997) 'The Voice that Outlasted Soviet Tyrants: Portrait Izvestia', *The European* (358) 20–26 March, 13

The Economist (1996) 'Beavis Comes to Budapest', *The Economist*, 6 July, 89–90

Freeland, Chrystia (1997) 'Russia Discovers the Tension Between Rights and Freedoms', *Financial Times*, 26–7 April, 2

Grabel'nikov, A.A. (1998) 'Bor'ba pressy za chitatelia', *Vestnik Moskovkogo Universiteta Seriia 10, Zhurnalistika* (5), 3–11

Grabel'nikov, A.A. (1998) 'O Rossiiskoi Gosudarstvennoi Ideologii i Informationnoi Politike', *Vestnik Moskovkogo Universiteta Seriia 10, Zhurnalistika* (6), 3–15

Matthews, Mervyn (1994) 'Pluralism and the New Press in Russia' in Carol R. Saivetz and Anthony Jones (eds) *In Search of Pluralism: Soviet and Post-Soviet Politics*, Boulder, CO: Westview Press

Mickiewicz, Ellen (1988) *Split Signals*, Oxford: Oxford University Press

Murray, John (1994) *The Russian Press from Brezhnev to Yeltsin: Behind the Paper Curtain*, Aldershot: Edward Elgar

Ovsenian, R.P.(1998) 'Zhurnalistika Natsional'nykh Regionov Rossiiskoi Federatsii', *Vestnik Moskovkogo Universiteta Seriia 10, Zhurnalistika* (2), 8–15

Resnianskaia, L.L., Svitich, L.G., Formicheva, I.D. and Shiriaeva, A.A. (1996) 'Perspektivy razvitiia regional'noi pressy', *Vestnik Moskovkogo Universiteta Seriia 10, Zhurnalistika* (2), 3–15

Skillen, Daphne (1996) 'Media Coverage in the Elections', in Peter Lentini (ed.) *Elections and Political Order in Russia: The Implications of the 1993 Elections to the Federal Assembly*, Budapest, London and New York: Central European University Press

Troshkin, Iu.V. (1997) 'Prava Pressy: Pechat' i Vlast', *Vestnik Moskovkogo Universiteta Seriia 10, Zhurnalistika* (2), 3–17

Urban, Michael E. (1993) 'The Russian Free Press in the Transition to a Post-Communist Society', *Journal of Communist Studies* 9 (2) June, 20–40

Wedgwood Benn, David (1992) *From Glasnost to Freedom of Speech: Russian Openness and International Relations*, London: Pinter

Chapter 10. Russian foreign policy: from superpower to great power

Achcar, Gilbert (1998) 'The Strategic Triad: The United States, Russia and China', *New Left Review* (228) March–April, 91–126

Adams, Jan S. (1989) 'Change and Continuity in Soviet Central American Policy', *Problems of Communism* 38 (2–3) March–June, 112–120

Adams, Jan S. (1996) 'Russia's Foreign Policy Under a President Zyuganov', *Post Soviet Prospects* 4 (6) April, http://www.csis.org/

Adomeit, Hannes (1995) 'Russia as a "Great Power" in World Affairs: Images and Reality', *International Affairs* 71 (1), 35–68

Akaha, Tsuneo (1995) 'Russia in Asia in 1994: An Emerging East Asian Power', *Asian Survey* 35 (1) January, 100–110

Azizian, Rouben (1995) 'Russia's Asia-Pacific Dilemma', *New Zealand International Review* 20 (4) July–August, 13–17

Baev, Pavel K. (1998) 'Bear Hug for the Baltics', *The World Today* 54 (3) March, 76–79

Baranovsky, Vladimir (1995) 'Russian Foreign Policy Priorities and Euroatlantic Multilateral Institutions', *The International Spectator* 30 (1) January–March, 33–50

Bielen, Stanislaw (1994) 'Poland's Expectations Towards Russia', *Polish Political Science* (24), 183–192

Birch, Julian (1995) 'Ossetia: A Caucasian Bosnia in Microcosm', *Central Asian Survey* 14 (1), 43–74

Blank, Stephen (1994) 'Russia, the Gulf and Cental Asia in a new Middle East', *Central Asian Survey* 13 (2), 267–281

Blank, Stephen (1995) 'Energy, Economics and Security in Central Asia: Russia and its Rivals', *Central Asian Survey* 14 (3), 373–406

Blum, Douglas W. (1994) 'Disintegration and Russian Foreign Policy', in Douglas Blum (ed.) *Russia's Future: Consolidation or Disintegration*, Boulder, CO: Westview Press

Bratkiewicz, Jaroslaw (1994) 'Relations with Russia, Ukraine and Belarus', *Yearbook of Polish Foreign Policy 1993*, 129–138

Brill Olcott, Martha (1995) 'Central Asia: The Calculus of Independence', *Current History* 94 (594) October, 337–342

Brzezinski, Zbigniew (1995) 'A Plan For Europe', *Foreign Affairs* 74 (1) January–February, 26–42

Buszynski, Leszek (1993) 'Russia and Japan: The Unmaking of a Territorial Settlement', *The World Today* 49 (3) March, 50–54

Cross, Sharyl (1993) 'Gorbachev's Policy in Latin America: Origins, Impact, and the Future', *Communist and Post-Communist Studies* 26 (3) September, 315–334

Dawisha, Karen and Parrott, Bruce (1994) *Russia and the New States of Eurasia*, Cambridge: Cambridge University Press

Derleth, J. William (1996) 'The Evolution of the Russian Polity: The Case of the Security Council', *Communist and Post-Communist Studies* 29 (1) March, 43–58

Dolan, A.R. (1990) *Undoing the Evil Empire: How Reagan Won the Cold War*, Washington, DC: Washington Institute Press

Duran, Khalid (1992) 'Rivalries Over the New Muslim Countries', *Aussenpolitik* (English-language edn), 43 (4), 373–380

Eberle, Sir James, (1992) 'Russia and Ukraine: What to do with the Black Sea Fleet?', *World Today* 48, August–September, 158–160

Gerhardt, Simon (1997) 'Russia's Identity and International Politics', *Aussenpolitik* (English-language edn), 48 (3), 245–256

Ginsburg, Tom (1995) 'Political Reform in Mongolia: Between Russia and China', *Asian Survey* 35 (5) May, 459–471

Halbach, Uwe (1992) 'World Politics and Indigenous Development in Central Asia', *Aussenpolitik* (English-language edn), 43 (4), 381–391

Halliday, Fred (1995) 'The Empires Strike Back? Russia, Iran and the New Republics', *The World Today* 51 (11) November, 220–221

Haslam, Jonathan (1998) 'Russia's Seat at the Table: A Place Denied or a Place Delayed?', *International Affairs* 74 (1), 119–130

Hiro, Dilip (1995) *Between Marx and Muhammad: The Changing Face of Central Asia*, London: HarperCollins

'Historic Agreement to Launch New NATO – Russia Relations' (1997) http://www.lubbockonline.com/news/052797/historic.htm

Ikenberry, G. John (1996) 'The Myth of Post-Cold War Chaos', *Foreign Affairs* 75 (3) May–June, 79–91

Inder Singh, Anita (1995) 'India's Relations with Russia and Central Asia', *International Affairs* 71 (1) January, 83–102

Karaganov, Sergei A. (1992) 'Russia I: A Moscow view on the West's Role', *The World Today* 48 (7) July, 122–124

Keen, David (1996) 'Organised Chaos: Not the New World Order', *The World Today* 52 (1) January, 14–22

Kemp, Walter (1994) 'Giving teeth to the CSCE?', *The World Today* 50 (10) October, 183–185

Kenet, Roger E. and Birgerson, Susanne M. (1997) 'The Domestic–Foreign Policy Linkage in Russian Politics: Nationalist Influences on Russian Foreign Policy', *Communist and Post-Communist Studies* 30 (4) December, 335–344

Kerr, David (1995) 'The New Eurasianism: The Rise of Geopolitics in Russia's Foreign Policy', *Europe–Asia Studies* 47 (6), 977–988

Khan, Rashid Ahmad (1994) 'Pakistan's Relations with the Central Asian Republics: Problems and Prospects', *BISS Journal* 15 (3), 237–253

Kimura, Hiroshi (1997) 'Primakov's Offensive: A Catalyst in Stalemated Russo-Japanese Relations?', *Communist and Post-Communist Studies* 30 (4) December, 365–377

Kirby, David (1995) *The Baltic World 1771–93*, London: Longman

Lakis, Juozas (1995) 'Ethnic Minorities in the Postcommunist Transformation of Lithuania', *International Sociology* 10 (2) June, 173–184

Lipovsky, Igor P. (1995) 'The Russian Problem in Central Asia', *Orient* 36 (3), 499–517

McCausland, Jeffrey D. (1996) 'Conventional Arms Control and European Security', *Adelphi Papers* (301) Oxford: Oxford University Press

Macfarlane, Neil S. (1995) 'The Structure of Instability in the Caucasus', *International Politik und Gesellschaft* (4), 380–393

Maley, William (1995) 'Does Russia Speak for Baltic Russians?', *World Today* 51 (1) January, 4–6

Malcolm, Neil and Alex Pravda (1996) 'Democratisation and Russian Foreign Policy', *International Affairs* 72 (3) July, 537–552

Mandelbaum, M. (1995) 'Preserving the New Peace. The Case against NATO Expansion', *Foreign Affairs* 74 (3) May–June, 9–13

Martin, Laurence (1992) 'National Security in a New World Order', *The World Today* 48 (2) February, 21–26

Matlock Jr, Jack F. (1996) 'Dealing with a Russia in Turmoil', *Foreign Affairs* 5 (3) May–June, 38–51

Medish, Mark (1994) 'Russia: Lost and Found', *Daedalus* 123 (3), 63–89

Mendl, Wolf (1991) 'Japan and the Soviet Union: Towards a Deal?', *The World Today* 47 (11) November, 196–200

Menon, Rajan (1989) 'New Thinking and Northeast Asia Security', *Problems of Communism* 38 (2–3) March–June, 1–29

Mesbahi, Mohiaddin (1993) 'Russian Foreign Policy and Security in Central Asia and the Caucasus', *Central Asian Survey* 12 (2), 181–215

Moltz, James Clay (1995) 'From Military Adversaries to Economic Partners: Russia and China in the New Asia', *Journal of East Asian Affairs* 9 (1) Winter–Spring, 157–182

Moltz, James Clay (1995) 'Regional Tensions in the Russo-Chinese Rapprochement', *Asian Survey* 35 (6) June, 511–527

Mroz, John Edwin (1992/3) 'Russia and Eastern Europe: Will the West Let Them Fail?', *Foreign Affairs* 72 (1), 44–57

Paye, Olivier and Remacle, Eric (1994) 'The United Nations and the CSCE: Facing Conflicts in Abkhazia and Nagorno-Karabakh', *Peace and the Sciences* September, 1–18

Pi, Ying-hsien (1996) 'The Dynamics of Sino-Russian Relations', *Issues and Studies* 32 (1) January, 18–31

Pravda, Alex (1997) 'The Politics of Foreign Policy', in Stephen White, Alex Pravda and Zvi Gitelman (eds) *Developments in Russian Politics 4*, Basingstoke: Macmillan

Rich, Vera (1995) 'An East Slavic Union?', *The World Today* 51 (3) March, 48–51

Rogov, Sergei (1995) 'This Dangerous Crisis Over Arms Control', *European Brief* 3 (1) October, 34–36

Roucek, Libor (1991) 'USSR/Eastern Europe: A Wary Damage-Limitation', *The World Today* 47 (6) June, 95–96

Roychowdhury, Rajyasri (1995) 'Nato's Eastward Expansion: An Institutional Challenge', *Strategic Analysis* 18 (1) April, 73–90

Rubinstein, Alvin Z. (1994) 'Russia and North Korea', *Korea and World Affairs* 18 (3) Fall, 486–508

Sagadeev, Arthur (1993) 'Russia and the Great Power Ideology', *Central Asian Survey* 12 (2), 169–179

Sarkisov, Konstantin (1997) 'The Northern Territories Issue after Yeltsin's Re-election: Obstacles to a Resolution from a Russian Perspective', *Communist and Post-Communist Studies* 30 (4) December, 353–363

Segal, Gerald (1991) 'Gorbachev in Japan: The Territorial Issue', *The World Today* 47 (4) April, 59–61

Seung-Ho, Joo (1995) 'Soviet Policy Toward the Two Koreas, 1985–1991: The New Political Thinking and Power', *Journal of North East Asian Studies* 14 (2) Summer, 23–46

Shad, Tahir I., Boucher, Steven and Gray Reddish, Jennifer (1995) 'Syrian Foreign Policy in the Post-Soviet Era', *Arab Studies Quarterly* 17 (1–2) Winter–Spring, 77–94

Sherr, James (1996) 'Doomed to Remain a Great Power', *The World Today* 52 (1) January, 8–12

Shigeki, Hakamada (1997) 'Building a New Japan–Russia Relationship', *Japan Echo* 24 (5) December, 22–25

Shlapentokh, Vladimir (1995) 'Russia, China, and the Far East: Old Geopolitics or a New Peaceful Cooperation', *Communist and Post-Communist Studies* 28 (3) September, 307–318

Shlapentokh, Vladimir (1998) ' "Old", "New" and "Post" Liberal Attitudes Toward the West: From Love to Hate', *Communist and Post-Communist Studies* 31 (3) September, 199–216

Singh, Rai (1994) 'Russia and its Southern Flank', *India Quarterly* 50 (3) July–September, 71–82

Volk, E. (1995) 'Report From Russia: Politics, Economics, and the NATO Expansion Issue', http://www.heritage.org/

Wallander, Celeste A. (1992) 'International Institutions and Modern Security Strategies', *Problems of Communism* 41 (1–2) January–April, 44–62

Wallenstein, Peter and Sollenberg, Margareta (1995) 'After the Cold War: Emerging Patterns of Armed Conflict 1989–94', *Journal of Peace Research* 32 (3), 345–360

Wehling, Fred (1993) 'Three Scenarios for Russia's Middle East Policy', *Communist and Post-Communist Studies* 26 (2) June, 182–204

Winrow, Gareth (1995) *Turkey in Post-Soviet Central Asia*, London: RIIA

Yemelianova, G.M. (1995) 'Russia and Islam: The History and Prospects of a Relationship', *Asian Affairs* 82 (3), 278–290

Zviagelskaia, Irina (1995) *The Russian Policy Debate on Central Asia*, London: RIIA

Chapter 11. Reforming the economy

Adams, Walter and Brock, James W. (1993) *Adam Smith Goes to Moscow: A Dialogue on Radical Reform*, Princeton, NJ: Princeton University Press

Åslund, Anders (1995) 'The Russian Road to the Market', *Current History* 94 (594) October, 311–316

Åslund, Anders (1998) 'Rouble Trouble', *The World Today* 54 (7) July, 185–187

Åslund, Anders (ed.) (1992) *The Post-Soviet Economy: Soviet and Western Perspectives*, London: Pinter

Åslund, Anders (ed.) (1994) *Economic Transformation in Russia*, London: Pinter

Åslund, Anders (ed.) (1994) *Russian Economic Reform in Jeopardy*, London: Pinter

Åslund, Anders (ed.) (1997) *Russia's Economic Transformation in the 1990s*, London: Pinter

Åslund, Anders and Richard Layard (eds) (1993) *Changing the Economic System in Russia*, London: Pinter

Barnes, Andrew (1998) 'What's the Difference? Industrial Privatisation and Agricultural Land Reform in Russia, 1990–96', *Europe–Asia Studies* 50 (5) July, 843–857

Brada, Josef C. (1993) 'The Transformation From Communism to Capitalism: How Far? How Fast?', *Post-Soviet Affairs* 9 (2) April–June, 81–110

Boycko, Maxim, Shleifer, Andrei and Vishny, Robert (1995) *Privatising Russia*, Cambridge, MA, and London: MIT Press

Braginskii, M.I., Butler W.E. and Rubanov, A.A. (1993) *Foreign Investment Legislation in the Republics of the Former Soviet Union*, London and Moscow: Interlist (trans: W.E. Butler)

Channon, John (1995) *Agrarian Reforms in Russia, 1992–5*, London: RIIA, Russian and CIS Programme

Christensen, Benedicte Vibe (1994) *The Russian Federation in Transition. External Developments*, Washington, DC: IMF

Clarke, Simon (1992) 'Privatization and the Development of Capitalism in Russia', *New Left Review* (196) November–December, 3–27

Conway, Patrick (1995) 'Currency Proliferation: The Monetary Legacy of the Soviet Union', *Essays in International Finance* (197) June, Princeton, NJ: International Finance Section, Department of Economics, Princeton University

Cooper, Julian (1991) *The Soviet Defence Industry: Conversion and Reform*, London: RIIA Pinter Publishers

European Bank for Reconstruction and Development (1995) *Transition Report 1995*, London: EBRD

Gaddy, Clifford G. and Ickes, Barry W. (1998) 'Russia's Virtual Economy', *Foreign Affairs* 77 (5) September–October, 53–67

Johnson, Juliet Ellen (1994) 'The Russian Banking System: Institutional Responses to the Market Transition', *Europe–Asia Studies* 46 (6), 971–995

Kirichenko, Vadim (1993) 'Sostoianie i perspektivy ekonomicheskikh sviazei v CNG', *Svobodnaia Mysl'* (3) February, 12–23

Kuznetsov, Andrei (1994) *Foreign Investment in Contemporary Russia: Managing Capital Entry*, New York: St Martin's Press

Laird, Roy D. (1997) 'Kolkhozy, the Russian Achilles Heel: Failed Agrarian Reform', *Asia–Europe Studies* 49 (3), 469–478

McAuley, Alastair (1991) 'The Economic Consequences of Soviet Disintegration', *Soviet Economy* 7 (3), 189–214

McFaul, Michael (1995) 'State Power, Institutional Change, and the Politics of Privatization in Russia', *World Politics* 47 (2), January, 210–243

McFaul, Michael and Perlmutter, Tova (eds) (1994) *Privatisation, Conversion, and Enterprise Reform in Russia*, Boulder, CO: Westview Press

Major, Ivan (1993) *Privatization in Eastern Europe: A Critical Approach*, Aldershot: Edward Elgar

Maltsev, Yuri (1992) 'Toward a Post Communist Economy', *Problems of Communism* 41 (1–2) January–April, 106–113

Marnie, Sheila (1993) 'The Unresolved Question of Land Reform in Russia', *RFE/RL Research Report* 2 (7) 12, 35–37

Medish, Mark (1994) 'Russia: Lost and Found', *Daedalus* 123 (3) Summer, 63–89

Minton-Beddoes, Zanny (1995) 'Why the IMF Needs Reform', *Foreign Affairs* 74 (3) May–June, 123–133

Morozov, Alexander (1996) 'Tax Administration in Russia', *East European Constitutional Review* 5 (2–3) Spring–Summer, 39–47

Murrell, Peter (1992) 'Evolutionary and Radical Approaches to Economic Reform', *Economics of Planning* 25 (1), 79–95

Nolan, Peter (1995) *China's Rise, Russia's Fall: Politics, Economics and Planning in the Transition from Stalinism*, Basingstoke: Macmillan

Noren, James H. (1992) 'The Russian Economic Reform: Progress and Prospects', *Soviet Economy* 8 (1), 3–41

Odling-Smee, John (1992) *Economic Review: Common Issues and Interrepublic Relations in the Former U.S.S.R.*, Washington, DC: IMF

OECD (1995) *Agricultural Policies, Markets and Trade in the Central and Eastern European Countries, Selected Independent States, Mongolia and China: Monitoring and Outlook 1995*, Paris: OECD

OECD (1995) *Taxation and Foreign Direct Investment: The Experience of the Economies in Transition*, Paris: OECD

OECD (1995) *Trade Policy and the Transition Process*, Paris: OECD

OECD (1998) *OECD Economic Outlook* (63) June, 149–151

Owen, Henry (1994) 'The World Bank: Is 50 Years Enough?', *Foreign Affairs* 73 (5) September–October, 97–108

Reisinger, William M., Miller, Arthur H. and Hesli, Vicki L. (1995) 'Political Norms in Rural Russia: Evidence from Public Attitudes', *Europe–Asia Studies* 47 (6), 1025–1042

Rutland, Peter (1996) 'Russia's Unsteady Entry into the Global Economy', *Current History* 95 (603) October, 322–329

Sabelnikov, Leonid (1996) 'Russia on the Way to the World Trade Organization', *International Affairs* 72 (2) April, 345–355

Smith, Alan (1993) *Russia and the World Economy: Problems of Integration*, London: Routledge

Van Atta, Don (1994) 'Agrarian Reform in Post-Soviet Russia', *Post-Soviet Affairs* 10 (2) April–June, 159–190

Wegren, Stephen K. (1994) 'Building Market Institutions: Agricultural Commodity Exchanges in Post-Communist Russia', *Communist and Post-Communist Studies* 27 (3), 195–222

Wegren, Stephen K. (1994) 'Rural Reform and Political Culture in Russia', *Europe–Asia Studies* 46 (2), 215–241

Wegren, Stephen K. (1996) 'Understanding Rural Reform in Russia: A Response to Reisinger', *Europe–Asia Studies* 48 (2) March, 317–329

Whitlock, Erik (1993) 'Obstacles to CIS Economic Integration', *RFE/RL Research Report* 2 (27), 35–38

Williams, Frances (1997) 'Funds Flow to Ex-Soviet Bloc', *Financial Times*, 26 February, 6

Chapter 12. The Russian people: degraded and insulted?

Adams, Jan (ed.) (1991) *Economic Reforms and Welfare Systems in the USSR, Poland and Hungary: Social Contract in Transformation*, Basingstoke: Macmillan

Anderson, Barbara A. and Silver, Brian D. (1990) 'Trends in Mortality of the Soviet Population', *Soviet Economy* 6 (3), 191–251

Badkhen, Anna (1999) 'Clashes Erupt at Disputed Paper Mill', *Moscow Times*, 15 October, http://www.trud.org/

Basi, Rajpreet (1995) 'Priroda and Priority Environmental Regulation in Post-Soviet Russia', *International Environmental Affairs* 7 (1), 3–21

Bobkov, Viacheslav (1996) 'Regional'nye programmy sotsial'noi zashchity naseleniia', *Chelovek i Trud* (5), 38–41

Borisov, Mikhail (1997) 'Obmanutykh vkladchikov vse bol'she', *Rossiiskaia Federatsiia* (6), 41–42

Braitsara, Liubov' (1997) 'Stoi, kto polzet pred"iabite pasport', *Sotsial'naia Zashchita* (2), 25–32

Brown, J. David (1996) 'Excess Labour and Managerial Shortage: Findings from a Survey in St Petersburg', *Europe–Asia Studies* 48 (5), 811–835

Connor, Walter D. (1996) *Tattered Banners: Labor, Conflict and Corporatism in Post-Communist Russia*, Boulder, CO: Westview Press

Council of Europe (1994) (7th edn) *Comparative Tables of Social Security Schemes in Council of Europe Member States not Members of the European Union, and in Albania, Australia, Canada, Latvia and the Russian Federation*, Strasbourg: Council of Europe Publishing

Denisova, Irina (1999) 'Social Policy in Russia: Employment Fund', *Russian Economic Trends* 8 (1), 6–23

Flemming, John and Micklewright, John (1999) 'Income Distribution, Economic Systems and Transition', *Innocenti Occasional Papers* Economic and Social Policy Series (70) May, 1–89 available to download as a pdf file from http://www.unicef-icdc.org

Granville, Brigitte, Shapiro, Judith and Dynnikova, Oksana (1996) 'Less Inflation, Less Poverty', *Royal Institute of International Affairs Discussion Paper* (68)

Jones, Anthony (ed.) (1994) *Education and Society in the New Russia*, London: Sharpe

Lawyers Committee for Human Rights (1993) *Non-Governmental Organizations and the Protection of Refugees and Displaced Persons in the Russian Federation: A Summary of a Conference and Meeting in Moscow (March 29 to April 3, 1993) Between Russian and Western NGOs*, New York: Lawyers Committee for Human Rights

Lebedev, S. and Shchipanov, N. (1990) 'Bezhentsy', *Dialog* (9) June, 88–89

Marnie, Sheila (1993) 'Who and Where are the Russian Unemployed?', *RFE/RL Research Report* 2 (33), 36–42

'Migratsiia: zona bedstviia' (1996) *Rossiiskaia Federatsiia* (9), 58–59

Opitz, Peter J. (1991) 'Refugee and Migration Movements', *Aussenpolitik* (English-language edn) 42 (3), 261–270

'Programma sotsial'nykh reform' (1997) *Sotsial'naia zashchita* 1 (6), 97–128

Romanova, Elena (1999) 'Pension Arrears in Russia: The Story Behind the Figures', *Russian Economic Trends* 8 (4), 15–24

Rybakovskii, Leonid (1997) 'Migratsiia ili massovyi iskhod?', *Rossiiskaia Federatsiia* (2), 48–49

Rybakovskii, L.L. and Tarasova N.V. (1994) 'Vnutrirossiiskaia migratsiia naseleniia: nyneshniaia situatsiia i prognoz', *Sotsiologicheskie Issledovaniia* (1), 31–38

Satter, David (1997) 'Russia's Non-Payment Problem', *Jamestown Commentary* 1 (2), 18 April, http://www.jamestown.org/

Smirnov, S. and Isaev, N. (1999) 'Sotsial'naia politika: novyi kurs', *Voprosy ekonomiki* (2) February, 65–73

'Sotsial'naia Politika. Sil'naia sotsial'naia politika nachinaetsia s proizvoditel'nogo truda' (1997) *Chelovek i Trud* (3), 4–9

Standing, Guy (1997) *Russian Unemployment and Enterprise Restructuring: Reviving Dead Souls*, Geneva: ILO

Starkov, Anatoly (1996) 'Migratsionnye protsessy na postsovetskom prostranstve', *Otkrytaia Politika* 1–2 (11) January–February, 15–22

Titarenko, L.G. (1998) 'Spid kak ugroza sostial'noi katastrofy', *Sotsiologicheskie Issledovaniia* (9), 44–50

Trade Unions of Russia on the Internet (2000) 'Russian Trade Unions Demand to Stop Violence Against Workers: Parliamentary Hearings', 11 April, http://www.trud.org/

Travin, Dmitry (1997) 'Kuda delis' pensionnye den'gi?', *Argumenty i fakty* (St Petersburg) 3 (848) January, 4

Voinova, V.D. and Ushkalov, I.G. (1994) 'Sovremennye emigratsionnye protsessy v Rossii', *Sotsiologicheskie Issledovaniia* (1), 39–49

Waller, Michael, Courtois, Stephanie and Lazar, Marc (eds) (1991) *Comrades and Brothers: Communism and Trade Unions in Europe*, London: Frank Cass

Websites

Website servers in the FSU
http://www.smartlink.net/~migre.v/russian.FSU.servers.html

The following websites provide information and analysis about contemporary Russia from a range of view points:

Carnegie Endowment for International Peace
http://www.ceip.org/

CIA site on Russia
http://www.odci.gov/cia/publications/factbook/geos/rs.html

Center for Nonproliferation Studies, Monterey Institute of International Studies
http://www.cns.miis.edu/

Center for Political and Strategic Studies
http://www.cpss.org/focus.htm

BBC On-Line News
http//news.bbc.co.uk

BBC Monitoring (translations from the media of 150 countries including Russia)
http://www.monitor.bbc.co.uk

Financial Times
http://www.FT.com

Institute for the Study of Conflict, Ideology, and Policy, online journal *Perspective*
http://www.bu.edu/iscip.html

Jamestown Foundation (produces bulletins and the journal *Prism*)
http://www.jamestown.org/

NUPI Centre for Russian Studies Database (provides regularly updated information about institutions, personnel, political parties, chronology; add linker.exe/listalle to the URL for a list of additional links to other websites on Russia)

http://www.nupi.no/RUSSLAND/DATABASE/start.htm

The Political Reference Almanac
http://www.polisci.com/almanac/almanac.htm

Radio Free Europe–Radio Liberty
http://www.rferl.org/

Russian Politics (provides information about political parties and organisations, elections, federalism, as well as biographies of key figures, and a copy of the Constitution)
http://www.russia.net~oldrn/politics.html

US–Russia Binational Commission
http://www.usia/gov/regional.bnc/usrussia/gcchead.htm

Index